The émigrés who left, or were driven from, Revolutionary France included a large part of the officer corps of the former royal army. Joined by others who wished to fight for the restitution of the monarchy in their homeland, these officers soon served this cause in the pay of countries facing the common enemy. With its origins at the 1793 Siege of Maastricht, one unit of such men, and one woman, was raised by Etienne de Damas-Crux for the service of the United Provinces and was to comprise of both infantry and cavalry. After the United Provinces were defeated and invaded in 1795, the unit transferred to the service of Britain. Its infantry companies were destroyed in the ill-fated Quiberon expedition while the cavalry, which grew to a regiment, joined in early 1796 the last émigré army, that of the Prince de Condé, and served alongside the Austrians in Southern Germany. Finally, the Damas Hussars disappeared when the Armée de Condé was reorganised in Russian service.

This is a comprehensive and detailed history of the Légion de Damas which provides a case-study of the French military emigration and thus an alternative view point of the Revolution that caused it and the wars that followed. By drawing in particular on memoirs of members of the unit and contemporary material in archives across Europe, from Britain to Russia, the story is told of those who remained steadfast to God and their King.

Hughes de Bazouges is a retired colonel in the French Army. His interest in military history and modelling became centred around the history of the French military emigration in which a direct ancestor took part during the Revolution. He pursued this passion when studying for his MA at La Sorbonne, Paris, and in several articles dedicated to the émigrés at arms. Along with research and his activity with La Sabretache, he currently teaches geo-politics and the history of Africa at ICES (Vendée) and the Military Academy of St Cyr (Brittany).

Alistair Nichols is a retired police officer. His interest in military history emerged after the realisation that he was not very good at painting models. He has studied in particular the history of the foreign units in the British Army during the era of the French Revolutionary and Napoleonic Wars. His published works include histories of the Chasseurs Britanniques and the Watteville Regiment and his most recent is *They Turned Out So Ill! The Independent Companies of Foreigners 1812–1814.*

For God and King

A History of the Damas Legion (1793–1798): A Case Study of the Military Emigration during the French Revolution

---

Hughes de Bazouges and Alistair Nichols

Helion & Company

To our wives, Jane and Marjorie, for their support and patience, and to those who came before us and those who follow.

Helion & Company Limited
Unit 8 Amherst Business Centre
Budbrooke Road
Warwick
CV34 5WE
England
Tel. 01926 499619
Email: info@helion.co.uk
Website: www.helion.co.uk
Twitter: @helionbooks
Visit our blog at http://blog.helion.co.uk/

Published by Helion & Company 2021
Designed and typeset by Mach 3 Solutions Ltd (www.mach3solutions.co.uk)
Cover designed by Paul Hewitt, Battlefield Design (www.battlefield-design.co.uk)

Cover: Infantry of the Légion de Damas in Dutch service (1793–1795). (Artwork by Giuseppe Rava, collection of *Colonel* (retd) Hughes de Bazouges).

ISBN 978-1-913336-60-8

British Library Cataloguing-in-Publication Data.
A catalogue record for this book is available from the British Library.

For details of other military history titles published by Helion & Company Limited, contact the above address, or visit our website: http://www.helion.co.uk

We always welcome receiving book proposals from prospective authors.

Contents

List of Colour Plates

List of Maps

Acknowledgements

No work such as this can be completed without the help of very many people. This is particularly true in this case, where research has taken place over such a long timescale. Among them are the staff of various archives, collections and libraries, fellow enthusiasts who have willing contributed and advised even if the only contact is by e-mail and friends, new and old. Thanks to them all for their kindness and help.

Special thanks are due to Andrew Bamford and Helion for providing the means for this work to see the light of day.

Authors' Notes

The authors of this book come from different traditions, backgrounds and academic principles. Largely because of this, they have, of course, their own individual styles. In writing this book a consistency of approach has been applied but differences will be discernible between sections according to the contributor. This is intended, reflecting that this is indeed a collaborative effort bringing together these viewpoints with the intention to provide a wider perspective to the story to be told.

In the text place names have been given in their current vernacular form such as, for instance, Liège. However, some exceptions have been made where other versions will be so familiar to English-speaking readers, such as Brussels (Bruxelles), Brunswick (Braunschweig) and Dunkirk (Dunkerque).

Preface

The present work has its origin in a discovery made in Paris around 1975. Specialists in the Wars of the French Revolution and Empire would not recall it; it was neither the discovery of an original manuscript which had suddenly enlightened us on the history of the Légion de Damas, nor the sale of a miniature or portrait of one of its officers, recorded in the catalogue of an auctioneer such as Drouot or Christie's, nor even the uncovering of the still ardently sought archives of the Duc de Damas-Crux who had been its proprietor.[1] The unique and unusual piece that caught my attention measured 54 mm without its headgear, and beckoned in the window of the Model department of the *Paquebot Normandie*, then the largest shop for toys, models and figurines in Paris, situated at the end of the Rue de Tolbiac (XIIIe), near the Parc Montsouris. More than the nonchalant attitude of this little soldier, his weapon slung over one shoulder and his other arm dangling down by his side, it was without doubt other details that had made me notice him: the sky blue colour of his uniform, even its cut and finally his strange headgear, a black felt hat the brim cocked at right angles on one side, a style reminiscent of the contemporary Pontonniers de Strasbourg, the Austrian artillery or even Jägers, whether Hanoverian or others of the Duke of Brunswick. Yet the name on the base 'Chasseur émigré de Damas (1795)' evoked, for the novice that I then was, the vague recollection of the military emigration (1791–1801) and of the unfortunate Quiberon expedition (1795). However, fate had determined that as a teenager I would become the custodian of my family's archives, stored in a large cardboard box itself religiously deposited at the bottom of an antique sixteenth century chest, the only surviving piece of furniture from the shipwreck that led, in 1910, to the sale of the family château. For the military history enthusiast that I already was, these 'old papers' taken from an 'old house' to quote a title dear to the historian Gaston Lenotre,[2] concealed a treasure or at least several docu-

1 Nevertheless, the sabre that he possessed when he was proprietary colonel of the Etienne-Damas hussar regiment with the Army de Condé (1796–1798) was recently discovered when put on sale in Paris in November 2018. It is a British hussar officers' sabre of the new 1796 model: 'blade etched *Vive le Roi* with the French Royal Arms on one side and on the other the Damas family's coat of arms and motto. GILL of London makers' mark. 97 cm long' (*Souvenirs historiques chez Million & Associés Paris*). In addition, a miniature that we believe to be an officer of the chasseurs of the Damas Legion's infantry was sold during the winter of 2018–2019.

2 Under his pen name of Gaston Lenotre, Théodore Gosselin, member of the *Académie française*, was around 1900, considered as one of the most prolific and popular historians of his time, and the six volumes of his collection *Paris révolutionnaire. Vielles maisons, vieux papiers* were a great book shop success that contributed in this era to a growing interest in French history. His work has been reissued by the Editions Grasset, Perrin and Tallandier. In Volume Six he related the astonishing story

ments that set me on a hunt: thanks to ten or so certificates of various kinds, it was in fact possible to reconstruct the story of a certain François Aumont de Bazouges (1747–1808), 31st and last *seigneur* of Bazouges-sur-Loir, whose military career would in 1791 doubtless not have passed beyond the rank and employment of cavalry captain if the French Revolution had not led him to emigrate and fight for ten years across Europe *pro Deo et Rege* (for God and King). If one is indebted to Théodore Muret, author of the *Histoire de l'Armée de Condé* (Paris: Dentu, 1844), for the only bibliographic mention known of this person, it was at least eulogistic: 'The hussars of Etienne de Damas, who included among their best officers Monsieur de Bazouges, former capitaine in the régiment de cavalerie d'Orléans ...'

In addition to the quality of the painting and finish of this little figurine that had suddenly excited me, it was for many years my only link with this ancestor as well as the Légion de Damas that remained to be discovered, so I did not fail, up to my last visit to the *Paquebot Normandie*, in 2005 (it was to close in 2007), to regularly go to greet him. His presence seemed all the more unusual, even incongruous, as the Damas Chasseur was the only representative of the military emigration, a subject then still largely unknown, isolated amidst others of the Empire or the Second World War that made up the bulk of the subjects displayed and some of which eyed him up and down loftily from their heights of 77, 90 or 120 mm.

During the 20 years that followed, I managed to amass together the existing documents on the subject, or at least those within my reach, and to discover the extremely tight circle of artists and historians who have been passionate in the field of the history of the military emigration. If Vicomte Robert Grouvel (1900–1965), author of the monumental *Histoire des Corps de Troupes de l'émigration* in three volumes (Paris: La Sabretache, 1961–1965), was dead by this time, his son, the late *Lieutenant-colonel* François Grouvel, opened the contents of his archives to me in 1993, and the work of my friend Patrice Courcelle, talented illustrator specialising in the uniforms of the wars of the Revolution and Empire, aroused a new interest for the subject thanks to the first colour magazines dedicated to uniformology, in particular *Uniformes* then *Tradition*, and the Men-at Arms collection from Osprey, which popularised this field of study.[3]

I soon discovered that the figurine which had been the catalyst for my quest, was in fact the true reproduction of one of two illustrations of soldiers of the Légion de Damas by JOB (Jacques Onfroy de Bréville), published in Issue No.15 of the *Tenues des troupes de France* (Paris: Martin, January 1903) in a collection of forty-eight plates by this celebrated artist then considered an international reference because of his authority in the field of uniformology. We know that the text accompanying each of these plates was not written by the artist himself but by a member of La Sabretache, the oldest learned society for French military history, founded in 1893 and then well renowned. The other plate represents a cavalryman of the Damas Hussars, the unit in which François Aumont de Bazouges served from its creation, for Dutch service in 1794, until its disbanding in 1798 when the Armée de Condé passed into the service of Tsar Paul I. During one of my visits, I was to discover that the figurine, a Historex conversion (the equivalent of the 54 mm Airfix figurines), had been

of Madame de Bennes, *homme d'armes*, the only woman to have served during the emigration in the dress of a man, within, precisely, the Légion de Damas.

3 René Chartrand and Patrice Courcelle, *Emigré & Foreign Troops in British* Service *(1) 1793–1795* and *(2) 1803–1815* Men-at-Arms Nos.328 and 335 (Botley: Osprey, 1999 and 2000).

created by the head of the *Paquebot Normandie's* Model department, who was the son of the store manager and himself a member since 1961 of the *Société des collectionneurs de figurines historiques* (SCFH) then, since 1970, of La Sabretache after the amalgamation of the two associations. The Vicomte Grouvel had joined this scholarly society for the study of military history in 1926 and, over many years, he had been the director of its publication, *le Carnet de La Sabretache,* before taking on the role of vice president until his death.

With these discoveries enriched by new publications and, above all, the reading of the work of René Bittard des Portes, *Les émigrés à la cocarde noire* (Paris: Emile Paul, 1908), I laid in 1994 the first stone of the present edifice in the form of a thesis for a master's in history, *La Légion de Damas au service des Provinces-Unies, 1793–1795*, produced under the authority of *Professeur* Jean-Paul Bertaud (1935–2015), then Director for the Studies of the French Revolution at The Sorbonne (Paris). The subject would perhaps have remained at that without the arrival of the internet and without reading the work of a British alter ego. In 2012, I passionately devoured the work of Alistair Nichols, *Wellington's Mongrel Regiment: A History of the Chasseurs Britanniques Regiment, 1801–1814* (Staplehurst: Spellmount, 2005), both delighted and surprised that a new British historian was interested – since Cecil C.P. Lawson and Robert W. Gould[4] – in the history of the émigrés in foreign service, and in particular of the last royalist combatants of the Armée de Condé who refused in 1801 to lay down their arms and return to France. Among the officers of this unit, I was to find a former Damas Chasseur.

My quest was continuously enriched with new sources published online – mainly of archives, old books or again references from hard-to-find works but also old papers, an antique weapon, miniature or portrait, decoration ... The internet is also, for the insatiable researcher, a formidable tool of communication allowing one to enquire of archivists, military history museums, local associations, etcetera as well as other enthusiasts across the planet. In this way I managed, in 2013, to get in touch with Alistair Nichols, member of the prestigious Society for Army Historical Research, thanks to the kindness of the local library in which he had given a talk.[5] We then communicated by email until he accepted, with the natural enthusiasm which he has never lost, my invitation to France to bring about a possible collaboration of which this is the result, enhanced by the talent of André Jouineau who I also thank wholeheartedly.

The *alliance cordiale* rapidly gave way to a warm friendship from which we can hope for further fruit.

On 3 December 2016, chance, if indeed it was, caused me to meet on the occasion of the international exhibition of the *Figurine historique de Sèvres*, at the gates of Paris, M. Joël Falconnet, the creator of the figurine of the Damas Chasseur. He remains a member of La Sabretache, fidelity that I always wanted to salute.

Colonel (retd) Hughes Lelouvier Aumont de Bazouges
Membre de La Sabretache

4 Respectively *A History of the Uniforms of the British Army*, (London: Norman, 1966) Vol.V; *Mercenaries of the Napoleonic Wars* (Brighton: Donovan, 1995).

5 The author since of two works dedicated to other foreign corps in British service: *Wellington's Switzers – The Watteville Regiment in Egypt, the Mediterranean, Spain and Canada* (Godmanchester: Ken Trotman, 2015) and *They turned out so ill! The Independent companies of Foreigners 1812–1814* (Peterborough: FastPrint Publishing, 2018).

1

'We must set fire to the four corners of Europe, there is our salvation!'

On the 5 and 6 October 1789 a Parisian mob marched on the Château of Versailles, pushed aside the guard and forced its way into the apartments of the Queen who only had time to flee into those of her husband. After the former Marquis de La Fayette, the commander of the Parisian National Guard, had intervened, the people returned to the capital carrying on pikes the heads of eight murdered members of the King's noble guards, the Gardes du Corps. Many considered the Duc d'Orléans, Louis-Philippe (1747–1793), as the principal architect of these events. He was the cousin of King Louis XVI and one of the leaders of political liberalism which was influenced by the British, constitutional, model. In order to remove him from France, a week later Louis charged him with a secret diplomatic mission to Britain. Its object, was to find out the British attitude towards events in France but also what was happening in the Austrian Netherlands.

> The Duc d'Orléans is not unaware of the severe agitation that reigns in the Belgian provinces; the spirit of insurrection, which has manifested itself among the inhabitants, and the dispositions in which they appear to be throwing off obedience to the Emperor. We are led to believe that the Brabanters have been strengthened in their stance, by the Courts of London and Berlin, and the States-General or rather the Stadholder; but one has in this respect only suspicions … The aim of the London Court must be either to unite the Netherlands with the Confederation of the United Provinces or form an independent republic or finally to submit them to a prince outside of the House of Austria …'[1]

After the United Provinces, equivalent to the modern-day Netherlands, the Austrian Netherlands, today Belgium and Luxembourg, had emerged as the new theatre of revolutionary troubles, the nature or scale of which no one at the time recognised, each power preoccupied by the pursuit of its own agenda without apprehending the holistic nature of the events which unfolded in front of their eyes. Defeated by the insurgents, the Austrians

1 Louis-Philippe d'Orléans, Duc de Chartres, *Mémoires (1789–1793)* (Paris: Plon, 1973), Vol.1 p.107: memorial to serve as instructions, 13 October 1789.

were driven from Turnhout on 27 October 1789 and on 12 December the commander of the Imperial forces at Brussels capitulated before being permitted to withdraw to Namur. On 11 January 1790 the Confederation of the United Belgian States, or Provinces, was proclaimed and two weeks later the citadel of Antwerp fell into the hands of the revolutionaries. The Imperial forces, facing the desertion of their Walloon troops, were forced 'to retire into Luxembourg, the only one of the ten provinces that still remained under the dominion of Austria.'[2]

One of the first measures taken by the Congress of the United Belgian States was the creation of a fairly heterogenous national army made up of line regiments raised in each of the cities and provinces, as well as numerous free corps and units of volunteers. Soon, realising that this force would be insufficient and wishing to internationalise the conflict, but without official support from any power, the congress supported the raising of foreign volunteer corps. One was the British Legion, but, with recruitment prohibited in Britain, the vast majority of the soldiers were, in reality, Germans and Belgians in red coats.[3]

The new army's principal military leaders included the Prussian Baron von Schoenfeld and the British officer, George Koehler, providing evidence that these countries encouraged the 'Brabant revolution' as part of an indirect strategy to weaken Austria. In France, this revolution certainly evoked real sympathy as it 'evinced neither disorder, nor tearing down, nor destruction. The three orders of the nation were united in the same spirit of liberty. Everyone was armed, money abounded, and a Prussian general, of repute, commanded … an army, not of National Guards, but of regimented and regular troops. It was thus that the Belgian Revolution was seen from afar.'[4] Although no intervention took place as Louis XVI had no wish to quarrel with his wife's family, and his Minister of Finance, Necker, opposed any expensive military adventure.

In March Emperor Leopold II marched into the Austrian Netherlands at the head of 40,000 men and his sovereignty was recognised by Britain, Prussia and the United Provinces in the Convention of Reichenbach of 27 July 1790. The Congress's response was hampered by internal division while Baron Schoenfeld worked in support of Prussia's new stance, favouring the surrender of Namur, on 24 November 1790, and the disbanding of a part of the confederation forces before fleeing to France. The rapprochement with Austria, Prussia's 'natural enemy' throughout the eighteenth century, driven by the latter's designs on Poland did not bode well for the future. Finally, with Namur retaken, the Austrian troops made their entry into Brussels on 2 December, the same day as the Congressional troops were dissolved. Like their Dutch cousins, who had fled their homeland after the suppression of the Dutch Revolution in December 1787, the Belgian patriots took refuge in the north of France. There was a risk that the conflict would spread into French territory. The Marquis de Bouillé commanded in the north-east, including Lorraine and Alsace, while Jean-Baptiste-Donatien de Vimeur de Rochambeau, a veteran of the War of Austrian Succession, the Seven Years War and the American War of Independence, headed the Armée du Nord. He was sent to the frontier:

2 Charles François Dumouriez, *La vie et les mémoires du général Dumouriez écrits par lui-même*, (Paris: Librairie Historique, 1822), Vol.II, (1792–1793), p.79.

3 Théodore Juste, *Histoire de la Révolution belge de 1790* (Brussels: Jamar, 1846), Vol.II, p.146.

4 Dumouriez, *La vie et les mémoires*, Vol.II, p.79.

> A tide of these fugitives flowed onto our frontiers, pursued by the Austrians, and caused great anxiety there. I was sent, in the month of December 1790, to go to reassure all the garrisons and to return to order, in our interior, all the Frenchmen who had joined these revolutionaries without the government's consent. I was expressly ordered, by the same decree, to avoid anything which might compromise us with the Emperor, with whom we then wished to arrange an alliance, at a time when our own affairs did not permit us to busy ourselves with those of our neighbours ...[5]

In France the progress of the revolutionary party was checked by the constitutionals who were distinguished above all by their fidelity to the Constitution and, by extension, to the constitutional monarchy. However, these liberals, who claimed to be defenders of the throne, became its grave-diggers, unable to extinguish the fire which they themselves had helped to light in 1789, at the convocation of the States-General. The three principal pillars of the monarchy – the nobility, clergy, and army – had all been systematically undermined. After the slaughter, from July 1789, of some representatives of the high aristocracy who were hostile to the new ideas, the nobility had been forced to abandon their privileges on 4 August 1789 and then to retreat to the provinces where their châteaux were attacked and sometimes burnt along with their charters of ancient feudal rights. To counter the constitutionals, the hard line, or true, royalists finally but belatedly engaged in the political arena in Paris to defend the dignity and independence of the sovereign as well as ensure the safety of their relatives, homes and properties in the provinces. Only a few members of the Royal Family and high aristocracy had emigrated. The Prince de Condé and the Comte d'Artois, the youngest of the King's two brothers and future King Charles X, had quit France after 15 July 1789. Considered as obstacles to the progress of the 'new ideas', they took refuge in Brussels and then Turin, where other conservatives joined them. There had been no international reaction to the assassination of a few gentlemen, Gardes du Corps or provincial squires, but the seizure of German princes' property in Alsace provoked diplomatic tension on the European stage.

Desperate to save the Bourbon monarchy and perhaps to buy time, Louis XVI had finally agreed to become the citizen-king and on 4 March 1790 'Louis, by the Grace of God, and the Constitutional Law of the State, King of France' took the civic oath. Then, on 29 May, he had to ban the white cockade, the traditional insignia of the French monarchy, to be replaced by La Fayette's new tricolour cockade. On 12 July 1790 the National Assembly also adopted the Civil Constitution of the Clergy which not only reduced the number of bishops from 134 to 83, one for each of the new *départements* that had been created in January, but also stipulated that their nomination was to be by assemblies and no longer by the Vatican following a proposal by the King. This decision, condemned by the Pope, split the clergy between juror and refractory priests; only four of the 134 bishops took the required oath and 46,000 of the 70,000 priests also refused. Retaliatory measures against the Church of France followed: the closure of convents, expulsion of the nuns and monks and the destruction of religious monuments and buildings sold at auction, sometimes just for their stone.

5 Jean-Baptiste Donatien de Vimeur Rochambeau, *Mémoires militaires, historiques et politiques* (Paris: Pillet Ainé, 1809), Vol.I, p.375.

On 14 July, a great celebration, the *Fête de la Fédération*, was held in Paris to mark the first anniversary of the taking of the Bastille and it was considered a great success.[6] La Fayette, famous for his role in the American War of Independence, commanded the 60 battalions of the National Guard of Paris and was nominated to lead all the National Guards of the kingdom. This force had been established since August 1789, initially only in Paris where it was an independent corps of 24,000 resident citizens along with 6,000 guards housed in barracks and 1,200 cavalrymen, soon joined by six companies of chasseurs recruited in part from disbanded former French Guards. La Fayette had seen the *Fête de la Fédération*, at which delegations from the army and the National Guards would attend, as the occasion to seal the union between the two institutions. The army, still under the authority of the King, remained responsible for the protection of the nation's frontiers while the National Guards, a new 'Civic and National' force, organised in cities and then *départements*, was now responsible for the internal security of the kingdom and guiding the Revolution by ensuring compliance with the decrees of the Constituent Assembly. To counter the most extreme revolutionaries, the latter had decided that the status of citizen, and therefore the right to vote, would be based on a census and only such 'active' citizens would form the National Guard.

The consequence of the *Fête de la Fédération* was that the army was increasingly exposed to agitation stirred by municipal revolutionary clubs and soon there was indiscipline throughout, especially in the infantry and the 'scientific branches' of artillery and engineers, whereas 40 percent of the cavalry, in particular the hussars and foreign or princely regiments such as Royal-Allemand (Royal German) or Dauphin, remained loyal to the King. Soldiers' committees were created in the barracks to claim their rights, arrears of pay, even custody of the regimental pay chest and flags, traditionally kept in the colonel's quarters. The authority of the officers, striving to retain loyalty 'to the Nation, Law and King,' was increasingly challenged and they were often physically menaced as aristocrats.

The prospect of a European conflict remained unlikely as the Revolution in France remained a strictly internal affair, much to the satisfaction of several countries which saw it enfeebled on the international stage. However, in mid-July 1790 the investigation committee of the Paris Municipality published a report denouncing a counter-revolutionary plot by army officers to free King Louis XVI from the control of the National Assembly and bring him to the frontier. Then three armies, raised with money and troops from Sardinia, Spain and German princes who had lost property in Alsace, would march on Paris to blockade the city, while a manifesto from Louis was published. Although nothing came of it, this project set the stage for the tragic events which would go on to push France into renewed civil strife and Europe into chaos.

The indiscipline of the royal troops came to a head in the middle of June 1790 at Nancy, in Lorraine, where the garrison was formed by the Swiss Régiment de Lullin de Châteauvieux, the infantry Régiment du Roi and the cavalry Régiment de Mestre de Camp. Jean-Victor de Constant-Rebecque, later a general who was to play a decisive role in the Waterloo campaign, was then a very junior officer in the Swiss regiment, having been commissioned

6 14 July is today the date of the French National Day (Bastille Day in English).

sous-lieutenant on 22 September 1788, his 15th birthday. He left a detailed account of the lead-up to what was to be called the 'Nancy affair' in his journal:

> 16 June: We find the city in turbulence, the Régiment du Roi is in continual insurrection; we had not yet worn the tricolour cockade, here we are given the order for it. Our regiment alone is employed to maintain the peace in the city against the disorders of the French soldiers who spare no means to put ours into insurrection.

Then, dated 20 July:

> The trouble at Nancy, stimulated by the Jacobins, grows day by day; we are continually on alert to contain the rebels and the soldiers of the Régiment du Roi, who imprison their officers, plunder the chests and commit a thousand disturbances. All possible means of seduction are employed towards our soldiers and manage to win over some of our grenadiers.[7]

The Régiment de Lullin de Châteauvieux was particularly vulnerable to such attempts as the men were almost all Francophone. Two weeks later two of the regiment's grenadiers were convicted of sedition, had their hair cut off and were imprisoned, to be driven out of the regiment at night. As soon as this was known, a mob from the town went to the Châteauvieux's quarters and the Swiss were assailed with stones in the streets. The people, mixed with soldiers from the French regiments, then forced their way into the barracks and liberated the detainees. Threatened, the Swiss officers were forced to reinstate the condemned men who then proceeded in triumph through the streets of Nancy. The following day, 12 August, 'at four in the morning, the general alert drum call beats everywhere; the garrison parades on the Royal Square where a proclamation of the National Assembly and the King against unlawful assemblies and seditions and for the return of military discipline is read out.' It had the opposite effect, as soon as the regiments had returned to their quarters the Swiss officers were shut in a room by their men, 'the soldiers establish amongst them a committee which governs the regiment. Afternoon, a crowd of soldiers, pell-mell from the three regiments, arrive armed and with sabres unsheathed.' At the point of the sabres, the officers had not only to sign the two guilty men's discharges but also to give them 200 louis each, then, the following day, the regiment's soldiers demanded the sum of 27,000 livres 'to purchase their lives and liberty'. The money was distributed among the soldiers who quickly partook in a drunken orgy of disorder: however, once they had slept off the effects of their wine, they rather sheepishly returned to renew their oath of fidelity to their officers.[8] All seemed to have returned to order, but it was only the calm before the storm.

A week earlier, the National Assembly had ordered the Marquis de Bouillé to suppress the insurrection. For many this was not simply to be a local operation to snuff out the mutiny of a few troops. La Fayette, for one, considered it '... the moment when we can begin to establish institutional order, which must replace revolutionary anarchy ... we have to strike

7 National Archief, The Hague (NA), 2.21.008.01/IN – 19: *Journal de Constant-Rebecque*, Vol.1.
8 NA, *Journal de Constant-Rebecque*, Vol.1.

an imposing blow for the whole of the army and halt, by means of an example, the general disbandment that is afoot.'[9] Supported by the Jacobins, the mutineers at Nancy sent emissaries to the Assembly and also deputations to the garrisons of the whole region to try to win over new rebels or at least to ensure that units would not march against them. Constant-Rebecque was getting ready to leave the city for Paris to take his post as *second sous-lieutenant*, with the rank of *capitaine*, in the prestigious Swiss Guards, but noted on 15 August that 'Nancy's calm did not last long; the same scenes recurred; money was again demanded; officers were disarmed by their soldiers; Monsieur de Noue [La Noüe], commandant of Nancy, and Monsieur de Malseigne, both generals, were placed in the dungeon by the rebels and ill-treated; the garrison went as far as to entice the Carabiniers from Lunéville.'[10] Bouillé's situation was critical as the numbers that opposed him, the rebel soldiers and a large section of the population that had embraced their cause, were four or five times larger than his own and, if he failed, the insurrection would doubtless trigger a more significant civil conflict. Though from the first the Régiment du Roi had left the city in compliance with the Assembly's decrees, the other rebel units opened fire on the Marquis de Bouillé's troops who immediately took the city by force on 31 August 1790. The assault cost the assailants 300 killed and wounded, including 35 officers. The guilty were then immediately tried and the three regiments were sent to new garrisons. The Swiss Régiments de Castella and Vigier, part of Bouillé's force, tried their rebel compatriots on the Place de Grève (now the Place Carnot); 'there, of 113 prisoners from Châteauvieux, one was condemned to be broken, twenty-two to be hung and forty-four to be sent to the galleys.'[11]

Bouillé was at first unanimously thanked for his energetic intervention but very quickly, through the instrument of the media of the period, the 'Nancy Affair' was transformed into a political battle between the constitutionals, partisans of the established order, and the relentless revolutionaries, the virtuous defenders of democracy who portrayed the mutineers as citizens who had legitimately risen up against the tyranny of royal authority. Following the event, a decree was issued in September forbidding soldiers from visiting the revolutionary clubs and their members from receiving them however, under pressure from the Jacobins, the decree was to be revoked in March 1791. Bouillé placed himself at the disposal of the King who, from the end of October, planned to flee Paris and reach a stronghold on the frontiers, where he could rally all his loyal subjects and win back his throne, 'proposing to only resort to arms when his bounty had been exhausted.'[12] Louis XVI wanted to get his brothers to join him, and thus neutralise competing projects, uniting the still loyal troops and the émigré nobility around him. The King decided that Montmédy on the border with the Austrian Netherlands, close to Liège and Luxembourg, would be the best place for his purposes. However, he warned the faithful Bouillé that he would attempt nothing before next spring.

9 Gilbert de La Fayette, *Mémoires, correspondance et manuscrits du général Lafayette* (Paris & London: sa famille, 1837), Vol.III p.135.

10 NA, *Journal de Constant-Rebecque*, Vol.1.

11 NA *Journal de Constant-Rebecque*, 31 August 1790. As galleys were no longer in service, this last sentence meant hard labour.

12 François Barrière, *Mémoires du Marquis de Bouillé, avec une notice historique sur sa vie, des notes et des éclaircissements historiques* (Paris: Didot, 1859), p.183.

However, through the autumn the King found himself increasingly isolated politically and he now decided to carry out his escape plan. In January 1791, he informed Bouillé that Emperor Leopold II had assured him that 12,000 to 15,000 men would be ready to march to the frontier as soon as the Royal Family was approaching Montmédy. The situation again changed when the project to dissolve the Assembly and reconstitute one more favourable to the King, collapsed on the unexpected death of its author, Mirabeau. Radicals then sought, by a coup on 28 February, to have La Fayette replaced at the head of the Parisian National Guard by the brewer Santerre, chief of the Jacobin club of the Faubourg Saint-Antoine. These events only strengthened the King's resolve to escape to Montmédy, and to use the Varennes road for fear of being recognised at Reims, at the end of April or more likely at the beginning of May 1791, giving Bouillé all the instructions and means necessary to facilitate his escape.

From February the weakness of Louis's sovereignty was illustrated when on 18 April he was prevented, by the National Guard and the populace, from leaving the Tuileries Palace to take Easter service from his confessor at Saint-Cloud, in the suburbs of Paris. Desperate, Louis, with the Comte d'Artois as intermediary, approached the Austrian Emperor Leopold, Friedrich Wilhelm I of Prussia, Empress Catherine of Russia, as well as the Kings of Sweden and Spain, to gather the European powers in an armed congress to bring the French to their senses and restore the position of the crown, and so protect the Constitution. Louis XVI's manifesto became known as the 'Mantuan' declaration, Article III of which stated:

> The Emperor will send thirty-five thousand men onto the frontiers of Flanders and Hainault; the troops of the Circles [the ten regional divisions of the German Empire] will bring fifteen thousand men towards Alsace; the Swiss will demonstrate on their frontier; the King of Sardinia will enter Dauphiné with fifteen thousand men; the twelve thousand men from Spain will be increased to twenty thousand to threaten the southern provinces ...[13]

The failure of the Royal Family's flight, halted on 21 June 1791 at Varennes, was a disaster for both the constitutional and the royalist parties. The former was weakened within the Assembly and the latter was excluded from the political debate, henceforth being treated as 'enemies of the people.' The Gardes du Corps du Roi were dissolved and, later, in January 1792, replaced by a 3,000 men strong Constitutional Guard. These different events led to an unexpected coalition.

On 27 August Emperor Leopold and Friedrich Wilhelm of Prussia met at Pillnitz Castle in Saxony, purportedly to discuss the conflict with the Ottoman Empire and the further partition of Poland. That country had already been drastically reduced by Russia, Prussia, and Austria in 1772 and the adoption of a liberal constitution in Poland, on 3 May 1791, led the sovereigns to fear another revolution, this time in the heart of Europe. Their reaction would lead, in 1793, to further partition and the destruction of the country. However, the Austrian Netherlands and France were the matters to be discussed at the meeting which the

13 Bertrand de Moleville, *Mémoires particuliers pour servir à la fin du règne de Louis XVI* (Paris: Michaud, 1823), Vol.II, p.524.

Comte d'Artois also attended. In a secret treaty, at Pavia in July 1791, the Empire, Prussia, and Spain agreed that the Austrian Netherlands would be enhanced, by the recovery of former territories, to form a new country, Austrasia, to be united to the Austrian crown, that Alsace would return to the German Empire and the Duchy of Lorraine to the Austrian Royal Family.[14] As for France, the two sovereigns, supported by Sweden and Russia, declared themselves ready to take every step necessary to restore Louis XVI.

This declaration enabled the Jacobins to impose, in September 1791, a new constitution on Louis but they had already required the troops to swear a new oath which no longer included the King. The majority of the noble officers chose to resign, to retire to their homes or emigrate, to escape the malice of the revolutionary clubs that openly called for the dissolution of the former royal army and even the murder of those who, refusing to scorn their previous oath to the King, were denounced for 'incivism'. In the first days of July 1792, Prince Louis-Philippe, Duc de Chartres, was the *colonel* of the 14ème Régiment de Dragons, formerly the Dragons de Chartres, and he took the new oath, with his troops, the day after the Assembly's decree was received. However, all the noble officers left the corps the same day, '… a dragoon regiment was then of three squadrons and twenty-eight officers. Only eight took the oath, they were all, except me who I count in the eight, those who were then called officers of fortune, that is to say officers who had begun by being ordinary soldiers.'[15] Despite his youth, the young *colonel* was to be *maréchal de camp* on 2 May 1792 and was soon known under the name of '*Général* Égalité' just as his father, the Duc d'Orléans, was known as Philippe-Egalité.

Almost 2,000 officers quit the army between 15 July 1789 and the end of June 1791, many gave the reason for doing so as personal reasons or to retire but 900 departures were registered for political reasons and 200 officers had been forced to leave the service because of the insubordination of their troops or having been subject to menaces. Until this time, the term *emigrette*, referring to a yoyo, had derisorily described the vacillations of a number of aristocrats who had left France but then had returned when their hold on property or position was threatened. However, émigré now described all the French who decided to quit their homeland due to their loyalty to their king and religion or simply to escape the excesses of the Revolution. In the space of a few months,

> [A]lmost all the officers of the army quit their colours, and came to join the French princes [the King's brothers, the Comte de Provence and Comte d'Artois, as well as his cousin, the Prince de Condé] who had retired to Koblenz; the provincial nobles, the majority followed by their wives and children, sought sanctuary abroad; fleeing a country where proscription resounded on all sides. The clergy of France almost in their entirety, came to remove themselves from the shadow of persecution, as well as the more illustrious members of the magistracy; the grandees, for the most part, had long since left the kingdom.[16]

14 John Debrett *A Collection of state papers relative to the war against France* (London: Debrett, 1794), Vol.I p.1.

15 Orléans, *Mémoires*, Vol.I pp.231–232.

16 Barrière, *Mémoires du Marquis de Bouillé*, p.268.

The King was thus deprived of his most profound defenders who had not only been driven over the frontiers but had their flight made a crime. Although he still had a right of veto, Louis found himself reduced to simply registering the Assembly's decisions, defenceless in the face of the new representatives of the nation, much more radical than their predecessors. The revolutionary deputies, largely Jacobins and Girondins, now had a free hand to put in place the legislative and legal framework that would allow them to finally rid themselves of the nobles by designating them as enemies of the people. A law on emigration had been discussed as early as 21 February 1791 with the debate being adjourned, but it was now that measures designed to strike at those identified as the leaders and architects of the Counter-Revolution were taken. Thus, on 5 March a tribunal was established at Orléans to try crimes of *lèse-nation*, literally treason against the nation, rather than against the monarch, and, on 5 June, the King's right of pardon was withdrawn.

The army was always suspect in the eyes of the most ardent revolutionaries who were concerned about its loyalty if not to the King but at least to the Constitution. Failing to have it disbanded, they managed on 12 June 1791 to have 83 battalions of National Volunteers raised to act as a populist counter-weight to the bourgeoisie National Guard. Then, on 4 August, they succeeded in having the paid element of the Parisian National Guard suppressed, and formed into line regiments; in the same month the National Volunteers were to be increased from 26,000 men to 100,000.[17] The same day as the attempted flight of the King, 21 June, the Assembly had ordered the arrest of everyone leaving the kingdom and, a week later, established the need for a passport. In response to the Declaration of Pillnitz, and the first armed gatherings of émigrés in the Austrian Netherlands and on the Rhine, the revolutionary club, *La Société fraternelle des Halles*, proposed on 22 October to declare the country in danger, a project that was then rejected. Three days later, 25 October, a surveillance committee was established in order to watch the activities of the relatives of émigrés and, more widely, the nobility and refractory priests against whom coercive measures multiplied.

On 31 October, the new Legislative Assembly, which had replaced the National Constituent Assembly on 1 October, ordered the émigrés to return before 1 January 1792 on pain of being declared rebels and deprived of their rights. However, it was still quite easy to cross the border with a false identity or with the help of smugglers using routes unguarded by the National Guard, therefore military officers continued to join the emigration throughout the autumn, but in smaller numbers. So, on 9 November, the Assembly declared that the émigrés were 'suspected of conspiracy against the country' and if they were still 'in the state of assembly' on 1 January 1792 they would be declared guilty of conspiracy and punished with death.[18] To ensure equality, Article 3 of the new penal code of 25 December had decreed that 'everyone condemned to death will have their head cut off' by the newly adopted guillotine.

Louis XVI, despite stalling, finally had to go to the Assembly on 14 December 1791 to announce that, if the Elector of Trier had not put an end to the activities of the émigrés in his territories by 15 January 1792, he would declare war on him. Yet the flow of officers from

17 It was thus that the 104ème Régiment d'infanterie was created; the future *Général de division* Louis Lazare Hoche, who we shall encounter later in this story, then served in it as a non-commissioned officer, being one of the unit's two *adjudants*.

18 General decree of 9 October 1792 against the émigrés.

France, after a lull in the autumn, swelled anew during the winter 1791–1792. Narbonne, since 7 December 1791 the new Minister of War, 'was not long in realising how much indiscipline and insubordination, then openly protected by the popular societies and as a result the legislative body [the new Assembly], had disorganised our troops. The emigration of the officers, which grew each day, was for this minister the task of Penelope; it defeated the next day all his work of the day before.'[19] Of the 9,000 officers of the former royal army, only 4,000 were left in the spring of 1792 and perhaps only a thousand or so, even several hundred, by the summer.

On 31 December 1791 the Jacobins forced the Legislative Assembly to give an amnesty to the forty Châteauvieux soldiers, who had been condemned only a year before, although the King at first opposed it, he had no other option but to provide it on 12 February 1792. Leaving prison at Brest on 13 March, they arrived at Versailles on 28 March and finally Paris on 9 April where they received honours at the session of the Assembly and were lauded, on 15 April, at the first *Fête de la Liberté* organised in their honour.

> ... their revolt was presented as a victory for liberty, and the guilty but amnestied soldiers were paraded in triumph, and offered to the people as victims who had escaped the fury of despotism. Invitations, carried by deputations, were sent to all the barracks for the non-commissioned officers and soldiers to be at the feast; it was to invite an insurrection.[20]

It was at the *Fête* that the mutineers were crowned with the Phrygian bonnet, a symbol in ancient Rome, of former slaves who had been freed, it had thus gained favour within the revolutionary clubs and assemblies, and later became emblem of the French Republic.

The new Assembly, dominated by radical parties, became more bellicose so Louis had no other choice but to opt for war to break the political impasse with the extremists who no longer concealed their desire to topple the monarchy, by adding to the affronts against the King and still more Queen Marie-Antoinette, *l'Autrichienne*.[21] The radicals saw war as a means to mobilise the people and relaunch the Revolution by not only ridding France of internal enemies but also exporting a sacred crusade for the liberty of peoples abroad. The King had few supports left to him, politically there was Narbonne and a few other politicians who remained loyal to both him and the Constitution and, physically, there was only the new Constitutional Guard, the Swiss Guards and, finally, about 7-800 gentlemen ready to come to the defence of the Royal Family. Louis gambled that in the case of a French victory, the glory would reflect on the sovereign and reconcile him with the army and the moderates led by La Fayette and, in case of defeat, that the advance of the Austrians, who had engaged to restore the French monarchy, would rally to him the French people who were still loyal but paralysed by the Revolution. The King's enemies, when the time came, were ready to profit from either scenario by unveiling some treason.

19 Rochambeau, *Mémoires militaires*, Vol.I p.394
20 NA *Journal de Constant-Rebecque*, Vol.1.
21 Literally meaning 'the Austrian woman' but, if *chienne*, is given significance can, conveniently, end as 'bitch' – so 'the Austrian bitch'.

The unexpected death of Leopold II, Marie-Antoinette's brother, on 1 March 1792 suddenly changed the situation, his successor, his son, Francis II, was known to favour the counter-revolutionary crusade of the émigrés, fearing that the fever of revolt that had already emerged in his Belgian provinces would infect the rest of Europe. In Paris steps continued to be taken to weaken and isolate the King; on 9 March Narbonne was replaced as Minster of War and, six days later, *Lieutenant-général* Charles François Dumouriez was named Minister of Foreign Affairs, imposing from the outset his views on the Comte de Grave, the Minister of War. A segment of the revolutionaries, which included Dumouriez, was favourable to Prussia and sought by every means to detach it from Austria, so that it was even secretly proposed to give Karl Wilhelm Ferdinand, Duke of Brunswick, command of the French forces.[22] The majority of the leading soldiers, such as La Fayette, on the other hand hoped that military success would permit the constitutionals to recover their former influence, something of course the most fervent revolutionaries feared.

The next weeks saw a race to the precipice. Francis II was more and more threatening, in particular to the Jacobins who were considered responsible for all the plots to bring down the monarchy, and the Legislative Assembly sent him an ultimatum demanding he withdraw his troops from the border and dissolve the émigré assemblies. The threat was unanswered and on 18 April Dumouriez demanded that war be declared on Austria and the 1756 pact between the two states ended. Dumouriez and the ministers relied on reports 'of general desertion in the Austrian army … of an emigration of more than thirty thousand men,' of whom five thousand had already arrived in the North but there were in fact only about 20 Austrian deserters and the corps of émigré Brabanters consisted of only 5-600 men.[23] Two days later, Louis XVI proposed declaring war against the King of Hungary and Bohemia, as Francis was yet to be crowned Emperor and this maintained a distinction between the ruling House of Austria and the German Empire thus preserving relations with Prussia. The decree declaring war was adopted the same day, 20 April 1792, and immediately sanctioned by the King, France had only taken up arms to maintain her liberty and independence against the unjust aggression of a despot.

This statement reflected the guarantee given to Britain some weeks earlier that the conflict was to be purely defensive and that France undertook to not seize the Austrian Netherlands. On the other hand, Dumouriez had made it clear that if Britain did not observe the desired neutrality, the victorious armies would carry revolution into Holland and Belgium, the latter to be united to France. This threat simply articulated a project he had been planning for two years since he had been sent, in June 1790, as an observer attached to *Colonel* Jean-André Van der Meersch, a former officer of the Régiment de La Marck in French service, who held a command in the Belgian 'patriot' army. There Dumouriez formed friendships that added to those he had with émigré Dutch 'patriots', of whom a great number had taken refuge in France, in Flanders and Artois, a region with which Dumouriez retained a strong affinity having been born there. Since then, he had sought to open a new front in Belgium, to weaken, as he later claimed in his memoirs, the power of Austria which alone constituted the principal threat to the French Revolution due to its support for the émigrés. He stated

22 He was Duke of Brunswick-Lüneburg, the electorate generally called, after its capital, Hanover, and Prince of Brunswick-Wolfenbüttel, of which Brunswick was the capital. The familiar versions are used.

23 Rochambeau, *Mémoires militaires*, Vol.II, pp.400–401.

that, 'his desire was, if it were possible, to carry out a great diversion in this country, to force the court of Vienna to no longer meddle in the French Revolution or, in its turn, to give it great perplexity, should it continue in its counter-revolutionary activity.'[24]

When Jacques Pierre Brissot had formed a new government, Dumouriez was appointed Minister of Foreign Affairs on 15 March 1792 for his knowledge of the Austrian Netherlands as well as secret diplomacy. On 20 April 1792, having got the Assembly to vote for war, Brissot wrote, 'Pikes started the Revolution, pikes will achieve it. We must set fire to the four corners of Europe, there is our salvation!'[25] In order to swell the ranks of the revolutionary armies, the National Assembly, guided by Dumouriez, stated in the declaration of war that France would welcome 'all foreigners, who abjuring the cause of her enemies, will join ranks beneath her standards, and devote their efforts in the defence of her liberty …' Without international allies, the constitutional monarchy welcomed foreign volunteers, particularly in the first six legions created by the law of 29 April 1792. One source were the Dutch 'political refugees' already in France after the 1787 Revolution many of whom had already enrolled in the National Guard company at Watten, Artois, which rapidly became, in effect, a regiment or free corps.

The French army was organised into three principal corps: The Armée du Nord, commanded by Rochambeau and stationed from the English Channel to the Ardennes, *Maréchal* Luckner's Armée du Rhin and finally that of the Centre, under the orders of *Lieutenant-général* La Fayette.[26] This last appointment had no other purpose than to keep La Fayette from Paris to weaken his position, as well as that of the King, having to relinquish command of the National Guard to accept that of the Armée du Centre. He was not replaced and the post of commander-in-chief of the National Guard was suppressed, the role was hence exercised alternately, each fortnight, by the divisional commanders.

The French Guards had been disbanded on 1 September 1789, because of their conduct during the first events of the Revolution, followed by the Gardes du Corps on 25 June 1791, to be replaced by the Constitutional Guard, and two thirds of the officers and a few thousand soldiers had emigrated but nevertheless the structures of the French army were almost intact on its entry into the war. Indeed, it had even been reinforced by the creation of the horse artillery and the first legions of foreign volunteers, some of the last decrees signed by King Louis XVI 17 and 29 April 1792. However, the line, infantry together with cavalry, lacked 51,000 men including almost 10,000 officers who were soon replaced by former NCOs or by young men from the bourgeoisie or National Guard. The army had 120,000 men, including 40,000 in garrisons, and, on 1 June, it still required 27,000 to bring the infantry, alone, up to strength. The officers of noble birth who remained with their regiments were systematically accused of incivism, even treason, while those from the National Guard and

24 Charles François Dumouriez, *Vie privée et politique du général Dumouriez, pour faire suite à ses Mémoires* (Hamburg: Hoffmann, 1794), p.88.

25 *Abbé* Auguste de Barruel, *Mémoires pour servir à l'Histoire du Jacobinisme* (London: Boussonier, 1798), Part IV p.420.

26 It was in honour of Luckner that engineer *Capitaine* Rouget de Lisle composed in the night of 25/26 April 1792, at Strasbourg, the *Chant de guerre pour l'Armée du Rhin* (War Song for the Armée du Rhin) which some weeks later became known as *La Marseillaise* when it became the hymn of the *Fédérés* from Marseille ordered to Paris to overthrow the monarchy.

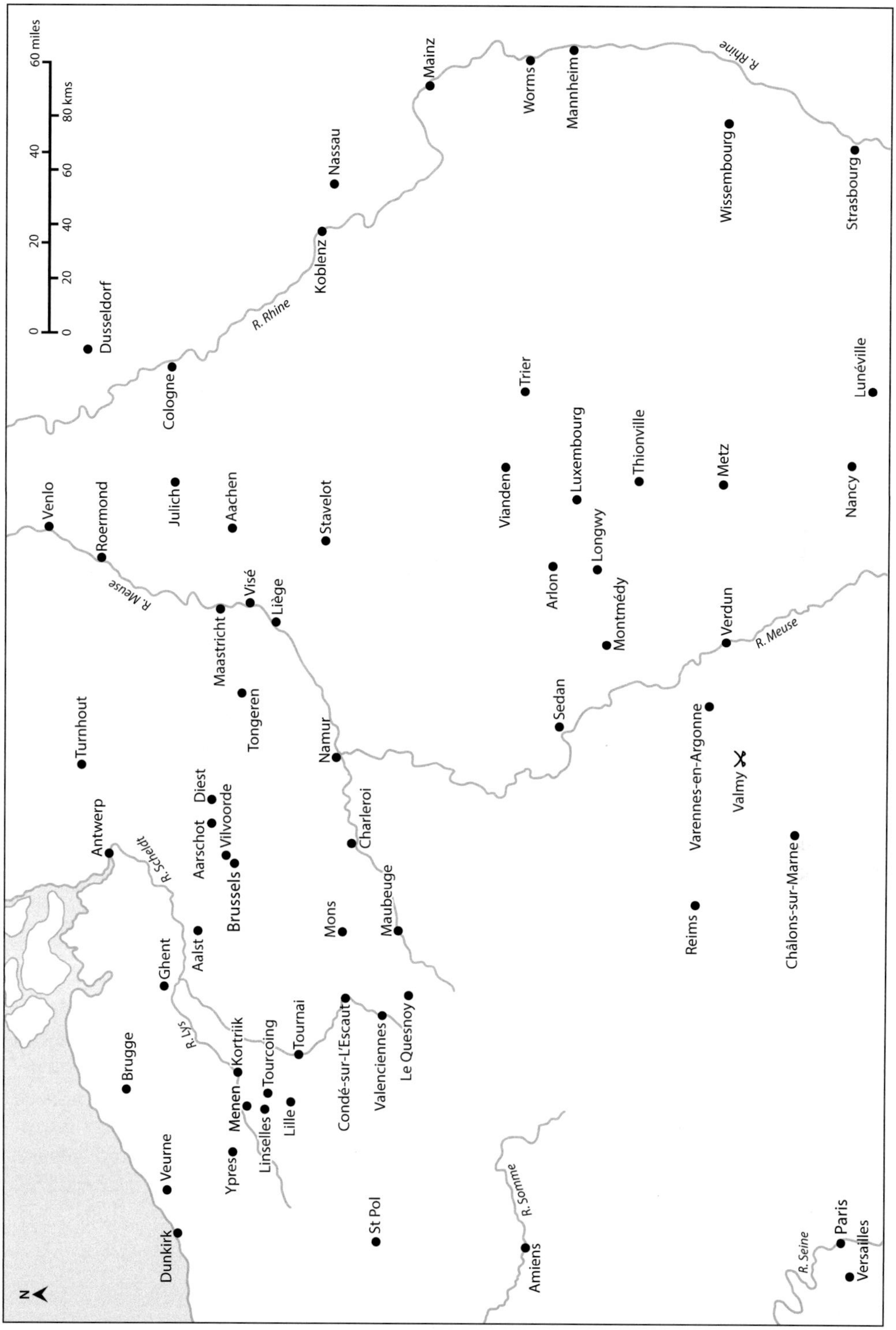

Northern France and adjoining regions.

the battalions of Volunteers were elected by their comrades. In turn, the National Guard was considered too conservative for the new Assembly, the political preference henceforth went to the battalions of National Volunteers. Little by little, the battalions of the National Guard were blended into those of the National Volunteers, nicknamed *les Bleus* due to the colour of their uniform, in contrast to the white of the royal infantry.

Rochambeau was concerned about the state of the army and asked for hostilities to be delayed until 15 May so he could assemble his troops in great entrenched camps backing onto the principal strongholds of the defensive system in the north of France. But on 24 April he received orders to prepare three columns to march at once in order to be 'on the 29 April, before Mons, Tournai and Veurne, to back a general insurrection in Brabant on which they relied.'[27] For his part, La Fayette was to be at the gates of Namur on 30 April. Rochambeau was to collect all the available troops at Valenciennes to form a reserve which would exploit the breakthroughs. He was then to continue to link with the other armies, between Liège and Roermond, and then march '... into Germany to fight the coalition armies of the Emperor and King of Prussia. It was forgotten that Maastricht, the Dutch's strongest position, was between these two cities and intercepted communication.' In addition, 'the height of insanity or treason', the 50,000 men that the Emperor had available and could probably be at Brussels on 3 or 4 May were ignored.[28] Events began very badly when the column that Comte Théobald Dillon, an officer of Irish extraction, led from Lille was routed by the Mons garrison and driven back whence it came: already wounded, Dillon was murdered by the populace who burned his body. The force under the orders of *Lieutenant-général* Biron, the former Duc de Lauzun, instructed to march on Mons, was also beaten and fell back on Valenciennes in the greatest disorder, the troops killing several officers who attempted to rally them during the retreat. Only the column that marched from Dunkirk succeeded and entered Veurne but, alerted to the destruction of the other two columns, it fell back in good order. La Fayette only escaped a similar disaster when, having encountered serious difficulties in his command, his advance was delayed. Rochambeau, on the grounds of ill-health but principally disgusted with the intrigues of Dumouriez who had dictated this offensive, presented his resignation to the King which was accepted and was immediately followed by that of the minister, Grave. At the end of May, the Constitutional Guard, suspected of counter-revolutionary projects, was disbanded and its commander, the former Duc de Cossé-Brissac, accused and arrested.

Reluctantly, Luckner agreed to replace Rochambeau who was on the point of leaving when the Austrians seized the position at Bavay on 11 June and attacked the camp at Maubeuge held by La Fayette. The troops' confidence was such that it required both *maréchaux* to command the relief force: on 20 June, Rochambeau led a column of 3,000 infantry, supported by cannon and howitzers, to dislodge the enemy while Luckner commanded the vanguard of light troops. At Bavay, the enemy were found to have already withdrawn to Mons, nevertheless Rochambeau continued his offensive and managed to occupy Kortrijk and Menen. On the same day, 20 June 1792, the people of Paris, stirred by professional agitators, seized

27 Rochambeau, *Mémoires militaires*, Vol.1 p.405.
28 Rochambeau, *Mémoires militaires*, Vol.1 p.406.

control of the Tuileries Palace and forced King Louis, wearing a Phrygian bonnet, to drink the health of the Assembly and to remain standing for the parade of rioters who had come to force him to revoke his veto in opposition to two decrees.

One was for the deportation of refractory priests which was, as a result, adopted on 26 August 1792 and led to almost 2,400 priests being sent to French Guiana between 1792 and 1795. Of the 120,000 ecclesiastics who were in France in 1789, nearly 25,000 had refused to submit and were thus forced into exile, to live clandestinely, or were murdered, guillotined, or deported. More than 20,000 found sanctuary abroad: 8,000 in Britain, 5,000 in Spain and Portugal, 3,000 in the German Empire and Austria. The other was for the establishment in Paris of a camp of 20,000 National Volunteers, who were soon to be called *Fédérés*, summoned by the Jacobins and Girondins to deal the final blow to the monarchy.

In an act of premonition, La Fayette had written on 16 June to the Assembly to denounce the proceedings of the Jacobins and their plots to not only overthrow the monarchy but also to destabilise the army. On 28 June, after having conferred with Luckner, he came to Paris to attest to the authenticity of his letter and condemn once more, in the name of the armies, the Jacobin faction, considered responsible for the events of 20 June, and to call on those guilty for the injuries inflicted on the King and Queen to be severely punished. He hoped to save the monarchy, although accused of aspiring to be a dictator by his political enemies, as the constitutionals were still in the majority and he retained a tranche of personal support within the National Guards. However, he was received very coldly at the Tuileries, the sovereigns refusing to place their salvation in the hands of the man who, according to them, was one of the principal causes of their woes; they preferred to await the arrival of the coalition troops and émigrés in Paris, as recommended in a letter from the Duke of Brunswick, appointed to lead the invasion force that was being organised.

The principal assembly points of the royalists were at Koblenz, where an extravagant court was established, and at Worms where, in contrast, the Prince de Condé oversaw the so-called 'camp' or 'barracks;' those who had gone to the Austrian Netherlands had been forced remain in semi-secrecy. Nevertheless, at the end of 1791 the émigré army had been organised, at least on paper. All the courts of Europe were approached for financial support to raise mercenary troops, and pay those who had already been collected, as well as to order, among other things, arms, equipment and horses. The uniforms for the regular troops, companies made up of infantry and cavalry officers from the former royal army joined by gentlemen who had never served as well as retired officers, followed the pre-Revolution 1786 regulations. The émigré officers wore a sword belt plaque decorated with a fleur de lys, often accompanied with the Latin motto: *Pro Deo et Rege* (For God and King). The uniforms were also set for the different legions and regional coalitions which had been formed on their own initiative. To enhance the prestige and splendour of the court at Koblenz, the Household troops of the King and his brothers had been resurrected, with the French Guards replaced by a new corps, the Hommes d'armes.

> The first infantry corps created under the denomination of the Hommes d'armes à pied [Foot Men at Arms] had been formed through the interest and at the expense of the officers of the Régiment des Gardes Françaises … The staff as well as the *capitaines, lieutenants* and *sous-lieutenants* were taken by seniority from among

> the officers of those ranks. The core of the companies was formed from the small number of non-commissioned officers and soldiers of the French Guards who remained true to the laws of duty and honour. They were joined by many volunteers drawn from the upper classes and the loyal bourgeoisie whose principles and conduct gave them such rights ...[29]

Moreover, recognition was to be given to the few corps which had, in part only, followed their colonels. Indeed, only the cavalry Régiment de Royal-Allemand had emigrated, in the spring of 1792, as a whole, with their arms and baggage, under the command of *Lieutenant-colonel* the Chevalier de Mandell; it was then cantoned in Luxembourg, 'in the small town of Vianden, capital of the county of that name, belonging to the Prince of Orange, Stadholder of the United Provinces.'[30]

Two *maréchaux*, de Broglie and de Castries, had been appointed to lead the Armée des Princes that had placed senior officers in all the towns where émigrés may join its ranks – Luxembourg, Brussels, Tournai, Mons, Trier, Liège, Frankfurt, Aachen, Maastricht, Cologne and Antwerp – to organise the cantonments of the various assemblies and impose military order.

> [O]ne of the principal functions of all these commissioners from the French nobility was to examine the claims of loyalty and authenticity of the émigrés who arrived in their respective districts, to assure themselves of the principals and conduct that had since the Revolution been manifested by those who came in crowds to all points of the frontier to join the assemblies which the Princes were forming and to incorporate them in various units that they were organising at the time, gentlemen, officers, non-commissioned officers, volunteers and soldiers who hastened from within to fight.[31]

However, it was only in the first days of July that the long-awaited arms and equipment arrived from Germany and Liège enabling the émigré troops, infantry and cavalry, to train.

The coalition army was under the orders of the Duke of Brunswick. It had, '42,000 Prussians supported with 200 cannon, 6,000 Hessians raised by the Landgrave George-William of Hesse-Cassel and 2,000 men kept ready by the Elector of Mainz.'[32] these German troops would be joined by Austrian forces, 30,000 men stationed in the Netherlands under the command of the Albrecht Casimir von Sachsen-Teschen and 34,000 deployed on the Rhine. The émigré contingent amounted to more than 20,000 men, divided in three corps: the most important, the Armée du Centre, under the direct orders of the Royal brothers (about 12,000 men) at Koblenz;[33] 5-6,000 men commanded by the Prince de Condé on the

29 Jean-Antoine de Brons, *Journal d'émigration* (Saint-Quentin-de-Baron: Entre-deux-mers, 2014), pp.48–49.
30 Brons, *Journal d'émigration*, p.34.
31 Brons, *Journal d'émigration*, pp.36–37. He served in this role in Luxembourg.
32 Jean Tranié & Juan Carlos Carimagni, *La Patrie en danger* (Paris: Lavauzelle, 1987), p.30.
33 For the organisation of the Armée du Centre, see Appendix I

Rhine and, between them, the army of the Duc de Bourbon, Condé's only son, with 4-5,000 men assembled in the Liège region.

Faced with invasion, on 11 July the Assembly decreed *la Patrie en danger*. This equated to a general mobilisation, all men able to serve had to join the battalions of National Volunteers on the frontiers, from which delegations were invited to Paris to participate three days later, on 14 July 1792, in the new *Fête de la Fédération*, giving rise to the name, *Fédérés*. That very day, at Frankfurt, Francis II was crowned Emperor of Germany which authorised him to mobilise the German troops of the Rhineland. Some alterations were, meanwhile, made to the deployment of the French army, La Fayette's Armée du Centre was transferred to Lorraine, deploying on the frontier at Stenay on 19 July and, on 2 August, *Lieutenant-général* Custine was appointed to command the Armée du Rhin.

On 25 July the Manifesto written by the Duke of Brunswick was circulated, in it he threatened the Assembly and the city of Paris with bloody reprisals if the King or Queen were subjected to the least insult or menace:

> His Majesty the Emperor and His Majesty the King of Prussia call for and invite the return without delay of the voices of reason and justice, of order and peace. It is with these views that I, the undersigned general commander in chief of the two armies declare:
>
> That the generals, officers non-commissioned officers and soldiers of the units of the French line are all summoned to return to their former loyalty and to submit at once to the King their legitimate sovereign.
>
> That the city of Paris and all its inhabitants without distinction will be bound to submit immediately and without delay to the King, to put this prince in full and entire liberty and to assure him, as well as all the royal persons, the inviolability and respect to which the laws of nature and men oblige of subjects towards sovereigns …
>
> That if the château of the Tuileries is forced or insulted, that if there is the least violence, the least outrage towards Their Majesties, the King, Queen and the Royal Family, if their security, their preservation and their liberty are not immediately provided, they will extract an exemplary and unforgettable vengeance by delivering the city of Paris to a military execution and total destruction, and the rebels guilty of outrages to the punishments that they will have deserved.

The main consequence of this threat was not what the coalition had hoped. The initial appeal for volunteers of 5 May 1792, like that of 11 July, had aroused little enthusiasm and only 45 battalions were raised, the Manifesto alone ensured the enlistment of a hundred battalions. It was also blamed for the tragedy of 10 August which saw the fall of the Tuileries Palace and the massacre of the monarchy's last defenders.

> [Unlike] the great revolutionary days, the attack on the Tuileries was not improvised but prepared over several weeks, as soon as it appeared vain for the Jacobins with a hullaballoo to call for the fall of the King by lawful means. The Motherland had been declared in danger on 11 July and on the 21st a secret directory was put into place. On the 25th, the sections that made up the revolutionary movement in

> Paris were authorised to sit permanently. A first plan of attack was postponed to wait for 500 Marseillais, who entered Paris on 30 July.[34]

The people then gave free reign to their hatred of their sovereigns and in particular against the *Autrichienne*. On 27 July, Constant-Rebecque and two other Swiss officers accompanied her, the Dauphin and the king's sister, Madame Élisabeth, with their lady companions, into the Dauphin's garden, on the side of the Tuileries. A unit of *Fédérés* passed by keeping their hats on their heads, and, soon joined by the mob, began to insult the Queen. The three officers managed to force the *Fédérés* to go away, after having thrown off some of their hats, and the Queen was able to return to her apartments where she remained. As early as 5 August, the Régiment des Gardes Suisses, about two thirds of its official strength, had been marched into Paris to reinforce its two companies which were already on duty there alongside the Grenadiers of the National Guard who were responsible for the protection of the Tuileries Palace but whose defection was feared. The danger having passed, the regiment returned to their barracks in the suburbs. The same day, 'the section of revolutionaries called Mauconseil was the first to demand the overthrow of the King. Finally, it will be forty-seven of the forty-eight Paris sections that vote for his deposition. In the meantime, the Mayor of Paris, Pétion, postponed the start of hostilities in order to better prepare the plan.'[35] Tension was extreme but the sans-culottes were appeased with some sacrificial victims: 'They contented themselves with walking some royalist heads in Paris, fixed on the tips of their pikes.'[36] Three days later, in the night of 8/9 August, the 600 Swiss Guards received the order to once again come to the Tuileries Palace, and quickly. However, it was only the following day, around midnight, that the tocsin sounded, calling all the Parisian sections to unite with the *Fédérés*, their ranks soon swollen by the mob as well as many of the National Guardsmen who abandoned their posts. Facing this mass of several tens of thousands who would soon overwhelm them, were the Swiss, little more than 800, reinforced by about 200 French gentlemen, among them many former Gardes du Corps.

At 8:30 a.m. on 10 August, the King finally agreed to leave the palace and go to the Salle du Manège where the Legislative Assembly was sitting, to put himself under its protection. Furious at seeing their prey escape, the rioters then went on the assault, driving before them the Swiss who, after having defended the gates then the courtyards of the Palace, fell back to the entrance where 400 to 450 among them fought a final battle, in the vestibule and the formal staircase, refusing to lay down their arms. When the order to do so from Louis XVI finally reached them, the mob threw themselves on the unarmed Swiss; the massacre, and the barbarous atrocities that followed against those in the palace, prisoners and civilians, men, women and children, were among the unspeakable crimes that were to sully the history of the French Revolution. A young artillery captain, Napoleone Buonaparte, then on leave in Paris, observed these events and followed the crowd as far as the Tuileries Palace arriving when the carnage was coming to an end. Twenty-five years later, he retained a clear memory of it:

34 Alain-Jacques Tornare, *10 août 1792 – Les Tuileries. L'été tragique des relations franco-suisses* (Lausanne: PPUR, 2012), p.118.

35 Tornare, *10 août 1792*, p.118.

36 NA *Journal de Constant-Rebecque,* Vol.I.

> The Palace forced, and the King brought into the Assembly, I ventured to enter the garden. Never since has any of my battlefields given me the notion of so many corpses, as I was presented by the masses of Swiss; either the confines of the site made the number stand out, or if it was the result of the first impression that I experienced of this kind. I saw women well placed to give themselves over to final indecencies on the corpses of the Swiss...[37]

Around 5:00 a.m., an insurrectional commune took the place of the legal authority and immediately decreed the dismissal of the King who was then, along with his family, considered a prisoner.

Fearing the reaction of the troops and in particular of the constitutional generals, the Assembly immediately despatched representatives named Commissioners of the National Assembly to the different armies. Getting the troops of the Armée du Nord to take the new oath was seen as a priority as it was the nearest to Paris, and thus the greater potential threat. Present in this army was *Lieutenant-général* Dumouriez, who, after having relinquished in turn the Ministries for Foreign Affairs then that of War, where he had been in office from 13 to 17 June 1792, had joined Luckner's army, at the moment when it retreated from Kortrijk and Menen, and now commanded the Maulde Camp. On 15 August he was the first to take the required oath, displaying a total submission to the Parisian decrees and so giving him the opportunity to replace his commander, *Lieutenant-général* Arthur Dillon. The latter, Théobald's brother, had immediately opposed the new decrees, as Dumouriez described in a letter to a friend, dated 14 August:

> Dillon has just lost himself by a royalist declaration, that he signalled in the order of his camp at Pont-sur-Sambre, and which he ordered me to publish in mine. I formally disobeyed him, and I have delivered these documents to the Assembly's Commissioners who have just arrived at the camp. I hope finally to render great services to the cause of the sovereignty and liberty of the French people. I will work for it with all my strength, as well as to restore Belgian liberty.[38]

La Fayette had already, on 8 August, been threatened with arrest so, learning that four deputies were on their way to demand the troops' oath as well as his dismissal, he requested that the civil authorities at Sedan arrest them. They were provisionally detained but the troops demanded their release and in the evening of the 19 August, La Fayette fled accompanied by 40 or so others, including part of his staff, 24 officers and their servants, to seek refuge abroad. The fugitives were detained at nightfall by a party of volunteers from Limburg in Austrian pay and, when questioned, La Fayette declared that he sought to bypass the Austrian troops to get to Maastricht and from there go to Holland, England and America. The ordinary officers were imprisoned in the fortress at Antwerp while the constitutionals

37 Emmanuel-Auguste-Dieudonné de Las Cases, *Mémorial de Sainte-Hélène: Journal de la vie privée et des conversations de l'Empereur Napoléon, à Sainte-Hélène* (London: Colburn, 1823), Vol.III p.168.

38 Jean-Gabriel Peltier, *Dernier tableau de Paris, ou Récit historique de la Révolution du 10 août 1792, des Causes qui l'ont produite, de Événements qui l'ont précédée, et des Crimes qui l'ont suivie* (London: Chez l'Auteur, Hôtel de la Sablonière, Leicester-fields, 1793), Vol.II, pp.151–152.

were successively taken to Namur, Luxembourg and then Wesel, finally being detained at Magdeburg, in Eastern Prussia. La Fayette protested, claiming that they should not be considered as enemy soldiers since, in taking flight to escape the factions that had violated the constitution, they had relinquished their places in the French army and should be considered as simple travellers who, although not having been able to remove their uniforms, only sought to go into exile. In 1794, La Fayette was to be transferred to the fortress at Olomouc, now in the Czech Republic, where he remained imprisoned until 1797.

On 19 August 1792, the coalition forces entered France in three columns, that on the left was the Austrian corps of the Freidrich William Fürst zu Hohenlohe-Kirchberg which was to cross the Rhine at Mannheim and to march on Thionville while that on the right, under Sachsen-Teschen, the Governor of the Netherlands, was to advance on Lille and Maubeuge In the centre were the Prussians who had assembled at Koblenz, reinforced by French émigrés and Austrians from Namur, who were to seize Longwy and Verdun and so separate the French Armée du Nord from that of the Centre.[39] While the émigré Armée de Condé would remain on the Rhine and Bourbon's corps in reserve in the Liège area, the Armée des Princes, also called that of the Centre, would join the Prussians to march through Lorraine and Champagne on to Paris. The émigrés themselves had sought this arrangement as they hoped that French troops would then rally to their cause, joining their officers and other monarchists on the three frontiers, in the North, Lorraine and Alsace. Yet despite the protests of *Maréchal* de Castries, the Armée des Princes found itself relegated to the second rank, that of supplementary troops, to make an inglorious return in foreigners' waggons.

Lack of money had delayed the organisation of the émigré army and it had only started to receive, due to the already heavy rains, tents around 15 August, but above all it severely lacked artillery. The Armée du Centre had been reviewed at Trier, by the King of Prussia himself who, strongly impressed, had remained hat in hand throughout the march past by the units composed of the French nobility, 'never had one seen a finer, better dressed, better disposed army; the cavalry, above all, was magnificent and superiorly mounted.'[40] This corps had as many officers or gentlemen as soldiers, and as much cavalry as infantry; beside the former Household troops of the King and his brothers, there were many companies of officers and gentlemen, from the infantry and cavalry but also the navy, along with regional coalitions of volunteers. There were also several foreign units formerly in the French army such as the Bercheny hussars, that officers from the other hussar regiments had joined, and remnants of the Irish Brigade as well as some others paid for the duration of the campaign, like the Régiment de Wittgentsein and the Chasseurs étrangers de Polignac. Among the cavalry, the corps of Hommes d'armes à cheval, commanded by the Marquis d'Autichamp, was especially remarkable being the reconstitution of the former Gendarmerie, the élite unit of the royal cavalry. Only the Régiment de Vexin represented the former royal French infantry although in truth the few hundred French soldiers in it were joined by French-speaking Belgians and Liégois. Nevertheless, the regiment's emigration was considered highly symbolic and the Princes had insisted on attaching it to the vanguard of their troops, in the hope of rallying other infantry regiments to their cause.

39 Tranié & Carimagni, *La Patrie en danger*, p.38.

40 Maurice de Barberey, *Dix années d'émigration – Souvenirs et correspondance du comte de Neuilly* (Paris: Douniol, 1865), p.49.

After the fall of Longwy, which surrendered on 20 August, then that of Verdun on 2 September, the allies laid siege to Thionville which was summoned on 4 September. The investment was confided to the royalist troops, reinforced by some Austrian artillery. The celebrated writer and politician François-René de Chateaubriand, then an ordinary volunteer in the 7th Breton company, found himself working as a navvy:

> These earthworks went slowly because we were all officers, young and old, little accustomed to wield the shovel and the pickaxe. We lacked wheelbarrows and we carried the earth in our coats which served us as sacks. The fire from a lunette opened up on us; it bothered us all the more as we could not reply: two eight-pound pieces and a Coehorn mortar that did not have the range were all our artillery.[41]

Thus, the majority of the Armée des Princes were tied down uselessly under the walls of the city and exposed to its fire.

At the head of the combined Armées du Nord and du Centre, the latter renamed Armée des Ardennes, Dumouriez had immediately concentrated his efforts on the Belgian coast, to chase the Austrians from the adjoining provinces and then drive them across the Maas and then the Rhine. He was determined to make up for a lack of French troops by enrolling as many foreign volunteers as he could to join the revolutionary crusade which was to set Europe on fire:

> The Swiss regiments had just been disbanded, he had three of them in garrisons in the North, he gave orders to employ all the NCOs and soldiers who would present themselves, and to make them the basis of eight free battalions, each of eight hundred men, admitting Austrian deserters into them as well … He also ordered the Belgians' corps which was to serve in his advance-guard to be brought up to six thousand men. He asked the Minister of War for an increase in troops and arms …[42]

However, the situation demanded that he organise the defence of Sedan, on 28 August, while the allies besieged Thionville and Verdun, nevertheless he 'announced that he would return in six weeks, and that he would make the expedition to Belgium this year, which no one believed'.[43] Knowing Verdun to be difficult to defend, he held a council of war at which it was decided that his army of 5,000 cavalry, 18,000 infantry and a strong artillery arm of 60 pieces, excluding the cannons with the infantry battalions, would withdraw by marching rapidly on Châlons, crossing the Forest of Argonne, then on to Sainte-Menehould before finally halting on the immense plain of Champagne Pouilleuse, or perhaps behind the Marne, to give time for reinforcements to arrive and so balance the opposing forces. On 3 September, he put himself at the head of 17,000 men at Grandpré in the Forest of Argonne and ordered Beurnonville and Kellermann to join him in Champagne on the axis of the enemies' advance.

41 François-René de Chateaubriand, *Mémoires d'outre-tombe* (Paris: Penaud, 1849), Vol.1, pp.58–59.
42 Dumouriez, *La vie et les mémoires*, Vol.II, p.380.
43 Dumouriez, *La vie et les mémoires* Vol.II, p.380.

The news of the fall of Verdun, redoubled the fury of the Parisians who, in answer to the call of Danton, the Jacobin Minister of Justice, gathered the following day on the Champ de Mars to march on Lorraine to retake the city. Profiting from the political vacuum created by the fall of the King, the Paris Commune installed on its own authority a Surveillance Committee that decided to use this armed mass to cleanse the capital of internal enemies. At the toll of the tocsin, bands marched on the prisons and began to slaughter refractory priests and aristocrats, men and women of any age. One of the first victims was the Princesse de Lamballe, close friend of Marie-Antoinette, who was assassinated on 3 September 1792, in the street, by a frenzied mob that decapitated her and abused her corpse; her head was then carried on the end of a pike under the window of the Queen, incarcerated with her family in a tower of the Temple Prison. The massacre was to last four days and nights, and extended on 9 September to Versailles where a convoy of prisoners from Orléans was intercepted, 44 of the 52 detainees, including the Duc de Cossé-Brissac, were murdered and their heads stuck on the railings of the palace where 13 more people were slaughtered in the evening in the Queen's stables which was being used as a prison.

On 9 September, doubtless due to this terrible news, the Duke of Brunswick held a meeting at Verdun with the Comte de Provence, who had taken upon himself the title of Regent of France due to the captivity of his brother Louis XVI although, at this time, the allies refused to recognise it. Brunswick informed him that he was abandoning the siege of Thionville, leaving some émigré infantry in observation, and marching on to Champagne. On 10 September, the Comte d'Artois, at the head of a light corps of nearly 6,000 cavalry in 56 squadrons; the emigrated part of the Irish Brigade; some cannons of the former colonial artillery; the Régiment de Vexin and the Compagnie des Gentilshommes de Rouault, about 7,000 in all, joined him and was attached to the Austrian corps of Belgian-born *Feldzeugmeister* Charles-Joseph de Croix, Comte de Clerfayt.

Forced to abandon his position at Grandpré, Dumouriez retreated onto Champagne Pouilleuse to block the Paris road, from Verdun and Châlons, by occupying the heights behind Sainte-Menehould. The allies followed more than pursued him, already anticipating victory. The poet Johann Wolfgang von Goethe was with the staff in the vanguard of the Prussian army which in turn led the coalition forces, and described the eve of, what was to be named, the Battle of Valmy, 'During this march, I was brought by chance into the suite of the King [of Prussia], then into that of the Duke of Brunswick; I conversed with the Prince of Reuss and other military diplomats of my acquaintance. These groups of riders populated the scenery nicely. One would have wanted a Van der Meulen to immortalise this march.'[44]

Instead of pushing on, the Prussians established their headquarters at Somme-Tourbe on 19 September, so giving time for Kellermann's force to join Dumouriez and form his left wing. The following day, 20 September 1792, the thunder unleashed by the French and Prussian artillery had no other result than to keep the two opposing forces at a respectful distance. The émigré corps, held in reserve behind La Croix-en-Champagne, was the flank-guard on the right of the coalition position, drawn out from Somme-Suippe to Suippe, with its headquarters still at Somme-Tourbe. On the same day, the royalist troops around

44 Johann Wolfgang von Goethe, *Campagne in Frankreich* (1822) translated as *Campagne de France* (1898) (Lausanne: Guild du Livre, 1968), p.35.

Thionville received the order to march on Etain and Verdun where they found it very difficult to obtain food and lodging from the Prussians.

At dawn on 21 September, each side observed the other. The Prussian position was closer to Paris than that of Dumouriez and when Austrian reinforcements under Clerfayt arrived the émigrés demanded that they be authorised to march west, thinking they could rally royalists as well as constitutionals desirous to put an end to the bloodbath and re-establish the monarchy. However, nothing came of it and, on 22 September, the German generals went to Dumouriez's headquarters not to negotiate the surrender of the French troops but to arrange the conditions for their own retreat to the frontiers. The Duke of Brunswick succeeded in convincing the King of Prussia to abandon the plains of Champagne, despite the exhortations of the émigrés who were kept in inactivity, by painting the bleakest picture to him. On 20 September the Prussians had had 1,200 men killed and fired 10,000 cannon balls to no effect but because of deplorable logistics, the troops were without drinking water, food and very often camping equipment with their supply line vulnerable to raids by the French hussars in the Argonne Forest. Finally, under the cover of the night of 25/26 September, Brunswick beat a retreat in appalling conditions. Continual rains not only destroyed the roads but also exhausted the horses, dysentery ravaged the Prussian army and hostility within the allied army would henceforth hold the émigrés responsible for these reverses. Outwitted by Dumouriez, the King of Prussia was pleased to find a plausible excuse to accept Brunswick's plan to withdraw his exhausted and disgusted army to Sedan and Montmédy, to recoup their strength and be in a state for a new campaign.

The royalist infantry had in turn to retreat to join the rest of the Armée du Centre at Arlon, and Chateaubriand, who had remained in Lorraine, was witness to this disastrous retreat.

> We quit Verdun. The rains had broken down the roads, everywhere we came across caissons, gun carriages, cannons, carts overturned, *vivandières* with their infants on their backs, soldiers dying or dead in the mud. On crossing a ploughed field, I was stuck sunk to the knees; Ferron and another of my comrades dragging me out despite me: I begged them to leave me there, I preferred to die.[45]

The debacle had become total because of the throng that followed the émigré army: women, children, domestics, churchmen and common people despairing of the fall of the monarchy, the Republican proclamation of 21 September and the slaughter of its enemies, establishing the Terror. Keeping the best routes for themselves, requisitioning lodging and forage, the Prussians, who abandoned their wounded and sick at the sides of the roads, stole from the baggage of the Armée des Princes. The Comte d'Espinchal, who had been in Champagne with the émigré cavalry, noted in his journal, on 30 September: 'The Prussian hussars came, in the night, to pillage our baggage and we cannot get satisfaction from their generals.' The deplorable weather persisted and turned the retreat into a disaster.[46]

45 Chateaubriand, *Mémoires d'outre-tombe*, Vol.I pp.58–59.

46 Ernest d'Hauterive, *Journal d'émigration du comte d'Espinchal* (Paris: Perrin, 1912), p.431.

> 6 October – Stay at Lion [Lion-devant-Dun]. Frightful weather, rain. The King of Prussia arrives at Dun with his army the camp of which we see, from our village. The Prussian army is full of sick and in a state of ruin that cannot be conceived. The roads are full of soldiers who are dying and those unable to follow.
>
> 8 October – ... we all have the appearance of being in complete rout and the most disastrous battle would not produce more unfortunate effects. Moreover, the Prussians are in the same state. Their army is in confusion ... We see a quantity of baggage stopped in the mud, horses broken down, men dying of exhaustion or dysentery ...[47]

Before long, it was clear that the Prussians had promised to restore Verdun and Longwy to the republicans in exchange for their slack pursuit but, as a consequence, the line of retreat avoided the main routes, and the important towns, making it even more difficult and destructive. Finally, the Prussian troops found refuge in the Austrian Netherlands from 12 October.

Hope of a successful return to France for the émigrés was lost. The majority of the royalists taken prisoner during this campaign had been immediately shot and several gentlemen had preferred to take their own lives rather than fall into the hands of the republicans. Their fate was sealed by the Law of 9 October 1792:

> Art.1. In enforcement of the decree that pronounces the sentence of death against the émigrés taken with arms in hand, they will be, within twenty-four hours, delivered to the executor of justice and put to death, after it has been declared by a military commission composed of five people and nominated by the headquarters of the army, that they were émigrés and that they had been taken with arms in hand, or that they had served against France.
>
> 2. It will be the same with regard to all foreigners who, since 14 July 1789, left the service of France, and, after having abandoned their post, joined the émigrés or enemies.
>
> 3. The official reports of execution will be sent, within the week, to the Minister of War, who will pass them without delay to the National Convention.
>
> 4. The enemy powers will be responsible for any violation of quarter that, by a false application of the right to reprisals, could be committed by the French émigrés.

Thirteen émigrés taken prisoner during the retreat were sent to Paris to be immediately guillotined. The Armée du Centre, finally reunited on 12 October, was no longer able to provide for the needs of its soldiers, so from that date certificates and passports were issued to those who wished to flee with their families to England, Holland or Germany. What is

47 Hauterive, *Journal d'émigration du comte d'Espinchal*, pp.444–445.

more, an Imperial edict ordered émigrés who were not part of the Armée des Princes to leave the Austrian Netherlands in eight days, under pain of being expelled *manu militari*. The émigrés however were never to know quite how badly they were regarded by the courts of Vienna and Potsdam; this was revealed by a letter of Baron Thugut, the future Austrian director of Foreign Affairs, dated 23 October 1792:

> The experience of this campaign appears to have proved that the very nature of the émigrés renders them hardly combinable with our troops and as well only renders them subjects to often become encumbrances in the subsistence, mobility and the operations of the armies of His Majesty, so that in considering the little service that had been got from them and might be promised for the future, it seems evident that in this regard, any future expense for them, even was it to be less considerable, will be always badly spent. It appears, in consequence, that one should know not to hesitate to cut them off, for the future, from all hope whatever of help, if until now it was impossible to imagine some means to break them up or to disencumber the allied courts of them in another means whatever.
>
> But these émigrés find themselves in so deplorable a misery that a great part, ready to perish from hunger in the full force of the term, without coats, without shoes, will be, I think, not physically in a state to follow the order which may be given to disperse them. It is to be feared that despair and absolute destitution of everything will soon lead them to great excesses, to throw themselves into the woods, to infest the highways, and if one wished to take the steps to expel them by armed force, the neighbouring States refusing to receive them, one would end up by being forced to exterminate them.
>
> As it appears desirable that one should avoid coming to such disagreeable extremes, I can only submit to Your Excellence's consideration if it would be possible to reach an agreement with the Prussian court to still provide in these circumstances, with the strictest and most severe economy, for the most pressing needs of the émigrés who make up the former royal army until it is possible to settle upon some sort of project to rid His Majesty's States of them.[48]

After being greeted in triumph in Paris, including by his political enemies, on 15 October, Dumouriez returned abruptly to Flanders to invade the Austrian Netherlands. On 6 November 1792, his forces threw back the Imperial troops of Sachsen-Teschen at Jemappes, west of Mons, and, a few days later seized Bruges and Brussels, which he entered on 14 November, then Liège on 28 November and finally Antwerp, which surrendered on 29 November. Dumouriez then took up winter quarters in the expectation of receiving the means, which he sorely lacked, to pursue the Austrians beyond the Maas. Only the troops with his deputy Miranda, who had just seized Antwerp, were in a state to march on the Maas.

48 Cited in Ernest Daudet, *Histoire de l'Émigration pendant la Révolution Française* (Paris: Hachette, 1905), Vol.I, p.212.

Born in 1750 at Caracas in Venezuela, Francisco Miranda was a South American adventurer who, like so many other foreign volunteers, had placed his sword at the service of the Revolution. He had served in North Africa as an officer in the Spanish army but with a brilliant, but independent and irreverent, humanist mind he fell afoul of the authorities and spent some time in prison. Released in 1780, he served in the American War of Independence in Cuba and Florida, despite being imprisoned again. Fearing once again for his liberty, Miranda fled in 1783 to the United States where he met the Marquis de La Fayette with whom he formed a friendship. He then travelled to and throughout Europe, acquiring a mastery of English, Italian and French, and served France, apparently, as a secret agent. Losing his employment due to the Revolution, he went in 1791 to England where he tried to gather support, including from William Pitt, for his project to create an independent empire stretching from the Mississippi to the Cape Horn. Appointed to the French army in the summer of 1792 as *maréchal de camp* 'he had gone to join Général Dumouriez in Champagne at the camp at Grandpré, attached himself to him, and had been extremely useful in the different attacks of the Prussians, and notably in the retreat of 15 September, onto Sainte Ménehould [sic].'[49] He was then named *lieutenant-général* at the beginning of November.

An offensive by *Général en chef* Custine had also been successful, he took Mainz on 20 October, crossed the Rhine and entered Frankfurt three days later. Dumouriez, however, wrote to the Minister of War, Pache, to express his opposition to such an advance:

> I am very opposed to any offensive and external war, above all to any war that takes us out of our natural frontiers, that is to say to the south, the Pyrenees and the Alps, to the east and north-east the Rhine. I would be equally opposed to the invasion of the Low Countries, if I would not see in the liberty of our neighbours a defence more solid than that of strongholds, and much less expensive ...[50]

The Batavian revolutionary committee, created in November 1791, advocated the invasion of the United Provinces and the legion of Dutch patriots had been one of the first foreign units raised following the decree of April 1792. It was proposed on 8 July by Herman Daendels, of the Batavian committee, and the Assembly had decreed its formation on 26 July. Although it was called the Légion Franche étrangère, as it had been completed with Swiss and Flemish, Dumouriez described it as the Légion Hollandaise. In August 1792 the new unit joined the legions of volunteers from Brabant and Liège already employed within the Armée du Nord. It was intended to be a legion of light troops with 2,822 men organised in four infantry battalions of fusiliers and chasseurs, one of chasseurs à cheval, and two artillery batteries.

The small royalist army of the Duc de Bourbon, hitherto unemployed, assisted at Jemappes, without taking part, and was with the coalition troops in their withdrawal to Fleurus and Brussels. Bourbon's troops then retreated eastwards towards the Liège region where they were to find their comrades in arms of the Armée du Centre. In the face of the

49 Dumouriez, *La vie et les mémoires*, Vol.IV (1792–1793), p.17.

50 Charles François Dumouriez [Dumourier], *Correspondance avec Pache, ministre de la Guerre, sur la campagne de Belgique en 1792* (Paris: Denné, 1793), p.66, tenth letter from Dumouriez to the Minister of War, 10 November 1792.

republicans' advance, the retreat became a desperate flight, the Austrian and royalist troops along with thousands of émigrés who had taken refuge in Belgium pell-mell on the roads to Holland or Germany. The Chevalier de Mautort recalled his arrival at Tongeren.

> [A] small and strong walled town ... It was so packed with carriages and people from Brussels that all the inns, all the houses were full, and what is more the square was covered by more than 200 carriages whose horses had passed the night attached to the traces; many people had slept in their carriages and had only been able to procure some bread to eat and a little wine to drink. The corps of Gendarmerie had been based there since its retreat from France; it was paid and fed by the Emperor. It was commanded by M d'Autichamp.[51]

Having reached the Liège region, what remained of the émigré army crossed the Meuse (Maas) at Visé between 19 and 22 November 1792. On 23 November, the King of Prussia informed the French King's brothers that from 1 December he would cease to provide the royalist troops with subsistence. Austrian assistance was also suddenly withdrawn by the Viennese court, which moreover forbade the admission of French gentlemen into its forces but negotiated to take the paid regiments into its service, notably the Hussards de Saxe and de Bercheny as well as the Régiment de Royal-Allemand, in which many of the soldiers originated from lands in Alsace and Lorraine previously owned by German princes. The émigrés, now treated like plague victims, were refused permission to stay in German states, for fear of attracting the fury of the revolutionary troops. Consequently, the Princes resolved to disband the army, or rather what remained of it, gathered in the area around Jülich, Aachen and the Principality of Stavelot. On 23 November, the Comte de Provence drafted a letter to all the émigré troops:

> Gentlemen, since the beginning of our misfortunes, no situation has affected us more painfully than that in which we now find ourselves. The powers for whose kindness or efforts in favour of our cause we should never forget, require, for the present time, our dispersal and disarmament. It is not to the entire body of the nobility, it is not to the loyal troops, it is not to the French who after all have sacrificed all for honour, their attachment to Religion, their love for their King, that we will do the injustice of recommending courage in adversity. Ours is not to succumb under the weight of misfortune. Nothing will shake our fidelity to the sacred principals which we have undertaken to defend. Nothing will ever weaken the sentiments which unite us to you and, if we withdraw for some time, this will only be to solicit new means and to make ourselves useful to the King and the Motherland. The agents who we will leave in the different States where you will have retired will render us a faithful account of your situation, inform you of the results of our steps and provide you with the help we may obtain. Your patience and your courage will finally vanquish all obstacles and the esteem of the entire world will be the reward

51 François, duc de La Rochefoucauld, *Souvenirs du 10 août et de l'Armée de Bourbon* (Paris: Calman-Lévy, 1929), pp.206–207.

> for noble and sustained conduct. As for us, Gentlemen, devoted to work without rest to prepare this happy event, all our cares will be aimed to procure you a destiny worthy of your sacrifices. Our only ambition will always be to live for you or die with you.[52]

With no income or compensation, the émigrés had to raise money by whatever means they could. Claude-Augustin de Tercier, former *capitaine* in the Régiment de la Martinique, then one of Monsieur's Garde du Corps in which he had served in the last campaign under the orders of the Comte Charles de Damas, was one:

> The two squadrons of the Gardes du Corps of the Princes were kept on for a month and sent into the land of Jülich, a principality of the Elector of Bavaria. We came to be cantoned in the small village of Rauderadt and were disbanded fifteen days later. I was then obliged to sell my horse and all my military equipment for a very modest price.[53]

In mid-December, the King's brothers had to leave the remains of their army, having been permitted by the King of Prussia to settle in Hamm, in Westphalia, which the Comte d'Artois later described as a 'trap pit.' They provided their agents with 320,000 livres, for the relief of their beloved nobility, taken from the 750,000 livres of aid they had been granted by the King of Prussia and the Empress of Russia.

For the survivors of this wretched campaign, it was now a question of finding shelter, some joined the Prince de Condé but the majority chose to remain in the United Provinces, which was closer and still neutral, or in the Rhineland cities they had access to. One of those who went to Germany was the Comte d'Haussonville whose son later wrote,

> At Düsseldorf, my father met with many of his acquaintances who had left Paris after him, and with the mass of émigrés driven back from all parts by the invading march of the French armies. The small towns of Germany were congested with them. There were officers of all ranks who had left their units, gentlemen abandoning their lands, courtiers expelled from the Court, and mixed with them, many wives who had come to re-join their husbands.[54]

The Republic of the Seven United Provinces was then, like Britain, neutral and the French royalists who sought refuge there were variously welcomed, warmly at Utrecht or Nijmegen, or with some hostility at Amsterdam and Rotterdam. They found that society was often Francophile due to the Huguenots who had themselves fled France at the end of the

52 Comte de D.P. (Laroche-Poncié) *Correspondance condéenne précédée d'une notice sur l'armée de Condé, de Lettres et Proclamations des princes étrangers pendant leur émigration et d'autres documents authentiques et importants* (Paris: Dentu, 1850), pp.15–16.

53 Charles de La Chanonie, *Mémoires politiques et militaires du général Tercier, (1770–1816)* (Paris: Plon, 1891), p.93.

54 Paul Gabriel de Haussonville, 'Souvenirs de l'émigration et de l'Empire', *Revue des Deux Mondes* (Vol. XXV, 1878), p.100.

Seventeenth Century after the Revocation of the Edict of Nantes. They also discovered that the banks and commercial houses remained in contact with France which allowed those with capital the ability to realise it.

Many did not go so far, seeking safety within the walls of Maastricht, despite it being somewhat remote from the industrial and mercantile cities of the United Provinces. At the end of 1792, there were nearly ten thousand Brabant, Liégois and French émigrés in the city after the French invasion of Belgium and the disbanding of the émigré troops. François de La Rochefoucauld, a former *capitaine* of the Chasseurs de Champagne, who had served as an ordinary soldier in the company of the Volontaires des Champagne in the Armée de Bourbon, arrived there on 10 November 1792:

> All the French scattered a short time before in Germany had made their way, in this first moment of despair, to Maastricht, being the first city where they could safely halt, look behind them and take a carefully considered decision on their situation. Those who were absolutely without means were in the cantonments of the Princes at Liège, others had remained with the debris of the Armée de Bourbon; finally, others had returned to France. But all who were back from the Armée des Princes and in the neighbouring towns were at the time at Maastricht.[55]

For those who were penniless or who had no family to join, it was preferable to remain together in adversity rather than disperse, protected not only by Maastricht's defences but also the prevailing Dutch neutrality.

55 La Rochefoucauld, *Souvenirs*, p.209.

2

Dumouriez Checked: the Remnants of the Armée des Princes at the Siege of Maastricht

Built on the left bank of the Maas, the city of Maastricht stands at the junction of what was then the Bishopric of Liège region to the south, Dutch Limburg and the Prussian possession of the Duchy of Kleve to the north, Flanders to the west and finally the Rhineland states to the east. Its strategic position had seen the French lay siege to it on several occasions in the last two centuries indeed Charles de Batz de Castelmore, seigneur d'Artagnan, *capitaine* of the Mousquetaires du Roi, later to be immortalised by Alexandre Dumas, had died under its walls in 1673. In 1792 it was protected on the eastern side by the wide river, and on the three others by ramparts that were well-constructed and generally in a reasonable state. From the right bank access was by a stone bridge defended by a fort, forming the important suburb of Wyck; the bridge's three arches were permanently mined so communication to the city could bc cut. Islands in the river had defensive works and around the whole perimeter, except where covered by the river, there were ditches that could be easily flooded. Generally, the city was surrounded by meadows which provided clear fields of fire but to the north hills closed in on the river around the village of Smeermaas and a significant hill, Caberg, dominated this part of the city but was only to be fortified in the next century. To the south, there was a steep plateau which extended, along the Mass, as far as Liège, and so from 1701 Fort Sint Pieter, taking its name from that of the plateau, was constructed to complete the city's defences in this sector; it had been strengthened over time and was connected to the city by underground passages providing shelter for its citizens.

The city's governor was Prince Friedrich of Hesse-Cassel, brother of the reigning landgrave and *Lieutenant-Generaal* in the service of the United Provinces, who, if he did not have a great deal of experience, was to prove himself both courageous and humane. There were only 1,800 men in the garrison in early November 1792 but its strength soon grew to more than 4,000 men, with contracted Brunswick units alongside those of the army of the United Provinces. The Dutch army units were the:

1st and 2nd Squadrons of the Hesse-Cassel Dragoons;[1]
2nd Battalion of the Waldeck Regiment of German infantry;
2nd Battalion of the Schmid Regiment of Graubünden (4th Swiss) infantry;
2nd Battalion of the Schepper Regiment of infantry (national);
Two companies of the Regiment Artilleristen (commanded by *Major* Frederik Lombach);
Mineurs en Sappeurs (brought up to 2,000 men by recruiting labourers, *handlangers*, locally)

The Dutch units were understrength as 'a part were absent, either through leave, as is always [customary] in times of peace among the troops of the Republic, and another part recruiting to work towards the augmentation of the units, that had been agreed in order to put the army on a respectable footing.'[2] The Brunswick corps had been in the pay of the United Provinces since 1788:

Two squadrons J.C. von Riedesel Dragoons, about 200 men;
Grenadier Battalion, four companies;
Infantry Regiment F.A. von Riedesel, two battalions;
Infantry Regiment Prinz Friederich, two battalions;
Jäger Company (*Hauptmann* Henneman), about 200 men;
artillery detachment (*Hauptmann* Knoch and Mohelmi), 100 men.[3]

Military opinion indicated the garrison should have over 6,780 men to be effective, due to the extent of the city's fortifications, and it was especially short of artillerymen.

The advancing French republicans, despite Dutch neutrality, immediately tried to gain control of the city by bluff:

> [T]he taking of Liège that had taken place on 28 [November], an officer arrived at Maastricht with a trumpeter, charged with an official letter on behalf of Maréchal de camp Eustace, commanding the light troops of the French army. He demanded from the Prince passage through the city for 1,500 men and that of artillery and ammunition by water, adding to it menacing insinuations which did not prevent the Prince Governor refusing all positively.[4]

John Skey Eustace was an American adventurer and merchant who had obtained the rank of *colonel* on 20 April 1792 and commanded a forward light infantry brigade. He demanded, in particular, that the émigrés at Maastricht be delivered to him, doubtless in pursuit of the

1 This was a Dutch national regiment of which Prince Friedrich was the colonel, since 1768, thus it bore his name.
2 Stichting Historische Maastricht (SHM), Anonymous account of the Siege of Maastricht.
3 R. Lavergne, 'Les émigrés au siège de Maëstricht', *Revue des questions historiques*, Vol.n°63, 1 January 1898, pp.516–531. Also Paul Demet *'We are accustomed to do our Duty': German Auxiliaries with the British Army 1793–95* (Warwick: Helion, 2018), Table 21, p.200.
4 SHM, Van Dijk Manuscript.

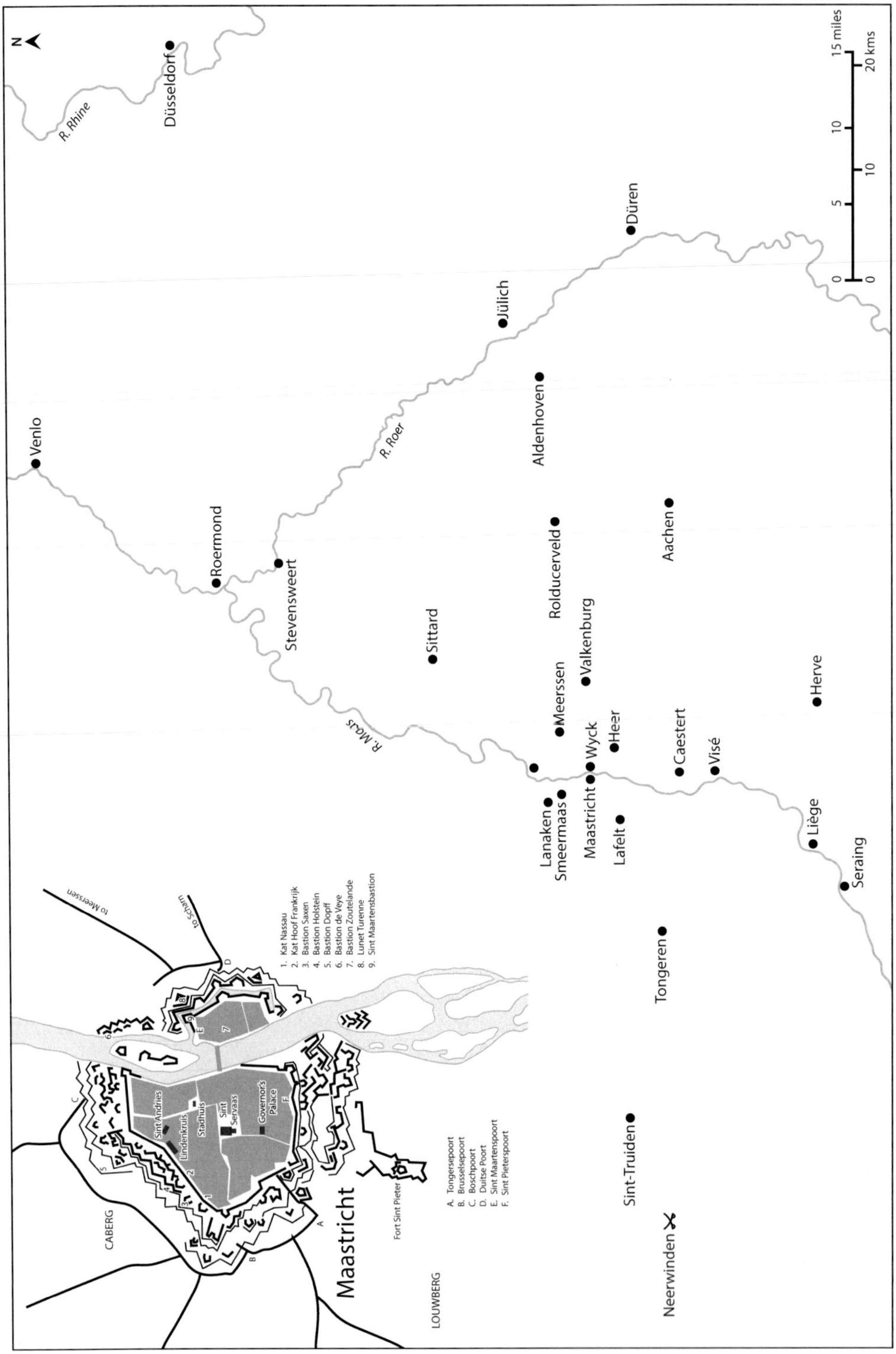

The siege of Maastricht.

Law of 9 October 1792. The Prince of Hesse rejected the threats and would not permit the city to be approached. On 30 November, the American returned to the city, this time the prince received him but refused his demand to authorise the baking of bread for the republican troops. He nevertheless agreed to allow French officers with passports to enter the city but after they had used this permission to preach the principles of liberty and equality as well as hatred for the émigrés in the inns and cabarets, the governor ordered the city's gates to be shut to them. The Prince of Hesse, like many others, expected the French to immediately invest the city, their cavalry now regularly interfering with its provisioning such as diverting approaching convoys to Liège. The capitulation of Antwerp, on 29 November, enabled the French to declare the Scheldt free for navigation despite international agreements to which France had hitherto been a guarantor; in response, the United Provinces and Britain felt compelled to arm. As early as 30 November, Dumouriez submitted his analysis of the situation to the Minister of War:

> You will observe moreover, Citizen Minister, that I am very far from being sure of the Dutch; the opening of the Scheldt can only infinitely displease them. I would not be surprised if England and Prussia urged the Stadholder to declare his resentment. There is a garrison of 9,000 men at Maastricht and preparations for its defence made which at least indicates ill will. I cannot begin to advance without knowing the stance of the Dutch; for if they fell on my left, while the Austrians were to fall on my right, the army of the Republic would be irretrievably lost, and it would be all up for the liberty of Belgium and Liège for ever …[5]

As part of the preparations, on 9 December the Prince of Hesse invited property owners in the city and the Overmaas region to place their goods and provisions, in particular grain and livestock, within the shelter of the city's fortifications. Already the republican troops were no more than a few leagues from Maastricht, having taken Aachen on 8 December and 10 days later they occupied Valkenburg, about 15 kilometres east of Maastricht on the right bank of the Maas, and nearby villages. The prince protested about this violation of the territory of the United Provinces but Dumouriez excused it as a mistake caused by a lack of maps. A week later, with more incidents, Dumouriez gave the governor the option to share policing measures, proposing that his garrison be posted at different locations to mark the territory of the Republic and so avoid such unfortunate incidents. The governor did not fall for this attempt to disperse and so weaken his garrison and continued preparations for Maastricht's defence.

> The basins of Sint Pieterspoort [gate] and the ditches susceptible to flooding were filled, the parapets of the Fort raised by woolsacks, the batteries repaired and provided with cannons and mortars. The latter were placed in the advance works. They charged fire pots to illuminate places as needed. Wyck's Sint Maartenspoort was firstly barricaded, then blocked with manure. Having received positive orders from The Hague to guard against surprise, continual patrols from one advance post

5 Dumouriez, *Correspondance*, Dumouriez to Pache, Liège, 30 November 1792 (Year I of the Republic).

> to the next guarded the covered way during the night. The those of dragoons observed during the day what was happening in the neighbourhood of the city. The artillery worked with as much ardour in the arsenals as in the batteries. The miners made fougasses and brought on the mines. The workmen and peasants made fascines and gabions, and platforms and merlons. The magazine of victuals already formed in December was augmented.[6]

Meanwhile, Dumouriez continued to vehemently oppose the Convention's order to drive the Austrians and Prussians beyond the Rhine, blaming logistical problems, above all he rankled at Custine's advance and the latter's criticism.[7] Dumouriez described his problems:

> The army shrinks day by day in a frightening manner. I have no more than twenty-one thousand men under my orders. There are very few battalions that amount to 300 men. Companies are reduced to seven or eight men. The decree that declared the motherland out of danger makes most of the volunteers think that they are free to go. A very great number left without asking for leave. Among those who remain with me, most, and some almost entire battalions, having made their declaration two months ago, demanding to leave on 1 December, that is tomorrow, and if the National Convention does not take a very prompt measure, I will not be able, under the terms of the decree, to retain any.[8]

On 3 December, Custine had to fall back to Mainz to spend the winter there and to abandon his projects of conquering Trier and Koblenz. Dumouriez had conceived a plan to invade the United Provinces but the Convention stuck to its decision that the priority was action on the Rhine. From 7 December Dumouriez clashed with, and sought to undermine, Pache, the Minister for War, who he had previously considered as his place-man, but on 15 December he had to submit to the final decision of the provisional Executive Council at the risk of being dismissed: 'It has not adopted the project to march into Holland, and it still considers that it is preferable that you place yourself around the Rhine, to push the Austrians across this river.'[9] Dumouriez was unaware that on the same day the Convention had recognised the liberty and the sovereignty of the people whose lands republican troops had entered by placing them under the guardianship of the French Republic.

In accordance with these instructions, Dumouriez issued orders to his subordinates for an advance into Germany but three days later, none of the troops had made the slightest movement, apparently waiting for a counter-order.[10] He also excused himself from compliance with the decree of the 15 December on the grounds that neither he or any of his subordinates had the capacity to administer the invaded territories as guardians.[11] He was summoned to Paris, on 29 December, to explain himself before the Executive Council of the Convention

6 SHM, Van Dijk Manuscript.
7 Dumouriez, *Correspondance,* Custine to Pache, Mainz, 19 November 1792 (Year I of the Republic).
8 Dumouriez, *Correspondance,* Dumouriez to Pache, Liège, 30 November 1792 (Year I of the Republic).
9 Dumouriez, *Correspondance,* Pache to Dumouriez, Paris, 13 December 1792 (Year I of the Republic).
10 Dumouriez, *Correspondance,* Dumouriez to Pache, Liège, 15 December 1792 (Year I of the Republic).
11 Dumouriez, *Correspondance,* Dumouriez to Pache, Liège, 21 December 1792 (Year I of the Republic).

and defend his plans of campaign. The conquest of the Austrian Netherlands had been achieved, except in the east, between the Maas, Roer,[12] and Rhine, where Austrian troops under *Feldmarschalleutnant* Johann Peter Beaulieu de Marconnay remained. French republican troops occupied Belgium, with no intention of leaving, and Dumouriez resolved to use it as a springboard to swoop on the United Provinces. The latter would then be transformed into a sister republic in which he knew he could find everything that his army lacked: 'arms, clothing, horses, provisions, money, everything was in Holland'.[13] It was a matter of him convincing the Convention of the strength of his strategic plan as war with both Britain and the United Provinces, called for by the radicals, was already in the wind. The initiative had to be seized from the start by surprising the enemy with the speed and ferocity of the attack.

Then on 4 January the political situation changed, the radical Girondins secured control over the direction of the war and soon afterwards, on 22 January, Pache resigned to be replaced by *Lieutenant-général* Beurnonville. There was nothing now to prevent Dumouriez from pushing to secure the United Provinces before a British expeditionary corps was dispatched. Maastricht would have to be taken to prevent any intervention by Austrian or Prussian forces; then he could march on Nijmegen and Utrecht folding back the defences of Holland and maritime Flanders. Urgency was required with news of the Stadholder's plans for the defence of the United Provinces. These entailed the replacement of the garrison at Venlo, on the right bank of the Maas, by Prussians and that of Maastricht by allied troops to allow the assembly of a field army of 20,000 men to defend the interior of the country, from Bergen op Zoom to Nijmegen, until the disembarkation of British troops. In response, Dumouriez ordered Miranda, at Liège, to advance on Venlo, to at least stop its evacuation, while La Noüe's army would secure 'the complete investment of Maastricht.'[14]

To carry out his plans, Dumouriez had to immediately to reorganise his depleted forces and he also secured the advice and services of *Général de brigade* d'Arçon, an engineer officer who was considered an expert on fortifications, to deal with the line of Dutch strongholds. In the meantime, after proposals from the Dutch patriots, Dumouriez secretly decided to modify his plan. He now was to thrust into the Netherlands, blockading the major fortresses in his way and cross the Hollands Diep estuary to Dordrecht from where he would thrust into the heart of Holland. At the same time, Miranda, now commanding the Armée du Nord, was to cover these operations by attacking Maastricht and Venlo and then, once the landing at Dordrecht took place, handing over to *Lieutenant-général* Valence while he, with 25,000 men, marched on Nijmegen where Dumouriez would join him via Utrecht. Maastricht was to be taken by swift, decisive action, as prescribed by d'Arçon:

> As soon as the first troops will have arrived, trenches will be opened and batteries will be prepared, … One should avoid as much as possible, becoming involved in

12 This river is known as the Rur in German and Roer in Dutch and is a tributary of the Maas (Meuse in French). Given the particular relevance of its position to the Maas, which it joins at Roermond, in this text, the Dutch version of the name has been used throughout for consistency. The Maas is used for the river flowing in the Netherlands and Meuse in Belgium, as it is referred to at several locations in both countries.

13 Dumouriez, *La vie et les mémoires,* Vol.II, Year 1793, p.5.

14 Dumouriez, *La vie et les mémoires,* Vol.II, p.5.

> a miners' war, the laborious processes of which make sieges so long, so disgusting and so murderous. … it is necessary to ensure success … to take all physical and moral means to astonish, to impose and to cast terror among the defenders …:[15]

While this was going on, between 10 and 26 December, King Louis XVI was prosecuted for treason and conspiracy against the State and then guillotined on 21 January 1793. Three days later, after the news had reached London, the French Embassy's passports were withdrawn and they were instructed to leave British soil within five days. Despite the diplomatic rupture between Paris and London, the United Provinces still tried to maintain relations which, if not cordial, at least conformed to the rules of neutrality. This included the passage of Dutch troops through the French-held territories to and from Holland, Maastricht and Roermond.[16]

On 1 February 1793, the Convention declared war on Britain and the United Provinces but it took three days for news of this to reach Liège and Maastricht. Although Miranda had not been warned of the declaration, he was able to report on 7 February that he had secured the fort of Stevensweert on the right bank of the Maas, south of Roermond, and that of Sint-Michiel, on the left bank opposite Venlo. When the territory of the United Provinces had been invaded, Prince Friedrich recalled his detachments, although some were caught at Tongeren and Stevensweert, and had his cavalry bring into the city all the cattle and horses that could be found in the surrounding villages. Nevertheless, the republicans succeeded in seizing a convoy of wine, corn and coal near the village of Heusden, a league and a half from Maastricht.

One of the first units to appear in front of Maastricht was a battalion of the Volontaires de Haute-Vienne, in Valence's command, as noted in the journal of Bricard, one of its soldiers:

> On 10 February 1793, departed to go to canton in a village close to Maastricht. The French émigrés who occupied this place had only the time to save themselves on their horses bare-back. Our grenadiers entered a grand house and found a table laden with a magnificent meal that had just been served, trunks full of precious possessions, very valuable swords and pistols, as well as the clothes of former guards of the King of France. Our soldiers took the precaution to not eat the prepared meal.[17]

The event is confirmed by an émigré priest, 'we thought so little of an invasion that a party of French émigrés was surprised in a village very close to the city.'[18] The following day Bricard's battalion moved forward to the village of Itteren, at the northern gates of Maastricht and on the banks of the Maas.

15 A de Raichas d'Aiglun, 'D'Arçon, sa vie et ses écrits', *Mémoires de la Société d'émulation du Doubs*, Series 4, Vol.2 (1867), pp.311–312.

16 Archivo del General Miranda (MIRANDA), Lamarlière to the Prince of Hesse, 24 January 1793.

17 Alfred & Jules Bricard, *Journal du cAnon.nier Bricard (1792–1802)* (Paris: Delagrave, 1891), pp.26–27.

18 G. Jacques Martinant de Préneuf, *Huit années d'émigration: souvenirs de l'abbé G.-J. Martinant de Préneuf, curé de Vaugirard, de Sceaux et de Saint-Leu, 1792–1801* (Paris: Perrin, 1908), p.86.

That day, 11 February, Dumouriez notified Miranda that he was going to launch his attack on 18 or 19 February; the success of the overall plan was, to a large extent, to depend on the siege of Maastricht which should begin simultaneously:

> It is necessary that you hasten this attack: for this is neither the season nor the time to open a regular siege. All depends moreover on the alacrity with which you extricate yourself from this siege to be able to, immediately, march on Nijmegen with twenty-five thousand effective men. … I authorise you to take into our pay all the Dutch, Germans and Swiss from the garrison of Maastricht who wish to join you.[19]

On 13 February, Dumouriez wrote again insisting on the 'infallible' steps that were to be taken to obtain a rapid surrender:

> I am also persuaded that before the seventeenth you will be on the march, & that already the mortars would have fired on Maastricht. The Prince of Hesse-Philippstahl [sic] who commands there is not in any way a soldier. He will perhaps propose to you to evacuate the place & and to retire with his garrison; for the project of the Dutch is to form a small army corps, while waiting for the Prussians; & the 6,000 men of the Maastricht garrison, if we let them leave, will serve as core of this small army, or to reinforce the garrisons of Arnhem and Nijmegen: this is what is to be absolutely avoided, by intimidating the governor who you will make personally responsible to the inhabitants for the damage from the bombardment. If the siege of Maastricht appears to you to be prolonged, leave it to be achieved by my army & that of Valence, & march yourself on Nijmegen … In the summons that you will make to the city of Maastricht, do not forget, independently of the governor, to summon the magistrates, & render them personally responsible for the damage from the shells. Warn them, & through them the inhabitants, that you only wish to pursue with all vigour the partisans of the Stadholder; but that you have, like us all, only friendship for the Dutch nation … You will put this advice in writing with your fiery style … I learn that the Brunswick troops in the service of Holland, have no intention at all of fighting.[20]

Despite Fort Sint-Michiel having been taken, Venlo had already been secured by Prussian troops and Miranda recognised that a successful attack on Maastricht, and the prevention of a junction between the Prussians and Austrians relied on the covering French troops, under Valence and La Noüe, deployed along the Roer. Nevertheless, Dumouriez continued to be insistent and optimistic:

> [I]t is important that the attack on Maastricht is sharp & that you can from the first day establish your mortar batteries … I wish and even dare to hope that this place will hold you up no more than two or three days, & that you will be able to march

19 MIRANDA, Dumouriez to Miranda, Antwerp, 11 February 1793.
20 MIRANDA, Dumouriez to Miranda, Antwerp, 13 February 1793.

> at once on the Prussians, only stopping twenty-four hours in Maastricht, & immediately putting your columns on the march.[21]

He was then to leave troops to attack, or at least cover, Venlo and Roermond, as well as Grave, in order to pin the Stadholder's forces down, and push or draw the Prussians to Nijmegen where they would be trapped between the two French armies.

Lieutenant-général Égalité joined Miranda at Liège, on 14 or 15 February, to take command of a division and to become second-in-command of the forces designated to invest the place.

> The army of Général Miranda was charged with this operation on the left bank of the Maas, where the city of Maastricht is situated and Fort Sint Pieter, which is its citadel; while on the right bank, the suburb of Wyck, also fortified and forming part of the place, was to be invested by a division of the Army of the Ardennes, under the order of Général Leveneur [sic] in the absence of Général Valence commander in chief of this army ...[22]

On the same day, Le Veneur, having made an inspection of his positions before Wyck and to cover the siege, reported his plans to Miranda, still at Liège, as well as significant intelligence, '... I am almost certain that d'Autichamp is in Maastricht, with a certain number of émigrés. There were some in the cantonments that we occupy. Several were nearly surprised when we arrived ...'[23]

Jean-Thérèse-Louis-Joseph de Beaumont, Marquis d'Autichamp, born in 1738, had entered service aged 11 and had served throughout the Seven Years War. *Maréchal de camp* in 1780, he had commanded the Gendarmerie Rouge, at Lunéville, from 1770 until its dissolution in 1788. A *grand seigneur*, tall, with a fine military appearance and a superb horseman, he was considered as one of the best cavalry officers of his time. Emigrating in 1790 with the Prince de Condé to whom he was equerry, he had, in December 1791, proposed to the Princes the re-establishment of the Gendarmerie as seven companies with the name Hommes d'Armes à Cheval. This unit, recruited from former Gendarmes Rouges and of the Royal Household as well as gentlemen and bourgeoisie of the First Estate, was joined by a foot company, raised, as described above, from the former Gardes Françaises, so at the start of the campaign the corps had almost 700 men, infantry and cavalry. On 24 November 1792, the corps had been dissolved at Visé, south of Maastricht, but a number of its members remained with d'Autichamp and followed him to Maastricht.

Towards the end of February, the encirclement of the city was complete, which meant that it could no longer receive any news, reinforcements or help. However, the garrison still carried out raids to bring more livestock and grain into the city and they enjoyed this relative liberty of movement until the morning of 19 February. Miranda knew that Clerfayt, with about 40,000 men, was around Cologne but was also aware that problems with logistics meant that this force, which was observed by Le Veneur's troops on the Roer, was unable to

21 MIRANDA, Dumouriez to Miranda, Antwerp, 15 February 1793.
22 Orléans, *Mémoires*, Vol.II, p.330.
23 MIRANDA, Le Veneur to Miranda, Valkenburg, 15 February 1793.

move. He was optimistic of success, writing on 17 February, that the bombardment of the city would be completed 'within six or seven day'.[24]

Miranda felt that he lacked precise information on Maastricht, its defences, the nature and strength of the garrison as well as the number of refugees. This was despite receiving the plan drafted by Arçon as well as the help of a Saxon spy, sent by Dumouriez, in whom, however, he did not have confidence. Reports prepared by the Saxon, named Thuring, were however thorough and appear to have been accurate. That of 14 January, not only dealt with the defences but also the state of provisions and the attitude of the garrison's troops to the French:

> The works of the fortifications of Maastricht are developing with the greatest activity. The redoubts constructed at the Brusselsepoort [Brussels Gate] are completed. All the advanced works are armed or ready to be. The mines have received their charges of powder. Fort Sint Pieter is likewise put in a state of defence, fascines have been placed on the parapet … The émigrés are still there numbering 1,200 to 1,300, without arms and the majority without shoes. And without food. The distinguished men are still so insolent and also extravagant as before. New magazines have been formed of food-stuffs and forage … The Brunswick dragoons are quite disposed to us. As well as some of the artillery.[25]

Le Veneur, meanwhile, continued to gather information.

> The letters that I have intercepted are almost all from émigrés who, under assumed names, write to other émigrés who are in Maastricht. They are all of the same style: great lamentations on their fate. In general, they announce little hope, except two or three which speak of this movement of the Austrians to reinforce the Prussians from the direction of Roermond. … I approached to the distance of a bit less than 500 toises [just under 1,000 m] of the glacis of Maastricht. We saw distinctly that there were at no point cannons on the ramparts, and the locals told me that for three days they have not patrolled outside the city as they had been accustomed to do. … they are working hard at Fort Sint Pieter …[26]

On 18 February 1793, on the eve of Dumouriez's invasion of the United Provinces, Miranda reported some difficulties which meant the bombardment of Maastricht would not commence for a few days and so he could not be at Nijmegen until 26 or 28 February.[27] His commander however felt that Maastricht was there for the taking.

> [M]ost of the troops of the garrison have little will to fight; that the less you use regular methods for this siege, the more you will succeed, because bombardment will disgust the garrison & frighten the inhabitants. The very émigrés who retired

24 MIRANDA, Miranda to Beurnonville, Minister of War, Liège, 17 February 1793.
25 MIRANDA, Thuring to Miranda, 14 January 1793.
26 MIRANDA, Le Veneur to Miranda, Valkenburg, 17 February 1793.
27 MIRANDA, Miranda to Dumouriez, Liège, 18 February.

> there, will be more of an embarrassment that will facilitate the surrender of the city ...[28]

Everyone, except Le Veneur, who Miranda despised, underestimated their adversaries and especially the émigrés who were trapped in Maastricht. They were useless mouths to be fed, hated by the republicans who sought to slaughter, wholesale, any who had borne arms against France during the previous campaign. The Convention intended to terrify the counter-revolutionaries and drive the surviving royalists still further away, even as far as Russia. The émigré population at Maastricht was made up of three categories: former soldiers of the Armées du Centre and of the Duc de Bourbon, priests and, finally, civilian non-combatants including the former soldiers' wives, children and parents as well as their loyal servants. The Prince of Hesse faced a dilemma: 3,000 or so proscribed royalists, including more than 500 priests, would eat into his reserves of food and also excite the fury of the new Republic. However, to drive them from, or house them outside, the city amounted to delivering them to their enemies who had made it known 'that all the French and Brabant émigrés who had borne arms for the defence of the place would be shot and the women and priests would have their noses and ears cut off.'[29]

As early as 5 February, when routes to Germany and Holland were still open, the governor had warned the Marquis d'Autichamp, with whom he enjoyed the most cordial relations, that he 'was resolved to send away the foreigners ... that he would only make an exception in favour of those who had a family and had been admitted for a long time, and engaged him to warn the French that this measure applied to them ...'[30] Autichamp apparently replied that his companions would be ready to die armed in defence of the city if he authorised it, but 'that in the other case, they would prefer to be shot in the city than to have to suffer persecution by their cruellest enemies'.[31] The governor reconsidered, as Autichamp notified the Comtes du Rosel de Beaumanoir and de Blangy, both *lieutenant-généraux* and considered as natural leaders of the émigrés in the city, who, on 7 February, called an assembly attended by all the *maréchaux de camp* present. They decided to propose that the refugees take up arms to assist with the defence of the city, the United Province and the Stadholder, de facto allies of the French monarchy after the declaration of war. A message was sent to the Stadholder to ask him to authorise the raising of an infantry regiment as well as an artillery corps to contribute to the defence of Maastricht and two days later the Prince of Hesse was presented with a draft regulation for the organisation of this corps. After an initial refusal, the governor consented to the raising of the corps but insisted that it was not to interfere in any way with the garrison, 'these gentlemen only offering their service to advertise their

28 MIRANDA, Dumouriez to Miranda, Antwerp, 19 February.

29 Charles-François de Cézac de Belcayre, *Dix ans d'émigration (1791–1801), Souvenirs de François de Cézac, Hussard de Bercheny, Volontaire à l'Armée de Condé* (Paris: Paul, 1909), p.71.

30 Félix de Romain, *Souvenirs d'un Officier Royaliste, contenant son entrée au service, ses voyages en Corse et en Italie, son émigration, ses campagnes à l'armée de Condé, et celle de 1815, dans la Vendée*, (Paris: Égron, 1824), Vol.II, p.380. The author himself cites the journal of the siege which was confided to him.

31 Archives du Musée Condé, Château de Chantilly (AMC), Fonds Grouvel, GR045: Baron d'Assignies *Souvenirs d'émigration (1789–1801)*.

courage in case of an attack or sortie.'[32] This led to the establishment of an 'office for the registration of the French émigrés who were obliged to go to register there and to take a certificate under pain of being removed from Maastricht as suspect ... and each French gentleman was to be obliged to present a certificate from a general officer from his province or of the Corps in which he had served.'[33] The 27 *maréchaux de camp* in the city were made responsible for the province from which he had originated, sharing others between them.

The assent of the Prince of Orange having been received on 13 February, the 'Régiment de Maëstricht' was at once established and on 18 February its volunteers took the oath prescribed by the Prince of Hesse himself:

> You swear and promise on your word of honour fidelity to Their Mightiest Lords the States-General of the United Provinces that you desire to serve as volunteers to work with all your ability for the safety, preservation and defence of the city of Maastricht, obedience to the Governor and to all Commanders under him and for him in the aforementioned city, to denounce and reveal any conspiracies and suspect people that you may know or discover as long as you are in the States of the Mightiest Lords.[34]

The organisation of the unit, of 1,174 volunteers, a great number being officers and gentlemen, but also NCOs, soldiers and bourgeoisie, was entrusted to the Comte de Blangy. Aged 71, he had commanded one of the two infantry brigades of the Armée de Bourbon, then been commissioner of the Princes at Mons before taking refuge at Maastricht with his two sons, the eldest being Vicomte Henri de Blangy, formerly *capitaine-lieutenant* of the 4th Company of the Hommes d'Armes à cheval (Gendarmes de Flandre), and his younger sibling, the Chevalier Gabriel, aged 17. The Régiment de Maëstricht had two divisions, of nine infantry companies, the first commanded by *Lieutenant-général* the Marquis du Rosel de Beaumanoir and the second by the Comte de Blangy. Each company had two platoons, and the platoons, two sections. The posts were distributed by seniority, the appointments to the staff and companies were chosen by the *lieutenant-généraux* and those within the companies by the *capitaines*. The staff officers of the regiment were:

1st Division: *Major* – Chevalier Etienne de Damas-Crux (*colonel*); *aide-majors* – Marquis de La Haye (*lieutenant-colonel*) and Chevalier de Saint-Sauveur (*lieutenant-colonel*); Chevalier de Harlay (infantry *major*), charged with clothing detail.

2nd Division: *Major* – Monsieur du Hall (*lieutenant-colonel*); *aide-majors* – de Bertrix (*major*) and Comte Antoine d'Allonville (chasseur *capitaine*).

The companies were to have 30-60 men but no two had the same strength because the émigrés were grouped by their former corps in the Armée des Princes or by regional

32 Lavergne, 'Les émigrés au siège de Maëstricht', pp.523-524.

33 Cacqueray de Valménier, 'Mémoires inédits', Vol.II, p.81.

34 Lavergne, 'Les émigrés au siège de Maëstricht', pp.524-525; the collective name for the States-General was their *Hoogmogende Heren* (Mightiest Lords).

coalition. The 6th Company of the 2nd Division (Anjou Coalition) only had 40 men, one of whom was François Aumont de Bazouges, the author's ancestor. *Capitaine* in the Régiment d'Orléans Cavalerie and emigrating in November 1791 from Valenciennes, he had served in the preceding campaign in the Armée des Princes as *maître* (gentleman trooper) in the Compagnie des officiers de Lorraine et d'Orléans Cavalerie. The 4th Company of the 1st Division, on the other hand, that of the Marquis d'Autichamp's Hommes d'Armes, was 104 strong.

The Marquis was responsible for organising the 28 companies 'to do duty in different quarters and diverse points of the fortifications',[35] and he arranged that in case of alarm, the two divisions would muster on the Stadhuis, City Hall, square 'opposite the Grote Gracht street; the artillery company on the left of the first division, and that of the marine [artillery] on the left of the second'. It was here that their arms were to be distributed, as well as deposited and cleaned after each action.[36] The municipality demanded that the émigrés be dressed like the national troops so their coats were blue with a red collar and they bore the orange cockade in their hats.[37] The expense being beyond the means of the majority of the émigrés, the governor sent some money to the Comte de Blangy, but it being insufficient, and no one wishing to advance credit to the refugee Frenchmen, it was necessary to go to the second-hand clothes dealers to buy old abandoned uniforms.

At the same time, 'Monsieur de Gilaudon, commissary of war, an émigré, had established, in concert with Monsieur Jacoby, mayor of the city, an infirmary for the French, where one saw prelates, venerable priests performing the functions of nurses, and acquitting them with a completely Christian ardour and charity.'[38] Under Cardinal de La Rochefoucauld, 559 French clergy registered either as nurses to serve in the hospital, as stretcher-bearers or as firemen to warn of and fight fires ignited by bombs. The Prince of Hesse, who had accepted their offer gladly, nevertheless compelled hem to comply with the same requirements, in terms of identity and guarantee, as the laity. The women assisted the 11 French doctors and surgeons from the Régiment de Maëstricht by preparing dressings and bandages, as well as making cartridges; the Princess of Hesse joined them in this work.

The artillery defending the city comprised of only five batteries, three Brunswick and two Dutch, which an émigré described as well provided but 'most defective and the ramparts abandoned since the Seven Years War, presented a unfortunate appearance'.[39] The Dutch artillery was commanded by *Major* Lombach who was considered as well intentioned, poorly trained, although ready to learn, and rather too fond of alcohol. On 15 February he

35 Cézac de Belcayre, *Dix ans d'émigration*, p.69.

36 Romain, *Souvenirs d'un Officier Royaliste*, Vol.II, p.384.

37 This detail is provided by a letter from an eyewitness cited by Jean-Gabriel Peltier in *Histoire de la Restauration de la Monarchie française ou La Campagne de 1793. Publiée en forme de correspondance sur les affaires du tems, et servant de suite à l'Histoire du 10 Août et du 2 Septembre 1792* (London: Unknown Publisher, 1793), p.37. The Baron d'Assignies, who had lodged with a coal merchant, recalled that his host offered him 'on a plate an orange cockade in the middle of which was a white one' (AMC, Fonds Grouvel, GR045).

38 Antoine de Saint-Gervais, *Histoire des émigrés français depuis 1789 jusqu'en 1828* (Paris: Hivert, 1828), Vol.II, p.40.

39 Paul and Martial de Pradel de Lamase, *Nouvelles notes intimes d'un émigré (le chevalier de Pradel de Lamase, officier à l'armée de Condé)* (Paris: Paul, 1914–1920), p.92.

supported a proposal that six émigré artillery officers be posted at Fort Sint Pieter, three of them to be on duty in turn. The governor appeared to be reluctant at first, concerned that his own officers might take umbrage, but two days later, 'the artillery and naval officers having been permitted to do service jointly with those of the place, the prince required from them that they take the oath of fidelity to [Their Mightiest Lords], which they did'.[40] A special clause was added to the oath for the émigré artillery and naval officers, as with the engineer officers, engaging them to never divulge the city's means of defence and the secrets which would be confided to them, and, in the case of their passing into the service of an enemy army, to refuse to be employed against the place. These officers soon directed work:

> [W]ithin a week, the 24 engineers had repaired the ramparts in such fashion that they had protected them from a surprise. It is true that all our people, the majority belonging to the high nobility, had lent a hand, helped by a large part of the priests. Emulation took over the citizenry and it was with a febrile zeal, which did not relent during the whole length of the siege ... On their part, the 60 gunners repaired the old pieces that lay rusty on their carriages and put them into a serviceable state.[41]

When Dumouriez marched from Antwerp on 19 February, Miranda was still at Liège but remained optimistic. He had at his disposal around 30,000 men, excluding the 3,500 men with *Général de brigade* Lamarlière who covered his left and *Lieutenant-général* Le Veneur's 6,000 men on the right bank; his artillery was estimated at 22 heavy pieces, along with the infantry's guns, two 4-pounders with each battalion. The investment of Maastricht was tightened but Le Veneur lacked artillery and even entrenching tools, Miranda having directed that his artillery park be placed at Sint-Truiden. A letter from Brussels, dated 20 February, described troops and supplies being sent to the siege:

> As for the siege of Maastricht, it still has not begun; but Dumouriez is preparing to make this vast city fall. For four days, more than two hundred waggons with all sorts of munitions passed through here destined in part for the siege. Seven to eight hundred chasseurs from Hainault passed, on the 17th, to go towards Maastricht. This corps is a tribute to the Montois [people from Mons], both for the good appearance of the men as for their equipment. Other corps leave successively for the same destination.[42]

Le Veneur had, despite everything, started works to the north of Wyck and on 22 February he reported on the construction during the night of 'a redoubt in front of the castle of Geusselt, about 350 toises from the glacis of Maastricht' as well as 400 metres of communication trench. The garrison had tried to destroy the works with cannon fire and, although

40 Lavergne takes these details from the journal of the siege kept by an émigré who he identified as the Comte de Lardenoy, second in command of the 7th Company of the 1st Division.

41 Pradel de Lamase, *Nouvelles notes intimes d'un émigré*, pp.93–94.

42 *Moniteur universel n°58*, Wednesday 27 February 1793.

they had little success, he concluded that, 'It would be desirable that we would have mortars to suppress their fire a little.'[43]

The Prince of Hesse was cognisant of his garrison's weakness and thought the enemy was in strength, so he was reluctant to risk a sortie into open country or far from the city's defences. A sortie was, however, made on 19 February by Brunswickers from the garrison towards Lafelt but this only resulted in skirmishing by the light troops.[44] The émigrés resented this inaction, putting it down to Dutch laxity, while the republicans were left, undisturbed, to pursue their approach works on right bank of the Maas. Finally, Miranda arrived on 22 February, joining *Lieutenant-général* Égalité at Caestert; artillery and engineer officers arrived with him to direct the operations which would concentrate on establishing batteries to bombard the city from the north-west.[45] The same day, Dumouriez wrote to inform Miranda that Bergen op Zoom was blockaded and his advance guard was on the River Mark where it had seized boats ready to cross to Dordrecht. He also anticipated capturing Breda where, 'I will take artillery of all kinds which will serve me very well in Holland, & I will find all the [Dutch] Republic's pontoons'.[46]

Maastricht was now invested by 12,000 men as well as Le Venuer's men around Wyck; Miranda then established his headquarters at Hocht Abbey while *Lieutenant-général* Égalité, his deputy, moved to Pietershem Castle, both just outside Lanaken. The batteries erected on the height of Caberg, 800 metres from the city's covered way, were completed with 40 heavy pieces in the evening of 23 February and, on the next day, a mortar battery was armed before Wyck. The progress was seen from the city:

> Saturday 23 February: This morning one perceived that the enemy had worked through the night with much diligence to form a trench on Caberg and batteries a little below the belvedere of Mr Nyvar. Our batteries of Hoogfrankrijk, Nassau, Lindenkruis and Fort Holstein fired with great effect on the enemy's new batteries, albeit distant from the city. … In the plain of Wyck the enemy had worked with no less diligence to prolong and to perfect the trench. It began to take the form of a parallel, presenting an obtuse angle. They worked at the two ends, one of the extended lines would have reached the Maas under Fort Veye, the other went perpendicularly to the Aachen Road. The land being more elevated around the middle, it was presumed that a battery was formed there, but the majority of our shots being aimed there, this work was somewhat broken down and thrown into the trench.[47]

The city's batteries had been assisted by the French émigré artillery and naval officers of the Régiment de Maëstricht, formed in two distinct companies, the 28 volunteers from the Artillerie Royale, 27 officers and a gunner, commanded by the Chevalier de l'Ertère and that of the Marine Royale, 32 naval officers along with 10 officers and six volunteers, one of

43 MIRANDA, Le Veneur to Miranda, 22 February 1793.
44 MIRANDA, Égalité to Miranda, 20 February 1793.
45 Orléans, *Mémoires*, Vol.II, p.332.
46 MIRANDA, Dumouriez to Miranda, Groot-Klundert, 22 February 1793.
47 SHM, Manuscrit Van Dijk.

whom was a gunner, from the Régiment de la Marine, under the Comte de Cacqueray, *chef d'escadre*. In addition, due to the lack of artillerymen, the Comte de Vogüe organised his company (2nd Company 1st Division) for duty with the guns.

The Prince of Hesse now asked Autichamp to prepare a sortie, for the morning of Sunday 24 February. When the plan was presented the evening before to the council of war, despite support from the prince, its aims were reduced and it was decided that fire support would be provided by the city's artillery alone; the two 4-pounders which Autichamp had requested would not accompany the troops. The sortie was to take place at daybreak.

> Sunday 24 February: There was this morning a sortie by the Duitse Poort [German Gate] to destroy several houses on the Scharn and Meerssen road. The plan had been conceived by Monsieur the Marquis d'Autichamp and communicated by him to his chief, the Comte de Blangy, who had come to propose it to the Prince; he desiring to furnish the Émigrés the means to give proofs of their courage, gladly acquiesced to it the preceding day, and in order that nothing of it could leak out, he had called the Council of War at six o'clock in the evening after the closing of the gates, but the émigré aides-de-camp had been warned of it in advance. It spread among them and the sortie was betrayed. The detachment of émigrés destined for this sortie were commanded by the maréchaux de camp Marquis d'Autichamp and Comte [Louis] de Damas. It consisted of five hundred Frenchmen who were to be supported by a lieutenant-colonel from the garrison with about 600 dragoons, soldiers or jägers to cover the workmen; but on coming onto the highway, these troops were greeted by the masked batteries of the trench and when they then advanced on the great road (instead of going to the side), they sustained a discharge of cannons posted on the road. The surprised workmen threw themselves into the works and rendered the enterprise impossible. It was realised that the enemy were waiting and that it had been betrayed, and the detachment retired in good order, but without achieving anything, bringing back five or six wounded from the émigrés, of whom most died.[48]

The Chevalier Gabriel de Blangy, the younger of the Comte de Blangy's two sons, was killed by a cannon shot, the other casualties were '… Messieurs de Borda, St Florent, de la Vieville & Loudun, émigrés, capitaines in different regiments; the first three are since dead. There was no other loss'.[49] The disappointing result gave rise to recriminations, as indicated by the account left by an émigré.

> On 24 February, the French detachments were assembled at five o'clock in the morning. They waited until half past six for those from the garrison. The Dutch artillery officer, who commanded the advance batteries, had neglected to put them in readiness; he begged the Marquis d'Autichamp to only start his movement when he was ready. At last it was possible to issue out at seven o'clock. The Brunswick

48 SHM, Van Dijk Manuscript.

49 Peltier, *Histoire*, pp.16–17, quoting an émigré's letter; the source quoted by Lavergne presents only minor variations.

> dragoons and jägers formed the vanguard; they were followed by the workmen and the bulk of the troops. Two grenadier companies were posted near the house to protect the demolition. The rest of the infantry advanced in column on the Meerssen road and headed towards the second house, when the enemies fired from a battery of four 4-pounders that they had placed on the roadway. After the first shots, which nevertheless did not reach anyone, the dragoons turned bridle and regained at full speed the glacis; the jägers, in their turn, gave ground and fell back to the column. The Marquis d'Autichamp had to support his left behind the second house. They had been able to raze both of them, but the pioneers dispersed, not one of them was left.[50]

Baron d'Assignies who witnessed events from the ramparts provides another, perhaps more balanced account:

> [T]his sortie was composed of 1,000 men including 300 émigrés who had not had time even to put on uniforms. No more could sortie, the garrison being no more than 6,000 men. I do not know who had the unfortunate idea to do it at the break of day, which allowed the French to direct their batteries in a manner to hinder the demolition of the house and most of their discharges fell on the 300 émigrés who their costume made distinguishable. ... the workmen who were to demolish it could not continue their work. Besides, the loss suffered at each instant by the garrison and all these considerations engaged the generals to have their troops retire. The émigrés devoted themselves to retreat the last and thus experienced some losses. No wounded were abandoned, although all demanded that they be finished off rather than leave them in the hands of their enemies.[51]

Comte Louis de Damas-Crux, *maréchal de camp*, had led his column in the direction of Scharn in order to cover the main sortie. On its advance the French republicans threw skirmishers forward supported by horse artillery which fired twenty or so rounds. As soon as he received the order to withdraw, Damas-Crux did so in good order, without losing a single man. The city's artillery had remained silent during the sortie but once the enemy's battery had revealed itself the cannons in Wyck subjected it to fire all day.

Sortie or not, Miranda considered that by noon, that same day, 24 February, his dispositions were sufficiently threatening for him to summon the Prince of Hesse to surrender. *Colonel* Arnaudin appeared at the city gates at about 3:30 p.m. and received a hostile reception from the citizens when he was conducted, blindfolded, to the governor. He carried three messages, two from Miranda, to the governor and the city's magistrates, and another to the magistrates from the newly self-declared Batavian revolutionary committee.

Miranda's message to the governor called on him to surrender and that he would be subjected to 'capital punishment' if he resisted, while that to the magistrates took a different tone:

50 Romain, *Souvenirs d'un Officier Royaliste*, Vol.II, pp.396–397.

51 AMC, Fonds Grouvel, GR045.

> The French nation having been forced to declare war on the Stadholder, & his partisans, wishes to break the bonds of the Batavians; & we will enter your city as brothers & friends. Thus, it will not be against you, but for you that we make war. … Your duty, as representatives of the people, is to shield them from the disasters and calamities of a useless siege. I require you, in the name of humanity & for your personal preservation, to engage, or oblige the commander & officers to give up the place, without any delay, to the arms of the French Republic.
>
> I declare to you, magistrates of the people, that if unfortunately you force me to fire on the city, it is you who I will render personally responsible for the irreparable harm that your weakness, or your connivance with our enemies will have brought on your country; & your capital punishment will serve as an example to the satellites of despotism, & will purge the national injury.[52]

As Miranda informed the Minister of War, '… the response of the Prince of Hesse … was a refusal … having verbally said to me, through Colonel Arnaudin, that he found the aforementioned summons strange, since he did not know that the Dutch nation had declared war on France…'[53] The magistrates did not respond at all.

General service for the Régiment de Maëstricht commenced that evening, 24 February, with 125 men doing duty each day, 50 each at the Saxen and Dopff Bastions and 25 at Fort Sint Pieter. Each soldier was issued with a pound and half of bread, a half-pound of meat and some beer, and the casemates were provided with benches and straw. Later, the most advanced and exposed posts were regularly entrusted to the émigrés who were not going to desert and whose vigilance was all the sharper for fear of being captured.

At 11:00 p.m. that night the threatened bombardment commenced, immediately causing terror in the city, where 'the air lit up with the whistling of the shells, the bursts of them that exploded in the air or knocked the houses down, the violence of those that were shot from the batteries of the place, … the shouts which announced fires and conflagration, could only give rise to terror and confusion', accompanied by people's screams and the bellowing of cattle being dragged to cover.[54] The first bombs were fired from the batteries on Caberg, and at first chiefly fell on the city hall square and Bosch, Capucijn and Brusselsestraaten; moreover, the batteries the French had established 'on the Hertogenbosch bridge poured down in the streets of this name and around the hôtel de Tilly; the whole quarter was badly damaged.'[55] Cézac de Belcayre, formerly of the Hommes d'Armes à Cheval in the Armée du Centre, who served on the ramparts confirmed the sights and sounds of destruction and terror in the city and the response. 'Maastricht, from all its ramparts as well as its citadel, constantly blasted the trenches and all the enemy's works, finally the whole firmament was on fire and offered the most sinister aspect.'[56] One witness noted:

52 MIRANDA, Miranda to the Magistrates of Maastricht, 24 February 1793.
53 MIRANDA, Miranda to Beurnonville, Hocht, 25 February 1793.
54 SHM, Van Dijk Manuscript, 24 February.
55 AMC, Fonds Grouvel, GR045.
56 Cézac de Belcayre, *Dix ans d'émigration*, p.75.

> They threw about 1,500 bombs into the city, of which a part were loaded with incendiaries that damaged the houses situated beside the Boschpoort and caused fires several times, and which were extinguished immediately through the vigilance of the citizens and the émigré French priests who went there. The city responded to the fire in a very animated way.[57]

Another simply wrote '... I think that the devil that night sent into Maastricht a rain of fire: there was more damage than in the whole of the rest of the siege.'[58]

Miranda assisted in firing the first bomb, the only time that he was seen at the trenches during the siege, with him was one of the commissioners, sent to Belgium to apply the decree of 15 December 1792, who saw that the republican attackers immediately had difficulties:

> The trench was open; I accompanied the generals there; I saw the start of the bombardment; I was placed beside the mortar from which the first bombs were fired. I have to say that the fire was at first badly served; it was scant, interrupted and not heavy. The majority of the bombs did not go far enough, the others burst in the air. I remained in the trench for eleven hours until half past one in the morning ... I will add that the enemy's fire was very well served.[59]

In the morning the destruction was assessed, as well as the citizens' response after the initial terror had subsided:

> Monday 25 February: The Waldeck Regiment, several companies of Schmid, dragoons, jägers, grenadiers and miners were driven from their barracks of Lindenkruis and Sint Andries [Achter de Barakken] by the first bombs which fell there, set them alight and killed and injured several men in their beds. ...the damage caused by the bombs was not proportionate to their quantity. Many exploded in the air having a too distant target. Others did not explode and many fell in the exterior works or in the Maas. As soon as there were some cries of fire or conflagration, the citizen guards recovering from their first consternation ran to them with the greatest intrepidity and extinguished them despite the greatest risks.[60]

One of the wounded was from the Régiment de Maëstricht, M. Dubois, in the company of Hommes d'Armes, caused by an exploding bomb at the Saxen Bastion. The Marquis d'Autichamp made a tour of inspection on the morning of 25 February, according to an émigré who was consistently critical of the Dutch: 'He remarked, in almost all, the greatest negligence: the batteries were devoid of gunners and workmen; the Dutch officers were absent and they were no longer there, their soldiers themselves went or got themselves

57 Journal cited by Lavergne, 'Les émigrés au siège de Maëstricht', p.526.

58 Peltier, *Histoire* p.17.

59 Jean-Baptiste Publicola-Chaussard, *Mémoires historiques et politiques sur la révolution de la Belgique et du pays de Liège en 1793, etc.* (Paris: Buisson, 1793), p.428.

60 SHM, Van Dijk Manuscript.

drunk. The French artillery officers complained about the lack of obedience of the latter.'[61] In fact the Dutch workmen were exhausted and the Prince of Hesse had the French émigrés replace them with their servants.

The fire on the city continued on 26 February, especially targeting the Church of Sint Servaas and the governor's palace, in the centre of the city, meanwhile the abandoned Lindenkruis barracks continued to burn. Moreover, the besiegers had strengthened their works and made them deeper, so reducing the effects of the fire from the city.[62] Although the bombardment on Wyck had been weaker, mainly on the church and Turenne Bastion, it was feared that it was to be the target of the principal assault, the republicans 'advanced the works in zigzag as to enter into a second parallel and they commenced a second battery menacing the Duitse Poort'.[63] As a result, the Prince of Hesse had French engineer officers placed there, directly under his orders, to improve the defences and 'he thought it prudent to hold the two battalions of Brunswick infantry which were to be found in large part at this last point ready to march, to have the soldiers sleep fully dressed, and to give the order to a detachment of émigrés to go there at the first musket shot.'[64]

The bombardment continued for two long days when Miranda received an enthusiastic message from Dumouriez:

> I am persuaded, my dear general, that your first message will bring me the news of the surrender of Maastricht ... The news of the taking of Breda is going moreover to cast it [Maastricht] into dismay. Général Berneron this night took Klundert; tomorrow he will attack Willemstad: the day after tomorrow, I will attack Geertruidenberg ... I have for the crossing twenty-one decked vessels making up almost eight hundred tons, and five or six sloops ... The artillery from Breda and that from Klundert will serve for my batteries and provide me with covering fire during the crossing of my advance guard ... the artillery from Breda is very considerable; that from Klundert gives me five hundred good muskets, about ten cannons, out of fifty that I found there, more than two thousand ten-pound bombs, eighteen thousand pounds of powder and a good collection of ducats, both by the voluntary offers of the good citizens, as by the seizure of the Prince of Orange's property ... I have instructed Général Thouvenot to push on with the formation of twenty-five to thirty Belgian battalions ... I hope that before the month of May, we will have at least twenty-five thousand Belgian infantrymen to join to our army. Our volunteers will come back to join us in droves, once they learn of our successes ...[65]

Miranda at once sought to convince the governor, the garrison and citizens that all resistance was in vain, and that Maastricht would soon capitulate like Breda. Fire continued into the city through the night and throughout the morning of Wednesday 27 February, when, an hour after midday, Miranda sent another summons to the governor for him to follow the

61 Romain, *Souvenirs d'un Officier Royaliste*, Vol.II, p.400.
62 SHM, Van Dijk Manuscript, 26 February 1793.
63 Journal cited by Lavergne, 'Les émigrés au siège de Maëstricht', p.52.
64 Romain, *Souvenirs d'un Officier Royaliste*, Vol.II, p.403.
65 MIRANDA, Dumouriez to Miranda, Zevenbergen, 26 February 1793.

example of Breda and surrender. This time *Colonel* Arnaudin was not allowed to enter the city, the summons was again rejected and 'having received the response, he left at the gallop and scarcely had he reached the heights when all the enemy batteries began to make play again, as well as those of the place with a noise difficult to imagine for someone who has not yet found themselves in such a situation'.[66] Miranda reported the rebuff and his future plans which were to leave 10,000 troops raised in Belgium to take over the posts held by his own men to continue the siege of Maastricht, while he took his corps towards Grave, leaving 4-5,000 men to cover Roermond, as planned by Dumouriez.[67]

Although the bombs had not yet created sufficient damage for an assault on the city, Miranda wanted them to undermine the inhabitants' morale and perhaps give rise to an insurrection supported by Dutch patriots in the city. The magistrates had already faced demands to surrender from some citizens but these had been peremptorily rejected. Now, 27 February, there was evidence that the besiegers were running short of bombs:

> Around the evening the fire of the besiegers diminished a little ... The enemy still fired their mortars from the Caberg but often one heard two or three reports in succession and the bombs did not appear. From which one concluded that due to the lack of ammunition they fired rocks. ... At three o'clock in the morning the batteries on Caberg ceased to fire entirely. It was thought that the enemy had raised the siege but we were mistaken. They lacked ammunition and were waiting for it to arrive; they had used the interval to make or to consolidate a cannon battery and to construct an oven to set fire to the city with red shots.

The garrison was placed on alert, in case the slackening in the bombardment, was the prelude to an assault.[68] Miranda had decided to begin bombarding the city with red-hot balls, and to this end he ordered Le Veneur to get four 12-pounder cannons brought from Sint-Truiden or Liège and place them in a battery to fire 'red-hot balls by ricochet' into Wyck while the same was done on the other side of the city by 16-pounders.[69] His plans were delayed as no artillery officer present knew how to construct the oven required to heat the balls. However, the immediate shortage of bombs was overcome, as those in the city found out.

> Thursday 28th: This morning at three o'clock the enemy had ceased to fire from the batteries of Caberg, but at half past eleven they recommenced with a renewed fury. The ... field officer of the day at Wyck, had reported that a great train of artillery had been seen, coming from the direction of Visé and passing behind the village of Heer. From Fort Sint Pieter 17 wagons covered with canvas were counted, which indicated that the enemy had received new munitions. ... It had been thought for some days that the enemy were working on the heights of Louwberg behind the house of the Twelve Apostles [sic] on the side of Neercanne. Today this was confirmed by the quantity of people that could be seen occupied and by the already

66 SHM, Van Dijk Manuscript, 27 February 1793.

67 MIRANDA, Miranda to Beurnonville, Hocht 27 February 1793.

68 SHM, Van Dijk Manuscript, 27 February (continued).

69 MIRANDA, Miranda to Le Veneur, Hocht, 28 February 1793.

> very advanced fieldwork that can be distinctly seen from the top of the houses of Looiersstraat [Tanners' Street]. Some balls have been fired from the cavalier of the Tongersepoort; but without effect, the work being sunk behind the heights ... Fort [Bastion] Zoutelande was guarded this night by 50 French émigrés.[70]

Cézac considered that the aim of the renewed bombardment was to ignite fires and intensify civilian casualties so to add to the pressure on the magistrates, 'the besiegers directed precisely all their fury around the seats of these conflagrations to add to the disaster in thinking that, there especially, there were a greater number of people eager to extinguish them... The streets of the city were full of patrols constantly occupied to disperse gatherings of the people and citizens'.[71] There was also a need for vigilance against Dutch patriot sympathisers, both at the vulnerable points of the defences but also in the streets, for signs of treason or spies. From the beginning of operations, it had been noticed that the republicans directed their bombs on the *place d'armes* at just the time various guards assembled there and when the assembly point was changed in vain to the Theatre Square, the bombardment simply followed. It was soon discovered that messages had reached the republicans, placed in empty bottles and thrown into the river. The émigrés suspected the loyalty of several of the garrison's units, with the exception of the Swiss of the Schmid Regiment.

The bombardment continued:

> Friday 1 March: During last night and today the enemy threw bombs without interruption from all their batteries both at Wyck and the Caberg which ruined many buildings and wounded some citizens and soldiers. The fire from the city was very hot also, although the gunners were tired out from fatigues and voluntary watches. ...[72]

That same day, the Prince of Hesse requested that the émigrés send an extra fifty men to the outlying works at Wyck, raising the daily contingent from the Régiment de Maëstricht to 175 men, excluding the staff, artillery and engineer officers on duty. There was a general sense that a decisive moment of the siege approached but the garrison was starting to show signs of exhaustion:

> 1 March, the Marquis d'Autichamp came to Wyck, observed the enemy, saw that their progress was more and more noticeable, inspected subsequently the posts, and remarked less order as was customary there; that of Sint-Maartens was not numerous enough to be able to relieve all of the sentries there, and there was no officer there; gunners were in the batteries for thirty-two hours; Capitein Bischoff of the artillery was no longer up to it. Monsieur d'Autichamp sent word to the Prince that it was essential to replace him immediately, and to give him the rest to compose his spirits: Capitein Vinchebach [sic], commanding the pioneers of the place, present at the scene, appeared ground down with it. Major Lombach also

70 SHM, Van Dijk Manuscript.
71 Cézac de Belcayre, *Dix ans d'émigration*, p.76.
72 SHM, Van Dijk Manuscript.

> came to make his tour: unfortunately, it was not a day of abstinence, his ideas were not very lucid; he went along the ramparts, saw little, and took no action at all.[73]

The progress of the siege works in front of Wyck clearly showed the threat at this point. Two émigrés were wounded by bombs and the besiegers were readying to subject the city to red-hot shot on 2 March.[74]

Many participants of the Siege of Maastricht later observed that the constant noise, from 24 February to 1 March, made it impossible to hear anything else, reinforcing the feeling of isolation for the besieged who had no communication with the outside world. In fact, its relief had already been decided as early as 14 February when the new Austrian commander *Feldmarschall* Prinz Friedrich Josias von Sachsen-Coburg-Saalfeld had met his Prussian counterpart, the Duke of Brunswick, at Frankfurt. There they had established the general plan of future operations; the first step would be for the Austrians to drive the enemy from the right bank of the Maas and relieve Maastricht, while the Prussians assembled at Wesel along with the Hanoverians. Once the Austrians had succeeded, the Prussians would begin the second step, the relief of Mainz. Any move into Belgium would wait until this was completed, whether this be over the Maas, through Luxembourg or by opening a new front in the north of Alsace. However, at the time it still remained open whether the United Provinces would declare for the coalition. This question was answered by Dumouriez's invasion as well as the attack on Maastricht.

As soon as news of Dumouriez's invasion reached Britain it was decided to send an expeditionary corps to the United Provinces in support of the defensive alliance of 1788 between the two countries. However, the only infantry available for immediate deployment were the Foot Guards, posted in London:

> Thursday morning [21 February] the three regiments of foot-guards were drawn out upon the parade in St James's Park: the Duke of York appeared at their head, and intimated his intention of embarking for Holland, desiring such men as were willing to serve with him to declare themselves; 2,100 are to embark ... General Lake is to command this detachment, the destination of which is Holland. Some companies of dragoons, and some battalions of artillery, are likewise to be embarked, for the same service, without delay.[75]

The duke was to go ahead to the United Provinces, as commander-in-chief of British forces on the Continent and also the Hanoverian army.

Prussia was also allied to the United Provinces and, as part of the agreed plan, the Duke of Brunswick moved forwards to protect Prussian and Dutch Gelderland and, on 21 February, work began to throw a bridge across the Rhine at Wesel. Meanwhile in response to Dumouriez's invasion, the Dutch gathered a field force at Gorinchem and around Grave, although at least half of the army was committed in static garrisons. On 25 February the Prussians began to cross the Rhine and so drew closer to Clerfayt's Austrians; the next day

73 Romain, *Souvenirs d'un Officier Royaliste*, Vol.II, p.404
74 *Bulletin des Amis de la vérité* (Vol.I, 1793).
75 *Hampshire Chronicle*, Monday 25 February 1793.

Brunswick conferred at Kleve with the Stadholder's eldest son, the Erfprins (Hereditary Prince), Willem of Orange. Then the Duke of York arrived at The Hague on the night of the 27/28 February where he held discussions with the Stadholder and the British Ambassador; it was decided that the Brigade of Guards, as soon as it landed, would be sent to Dordrecht which had been identified as a strategic priority for the French invasion. Despite these developments, the campaign was still in the balance, if Maastricht fell, the other Dutch defences could collapse one after another. The British would be forced to re-embark and the French, with the aid of the Dutch Patriots, would very rapidly take the rest of country, then, reinforced by Miranda's troops and those raised amongst the Belgian, Liegois and Dutch Patriots, Dumouriez could turn east and fall on Clerfayt.

Conscious of this threat, the Austrians had, from 15 February, brought up corps to both Mannheim, under *Feldzeugmeister* Wenzel Graf von Colloredo-Mels und Wallsee, and the Breisgau, under *General der Kavallerie* Dagobert Sigmund Graf von Wurmser, while Mainz was in turn invested and soon besieged by Prussian and German Imperial troops as well as an Austrian contingent under the command of the *Feldzeugmeister* Hohenlohe-Kirchberg. Finally, on 1 March, Clerfayt, with 50,000 troops, launched his offensive to relieve Maastricht attacking the French on the Roer. That evening, the post at Aldenhoven was surprised and the French were chased from Düren and Jülich losing 1,400 men either killed or wounded and abandoning 600 prisoners; at the same time, Austrian cavalry entered Valkenburg from which the republicans had fled precipitously. The following morning the general offensive began on three axes: the principal corps on Rolducerveld, the vanguard under the orders of the *Generalmajor* Archduke Charles, younger brother of the Emperor Francis II, on Valkenburg, and finally the corps of *Feldmarschalleutnant* Ferdinand Duke of Württemberg on Aachen which was secured after severe fighting.

The French were apparently unaware of Clerfayt's preparations and on 2 March the Minister of War, writing to Miranda, remarked on the ongoing situation at Maastricht:

> I am not astonished by the resistance that this place makes: five or six thousand émigrés, at the head of which is d'Autichamp, and who on all sides only see death, must prevent the inhabitants from surrendering, as they perhaps wish. … An unrelenting fire ought to finally subdue this place; and we must burn as far as to the walls, if it persists to not cede.
>
> I approve your arrangements for the march which you command to Grave, to support the operations of Général Dumouriez, in leaving ten thousand men of the Army of Belgium …[76]

Despite this Miranda did not move north and in Maastricht, still cut from any communication, its defenders awaited a final assault. In the night of 1/2 March, the 4th Company, 1st Division, of the Régiment de Maëstricht was on duty in the fort at Wyck and nothing seemed to distinguish this night from any before, as described by Cézac, one of its members:

76 MIRANDA, Beurnonville to Miranda, Paris, 2 March 1793.

> [W]e had been strongly recommended to make frequent patrols in the various fortifications of this fort, above all to throw into the countryside many fire pots and to constantly keep our eyes and ears open. The night being very dark, our artillery did not stint to make frequent use of its projectiles. Meanwhile, we never saw anything with clarity, we were only astonished with the inaction of the trenches on the right bank, which we had facing us, while the left continued a terrible bombardment ...[77]

This stillness threatened an imminent attack, at least on this advance post, masked by the deafening din elsewhere as well as the darkness.

> Saturday 2 March: Some people claimed to have heard very lively distant cannonades, yesterday and in the morning today. They were probably not mistaken, but as impatience to be delivered from a pitiless bombardment had often caused similar things to be imagined, one did not attach belief to it; besides the wind which began to be very strong, prevented the discharges of the approaching Austrians being distinguished from those of the French. Far from reassuring itself the anxiety grew on seeing the enemy's works on the Mountain of the Twelve Apostles increased and improved. It was supposed that the enemy's intention was to bombard the city from the side which had been spared until then, to no longer leave any shelter for the garrison nor the inhabitants. ... The besieged and the besiegers today continued to make a sustained fire. The bombs caused all the more damage as there was less that exploded in the air.[78]

In the city, it was known that the besieging forces had received a new siege artillery train and that they were about to fire red-hot balls on the city. But, at 11:00 a.m., when the batteries were at last ready to pour in such fire, Miranda formally received the news that:

> [T]he enemy had attacked forward posts on the Roer, forced their way through the troops of the army of observation, commanded by Général La Noüe, who covered the investment of Maastricht, and that they proceeded rapidly, with a force of more than 35,000 men, towards Wyck to bring help to the troops at Maastricht and to save the place, forcing the investment and attack to cease.[79]

The French on the Roer were driven from the formidable fieldworks they had constructed by the Austrians, émigré regiments among them, 'The Royal-Allemand distinguished themselves & massacred all in the name of the late king.'[80] Eventually the news of the Austrian advance reached the besiegers at Maastricht and naturally Le Veneur's troops, in front of Wyck, were the first to hear it.

77 Cézac de Belcayre, *Dix ans d'émigration*, p.79.
78 SHM, Van Dijk Manuscript.
79 *Journal des débats et des décrets*, Vol.43, Miranda to the Minister of War, Liège, 4 March 1793, the second year of the French Republic; 10 o'clock in the evening, and finished at Sint-Truiden on the 6th.
80 Peltier, *Histoire*, p.20.

> The 2nd, alarming rumours spread in the trench: they stated that our troops, stationed in the area of Jülich, had been surprised in these regions by a much superior force and that many men had been slaughtered. Towards night, orders arrived which confirmed this unfortunate news. Several battalions left the trench in haste with orders to bring themselves up to encounter the enemy. Whether the besieged had been informed of our reverse by spies, or they had seen our retrograde movement, they redoubled their fire such that we lost many people. At seven o'clock in the evening, an order came to abandon the trench; the first battalion of the Haute-Vienne stayed to help to remove the remainder of the artillery...[81]

Valence hastily retreated on Liège, immediately begging Dumouriez to come and stem the Austrian breakthrough, so Miranda gave the order to Le Veneur to retire with his 5,000 men on Visé while he himself prepared to retreat, hoping to conceal it under cover of the night. He wanted to form a defensive line between Visé and Tongeren to protect the retreat of his artillery and hold the enemy, to do so too near Maastricht put the position at risk from a sortie.[82] Miranda was not strong enough to face the Austrians alone so needed to combine his forces with those of Valence, so he left for Liège to confer with the latter. Command of the retreat fell to *Lieutenant-général* Égalité. It was a tricky operation as:

> From Tongeren to Liège, there was a paved highway; but up to Tongeren there was only profoundly sodden earthen roads, at this time of year, and along which I feared that our heavy mortars and our artillery would not be able to be drawn ... The convoy for one column was of such length that it was not possible to be properly watched and escorted at any point ...[83]

Le Veneur's troops had barely arrived at Visé when they were attacked by the Austrian vanguard but they managed to hold their position and so allowed Miranda's troops to retreat from Maastricht. When the siege artillery reached Tongeren 7,000 men were placed there and another 7,000 were posted on the heights at Haccourt, on the left bank of the Meuse, opposite Visé, so covering the routes to Liège.[84] The defeat of the French armies had, in a day and a half, driven them over the Maas with the loss of 6 to 7,000 men killed, wounded or prisoners. For their part Miranda and his subordinates had achieved a successful retreat from Maastricht, having not only managed to save almost all the artillery and avoided contact with any pursuers but also, and above all, masked the operation by continuing a sporadic bombardment of the city until the night. Gunner Bricard recalled the retreat from his perspective:

> We set off on the march through a great wind and conditions so black that it was impossible to either see, or hear, each other even those who were alongside us. We

81 Bricard, *Journal du Canonnier Bricard*, p.30.
82 MIRANDA, Miranda to Valence, Hocht, 2 March 1793.
83 Orléans, *Mémoires*, Vol. II, p.339.
84 *Journal des débats et des décrets*, Vol.43, Miranda to the Minister of War, Liège, 4 March 1793, the second year of the French Republic; 10 o'clock in the evening, and finished at Sint-Truiden on the 6th.

> were able to cross the Maas two leagues above Maastricht, on a pontoon bridge; the army rallied on the other side of the Maas. The next day, at the break of day, all the troops had still not arrived; some had lost their way, many had been made prisoner.[85]

In the city, that night 2/3 March, they were unaware of what was happening, indeed when the republican's fire ceased, they expected an immediate assault. Cézac of the Régiment de Maëstricht, a sentry in a defensive outwork, was nervous.

> I thought I made out an individual who appeared to be moving about at the foot of the glacis; I shouted several times the German challenge: "Halt! Wer da?" No one replying, I meanwhile dared not fire, for fear of causing a false alarm; but I kept my musket playing on what appeared to me a living being, all the time of my duty. When the patrol came to relieve me, I showed the officer, as well as several soldiers, what I had seen for a long time and had even given me a certain anxiety. They then recognised that it was the hat of a soldier placed at this post which had been blown off by the wind.[86]

His mistake of course amused his comrades, but a few hours later, with daybreak, they saw a man approaching the glacis. He brought the news that the French were in full flight and so was taken immediately to the governor. It was about 6:30 a.m., and the Marquis d'Autichamp proposed to pursue the retreating troops along the Tongeren road:

> The Prince of Hesse was undecided for a long time; finally, at eight o'clock, he sent a squadron of his regiment, of about eighty men, an infantry battalion of three hundred men, one hundred and fifty to two hundred émigrés, and two 4-pounder pieces. This detachment went about a league from the city; it was preceded by sixty Brunswick jägers. They fired at a great distance on the tail of the enemy's teams, which went from here in the greatest disorder. The Dutch dragoons took some vehicles loaded with powder, camping equipment and eau-de-vie.[87]

After having passed through the village of Rechteren, the troops retired to the city, 30 of the émigré cavalrymen, with Autichamp at their head, then left to go onto Caberg where they discovered some cannon and mortar gun-carriages, as well as a large quantity of bombs and cannon balls, in the deserted entrenchments. Autichamp then sent his aide de camp to Smeermaas and Lanaken from where a number of waggons full of bread, forage and various effects were brought back. Republican soldiers were also found:

> Many stragglers were collected up whose lives were generously spared, although we knew that they would not have done so to us. These unfortunates falling into our hands thought themselves lost. It is remarkable that the citizens were the most

85 Bricard, *Journal du canonnier Bricard*, p.31.
86 Cézac de Belcayre, *Dix ans d'émigration*, p.80.
87 Romain, *Souvenirs d'un Officier Royaliste*, Vol.II, pp.407–408.

> embittered in comparison with the soldiers, for without the escort that led them, they would not have ceased to be insulted; they threw manure at them and mud in their faces, they threatened to hurl them into the river …[88]

In the middle of the morning, the heights on the right bank to the north of Maastricht were suddenly seen to be covered with troops, their weapons sparkling in the sun, while the French continued, in their retreat, to sporadically bombard the city from the left bank of the Maas. The citizens of Maastricht, already rejoicing at their deliverance, swarmed on the ramparts and numbers of them even forced the guard at the gates to go further forward. Riedesel's Brunswick dragoons were the most forward of the troops sent out on reconnaissance and, fearing that the retreat may be a ruse to draw the garrison from the city's ramparts, they did not hesitate to fire their carbines in the direction of the cavalry who advanced towards them. The citizens who had rushed out of the city now dashed back, creating panic. Fears were soon, however, dispelled when staff officers were seen at the front of the advancing troops waving white handkerchiefs, above their heads, fixed to the point of their swords. Archduke Charles, at the head of a regiment of Hungarian hussars and three grenadier battalions, was the first to enter the liberated city and he was soon followed by Coburg and Clerfayt, to be greeted by the noise of the city's artillery and bells.

> [T]he masses of people who crowded the fortifications, uttered the loudest cheers of joy in shouting with unanimity: "Long live the Emperor! Long live the Prince of Cobourg! Long live the brave Austrian army!" The appearance of all this world splashed with colour, heaped together, shouting all at once and in a deafening manner, could have truly made us think that they were tearing each other apart if we had not known that the clamour was on the other hand from delirium and joy. Meanwhile the Austrian army, advancing majestically in battle lines, came to deploy a quarter of a league from the city and presented a most imposing force; it saluted the place with a hundred cannons and, after this customary ceremony, its victorious phalanxes placed themselves in column and made a triumphal entry into Maastricht with their double eagles unfurled, drums and band at the head.[89]

Some of the garrison left the city, by the Brusselsepoort, to harass the republican rear-guard which was already pursued by the Hungarian hussars:

> [T]he garrison, 500 in number, of which the majority were French, made a sortie which was commanded by the Comte d'Allonville, general officer of the day, who having been as far as a league on the Tongeren road, had the villages searched and again took about sixty stragglers and waggons. He noticed an enemy column leaving the village of Lafelt, and had them fired upon, but could not reach them, being out of range. He returned at two o'clock, leading back his detachment …[90]

88 AMC, Fonds Grouvel, GR045.
89 Cézac de Belcayre, *Dix ans d'émigration*, p.85.
90 Lavergne, 'Les émigrés au siège de Maëstricht', p.528.

The city's population indulged in all sorts of demonstrations of joy:

> [E]ach citizen, at his door, distributed to the conquering soldiers, bread, eau-de-vie, beer and tobacco, in fact everything that could give them pleasure and comfort. The women, who not long since had been so dismayed, were those who showed the greatest joy and were the most unrestrained; they extended the sentiment of gratitude as far as to fling their arms round the Austrian soldiers' necks to thank them. In my life, I have not seen such excitement nor more extraordinary enthusiasm …'[91]

That evening, two of the French generals went to the Comte de Blangy to suggest sending an émigré to the Regent, the Comte de Provence, to announce the lifting of the siege and they requested, in the name of the whole corps, that Blangy's own son should be the bearer of the message. For the émigrés, the deliverance of Maastricht was a victory, but each knew that with it came the dispersal of the Régiment de Maëstricht and so a new episode of wandering, danger, misfortune and challenges. However, at least they had the honour of contributing to one of the finest feats of arms in the history of the counter-revolution.

91 Cézac de Belcayre, *Dix ans d'émigration*, p.86.

3

From the Régiment de Maëstricht to the Légion de Damas

At 7:00 a.m. on 4 March 1793 the Maastricht garrison paraded for the ceremony to mark the city's deliverance. Firstly, a *Te Deum* was celebrated at the Basiliek of Sint Servaas, in the presence of the Archduke Charles, Coburg and Clerfayt, then, after three salvoes from the city's artillery followed by rolling fire from all the infantry of the garrison, the troops, lining the roads in two files, were reviewed by the Austrian commanders and the city's governor. In front of the Régiment de Maëstricht, in Brusselsestraat, they 'gave them praise and testimonials of esteem which made them forget their fatigues, and which appeared to them the loftiest price that one could place on their services.'[1] At the conclusion of these ceremonies, Archduke Charles, with the Austrian vanguard, set off after Miranda's troops, pushing back the French republican advanced posts. Other Austrians marched out of the city by the Brusselsepoort and Tongersepoort to go into cantons in neighbouring villages; at midday only Coburg and his staff remained in Maastricht.

Next day, two émigrés who had been wounded during the 24 February sortie and since died were buried with military honours from the garrison's units.[2] The cost of the siege could now be assessed, 721 houses had been damaged, 120 severely, part of the City Hall collapsed and four religious buildings were seriously damaged. Of the 21 victims of the siege, 17 had been killed during the bombardments. The besieging troops lost in total about 800 men, while it was observed, 'As for us, émigrés, we only lost nine men, first and last, killed in two sorties.'[3]

The Prince of Hesse wanted to keep the Régiment de Maëstricht together, on 5 March he wrote to the two French émigré *lieutenant-généraux*:

> I beg you, Messieurs, to assure the French nobility who had assembled under your orders, of my satisfaction for the zeal that they illustrated in cooperating in the defence of Maastricht. The position being changed, it will be unnecessary that they continue their active service; but as the events of war are always uncertain,

1 Romain, *Souvenirs d'un Officier Royaliste*, p.410.
2 Romain, *Souvenirs d'un Officier Royaliste*, p.410, M. de Saint-Florent was buried at the Protestant church.
3 Pradel de Lamase, *Nouvelles notes intimes d'un émigré*, pp.97–98.

> I would desire that you continue to remain united as you have been, … so that, always relying on the same will which the French nobility has just given proof, I can employ them, if the maintenance of the place requires it; and begging you to continue your care to maintain amongst those who remain the discipline so necessary for such a great number of people assembled in the place.[4]

However, the majority declined this offer. Some simply wished to escape the theatre of operations while others sought to join the many foreign corps being raised by the Austrian, Prussian, and Dutch as well as the British armies. Fervent royalists also turned to the Armée de Condé which was now considered the only legitimate representative of the Royal army. As a result, on 6 March the *aide-majors* collected the muskets and cartridges that had been issued to the émigrés.

The ceremonies in Maastricht continued on 6 and 7 March with thanksgiving in the Dutch and Walloon Reformed Churches and a presentation of thanks by the citizenry to the Prince of Hesse; finally, on 8 March, the Stadholder's birthday was celebrated. However, the following day:

> [A]ll celebrations were suspended, and the garrison's order of the day, as well as all the bells, announced a funeral service for the repose of the soul of the so unfortunate King of France, who had perished some days before, victim of his devotion and bounty for his people … All those who could dress in black hurried to attend. The soldiers of all ranks and diverse powers who were at Maastricht also attended in full dress with black crepe on their arms and on the hilt of their swords.[5]

What role could the royalists now play in the counter-revolutionary crusade as the tide of the war had seemingly changed? A few engaged in the Austrian service, particularly in the regiments that had passed into that army following the disbanding of the émigré armies. François de Cézac, then 19 years old, joined, as a volunteer, the émigré Hussards de Bercheny, who rode through Maastricht to join the theatre of operations. Comte Louis de Bouillé, son of the Marquis de Bouillé who was *lieutenant-général* of the Royal armies, on the other hand wished to join the Dutch service 'as major of a regiment of French hussars, which was to be formed from the remnants of those who had emigrated', but the project got no further so he was happy to be accepted as a volunteer with the Prussian army, before raising a regiment of uhlans in British pay some months later.[6]

Among an émigré's most valuable possessions at this time were papers attesting to their service, evidence that could be presented to solicit a place in a corps, and, one day, in the ranks of the reconstituted Royal army, at least for those who lived long enough. Service in a campaign would also count towards a royal pension that they, or those who survived them, could hope for in the future. A certificate that showed they had taken up arms once again may strengthen a claim for a higher rank in a newly raised émigré unit. For the Catholic

4 Lavergne, 'Les émigrés au siège de Maëstricht', p.530.
5 Cézac de Belcayre, *Dix ans d'émigration*, p.89.
6 Louis-Joseph-Amour Marquis de Bouillé, *Souvenirs et fragments pour servir aux mémoires de ma vie et de mon temps* (Paris: Société d'histoire contemporaine, 1908), Vol.II, p.121.

officers, these documents would also give them the right to claim one day, after 22 years' service, the coveted cross of the royal and military order of Saint-Louis, established in 1693 by Louis XIV. This explains the particular importance of the certificates bearing the seal of the Prince of Hesse, distributed, from 8 March, by the company commanders to the members of the Régiment de Maëstricht.[7]

On the other hand, the Regent of France wanted to know about the émigrés who had not shared 'the glory of their companions in arms,' who they were and what they had done.[8] Such men were few and on 25 March he asked the Comte de Blangy to pass on his regard for the majority:

> I have been too pleased, Monsieur, with the manner in which the Émigrés have conducted themselves at Maastricht to not desire to make them acquainted with all my satisfaction. ... I beg you to say on my behalf to our companions in arms, that I will never at any time forget their noble devotion and I hope that I will be able one day to be at their head and with the aid of their valour, restore the altar and the throne. ...[9]

The same day, the Prince of Hesse passed on the thanks of the States-General and Stadholder to the Comte de Blangy as well as repeating his personal thanks.[10] Finally, to show its gratitude, the city of Maastricht decided to accord citizenship to all the French refugees who had contributed to its defence and found themselves homeless, as well as distributing a service certificate of their own. Augustin de Tourdonnet, who left to join the Armée de Condé, wrote: 'I had not wanted to quit Maastricht ... without having my diploma in my pocket. Here it is, duly sealed and initialled. I am as proud of it as my title of Marquis'.[11] These certificates were more prized as they were awarded by those who had shown no less bravery, one émigré paid homage to the city's magistrates who had 'lacked neither wisdom nor courage; they showed themselves at once disposed to act and acted since as men who love their country and are ready to serve it. It is to them that it is necessary in part to attribute the place's safety'.[12]

Meanwhile the fight for the survival of the United Provinces continued. The Stadholder had confided operational command of the republic's army to his eldest son, the Erfprins Willem, who was personally courageous and, if, at 21 years of age, he lacked experience, he had had a solid military education. Born in 1772, he had received honorific ranks from a very young age, such as *colonel* of the Hollandsche Gardes te Voet Regiment (Dutch Foot Guards) on 19 October 1784, before, in 1790, being appointed *generaal van infantery* and governor of Breda, one of the principal strongholds in the Dutch defences. Detached on 31 January 1793, to the King of Prussia, to represent the army of the United Provinces, on his

7 Bazouges family archives.
8 Lavergne, 'Les émigrés au siège de Maëstricht', pp.528–529, the letter appears to follow that of 25 March.
9 British Library, London (BL), Add MS 8069.
10 Lavergne, 'Les émigrés au siège de Maëstricht', pp.529–530.
11 Pradel de Lamase, *Nouvelles notes intimes d'un émigré*, p.98.
12 Jacques de Thiboult de Puisact, *Journal d'un fourrier de l'armée de Condé* (Paris: Didier, 1882), p.321.

return he was charged with placing the army on a war footing to resist the French republican forces.

As has been seen, Dumouriez had entered Dutch territory on 19 February and, from 22 February, attacked Breda, Klundert and Geertruidenberg which offered scant resistance, in contrast to Willemstad, commanded by *Lieutenant-Generaal* Carel Baron van Boetzelaer, 'Usefully assisted by the Chevalier de Verclay, *capitaine* of the corps royal de l'artillerie de France.'[13] The commander of Willemstad rejected all French summonses and resisted their bombardment, thus giving the Erfprins, and his younger brother Frederik, time to get to the Waal and Lower Maas to erect new defence lines along the rivers and canals. These lines were well provided with artillery with which some French émigré officers served, among them was Jean-Etienne Fourrier de Nacquard who, after seeking to raise an artillery company around a French cadre in January 1793, had been appointed *tweede capitein* (second captain) in the Dutch artillery on 22 February.[14] The Dutch prepared to place all the troops from Gelderland in the entrenched camp at Nijmegen while the bulk of their men were placed behind Gorinchem.[15] Men were also posted at Dordrecht where, 'the first regular companies of émigrés were organised in the service of the States-General,' these last were soon to form the Légion de Béon.[16] It was there that the Dutch were also joined by the British Guards Brigade and the Duke of York.[17]

Coburg's Austrians, on leaving Maastricht, had pursued the French republican troops as far as Leuven on 9 March, where Dumouriez joined them on 13 March. In difficult circumstances he gathered his dispersed troops and retook Tienen on 15 March but was defeated at Neerwinden three days later, losing a significant part of his army, 4,000 casualties and 10,000 fugitives. Dumouriez then sought time and space to retreat so he could re-establish the army in Flanders on the Vauban barrier fortresses. To do this, he engaged in direct negotiations with the Austrians to whom he agreed to give up Condé-sur-l'Escaut. As a result, Dumouriez was publicly accused by decree on 2 April and then confronted by commissioners tasked to bring him before the Convention, which would inevitably lead to condemnation and immediate execution. In response his hussars seized the commissioners to hand them over to the Austrians and, on 5 April 1793, Dumouriez attempted to get his troops to march with him onto Paris. However, they denounced him as a traitor and he fled to the Austrians, accompanied by some of his troops who went on to form a new émigré corps, the Légion de Bourbon, in Austrian service.

On 22 March the Duke of Brunswick had reached 's-Hertogenbosch at the head of 25,000 Prussians and Hanoverians and then headed for Antwerp. Then on 4 April he continued his advance from there to the French frontier, while the Prince of Coburg reached Quiévrain and from there threatened Maubeuge, Valenciennes and Condé. The Dutch retook Breda, then Geertruidenberg and Klundert. Then on 8 April, representatives of the coalition met at Antwerp to set its war aims and the new strategy to be adopted. The same day, the Erfprins

13 Jean-Baptiste-Louis de Crossard, *Mémoires militaires et historiques pour servir à l'histoire de la guerre depuis 1792 jusqu'en 1815 inclusivement* (Paris: Migneret, 1829), Vol.I, p.23.

14 Nacquard was later to serve in the British Army commanding the Dutch Emigrant Artillery.

15 Crossard, *Mémoires militaires et historiques*, Vol.I, p.24.

16 Brons, *Journal d'émigration*, p.136.

17 Bouillé, *Souvenirs*, Vol.II, p.130.

was officially named commander-in-chief of the Dutch corps which was to act as part of the coalition forces, under the overall command of the Prinz von Sachsen-Coburg-Saalfeld.

The following day, 9 April, the British and Austrians proposed that once the French had been driven from the invaded territory, including Nice and Savoy, they should be left to their own devices. France was in turmoil. Popular resistance to revolutionary changes had coalesced against conscription; political infighting, the settling of scores as well as local issues had combined into insurrection. Swathes of France was in revolt against the regime including major cities such as Marseille, Bordeaux and Lyon, as well as Toulon, along with significant rural regions especially in Western France, in Brittany and, most significantly, the Vendée. The hope was that the royalists and constitutionalists would bring down the Convention: if needed, with the aid of émigrés who could be disembarked on the Western or Mediterranean coast. The Prussians and Stadholder's view, which prevailed, was that the frontiers of France should be attacked to attract and fix the maximum number of French republican troops, so aiding the royalist insurrections. The coalition allies were thus to successively and methodically capture the frontier strongholds opening a wide corridor to expose Paris but without venturing much further, each mindful of the fate of the previous 1792 campaign in Champagne.

In pursuit of this plan, British troops, now numbering 4,000 men, set off from Antwerp on 12 April for Lokeren and then Ghent, while others were embarked for Oostende. The same day, the Prussians penetrated into French Flanders and advanced between Menen and the camp of Maulde to reach Tournai. Hanoverian troops moved up to join the British expeditionary corps in Flanders. Finally, on 20 April, one of the Dutch divisions camped near Breda, under Prince Frederik, marched south to join the Prussian troops camped under Tournai and support Coburg's right wing.

Due to the state and strength of the Netherlands' forces, the field army was formed of only two divisions, the first commanded by the *Generaal Major* Carel von Geusau, a 'brave, educated and wise officer,' with whom the Erfprins and his staff marched, and the second by the Stadholder's younger son, Frederik, barely 19 years old.[18] The land forces of the United Provinces had been 200,000 men strong at the opening of the War of the Spanish Succession (1702–1714) but they had shrunk to 35,000 at the time of the 1787 revolt. Since then, the Stadholder had tried, in the face of political opposition, to augment the army to 50,000 but in April 1793 only 16,000 combatants could be brought into the field as at least half of the army was committed to defending the numerous fortresses that formed, in this flat country, the first belt of defences. However, Baron de Crossard, an émigré officer with strong links with the Dutch army, considered that 'the troops were fine, the cavalry well mounted; and everything that applied to the equipment did not bear the impression of parsimony at all ...'[19] The Duke of York, for one, was less impressed by the Dutch in the field, describing them in a private letter of 14 May, as 'without exception the worst archpoltroons that have ever been seen'.[20]

18 Crossard, *Mémoires militaires et historiques*, Vol.I p.49.

19 Crossard, *Mémoires militaires et historiques*, Vol.I p.35.

20 Royal Archives, Windsor (RAW), De Budé Papers, GEO/ADD/15/0548, 14 May 1793; York to General Jacob de Budé (1737–1818), a Swiss officer, previously in Dutch and Sardinian service, who had been the duke's military tutor and subsequently his trusted confidant.

Already almost half the soldiers in the Dutch army were foreign and, even without the Dutch patriots, there was little enthusiasm to resist the invasion of the French armies amongst the general population. So, it was necessary to recruit new mercenary soldiers in an already very competitive market, as the different belligerent nations sought to expand their forces. Among them was Britain, her army, after years of neglect, was manifestly unprepared for conflict with France or even to intervene on continental Europe. Lacking men, training and equipment, with poor discipline, the government's hasty attempts to rectify the shortfalls, for instance, by raising new regiments, proved ill-conceived and even counter-productive. King George was also Elector of Hanover and so the troops of the electorate were drawn upon while the British government, as well as providing financial support to other allied nations, also paid for troops from other German states to serve with the coalition. In addition, new units of light troops were raised on the Continent in which émigré officers were to be found, the first of these was proposed in May 1793 by Captain George Ramsay and became known as the York Rangers or sometimes under his name.[21] The Austrians already had several 'French' units in their service but at the outbreak of the war the United Provinces only had some individual émigré artillery and engineer officers in their service.

Circumstances were favourable for émigrés who wished to offer their services to the Republic of the United Provinces. At the beginning of February 1793, the Comte de Bosen and Baron d'Oberlin-Mitterbach, officers of the Hussards de Chamborant and Bercheny, had together proposed to the Stadholder to raise a corps of 12 companies of hussars, eight of foot *chasseurs-carabiniers* and supporting arms, amounting to nearly 2,000 men.[22] At the same time, the Chevalier de Boissieu, *maréchal de camp*, offered to form another mixed corps but nothing came of these two projects.[23] The Comte de Béon, who was then living at Utrecht, solicited the French Regent's authorisation to propose to the Stadholder to raise an émigré unit of which he would be proprietor, describing himself as 'honoured with the confidence of a considerable number of good Frenchmen all devoted to honour.'[24] He asked the Stadholder for arms to assist in the defence of the United Provinces and sent the States-General a draft capitulation for the levy of an infantry unit. He seems to have had positive indications as on 1 March Béon, then at The Hague, requested that the Stadholder send him, 'the signature which [was] indispensably necessary to begin his assemblage and to carry out the complete formation of the corps.'[25]

Such an initiative was supported by *Lieutenant-Generaal* van Dopff who wrote to the Stadholder:

> In the critical state that the Republic finds itself, it is necessary to seize opportunities; this is to augment by all possible means our defence, in order to avoid the

21 For the deficiencies of the British Army see Hon. J.W. Fortescue, *British Campaigns in Flanders 1690–1794 being extracts from 'A History of the British Army'* (London: Macmillan, 1918) especially pp.185–190 and 197–198. For the York Rangers see Robert W. Gould, *Mercenaries of the Napoleonic Wars* (Brighton: Tom Donovan, 1995), pp.114–116.

22 Koninklijk Huisarchief (Dutch Royal Archives), The Hague (KHN), A31 Inv. 2120.

23 KHN, A31 Inv. 2120.

24 KHN, A31 2124.

25 KHN, A31 2124.

> depth of misfortune. This is why I have the honour to inform Your Serene Highness that the émigrés here assert that it would not be difficult to assemble before long a considerable corps of French émigrés. It is known that one was not happy with them in the previous campaign, but, Monsieur, the defensive war to which we have been reduced is a contest in which one cannot deny that they surpass other nations through the number of educated and experienced officers that they have in the engineers and artillery.
>
> Perhaps it would have been dangerous to take an ordinary chief with an individual corps; but in taking a general with reputation, a man of birth, the interest of his misfortune and that of the cause of his homeland depending more or less on the success of ours, these pressing motives ought to make him embrace the defence of our country as that of his own, and I persuade myself that he would do it in desperation.
>
> Moreover, one would be sure that he would only take with him and admit in his corps officers of recognised merit, seeing that his existence and reputation would depend on them ... There is no time to lose for I fear that the completion of our augmentation will be difficult.'[26]

Perhaps he was listened to, as on 4 March, the same day on which Maastricht celebrated its deliverance, the Stadholder agreed to the Béon's proposal.

François-Frédéric de Béarn, Comte de Béon, born in 1754 into an old family of the *noblesse d'épée* (literally, nobility of the sword) from the South West of France, brought the advantages of honourable service and the strong support of the Princes for such an enterprise. He had begun his career in 1770 as *sous-lieutenant*, with the rank of *lieutenant*, in the Carabiniers, and two years later he was *capitaine* in the Régiment du Roi cavalerie, In 1777 he joined the Gardes du Corps du Roi as *sous-lieutenant* in the Compagnie de Luxembourg but, that year, with the rank of *lieutenant-colonel* and then cavalry *mestre de camp* from 1780, followed by being a chevalier of Saint-Louis two years later.[27] At the time of the Revolution, Béon was still *sous-lieutenant* in the Gardes du Corps and continued to serve protecting his sovereign at Versailles, in particular during the events of October 1789. Emigrating in 1791 the day after the Varennes affair and the disbanding of the Gardes du Corps, he had then joined the King's brothers who, in June 1792, had sent him on a diplomatic mission to Spain. He served in the 1792 campaign with his company of the Gardes du Corps and was discharged on 26 November at Jülich. He had already considered raising a unit, in the name of the Gardes du Corps, for the service of an allied power as he requested permission from the Comte d'Artois to do so, on 22 November 1792; although this was granted, the project did not progress.[28] Although Béon had been at Utrecht, his unit's depot was placed at Nijmegen where the first of its officers' brevets were issued, dated 7 March 1793. That day, Béon had, with the first hundred volunteers, crossed the Hollands Diep to Moerdijk to co-operate in the defence of the Dutch batteries

26 Dated 2 March 1793, quoted in René Bittard des Portes, *Les émigrés à la cocarde noire, en Angleterre, dans les provinces belges, en Hollande et à Quiberon* (Paris: Paul, 1908), pp.14–15.

27 NAN, A31 Inv. 2124.

28 KHN, A31 4294.

after which the émigrés had advanced 'at the moment when Geertruidenberg and Breda were attacked'.[29]

Under the terms of the capitulation, the émigré unit, to be 'employed apart or attached to such corps of troops that Their High Authorities will find appropriate,' was to have six infantry companies formed exclusively of gentlemen and former officers who, 'armed lightly', would perform 'the duty of foot chasseurs.' The staff was to comprise the *colonel, lieutenant-colonel, major, adjudant, aalmoesenier* (chaplain), *quartiermeester*, and *chirurgien major* (surgeon major). As was the practice in the army of the United Provinces, the *colonel* was captain proprietor of the first company, the *lieutenant-colonel* the second and the *major* the third. Each company would have: a *capitein, commandant* in the place of the titular *capitein* in the first two companies, a *lieutenant*, a *tweede lieutenant* (second lieutenant) and a *vaandrig* (or ensign); the exception was the third company which had no *capitein* being commanded directly by the *major*.[30] The NCOs were *chefs de section* (section leaders) in lieu of sergeants and *chefs d'esouade* (squad leaders) for corporals. The émigrés were reluctant to have the ranks of *sergent* or *caporal* as these were *bas-officiers* in the royal army, only that of *fourrier* was acceptable, responsible for the management and quartering of his section and elected by his comrades. Initially the legion attracted recruits easily, so on 29 March it already had the first three chasseur companies complete while the fourth, that of the Chevalier des Aïgues, only lacked a drummer and three wagons. Nevertheless, it was never to exceed four infantry companies.

Doubtless the Chevalier de Damas-Crux, of the Régiment de Maëstricht, was well aware of the capitulation awarded to the Comte de Béon, and also decided, in turn, to become a military entrepreneur. Born at the Château de Crux-le-Châtel, in Nivernais, on 10 February 1754, the young Etienne-Charles had been appointed a Knight of Malta in the cradle then, at the age of 16, *sous-lieutenant* in the Régiment de Limousin which was then commanded by his elder brother and godfather, Louis-Etienne-François. He was promoted *aide-major* in 1772 before attending the Ecole d'Artillerie de La Fère. On his return to his regiment in 1776 he was nominated *capitaine en second* of a fusilier company, then *capitaine en second* of the grenadiers on 4 July 1777 and finally commander of the chasseur company two years later. After two brief stints on the general staff, he was promoted to second-in-command of the Régiment d'Aquitaine, on 3 October 1779, which was posted at Saint-Brieuc, on the north coast of Brittany. In an inspection of 1781, he was reported to be 'very applied; leads his battalion well, has a very good tone of command.'[31]

He accompanied his regiment's second battalion, as supernumerary *lieutenant-colonel*, when it embarked at Brest on 26 January 1781 for India, part of French support for Tipu Sultan of Mysore (1750–1799) in his wars against the British East India Company and globalisation of the American War of Independence. It was only after the Bailli de Suffren had defeated the British fleet, on 20 February 1782, that the battalion could disembark at Parangipettai

29 Comte de Béon to the Stadholder, dated 29 March 1793. The list of the names of the second company is attached to the document while the third is already assembled. KHN, A31 2120.

30 *Naamregister der Heeren militaire Officieren den Capitein Generaal…* 1793–March 1794 (The Hague: Unknown Publisher, 1794), p.224.

31 Alexandre Mazas, *Histoire de l'ordre royal et militaire de Saint-Louis depuis son institution en 1693 jusqu'en 1830*, second edition (Paris: Didot, 1860), Vol.II, p.393.

(then called Porto Novo), on the Coromandel Coast, on 10 March. Reinforced by 2,000 Mysorean troops, the French seized Cuddalore, 20 kilometres to the south of Puducherry (formerly Pondicherry) on 3 April and the Aquitaine battalion was stationed in the town. In June 1783, the British advanced from Chennai (Madras) and besieged Cuddalore and, on 13 June, assaulted the town; this was repulsed after fierce fighting in which the Chevalier de Damas-Crux commanded a unit of Indian sepoys. Twelve days later, the French made a sortie but were cut off and Damas-Crux, who was abandoned by his men, was taken prisoner. He was, however, soon released, after peace with the Treaty of Paris on 3 September 1783, and the Aquitaine battalion was sent to Puducherry where it remained in garrison for a year. In August 1784 it embarked for France but only reached Lorient, in Brittany, after almost a year, at the end of July 1785. Etienne-Charles had been appointed *mestre de camp*, that is to say colonel commandant, of the Régiment de Vexin, then in garrison at Saintes, near Bordeaux, in 1784 but, as a result of the lengthy voyage, he only joined his command at the end of 1785. On 2 April 1786 he was made a chevalier of Saint-Louis; that year the Régiment de Vexin was posted to Perpignan and then Marseille, in 1788, and its commander was noted as 'zealous, knowledgeable, in all regards a good chief.'[32]

At Marseille the Régiment de Vexin became embroiled in the progress of the Revolution in the South of France but the officers, along with some NCOs and men, remained resolute and had tried, in August 1791, to seize Monaco to rally the still loyal troops there. The plan failed but most of the Vexin officers remained together and joined the Armée des Princes, with their *colonel*. The King's brothers wished to make the unit a model and attached it to the vanguard of the Armée du Centre in the advance into Champagne, alongside the Compagnie des Chasseurs (or *gentilshommes*) de Rouault.

At the end of the disastrous 1792 campaign, both units were dissolved on 27 November in the Liège region: the Chasseurs de Rouault at Malmedy and the Régiment de Vexin at Noorbeek, east of Visé and Maastricht, unusually the latter still at the same strength as it had entered the campaign.[33] Many of the men found themselves in Maastricht when it was besieged by the French and took part in its defence. The Chevalier de Damas-Crux was employed on the staff of the Régiment de Maëstricht, as *major* for the First Division. His brother, the Comte de Damas-Crux, commanded the 4th Company of the Second Division (36 men), in which the Comte de Rouault was his second-in-command, and participated in the sortie led by Autichamp. In this same company there were 14 former Vexin officers serving in its ranks including *Capitaine* Pierre François Hugues de Burgault de Montfort, *Lieutenant* Jean-Baptiste du Crozet and *Sous-lieutenant* Pierre-Simon-Louis de Pindray d'Ambelles. The former *chirurgien-major* of the Régiment de Vexin and his *aide* also served through the siege.[34]

32 Mazas, *Histoire de l'ordre royal et militaire de Saint-Louis*, p.393.

33 A note conserved at the Chantilly Archives, (*AMC, Série Y, Carton VI, dossier 3, ff.86–88*) but undated, is without doubt the last roll drawn up when the regiment entered campaign, with a total of 80: 32 officers, 4 volunteers, 1 surgeon, 1 assistant surgeon, 3 NCOs, 1 *appointé*, 11 chasseurs, 25 fusiliers.

34 'Etat nominatif du Régiment de Maëstricht' *La Sabretache* <http://lasabretache.fr/produit/regiment-de-maestricht-1793/> (accessed 17 December 2019).

Etienne-Charles de Damas-Crux had a prestigious name, as well as his military service, to support his aspirations. The Damas family was of the old *noblesse d'épée* and claimed to trace its origins to the Crusader Kingdoms of the Middle East (Damas being French for Damascus). It had a number of aristocratic branches including the Crux branch that appeared in the second half of the Fourteenth Century when Philiberte de Crux had married Hugues de Damas in 1362 bringing with her a modest property in Nivernais. Nevertheless, the Damas-Crux retained the arms of the senior branch: *D'or à la croix ancrée de gueules* (Gold with the red cross moline) as well as its motto: *Et fortis et fidelis* (Both strong and faithful).

Thanks to its many offspring and therefore alliances, the Damas-Crux branch prospered through the centuries with members in senior ranks of not only the French army but also the ecclesiastical orders and its fiefdom became a county at the beginning of the Seventeenth Century. Its seat remained, until the time of the Revolution, the ancient château of Crux-Châtel, north-east of Nevers. Louis-Alexandre, the Comte de Damas-Crux, died there on 6 September 1763, at the age of 57, leaving his wife, Marie-Louise de Menou, and a large family. Their eldest child, Louis-Etienne-François (1735–1814), had entered the 1ère Compagnie des Mousquetaires at the age of 15 and was also appointed *menin* to the Dauphin, that is to say games companion of the future Louis XVI. *Capitaine* in the Régiment des Dragons de Flamarens in 1757, he distinguished himself during the Seven Years War and was nominated to the command of the Régiment de Foix in 1761 and then the Régiment de Limousin from 1762 to 1779. Chevalier de Saint-Louis in 1761, he had some command positions before being named *maréchal de camp* in 1780 and was later military governor of the Three Bishoprics (Metz, Toul and Verdun) until the Revolution. After emigrating, Louis-Etienne-François Comte de Damas-Crux served in the 1792 campaign in the Armée du Centre, as *adjudant-général* to *Maréchal* de Broglie. After the siege of Maastricht, he remained some months with the Comte de Blangy before being summoned in 1794 by Monsieur to accompany the Duc de Berry, the youngest son of the Comte d'Artois and thus the nephew of the future King Louis XVIII. He served alongside Berry in the campaigns of the Prince de Condé in 1794 to 1801 and stayed with him during his travels through Europe before sharing his exile in England until 1814. At the Restoration he was Peer of France and knight of honour to the Duchesse d'Angoulême, wife of the eldest son of the Comte d'Artois, in 1814. The second child of the Damas-Crux family, François, joined the clergy and it would have doubtless been the same for Etienne-Charles, as the fifth child, if his sibling, the fourth, a page to King Louis XV, had not died as a youth in 1763.

Yet at the time of the Revolution, the reputations of three other members of the Damas family eclipsed those of the Damas-Crux brothers. The youngest, Roger de Damas d'Antigny (1765–1858), had served in the French army before going to Russia, in 1787, to fight against the Ottoman Empire, distinguishing himself on many occasions. Serving until December 1790, he became a heroic figure, less than 25 years old, and attracted other compatriots to Russian service. He left Empress Catherine's service at the beginning of 1791 and joined the King's brothers at Koblenz. He was attached to the staff of the Comte d'Artois in the 1792 campaign and accompanied him when he went to Russia to solicit help from Catherine. Failing to persuade Artois to go to the Vendée, he served with the allies in Flanders in the spring of 1793 before joining the Armée de Condé, in which he bought the famous Légion de Mirabeau and served in the campaigns of 1795 to 1797, before passing into Neapolitan service. Later Napoleon was heard to speak of him with great respect, 'Every time that he spoke of the bravery of the émigrés, he always cited the Comte Roger de Damas'.[35]

Roger's older brother, Charles (1758–1829), a supernumerary *sous-lieutenant* in 1771, was named gentleman of honour to Monsieur, the Comte de Provence and the future Louis XVIII, in 1776 and chevalier of Saint-Louis in 1778. He served in the American War of Independence initially as aide de camp to the Comte de Rochambeau, September 1780, and then, after promotion to *mestre de camp* on 29 April 1781, as *colonel en second* of the Régiment d'Aunis on 27 January 1782. On his return from America he transferred to the cavalry, passing through different regiments until, in 1788, he received the command of the Régiment des Dragons de Monsieur in which he strove to maintain discipline during the Revolution. On 20 June 1791, the Comte Charles de Damas, at the head of 150 horsemen of the 13e Dragons (formerly Monsieur) which was stationed at Clermont, was to assist the flight of the Royal Family, but impeded by the municipal authorities and the inhabitants of the town, he only managed to join the King at Varennes with a single officer and some still-loyal NCOs and troopers. The next day he was imprisoned but was amnestied on 15 September and emigrated, joining the Comte de Provence at Koblenz. In November he was appointed to lead the company of émigré officers from the Dragons de Monsieur and, at the same time, offered by the Comte de Provence the command of one of the two companies of his own Gardes du Corps, it was in this latter position that he served in the 1792 campaign and remained in the prince's suite afterwards. So, when La Fayette tried to get the King's brothers to intercede on his behalf:

> [T]here was no communication at Hamm with these prisoners and the émigrés in the suite of the Princes, with the sole exception of Comte Charles de Damas whose loyalty is well known and who asked the Princes for approval. I have often heard him say that if he met La Fayette, whose conduct he could not excuse, he could not help but express his gratitude, believing he owed him his life after his arrest with the King at Varennes.[36]

Charles de Damas later served as aide de camp to the Comte d'Artois before joining the Armée de Condé in which he commanded the legion of his brother Roger. He then remained with the army until it was disbanded in February 1801, serving as *major* in the Dragons d'Enghien. Gaston de Damas, the youngest brother of Charles and Roger, after emigrating had served in the 1792 campaign and then became an officer in the Uhlans Britanniques.

The third Damas of note at this time was the Comte Alexandre de Damas whose early career testified to the decline of the family's oldest branch of which he was issue. He had been received as page to the Dauphine, the future Queen Marie-Antoinette, on 1 April 1771 and started his military career in the cavalry as *sous-lieutenant* in the Dragons d'Orléans on 7 April 1774. He later passed to the infantry, doubtless having given up buying a place as *colonel* in the cavalry as too expensive, and became *mestre de camp en second* of the

35 Laure Junot d'Abrantès *Mémoires de Madame la duchesse d'Abrantès, ou Souvenirs historiques sur Napoléon, la Révolution, le Directoire, le Consulat, l'Empire et la Restauration* (Paris: Mame-Delaunay, 1833), Vol.IV p.124.

36 Hauterive, *Journal d'émigration du comte d'Espinchal*, p.511.

Régiment de Soissonnais on 11 November 1782. Having married into a wealthy family in Saint-Domingue (now Haïti), he was promoted *colonel* of the Régiment de Beauvoisis on 10 May 1788 and named chevalier de Saint-Louis on 8 April 1789, at the age of 44. The upheaval of the Revolution, however brought him distinction after 27 officers of the Régiment de Beauvoisis had fought for more than four hours on 19 April 1791 against 700 mutinous soldiers at Wissembourg, in Alsace. After the Comte Alexandre de Damas had presented the officers on 16 June to the Prince de Condé, he, as their *colonel*, was honoured by being made the prince's first squire and aide de camp. Alexandre de Damas nevertheless was permitted to remain at the head of his officers in the 6th Company (Bourbonnais and Beauvoisis) of the Chasseurs Noble in the infantry of the Armée de Condé, with the rank of *premier lieutenant* in 1793. *Capitaine* in 1794, he was chosen, on 15 June 1795, to present the compliments of the Prince de Condé and his army to the new King Louis XVIII on his accession. That year when four new cadre regiments were raised in the Armée de Condé, he was given the command of one of them. The four *colonels* of these regiments were each appointed *maréchal de camp*, the Comte de Damas from 5 June 1795. Later promoted *major général* then *général*, he remained with the Prince de Condé until the end of his exile in 1814, a Peer of France, he retired in November 1816.

In the weeks that followed the lifting of the Siege of Maastricht, Etienne-Charles de Damas-Crux, if he was to succeed with his project, had to quickly exploit the advantages he currently possessed. The first was the role that he had played in the defence of the city with the Régiment de Maëstricht, in which his conduct had been noted by the governor, and the second was his proximity to the Comte de Blangy, allowing him to be informed of the progress of the different corps which were being established. He had much in common with the Comte de Béon: both had been born in 1754 into families of the old *noblesse d'épée*, they had begun their careers the same year, were *mestres de camp* and holders of the cross of Saint-Louis at the time of the Revolution, served side by side in the Armée du Centre during the Champagne offensive and had taken refuge in the United Provinces. From such similarities, rivalry would grow.

On 27 March 1793 Etienne de Damas-Crux, having travelled to The Hague, addressed a memoir to the Stadholder soliciting 'the favour of forming a corps in the manner of that which Their Mightiest have deigned to grant the agreement with the Comte de Béon' which would be named the Régiment de Maëstricht.[37] He suggested that the six infantry companies be at first of 50 men, so they could enter the campaign quickly, and then later be progressively raised to 100. He also recommended the addition of a seventh, artillery, company with three officers and 50 NCOs and men from the former Corps de l'Artillerie Royale armed with two field pieces. Willem V responded favourably assuring him 'that the Council of State would ratify the proposed capitulation and that the United Provinces accepted with readiness the assistance of brave soldiers who were already entitled to its gratitude.'[38] Three days later Damas had developed his project by proposing that the corps, to be called the Chasseurs nobles de Maëstricht, would have, like the national jager corps, two battalions each of 374 men, and he submitted a projected capitulation of sixteen

37 KHN, A31 Inv. 2120.
38 Bittard des Portes, *Les émigrés*, p.23.

articles.[39] Copying Béon's idea, he proposed that the six companies of chasseurs would be only of French émigré gentlemen and former officers, adding, in the proposed capitulation sent to the States-General the following day, that 'the title of Chasseurs nobles de Maëstricht will infinitely flatter all those who would form the corps, in that it will recall an honourable time for them; and would bear it with pride, as a memorial of their gratitude for the generous asylum that they have found in this part of Their Mightiest Lords' possessions.'[40]

Two days earlier, the Comte de Béon, without mentioning the Chevalier de Damas-Crux by name, denounced to the Stadholder the opportunism of new applicants whose activity would only hinder the recruitment of his own corps, 'they attract to them individuals who would have already completed the corps, they promise very great advantages. But reason ought to put an end to their hopes, and make known the danger of hearing these applicants.' He emphasised that his unit was being raised 'with the authorisation and support of the French Princes' but that recruitment had slowed with the risk that both corps would be 'two imperfect skeletons'.[41] Recruitment of French émigrés for Dutch service was in fact much harder than Béon suggested, as other opportunities existed in the pay of other countries as well as the Armée de Condé. Indeed, Béon's second company, established from 29 March 1793, included 13 former officers of the Brigade Irlandaise alongside 90 French volunteers and he pursued this source of manpower. So, on 1 April, the Comte de Béon entered into an accord, at Nijmegen, with the Duc de Fitz-James, representative of the former Brigade Irlandaise with the French Princes, for the former Régiment de Berwick to not only furnish him with these 13 officers but provide his 4th and 5th Companies in full:

> The Duc de Fitz-James proposes to attach to Monsieur the Comte de Béon's corps of French gentlemen, two companies of chasseurs which will have the same formation and number of officers and fusiliers as the other companies of the corps. The officers of these two companies will be taken from the eight most senior officers of the Régiment de Berwick, from the number of which is the lieutenant-colonel and major, the rest of the officers in addition of those who will be active will be in the ranks.[42]

The agreement covered recruitment, the promotion of the officers when vacancies occurred, particularly from amongst those serving as volunteers, and a distinctive uniform as well as a clause that the engagement would end should the Princes wish to resurrect the Régiment de Berwick.

By the time of the Revolution, the rank and file of the Irish Brigade were Belgians, Liégois, Luxembourgers, Germans and any nationality other than French, with the exception of German-speaking Alsatians and Lorrainers. In the military emigration the Régiment de Berwick had retained about 500 men while Dillon and Walsh, the other two regiments of the old brigade, kept 150 and 120 respectively. While these last two had broken up following their disbanding on 23 November 1792, the officers of the Régiment de Berwick, which

39 KHN, A31 Inv. 2120, letter of 30 March 1793.
40 NAN, 1.01.19 Inv. 2622.
41 NAN, 1.01.19 Inv. 2622, letter at The Hague, 29 March 1793.
42 KHN, A31 2124.

traditionally maintained a recruitment depot in Liège, had remained in the region until the French invasion when, together, they had retreated onto the Rhine.

The men for the two companies were to be recruited from 'among the former non-commissioned officers and soldiers who served in the last campaign with the Régiment de Berwick, that had been disbanded and who were known to still be in the Liège Region, very disposed to re-join their officers.' The accord also specified the officers' role in the formation of the companies:

> These conditions proposed by the Duc de Fitz-James and accepted by the Comte de Béon, it is further agreed that the Berwick officers will occupy themselves with the recruitment, armament, clothing and equipment, and that the Comte de Béon obliges them to furnish for this purpose sixty florins per man. These two chasseur companies will be on the pay scale of the Dutch national infantry. Without being able to pretend to the other advantages or gratifications accorded to the Comte de Béon for his corps, the Duc de Fitz-James and the officers who command these companies expressly renounce them by this agreement.'[43]

Eight officers were chosen for the two companies, their names being submitted by Béon on the same day as the accord, 1 April.[44] The two *capitaines* had been *lieutenant-colonels* and all the others were former *capitaines* in the Régiment de Berwick.

Fourth Company	
Capitaine	James ÔMoore [James O'Moore]
Lieutenant	Antoni Egan [Antony Egan]
Sous-lieutenant	John Geogehegan [James Geoghegan]
Enseigne	John Mulhalt [John Mulhall]
Fifth Company	
Capitaine	Thomas Macdermott [Thomas McDermott]
Lieutenant	Thadée ÔMeara [Thadée O'Meara]
Sous-lieutenant	Valter Grace [Walter Grace]
Enseigne	Williames ÔKennédy [Liam O'Kennedy, he also used the first names William and John]

Béon sought to expand his corps and, with the arrival of more French volunteers among whom were a number of former cavalry officers, he requested authorisation to add a cavalry unit of 200 men on 12 April, while the 4th and 5th Companies were organised.

Two days later, Damas reported to the Stadholder that, in accordance with his orders, he had seen the members of the Council of State and was confident about the proposed capitulation that he had sent them.[45] However, without news and seeing many of his former comrades from the Régiment de Maëstricht, without other means of support, preparing to leave the city to enlist as ordinary soldiers in the Austrian army or that of the Prince

43 KHN, A31 2124.
44 KHN, A31 2124.
45 KHN, A31 Inv. 2120. Letter of 14 April 1793, at The Hague.

de Condé, on 1 May Damas wrote another letter to Willem V. He openly explained his concerns, recognising that due to many such requests the Stadholder may not be able to fulfil his promise to give satisfaction to the émigrés who had distinguished themselves during the siege and also took a swipe at the, un-named, Comte de Béon:

> Far from me the idea to seek to be harmful to any one of my compatriots who offered their services… but in the end if he [the Stadholder] is obliged to make a choice, is it too much to presume of his bounty to assert a title that he has deigned himself to admit to my companions? Our rivals would have done what we have done, but envy is a sentiment below them, and I do not insult them by thinking that they do not blame anything else than fate that has placed us in happier circumstances than they have been able to obtain for themselves.[46]

He finished the letter by pressing for urgency as the campaign had started and the season was now advanced. On 15 May Damas wrote to the Grand Pensionary, who had expressed an interest, to ask him to bring his project before the Assembly of the States-General of the United Provinces that very day, on the grounds that any delay would certainly do irreparable harm to his efforts but doubtless still greater to the service of the Republic.[47] This was done as, on Saturday 25 May, the official decree of the States-General was published announcing both the creation of the two cavalry companies, initially designated *ligte Paarden* or light horse, of Béon's corps and of Damas's corps which would be six infantry companies strong, two of chasseurs and four of fusiliers, in all of 700 men including the staff. It is noteworthy that the French terms of chasseur and fusiliers were more commonly, but not exclusively, used in relation to the émigré units as opposed to the contemporary Dutch terms of *jager* and *musquettiers*, even in correspondence using the latter language; this was also true for ranks, French ranks being used more commonly than Dutch.[48]

Etienne de Damas, who at this time adopted the title of comte, had, from 1 June, handbills printed at The Hague. They included detailed information about the unit, drawn from the capitulation (see Appendix II), and were considered 'the best means by which the notice spreads with speed.'[49] On 7 June, Etienne's brother, Comte Louis sent a hundred handbills to the Comte de Blangy, at Brussels, and to the Vicomte de Brons, agent of the King's brothers at Luxembourg, from Maastricht asking them to furnish 'the gentlemen who proposed to serve in it the necessary advances for their journey.'[50]

Returning to Maastricht, which had been assigned as the depot of his corps, Comte Etienne de Damas-Crux had a résumé produced in French of the official journal of the States-General entitled 'Capitulation of an infantry corps for the service of Their Mightiest

46 KHN, A31 Inv. 2120, Letter of 1 May 1793, at The Hague.

47 NAN, 1.01.19 Inv. 2622, Letter of 15 May 1793, at The Hague.

48 NAN, 1.01.19 Inv. 2622, Letter of 15 May 1793, at The Hague; *Extract uit het Register der Resolutien van de Hoog. Mog Heeren Staaten Generaal der Vereenigde Nederlanden.*

49 Hauterive, *Journal d'émigration du comte d'Espinchal*, p.193.

50 Hauterive, *Journal d'émigration du comte d'Espinchal*, p.193. A note from the Comte de Blangy, in BL, *Puisaye Papers*, Add MS 8069, states 'An officer of the legion of the Comte de Béon received 12 francs to go to Nijmegen. M. Fonteau received from the Comte de Blangy 6 livres to go to join the legion of the Chevalier de Damas.'

Lords,' in the form of posters, to be displayed in all the important towns of the United Provinces, where the émigrés were to be found. The 14 articles of the capitulation are followed by a model of the act of engagement which applicants would have to sign.[51] Although the name initially proposed was Régiment de Maëstricht Article 1 added 'or such other name that H.S.H. will be pleased to choose' and the fusilier companies were to have the same establishment as in Dutch units, that is 116 men per company: *capitein, eerste lieutenant, tweede lieutenant, vaandrig*, three *sergeanten*, six *korporaals*, 100 fusiliers and two drummers. The structure of the noble chasseur companies was identical to that of the fusiliers except that hornists replaced the drummers and both companies would each have an additional *capitaine des armes* (armourer) with the rank of 'gefyrte' (as the German gefährte or corporal), 'as that of the Republic's chasseurs' (Article 2). The staff was to be composed of 'a *colonel*, a *lieutenant-colonel*, a *major*, an *adjudant*, a *tambour-major*, a *chirurgien-major* and an *aumônier* [chaplain]' (Article 3). The unit's military solicitor at The Hague was J.C.W. Daehne, he was the agent who acted as the interface between the corps and the States-General, especially in relation to payments, receipts, transfer of pay and other financial matters. His role is not to be confused with the *solliciteurs*, distributed throughout the corps, one per company, which were paid vacancies, equivalent to Warrant or Contingent Men in the British Army, the subsistence of which was used by the colonel and agent for expenses such as recruiting and administration. They continued despite, Damas, in his first proposal of 27 March, suggesting that their combined cost could be used to pay for an officer, appointed quartermaster.

Initially Comte Etienne de Damas-Crux wanted his corps to include a *bourgeoise* company of fusiliers, composed exclusively of former volunteers of the Third Estate and soldiers who had served in the 1792 campaign in the armies of the King's brothers, while the three others would be formed of deserters from the French Republic's army, Frenchmen or foreigners, as well as voluntary enlistment of foreigners. While the other soldiers would be engaged for a period of two years, those of the *bourgeoise* company could, like the gentlemen volunteers in the two chasseur companies, engage to serve only for the duration of the campaign. An annexe to the recruitment poster, stated that each soldier, whether fusilier or chasseur, would be issued with a knapsack of hide, two shirts, two pairs of shoes, a pair of black gaiters, a black stock (collar) with two flaps, a bonnet de police (a fatigue cap) and small utensils including a bag of hair powder, a comb, a clothes brush, two shoe brushes and a queue ribbon.

Articles one to four having established the unit's organisation, five to nine and 14, explained the financial arrangements. The disbursements would be made in three stages, as recruitment progressed. The first tranche was to be paid immediately after the signing of the capitulation thus acting as a working fund for the recruitment and equipping of the first third of the corps; the second was released once the first third was recruited and the third and last tranche was paid on the same basis, after the unit was at two thirds of its strength, so permitting the unit to be completed.

Only when complete, each company then the entire corps would be paid their 'appointments and pay', at the start of each 42-day month (named in Dutch *Heer Maand*). The unit

51 An example is to be found at BL, *Puisaye Papers*, Add MS 8069 folio 48.

had to be fully formed in two-and-a-half months, from the day of the payment of the first tranche of money, and could be employed once the first half was formed, even by company if the Prince of Orange considered it necessary (Article 8). This was the case for Béon, while the third and fourth companies were still forming at Nijmegen, the first two companies were in Flanders with the Dutch field army; the second company marching through Tournai on 28 May to join the first at Orchies.[52] Sent to reinforce the garrison of Menen in early June, Béon's two companies received their baptism of fire on 10 June between Wattrelos and Tourcoing, losing six men killed and several wounded.[53] Damas's two chasseur companies were to be paid for by the province of Friesland and the four fusilier companies by Zeeland, unlike the Légion de Béon which was, as a whole, paid by Holland

Article Five of Damas's capitulation stipulated the amount allocated for the recruitment of each man as well as the pay for each rank:

> To achieve the formation of the Régiment de Maëstricht … he will be paid by the Republic under the title of levy money, 60 florins for each chasseur non-commissioned officer, drummer and chasseur, and 100 florins for each fusilier non-commissioned officer, drummer and fusilier with nine weeks of the following pay …

Fusiliers cost more as it was difficult to find ordinary soldiers due to competition and they engaged for two years, receiving a bounty for doing so. The French gentlemen, on the other hand, engaged to serve for the duration of a campaign or the war, but with the option, a kind of gentlemen's agreement with the commander, to be able to leave at any time, particularly to take an opportunity of advancement in another corps, on the condition they had made a prior request to do so. In both the émigré corps in the service of the United Provinces, the term 'volunteer' was synonymous to those of 'chasseur' or 'noble chasseur' designating both a light infantry soldier and a gentleman serving as an ordinary soldier; this was also the case in the noble infantry of the Armée de Condé.

The situation of such gentlemen was further clarified in a letter from Comte Louis de Damas-Crux, who oversaw the unit's formation at Maastricht when his brother was away at The Hague, of 7 June 1793 to the Comte de Blangy, now in Brussels.

> [T]he number of officers or gentlemen who can enter the chasseur companies being rigorously fixed at 200, the first who will be registered will have preference to be placed in them and if there are others later, they can only be admitted in the bourgeoise company of fusiliers until in their turn they pass to the chasseurs, when places in it are vacated.[54]

52 *Le Mercure de France,* N°99/1793 p.355.

53 Jean Brumauld de Beauregard *Mémoires de Monseigneur J. Brumauld de Beauregard, évêque d'Orléans, précédés de sa vie, écrite sur des notes et des documents authentiques* (Poitiers: Saurin, 1842), p.59. In the same letter the author adds, '… the infantry companies are with the army, where they very often have actions and act like lions'.

54 BL, *Puisaye Papers,* Add MS 8069, f.12–13.

This happened as four gentlemen were shown in the second fusilier company and one in the fourth on 28 September 1793; they had no precedence over experienced men as non-commissioned officers in these companies and only a detail in uniform distinguished them from the other soldiers.[55] On the other hand there were to be some men in the chasseur companies who were of more humble origins such as Antoine Grange (number 11 in Rouault's company) and Joseph Grosjean (number 33 in Damas's company), both were former NCOs in the Gardes Françaises, who had served in the preceding campaign within the Hommes d'Armes à pied during the 1792 campaign and thus had gained their promotion to infantry lieutenants. They were exceptions, the majority of the volunteers in the chasseur companies were gentlemen or officers who had previously served in the various units of the Armée du Centre.

The Damas chasseurs' pay, 18 florins 1 sol, was not only higher than that of the Damas fusiliers, who received 14 florins 1 sol, but also that of their counterparts in Béon's chasseurs, also 14 Dutch florins 1 sol per 42-day month, amounting to a little more than 14 French sols per day, to which the Regent added 2 French sols. Naturally Béon could not let this disparity continue for long, so on 1 July 1793 he solicited 'an augmentation of pay equal to that which has been accorded to the legion of the Comte de Damas,' which could not be denied.[56]

Damas explained in a note of June 1796 the role and responsibilities of an effective *capitaine* (or *capitien* in Dutch):

> There were two types of capitaine in Holland: the effective, who has a company ... The effective capitaine (the senior officers of this corps are as the effective of companies) is proprietor of the totality of the subsistence funds of his company, likewise the officers' appointments which he is responsible for paying ... He administers his company as he sees fit. He himself supplies the clothes, the linen items and shoes, the horses, the equipment; he engages the men, gives them their leave, replaces them, etc. He is answerable for his company to such a degree that he undertakes by oath to the Council of State and to that of the Seven Provinces that pays him, to maintain his company at his own personal expense and even on his own credit, in the event that the indemnifying province to which he is [bound], would not have provided the necessary funds ...'[57]

The effective *capitein* received 158 florins pay per 42-day month, reflecting the personal financial risks involved, compared with the 83 florins for the *capitein commandant* in the first two companies, those of the *colonel* and *lieutenant-colonel*. The three senior officers, which included the *major*, received double pay, as field officers and the effective *capitein*, so their companies did not have a *tweede lieutenant* (Article Four). The salaries of the staff were paid annually and the rates were given in Article Six of the capitulation.

55 *AMC Fonds Grouvel, Légion de Damas.*
56 Bittard des Portes, *Les émigrés*, p.40.
57 AMC, Series Y, Carton XXIII, Piece 465.

Rank	Annual pay (florins)	Per 42-day month (florins)
Colonel	2400	277
Lieutenant-colonel	960	110
Major	360	42
Adjudant	840	97
Drum major	168	20
Chirurgien-major	480	55
Aumônier	600	70

It is noteworthy that there was no difference, in pay, between the chasseur and fusilier officers and every company had a *vaandrig*.

Comte Etienne de Damas was determined to maintain a high standard of discipline and conduct in his unit and so the recruitment poster, of June 1793, was supplemented with a firm address from the *colonel* to candidates. In it he recognised that, 'If the events of a disastrous campaign have left anything to be desired in our armies' it was behaviour 'essential to the service and of the subordination necessary for military order.' So that volunteers who acted against 'good order and discipline' by 'disobeying their superiors, or in making justly reprehensible remarks' would not only be dismissed but also have their conduct reported to the Regent. Once they had been presented with the extracts from the capitulation and this address, the volunteers would be asked to sign the following 'solemn' promise:

> I engage myself under on my word of honour to serve in the corps raised under the title of the Régiment de Maëstricht, in one of the companies, on the conditions set forth in the aforementioned capitulation, and to only leave it after having obtained, in writing, the permission of the commander in chief, declaring to submit myself to the rule of discipline mentioned above, of which I have perfect understanding.[58]

Thus, Damas reminded his compatriots that although the French nobility had sometimes been noted for insubordination and a Gallic spirit, prone to criticism and division, there would be no place for either in the Régiment de Maëstricht. Those dismissed and denounced to the Regent would not only suffer social disgrace and be prevented from entering other émigré units but would also be excluded from future royal honours, pensions and positions in case of the restoration of the French monarchy.

The first to engage as volunteers were three brothers, Joseph, Pierre and Théodore du Garreau de la Seinie, who all signed with the single name 'de Laseinie', boys then only 18, 16 and 14 years old, who were the sons of a former cavalry officer. After them was the Chevalier de Codine, sometimes shown as Godine; all four registered in *Major* de Rouault's chasseur company on 8 June 1793.[59]

Seniority in the unit, determined by previous rank and service, was established as from 15 July, after which any later entrants would join the general list. As a result, the la Seinie

58 BL, Add Ms 8069.
59 BL, Add Ms 8069.

brothers were numbered 90, 91 and 92 in Rouault's company and the Chevalier de Codine, fourth to register, as 37 of the same company. The places as *chefs de section* and *chefs d'escouade* in the chasseur companies were allocated to former officers who could then rise through the ranks, in strict seniority, so, Thomas de Pressac, the first of the *chefs de section* of the first chasseur company, replaced the Comte d'Havrincourt, *vaandrig* of the third company, when the latter resigned.[60] In the fusilier companies, however, the NCO posts were reserved for experienced soldiers, with their own opportunities for progression, so even if a gentleman served in a fusilier company, as a volunteer or a gentleman cadet, he could not aspire to be *chef d'escouade* or *chef de section* of fusiliers.

Of course, the downside of this system was that outstanding men were condemned to the prospect of desperately slow advancement, one of the most interesting examples being Charles-Augustin de Tercier (1752–1823). Not only was he early to engage, numbered 6 in the 1st Company, but he was also very experienced. He had entered the Régiment de La Martinique in 1772 and distinguished himself on land and sea during the American War of Independence. He was *capitaine* of the regiment's grenadiers and recipient of the cross of Saint-Louis, as well as a gratuity for bravery, before he returned to France after nine years and he joined Monsieur's Guards until their dissolution in 1790. Emigrating in 1791, he served in the 1792 campaign in Monsieur's reconstituted Guard, under the orders of Comte Charles de Damas. Although he doubtless had reason to expect an officer's post, Tercier was initially a *chef de section*, second in precedence, and had to wait until 1794 to be promoted. This perhaps explains a certain bitterness, even rancour, towards his *colonel* in his memoirs. Another effect was that two of the junior officers were old, when Thomas de Pressac was promoted *vaandrig* he was the oldest officer of the corps at 62 years old, the next oldest being Jean-Joachim de Borrasol, *eerste lieutenant* in the second chasseur company, at 58. Nevertheless, the average age of the officers was between 30 and 35 years old and the *colonel* himself was not 40.

Damas was particular about the principle of seniority. During an audience, in June, he heard the Stadholder praise the Légion de Béon and mention the seniority of the Comte de Béon in the rank of *colonel*, which would give him, if needed, the command of both units. The Comte de Damas-Crux wrote, on 12 June, a deft protest, thanking Willem V for his favours but pointing out:

> I am colonel in France before M. de Béon and I have served in this capacity in the last war in India, commanding a corps. I am going meanwhile to find myself under the orders of my comrade, my junior until this day, but who will become my senior by the circumstance of the date of his [Dutch] colonelcy, earlier by six days to that of mine.

60 Anne-Eugène-Louis de Cardevac d'Havrincourt, born 1770, is shown as having been appointed to the Hohenlohe-Chasseur Regiment when he died at Utrecht in 1794 (Anon. *Notice Historique sur La Maison de Cardevac d'Havrincourt avec ses alliances et sur la Terre d'Havrincourt* (Cambrai: Renaut, 1885), pp.111–113). Pressac was nominated on 15 February 1794 (KHN A31 Inv No 2120) and his promotion was backdated to 10 November 1793.

Damas suggested that he had entered the service of the United Provinces, at the Siege of Maastricht, so before Béon and requested that the latter's commission be dated after his.[61] This was not done and Damas's rank, like that of most of his officers, was dated from 31 May 1793.

The first stage of the formation of the corps concentrated on its officer cadre, essentially composed of those known personally to the Comte de Damas or his brother. That was certainly the case for the three former Vexin officers, André Boucher de Courson, Pierre de Burgault de Montfort and Jean-Baptiste du Crozet, who were joined by other experienced officers who had served alongside them in 1792 and then during the Siege of Maastricht. Foremost amongst these was the Comte Charles-Gabriel-Armand-Fortuné Comte de Rouault, *major* of the Chasseurs à Cheval de la Lorraine, and others in this category were Joseph de Savignac de Vaux, *capitaine* of the Régiment d'Artois; Jean-Joseph-Antoine Comte de Cardon de Vidampierre, *capitaine* of the Régiment de Touraine; Jean-Joachim-Anne de Borrassol, *capitaine* of the Régiment de Hainault; Jean-François-Louis-Charles Chevalier d'Hébert de Boulon, *major* of the Régiment de Lorraine; and César Justin Niel, former surgeon to the Gardes de la Porte.

If the *Abbé* Louis du Chilleau owed his position as chaplain to a family connection with the Damas-Crux, that of *Lieutenant-colonel* Stack, who brought some men of the Régiments de Dillon and Walsh with him, was due to his renown. Born in 1756 in County Kerry, Ireland, Edward Stack had entered the Régiment de Walsh as a cadet at the age of 16 and later, as a *lieutenant*, he volunteered to join the Americans fighting for independence. On 13 May 1779 three officers, Stack, James O'Kelly and Eugene McCarthy, along with 137 soldiers of the Brigade Irlandaise, joined John Paul Jones's squadron at Lorient, to serve in the American Continental Marine Corps. On 23 September, of the same year, in the North Sea, off Flamborough Head, East Yorkshire, Jones's squadron attacked HMS *Serapis* (44 guns) and the hired vessel *Countess of Scarborough* (20 guns), escorting a Baltic convoy to England. Jones, on board the *Bonhomme Richard* (42 guns) took on the more heavily-armed British warship and, once damaged, Jones attached his ship to the *Serapis* to board her and take advantage of his larger crew. James O'Kelly was killed; Eugene McCarthy was wounded and Edward Stack distinguished himself in the fight on the upper deck. This naval battle gained such repute that Stack and McCarthy were promoted *capitaines en second* by King Louis XVI and awarded a gratuity of 400 livres for life. After the war he re-joined the Régiment de Walsh and on 25 July 1791 he was appointed *lieutenant-colonel* in the 87e Régiment (former Dillon) but he emigrated before joining. Stack had joined Damas by 12 June, as on this date he was signatory, along with the *colonel*, to a letter authorising J.C.W. Daehne, the military solicitor and agent, to collect the pay on the part of the *capitaines* who were proprietors of the companies from the States-General.[62]

If posts as officers and chasseurs were rapidly filled, recruitment of soldiers for the four fusilier companies was comparatively slow. One man who did enlist in this period was Jean-Baptiste Catoire who joined Boulon's fusilier company. He was aged 28 and a native of Verdun, where his family had held minor administrative posts in the city. He had received an

61 Bittard des Portes, *Les émigrés*, p.39.
62 NAN, 1.101.19 Inv. 2622.

education for the clergy before joining the French infantry, as a cadet in the Régiment Royal des Vaisseaux, but, at the time of the Coalition's invasion of France in 1792, he deserted and later fled to Koblenz, where he remained until enlisting at Maastricht. The somewhat flexible principles he displayed in his eventful life were certainly to assist his later survival.[63]

This slow progress was doubtless dispiriting for the Comte de Damas-Crux as he faced competition from other émigré corps, in particular the Loyal Emigrant Regiment, under the command of the Comte de La Châtre, in British pay. An émigré noted 'June 1793 … That of La Châtre, formed in England, disembarked at Oostende to join the Duke of York's army. An officer of this legion came to Maastricht to raise recruits from amongst the émigrés, but, the Prince of Hesse showed him the door quite brusquely'.[64] The Governor's reaction can be explained by the 'four Companies of Colonel de Damas's Free Corps' being part of his garrison, as shown by a return dated 11 June 1793.[65] Being part of the garrison the unit had the right to lodgings in the city, the fusiliers occupied two granaries in the Lindenkruis while the chasseurs were lodged in two houses in Sint Pieterstraat, leading to the city gate of that name.[66] It had taken a little time for this to be arranged as Louis de Damas-Crux noted on 7 June when writing to the Comte de Blangy, 'We have already been given a very good quarter for the fusiliers, so you can send to me without inconvenience the bourgeois who come forward to serve. It is not the same for the chasseurs. We still do not have an establishment set up for them, and it will be too dear to keep them at the auberge.'[67] To discourage further interference with the unit, in July, the governor excluded French émigrés 'who were not in the Légion de Damas' from Maastricht 'under the pretext that there were too many French in the city'.[68]

The competition for recruits was, of course, not one sided and Damas obtained at least two recruits who had originally intended to join the Loyal Emigrants. François-Timoléon de Bennes, a gentleman from Normandy, and his wife, Louise-Françoise Claudine, escaping death, had fled France, leaving their two children behind. They had served side by side in the Armée du Centre, she using an adaption of her maiden name, the Chevalier de Haussay, and when the army was disbanded, they retired to Sittard. However, as the summer approached and their funds were exhausted, they decided to engage in the Loyal Emigrants. However, as she later recalled, '… we accidentally met the Major of the corps *de Damas* … He invited us to serve with him, and we readily complied, the corps we had first given the preference to, being a greater distance than the little money we had left could carry us'. They both engaged as noble chasseurs in the *major*'s company on 26 July 1793, Mme de Bennes noting that her 'sex now was generally known.'[69]

63 Listed as Catoir in the legion's 1793 register, he wrote an undated memoir in the Channel Islands shortly after returning from the Quiberon expedition in 1795: The National Archives, Kew (TNA) HO 69/31. It formed the basis of the article by D.K. Broster 'The Black Cockade' *The Cornhill Magazine* Vol.XVIII, May 1910; Catoire gave scant attention in it to his service in the unit before Quiberon.

64 Charles Georges Cacqueray de Valménier *Mémoires inédits – Tome II « L'émigration » 1791–1794* (Cholet: Pays & Terroirs, 2006), Vol.II, p.105.

65 MAASGOUW (Local history magazine) Vol.V, May 1907, p.39.

66 MAASGOUW, Vol.V pp.39–40.

67 BL, *Puisaye Papers*, Add MS 8069, f.12–13.

68 Cacqueray de Valménier *Mémoires inédits*, Vol.II, p.106.

69 Louise-Françoise-Claudine de Bennes *A Narrative of The Sufferings of Louise Francoise de Houssay, de Bannes …* (London: Unknown Publisher,1796), p.25.

It was at this time that the unit definitively took the name Légion de Damas so matching that of the Légion de Béon with which it shared a very similar structure and uniform. This reflected Netherlands military terminology, Colonel de Damas's first choice had been the Régiment de Maëstricht to attract veterans of the former unit as well as to maintain, or construct, continuation of its service but regiments were formed of two battalions of seven companies, six of musketeers and one of grenadiers, while a legion or free corps (*vrijkorps*), could be smaller or have a combined arms structure with infantry and cavalry, or even artillery, components.

At the end of July 1793, the legion was far from complete, and the difficulty in obtaining fusiliers continued, as the Comte de Cacqueray recalled:

> At this time, the Légion de Damas was almost entirely made up of two companies of Chasseurs, composed of émigré gentlemen, and of four fusilier companies in which were incorporated all the deserters who presented themselves. It was feared that this type of men accustomed to the notions of equality and indiscipline only brought a bad spirit into the corps. However, events proved that this fear was ill founded ...[70]

If the idea that the four companies of fusiliers would only be of doughty royalists had been abandoned with the recruitment of deserters, the number of these last should nevertheless not be exaggerated.

It was now that the Comte de Damas-Crux acquired Béon's Irish companies. Evidence does not show who made the first approach, Fitzjames and the Irish officers or Damas himself, or how the move came about, but it doubtless rested on Damas offering a better, or at least more secure, financial arrangement than his rival. The two companies had been fully formed, if not at full strength, at Nijmegen on 19 May when Béon asked for the officers' warrants and they were still there in June.[71] Although Cacqueray noted in his journal, on 9 September, that these companies had been incorporated into the Légion de Damas this appears to have actually taken place a few weeks earlier as, when 15 of the unit's officers wrote to their *colonel* on 26 August 1793, O'Moore was included in their number.[72] The signatories were *Lieutenant-colonel* Stack; *Capitaines* de La Basse Boulogne, de Boulon, O'Moore, de Chalup, David Barry and de Rancé, who was *aide-major*; *Lieutenants* de La Grange, de Burgault de Montfort, de Savignac, Richard Barry and de Borrassol and *Enseignes* de Cardon de Vidampierre and de Lavenne. Writing in a respectful but firm manner, the officers illustrated the practical difficulties émigré officers encountered on entering the service of another country:

> We see with the greatest satisfaction the speed with which your corps completes itself, and we all concur with the greatest eagerness to put it into a state to go to campaign at the earliest; we would wish that our resources matched our zeal but we know our situation; proscribed for four years from our unfortunate country, without the possibility of drawing any help from it, having exhausted all our

70 Cacqueray de Valménier *Mémoires inédits*, Vol.II, p.109.

71 KHN A31 Inv. 2124 and BL, *Puisaye Papers*, Add MS 8069, fol. 7.

72 Cacqueray de Valménier *Mémoires inédits*, Vol.II, p.112.

> resources, without credit in a foreign land … we have only our arms and our blood to offer to T.M.L.
>
> … it is to you, Monsieur Comte, as our chief, that we address ourselves with confidence to present to the States-General and HSH the Prince of Orange how cruel our position is. Barely for the most part have we had enough for us to provide uniforms … which will absorb several months of our salaries; moreover, we have no means of providing ourselves with what is absolutely necessary for us to join the army. … our well-known misfortunes … have taught us to live on little and the privations will cost us nothing if we can contribute to the punishment of the scoundrels who are tearing our country apart.
>
> … We are not in a condition to make any advance for the purchase of our effects of campaign; we do not blush about our penury, the principle of which can only honour us. Deign, Monsieur Comte, to assert our just claims … we have neither salary nor pension to hope for in peace, that being paid only for the time we will be useful, it is quite right that we have at least during our services what is strictly necessary for our maintenance and our subsistence, we do not desire more.
>
> … [we ask for] a sufficient advance to provide us with what is indispensably necessary for the war … our demands are solely founded on our needs. … we have to flatter ourselves that they will be received favourably. We have no doubt of your eagerness to assert them and it is principally on your solicitation that we base our hopes. If they are rejected, our condition will be infinitely less than that of an ordinary chasseur, and in the absolute impossibility … [of sustaining] the status of an officer, the majority of us will be obliged to resign our employ and to restrict ourselves to serve in the ranks, for we wish to serve at whatever price; this is the first and the only object of our desires.[73]

Émigré officers, having exhausted any money they may have brought from France and unable to raise credit in foreign countries, being without capital or firm future prospects, were often preoccupied with their precarious financial situations leading them to be frequently considered as money-grasping by both contemporaries and later historians. The letter, although couched in respectful terms, as required by personal regard and etiquette, nevertheless carried a threat as such a mass resignation would not only delay the formation, and deployment, of the unit but also severely damage it reputation, and that of its *colonel*, in the eyes of other émigrés.

The Légion de Damas now had two companies of noble chasseurs and four of fusiliers, three of which were 'Irish'. The first of these to have joined Damas was that commanded by Stack, the *lieutenant-colonel* or first fusilier company, composed largely of the debris of the Régiments de Walsh and Dillon, while the other two companies (McDermott's and O'Moore's) were drawn from the Régiment de Berwick with many of that regiment's junior officers and cadets serving as volunteer fusiliers, sometimes commanded by their former NCOs. One of these officers was James Nash who later applied for the cross of Saint-Louis, he attached a certificate with his services from the Duc de Fitz-James,

73 A31 Inv. 2124.

> [B]orn in Dublin on 1 February 1754, served as a volunteer in the Régiment de Berwick from 2 January 1770 until 3 March 1776 when he was made sous-lieutenant in the same regiment in which he continued to serve as lieutenant en second and substantive lieutenant. Served under the orders of the Marquis de Bouillé in the American campaigns of 1782, 1783 and 1784. Emigrated: served in the 1792 campaign with the Armée du Centre, those of 1793 and 1794 in the Berwick companies attached to Damas's corps ...[74]

The legion had homogeneity and diversity at the same time, with the chasseur companies of French gentlemen and fusilier companies with Irish officers serving in the ranks, French deserters and émigré commoners serving through duty or necessity alongside former soldiers. They were joined by young foreigners in search of adventure like 'Jean-Pierre Liben, son of the notary, prelate, bailiff Liben of Hocheporte' who was noted in June 1793 as going 'to Nijmegen to join one of the two Berwick companies which assemble there'.[75] Such a mixture of men had been true of the Irish Brigade for many years and Damas's 'Irish' companies can be considered as the final remnants of the brigade that had served the French monarchy, under its motto: *Semper et ubique fideles*.[76]

News of the war in the summer of 1793 was dominated by the surrender of Mainz at the end of July, the sieges on the frontiers of France and also the insurrections at Toulon and Lyon. In August news would have arrived at Maastricht of the capture of Valenciennes, the garrison marching out on 1 August, and the losses suffered by the Dutch troops at Linselles, on 18 August, but also the first success of the *Condéens*, two days later, at Wissembourg in northern Alsace. On 25 August, Saint-Louis's day, the Bishop of Auxerre led a Catholic service in the Basiliek van Onze Lieve Vrouwe (Basilica of Our Lady) with prayers for Queen Marie-Antoinette, still held prisoner in Paris, at which 'all the émigrés and the Légion de Damas attended'.[77] At the end of August Béon's two companies of chasseurs à cheval, 178 sabres, left Nijmegen for the front around Maubeuge. Meanwhile the legion 'exercised every day for three months' to be ready for service.[78]

The Comte de Damas-Crux at least twice sought permission to add to the regulated number of his officers but he was knocked back each time. On the first occasion he applied for two experienced officers to be attached to him as aides de camp but, although neither apparently applied for a salary only an allowance for a horse, this request was rejected. The second time, was for the appointment of a M. de Monternay, a former officer of the Corps royal de l'artillerie, in the expectation the legion would be equipped with two to four cannons.[79] However, over time, the Stadholder was to give ground to Damas by authorising the posts of quartermaster, instead of the *solliciteurs*, and a second adjutant, this last

74 AG, Order of Saint-Louis – Nominations in the emigration – Carton E.12 register n°3. It appears that Nash was known under the name of Nagle during his French and Dutch service.

75 BL, *Puisaye Papers*, Add MS 8069, fol. 7. Whatever the reason, there is no man with this, or a similar, name shown as serving in the Legion.

76 It is perhaps not by chance that that of the US Marine Corps is *Semper fidelis*?

77 Cacqueray de Valménier *Mémoires inédits*, Vol.II, p.111.

78 Bennes, *Narrative*, p.25.

79 Bittard des Portes, *Les émigrés*, pp.70–71.

post being taken by Marie-Jean-André-Claude Boucher de Courson, a *sous-lieutenant* of the Régiment de Vexin, whose brevet was dated 29 June 1793. In addition, doubtless through the intervention of his old comrade Stack, Eugene McCarthy was to later join the Légion de Damas as a second *major* attached to the first fusilier company; his brevet was dated 20 September 1793.

It is noteworthy that the legion's staff was as large as that of a line regiment so allowing it to operate separately in the field. In camp or in garrison, the corps was commanded by the *lieutenant-colonel* in the absence of the *colonel*, and the administrative roles, such as lodging, management and discipline as well as training was confided to the *major*, assisted by the two *aide-majors*, or *adjudants* and the *quartier-maître* who acted as treasurer or chief of administrative services. In combat, the entire corps was commanded by the *colonel* but if absent the *major* commanded the chasseurs and the *lieutenant-colonel* the fusiliers, assisted by the additional *major*. All the officers of the staff and commanding *capitaines* were mounted; the other company officers, *lieutenants* and *enseignes*, were on foot, wearing black gaiters, and were armed with a musket and sword in the fusiliers and a carbine and sabre in the chasseurs.

Finally, orders arrived to join the army in the field and on 28 September the legion was reviewed by the Prince of Hesse and executed several different manoeuvres and firing exercises with cohesion and precision.[80] It had 596 officers and men of whom at least 16 were sick and 31 on recruiting duties. The changes in organisation had not been worked through. Although the *quartier-maître* was in post, six *solliciteurs* were still listed with the companies: an *aide-chirurgien* in Damas's, *chef d'escouade* in Rouault's and a drummer in each of the fusilier companies; in addition McCarthy was yet to join.

Légion de Damas, at the review of 28 September 1793 at Maastricht

Compagnie du Colonel	
Capitaine	Comte Etienne de Damas-Crux
Capitaine commandant	Vincent-Joseph Chevalier de Chalup
Lieutenant	Joseph de Savignac
Enseigne	Jean-Joseph-Antoine Comte de Cardon de Vidampierre
Aide-major (capitaine)	Charles-Augustin Comte de Rancé
2e aide-major	André Boucher de Courson
Quartier-maître	François-Joseph Ducoux
Aumônier	Louis du Chilleau
Chirurgien-major	César-Justin Niel
Tambour-major	Jean Camen
Chefs de section	3
Trompettes (Hornists)	2
Chefs d'escouade	6
Chasseurs	99

80 Bittard des Portes, *Les émigrés*, p.71.

Compagnie du Lieutenant-colonel	
Capitaine	Baron Edouard Stack
Capitaine commandant	David de Barry
Lieutenant	Pierre de Burgault de Montfort
Enseigne	Anne-Eugène-Louis Comte d'Havrincourt
Sergents	4
Tambours	3
Caporaux	6
Fusiliers	69
Compagnie du Major	
Capitaine	Charles G A C F Comte de Rouault de Gamache
Capitaine commandant	François-Claude de la Basse Boulogne
Lieutenant	Jean-Joachim de Borrassol
Enseigne	Charles-Florimond de Lavenne
Chefs de section	3
Trompettes (Hornists)	2
Chefs d'escouade	6
Chasseurs	103
Compagnie de Boulon	
Capitaine	Jean-François-Louis-Charles Chevalier de Boulon
Lieutenant	Jean-Pierre-Alexis de Chateigner de la Grange
Sous-lieutenant	Richard Chevalier de Barry
Enseigne	Jean-Baptiste du Crozet
Sergents	3
Tambours	3
Caporaux	6
Fusiliers	91
Compagnie de McDermott	
Capitaine	Thomas McDermott
Lieutenant	Thadée O' Meara
Sous-lieutenant	Walter Grace
Enseigne	John O' Kennedy
Sergents	3
Tambours	3
Caporaux	9
Fusiliers	63
Compagnie d'O'Moore	
Capitaine	James O' Moore
Lieutenant	Antony Egan
Sous-lieutenant	James Geoghegan
Enseigne	John Mulhall
Sergents	3
Tambours	2
Caporaux	6
Fusiliers	68

On 4 October the Governor of Maastricht signed the unit's muster list and sent it to The Hague, accompanied by a report that the legion had left on its march to Vilvoorde where it was expected to have arrived on 3 October adding '… that the said Corps is in a very good state and set off in perfect order'.[81] The depot remained at Maastricht until the summer of 1794, serving in addition as its hospital.

81 *AMC Fonds Grouvel, Légion de Damas.*

4

The Belgian Campaign 1793–1794

Through the summer of 1793 the coalition allies had pursued their plan to take the French frontier fortresses, the successful capture of Condé-sur-l'Escaut (12 July) and Valenciennes (27 July) being followed by failure at Dunkirk. Despite this defeat and that of the Dutch around Menen, the Austrians captured Le Quesnoy on 13 September and the allied line was re-established three days later. The next target was Maubeuge on the banks of the Sambre: with the siege work being shared amongst the allies, the British having undertaken that of Valenciennes, it was now the turn of the Dutch. The arrangements for the Dutch army's move from Flanders were agreed at a conference held on 23 September, attended by the Erfprins and *Feldzeugmeister* Clerfayt. In preparation for the siege an Austrian corps crossed to the south bank of the Sambre, on 29 September, and drove the two French divisions covering Maubeuge to seek shelter in the entrenched camp, originally established in 1709 after the Battle of Malplaquet, that strengthened the city's defences by guarding the easiest river crossing and holding the higher ground to the south which dominated the town.[1] Now both the town and camp were surrounded.

The same day the main body of the Dutch infantry marched east, via Aalst, Brussels, Anderlecht and Braine-le-Comte, reaching Mons on 5 October and immediately moved onto Bettignies to begin the siege operations.[2] The Duke of York, a consistent critic of the Dutch army and its commander, suggested that there was some reluctance on the part of the Dutch about their change of role, writing in a private letter:

> The Dutch again behaved in their usual manner, after having lost so much time … they are camped on this side of the Sambre and have absolutely refused to cross it giving as the reason that they find themselves engaged to come to carry out the siege of Maubeuge and not the attack on the entrenched camp …[3]

1 Zéphy-Joseph Priérart, *La Grande Epopée de l'An II Souvenirs, Rapprochements, Rectifictaions et Faits inédits* … (Paris: Spiritualiste, 1864), p.28.

2 Victor Dupuis, *La Campagne de 1793 L'Armée du Nord et des Ardennes: D'Hondschoote à Wattignies* (Paris: Chapelot, 1909), p.72.

3 RAW, De Budé Papers, GEO/ADD/15/0560; York to General de Budé on 11 October 1793, he had previously remarked, 'You can have no idea how the Hereditary Prince of Orange is detested by the Dutch officers and soldiers …' (GEO/ADD/15/0557, 21 August 1793).

The Erfprins was joined by fresh troops, including the Légion de Damas. The legion had left Maastricht after its inspection and marched through Sint-Truiden, on 30 September, Diest and Aarschot, to arrive at Vilvoorde, north of Brussels, on 3 October where it passed to the command of the Erfprins and was given further marching orders by his staff. The Comte de Damas reported that the legion had been harassed on the march by recruiters seeking to attract men to units in Austrian and British pay and indeed, as a result, it had lost several men. These activities only ceased after one recruiter, acting for the York Rangers, had been chased and beaten.[4] An émigrée, Madame de Valon d'Ambrugeac, saw the legion on Thursday 8 October:

> At 11 o'clock in the morning the Légion de Damas, called the Régiment de Maëstricht, arrived at Mons … At 5 in the evening, they had the order to leave immediately to serve at Maubeuge. They gave shouts of 'Vive le Roy!' they were in great joy. The inhabitants of Mons had never seen such joy to go to the enemy.[5]

The unit joined the Dutch field army that same day.[6] The Erfprins, in overall command of the siege, had his headquarters in the Château de Gontroeul, about halfway between Bettignies and Gognies-Chaussée. The Dutch began to encircle Maubeuge itself, on the left bank of the Sambre, while about 14,000 Austrians blockaded the entrenched camp on the south bank of the river. The Dutch began by driving in the enemy's well-defended outposts and establishing their own siege works. This entailed small scale actions almost daily, resulting in casualties on both sides. The Légion de Damas was posted in one of three redoubts constructed in the Bois de Tilleul, west of the town and close to the north bank of the Sambre. There it was not only subject to sorties but also artillery fire from the garrison as *Chef de section* de Tercier of the Colonel's Chasseur Company, remembered, 'We were divided amongst the advance posts, and obliged …, to put ourselves in continual shelter from the fire of the French, to hollow out our bivouacs to five or six feet into the earth.'[7]

Alongside the Légion de Damas, the outworks were held by the 5e Battaillon Waldeck (*Colonel* Georg von Haacke), the Anspach Jagers and a Walloon infantry battalion; one participant recalled that it rained 'almost every day' during the siege.[8] The garrison made sorties on 6, 7 and 9 October, but the positions held by the legion came under the most sustained attack on 13/14 October. The republicans, spearheaded by three élite battalions, initially took two of the redoubts, and seized an artillery piece, but in the struggle the foremost men were fired upon by their support which caused them to fall into disorder and retreat, leaving 60 dead and 27 prisoners in Dutch hands. The defenders lost 13 men dead

4 KHN Archieven van Stadhouder Willem V, A31 Inv No 2120, report dated 3 October 1793 at 'Vilvorden.'

5 AMC AFII Carton 54 No.379 : Journal d'émigration de Madame de Valon d'Ambrugeac, née d'Erlach.

6 Report from the Erfprins dated 'Goutreuil', 8 October 1793 reproduced in *Nieuwe Nederlandsche Jaarboeken, of Vervolg der Merkwaardigste Geschiendenissen, die voorgevallen zyn in de Vereenigde Provinicien, de Generaliteits Landen, en de Volkplantingen van den Staat, MDCCXCIII* (Leyden and Amsterdam), p.1636.

7 La Chanonie, *Mémoires*, p.68.

8 Willem Pieter d'Auzon de Boisminart, *Gedenkschriften* (Gravenhage and Amsterdam: Cleef, 1841), Vol.I p.33; Auzon de Boisminart, of a Huguenot family, was serving as a cadet in the Dutch artillery.

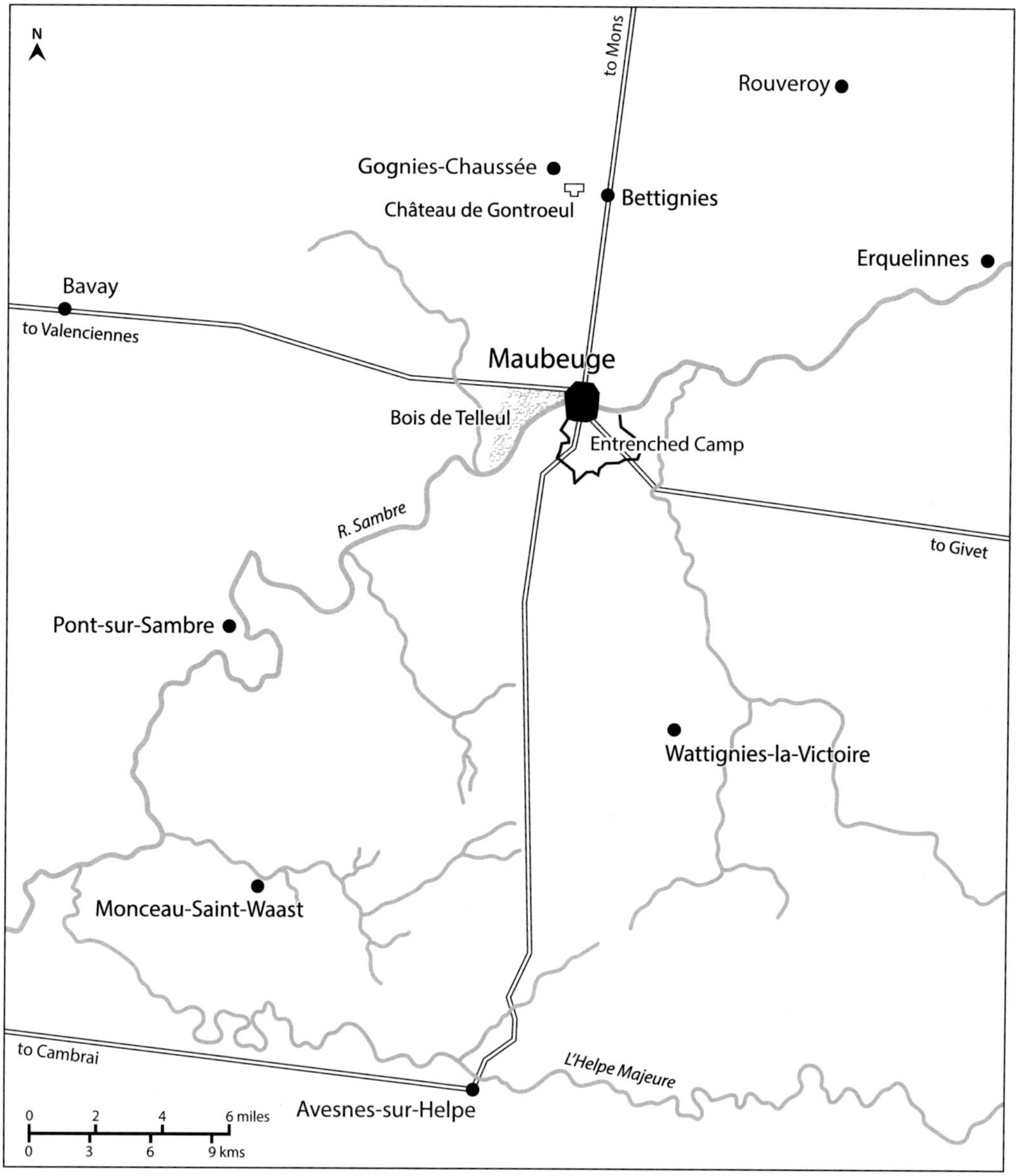

The siege of Maubeuge.

and 19 wounded, all from the Waldeck and Walloon battalions.[9] Louise Françoise de Bennes recalled the service at the siege, her first time under fire:

> [W]ithin cannon-shot of the ramparts. Several skirmishes ensued, and I will candidly confess, that when the first took place, I was frightened almost out of my senses. ... I trembled all over, but when I became sensible that none about me fell, my courage on a sudden returned, and never since have I experienced any emotion in similar circumstances.[10]

Jean-Baptiste Jourdan was the new French republican commander facing the allies, 'placed with the alternative of earning a crown of laurels or climbing the scaffold'.[11] The response of the politicians in Paris in the Reign of Terror to external and internal enemies, real or imagined, was merciless. Jourdan's first task was to relieve the besieged garrison of Maubeuge and his mission was considered so important that he was joined by a member of the Committee for Public Safety, Lazare Carnot. They recognised that if the Austrian covering force, under Clerfayt's command, was defeated, the siege would have to be lifted. On 13 October, the French army concentrated around Avesnes-sur-Helpe; Jourdan and Carnot arriving the next day. Maubeuge was in jeopardy, with the garrison running short of food and the allies unmasking batteries close to the town on the night of 14/15 October.

Clerfayt had deployed his army across the Avesnes to Maubeuge road, with his right wing extended to the Sambre around Saint-Waast and his left on the higher ground around Wattignies. On 15 October Jourdan attacked the Austrian positions, launching divisions against both wings as well as the centre. The French were in far superior numbers, with about double the number of troops, but their attacks were repelled, with significant losses, by the disciplined musketry of the Austrians, supported by cavalry. Nevertheless, Jourdan renewed the attack the next day, concentrating his forces on taking Wattignies; he was finally successful after a long and hard fight.[12] Nevertheless, Clerfayt could draw his army off and cross the Sambre, largely because Jourdan had received little support from the French divisions in the entrenched camp. As anticipated, the Dutch were compelled to lift the siege and to withdraw overnight.[13] Despite attempts to do so without being discovered, such as wrapping the wheels of the guns and munition wagons with rags and straw, the garrison was alerted and made a sortie, which was repulsed by the detachments left in the outposts to cover the retreat. The garrison had suffered such hardship during the siege that even when relieved, and supplied with food, many died of sickness.[14] By 17 October the Dutch

9 Antoine de Jomini *Histoire critique et militaire des Guerres de la Révolution, 1793–1797* (Paris: Anselin et Pochard, 1816–1820), Vol.I, pp.406–40 ; Dupuis, *La Campagne de 1793* p.87. Dr. P.J. Vermeulen *Tijdschrift voor oudheden, statistiek, zeden en gewooten, regt, genealogie en andere deelen der Geschiedenis van het Bisdom, de Provincie en de Stad Utrecht* (Utrecht: Kemink en Zoon, 1852), p.159 states that the Walloon unit was the 3e Battaillon, Nassau-Usingen, but with unreliable evidence which is contradicted by primary sources.

10 Bennes, *Narrative*, p.26.

11 Jomini, *Histoire critique et militaire*, Vol.I, p.93.

12 Hence the latter town is now called Wattignies-la-Victoire

13 Auzon de Boisminart, *Gedenkschriften*, Vol.I, p.35.

14 Louis-François, Baron Lejeune, *Souvenirs d'un Officier de l'Empire* (Toulouse: Viguer, 1851), p.29.

had reformed around Bettignies where they were joined by Clerfayt and his units; they then retreated north, unhindered by the French, and by 19 October the Dutch were deployed to the south of Mons.

In response to Jourdan's advance on Maubeuge, Austrian and British forces had been drawn from Flanders to support Clerfayt. The Erfprins, even in the changed circumstances, had refused to cross the Sambre leading to Coburg to call on York to assist.[15] Following Jourdan's victory, the French divisions in the west seized the initiative and advanced against the weakened opposition forces causing Coburg, on 24 October, to march westwards with 24,000 men. He left Clerfayt on the Sambre with about 20,000 Austrians supported by three detached Dutch brigades placed at Thuin, under the command of *Lieutenant-Generaal* Friedrich Fürst zu Waldeck und Pyrmont (Prince of Waldeck). They were joined by the Dutch infantry regiments Baden and Bedaulx, the Légions de Béon and Damas, the Jagers van Bylandt and the Hussaren van der Hoop, apparently brigaded under Guillaume-Anne Constant de Rebecque, whose cousin, Jean-Victor Constant de Rebecque, served as his aide de camp.[16]

Jourdan wished to place his army in winter quarters. He needed to organise and train it after the last campaign and the influx of raw recruits raised through the *levée en masse*, but his political masters demanded that all foreign invaders be driven from French soil. On 22 October, he was ordered to continue the campaign by attacking the lower Sambre so, despite heavy rain, by 28 October three divisions were concentrated on the right bank of the river, around Thuin and Solre-sur-Sambre. However, Jourdan baulked at making an unsupported advance across the river. The campaign petered out with a series of outpost actions between the French and Waldeck's brigades, on the south bank of the Sambre.

The Légion de Damas was fully engaged in these actions as it was posted in the rear guard at Thuin when the Republican divisions approached the river, Tercier wrote that they were alongside Dutch cavalry and light infantry, 'The Republicans came to attack us there. They were vigorously repulsed. It was a strong reconnaissance that they made. But they returned in force the following day, and we were forced to evacuate the town. We took up a position in the woods which covered this area.'[17]

Two men from the legion were wounded in this action.[18] On 29 October *Lieutenant-colonel* Stack commanded a detachment sent to dislodge a Republican post, about 400 strong, that had occupied the village of Ham-sur-Heure since the previous day. The detachment was made up of 200 from the Damas and Béon infantry, 50 of the latter's cavalry, 30 of the Van der Hoop hussars and 34 Bylandt Jagers. Tercier described the action:

> We left about midnight, and at the break of day we arrived at the village that we had been ordered to attack and storm. We entered it by two paths. The Republicans, surprised, rallied with confusion in the square, and sought to defend themselves

15 Coburg sent an aide de camp with the request, RAW, Budé Papers, GEO/ADD/15/0561; York to Budé on 15 October 1793.

16 Vermeulen *Tijdschrift voor oudheden*, p.160, future events indicate the brigading.

17 La Chanonie, *Mémoires*, pp.69–70. The memoirs of the legion's members differ as to the date of the actions in this period, the dates used reconcile all sources.

18 Bennes, *Narrative*, p.26.

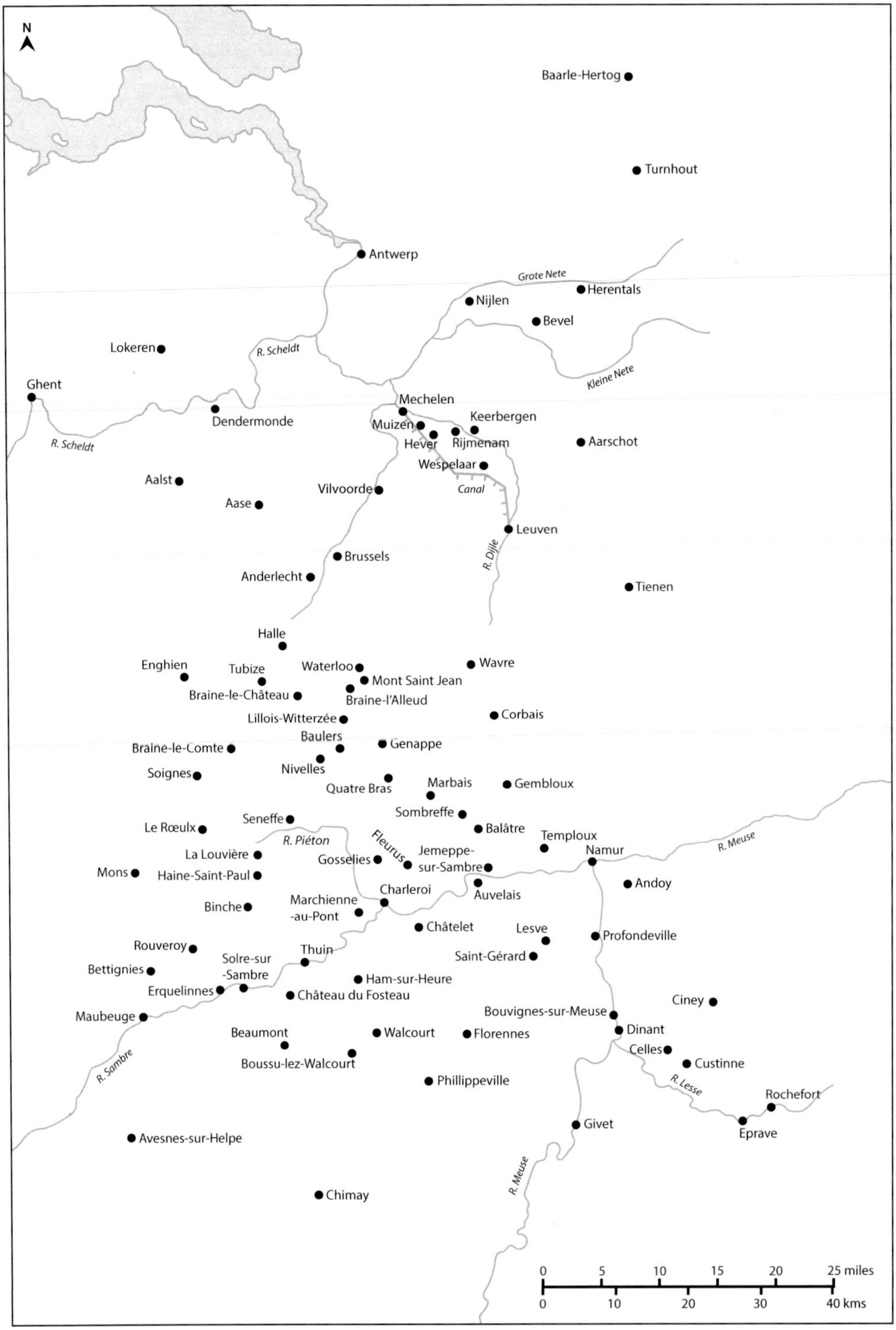

The theatre of war in Belgium.

> there, in the shelter of the baggage vehicles, behind which they reformed without success. Obliged to flee in disorder, they abandoned all their equipment, two field pieces and a caisson. They lost several men, and their wounded remained prisoners. Only a few of our men received minor wounds.[19]

On reporting the action to the States-General the Erfprins, wrote, 'The conduct of Lieutenant-colonel Stack, that of Captain van der Hoop, commanding the Hussars, as well as all the Detachment in general, merit the greatest praise, having all distinguished themselves extremely in this Expedition.' However, the enterprise, through no fault of Stack's detachment, was not a total success. The prince considered that all of the enemy would have been taken if total surprise had been achieved, but they had been warned by two pistol shots from a Dutch cavalry patrol which, presumably, had been part of a covering force.[20] Dutch troops were sent to hold the village, however, the republicans brought up superior forces and soon retook it. The Légion de Damas remained at the advance posts in the woods for some weeks, 'We bivouacked there for a month, facing the Republican posts with which we had daily engagements. We carried out a duty of continuous surveillance. They attempted many times to surprise us during the night, but they always found us on our guard.'[21] This duty was carried out by the chasseur and fusilier companies, as Catoire, a fusilier, recalled, 'during nearly a month we remained there, almost every day we had skirmishes with the Carmagnoles'.[22] However, the year's campaign was finally drawing to a close and the last engagement for the Légion de Damas was a desultory affair against French republican forces around the Château du Fosteau. Bennes simply remarking that 'our advanced posts exchanged a few shots with those of the enemy.'[23]

Although it did not come to fruition, there is evidence that some thought may have been given to using the Légion de Damas elsewhere. The coalition allies considered sending troops to support the insurrection in Western France and, in Flanders, troops were identified for this purpose, perhaps to be joined by émigré units, as described by *The Times* on 29 November 1793:

> Besides the 8 or 9000 [British] … 6000 Hessians and 2000 Austrian Hussars, are ready to sail from Ostend and follow them … It is believed, that the legions of *La Chatre*, *De Damas*, *Carneville*, and *Béon*, will be sent into Normandy and Brittany; for people seem generally convinced, that to put an end to the present war, and thereby restore tranquillity to Europe, more effectual means cannot be used …[24]

---

19 La Chanonie, *Mémoires*, p.70; Bennes, *Narrative*, p.26 stated that 22 republicans were captured along with 27 horses; Vermeulen *Tijdschrift voor oudheden*, p.160 that the republican loss was 38 men killed and 11 taken prisoner.

20 Dated Mons, 30 October, printed in *Nieuwe Nederlandsche Jaarboeken* p.1801.

21 La Chanonie, *Mémoires*, p.70.

22 TNA HO 69/31; although not specified, he was clearly describing this period.

23 Bennes, *Narrative*, p.26.

24 *The Times* Friday 29 November 1793.

Nothing came of such plans and in Belgium both sides retired to winter quarters. The Dutch forces were originally directed towards Nivelles and it appears that the Légion de Damas may have begun to march in this direction. Certainly, the Comte de Damas was at Ransart, just north of Charleroi, on 20 November, as it was there that he wrote to the Stadholder requesting his legion be augmented to 1,200 men by the addition of two or three squadrons of cavalry.[25]

In the winter, many of the Dutch units returned to the United Provinces. Those that remained were quartered so that they could defend the Principality of Liège; the émigré units, including the Légion de Damas, were part of this latter force. The unit marched to Liège, around 1 December, and the newly recruited chasseur Bernard de Corbehem recalled that it was quartered in the village of Seraing, on the banks of the Meuse, on the south-western outskirts of the city.[26]

The Légion de Damas's sojourn ended in January when it marched to Namur to serve in the garrison for a fortnight.[27] The legion then joined the outposts that covered the country to the south of Namur. The line ran from Saint-Gérard in the west, held by the cavalry of the Légion de Béon with a squadron of the Hussaren van Heeckeren, to Ciney, where the Anspach Jagers were posted along with three cavalry squadrons, two from the Hoeufft van Oyen regiment and one of Van Heeckeren hussars. The Légion de Damas was sent to hold the central position at Profondeville, on the banks of the Meuse.[28] Tercier recalled the march to this post.

> At the time of our departure, it snowed so heavily that after half an hour the side-roads were so thickly covered that no route could be discerned. Our guides got us lost. We often fell and rolled into deep ravines. Several of our young men had grave falls. Finally, after seven hours painful march, we arrived at the village which was designated to us, but worn with fatigue and cold.[29]

The legion remained at Profondeville only a short time, Tercier says eight days, before being on the move again.

Meanwhile, there had been another change of commander in the French republican Armée du Nord. Jourdan had been denounced, but he managed to avoid execution being permitted to retire from the army, a situation he was to enjoy for only a very short time. His replacement was Jean-Charles Pichegru who took over a large and widely dispersed command, of about 195,000 men. The pressures, operational and political, endured by the French army in the previous year along with its rapid expansion brought many challenges. However, limited operations, launched against the allied positions in Flanders from January through to March 1794, began to prove and test the units' military effectiveness.

---

25 Bittard des Portes, *Les émigrés*, p.74.

26 Bernard de Corbehem, *Dix ans de ma vie ou Histoire de mon émigration* (Paris: Delaforest, 1827), p.91, given as 'Serin'.

27 Bennes, *Narrative*, p.27.

28 Vermeulen *Tijdschrift voor oudheden*, p.275; the Jaarboeken for 1794, p.142, shows the legion at Profondeville on 10 February.

29 La Chanonie, *Mémoires*, p.69.

It was now that the Légion de Damas was expanded. On 14 February 1794, the States-General agreed that the legion should be augmented by two companies of light cavalry, chasseurs à cheval; at the same time the Légion de Béon was also enlarged by two chasseur, or jager, companies, so that both had the same establishment. *Colonel* Etienne de Damas-Crux, became *ritmeister*, or *capitaine*, of the first company and his nephew, Alexandre-Marie-Louis-Charles Lallemant, Comte de Nantouillet, formerly *major en second* in the Dragons du Duc d'Angoulême, was commissioned *ritmeister* of the second company on 22 February.[30] Damas had spent much of February in The Hague lobbying for this augmentation and then, once it was agreed, with administrative matters such as agreeing contracts with suppliers of uniforms and equipment. The following month he was at the legion's depot, at Maastricht, where the new companies were raised, overseen by Nantouillet. On 5 March Damas wrote to the Stadholder from the city about progress in raising the new companies. He expressed frustration that the funds had not been released for this purpose and he feared that any delay might prevent the troops being ready for the forthcoming campaign, as well as potentially causing him some embarrassment with his suppliers. He then expressed his desire to only have 'extremely distinguished' officers so that he sought 'former superior officers and chef d'escadrons of recognised talent. I still await two responses to this effect.' As for those he would nominate for positions as subalterns he assured the Stadhouder, '... I will only present him officers truly deserving of his bounty'.[31]

A census of French emigrants living in Maastricht on 1 April shows that at least 10 of the officers and volunteers were present in the city including *Lieutenan*t François Aumont de Bazouges, *Lieutenant* Henry de Conan d'Ocor (Aucors), former *capitaine* of the Artois cavalerie, and Nantouillet, who lived there with his wife, a chamber maid and four domestics.[32]

The Damas cavalry companies were organised on the same lines as those of the Béon Legion, described thus: 'the two hundred men form two companies which each have a capitaine, a lieutenant, a sous-lieutenant and an enseigne, two fourriers, two maréchaux-des-logis, six brigadiers, two chefs d'escouade'.[33]

Initially there were nine officers because, as in the infantry, the *colonel* was, to use the Dutch ranks, *ritmeister* of the first company which had a *ritmeister commandant*, a *lieutenant*, and a *cornet*; the officers of the second company comprised a *ritmeister*, a *lieutenant*, a *tweede lieutenant* and a *cornet*. Soon an adjutant was added along with a major, who took command of the two companies, in the absence of the colonel. It should be noted that the companies of the Damas, and Béon cavalry were frequently referred to as squadrons, this being the lowest tactical unit; such a designation was not, in fact, as misleading as it may seem because the legions' companies, each of a hundred troopers, were at least comparable

30 *Naamregister der Heeren Militaire Officieren* of 1794, p.268.

31 KHN Archieven van Stadhouder Willem V, A31/2120, letter 5 March 1794, Maastricht.

32 *List der Fransche Emigranten uit den Leekenstand te Maastrricht en 1794* or *Noms de Messieurs les Français habitant la ville de Maëstricht au 1er avril, dont les admissions ont été vérifiées et renouvelées d'après les ordres de S.A. le prince de Hesse à l'hôtel de ville en présence de MM. les grand-mayeur, vice-mayeur et ancien bourgmestre Munix et conseiller-juré Hollard, par Messieurs le comte de Damas, marquis de Belsunce, comte de Lambertye, maréchaux de camp, nommés et requis à cet effet par Mgr le prince de Hesse* in n°xxx of *Maasgouw*, 1883, Archives of the city of Maastricht.

33 Brumauld de Beauregard *Mémoires*, Vol.II, pp.58–59.

to a Dutch war squadron. Initially each Dutch cavalry or dragoon regiment of four squadrons provided three war squadrons, soon reduced to two, and those of two squadrons only one. A return of 21 September 1793 shows eight regiments, including the two from the guards, providing 20 war squadrons of, on average, five officers and 74 other ranks. Indeed, the two war squadrons of the Stavenisse Pous Regiment were comparatively strong, on 14 July 1794, when the first had seven officers and 87 other ranks and the second, five and 84.[34]

The expansion of the legion was shortly followed by Comte Louis de Damas-Crux being proposed as general commanding both the Béon and Damas legions. Having already raised this with the Erfprins, his brother, Etienne, wrote to the Stadholder on 3 March expounding the advantages of such an appointment, which he stated had been suggested by a third party, which would be so useful that he would welcome it even if another senior officer was selected and, of course, his elder brother's suitability for the role. Nothing came of the proposal.[35]

Damas pursued the interests of another relative with more persistence. On 8 February, he proposed that Nantouillet be placed as *colonel commandant* of the legion. To save expense Damas suggested that, once appointed, he should only receive the pay of *major* of the two cavalry companies, despite the former only submitting the nominations for the captaincies on 15 February. Damas soon returned to the subject, in another letter of 17 February, he asked for the appointment of, 'a colonel-commandant of his corps, to support him in the command of a corps composed of two arms, and reinforce his authority.' He again recommended Nantouillet for this post. Perhaps conscious that the rivalry between him and Béon was likely to irritate the Stadholder, he added that appointment of a colonel commandant to his legion would not cause any 'jealousy' on the part of Béon as the latter was going to make a similar proposal for his own legion. The captaincies were confirmed, dated 22 February.[36]

Encouraged that his proposal, while not acceded to, had not been refused, Damas returned to the same subject in a letter he wrote at Maastricht on 3 May. He again asked for his nephew to be appointed *colonel commandant* and, in pressing his case he shone some light on problems in the leadership of the legion. He described the appointment as a step 'of major importance for the order and harmony of the corps':

> I will not hide ... that M. Stack does not respond to what I thought ought to be expected from him, either a difference in characters, or difference of principles, or through any other reason that I do not wish to expand. My two absences have each time brought about in my infantry a change made to distress me after having exhausted all the means of patience and calm, I have convinced myself of the necessity to have a deputy with the principles, views and conduct on which I can count, and who strengthens my authority or respects it in my absence.[37]

34 François de Bas, *Prins Frederik der Nederlanden en Zijn Tijd* (Schiedam: Roelants, 1878), pp.644–5, 659.

35 NAN 1.10.19/1893, Raad van State correspondence.

36 KHN Archieven van Stadhouder Willem V, A31 Inv No 2120, letters dated 8 and 17 February 1794 at The Hague.

37 KHN Archieven van Stadhouder Willem V, A31 Inv No 2120, letters dated 3 May 1794 at Maastricht.

Damas wrote in glowing terms of Nantouillet's effectiveness in forming the legion's cavalry and his firmness in commanding its recruits. Despite his advocacy, nothing came of the proposal.

Meanwhile the infantry continued its active service in the Ardennes region, where Dutch and Austrian units, many of which were composed of émigrés, were deployed together. The left wing of the allied army, commanded by the Austrian general, Franz Wenzel Graf von Kaunitz-Rietberg, observed Maubeuge and Philippeville. Under his orders from Coburg, dated 26 March 1794, he was to hold a defensive line between Rochefort and the camp at Bettignies, with a front running through Dinant, Florennes, Boussu-lez-Walcourt, Beaumont and Erquelinnes.

Generalmajor Karl von Riese commanded 5,000 men holding the line of the small river, Lesse, between Rochefort and Dinant with the following units:

Austrian and Imperial troops:
Freiherr de Vins Nr. 37 Infantry Regiment (one battalion)
Salzburg Infantry Regiment, an Imperial regiment (one battalion)[38]
Carneville Frei-Legion Infantry (two companies)
Kaiser Nr.1 Light Horse Regiment (two squadrons)

Dutch troops:
Légion de Damas (one battalion)
Schmid (Swiss-Graubünden) Regiment (one battalion)
Hesse-Cassel Dragoons (two squadrons)

The other troops of Kaunitz's left wing were posted: at Florennes, including a company of the Carneville infantry; at Boussu-lez-Walcourt, with two squadrons from the Hussards de Saxe in the Austrian army; at Beaumont, including the Béon cavalry squadrons; at Erquelinnes, including the émigré Légion de Bourbon of four weak infantry battalions and four weak cavalry squadrons in Austrian service. His largest detachment, of about 10,000, was at Bettignies. There were also the garrisons of Charleroi and Namur, both with two battalions, one Dutch and one Austrian.[39] It is noteworthy quite how weak the Dutch battalions were, around 29 April Kaunitz wrote to Coburg stating that their effective strength equated to that of an Austrian company, and requested seven Imperial battalions and eight squadrons to replace them; a modern source estimates that Dutch battalions averaged about 220 men in their ranks at this time.[40]

For the Légion de Damas, this period of service required perpetual vigilance, as both sides sent out reconnaissance expeditions against the enemy's outposts. For example, on 26 March Riese led a reconnaissance towards Fromelennes, close to the French fortress of Givet, which was temporarily renamed Vedette-Républicaine by the republicans, and two

38 The Prince-Bishops of Salzburg were independent electors of the Holy Roman Empire.

39 Victor Dupuis, *Les Opérations Militaires sur la Sambre en 1794: Bataille de Fleurus* (Paris: Chapelot, 1907), pp.37–39; Bas, *Prins Frederik der Nederlanden en Zijn Tijd*, p.646.

40 Dupuis, *Les Opérations* p.77; Digby Smith, *The Greenhill Napoleonic Wars Data Book* (London: Greenhill, 1998), p.74.

days later there was a minor skirmish near Philippeville.[41] However, his Dutch contingent, including the Damas infantry, remained posted at Rochefort.[42]

At the beginning of April, the allied commanders agreed their strategy for the forthcoming campaign. It followed the same pattern as the previous year, concentrating in the centre of the line and starting with the taking of another stronghold, at Landrecies, to secure the potential invasion corridor into France. The Emperor, Francis II of Austria, joined the centre of the allied army, as supreme commander, and attended a grand review of the troops on 16 April. The following day the Erfprins, with the Dutch field army, reinforced with Austrian infantry and artillery, moved on Landrecies and began the siege; the entrenched camp protecting the town was stormed by Dutch troops on 20 April. Pichegru responded, on 26 April, with a general attack along his front, from Dunkirk to Philippeville, with emphasis on the wings. His left attacked the weakened allies in Flanders with some success but the centre failed against the Austrians covering the siege. The French republican right wing, which was considerably stronger than Kaunitz's forces, secured Walcourt and Boussu-lez-Walcourt and prepared to attack Beaumont which they found abandoned the next day.

Another attempt by the French centre to relieve Landrecies, on 29 April, failed and the town capitulated the next day. Pichegru, however, pushed on with his advance in Flanders securing the corridor along the River Lys by taking Menen and Kortrijk. On 30 April, the French, under the direction of Carnot, changed their overall strategy; whilst Pichegru was to continue operating in Flanders, a strengthened right wing was to drive towards Brussels and so split the allies. On 5 May, orders were given for the French divisions stationed around Maubeuge, reinforced to about 36,000, to join the 20,000 in the Ardennes, cross the Sambre and advance on Mons. Furthermore, the Armée de la Moselle, now commanded by Jourdan, was to be reinforced from the Armée du Rhin. He was to leave a corps observing Luxembourg and the Vosges, while he, with 45,000 men, was to join the forces on the Sambre. In response, the allied left wing, under Kaunitz, was given more support by moving the troops commanded by the Erfprins, released after the taking of Landrecies, eastwards.

The French forces on the Sambre front did not wait for Jourdan's arrival. On 10 May columns captured several bridges across the river, including that at Thuin. However, the attempt to secure and exploit this by attacking the entrenched positions, which were above the river and covered the route to Mons, was defeated at the Battle of Grandreng, or Rouveroy, on 12 and 13 May. A second attempt to secure a crossing by attacking the allied positions was again repelled at the Battle of Erquelinnes, or Péchant, 20-24 May. Being further to the east, the Légion de Damas was not immediately affected by these actions; in early May, it moved to the small village of Custinne, above the Lesse.

Meanwhile Jourdan, after being joined by the troops from the Rhine, had started his march towards the Sambre. On 21 May, his detachment was at Arlon and the following day it continued north in the wake of Beaulieu's Austrian corps which was too small to risk battle. Jourdan's original object was to reach and secure the entrenched position around Andoy, on the right bank of the Meuse and south of Namur. However, his corps was soon desperately

41 Vermeulen *Tijdschrift voor oudheden*, p.279.
42 NAN 2.21.008.01/19, Jean-Victor Constant-Rebecque Journal Vol.I, return dated 29 April 1794, Schmid is shown with two battalion.

short of food. So, he directed his advance division under François Joseph Lefebvre, which had reached Ciney, to march to the Meuse crossing at Dinant, and from there continue to Givet, to receive supplies there.[43] The Légion de Damas was directly in its path.

Having spent about three weeks of inactivity at Custinne, the legion was ordered to march to Eprave, 13 kilometres to the south east, where a party of French republicans had crossed onto the right bank of the Lesse. The enemy were in force and the legion, now only about 300 strong, was forced to retreat as far as Rochefort and then, as Madame de Bennes recalled:

> We returned to Custines [Custinne], and were encamped in a small wood, in the presence of the enemy for three days. At length, they being informed by their spies that we were but a very small number, they marched a considerable force, easily dislodged us, and we retreated under the protection of the fortress of Zell [Celles]. Not being permitted to pitch our tents, we remained here full twenty-four hours, on the bare ground.[44]

The next day the legion continued to retreat, harassed by French cavalry, until they were supported by a detachment of Salzburg troops and they drew up east of Dinant.[45] This town stands at the bottom of a cliff on the right, eastern, bank of the Meuse and its bridge spans the river to Bouvignes-sur-Meuse, on the opposite bank, which is, in turn, commanded by a steep hill behind it.

On 29 May, the Légion de Damas was posted on the edge of a wide plain to the east of Dinant; the sight left an impression on Corbehem:

> [T]here is a beautiful plain about a league in diameter, forming a kind of amphitheatre and surrounded by villages. Towards the northern extremity of this plain is placed an isolated farm, constructed in the midst of orchards bordered by living hedges. It was along these hedges and facing the plain that my legion was placed, about five hundred men strong … Our position … was very beautiful … nine o'clock in the morning, and in superb weather, pistol shots fired on our left, towards the edge of the plain, announced the presence of the enemy to us and the commencement of hostilities. … This spectacle, the first of this type that I saw, had much interest for me. Cavalrymen, lightly mounted and with uniforms of different colours and cuts, rode individually in the plain, … the squadrons ranged in battle lines … the charges … the fire of the horse artillery; such was the interesting scene which captivated my attention for more than three hours; but it ended by taking a more serious turn. … The fight that they had engaged with us was only a feint, and while they directed the weight of their troops against us to the right and left of the plain, the length of the villages which bordered it, in order to surround us and cut retreat off from us, taking possession of the tortuous path … which alone could return us to Dinant. … our commander … immediately ordering the retreat,

43 Dupuis, *Les Opérations*, pp.243–245.

44 Bennes, *Narrative*, p.27; the Château de Vêves stands just outside Celles, on the road to Dinant.

45 Bennes, *Narrative*, p.27.

> he made us do it at running pace, but in the best order. Despite the dispatch of our march, we would have been inevitably cut off, the retreat having been commanded too late, if the intrepid Saxe and Bercheny Regiments had not protected our movement with their sang-froid and customary valour. They managed to slow the enemy's pursuit, which left us just enough time to reach Dinant and to cross in haste the bridge over the Meuse, of which an arch was already cut. Our salvation was thus assured; but it was only achieved through a hail of balls and cannonballs, which were sent towards us on the other side of the Meuse ...[46]

Bennes described the barrage the unit endured in its retreat to the high ground on the left bank:

> The patriots, however, having taken possession of the heights near Dinan [sic], thundered upon us, if I may use the expression, for I am certain they fired no less than six hundred shots of their artillery. Our escape I look upon as miraculous, for had we been ten times the number, it seemed as if we must have been all destroyed by so heavy a cannonade. M. de la Basse-Boulogne, our Captain, had his right arm broke [sic], and fell: two of my comrades and myself had helped him up, and we were still holding him, when a second broke his left arm and a third three of his ribs, he expired an hour after. Five of my companions, who were behind me, were killed by one cannon-ball; my husband was wounded in two places, the head and thigh, and myself also in the left hand and leg, but very slightly.[47]

After the loss of his captain and recognising that the company, in close order, was suffering unnecessary casualties Tercier took responsibility to order the men to spread out, '"You are", said I to them, "a corps of light troops; thus on this occasion you should seek safety by your scattering"'. In this manner, the companies reached a wood beyond the range of the French republican artillery. *Major* de Rouault arrived demanding to know the reason for the apparent disorder, but was satisfied with Tercier's explanation.[48]

The legion continued to retreat north, parallel with the Meuse, into the night when the French ceased their pursuit. In the morning, the troops who had been expelled from Dinant reformed at the village of Bioul before retiring to Lesve where they bivouacked in the adjacent forest. The following day, 31 May, the Republicans appeared in strength and so the retreat continued that night to Namur, which was reached at daybreak on 1 June.[49] This withdrawal had been anticipated by Coburg, his order of 26 March stipulating that in the face of a serious enemy advance the troops posted along the Lesse were to retreat through Dinant and to take up a position in the defence of Namur. Jourdan crossed the Meuse

46 Corbehem, *Dix ans de ma vie*, pp.95–97; the description given in *Journal Général de la Guerre* No.159 (7 June 1794) suggests that this advance post may have been in the vicinity of Walzin.

47 Bennes, *Narrative*, pp.27–28; the *Journal Général de la Guerre* No.159 (7 June 1794) gives the legion's casualties as four men killed and 12 or 13 wounded.

48 La Chanonie, *Mémoires*, p.72.

49 *Journal Général de la Guerre* No.159 (7 June 1794).

between 31 May and 1 June; his main force continued west whilst his advance division marched towards Charleroi.

It had been the first serious action in which the legion had been engaged. The delay in retreating had placed it in jeopardy and indeed had caused unnecessary losses when it was exposed to the artillery fire on the west bank of the river. Both Corbehem and Tercier, in their later memoirs, apportion blame for the debacle. The former condemned the 'lack of talent in General Reiset [sic] who commanded us'.[50] Tercier, on the other hand, places the blame squarely on the shoulders of his own colonel:

> The Austrian general sent Comte de Damas the order to retire in all haste onto Dinant. But the colonel, well mounted wished to be a bit of a braggart by not executing this order to retreat at once; this swagger cost us dear a little later. A second very imperative order for our retreat was sent. … We lost many men in this fatal march, due to the non-execution of the orders given to the colonel, and to his lack of awareness, however so necessary for war, above all in a commander. If we had begun our march a quarter of an hour earlier, our retreat would have been accomplished without loss.[51]

Meanwhile Bennes found herself separated from the unit and alone. She had obtained a waggon for the wounded and, having assisted in dressing his head wound, she placed her husband in it. She then returned to the ranks but was ordered, by Damas himself, to get two more waggons. On her return she found the legion gone, having already retreated, and she took to the woods thinking that this was the route it would have taken. After some time, she reached the banks of the Meuse and 'could plainly hear somebody speaking French' but did not dare to approach. Learning from a villager that it was a republican she had heard, she instantly took to her heels. After walking further, she encountered a Carneville cavalry patrol and they directed her to Namur, where she knew the first waggon carrying the Damas wounded had been sent. She walked through the night to reach the town 'at six o'clock in the morning.' There she was reunited with her husband who was to be evacuated with the other wounded to Maastricht. The identities of two other chasseurs who were wounded is also known, they were Pierre-Abel de Savatte de Genouillé, of the same company, and Joseph du Garreau de La Seinie, the eldest of the brothers serving in Rouault's company.[52] Riese had reached Namur, with the legion, and the French approached the town, 'our drums were beating to arms, I saw my dear husband as far as the boat, and went, obedient to the duty of a soldier, to join my corps, … The enemy were not far distant, we engaged them, and fought very near five hours, without any material loss on either side.'[53]

Meanwhile, to the west, the French had crossed the Sambre again, the third attempt. This offensive was made despite a lack of supplies, low morale amongst the troops and the knowledge that Jourdan was not far away. The key difference between this attempt and

50 Corbehem, *Dix ans de ma vie*, p.97.

51 La Chanonie, *Mémoires*, p.71.

52 H. Beauchet-Filleau, *Tableau des émigrés du Poitou aux armées des Princes et de Condé* (Poitiers: Pichot, 1845), p.111 and AN, Dossier de la Légion d'Honneur, L0836063.

53 Bennes, *Narrative*, pp.28–29.

the previous ones was that the object was no longer to cross the river below Charleroi and to advance on Mons, it was now the capture of Charleroi itself. On 28 May, after securing Marchienne-au-Pont, the republicans crossed from the right, south, bank and took up positions around the city the following day. The siege began with trenches being opened on 1 June.

Kaunitz, with only about 27,000 men, had remained on the defensive while reinforcements arrived. On 30 May he was replaced in command by the Erfprins, who, on the same day, ordered Riese to march from Namur; the city now being covered to the south by Beaulieu in the entrenched camp at Andoy. Riese was directed to hold the Charleroi-Namur road at Sombreffe and he reached this position on 1 June with just over 5,000 men, including the Damas infantry.[54]

The Erfprins organised his strengthened army in five columns for the offensive to relieve Charleroi. These moved into position on 2 June ready for the following day's attack. He perceived the key to the Republican position to be the heights around Gosselies and four columns were assigned to secure them. The fifth column, which included Riese's command, advanced along the Fleurus road to cut the French line of retreat to the east of Charleroi, as far as the bridge at Châtelet. The infantry of both the Damas and Béon legions were at the front of this flanking column.

The young chasseur, Corbehem, remembered the night and the battle that followed:

> We spent the night without shutting an eye; but in a calm attitude and full of confidence. Our officers exhorted us to do our duty well; but they took unnecessary trouble: the sentiment of honour and the memory of the cause that we had embraced spoke loud enough to our spirit that we had no need of another incentive. … A little before daylight, a pretty big measure of eau-de-vie was distributed to each of us; a precaution which is sometimes necessary, and which we try not to miss whenever possible on such occasions, in order to add artificial means to the natural forces of man, so to spare him the horror of slaughtering in cold blood his fellow man and to help him brave death. As dawn broke, a cannon fired at the centre of the line gave the signal for the attack; a signal which was immediately repeated by the drummers and trumpeters. Then the tumult became general; we fell with impetuosity on the enemy that our audacity frightened. …the villages were seized by force; but in truth after very feeble resistance … all the enemy's positions were taken without costing us many men. Finally, the republicans, beaten, overwhelmed, chased in every direction, precipitately retreated behind the Sambre …[55]

After the battle there were no comforts for the Damas soldiers, '…to refresh ourselves, after our fatigues, we were indulged with the bare open fields, and a very heavy shower'.[56]

The engagement of 3 June, subsequently called the Battle of Gosselies or Charleroi, saw the French lose about 2,000 men and 12 artillery pieces; the allies suffered less than 500 casualties. In the evening the Emperor entered Charleroi in triumph. Subsequently he

54 Dupuis, *Les Opérations* p.200 and 202; Bennes, *Narrative*, p.29.
55 Corbehem, *Dix ans de ma vie*, pp.107–108.
56 Bennes, *Narrative*, p.30.

travelled back to the allied headquarters, being there overnight 10/11 June before he left at noon the next day for Germany. His departure, at this point, was regarded as signalling that the Austrians had lost interest in Belgium and might even abandon the country.[57]

Meanwhile, on the other side of the Sambre, Jourdan joined the defeated army and took command of all the French forces there.[58] The allies did not exploit the victory as attention was drawn to Flanders where Pichegru was gradually gaining the upper hand and had besieged Ypres on 1 June. The Erfprins was directed to concentrate his main force at the Rouveroy camp and he confirmed that this move had taken place on 6 June.[59] However the Damas infantry remained detached from the Dutch field army, and returned to the vicinity of Namur. Bennes recalling that, after staying in the fields on 3 June, they 'relished the comfort of pitching our tents at Andois [Andoy], where we continued four days'.[60]

On 12 June Jourdan, having reorganised his army which now consisted of about 90,000 men, crossed the Sambre and pushed the allies' weak cordon back and the next day he invested Charleroi. The bulk of the Erfprins's forces were posted to the west; only Beaulieu was to the east, near Namur, with Riese posted at Balâtre, on the road between Namur and Charleroi. The Erfprins had about 45,000 men in total, including outlying posts and the Charleroi garrison. Despite having contemplated retreat, he quickly brought his troops up to resist Jourdan and by 14 June those from Rouveroy had arrived at Nivelles while Beaulieu had moved up to Temploux to link up with Riese. The Erfprins planned for the attack to be delivered on 16 June, again by five columns: three columns were to assault the French centre while two others, under Beaulieu's command, were to take the positions held by the enemy's eastern flank. Amongst the troops with Beaulieu were both the cavalry and infantry of Béon and Damas, although apparently kept in reserve this was the first time that the latter's cavalry had been brought forward for active service.[61]

Beaulieu's right column was to start off from Balâtre to attack the French positions at Lambusart and his left from Point du Jour, just east of Sombreffe, to move against Fleurus. Once these initial objectives had been achieved both columns were to unite for an attack on Ransart whilst a detachment was sent to secure the bridges east of Charleroi, at Châtelet and Montignies-sur-Sambre. Beaulieu's columns began to march at 2:00 a.m. on 16 June, and launched their attacks three hours later. Success here assured victory on the day, after the attacks in other areas ran into stiffer opposition. Although the result of the battle, called the Battle of Lambusart or First Fleurus, was the same as on 3 June, it was evident that the enemy were not only more determined but also better commanded than before.

That morning *Major* Charles-Louis-Auguste Senarclens de Grancy of the Bylandt Dragoons commanded a small detachment that advanced along the left bank of the Sambre to clear opposition on Beaulieu's left flank. With him were the Damas infantry, about 500 men, commanded by *Major* de Rouault, the Comte de Damas being attached to Beaulieu's staff and *Lieutenant-colonel* Stack to that of the Erfprins; there were also 150 Béon infantry

57 Sir Harry Verney, *The Journals and Correspondence of General Sir Harry Calvert* (London: Hurst and Blackett, 1853), p.246.
58 Jomini, *Histoire critique et militaire*, Vol.V, p.93.
59 Dupuis, *Les Opérations* p.280.
60 Bennes, *Narrative*, p.30.
61 Jomini, *Histoire critique et militaire*, Vol.V, p.104a.

and 20 dragoons of the Hesse-Cassel Regiment. The detachment ran into a French republican advanced post at Jemeppe-sur-Sambre, a village standing on a small river, the Orneau, which flowed into the Sambre nearby. Two of the enemy were killed and seven were immediately taken prisoner.[62]

Clearing Jemeppe the detachment continued towards the bridge over the Sambre at Auvelais (known as Auveloix at the time). The Béon infantry, reinforced by 24 Damas chasseurs, were placed on the right and those of the Damas legion on the left.[63] The two small émigré columns advanced, in parallel, through a wide wheat field, pushing the enemy skirmishers before them, towards a wood that bordered the Sambre. As they approached the wood a fire fight began between the legions and the enemy's main body. The Légion de Damas, despite being in skirmishing order, lost several men before they could reach the shelter of the trees in the hedge fringing the wood, 'because the enemy, who were very close to us, made us out through the trees whose leaves were still not very developed, put us under continual fire by platoon and of grape-shot.' Corbehem owed his safety to an old trunk which soon became riddled with shot.[64]

The Légion de Damas halted for some time before following the enemy into the wood with the intention of turning their flank. However:

> [T]he Damas corps was halted in its pursuit for fear of firing on the right hand column, some voices having shouted … *they are the Béons*; to assure himself of this the Damas's major uttered that cry so dear to true Frenchmen, Vive le roi! at this cry repeated with enthusiasm by the whole corps, the Carmagnoles loosed a most lively musketry fire. Then the major ordered the bayonet charge; it was executed with impetuosity. The enemy did not wait for it, and under fire to their left from the Béon infantry, they took flight with such precipitation that a great number being unable to cross the bridge, congested with fugitives, threw themselves into the river.[65]

Tercier wrote:

> [C]arried away by our ardour, we thought it necessary to pursue the fugitives as far as musket range of the river. But four artillery pieces, that the enemy fired on us, forced us to fall back up to half-way up the hill. As we overlooked them by our position, all our musket shots told on their frightened and disordered troops, who moreover found themselves obstructed and congested in crossing the bridge. Several Republican soldiers only found safety by swimming across the river.[66]

The French republican cannon defended the bridge and although the émigré detachment, without artillery, were unable to respond in kind but continued to fire on the enemy causing severe losses, especially among the gunners who did not abandon their posts. Corbehem

62 *Journal Général de la Guerre* No.173 (20 June 1794).
63 La Chanonie, *Mémoires*, p 74.
64 Corbehem, *Dix ans de ma vie*, pp 101–103.
65 *Journal Général de la Guerre* No.173 (20 June 1794).
66 La Chanonie, *Mémoires*, p 74.

described that 'a very sharp and deadly fusillade' was maintained for up to two hours, the émigrés being able to find cover from the cannon fire behind a redoubt that had been constructed, but left undefended, until they had expended almost all their ammunition. Finally *Major* de Grancy ordered the detachment to retire and it did so without any interference from the enemy. The detachment re-joined Beaulieu's columns which had driven the enemy from their positions, at Lambusart and Ransart, where Corbehem, for one, was struck by the scene, 'All the ground that they occupied, ... was covered by mutilated cadavers'.[67]

Despite having been a minor action, and an adjunct to the main battle, the *Journal Général de la Guerre* stated that the émigré infantry 'displayed an ardour and courage above all praise.'[68] Furthermore, Tercier recalled that Beaulieu congratulated the two legions for their conduct in an order of the following day and he also noted that, 'Our four fusilier companies likewise showed a valour such that, if it were necessary to detail all the facts, they would have honoured the most celebrated armies.'[69] The Béon infantry lost three men wounded and the Légion de Damas about 10 killed and 30 wounded; amongst these last were *Capitaine* Thomas MacDermott grievously wounded and *Lieutenants* James Geohegan and Joseph de Savignac slightly.[70] The enemy they had faced had been about 2,500 strong: those posted at the bridge, on the left bank of the Sambre, and in the wood in front of Auvelais were the first battalions of the 172e Demi-Brigade de Ligne and the 9e Demi-Brigade Légère as well as 306 men of the 11e Chasseurs à Cheval,with the 2e bataillon du Nord (721 men) at the bridge on the right bank.[71] After the action, the commander of the 9e Demi-Brigade Légère was removed after having refused to rally his battalion.[72]

Despite the victory, once again the allies did not have sufficient numbers to press their advantage. They had to be satisfied with simply driving the French over the Sambre and no more. Initially it was intended that the allies would now concentrate on relieving Ypres and for this purpose reinforcements were to be sent from the left wing towards Tournai. The Erfprins was to remain covering the Sambre and on 17 June he concentrated his main force around Chapelle-lez-Herlaimont, whilst Beaulieu retired further to the east, on the road to Namur. A small detachment, commanded by an *Oberst* Spiegel, was placed between them, in the vicinity of Gosselies. The infantry units of this detachment were the six companies of the Légion de Damas and at least one battalion from the Austrian army; the cavalry appears to have been the Hussards de Bercheny and Saxe, that of the Légion de Béon along with an Austrian squadron, perhaps of Carneville.[73]

However, both the local and strategic situation changed very quickly when, early on 18 June, Jourdan responded to his recent defeat by sending his troops over the Sambre once again. Within hours of making the crossing their advance pushed north as far Gosselies. Spiegel's detachment found itself in jeopardy, Bennes remembered that it tried to reach

67 Corbehem, *Dix ans de ma vie*, p.103.
68 *Journal Général de la Guerre* No.173 (20 June 1794).
69 La Chanonie, *Mémoires*, pp.74–75.
70 Bennes, *Narrative*, p.30, stated the Damas infantry lost 40 men killed or wounded.
71 Dupuis, *Les Opérations* pp.274–275.
72 Dupuis, *Les Opérations* p.557.
73 Dupuis, *Les Opérations* pp.305–306. The memoirs and other contemporary sources are at odds with each other as to the detachment's commander and units.

the Erfprins's corps but was unable to do so, 'The patriots were in force, they attempted to blockade us, we were very near being surrounded, but providentially escaped, happy enough to retreat unhurt, and arrived safe at Quatre Bras'.[74]

Meanwhile Jourdan urgently pressed on with besieging Charleroi, as the allies were expected to respond without delay. However, the Erfprins feared that the true target of Jourdan's offensive was Mons and that his position at Chapelle-lez-Herlaimont could be easily turned so he retired with his main body to the camp around Rouveroy. He kept outlying detachments, one in his old position at Chapelle-lez-Herlaimont, another in front of Gosselies and Spiegel at Quatre Bras. Beaulieu was ordered to move up to Gembloux and keep in touch with Spiegel.

Although Coburg had planned to take the Austrian corps from the centre, around Tournai, to join Clerfayt and counter Pichegru, he now resolved to join the left wing by marching to Nivelles and placing it between the Erfprins and Beaulieu. On 21 June, he marched east, leaving York's corps to cover Tournai, and reached Nivelles two days later. Significantly he had declined to leave Austrian troops under York's direct command, those left in Flanders were either in garrison or under the command of the Austrian general Clerfayt, and the apparatus of the Imperial administration retired to Brussels, all signs of disengagement.[75]

Meanwhile the French covering the siege of Charleroi carried out a number of operations to press and harass the allies. On 20 and 22 June, they attacked the detachment the Erfprins had left at Chapelle-lez-Herlaimont, and on the fine and warm morning of 21 June, a division of nine infantry battalions and six cavalry squadrons, supported by two cavalry brigades, 18 squadrons, advanced on Spiegel's detachment at Quatre Bras. The Damas infantry, according to Corbehem, was:

> Camped on the left of the [Brussels] road, and facing the enemy, [the legion] occupied an eminence which dominated the plain, having before it a marsh of small extent, at its left a wood abutting a village; on its right, and beyond, as well as to its rear, a continuity of open country cut at intervals by clumps of woods and hamlets which broke the uniformity, and offered the finest positions for the deployment of cavalry.[76]

At about 10:00 a.m. the enemy appeared, advancing on the position and driving the allied cavalry screen in front of them, while their own cavalry began working around the flanks. Finally, as the situation became critical Spiegel ordered a retreat, which became precipitous. The French republicans pressed the detachment closely; the Comte de Damas offered to place his infantry to act as the rear guard, but according to Tercier, Spiegel replied:

> "No, no, Monsieur Comte, you, you have a good horse between your legs, by which you can save yourself; but your émigrés are on foot, and there is no chance of mercy for them if they are made prisoners. In consequence, they will open the march

74 Bennes, *Narrative*, p 30.
75 Verney, *Journals and Correspondence of General Sir Harry Calvert*, pp.257–258.
76 Corbehem, *Dix ans de ma vie*, p.114.

> in retreat, which I will protect by my regiment and the cavalry I have under my command. March."

Corbehem also mentioned Spiegel's consideration as an exception, regarding it as common practice for coalition generals to place the émigrés at the rear despite the fate that awaited them if captured.[77] Tercier continued:

> We were scarcely on the Brussels highway, which the French skirmishers already occupied on both sides. They did us a lot of harm by their crossfire. But our brave hussars soon made them retire. We did not march, we ran. The heat was excessive, and the dust bothered us to excess. Our rapid march was protected for three leagues by our Hussards de Saxe and Berchini [sic], who continually charged along the wide road, and forwards and backwards by their different charges, delayed the enemy's march, …[78]

On reaching Genappe the Austrian infantry deployed the single field gun they had with them; two discharges of case shot ensured their pursuers kept a greater distance. Indeed, it was here that the French infantry stopped, leaving the cavalry to continue the pursuit. Spiegel's detachment continued to retreat for nine kilometres along the Brussels highroad. The republican cavalry continued to harass the infantry column but were kept at bay by the cavalry that accompanied it; the Hussards de Bercheny were particularly distinguished in this task. Finally, at a defensive position on the edge of the Forest of Soignes, along the ridge in front of Mont-Saint-Jean, four and a half kilometres south of Waterloo, the retreat was halted. The enemy cavalry rode off. Corbehem recalled that this position of safety had been reached after, 'four hours of a forced retreat, made at the most hastened pace, without a moment of halt and during the greatest heat of one of the hottest days of the year, … covered with sweat, dust and consumed with thirst'.[79] Tercier was more succinct. 'We were exhausted, wiped out.'[80] The legion had lost 30 men as casualties.[81] Some of the soldiers, including Corbehem, went to a local church to give thanks for their deliverance, at a service led by the *Abbé* Louis du Tertre, chaplain to the Légion de Béon and a former an army officer. After the trials of the day the troops camped overnight at Mont-Saint-Jean before returning the following day to resume their previous position at Quatre Bras, the enemy having retired.

With the arrival of Coburg, the coalition forces, amounting to 46,000 men, were reorganised ready to attack the republicans around Charleroi. According to Tercier the Austrian *Reichs-Generalfeldmarschall* reviewed the Légion de Damas on 23 June and commented on it in the most flattering terms to the Comte de Damas.[82] The importance of the

77 Corbehem, *Dix ans de ma vie*, p.116.

78 La Chanonie, *Mémoires*, p.76; the distance between Quatre Bras and Genappe is 4.6 kilometres.

79 Corbehem, *Dix ans de ma vie*, p.118.

80 La Chanonie, *Mémoires*, p.76.

81 *Nieuwe Nederlandsche Jaarboeken* p.747. The casualties from all the outpost actions are combined, including the thirty men of the Légion de Damas and four from Béon – unfortunately the arm of the legion is not specified in either case.

82 La Chanonie, *Mémoires*, p.76.

impending contest was widely recognised. In Flanders Sir Harry Calvert, the Duke of York's adjutant-general, wrote, 'The event must decide the fate of this country, on which you may rely that the happiness of our own materially depends.'[83]

Coburg's attack was scheduled for 26 June, giving time for preparations and for the troops to get some rest. Meanwhile Jourdan, apparently aware of the date of the planned attack, pushed ahead with the siege, the bombardment of the city commencing on 24 June, while ensuring that his 77,300 men were in the best possible state to resist the onslaught. The covering force strengthened its positions with field works, the local population being requisitioned as labourers.[84] Furthermore, a static balloon, *L'Entreprenant*, arrived on 23 June and was stationed at Jumet, to observe the coalition's future deployments and movements; it also had a psychological effect, as Corbehem observed, 'this fatal balloon; the aspect of which, foreign to the majority of the army's soldiers, seemed to them to be marvellous.'[85] Finally, when Charleroi's garrison surrendered on 25 June, not only were the 16,000 men and the artillery, previously committed to the siege, available to Jourdan but also the risk from a sortie during the ensuing battle was removed. Coburg, however, did not know if Charleroi was still in coalition hands; in the evening of 25 June he had to send a staff officer to go through the lines to discover the situation.[86]

Coburg's offensive was to be delivered by a number of simultaneous assaults on the enemy positions which were in a rough semi-circle around Charleroi with both flanks resting on the Sambre. To the east, Beaulieu was to seize those between the Sambre and the Namur-Nivelles road while Archduke Charles advanced down the road from Gembloux to take Fleurus; they were then to combine their forces to attack the position around Lambusart. Quosdanovich, coming down the Brussels road, had Gosselies as his objective; between him and Archduke Charles, Kaunitz was to clear some outlying positions before attacking Heppignies. Finally, the right wing, commanded by the Erfprins, was to operate to the west of Charleroi and head for the Sambre, in particular the crossing at Marchienne-au-Pont; he was isolated from the other coalition forces by the Bas Piéton (the course of which now forms the Brussels-Charleroi Canal).

The Erfprins's wing consisted of the Dutch field army, which assembled on 25 June at Chapelle-lez-Herlaimont, to which some Austrians were added. It was formed into two divisions, commanded by the Fürst zu Waldeck and Prins Frederik, as well as a vanguard of light troops under *Generalmajor* Graf von Riesch.[87] Both arms of the Légion de Damas were involved, the cavalry appear to have been with Prins Frederik's division while the infantry were in Riesch's vanguard, alongside two battalions of the Hungarian Infantry Regiment Gyulai No.32 and a battalion each from the Légion de Béon and Bylandt Jagers.[88]

83 Verney, *Journals and Correspondence of General Sir Harry Calvert*, p 265.

84 See note of the report by Lieutenant Franceschi cited in Lucien Cécille, Philippe Charlet and Jean-Jacques Pattyn, *La Bataille de Mont-Saint-Jean 6 & 7 juillet 1794* (Plougastel: Historic'One, 2015), p.19.

85 Corbehem, *Dix ans de ma vie*, p.121.

86 Dupuis, *Les Opérations* p.321; the staff officer was Josef Radetzky (1766–1858), later to be immortalised in the march composed by Johan Strauss I.

87 Johann Sigmund von Riesch (1750–1821) should not be confused with the previously mentioned Karl von Riese (c1730–1806).

88 Alain Arcq, *Fleurus, 26 juin 1794* (Plougastel: Historic'One, 2007), p.24 and Smith, *Data Book*, p.86, there is some divergence amongst other sources.

Prins Frederik's division, on the right of the wing, set off from Chapelle-lez-Herlaimont at 2:00 a.m. for Anderlues; from there it easily drove a French detachment from Fontaine-l'Eveque before being brought to a halt before the camp of l'Espinette, that covered the Sambre behind Leernes. There a three-hour artillery duel began, while troops from the division captured the fortified farm of Wespes, or la Pisselotte, and worked their way into the woods at Landelies, on the enemy's left flank, alongside the river.

Waldeck's division had crossed the Haut Piéton at 1:30 a.m., formed up and then advanced on the French position about Trazegnies. An artillery duel commenced but after about an hour Waldeck launched an infantry attack. This apparently had an immediate result, enemy resistance collapsed and they retreated, in some haste and disorder. On Waldeck's right Riesch's light troops moved up into the woods before Monceau-sur-Sambre, penetrating almost as far as the village. The pursuit of the fleeing French republicans continued and soon, by about 9:00 a.m., Waldeck's troops were on the heights above Monceau from where they were able to cannonade the enemy at Marchienne-au-Pont.

This rapid progress however put his troops in a precarious position, the Erfprins became concerned that Waldeck's right flank was unsupported as his brother, Frederik, had not linked up with him yet; furthermore, his rear and left flank were vulnerable from attack across the Bas Piéton. Indeed, the French commander on the other bank, Kléber, had already sent a detachment across the river to assist at Trazegnies; when it returned having found the defenders in flight, he ensured all the river crossings, from Roux to Marchienne were reinforced. Then at around midday he had his artillery open up on Waldeck's positions, including howitzers which bombarded the wood of Monceau. Kléber had been able to make this counter-attack because Quosdanovich's advance, in the face of strong resistance, was making slow progress. Kaunitz, similarly, was having difficulty. However, both Archduke Charles and Beaulieu had achieved their initial objectives and by about midday were combining ready to attack the well defended position around Lambusart.

Prins Frederik's attack on the camp of l'Espinette remained stalled and when a French brigade arrived on his left flank he was forced to retreat; he reached Anderlues at 3:00 p.m. Meanwhile substantial French counter-attacks were being sent over the Bas Piéton, and a force of about 6,000 entered the woods of Monceau, nevertheless Waldeck and Riesch's units retained a hold in the woods and along the Bas Piéton. Finally, about 5:00 p.m. the Erfprins ordered a retreat to heights around Forchies-la-Marche.

Elsewhere Quosdanovich had eventually forced the enemy to fall back on Gosselies and was preparing to advance; Kaunitz had driven those facing him back to Ransart; the other corps were engaged in assaulting Lambusart. Despite these signs of success, it was now that all the commanders received Coburg's order to break off any engagement and retreat. Although some French generals, in the centre and left wing, were to claim to have driven their opponents off with counter-attacks, the coalition forces' retreat was not seriously interfered with and they were permitted to reach their encampments, and stay there, undisturbed, overnight. Indeed, the French did not move on 27 June, apparently exhausted by the battle in which they suffered about 5,000 casualties. Those for the coalition forces were very light in comparison: the Austrians had 208 killed, 1,017 wounded and 361 captured or missing while the Dutch suffered a total of 700 casualties.[89] The comparatively light losses, for a force of around 46,000 men in a full day's battle, added to the suspicion that the Austrians had only engaged in battle to preserve their honour, Coburg calling off the attack once he had heard of the fall of Charleroi.[90]

It appears that, once again, the Damas cavalry, with Prins Frederik's division, were not engaged in the battle but were held in reserve. In contrast the Damas infantry companies were in the thick of the action, Corbehem recalled the eve of the battle, 'We spent the night under arms, without a thought of giving ourselves up to sleep; too great interests occupied us. In the morning, battle commenced; the greatest enthusiasm was amongst us, and especially in my legion, as we were burning with desire to avenge our last retreat.' Jumet was directly in view on Waldeck's initial line of attack, 'we advanced always in the direction of the perfidious balloon, which seemed to move off at the same speed that we approached it.'[91]

At times the artillery fire, which dominated the battle, was intense and, for Corbehem, every step was dearly won. Tercier wrote, 'We advanced successively and congratulated ourselves on the success of a battle that was finally going to end this horrible Revolution.'[92] They were involved in heavy fighting to capture a village, presumably Monceau-sur-Sambre:

> [W]e reached a village the possession of which was important. Here the combat redoubled; but despite the efforts and murderous fire of the enemy, we seized the entrance to the village, we penetrated as far as the centre; the area around the church became the theatre of a bloody mêlée.[93]

Tercier remembered that after the village had been taken the republicans made an attempt to retake it half an hour later; both actions cost the legion several casualties. The battle lasted all day. 'We were famished, doubly exhausted. The colonel sent for several barrels of beer to refresh us.'[94] The order to retreat, after the legion's hard-won success, came as a shock and it was obeyed with consternation. 'Then, as skirmishers that we were, we formed ourselves in platoons, and retired with heavy steps, leaving the enemy to reap the fruits of a victory they had not won. Our retreat was not troubled at any point, and we quietly resumed our positions of the day before.'[95]

---

89 Dupuis, *Les Opérations* p.372, the allied losses are sometimes given as about the same as the French but this is by including the 2,800 already taken prisoner when the garrison of Charleroi surrendered on 25 June.

90 This is the view taken by many contemporary commentators, and followed by subsequent historians, many, like Calvert, blaming the Emperor's advisors rather than Coburg himself. Guillaume-Anne Constant-Rebecque-Villars, commanding a brigade in the battle, however was scornful of the suggestion that Coburg only became aware of the surrender of Charleroi after noon on 26 June (NAN 2.21.005.41/32).

91 Corbehem, *Dix ans de ma vie*, pp.121–122.

92 La Chanonie, *Mémoires*, p.78.

93 Corbehem, *Dix ans de ma vie*, p.122.

94 La Chanonie, *Mémoires*, pp.77–78, Tercier identifies the village as 'Sainte Barbe' whilst Corbehem, does not name it.

95 Corbehem, *Dix ans de ma vie*, pp 122–123; Tercier states that the final order to retreat was received at 8:30 p.m.

Tercier initially thought it was a tactical move to turn an enemy position while Corbehem thought it was a mistake or, indeed, an act of treachery.[96] Even if it is a moot point whether Jourdan had indeed won the battle, he was the victor as he was left in possession of Charleroi and his positions around it.

The coalition allies continued their retreat in good order, the bulk of the Austrians to Marbais and the Erfprins, with some Austrians under *Feldmarschalleutnant* Latour, to Haine-Saint-Paul, just south of La Louvière, and then towards Nivelles. On 28 June, the Erfprins established his headquarters at Le Rœulx in support of the defence of Mons which was held by troops that had abandoned positions further south. The same day Coburg's centre was deployed in front of Braine-l'Alleud, with outposts placed on the two highroads to the south at Nivelles and Genappe. The coalition's left, under Beaulieu, still defended the route to Namur having only moved back to Gembloux, with a post at Sombreffe. The memoirs of those serving in the Légion de Damas, that took part in the Dutch movement from Nivelles to Le Rœulx, are somewhat confused in this period. This is to be expected at a time of retreats, counter-marching and skirmishes.

Although the coalition forces had not been pressed, the Austrian army was demoralised and their headquarters was in confusion; Coburg resolved to take a defensive stance. On 1 July, a conference of the allies' senior commanders was held at his headquarters at Braine-l'Alleud. There, after Coburg had given unequivocal assurances that the Austrians would not abandon the province, it was decided the allies, in the face of the French armies' success not only at Fleurus but also in Flanders, should take up positions in a wide arc covering Brussels. These were to extend from Dendermonde, held by the Hanoverians, through Geraardsbergen, York's command, to Anderlecht, closer to the western fringes of Brussels, where Clerfayt was to be placed. The line was to continue through Tubize, to be held by the Erfprins, and then the main Austrian army at Mont-Saint-Jean to Beaulieu and Quosdanovich's positions around Gembloux. The allied movement was scheduled to take place five days after the conference. However, Jourdan had already seized the initiative.

Initially, whilst a part of his army observed Beaulieu and Quosdanovich, divisions under Kléber advanced on Mons. On 1 July, the entrenched camp, on the imposing high ground of Mont Panisel, southeast of the city, was seized after heavy fighting and the city was itself soon occupied unopposed. Late in the afternoon the French, after some resistance by the Dutch, turned the Erfprins's position at Le Rœulx forcing him to retreat via Soignies and Braine-le-Comte, to Tubize which he reached by 3 July. The main Austrian force also withdrew, reaching Mont-Saint-Jean on 2 July.

The Légion de Damas saw action during these operations including the engagement at Le Rœulx. Although Bennes simply observed that 'some few shots were twice exchanged at the advance posts' Tercier indicates that it was more serious, 'There were different engagements,

96 The Duke of York, although accepting that Coburg called off his attacks due to their lack of progress, considered the immediate decision to retreat to be treacherous on the part of the Austrians (RAW, De Budé Papers, GEO/ADD/15/0589; York to Budé on 28 June 1794). Given his previous observations it is noteworthy that, at the same time, he observed that the Erfprins had conducted himself 'perfectly well'.

in which our legion and that of Béon continually took part. We had one of them near Rœulx, ... It lasted until night, of which we took advantage to make our retreat.'[97]

The French offensive forced the hands of the coalition commanders and another conference was held, on 5 July, at Coburg's headquarters, now at Waterloo. It was decided that Brussels would only be defended until 7 July, giving sufficient time for the stores kept there to be moved. The allies would then withdraw to a new defensive line running north to south, from Antwerp to Namur, through Leuven, Wavre and Gembloux, to safeguard Liège and the Maas crossings into Germany. Coburg assured those at the conference that the Antwerp-Namur line would be maintained unless the coalition were 'completely defeated.'[98] To make the move to this line the main Austrian force was to move off the Brussels road and march eastwards towards Wavre, this move was to be covered by the Erfprins, who would leave the area of Halle and take over the key defensive position at Mont-Saint-Jean during the morning of 6 July. He, in turn, was to follow Coburg in the night of 7/8 July. Meanwhile the Duke of York and Clerfayt, to the west of Brussels, were to remain in place until 7 July and then retreat north of the city to the new line.

At the same time, Jourdan, who was receiving contradictory instructions from the Committee for Public Safety, consolidated the positions around Mons and sent cavalry patrols to reconnoitre the allied positions resulting, notably on 4 July, in some skirmishing across the front.[99] On 5 July Jourdan decided, on his own initiative, to push forward. A division, commanded by François-Joseph Lefebvre, moved up to Nivelles and another two to Quatre Bras, with Paul-Alexis Dubois's cavalry division linking and supporting these columns. This coincided with the Austrians concentrating on Mont-Saint-Jean before Coburg moved off, in the early hours of 6 July; his headquarters left Waterloo at 3:00 a.m. to reach Corbais at 1:00 p.m. His three columns marched across a broad front, extending from Wavre to Gembloux, and his rear guard, at Lillois-Witterzée, was to head for Genappe to provide a link with his southerly column and the Dutch advance.

At the same time, Lefebvre's division set out from Nivelles and, pushing on through Lillois-Witterzée, saw enemy troops moving in front, which was the Dutch taking over positions from the Austrian rear guard. The first Dutch troops had marched overnight from Tubize and had begun to arrive while others, from further afield and who had only left their positions mid-morning, would arrive late in the afternoon. As Lefebvre's men approached Braine l'Alleud they were brought to a halt by the Dutch artillery, established in earthworks constructed earlier by the Austrians. Dubois, on Lefebvre's eastern flank, heading to attack the Dutch, and the Austrians they were taking over from, on Mont-Saint-Jean deployed his light artillery near the Hougoumont Wood. Prins Frederik, commanding the Dutch advance, reached Waterloo at about 7:00 a.m. and, hearing the cannonade, went to the field. He brought up his cavalry that charged Dubois's guns forcing them to withdraw, Dubois counter-charged, in turn driving the Dutch off. The success of his cavalry permitted Dubois to place all his guns on the left of the Dutch artillery at Braine l'Alleud and their enfilading fire supported Lefebvre

97 Bennes, *Narrative*, p.31; La Chanonie, *Mémoires*, p.79, he is supported by Jean Baptiste Catoir (or Catoire) who in a later memorial listed this action amongst those that were of significance in the history of the Damas infantry, TNA HO 69/31.

98 RAW, De Budé Papers, GEO/ADD/15/0590; York to Budé on 8 July 1794.

99 Cécille et al, *La Bataille de Mont-Saint-Jean*, pp.48–50.

as he eventually advanced and seized the position. In the cavalry action Prins Friedrich of Hessen-Philippsthal was killed at the head of the Bylandt Dragoons when they clashed with the cuirassiers of the 8e Régiment de Cavalerie during the French counter-attack. The Damas cavalry appears to have been with the Dutch cavalry but were again held in reserve.[100]

To secure the position on the ridge at Mont-Saint-Jean the Damas infantry were sent to occupy a forward position between the opposing forces, the substantial Hougoumont farmhouse and outbuildings, otherwise called the Château de Goumont. This stood on the eastern side of the Nivelles road at the bottom of the forward slope of the ridge and its defence in a subsequent battle for the same ridge, the Battle of Waterloo, 20 years later was to become famous. The Damas infantry were joined, at the farm house, by the Slavonisch-Serbisches Corps, a free corps in Austrian service, raised in 1792 by the Croatian *Oberst* Stephan Mihaljevich. The Béon infantry were placed in support, in the wooded area behind, to the north of, Hougoumont. As the Damas infantry took possession of the farm, they came under artillery fire from the higher ground opposite and Corbehem had a lucky escape:

> On arriving at the château … we had to endure fire from a light artillery piece that the enemy had placed on the height which dominated it on the southern side … As we marched, two abreast, in front of the outer wall of the main building, and we presented the right side to the piece of which I have spoken, a cannon ball, thrown at the height of my waist, and passing about a foot in front of me and behind the file which preceded me, pierced the wall which was to my left.

The farm buildings stood in substantial grounds and the soldiers lined the boundary hedge, facing Dubois's position, until nightfall.[101]

However, the anticipated French attack did not materialise and each side remained in their positions, on the evening of 6 July, wary of being attacked. The Dutch retained the position at Mont-Saint-Jean, as planned, with their headquarters immediately behind it, at Waterloo; the two French divisions bivouacked around Hougoumont Wood. Their compatriots that had launched their attacks from Quatre Bras, as well as those operating further south, had not been as successful and all the French troops were short of ammunition. Furthermore, that evening, Jourdan received instructions from his political masters indicating he should take a defensive stance. The French had had the best of the fighting but they had not taken the coalition forces' main position, made them change their plans or split the Dutch from the Austrians. The action at Mont-Saint-Jean was not a French republican victory that led to the capture of Brussels despite recent attempts to portray it as such.[102] There were a number of men present who would have a prominent role in the Waterloo campaign of 1815, including Soult, Ney, Drouet d'Erlon, and Duhesme.

---

100 Bittard des Portes, *Les émigrés*, pp 176–177; Bas, *Prins Frederik der Nederlanden en Zijn Tijd*, p.289; Paul Marmottan, *Le Général Fromentin et l'Armée du Nord (1792–1794)* (Paris: Dubois, 1894), report of General Dubois pp.236–238; Louis Jouan, *La Campagne de 1794–1795 dans le Pays-Bas* (Paris: Fournier, 1915), Vol.I p.284; NAN 2.21.008.01/19, Jean-Victor Constant-Rebecque Journal Vol.I.

101 Corbehem, *Dix ans de ma vie*, p 126.

102 For example Philippe Charlet, '1794 Les Français Victorieux à Waterloo', *Traditions: Guerriers et Militaires de l'Époque Moderne* (February 2018), pp.26–39.

Although not attacked, the farm's defenders, over the two days they remained there, were occasionally harassed by the enemy's light cavalry and horse artillery. The weather was particularly hot, indeed Constant-Rebecque-Villars noted that 'the heat during the 5,6,7 and 8 was so insupportable that it was the cause of the death of several unfortunates' and Auzon de Boisminart, with the Dutch artillery, remembered the 'burning sun' and being unable to get fresh water, so being forced to rely on ditch water to quench his thirst.[103] The defenders also lacked supplies and the ensuing hunger affected all, but the Balkan soldiers, described by Tercier as 'bad troops, plunderers, so undisciplined and so uncivilised', took the situation as licence to pillage. Nevertheless, he was struck by the severity of the punishments imposed by their officers including the brutal hanging of two soldiers.[104] Corbehem recalled:

> These Croats therefore, thinking themselves permitted everything, decided to plunder from top to bottom the rich dwelling that we occupied. In an instant the doors and the windows were broken open ; the frightened animals came out headlong from their stables, and were pursued in the vast farmyard by the Croats who, their great sabres in hand, slashed to right and left, and ran off in triumph with scraps of flesh and palpitating limbs: a frightful spectacle and what rendered it still more terrible the plaintive cries of the animals and the blood that ran everywhere.[105]

One of the marauders discovered a cache of silver coins in the farmhouse only to be unceremoniously relieved of his burden by a mob of his comrades. Corbehem was at pains to state that members of the Légion de Damas did not have a hand in these events.

The French inactivity permitted the Erfprins to quit his position, as planned, unmolested. His corps entered the edge of the Forest of Soignes and marched to join Coburg over the night of 7/8 July; the junction taking place by 8:00 a.m. Lefebvre followed, entering Waterloo very late on 7 July, and cautiously continued towards Brussels which his foremost troops entered on 9 July. Meanwhile the French had finally forced Beaulieu to abandon his positions covering Namur. With this news, Coburg, who was soon joined by Clerfayt, moved north to Leuven, and, on 9 July, placed his headquarters at Tienen. His line of retreat to Maastricht was secured.

The Erfprins continued his retreat east of Brussels and then on to the far side of the Leuven-Mechelen canal on 10 July. He established a chain of posts to defend the east bank of the canal, between it and the River Dijle, a defensive line which was to be shown to be 'as illusory as dangerous'.[106] The rest of the Erfprins's troops camped around Keerbergen, east of Mechelen and behind the Dijle. Reflecting the movements of his coalition allies, the Duke of York withdrew from Aase, crossing the Nete, to take up positions south of Antwerp.

103 NAN 2.21.005.41/32, Guillaume-Anne Constant-Rebecque-Villars Journal 1794–95; Auzon de Boisminart, *Gedenkschriften*, Vol.I, p.37. Also see Robert Brown, *Corporal Brown's Campaigns in the Low Countries: Recollections of a Coldstream Guard in the Early Campaigns Against Revolutionary France 1793–1795* (Milton Keynes: Leonaur, 2008, first published 1795), p.128.

104 La Chanonie, *Mémoires*, p.79.

105 Corbehem, *Dix ans de ma vie*, p.128.

106 Jomini, *Histoire critique et militaire*, Vol.VI, p.137.

The Hessians, under Dalwigk, provided the link between York and the Erfprins by holding Mechelen.

The retreats and the service both the Damas and Béon Legions had performed had had its effects on their personnel: 'We had many sick in our two legions, so that by the diminution of our soldiers put out of service we found ourselves cruelly fatigued. The foreign generals did not spare us, and, to save their troops, made us bear the full weight of the fatigues of the war.'[107]

The French armies of Pichegru and Jourdan made their junction at Brussels and on 11 July they formed a united line from Vilvoorde, north of Brussels, southwards, almost to Namur. The French commanders wanted to press the coalition armies further and force their dislocation. Jourdan was to drive Coburg onto the Maas while Pichegru's Armée du Nord prevented any interference from York by applying pressure around Mechelen.

An order of battle of 11 July shows that the six companies of the Damas infantry were part of a small brigade at the advance posts, commanded by *Colonel* Christiaan Reinhold van Bylandt of the Bylandt Jagers, comprising a company of jagers of the 5e Waldeck, three companies of Bylandt Jagers, three companies of the Béon infantry and the three companies of the Matthieu Corps. Their supports were posted at Hever (*Colonel* Mollenbruyn with two grenadier battalions: Mollenbruyn and Panhuijs) and Wespelaar (the recently promoted *Generaal Major* von Haacke with the rest of the 5e Waldeck Battaillon and the field battalions of the Welderen, Petit and Wartensleben infantry). The advance posts and their supporting units were commanded by *Gemeraal Major* von Geusau.[108]

On 11 July, the Hessian positions were attacked and two days later the Dutch line of advance posts were tested, 'There is constant shooting at our advance posts. General von Geusau commands them and defends the passage of the Leuven Canal which the enemy threatens to attempt with large forces.'[109] On 14 July, the Dutch extended their line from Muizen and Hever, just outside Mechelen, to Wespelaar. It was early the following day, 15 July, that the French launched an attack to the west and south of Mechelen with the aim of securing the area between the canal and the Dijle south of the city. It was to be a day that cost the Légions de Damas and Béon dearly. Tercier remembered:

> [O]ur two legions received the order, at six o'clock in the morning, to rapidly proceed to the Leuven canal to defend the crossing … We arrived at the canal at about eight o'clock, and we had the whole length of the road to endure the republicans' fire. We counted in this journey several killed and wounded. Arrived at the canal, we found the French established on the other side … We held them in check for four hours.[110]

Baron de Crossard, serving with the staff, wrote:

107 La Chanonie, *Mémoires*, p 80.

108 NAN 2.21.005.41/31, Guillaume-Anne Constant-Rebecque-Villars correspondence and 2.21.008.01/19, Jean-Victor Constant-Rebecque Journal Vol.I (dated 14 July).

109 NAN 2.21.008.01/19, Jean-Victor Constant-Rebecque Journal Vol.I, 13 July.

110 La Chanonie, *Mémoires*, p.80.

> The combat was, for the Dutch, only a fire fight; it would have been impossible to come to blows, as the width of the canal separated the two sides, who covered the natural banking created by its excavation. The fire was sustained, on both sides, with vehemence and obstinacy; but the proximity of the combatants and the banking … rendered the losses less considerable than would have been believed. From this proximity, and from the degree of elevation that the shape of the banking caused to the fire, resulted in the projectiles passing over the men who lined the canal…[111]

Corbehem recalled:

> The defence was no less lively than the attack; we fired at half musket range. I recall that a cannon close to where I was placed, wreaked deadly havoc in the enemy's ranks, in which the voids were immediately filled by new victims. We fought thus for half the day … we were forced to retire in haste, abandoning part of the equipment, and, what is worse, all our wounded.[112]

The French gained footholds on the far side of the canal forcing Geusau to issue orders for a retreat before his force was encircled. Tercier explains that the unnamed officer from the legion with the order did not arrive, 'This order did not reach us, and the general, informed of its non-execution, railed against the negligence of this officer, which was the cause in part of the losses that we suffered. The general then sent a second order by one of his aides de camp.'[113]

Not only the canal but also Mechelen was abandoned that day, as the British adjutant-general, Calvert, curtly observed, 'The Dutch army, which was on the Dyle [sic], retired from their position … Lieutenant-general Dalwig [sic] retired from [Mechelen]. Which of these corps first quitted their position is uncertain; as they respectively throw the blame on each other'.[114]

Tercier described retreating under enemy fire and marching towards the Dijle. Here the fault of the Dutch position, extended along the canal with the river immediately to the rear, was made clear as there were only a few bridges over the river. The swing bridge at Rijmenam became a scene of confusion as units tried to get to safety on the other side of the river. Fortunately, the Légion de Damas was able to make use of a quickly-established pontoon bridge and so crossed the river without delay. It was only when the legion reached the far side that losses could be counted, they were the worst the legion was to suffer in the campaign. 'Our first company of noble chasseurs had lost half its effective strength'.[115] Madame de Bennes went into the action alongside her husband who had returned after being wounded at Dinant, it was to be a day of personal tragedy, 'The action of the 15th of July, called the affair of the Leuven Canal, I shall remember as long as I live. We fought

111 Crossard, *Mémoires militaires et historiques*, p.109.
112 Corbehem, *Dix ans de ma vie*, pp.130–131.
113 La Chanonie, *Mémoires*, p.81.
114 Verney, *Journals and Correspondence of General Sir Harry Calvert*, p.278.
115 La Chanonie, *Mémoires*, p.81.

desperately for nearly seven hours, our corps lost 130 men, my husband was one of the number. I was carried away motionless ... Oh! that I had never recovered my senses!'[116]

Her husband had been killed by a cannon ball and she was wounded by a musket ball in her left leg and a bayonet-thrust to her right hand, the only evidence that some, at least, of the legion took part in close quarters fighting.[117] Although she may not have considered it at the time, Madame de Bennes was fortunate to be evacuated early in the action and then sent to recover at Breda. The legion's wounded who had to be abandoned in the precipitous retreat, were dealt with mercilessly, 'transported to Brussels and inhumanly shot, victims of an atrocious law and sectional fury'.[118]

The Comte de Chalup, *capitaine commandant* of the first chasseur company, commanded the legion that day. Geusau wanted him to return the unit to action to counter the French approaching the Dijle, despite the fatigue of the soldiers and fresh troops being available. Chalup explained it was physically impossible to do so but the general persisted, leading to the following exchange:

> – General, we do not have a single cartridge.
> – And what have you done with them?
> – General, we have consumed them to save you, as well as your army. Our caissons are now in the hands of the enemy.

On verifying this, Geusau permitted the legion to withdraw and other units were brought up to defend the river.[119] The 'largest share' of the action had fallen to only three units of the army, the Damas and Béon infantry and the Bylandt Jagers.[120] The commitment of all the Damas companies is indicated by the six other wounded who have been identified. These were *Chasseurs* Thomas-François de Ronnay and André de Saulnier of the colonel's company, *Chef d'escouade* François-Philippe d'Angély de Rochebrune, who died of his wounds, and *Chasseur* Jean-Joseph Grenier de Montgaillard both of Rouault's company, *Sergent* Jean-Baptiste Jessel of Stack's company and volunteer Charles MacCarthy of O'Moore's company.[121]

Constant-Rebecque summarised the events of the day thus:

> This morning the enemy attack us at every point, the length of the Leuven Canal, with great strength; the fusillade and the cannonade have been very lively; we fight from three o'clock in the morning until the evening. The French cross the Canal, make our advance posts retire; the Hessians evacuate Mechelen, the enemy enter

116 Bennes, *Narrative*, p.31.
117 Service historique de la Défense, Vincennes (SHD) GR1 Yi3. This episode was later celebrated, with hyperbole, by Comte Gerard de Contades, *Émigrés et Chouans* (Paris Perrin, 1895), pp.4–5.
118 Corbehem, *Dix ans de ma vie*, p 131.
119 La Chanonie, *Mémoires*, p 82.
120 Auzon de Boisminart, *Gedenkschriften*, Vol.I, p.39; see also Crossard, *Mémoires militaires et historiques*, p.109.
121 Beauchet-Filleau, *Tableau des émigrés du Poitou*, p.84, D.D. Daly, 'Brigadier-General Sir Charles MacCarthy, KT. 1764–1824', *Journal of the Society for Army Historical* Research, Vol.X No.39b (July 1931), pp.143-149; *AMC Fonds Grouvel, Légion de Damas.*

> it, and come to shoot on the banks of the Dijle as far as into our camp; the bridge at Muizen is taken and retaken several times; we have lost a lot of men; our light troops have suffered a lot … The Columns leave this evening for their new destination, the camp at Bevel.[122]

That same day, 15 July, the Austrians were driven from the strong Ijzerenberg (literally Iron Mountain) position north-west of Leuven and the city was abandoned. Their centre was attacked south of Tienen and Namur was evacuated, with only a small garrison left in the castle. Coburg, fearing for his line of communications, began to retreat over the Maas at Maastricht and other crossings, a manoeuvre which he covered with his left wing. The latter subsequently crossed the river at Liège and the French, by the 27 July, faced them on the opposite bank. These movements severed the link between the Dutch and Austrians, the Duke of York observed bitterly, 'the unfortunate situation in which we find ourselves at this time is not begun through defeats or through losses we have suffered but by the treachery and the infamous conduct of the Austrians.'[123]

The Dutch were now over the Nethe at Bevel in front of Nijlen; York's army held the same river line, south of Antwerp. However, in light of Coburg's movement, the Erfprins abandoned his positions and his army marched in three columns towards the United Provinces. The Damas and Béon infantry and cavalry were together in the third column commanded by Geusau.[124] The Légion de Damas marched through Herentals and Turnhout and on 22 July it was at the field army's camp at Baarle-Hertog. There the infantry formed part of the army's vanguard, still under the command of *Colonel* van Bylandt with the same units as on 11 July, and the 'Hussards de Damas' [sic] were in *Generaal Major* Anthony Louis van Oyen's cavalry brigade of the main body, First Line, of the army along with the Carabiniers, two squadrons, Gardes Dragonders, two squadrons, Gardes Holland, two squadrons, and Légion de Béon.[125]

The following day, 23 July, the Damas cavalry left the Dutch field army to join the garrison of Grave, on the west bank of the Maas. The squadron was now commanded by *Major* Louis-Marc-Antoine Bardon, Chevalier de Segonzac, former *Lieutenant-colonel* of the Royal Piémont Cavalerie, replacement for the Comte de Nantouillet who had left to join the suite of the Duc de Berry.[126] The depot for the legion, as a whole, was also established at Grave so some attached infantry accompanied the cavalry.[127]

122 NAN 2.21.008.01/19, Jean-Victor Constant-Rebecque Journal Vol.I, 15 July.

123 RAW, De Budé Papers, GEO/ADD/15/0590; York to Budé on 8 July 1794.

124 NAN 1.10.19/1894, Raad van State correspondence, order of march dated 17 July. Due to the date of this order Jomini, *Histoire critique et militaire*, Vol.VI, p.139 gives the date of the Erfprins's retreat as 17 July, however, Calvert, in a letter of 22 July (Verney, *Journals and Correspondence of General Sir Harry Calvert*, p.280) stated that it actually happened on 20 July.

125 Bas, *Prins Frederik der Nederlanden en Zijn Tijd*, p.653.

126 Bittard des Portes, *Les émigrés*, p 237, suggests that an officer by the name of Van Raveld succeeded Nantouillet, and that Segonzac was promoted after Van Raveld had died of his wounds. No other source mentions Van Raveld.

127 Frederick Henri Alexander Sabron, *De oorlog van 1794/1795 op het grondgebied van de Republiek der Vereenigde Nederlanden* (Breda: Koninklijke Militaire Academie, 1892), Vol.II, p.59.

Exposed and over-extended, the Erfprins could not renew links with the retreating Austrians so he continued to withdraw into the United Provinces. He finally established his headquarters at Breda, with his army camped at Vijf Eiken, east of the stronghold, just outside Rijen; his outposts lined the border to the south. His retreat, in turn, made the Duke of York's position around Antwerp untenable; on 23 July, the city was evacuated and he also withdrew northwards into the United Provinces.

5

In Defence of the United Provinces 1794

By the end of a day's march on 25 July the Duke of York's army was encamped west of Breda, around Roosendaal, the main body at Rucphen to the east, with a corps at Wouw, between Roosendaal and Bergen op Zoom. The area in which his army, and that of the Erfprins, camped was bleak:

> Here again are vast plains, hardly half covered with heath, and small patches of wood here and there, which never arrive to any considerable growth; and where there happens to be a cottage, the ground they occupy bears so little, that one would think it hardly repays them for the cultivation.[1]

The allies were concentrated on a narrow front to block the route previously taken by Dumouriez, only 18 months or so before, which was now threatened, in turn, by Pichegru who was at Antwerp. However, after their string of successes, the French did not move; time was needed to consolidate their victories. Substantial efforts were dedicated to the recapture of the places that the coalition still held: Landrecies was retaken on 17 July, Le Quesnoy on 15 August, Valenciennes on 27 August and finally Condé-sur-l'Escaut on 30 August. Furthermore, a corps under Jean-Victor-Marie Moreau was clearing the Flanders coast of allied posts; it was during one such operation, the capture of Nieuwpoort, that about 200 émigrés in the Loyal Emigrants were slaughtered. At the same time, there was political upheaval in Paris; Maximilien Robespierre, architect of the Reign of Terror, dramatically fell from power and was immediately executed on 28 July.

On 27 July, a conference was held at Breda to discuss and concert plans to defend the United Provinces, attended by the Stadholder, his son, the Erfprins, and the Duke of York, the reduced attendance reflecting the changed situation for the allies. The survival of the United Provinces now relied on the Republic's traditional defences of water and fortifications, as well as the allied armies of the two princes. However, years of neglect had left the fortresses not only in a poor state of repair but also inadequately garrisoned, for instance Calvert noted that there were only 27 artillerymen at Bergen op Zoom.[2] The Dutch army which had been under strength from the start, had not only suffered losses from fighting in the campaign but also endured the

1 Brown, *Corporal Brown's Campaigns*, p.132.
2 Verney, *Journals and Correspondence of General Sir Harry Calvert*, p.289.

The United Provinces.

corrosive effect of retreat, defeat and political insecurity. The successes of the French Republic's armies and the activities of its agents emboldened the House of Orange's political opponents and attempts to strengthen the Dutch forces were frustrated. At the conference it was decided that the Dutch would defend the direct line towards the provinces of Holland and Utrecht, especially the principal fortifications of Bergen op Zoom, Breda and 's-Hertogenbosch – 'the key to Holland'.[3] The Duke of York was to keep his force together and move inland to a position behind the River Aa; his right was to rest on the flooded lands, the inundation, surrounding 's-Hertogenbosch and his left on an immense peat bog or marsh, De Groote Peel. The choice of the latter was made as York was assured that it was 'impracticable for cavalry or artillery, and may, without much difficulty, be rendered equally so for any considerable force of infantry.'[4] York's position would not only screen the easterly strongholds, of Grave and Nijmegen, but also mean he could readily support any point of the Dutch line that came under attack.

Despite the confidence this deployment may suggest, the Duke of York's command was in a poor state to fulfil what was hoped of it. To replace his losses during the campaign, recruits had been sent out from Britain, untrained and unequipped. The provision of transport and hospitals was woefully inadequate and 'the Duke of York's corps was in a worse state in respect of clothing than had been hitherto recorded of any British army.'[5] The Duke issued orders to halt plundering of the local population, and other such abuses, but he was short of the means to ensure proper levels of discipline in the army. The rapid expansion of the British Army had seen many officers promoted to senior regimental commands with little knowledge of their profession let alone any experience of it; to make matters worse York had only four general officers, one of whom was employed as Quartermaster General, available for a corps of four cavalry and seven infantry brigades.[6]

The Dutch do not appear to have prepared accurate maps of the frontier or arranged for reliable intelligence to be collected and disseminated.[7] It was worse for the British who were hampered by their lack of knowledge of Dutch, French having been adequate in Belgium, and they soon found they were not necessarily defending friendly territory. In September Calvert visited *Lieutenant-Generaal* Robert Douglas, a Dutch officer of Scottish descent, at 's-Hertogenbosch:

> [T]o represent to him that, owing to the change of language and other circumstance, I am apprehensive that our intelligence may be very defective, and to request his assistance in procuring some new channels of information. General Doughlas [sic] assured me that he was very willing to give us any assistance in his power; but that the disaffection of the people in this part of the country was so great, that it was entirely out of his power to be of any service to us in the present instance.[8]

3 La Chanonie, *Mémoires*, p.82; Bois-le-Duc in French.
4 Verney, *Journals and Correspondence of General Sir Harry Calvert*, p.285, Calvert to St Helens, 29 July 1794.
5 Fortescue *British Campaigns in Flanders*, p.373.
6 Fortescue *British Campaigns in Flanders*, p.377, 373 and 371.
7 Verney, *Journals and Correspondence of General Sir Harry Calvert*, p.318.
8 Verney, *Journals and Correspondence of General Sir Harry Calvert*, p.324, Calvert to St Helens, 13 September 1794.

The Duke of York was due to start the move eastwards on 30 July; however, it was learnt that, two days earlier, Moreau had seized the island of Cadzand in preparation for siege operations against Sluis. This fortress stood on the southern point of the Scheldt where it met the North Sea; it was the first Dutch stronghold to be threatened. Its fall would not only threaten Vlissingen (Flushing), on the opposite bank, and so the province of Zeeland, but also the navigation of the estuary. The Erfprins wished to relieve Sluis, as well as to support his other forts on the southern side of the Scheldt, so he requested that York postpone his march. On 4 August, the British moved camp to the plain in front of Oosterhout, between Breda and Geertruidenberg, which stood on the banks of the Maas just before the estuary of the Hollands Diep; the move was to cover both these strongholds as they were put into a better state of defence. The Erfprins now decided to evacuate his posts south of the Scheldt and, on 7 August, the Hessian corps was detached to west of Breda to cover the Dutch retreat. Finally, any attempt to relieve Sluis was abandoned and the fort surrendered on 26 August. Although there were no émigré units present, any such individuals were left to face the Republican fury, the commander, *Generaal Major* Willem Hendrik van der Duyn, managed to have the two Hanoverian units, Infantry Regiments 11 and 14, in his garrison included in the capitulation despite Moreau's objections but the agreement specifically stated, 'The Émigrés are allowed no capitulation'.[9]

While this was happening the Damas infantry remained in the advance posts in front of Breda. There they faced Pichegru's corps which had been strengthened and had renewed operations in skirmishing with the Dutch and British outposts. So, on 9 August *Major* de Rouault reported that his command, made up of the Damas infantry and the Bylandt Jagers, had occupied posts along the edge of the Mastbos, a large pine forest that extended south of Breda. The forest stretched far to his right so he was unable to patrol as well as he would have wished. Having established his posts, he had gone to Meersel, where he found about 40 Dutch dragoons, rather than the Hanoverians he had expected; they informed him that French had been present but, according to patrols, were now in retreat. Rouault intended to keep his men active and alert, 'I will take care to scout the edge of the wood during the night by continual patrols.'[10] On 18 August, the French made a serious incursion into the allied line of outposts, penetrating it between Alphen and Chaam, and driving the British cavalry back; it was only in the evening that the allied outposts were re-occupied.[11] At least some of the Damas infantry were present, but not involved, as the action was witnessed by Corbehem who stated the British cavalry were 'bivouacked in a plain before us'.[12]

On 28 August Pichegru finally advanced towards Breda and 'before noon, they carried and established themselves at the post of Strybeck [Strijbeek].'[13] The allied forces withdrew from their outposts and the Damas infantry entered Breda itself. York, concerned that the Republicans were aligned to turn his flank, and so cut him off from 's-Hertogenbosch, and satisfied that sufficient time had been bought for the Dutch defences to be ready, began his planned move inland. On 30 August, having already been re-joined by the Hessians, he

9 Sabron, *De oorlog van 1794/1795*, Vol.I p.63 and Appendix IV.
10 KHN Archieven Prins Frederik A34 Inv No 256; letter to his general, timed at 9:00 a.m.
11 Verney, *Journals and Correspondence of General Sir Harry Calvert*, p.305.
12 Corbehem, *Dix ans de ma vie*, pp.133–134.
13 Verney, *Journals and Correspondence of General Sir Harry Calvert*, p.307.

arrived on the Aa; he chose Uden for his headquarters and placed his advanced posts along the Dommel, which flowed south of 's-Hertogenbosch. His position was however immediately under threat as a French corps pressed towards Eindhoven and De Groote Peel was found not to be a serious barrier, despite the earlier assurances; dry weather having rendered it passable.

The Damas infantry's stay in Breda was brief. On 29 August *Generaal Major* von Geusau took over command of the stronghold itself, while divisions had been organised to operate in support, outside the city. *Generaal Major* von Haacke had command of one of them, which comprised:

Bylandt Jagers (one battalion)
Damas infantry (six companies)
Béon infantry (three companies)
Matthieu Corps (three companies)
Jagers, 5e Waldeck (one company)
Hesse-Cassel Dragoons (two squadrons)
Heeckeren Hussars (one squadron)
Horse artillery (2 × 6-pdrs and a howitzer)[14]

Haacke's orders were to hold positions between the Mark just north of Breda and the Donge near Rijen, with a line of retreat through Teteringen, Oosterhout, Den Hout to Steelhoven in front of Geertruidenberg. The Damas infantry appears to have been placed, initially, in reserve in the last city.[15] The following day, 29 August, the French advanced to the outskirts of Breda as the first stage of its investment engaging Geusau's outposts at Princenhage and Ginneken and burning houses; Haacke withdrew, placing his advance posts at Den Hout, where a defensive line of earthworks had already been constructed, and Teteringen.[16]

On 4 September, the Erfprins left his troops to travel to The Hague and entrusted the command to *Generaal Major* Guillaume-Anne de Constant-Villars, whose headquarters were at Waspik. The latter wrote to the officers commanding posts and units, informing them of the change in command. Haacke's reply, of 5 September, indicates that he felt far from secure. He reported that the enemy had been reinforced as well as his concern about his final retreat to Steelhoven, before continuing:

> Besides, my General, I am to be pitied if the enemy undertakes something against me, having no other infantry than the Damas and Béons who will not hold for a moment carrying the notion of the Guillotine on their backs, a precipitative retreat will be my fate, I wish to be extracted with honour from so disagreeable a position.[17]

14 NAN 1.10.19/1894, Raad van State correspondence and 2.21.005.41/41, Constant-Rebecque-Villars correspondence. Sabron, *De oorlog van 1794/1795*, Vol.I pp.178 and 402 gives the following list for the division, dated 4 September: Perez Walloon Guards (one battalion), Bylandt Jagers, Damas infantry, Béon infantry, Matthieu Jagers, Hesse-Cassel Dragoons, Bylandt Dragoons (one squadron), Horse artillery (detachment).

15 Corbehem, *Dix ans de ma vie*, p.135; Bennes, *Narrative*, p.32.

16 NAN 2.21.008.01/19, Constant-Rebecque Journal Vol.I.

17 NAN 2.21.005.41/41, Constant-Rebecque-Villars

The next day, Haacke wrote a second letter in which he made it clear that he wished to retreat to Steelhoven. Constant-Villars replied that he should not fall back without positive orders from the Erfprins or a pressing reason to do so. However, later that day, when Constant-Villars was inspecting the defences of Geertruidenberg, he learnt that Haacke had not only left Den Hout but was in the city to report that his advance posts had been repulsed. In response Constant-Villars ordered that the Bylandt Jagers and Damas infantry hold Steelhoven. The following day, 7 September, Constant-Villars broke up Haacke's division and redistributed the troops in his command; the Damas and Béon infantry temporarily remained at Steelhoven and the rest were posted further east. On 8 September Constant-Villars instructed the Comte de Damas (showing that the latter was then with his infantry) that they would move to an entrenched defensive position at Waspik; but later that day the general received instructions from the Erfprins which included the order to send the Damas infantry to join the legion's cavalry at Grave while the Béon infantry were to join the garrison of 's-Hertogenbosch.[18] The governor of this latter stronghold was the 68-year-old Wilhelm, Landgrave of Hessen-Philippsthal whose family had already paid a heavy price in the war, his eldest living son, Karl, had been killed serving with the Dutch in Flanders in 1793 and the next in line, Friedrich, had met the same fate in 6 July at Waterloo.[19]

Pichegru continued to press his advantage. In the afternoon of 14 September his forces attacked and seized York's advance post at Boxtel, on the Dommel, then crossed the river at Sint-Michielsgestel and advanced on the Aa. York recognised that the latter line was untenable without the outposts on the Dommel, so at midnight on 15 September Lieutenant General Abercromby led the reserve out to retake Boxtel. However, the attack on the Dommel was not Pichegru's main thrust and Abercromby stumbled into the bulk of the French corps, estimated at 80,000, marching to turn York's left wing. Abercromby managed to abstract his troops from the predicament with comparatively few losses but York, with only about 20,000 under arms, could not attempt an action and retreated in the face of the superior numbers. On 16 September, he crossed the Maas at Grave; the bulk of his army followed over the next two days and deployed behind the Maas, only some outposts were placed over the river, close into Grave.

The siege of 's-Hertogenbosch commenced on 22 September with the three companies of the Béon infantry still part of the garrison. Whether this was due to an oversight or indifference is not clear but the fate of any émigré who fell into republican hands when a garrison capitulated was well known. Indeed, elsewhere steps were taken to avoid this, for example, émigrés in the garrison of Maastricht were ordered to leave the city before it was besieged on 19 September.[20]

18 NAN 2.21.005.41/31, Constant-Rebecque-Villars correspondence, order dated 8 September 1794 and 2.21.005.41/41, Constant-Rebecque-Villars Journal 1794–95.

19 Only three of Wilhelm's (1726–1810) nine children remained alive: a daughter, Juliane (1761–1799), and two sons, Ludwig (1766–1816) and Ernst Constantine (1771–1849). Ludwig however had married a Roman Catholic, Countess Marie Franziska Berghe von Trips, in 1791 and his family did not recognise the union which also led to him having to quit the Dutch service. He later served in the Neapolitan army with some distinction.

20 Verney, *Journals and Correspondence of General Sir Harry Calvert*, p.330.

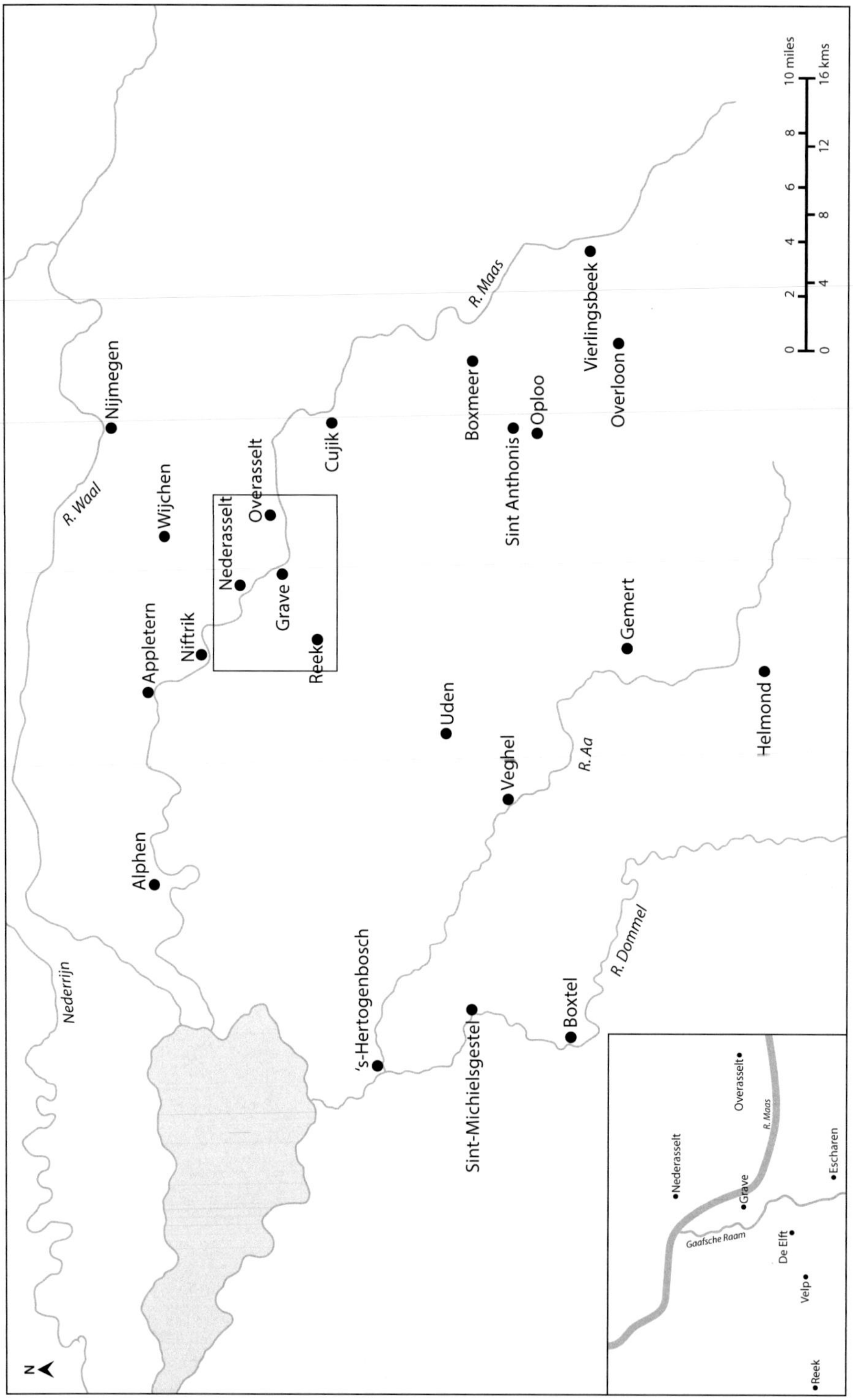

Operations around Grave.

The defence of the Maas now became crucial to the allied strategy. As early as 1 September a conference had been held with the new Austrian commander, Clerfayt, with a view of concerting action and maintaining a link along the river. The defensive line now extended from Bommelerwaard, a near island lying between the Maas and Waal rivers, through Grave and Venlo towards Maastricht. Grave was being put into a state of defence but it had only been on 16 July that the Council of State of the United Provinces had granted the governor, the elderly *Generaal Major* Andreas de Bons, permission to do so.[21] Originally his garrison only comprised of the depots of the Hessen-Darmstadt (German) and May (Swiss) Infantry Regiments and a few gunners. On 23 July, the Damas cavalry, about 200 strong, had been ordered to join it along with the legion's depot and a few days later a company of the Bylandt Jagers arrived. In addition, *Major* Albrecht de Gros of the May Regiment arrived to be deputy to de Bons and he wrote a detailed journal of the siege, and critique of the campaign, which was to be published a year later.[22]

On 29 July two thirds of the legion's cavalry, and 20 chasseurs from the depot, were deployed from Grave to cover the region of Cuijk, south east of Grave, and maintain communication with the outposts sent out from the 's-Hertogenbosch garrison. After some adjustment, the posts were, on the Maas side of the Peel: at Boxmeer, a reserve, with infantry holding the ferry; at Vierlingsbeek, one officer with cavalry and infantry, with an outpost at Overloon; at Oploo, with an officer posted at Sint Anthonis to observe the path over the Peel; these posts were to provide, alternately, patrols as far as Venlo. On the other side of the Peel, an officer and 20 cavalrymen were posted at Uden to patrol the area as far as Gemert, where cavalry from 's-Hertogenbosch were placed. Finally, communication between Grave and Venlo was maintained by cavalry stationed along the route. On 4 August, the cavalry provided a strong patrol as far as Venlo, to cover the march of three battalions reinforcing the garrison there.[23]

Around 25 August there was a false alarm caused by a patrol. Apparently when French patrols had approached Helmond, on the far side of the Peel, some priests and merchants, who had taken refuge there, had taken flight and crossed the marsh heading towards Sint Anthonis, joined on the way by some peasants and their livestock. The outpost there, in the darkness, thought themselves under attack from enemy cavalry and infantry and so took the necessary defensive steps, including the cavalry assembling at their rendezvous point, as well as reporting the attack to Grave. There the remaining 40 cavalrymen, with a strong infantry detachment and two artillery pieces were readied to leave before the break of day; a second, supporting, detachment was also prepared. Then the news arrived that the original report was a false alarm. It is not stated whether those responsible were from the Légion de Damas or not but *Major* de Gros, not for the only time, was critical of the light troops in general:

21 Sabron, *De oorlog van 1794/1795*, Vol.II, p.59.

22 Albrecht David Gabriel de Gros (or von Gross), *Journal des Principales Opérations de la Campagne de 1794 dans les sept Provinces-unies et pays de la Généralité* (1795). Andreas de Bons (1720–1800) had apparently asked to retire before the campaign.

23 Gros, *Journal*, pp.20–22.

> The officer who had given the first report was punished, but this example & several others in the preceding campaigns have made me see the inconvenience of the newly raised light troops, of which the soldiers are not experienced for the *petite guerre* & of which the officers, though very brave moreover, have not the developed awareness.[24]

As soon as the news of York's imminent retreat reached Grave, orders were given for the Damas cavalry to withdraw to the bridge at Escharen, over the Gaafsche Raam which flows towards the city from the south, as the allies had abandoned the post at Gemert. The Damas infantry, which had joined the garrison by now, was to bring the Maas ferry boats into Grave and as many peasants as possible from the area around Cuijk, along with as much produce and livestock as they could, on the promise of payment by the state. Furthermore, that evening, the 40 remaining cavalrymen, 'under the direction of an intelligent officer', with 20 chasseurs and 20 infantrymen, were sent down river as far as Alphen to burn the small boats and bring to Grave the larger ones along with the ferries from that stretch of the river. They were also to furnish posts, as best as possible, until the arrival of the allied troops; it was to be three or four days later that they were relieved.[25] This last mission could not have been carried out by the Damas infantry as on 15 September an order arrived for them to march to Venlo; they left Grave that same day. The Comte de Damas wrote, that day, to the Stadholder to ask that both van Mönster at Venlo and de Bons at Grave be informed of Willem's wish that no émigré corps be kept in garrisons that were likely to have to surrender which would 'expose [them] to the horrors of capital punishment.'[26]

As has been described, of York's army only the 54th Foot, which temporarily reinforced the Grave garrison, and its outposts remained on the west bank of the Maas. These occupied field works with a light cavalry screen in a semi-circle in front of Grave, from the windmill at Reek to the river, its left joining up with the Damas cavalry at Escharen.[27] This screen was attacked on 22 September, the day that 's-Hertogenbosch was invested, by a French force of about 500–600 cavalry and infantry, with two horse artillery guns. They advanced on Grave to test the defences and, at the same time, reconnoitre a suitable site for their forces covering the siege of 's-Hertogenbosch. The allied outposts, including the Damas cavalry at Escharen, were superior in numbers but without artillery. The French skirmishers, supported by their artillery, reached the windmill at Reek between 1:00 and 2:00 p.m.; there the guns were brought to bear on the allied light troops who withdrew steadily. A party had already reached Grave and the firing was closer when:

> General de Bons gave the order to the 40 or 50 horsemen of Damas who remained with us, to go to support them, after which we went to load some pieces on the rampart. Major de Segonzac who commanding this little troop, encountered the

24 Gros, *Journal*, pp.36–37.

25 Gros, *Journal*, pp.60–61; this is the only indication the infantry companies had arrived at Grave, Gros does not give their movements, as he does for other units, at any stage.

26 KHN Archieven van Stadhouder Willem V, A31/2120, letter from the Comte de Damas to the Stadholder, dated Grave 15 September 1794.

27 Gros, *Journal*, p.64.

> enemy a little beyond the New Society on the 's-Hertogenbosch road, & after having had the charge sounded, it attacked them so willingly that it cut down more than twenty-five of them on the spot; but as his squadron was a little separated from him in their pursuit & engaged too far in advance, he received all the fire of the skirmishers hidden in the bushes, & the brave major himself was thrown to the ground from his horse by a gunshot & brought back into town; his troopers received like the others the order to retire, & the enemy who followed them on their heels, had the time to bring their two pieces the one behind the Elft Auberge, the other beside the New Society, & fired two or three shots from them at us into the exterior drawbridge & into the parapet of the ravelin of the Ham gate, until we answered them with our 24 pounders, a ball from which went straight under one of their cannons & covered them with earth without wounding anyone; this ended the pleasantry, the enemy turned his guns & peacefully withdrew without being pursued.[28]

A British soldier described the day's events in his journal of the campaign:

> Monday 22d September. ... This day the French made their first attack upon the out posts, about six miles from Grave, upon the Great road leading towards Bois-le-Duc [sic]. They sent immediately from the out-posts to Grave for a reinforcement, the garrison beat to arms and every man flew to his post, a heavy cannonade and discharge of musquetry took place in front, from which the firing afterwards proceeded to the right and left of the out-posts in a semicircle, it was therefore supposed that the enemy were approaching to invest the place, and the miserable inhabitants, greatly alarmed, fled in crowds towards Nimeguen [sic], carrying away with them their young children, and any little bundle they could bear; it was certainly a very affecting sight; ... A reinforcement of cavalry was sent out on the first alarm, and the Emigrant regiment of Damas, ... behaved very gallantly in their skirmish, charging the enemy sword in hand and at the same time crying out "Vive-le-Roi" they killed twenty two French dragoons, and brought in several prisoners and horses, without the loss of a single man: their Major was slightly wounded, having his knee shattered by a musquet ball; this action gained the regiment very great applause.[29]

Segonzac died of his wound and more dramatic versions of his loss were told. For instance, Corbehem, who was not present, being at Venlo, related that the charge of the Damas detachment routed an infantry battalion and Segonzac spared a soldier who had thrown his musket down begging for mercy on his knees. Segonzac granted quarter, telling the soldier to get up and follow him, when the soldier took up his musket, shooting and killing the major.[30]

---

28 Gros, *Journal*, pp.69–70.

29 Anon., *Journal kept in the British Army, from the landing of the troops under the command of Earl Moira, at Ostend, in June 1794, to their return to England the following year* (Liverpool: Unknown Publisher, 1796), pp.81–82.

30 Corbehem, *Dix ans de ma vie*, pp.136–137.

The threat to Grave increased, as the French established posts to the west, with two brigades around Reek and another further back at Veghel. The garrison was now restricted to sending out some pickets as well as providing cavalry and infantry escorts for the working parties clearing woods and buildings around the fortifications. As Gros explained, not only was the garrison lacking in numbers, but also, 'our chasseurs were new, did not know the terrain, & we perceived a type of scruple to compromise our cavalry corps, entirely composed of émigrés.'[31] In the afternoon of 26 September, a very strong enemy patrol attacked the outposts in front of Grave, manned by only 20 chasseurs with a cavalry NCO and four troopers, forcing them to fall back into the city. Although pickets, of chasseurs, were placed at night outside the walls, they were withdrawn before the enemy patrols began in the morning. It was clear that no attempt was going to be made to prevent Grave being invested or to relieve 's-Hertogenbosch.[32]

The Erfprins, by 26 September, had already issued orders that the Damas cavalry were not to be kept in Grave; *Generaal Major* de Bons only retained a *maréchal des logis* and 20 volunteers for service within the city. In addition, the legion's depot had already been removed to the entrenched camp outside Nijmegen where it bivouacked. In a letter, of 26 September, written on the glacis at Grave, the Comte de Damas asked the Stadholder to allocate a town for the depot as 'all the possessions of the store which are on the carts are lost to the rain, and the men as well as the horses infinitely suffer.'[33] On 3 October the depot moved into Nijmegen itself.[34]

In the same letter Damas expressed his concern for the fate of his infantry should Venlo capitulate. However, that very day, *Major* de Rouault arrived at Grave having been sent by *Lieutenant-Generaal* van Mönster to obtain permission from the Erfprins to send the Damas infantry from the city. A French advance had given the general grounds to fear Venlo would be invested imminently. Of the service outside Venlo, Bennes simply remarked that the Damas infantry were in the advanced posts but 'the few skirmishes which took place … are not worth mentioning.'[35]

Mönster appears to have received instructions from the Erfprins to send the Damas infantry away when necessary, although the critical moment came later than he first expected, as Corbehem related:

> Arrived at Venlo … we had almost immediately to defend the approaches of this place against a division detached from the army that laid siege to Maastricht, and which sent parties as far as under the cannon of Fort Sint-Michiel. We were witnesses of the preparations which were made for the defence of the town, formidable preparations, which only served to ruin the proprietors of the houses neighbouring the fortifications, and which really only delayed its occupation for a few days. Finally, about 21 or 22 October, the day before or the day preceding that of

31 Sabron, *De oorlog van 1794/1795*, Vol.II, p.65; Gros, *Journal*, pp.71–72.

32 Gros, *Journal*, pp.75–76.

33 KHN Archieven van Stadhouder Willem V, A31/2120.

34 The depot's move is noted in the Evert Kam (ed.) *Dagboek van Nijmegen 1794–1795* p.6, at < http://www.noviomagus.nl/Gastredactie/Kam/Hulst/Hulst.htm> (accessed 13 April 2015).

35 Bennes, *Narrative*, p.32.

> its entire investment, the order arrived for my legion to evacuate Venlo, an order which was executed immediately…[36]

The Damas infantry marched for Nijmegen. Venlo only sustained the briefest of sieges, surrendering on 26 October.

Although little movement took place along the line of the Maas held by the Erfprins and Duke of York, the Austrians had been continually pushed back behind that river and, after being defeated at Roermond on 2 October, they crossed the Rhine. York had initially extended his forces southwards to support the Austrians but then, in response to their retreat, he prepared to retreat over the Waal, the main distributary or branch of the Rhine, at Nijmegen.

Major de Gros was advised, on 4 October, to make final preparations for the siege that would inevitably follow York's retreat. One of these was to issue secret orders to send out all the Damas cavalry to bring in 800 to 1,000 peasants to finish the work on the defences. Gros was critical of the advice, in particular about the legion's suggested mission which he felt was impractical, 'particularly by the agency of the Damas corps, who did not speak the language, & were hardly loved by the inhabitants.'[37]

Although much of York's army had already crossed the Waal, there was a fleeting sign of more active operations when, on 10 October, Lieutenant General Abercromby retook Fort Sint Andries, which had previously been abandoned. However, this action was rendered useless as, the same day, the Landgrave of Hessen-Philippsthal surrendered 's-Hertogenbosch. This was considered ignominious. Calvert wrote:

> Not a shadow of excuse has his Serene Highness of Hesse-Phillipsdorf [sic] for surrendering … and I fear that many emigrants were put to death in cold blood when the enemy took possession. Of all the disgraces which have fallen on the Allies in this campaign, surely it is the most deplorable that those who had thrown themselves upon our protection, whom we were bound by every tie of honour and humanity to defend, have, in almost every instance, been sacrificed.[38]

At Grave the first they knew of the surrender was when, on 11 October, Hessen-Philippsthal's adjutant arrived on his way to The Hague; he was accompanied by a French officer to arrange the arrival of the defeated garrison the next day. There was to be a temporary cessation of hostilities, while the garrison marched; it did so under strict conditions, including a prohibition on communicating with anyone until it had crossed the Maas and each of its units had to march separately, 500 paces apart. The 's-Hertogenbosch garrison was delayed and only arrived at Reek at nightfall on 12 October. The French attempted to have the soldiers received, and fed, in Grave, but this demand was refused, seen as a ploy to deplete the garrison's food supplies immediately before a siege. The following morning the Damas cavalry

36 Corbehem, *Dix ans de ma vie*, pp.137–138.
37 Gros, *Journal*, p.100.
38 Verney, *Journals and Correspondence of General Sir Harry Calvert*, p.367: Calvert to Major General Sir Hew Dalrymple, 22 October 1794.

escorted the column, still with each unit 500 paces apart, over the Maas; on the right bank, the soldiers were provided with bread and assigned quarters in surrounding villages.

It was only now that the circumstances of the surrender and the fate of the men of the Légion de Béon emerged. The Duke of York immediately informed the British Government having received the testimony of an eye witness, who was independent of the 's-Hertogenbosch garrison.

> According to the Account I have received from a Hessian Officer, who being sent upon some regimental Business into that Town was shut up in it, the loss of the Garrison was very small, being only six Men killed and seven wounded, besides two Officers. The Reasons of the Surrender seem to have been the Smallness of the Garrison which consisted of only Eleven hundred and sixty Men from the beginning of the Siege, who were totally inadequate to the Manning of the Works, from the Moment that the Enemy, by the possession of Crevecoeur were able to draw off Waters which formed the Inundation. The French refused to admit the Emigrés, of whom there were three hundred in the Garrison, to the Benefit of the Capitulation, but Pichegru acquainted the Governor under hand, that if they were disguised, no search should be made after them, upon which they marched out mixed with the Soldiers of the Garrison but unfortunately some of them being known and pointed out by two Emigrant Deserters, they were immediately torn out of the Ranks and massacred...[39]

Subsequently, after the garrison had marched through Nijmegen on 14 October, the duke could provide more details.

> At the same time no Excuse whatsoever is offered for their [the garrison's] shameful Conduct towards the Emigrants, of whom there were four hundred in the Town, and who at first entreated to be allowed to make a Sortie before the Place was given up, and to endeavour to cut their Way through the Enemy, or otherwise to have one of the Forts given up to them, in order that they might defend themselves to the Utmost; both of which Proposals were peremptorily refused; and the Consequence was that only eighty of them escaped, the Rest having been seized upon and torn out of the Ranks as they marched out of the Place.[40]

An émigré, Louis-Gabriel de Villeneuve-Laroche-Barnaud, was serving in the Bedaulx Infantry Regiment of the Dutch Army, the depot of which formed part of the garrison. His unit was at the rear of the column as it marched from the city, he later wrote:

39 TNA WO 1/170, Duke of York to Henry Dundas, 13 October.

40 TNA WO 1/170, Duke of York to Henry Dundas 16 October. A Swiss soldier, serving with the Gumöens Regiment, describes taking part in a sortie, with some émigrés, on 7 October, in which he was wounded and then captured. He mistakenly stated that the émigrés were from the Légion de Damas, rather than Béon. Abraham Rösselet and Rudolphe de Steiger, *Souvenirs de Abraham Rösselet* (Neuchatel: Attinger, 1857), p.60.

> The regiment of Hessen-Philippsthal, cavalry, marched first, between the two rows of the besieger's army, and after it the other corps. … Be that as it may, an extraordinary agitation manifested itself amongst the enemy soldiers, successfully as the garrison's column passed before them. The French émigrés soon perceived that they were the object of this clamour, that several amongst them had been recognised, and that they sought to recognise others, in the midst of the foreigners who wore the same uniform.

He learnt that 'the Republicans slaughtered, with sabre and bayonet blows, the émigrés included in the ranks of the Hessen-Philippsthal Regiment.' As the noise approached, he expected to suffer the same fate but, as he related, Pichegru and his staff arrived and restored order, 'he then gives his orders for them to return to the ranks along the whole extent of the two lines. For his part, our general re-establishes his column: he had loaded on baggage wagons, the mutilated corpses of our unfortunate companions, and we continue to march, heading to Grave.'[41]

The fate of their fellow émigrés, and long-time brothers-in-arms, must have had a significant impact on those of the Légion de Damas. Tercier, serving with the depot, saw the survivors arrive at Nijmegen and learnt what had happened:

> Eighty émigrés were taken and shot on the spot. The lieutenant-colonel and the major of the Légion de Béon had joined the ranks of a regiment of Dutch grenadiers who would not permit that the least search being made among them. I saw these two unfortunate officers arrive at Nijmegen with their grenadier uniform and bearskin …[42]

The grenadiers were of the Hessen-Philippsthal Battalion, formed of the grenadier companies from the Van Welderen, Bosc de la Calmette and Des Villattes Regiments. Between 22 September and 12 October, the Béon infantry had lost 272 of its 494 men.[43]

The same day that the 's-Hertogenbosch garrison passed through, 13 October, the French invested Grave and occupied Velp, Escahren and the advance posts with three infantry battalions and a regiment of chasseurs à cheval. The link with the east bank of the Maas remained open and the Damas cavalry were cantoned on that side, at Nederasselt, and supplied no more than a picket in Grave itself.[44]

On 19 October, the morning patrol of Damas cavalry reported the approaching sound of combat, between the Maas and Waal. *Major* de Gros passed an order for the Comte de Damas to send:

41 Louis-Gabriel de Villeneuve-Laroche-Barnaud, *Mémoires sur l'expédition de Quiberon précédés d'une notice sur l'émigration de 1791, et sur les trois campagnes des années 1792, 1793, 1794* (Paris: Trouvé, 1819), Part I, pp.153–156.

42 La Chanonie, *Mémoires*, p.83.

43 KHN Archieven van Stadhouder Willem V, A31/2124, report by Béon dated 18 October 1794.

44 Gros, *Journal*, pp.109–125.

> [A] very strong patrol, under an intelligent officer, as far as Niftrik & beyond, to learn positive news of the engagement. But around midday, Colonel de Damas came himself to me, & I saw from his demeanour that he brought us bad news. He took me aside & said to me that he was going himself to General de Bons, to ask him for orders to retire to Nijmegen, ...[45]

Damas reported that the officer commanding the patrol had returned and, 'that they, Damas chasseurs [à cheval], had seen the enemy advance along two narrow dykes, singing the *Ça ira*, each with a 4-pound piece at their head, that many of them had been killed, but that that had not prevented them forcing under their eyes the post at Appeltern,'[46]

The legion's colonel was anxious to leave immediately, 'all the corps was ready to march & horses saddled.' However, de Bons decided to wait for orders from Prins Frederik, who was at Nijmegen, and *Major* de Gros assured Damas that there was no appearance of an immediate attack, as the day was well advanced, the combat was continuing and the enemy far away, advising him to have his men eat and rest. Finally, towards the end of the day, Frederik's order for the Damas cavalry to withdraw arrived and the corps marched that night, 19/20 October, as far as Wijchen, the site of an allied outpost.[47]

On 21 October, the allies withdrew their advance posts to within a league of Nijmegen; the following day the French forced them back, closer to the lines around the city. The Duke of York had established his headquarters at Arnhem on 21 October, as part of the withdrawal over the Waal, in anticipation that this river line would be maintained when operations ceased for the winter.[48] Nijmegen was regarded as untenable against a sustained attack, particularly from artillery, the fortifications had been neglected and steps to rectify this had been inadequate. On 11 October, Johann Ludwig Reichsgraf von Gimborn-Wallmoden, illegitimate son of King George II of Britain, the Hanoverian general entrusted with its overall defence, had written:

> Nijmegen still lacks at this time almost everything. The Artillery and Munitions have not arrived. There is no Arrangement for the Provisions. There is an immensity of Works still to do; there is not a single Casemate for the troops which will be completed, and I do not think, that with the greatest Efforts, the most indispensable of these Works can be finished in less than 4 or 5 Weeks, whilst one cannot answer how many days the Enemy will leave us to be able to work here.[49]

Furthermore, the entrenched camp, designed to hold the field army covering the city, was commanded by high ground, marked by a windmill, to the east and any defence of the town relied on the pontoon bridge, over the Waal, which was about 365 metres wide, that

45 Gros, *Journal*, pp.132–133.
46 Gros, *Journal*, p.133.
47 Gros, *Journal*, pp.132–135.
48 See Verney, *Journals and Correspondence of General Sir Harry Calvert*, p.365.
49 KHN Archieven van Prins Frederik 1774–1799, A 34/98, correspondence between Duke of York and Prins Frederik.

would be dominated by enemy batteries should the town be surrounded.[50] Preparations were made to abandon the city; Corbehem described the ramparts being disarmed and the cast iron cannon being thrown into the dock basin.[51] A resident of Nijmegen noted that on 21 October:

> The passage of people took all night and early morning, though after midday it is completely quiet, because there are no people on the fortified works. The entire army has crossed the river, except for a few hundred or so, who remain on the city walls and bastions below the walls and several Hanoverian cavalrymen, who ride here and there. The walls have only field guns of the units (50 or 60 pieces both cannons and howitzers). The troops in the bastion also have some field guns. For the rest there are very few troops in the city, apart from the Emigrants of Damas, who keep watch, but they have already three times received an order to prepare for marching. The French are approaching, mostly from the south and their advance posts are already at Neerbosch.[52]

In the meantime, Grave was completely invested when, on 22 October, the French took Overasselt and Nederasselt and occupied the far bank of the Maas.

Meanwhile the political disunity of the United Provinces was causing increasing concern. In the provinces in which the campaign had already been fought, the population's lack of loyalty for the incumbent regime had already manifested itself, as *Lieutenant-Generaal* Douglas had observed at Breda. It also took more active forms, as the 78th Highlanders had found near the Maas:

> While the troops lay at this post … much attention was excited by the regularity with which a battery on the other side of the river opened a smart fire whenever any portion of the troops happened to be under arms, although not seen by the enemy. At last it was observed, that, before the fire commenced, a wind-mill, on the same side with the British, always put its wings in motion. This excited suspicion, and it was discovered that the miller had concerted signals with the enemy.[53]

Early in October the Stadholder became particularly concerned about the northern provinces of Groningen and Friesland, telling the Duke of York that he doubted the loyalty of these provinces' political leaders so much so that he would not be surprised if they had already sent deputies to Pichegru. York undertook to try to hold the Rhine and so cover the provinces but the Stadholder felt it was necessary to allocate Dutch troops to the provinces. This was done on 16 October and the troops identified were:

50 See Verney, *Journals and Correspondence of General Sir Harry Calvert*, pp.357, 361, 366 and 369.
51 Corbehem, *Dix ans de ma vie*, p.140.
52 *Dagboek van Nijmegen 1794–1795*, p.38.
53 David Stewart, *Sketches of the Character, Manners and Present State of the Highlanders of Scotland; with details of the Military Service of the Highland Regiments* 2nd Edition (Edinburgh: Constable, 1822), Vol.II, p.183.

Cavalry *Generaal Major* van Boetzelaer	**Infantry** *Generaal Major* von Haacke
Gardes Holland (field squadron)	Stuart Regiment (musketeer companies)
Gardes Dragonders (field squadron)	Van Randwijck Regiment (musketeer companies)
Van Tuyll Cavalry (field squadron)	Bentinck Regiment (musketeer companies)
Orange-Friesland Carabiniers (one squadron)	Gumoëns (Swiss) Regiment (field battalion formed from the second battalion)
Heeckeren Hussars (one squadron)	Légion de Damas
Légion de Damas	
Horse Artillery (detachment)	

The corps was to be formed at Zutphen, under the orders of Prins Frederik, to act wherever required including protecting the part of the province of Gelderland most under threat.[54] Thus the Légion de Damas marched from Nijmegen on Sunday 26 October to make its way to Zutphen.[55] The cavalry depot, 'the lame horses and sick men', since leaving Grave, had been sent to Zeist, just east of Utrecht, and, at the same time, its baggage had been sent to Gorinchem, Damas was once again to write to the Stadholder as the depot was bivouacked in the open which, especially at this time of year, was detrimental to both men and horses and asked that it be quartered at the nearby village of Amerongen.[56]

On 25 October, the Stadholder and Prins Frederik arrived at Arnhem, and, two days later, they visited Nijmegen in the morning accompanied by the Duke of York. The same day, 27 October, the French made a general attack driving the allied troops from their outposts into the entrenched camp and surrounding the town overnight. The next day they tried to take possession of a dyke to the east of the town, apparently to establish a battery there, but were frustrated after a determined fight. Clerfayt arrived at Arnhem that day, 28 October, to arrange co-operation for the next phase of the campaign. Nijmegen was the only bridgehead on the left bank of the Rhine that remained in allied hands and so it was now decided to attempt to hold and exploit the position with the 13,000 troops available. The crossing would be the gateway for future operations against the French promised by the Austrian's renewed activity as well as, more immediately, the means to relieve Grave. Most of Prins Frederik's units, including the Légion de Damas, were assigned to help hold the town. An Austrian corps, 10,000 strong, under *Feldmarschalleutnant* Franz von Werneck, was to be immediately available to co-operate with the allied forces around Nijmegen; his troops were to be followed by substantial reinforcements to make this the scene of the main allied effort. The renewed activity of the Austrians in the defence of the United Provinces had been secured by further payments by the British government and Prussia was also being encouraged to participate by the same means. Prussian involvement was regarded with a jaded eye and Calvert, on 27 October, pithily observed, 'The main object, I am persuaded, with some of our Allies is not to beat the French, but to cheat the English.'[57]

54 Sabron, *De oorlog van 1794/1795*, Vol.II pp 7–8.
55 *Dagboek van Nijmegen 1794–1795*, p 56.
56 KHN Archieven van Stadhouder Willem V, A31/2120, letter dated [?] October 1794.
57 Verney, *Journals and Correspondence of General Sir Harry Calvert*, p.371, observation made on 27 October.

On 27 October the infantry of the Légion de Damas was reviewed by the Stadholder at Arnhem. There were a total of 329 officers and men present.

Légion de Damas, at the review of 27 October 1794 at Arnhem

Compagnie du Colonel	
Capitaine	Comte Etienne de Damas-Crux
Capitaine commandant	Vincent-Joseph Chevalier de Chalup
1er Lieutenant	Joseph de Savignac
Enseigne	Charles-Augustin de Tercier
Sergents	3
Corporauux & Chasseurs	54
In exterior hospitals	21
With the baggage	1
Petit Etat Major	
Adjudant	André Boucher de Courson
Quartier-maître	François-Joseph Ducoux
Aumônier	Louis du Chilleau
Chirurgien-major	François Couturier
Tambour-major	Jean Camen
Prévôt	Gaspart Gerard
Fraters (artisans)	3
Compagnie du Lieutenant-colonel	
Capitaine	Baron Edouard Stack*
Capitaine commandant	David de Barry*
Lieutenant	Pierre de Burgault de Montfort
Enseigne	Thomas de Pressac
Sergents	3
Corporauux & Mousquetaires	22
Sick in quarters	2
In exterior hospitals	12
With the baggage	3
Compagnie du Major	
Capitaine	Charles-G-A-C-F Comte de Rouault de Gamache*
Capitaine commandant	Jean-Joachim de Borrassol
Lieutenant	Jean-Joseph-Antoine Comte de Cardon de Vidampierre
Enseigne	Charles-Florimond de Lavenne
Sergents	3
Trompette	1
Corporauux & Chasseurs	56
In exterior hospitals	7
With the baggage	2

Compagnie de Boulon	
Capitaine	Jean-François-Louis-Charles Chevalier de Boulon
Lieutenant	Jean-Pierre-Alexis de Chateigner de la Grange
Sous-lieutenant	Richard Chevalier de Barry
Enseigne	Jean-Baptiste du Crozet
Sergents	3
Chirurgien	1
Corporauux & Mousquetaires	29
Sick in quarters	7
In exterior hospitals	5
With the baggage	3
Guard	2
Compagnie de McDermott	
Capitaine	Thomas McDermott
1er Lieutenant	Thadée O' Meara
2e Lieutenant	Walter Grace
Enseigne	John O' Kennedy
Sergents	3 (1 sick)
Corporauux & Mousquetaires	18
Sick in quarters	3
In exterior hospitals	6
With the baggage	3
Guard	1
Compagnie d'O'Moore	
Capitaine	James O' Moore*
1er Lieutenant	Antony Egan*
2e Lieutenant	James Geoghegan
Enseigne	John Mulhall
Sergents	2
Tambour	1
Corporauux & Mousquetaires	6
Sick in quarters	5
In exterior hospitals	4
With the baggage	3
At the depot	2

* These officers did not sign the return, signifying they were not present at the review.

The companies appeared, at the review, in a different order, or differently numbered, than on 28 September 1793 but this earlier structure has been retained in the above table to enable comparisons to be made more easily. At this review, 27 October 1794, the companies were numbered in the following order: 1 – *Colonel*, 2 – *Lieutenant-colonel*, 3 – McDermott, 4 – O'Moore, 5 – Boulon, 6 – *Major*. This may have only been used for the purposes of the review, with the strongest companies being on each flank and the weakest in the centre.

*Chasseur nobl*e of the Légion de Damas by JOB. (Courtesy of Yves Martin)

Hussard of the Légion de Damas by JOB. (Courtesy of Yves Martin)

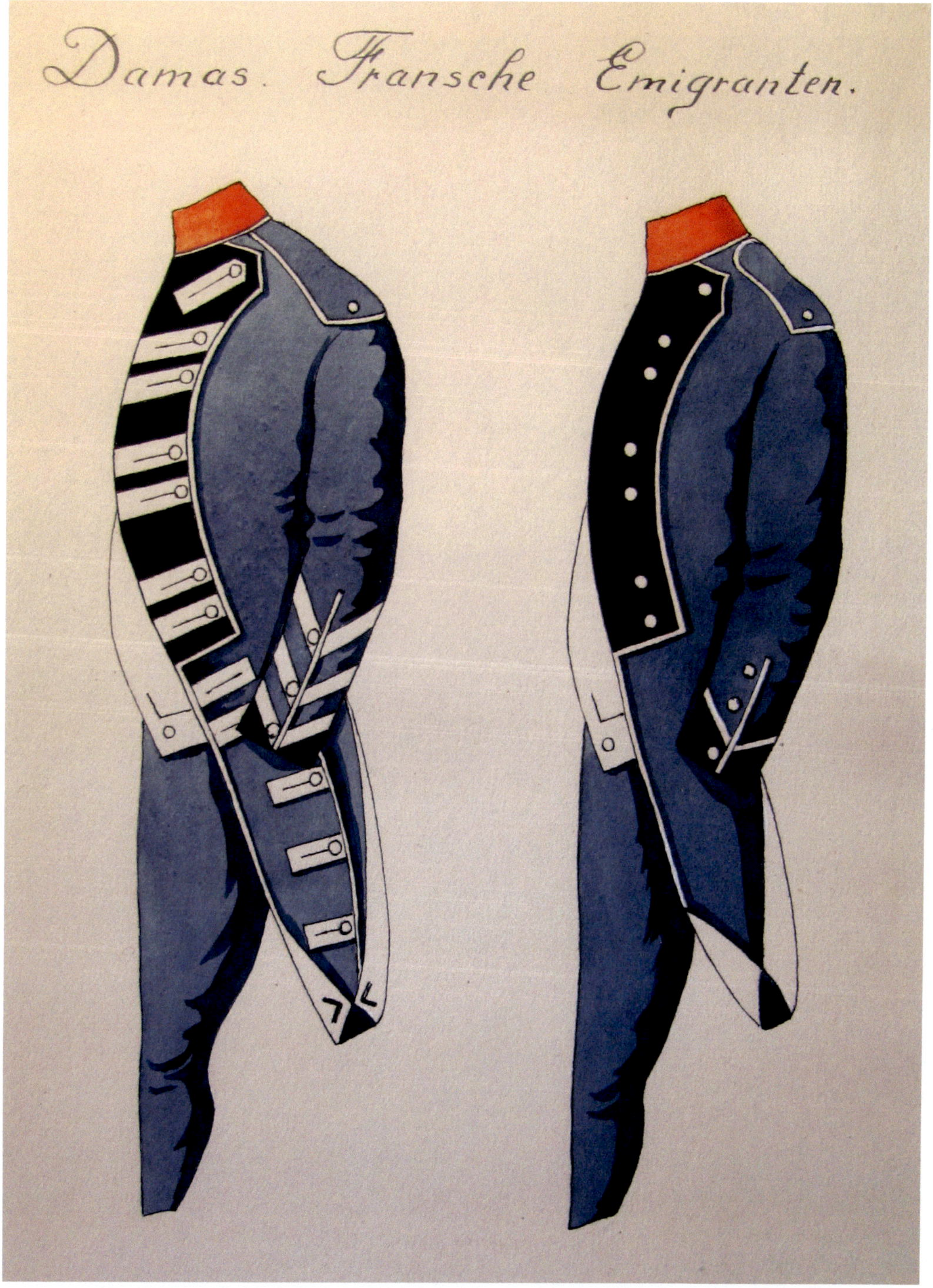

Sketch based on the *Jassenboekje* (Military Coats Book) in the Grouvel family collection.
(Image courtesy of Hughes de Bazouges)

Infantry of the Légion de Damas in Dutch service (1793–1795)
Top L–R: *Fusilier* officer, *Chasseur* hornist; Bottom L–R: *Fusilier*, *Chasseur* officer, *Chasseur*.
(Artwork by Giuseppe Rava; collection of Hughes de Bazouges)

Le comte Etienne-Charles de Damas-Crux,
colonel de la Légion de son nom au Service des Provinces-Unies (1793-1795),
et capitaine de la 1ère compagnie des Chasseurs .

Collection : Colonel (ER) Hughes de Bazouges
Infographie : André Jouineau

Comte Etienne-Charles de Damas-Crux, *colonel* of the legion under his name (1793–1795) and *capitaine* of the 1ère compagnie des Chasseurs. (Artwork by André Jouineau; collection of Hughes de Bazouges)

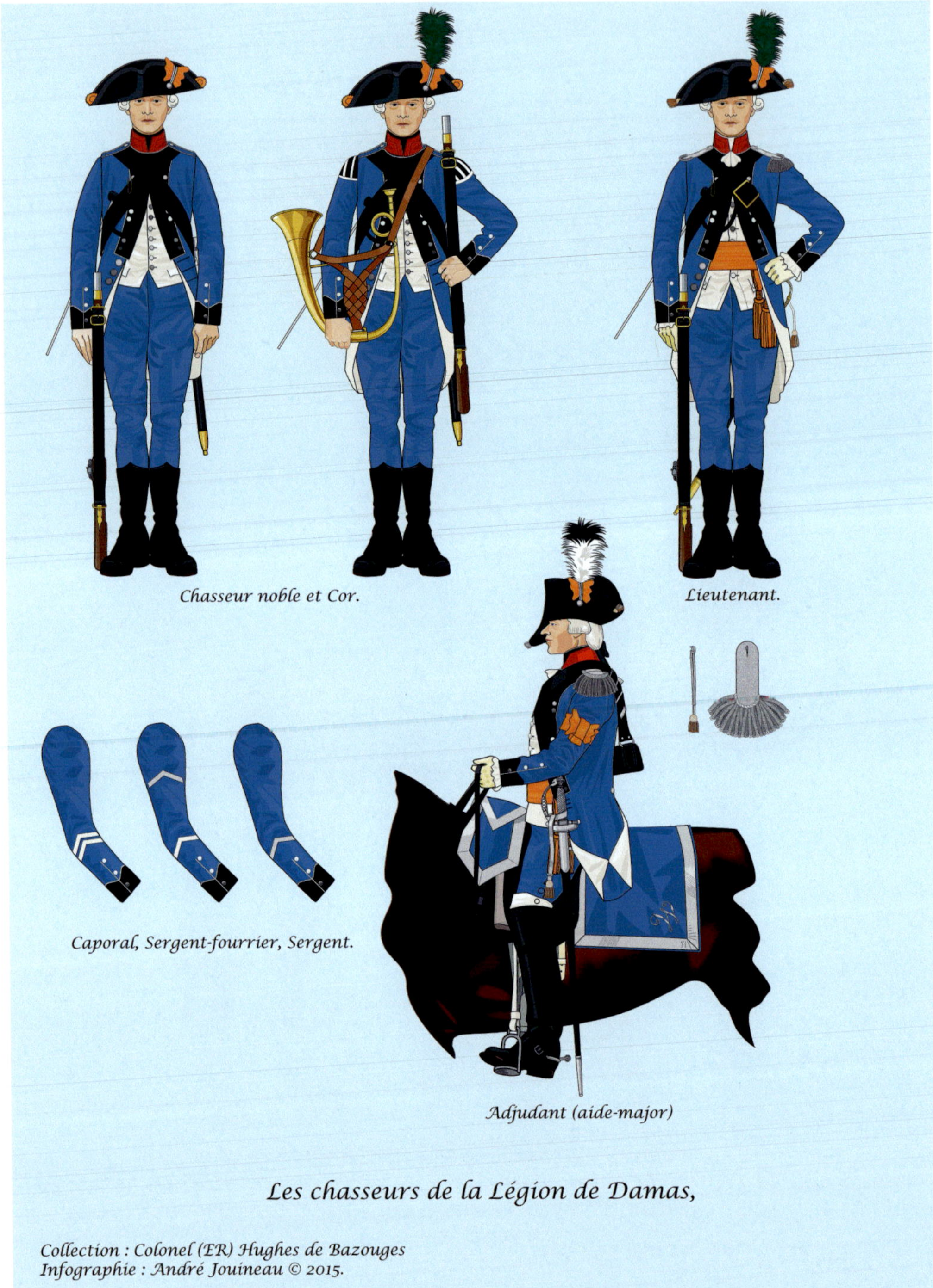

Chasseurs of the Légion de Damas in Dutch service (1793–1795).
(Artwork by André Jouineau; collection of Hughes de Bazouges)

Fusiliers of the Légion de Damas in Dutch service (1793–1795). (Artwork by André Jouineau; collection of Hughes de Bazouges)

Fusiliers of the Légion de Damas in British service at Quiberon (1795); bottom right – *Fusilier* in Dutch colours in Germany, February–April 1795. (Artwork by André Jouineau; collection of Hughes de Bazouges)

Chasseurs of the Légion de Damas in British service at Quiberon (1795); bottom-right– Urbain-Claude Vimar, *Chirurgien-major* (Surgeon) of the Damas infantry, shot at Auray on 11 thermidor An III (29 July 1795). (Artwork by André Jouineau; collection of Hughes de Bazouges)

Le comte Etienne-Charles de Damas-Crux,
Capitaine propriétaire de la 1ère compagnie des Hussards de la Légion de Damas au service des Provinces-Unies.

Collection : Colonel (er) Hughes de Bazouges
Infographie : André Jouineau

Colonel de Damas-Crux, *capitaine commandant*, 1ére compagnie de hussards in the service of the United Provinces (1794–1795). (Artwork by André Jouineau; collection of Hughes de Bazouges)

Hussards de Damas

au service des Provinces-Unies

Collection : Colonel (er) Hughes de Bazouges
Infographie : André Jouineau

Hussards de Damas in the service of the United Provinces (1794–1795).
Top: LH *Adjudant* RH *Sous-lieutenant* ; Centre: *Hussard*; Bottom: LH *Trompette* RH *Sergent*.
(Artwork by André Jouineau; collection of Hughes de Bazouges)

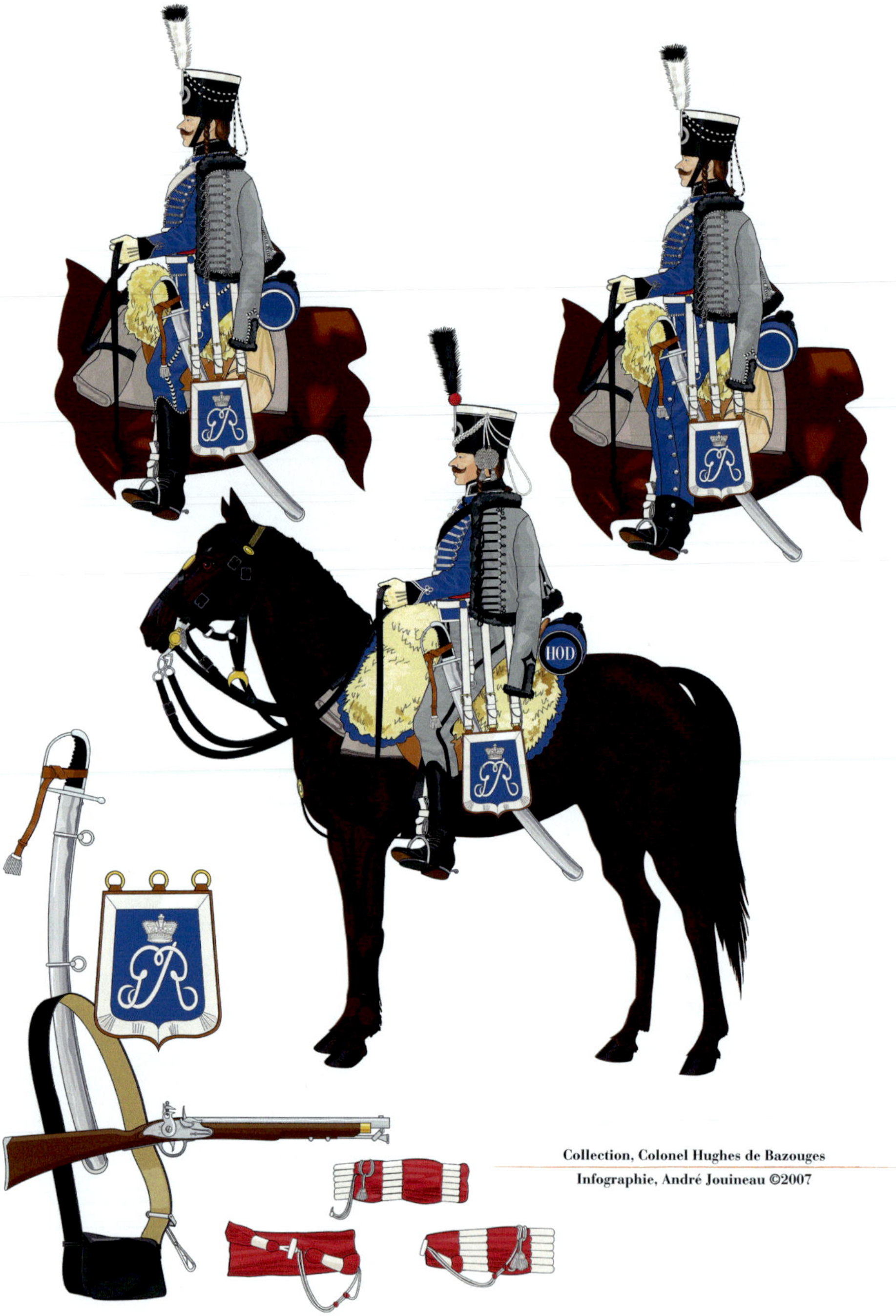

Hussards de Damas in British service (March 1795–March 1796).
Top: *Hussards* after the Berlin Album (Anne S.K. Brown Military Collection); Bottom: *Hussard* after Hamilton Smith (National Library, Paris). (Artwork by André Jouineau; collection of Hughes de Bazouges)

Hussards de Damas in the Armée de Condé (1796–1798) (1).
Top L–R: *Trompette*, *Hussard noble*, *Sergent noble*; Bottom: *Hussard* as a vedette.
(Artwork by André Jouineau; collection of Hughes de Bazouges)

Hussards de Damas in the Armée de Condé (1796–1798) (2).
Top: LH *Capitaine* RH – *Porte-étendard* (Standard-bearer) ; Bottom: LH *Colonel* Comte de Nantouillet RH *Chirurgien-major* (Surgeon-major). (Artwork by André Jouineau; collection of Hughes de Bazouges)

Hussards de Damas in the Armée de Condé (1796–1798) (3).
Comte de Damas-Crux, colonel-proprietor of the *Régiment d'Etienne-Damas Hussards* and *maréchal de camp* (brigadier), personally attached to the Duc de Berry, second son of the Comte d'Artois. (Artwork by André Jouineau; collection of Hughes de Bazouges)

Croix de Saint-Louis (Cross of the Royal and Military Order of Saint-Louis) awarded to François Aumont de Bazouges. (Collection of Hughes de Bazouges)

The return also compared the strengths of each company with those recorded in a review that had taken place in 1 April 1794.

Changes in company strengths, Damas Legion Infantry, 1 April to 27 October 1794

Companies	Strength on 1 April 1794 (all ranks)	Recruits	Losses (all reasons)	Strength on 27 October 1794
Colonel	109	16	42	83
Lieutenant-colonel	76	10	40	46
Major	107	15	48	74
Boulon	75	22	43	54
McDermott	92	4	58	38
O'Moore	85	19	71	33
Total	544	86	302	328

Source: NAN 1.10.19/1893, Raad van State correspondence.

Three days later, 30 October, the Comte de Damas wrote to the Stadholder, reporting on the loss of personnel and suggesting ways to remedy the situation.[58] He began by describing his efforts to raise and maintain his corps, noting that the two companies of chasseurs had been raised 'with surprising dispatch' and he and Rouault had kept them up to strength. He explained that former Berwick officers had offered him two companies which, they had suggested, would be 'formed from the remains of this old and brave Regiment'. He accepted the offer, at some expense, perceiving it as good for the service but the resulting recruitment did not live up to the promise. The companies 'have never been complete, and were composed in great part of Liegois' and they 'had not been slow to experience considerable desertion.' He complained that his orders to rectify things had not been followed and the situation in the other two musketeer companies, those of Stack and Boulon, was little better.

Damas portrayed his infantry as having suffered 'the blows from the enemy or the fatigues of one of the most arduous campaigns' in memory. He estimated that 150 men had been killed or died through illness. However British activities were a significant factor. He depicted the regiments which were being newly raised in British service as 'publicly' appropriating men from the musketeer companies; he knew of twenty-three who were in the Salm Regiment, alone. In addition, many of the chasseurs, from the companies formed of gentlemen, had also left to join these regiments where they often received commissions as officers.

The effect on the Berwick companies was particularly significant. Britain was understood to be preparing to raise a Catholic Irish Brigade, evoking the traditions of the former brigade in French service, which would offer better prospects to the officers, and volunteers, in these companies. Indeed, *Capitaine* O'Moore had already applied, on 15 October, for leave to travel to England for this purpose.[59] Damas knew that *Lieutenant-colonel* Stack and

58 NAN 1.10.19/1893, Raad van State correspondence.

59 KHN Archieven van Stadhouder Willem V, A31/2120; Damas was not unsympathetic to O'Moore's request as he had formerly been *lieutenant-colonel* in the Régiment de Berwick.

Capitaine McDermott had similar intentions. In time, all the officers and volunteers of Irish extraction followed; those that requested leave were granted it until 1 February 1795 by which time they were to have returned or resigned. In the end every officer and 27 volunteers from the Berwick companies, one volunteer from Stack's, as well as Stack, David Barry and Eugene McCarthy, were among the first appointed in the new Irish Brigade, their commissions dated 1 October 1794. Although the brigade proved to be fairly short-lived, several continued careers in the British Army, notably Edward Stack who, although not holding an active command, was general in 1830 before his death in 1833; Charles MacCarthy who became brigadier and Governor of Sierra Leone; and Bryan O'Toole who, detached to the Portuguese army, commanded regiments of caçadores in the Peninsular War, earning him the Gold Medal for four actions and investiture as Companion of the Order of the Bath.

In the final part of his report, Damas recognised that the corps faced dissolution and suggested ways to reorganise it. The first step was for him to become proprietor of all six companies allowing him to take steps, which were beyond the means of individual captains, such as establishing a recruiting depot in a German princedom, Switzerland or even Italy. He also recognised the aspirations of the gentlemen serving in the corps. Thus, he suggested disbanding the chasseur companies and dispersing their personnel amongst the six new companies, 12 apiece, under the title of cadets at the same rate of pay as at present. Nothing came of these proposals, whatever their merits they were overtaken by events.

On the same day, 30 October, Damas submitted nominations for promotion in his cavalry companies:

> Guilluame-Catherine-Judith Vicomte de Montjustin, formerly *capitaine* in the Royal-Lorraine cavalerie, to be *major*, and *capitaine* of the second company, in lieu of Segonzac and Jean-François-Marie Marquis de Bongars, *capitaine* in the Noailles dragons, to be *capitaine commandant* of the first company.

The following were nominated to the consequential vacancies:

> Conan d'Ocor to be *premier lieutenant*;
> Guillaume-Louis-Calixte Brandin de Saint-Laurent, former Garde du corps and cavalry *capitaine*, to *lieutenant en second* and
> Louis-François-Dominique Vicomte de Lentilhac, *sous-lieutenant* of Royal-Pologne cavalerie, to *ensigne* [sic].[60]

Montjustin, however, soon found that he did not have sufficient 'pecuniary means' to maintain his company and so, on 22 December, he renounced his proprietary rights and financial responsibilities in favour of the Comte de Damas, while continuing as *major*.[61]

The legion had returned to Nijmegen on 28 October to take part in its defence, arriving at 1:00 p.m.[62] However any optimism that may have been evoked by the allies' new plans was soon cooled when, on 30 October, Werneck visited York's headquarters. He not only

60 Bittard des Portes, *Les émigrés*, p.237.
61 AMC, Series Y, carton XXII - f.487.
62 *Dagboek van Nijmegen 1794–1795*, p.63.

announced that he would not be marching directly to Nijmegen but crossing the Rhine at Wesel, much further upriver, but also that he could not do so until the 7 November. Nijmegen still needed to be defended. By 4 November the siege works had approached to within 450 metres of the outer defences. A sortie was planned for that night to attack the siege works on the high ground east of the city, a parallel with three batteries which were yet to be armed. It was to be a significant affair drawing on units from all the allies at Nijmegen and led by the British Major General de Burgh:

Infantry	Dutch – Gumoëns (Swiss) Regiment, detachment
	Hanoverian – 1st Infantry (von Stockhausen), two battalions
	British – 8th (King's), 27th (Inniskilling), 28th (North Gloucestershire), 55th (Westmorland), 63rd (West Suffolk) and 78th (Highlanders) Foot
Cavalry	Dutch – Damas cavalry
	Hanoverian – Leibgarde Regiment, two squadrons; 2nd (von Hammerstein) Cavalry, one squadron; 5th (von Ramdohr) Dragoons, one squadron; 10th (Prinz von Wallis) Light Dragoons, one squadron
	British – 15th (King's) Light Dragoons, two squadrons
Reserve and supports	Dutch – Bentinck Regiment, 200 men carrying spades accompanied by engineers
	Hanoverian – Horse Artillery, detachment; 9th (Königin) Light Dragoons, two squadrons
	British – 7th (Queen's Own) Light Dragoons, two squadrons; Choiseul Hussars

A British account describes the attack of the main column:

> Tuesday, Nov. 4. As the enemy's works were now so far advanced, that with their guns and mortars, they could command any part of the town; it was resolved upon to make a sortie this evening, and endeavour to destroy some of their nearest works, and if possible, to surprise them in their entrenchments…
>
> The troops paraded in the dusk of the evening, and marched out with utmost silence, while the town batteries were playing very heavily from another quarter, in order to draw the attention of the enemy that way. The enemy's advance sentries were surprized before they could give the alarm, and everything had the greatest appearance of success. Our troops had positive orders to avoid firing and to use only the bayonet; they had now reached the enemy's lines without being discovered, and with the greatest intrepidity were proceeding to take possession, when one of our soldiers fired his piece, (whether by accident or design was not known) which immediately gave the alarm to the enemy, who instantly beat to arms, turned out, and began a very heavy fire upon our troops, who undauntedly leaping in upon the French in their works, began the dreadful carnage.
>
> It is impossible for description to give an adequate idea of a scene of this kind, where quarter is neither given or expected by either party; … The slaughter this night was very dreadful during the short time it lasted, but from the universal alarm given in the French camp, the whole of their army was soon marched to their works which were attacked, and fell upon our troops who were occupied in

> destroying them. The conflict was now very severe, and numbers fell on both sides; the troops were at times so intermixed, it was very difficult to distinguish a friend from an enemy, and it was supposed that the French actually killed a number of their own people, by their rash and undisciplined firing in all directions.[63]

This attack, of the main column, was succinctly described in the Duke of York's published despatch, dated 7 November, 'The Sortie had every Success which could be expected from it. The Troops advanced to the Enemy's Trenches under a very severe Fire, and jumped into them without returning a Shot. The Loss of the Enemy was almost entirely by the Bayonet, and amounted to above Five Hundred Men.'[64]

Most of the British infantry had marched from the Hertogpoort and around the city to attack the front of the works, while the 8th and 55th Foot had left the eastern gate, the former to join the main attack and the 55th to attack the flank of the parallel; covering Dutch infantry also marched from this gate. Simultaneously Hanoverian light infantry left the western gate to engage French outposts in that vicinity. The cavalry swept out to the left flank of the works, driving off some cavalry pickets and then engaging French infantry in the communication trench to the rear.[65] Lieutenant Charles Stewart, 28th Foot, noted in his journal:

> [T]he Troops … stormed and carried the Enemies trenches with the point of the bayonet by this time the Cavalry had cut of [sic] their retreat and the few who escaped the bayonet were sabered [sic] by the Dragoons about the time we gained their batteries the Enemy opened their batteries from their camp and played very heavy with round & grape on our men they cease when their reserve which had advanced from Lines becoming engaged with us …[66]

On the right the soldiers with tools set to work, destroying the enemy entrenchments, covered by the Damas cavalry, 15th Light Dragoons and the horse artillery. Once they had achieved their aims the units withdrew into the entrenched camp. Corbehem related that:

> This affair did much honour to the Scottish highlanders; the squadron of my legion distinguished itself there also, its colonel, the Comte Etienne de Damas, above all showed admirable sang-froid and great intrepidity. His horsemen, exposed for a long time, to the fire of the Republican artillery, without being able to make the least movement, endured it with a firmness and resignation above all praise. They proved, anew, on this occasion, that French blood ran through their veins: also, costing the squadron some men and many horses.[67]

---

63 Anon. *Journal* pp.101–104.

64 *London Gazette*, 11 November 1794.

65 Details from map 17, Atlas des Cartes et Plans Relatifs au Mémoire Historique et Militaire des Campagnes de l'Armée Britannique aux Ordres de Son Altesse Royale Monseigneur le Duc d'York sur le Continent pendant les Années 1793–1794 et Commencement de 1795 (TNA MPH 1/139).

66 R. M. Grazebrook 'The Campaign in Flanders of 1793–1795: Journal of Lieutenant Charles Stewart, 28th Foot', *Journal of the Society for Army Historical Research*, Spring, 1951, Vol. 29, No. 117, p.15.

67 Corbehem, *Dix ans de ma vie*, pp.141–142.

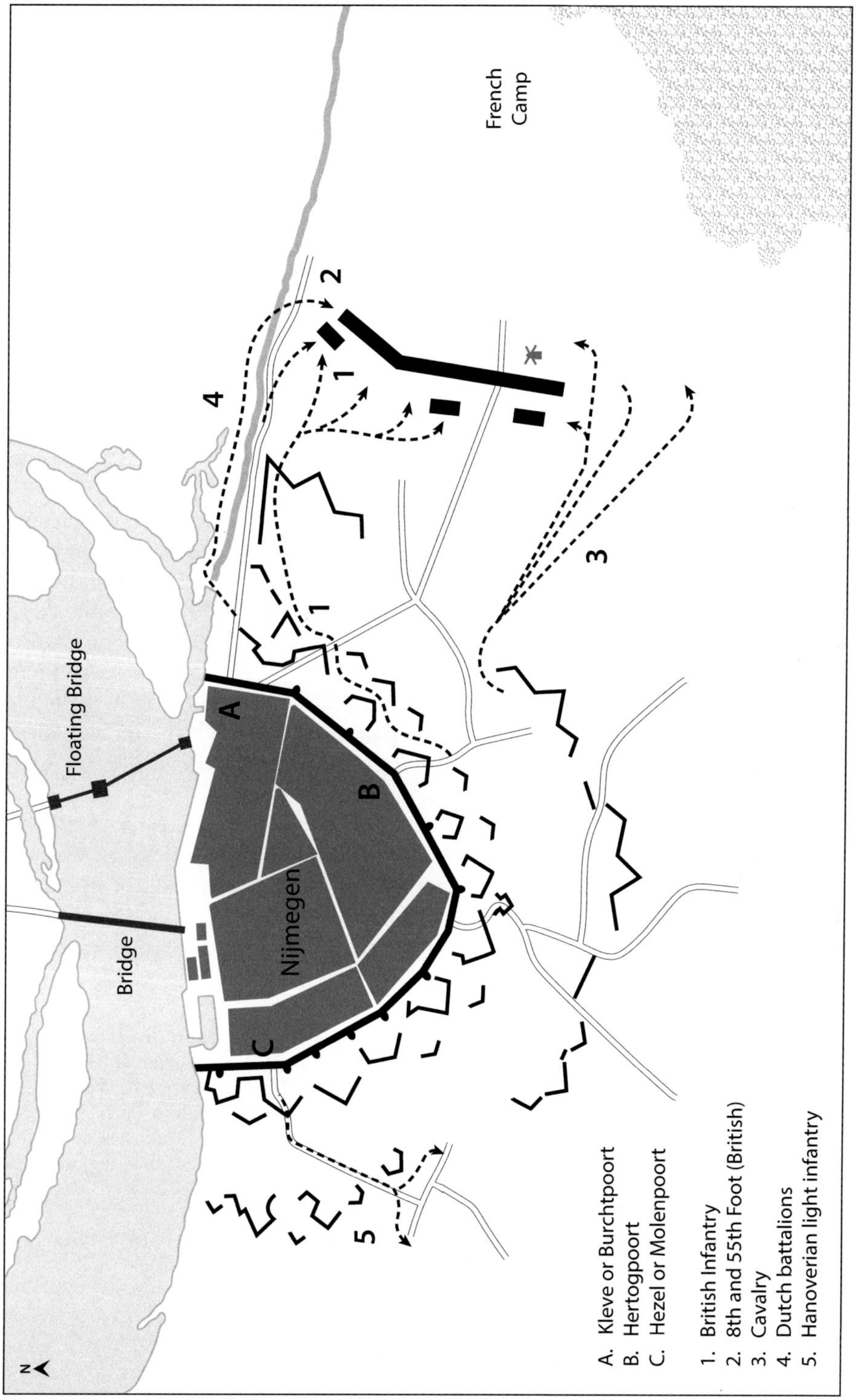

The sortie from Nijmegen.

According to one writer *Colonel* Etienne de Damas, had his horse killed under him and another that *Lieutenant* de Bazouges, 'among their best officers', was distinguished, along with *Chasseur Noble* Guillaume-Anne-Chrysogone Guigné de Maisod who was wounded in a shoulder by a gunshot, in this affair.[68] The British and Hanoverian units had 21 killed, 175 wounded and 22 missing.[69] Those suffered by the Dutch units were not produced; however, the significance of this single action for the Légion de Damas is illustrated by a later return of *Chasseurs Nobles* of the cavalry who had been disabled and unable to serve. Of the four men listed, three had received their wounds, all from gunshots, at the sortie, they were Maisod, Louis-Alexandre Cavié d'Asniérel, right hand, and Jean de Vauvillé, shoulder.[70] The Damas cavalry left Nijmegen immediately after the night of the sortie.

The fortitude and losses of the troops were largely in vain as Calvert observed, 'Brilliant as this affair may be in itself, I am sorry to say that the effect it produced was a trifling delay in the enemy's operations.'[71] However, Lieutenant Stewart noted, 'although the great objective of the Sortie was not accomplished to the extent that was expected it had one great and good effect by proving to our Soldiers that superiority alone of numbers had caused the unfortunate Campaign of 1794.'[72]

Despite heavy fire from Nijmegen, on the 6 November the enemy managed to open up two batteries which commanded the pontoon bridge and during a three-hour bombardment a great deal of damage was caused including the sinking of one of the pontoon boats. The bridge was under the superintendence of a British naval officer, Lieutenant Home Popham, who had arrived at Oostende in September 1793 as Agent for the Transports for the British army, and joined the Duke of York's headquarters by March 1794 where he particularly assisted with matters relating to the waterways. He, with a hundred British sailors, soon set to work on the bridge, 'This, however, we repaired by 7 o'clock in the evening [of 6 November] when 9000 men of the Garrison, and all the British and Hanoverian Artillery were retreated; leaving about 4500 men behind.'[73]

The Damas infantry crossed the bridge at 9:00 p.m. and continued on to Arnhem; the passage was not without risk, 'When our turn arrived, the pontoon bridge … was cut; we had to wait until it was repaired. While we were crossing, the enemy did not stop firing on the bridge; but it rarely happened that their cannon balls reached it, so our crossing was achieved without loss.'[74] The situation must have been particularly remarkable as all three

68 Crossard, *Mémoires militaires et historiques*, p.132 and Théodore Muret *Histoire de l'Armée de Condé* (Paris: Dentu, 1844,) Vol.I pp.253–254, who gives the second named as 'M. Guigue de Maisod.'

69 *London Gazette*. Anon. *Journal*, p 105, gives the losses of the 'British Troops' as 12 (and five horses) killed; 172 wounded and 20 missing and of the 'Foreign Troops': eight killed; four (and 22 horses) wounded. It is not clear in which category the Légion de Damas would have been listed as the author, who also ascribed to officers ranks that they only received after the events, described the unit as being in British pay.

70 BL Add MS 46710, undated return.

71 Verney, *Journals and Correspondence of General Sir Harry Calvert*, p.380, letter to Major General Sir Hew Dalrymple, 7 November 1794.

72 Grazebrook 'The Campaign in Flanders of 1793–1795', p.15.

73 Letter dated 9 November, quoted in Hugh Popham *A Damned Cunning Fellow, The Eventful Life of Rear-Admiral Sir Home Popham KCB, KCH, KM, FRS, 1762–1820* (Tywardreath: Old Ferry, 1991), pp.47–48.

74 Corbehem, *Dix ans de ma vie*, p.142 and *Dagboek van Nijmegen 1794–1795*, p.99.

members of the unit who produced memoirs noted this event. Bennes wrote, 'When we retreated the bridge was partly cut down; the enemy had erected two batteries, from which they kept continually firing, but it so happened, that every one of our men escaped unhurt, though the English were very great sufferers.'[75]

The sailors continued to try to keep the bridge operational, but the next morning the French artillery 'had so completely got the reach of the north end of the Bridge that they prevented our working'; seven boats, in a section, were sunk. As night fell, on 7 November, the sailors erected a platform over the damaged section of the bridge as well as maintaining the floating bridge, a ferry on which the occupants pulled themselves across the river by a hawser. At 9:00 p.m. orders were finally issued for the withdrawal of the last of the garrison. The remaining British infantry, picquets from different regiments, crossed first to be followed by the Dutch. The French received help from within the town, with the evacuation at midnight 'a light was hoisted on the top of the church steeple. From that instant not a shell fell into the town. The whole of the enemy's fire was directed to the bridge'.[76] The pontoon bridge was set on fire and, when the hawser broke on the floating bridge, the Dutch soldiers who were in mid-stream, preferred to be left to be taken prisoner than trust the skills of the sailors to gain the far bank and safety. These final events soured relations between the British and Dutch, some of the latter considered that the men of the Bentinck and Stuart Regiments had been abandoned by the British, and of course the French and their Dutch political allies, the Patriots, in their reports tried to add fuel to the fire. The pontoon bridge had been either set ablaze by hostile artillery fire or deliberately set alight too soon, with spectacular results. Confusion was caused by *Generaal Major* von Haacke and his apparent cowardice. He had peremptorily handed his command to *Colonel* Balneavis of the Stuart Regiment and abandoned the town, and its garrison; in doing so he indicated that the pontoon bridge was no longer needed, giving the impression that only the rear guard was left to cross which would use the floating bridge.[77] Given Haacke's conduct before at Geertruidenberg, only two months before, it is curious that he was entrusted with such a command so soon afterwards.

Although the enemy's activity had forced the immediate evacuation of Nijmegen its fate had already been sealed when, the day after the sortie, and when pressed, Werneck had declared he would not be anywhere near the town before 16 November. This was interpreted as, in fact, meaning he was not going arrive at all. Despite being effectively abandoned, the remaining garrison at Nijmegen were permitted to capitulate under terms and, once again, the republicans sought out any émigrés that may have been left behind, ordering the inhabitants to immediately deliver them up.[78]

---

75 Bennes, *Narrative*, p.32; Tercier also remarked that the Damas infantry crossed without loss, La Chanonie, *Mémoires*, p.84.

76 Norfolk Record Office (NRO) ACC 2011/219, Journal of Lieutenant Colonel Frederick Keppel (1762–1830) and transcript 'Keppel: Journal of Lt. Colonel Fred. Keppel Commanding 88th Regiment 1794 & 1795' by Kay Neville-Rolfe, Anne Glenister, & Patrick Morriss.

77 Popham p.48, Bittard des Portes *Les émigrés*, pp.243–246; James Ferguson, *Papers illustrating the history of the Scotch Brigade in the service of the United Netherlands 1572–1782* (Edinburgh: Scottish History Society, 1899), Vol.II pp. xx, xxi and 565. The Stuart and Bentinck Regiments had formerly been part of the Scotch Brigade.

78 Bittard des Portes, *Les émigrés*, pp.246–247.

Maastricht, left behind by the Austrian retreat over the Rhine, had surrendered on 4 November. Amongst the strongholds left defended by the allies, Breda held out until 22 December and Grave only capitulated on 29 December. *Generaals* von Geusau and de Bons, with their garrisons, had shown the constancy and courage that had been sadly lacking by others. Each fortress that was given up not only released enemy troops to join their field army but also contributed more artillery and ammunition for its use. There were French émigrés at Breda, particularly in the artillery, but many escaped after the capitulation, by marching out with the Stockar de Neuform (Swiss) Regiment which readily provided uniforms for their use. Disguise as Swiss soldiers had the added advantage that they, when prisoners, had the prospect of being returned home.[79]

All the armies in the Netherlands were exhausted by the continuous campaigning, with the winter setting in they needed a break in operations to recuperate and the allies settled into their defensive line on the Waal. The main Dutch field army was concentrated on Gorinchem, with an advance holding the Bommelwaard, while the British and their German allies held the easterly end, particularly around Arnhem, with the bulk of their cavalry placed in cantonments across the Ijssel. The Duke of York left the army to return to London, on 2 December 1794, and his command was split between Wallmoden-Gimborn and Lieutenant General William Harcourt.

The defects of the allied armies became ever more apparent as the winter weather and a habit of retreat set in. The effective strength of the Dutch units continued to shrink as men left the ranks from sickness or desertion. The British army's support services had proved inadequate in the campaign and now, after a month of rain, typhus swept through the ranks. Calvert observed, 'The sickness increases … I fear that the winter, which is generally supposed to afford ease and comfort to the soldier, and recruit him after the fatigues of the summer, will prove more destructive to this army than the campaign has been.'[80] On 27 November there were 21,000 infantry in British pay and nearly 11,000 of them were sick, further reductions were made when seven battalions were ordered to leave for service elsewhere.[81]

As soon as the Légion de Damas had reached Arnhem, on 8 November, orders were issued for it to march the next day to Utrecht to be placed in winter quarters.[82] Its arrival in that city was reported thus:

> Utrecht, November 12 – The legion of Damas, a corps of French emigrants, in the pay of the United Netherlands, arrived here the day before yesterday; and after having sworn allegiance to the States provincial, as well as to the magistrates of this place, they were quartered in the town; as this corps, since the 22d of September, has been almost daily engaged with the enemy, its outward

79 Crossard, *Mémoires militaires et historiques*, p.146; Gros, *Journal*, p.183.

80 Verney, *Journals and Correspondence of General Sir Harry Calvert*, p.415, letter to Major General Dalrymple 20 December 1794.

81 Fortescue, *British Campaigns in Flanders*, pp.391 and 393.

82 La Chanonie, *Mémoires*, p.84 and Het Utrechts Archief, Staten van Utrecht (HUA) inv. nr. 265-192, dated 10 November.

> appearance has exceeded the expectation, which might be formed from the above circumstance.[83]

The legion's infantry was provided with quarters within the city whilst the cavalry was housed in the surrounding villages, this appears to have been done in stages as quarters were provided for 10 officers and 81 men of the legion in the neighbouring villages of Leersum and Zuilenstein, east of the city, on 9 November and an oath was taken near De Bilt, on the eastern outskirts of Utrecht on 11 November.[84] Sympathetic citizens in the city opened their doors to the émigrés:

> During our stay in this city, we received many compliments and civility from the distinguished persons of the area. We were invited to be party of one of their societies, which was composed of the most outstanding men of this great city. It is a meeting of members who come to drink, smoke, play cards and discuss politics. We took part in their entertainments.[85]

Although the depot remained there, for most of the men the stay in the city was to be brief. On 27 November, a detachment of Damas cavalry, consisting of a captain, two subalterns, two sergeants, three corporals and 26 troopers was sent towards Amersfoort, as part of the troops ordered to the province's borders. A Damas cavalry detachment was maintained near this last town for some time, being noted there on 3 and 12 January.[86] In the first days of December 1794 the legion's infantry was posted to the Grebbe Line, on 2 December three waggons were provided for a detachment's march to the line, although it is known some remained in Utrecht as, on 10 December, they were to be given an allowance, of six *stuivers*, issued to all infantry posted there.[87]

The Grebbe Line ran along the provincial border of Gelderland and Utrecht, between Rhenen on the river Lek to the Zuiderzee, with Amersfoort just behind the line. It defended the western approach not only to Utrecht but also the cities of Holland, the heart and treasury of the United Provinces. Constructed in phases, starting from 1744, it consisted of a series of inundations, areas which could be flooded, with the areas between, and other vulnerable points, defended by fieldworks and strongholds, one of the largest and most important of the latter was Fort aan de Buursteeg, built in 1786. A British officer visited the area and described that part of the line as, 'a chain of Strong Earth works extending … to the Inundation. They are all connected by a breast work & secured in front by a wet ditch – The Country in their front is open Meadow & behind them are very fine bold hills the Inundation reaches to the left further than I could see'.[88]

83 *The Times*, London, 20 November 1794; the report was taken directly from Dutch newspapers such as the *Ommelander Courant*, 14 November 1794.

84 Het Utrechts Archief, Staten van Utrecht, inv. nr. 265-192.

85 La Chanonie, *Mémoires*, pp.84–85.

86 27 November 1794, HUA 265-192, 3 January 1795, HUA 265-193 and letter from the Comte de Damas, dated 12 January 1795, quoted by Bittard des Portes, *Les émigrés*, p.263.

87 HUA 265-193.

88 Peter Harrington (ed), *With the Guards in Flanders; The Diary of Captain Roger Morris 1793–1795* (Warwick: Helion, 2018), p.145. Morris visited the line on 12 January 1795. The Grebbe Line

Despite the comparative lull in offensive operations the French, denied rest by their political masters, sent forces over the Waal by boat to attack the sector held by the Hanoverians, notably on 11 December; all were repulsed. They then concentrated their forces in front of the allied centre which was screened by Dutch outposts on the Bommelerwaard. Soon the weather conspired to give them the opportunity to attack when it turned 'intensely cold'.[89] The Waal began to freeze and, from 18 December, sentries were posted on the ice, at night, as close to the edge as safety allowed. Three days later the river was 'frozen so thick and firm at the sides and for a considerable way across that our sentries and those of the enemy, were in some places within twenty yards of each other upon the edge ice.'[90] On 27 December, with the ice now thick enough, the French crossed the Maas and drove in the Dutch outposts on the Bommelerwaard. They continued over the Waal and seized Tuil, but their further advance was halted by the Hessians at Meteren. They were finally driven back over the Waal on 30 December with the arrival of British reinforcements.

The Damas infantry remained in the Grebbe Line. The particularly severe winter of 1794–5 was the first time the line was made operational and the sluices were opened to inundate the land. However, the extreme cold, although periodically marked by short but sharp thaws, meant that the water froze so that it, in common with all such defensive schemes, was, at best, compromised. An indication of how severe the winter was in North-west Europe is given by the Central England Temperature Series, the longest continuous series of surface temperature readings, taken at several locations in England from 1659, in which 1795 was the coldest January recorded, with the average reading never exceeding – 3.1° C.[91]

The Damas infantry was posted not only at Fort aan de Buursteeg but also in surrounding villages. Tercier wrote:

> [W]e were sent to occupy the Grebbe lines. They are strong entrenchments, easy to defend, and which protect Holland on this side. They are surrounded by water, and their position by this means is inaccessible. We were quartered in a village in the middle of the marshes. Half the legion each day mounted guard in the lines, tiring unhealthy duty, and which yielded us many sick. We had no hospitals.[92]

The Comte de Damas was concerned about the conditions in which his infantry was serving. On 20 December, he wrote from Utrecht to the Stadholder, concerned about:

> [T]he distressing situation of my Infantry – scattered the length of the Grebbe Line in bad houses, it does an extended duty in regard to its number. The fatigues of the campaign have not had time to recover – still add to the difficulty they have; maladies begin to overcome them, and the number of those who can serve diminishes

continued to be developed through time, up to and including World War II; see <http://www.grebbelinie.nl/page/home> (accessed 2 January 2020).

89 Anon., *Journal*, p.119, entry for Sunday 14 December 1794.

90 Anon., *Journal*, p.124.

91 Georgina Endfield, 'Cold weather records: reflections from the bus stop' *University of Nottingham*, at <http://blogs.nottingham.ac.uk/weatherextremes/2015/01/19/> (accessed 20 June 2017).

92 La Chanonie, *Mémoires*, pp.87–88.

> accordingly. It is impossible for me to occupy myself with repairs nor with training …[93]

As Damas stated the soldiers were inadequately housed in sheds. The area around Amersfoort was particularly noted for the cultivation of tobacco. The sheds had been constructed for drying, or curing, the leaves and so were well ventilated, troops, trying to make the best of a severe winter, had very different requirements. The level of sickness is indicated by the provision of six waggons on 7 January to bring the sick of the legion back from the line to Hoevelaken, east of Amersfoort, although from 10 January the soldiers received a daily allowance of coal whilst they were housed in the sheds at the Fort and elsewhere along the Line.[94]

The main body of the Damas cavalry had left the vicinity of Utrecht to join the Dutch field army during the crisis when the Bommelerwaard and the line on the Waal had been attacked. Constant-Villars had been tasked to establish a reserve line on the far side of the river Linge, north of the Waal, with an assortment of units. On 30 December he was joined by the Damas cavalry, which he posted along the length of the river, as far as Heukelum.[95] With the Waal re-established as the defensive line, on 31 December, Prins Frederik ordered Constant-Villars to take command of the left wing on its north bank, between Gorinchem and Hellouw, and the latter placed his headquarters in the fort at Vuren. The Damas cavalry, along with two battalions of the Hohenlohe Regiment and one of the Löwenstein Jägers, was posted at Herwijnen with a detachment at Hellouw, where it linked with the British sector. The rest of this weak line was manned by the Van Raesfeldt Grenadier Battalion and the field battalion of the Orange-Friesland Regiment at Dalem and Vuren respectively. The cavalry took up its posts on 2 January and the next day the Comte de Damas, after making a short tour of inspection of the area and visiting the adjacent British positions, recommended to Constant-Villars that the British take over Hellouw, a 'weak post that … extends all the more our weak cordon and does not strengthen it'. He did so on the grounds that it would reduce the over-extension of the Dutch units and recommended that Harcourt be asked to place the Loyal Emigrants at Hellouw, Damas having apparently conferred with their colonel, La Châtre. His request that his cavalry's forage waggon and campaign forge be placed at Arkel, behind Gorinchem, indicates that he was not impressed with the strength of the position.[96]

On 30 December emissaries, sanctioned by the Stadholder, had met Pichegru at 's-Hertogenbosch to negotiate a peace but he informed them that he was not authorised to deal with them and they would have to continue to Paris. The Dutch concern now was to hold out, so that peace could be bought at the best price. Wallmoden, who suspected that the Dutch were likely to make a separate peace, was in a difficult situation as he had to preserve the army, he had been entrusted with, in and allied to a country which was

93 KHN Archieven van Stadhouder Willem V, A31 Inv No 2120.
94 HUA 265-193.
95 NAN Constant-Rebecque Journal Vol.I 2.21.008.01/19.
96 NAN 2.21.005.41/31 journal entry and copy of order of 31 December 1794, letter to Constant-Villars and daily report of 3 January 1795 and 2.21.008.01/19 Constant-Rebecque Journal Vol.I.

negotiating with, if not yet submitting to, its conquerors.[97] On 3 January 1795 he moved closer to the Dutch army, transferring his headquarters from Arnhem to Amerongen, on the north bank of the Lek. The following day, 4 January, taking advantage of a renewed spell of cold weather, the French again attacked over the Waal. They took Tuil and drove a wedge between the Dutch and Wallmoden's British and German forces, but were halted on the river Linge. Nevertheless, realising that this line was untenable due to the frozen conditions, Wallmoden ordered a retreat over the Lek. With a thaw, the allies counter-attacked to try to re-establish the defensive line on the Waal, but this stalled, as the cold became worse and the enemy regained the advantage, and on 10 January they returned to the line on the Lek. Wallmoden had wished to continue to retreat over the river Ijssel, but, under diplomatic pressure and with another thaw, he remained, temporarily, where he was on the Lek. However, another hard frost enabled the French to attack over the Lek on 14 January and the next day Wallmoden ordered the withdrawal of his forces over the Ijssel.

In the days of confusion in early January, as the front line shifted back and forth between the Waal and the Lek, the Damas cavalry was continually on the move. Its main role was to keep the Dutch commanders informed of the movements of the British troops on their flank and they do not appear to have had any direct contact with the enemy. It was now suggested that they carry out another duty. Caroline of Brunswick was due to travel across the United Provinces on her way to England for her marriage to the Prince of Wales (the future King George IV), and the Damas cavalry was to be her escort during her overnight stay at Soestdijk Palace, just west of Amersfoort, while the Salm-Kyrburg Hussars provided the guard. However, she never made the journey: the closest she got was Delden, just outside Hengelo, on 9 January, when the Earl of Malmesbury, who accompanied her, decided to turn back due to heavy fighting around the Waal. The princess, herself, as befitted the daughter of a Duke of Brunswick, was reportedly unconcerned about the sound of the artillery. She finally sailed from Stade, on the Elbe, on 28 March.[98]

On the initial attack and the retreat of Wallmoden's troops, on 4 January, Prins Frederik ordered Constant-Villars to bring his brigade towards Gorinchem and the Damas cavalry appear to have concentrated at Arkel, on the north bank of the Linge. The brigade was then broken up and the Damas cavalry was posted in reserve. By 6 January it was at Almeide, under the command of *Major* de Montjustin, with a detachment at Lexmond. Early on 7 January the unit received orders to return to its previous post, to coincide with the counter-attack by the British and Germans, however they did not specify if this was at Arkel or Herwijnen requiring Montjustin to write for clarification.[99] On 11 January the unit is shown as being at Everdingen.

---

97 TNA WO 1/171, the Duke of York informed Evan Nepean, the Under Secretary of State for War, on 25 December 1794, of Wallmoden's suspicions.

98 Third Earl of Malmesbury (ed.), *Dairies and Correspondence of James Harris, First Earl of Malmesbury* (London: Bentley, 1844), Vol.III, pp.232–234; Alison Plowden, *Caroline and Charlotte Regency Scandals 1795–1821* (Stroud: Sutton, 2005), p.15. Bittard de Portes *Les émigrés* p.262 refers to a letter sent by the Stadholder to Bentinck, on 8 January, which described the arrangements and implies the journey took place. Captain Morris confirms the planned overnight stop that did not happen; see Harrington (ed), *With the Guards in Flanders*, p.149.

99 KHN Archieven Prins Frederik, A34/256, reports from Montjustin and Moizes, the adjutant, on 6 and 7 January.

The days were numbered for the United Provinces and resignation to defeat prevailed. On 6 January the States-General had voted that, once the Lek was crossed, no further resistance should be offered in the province of Holland and steps were to be taken to sue for peace. Even staunch Orangists wished to display their national credentials by distancing themselves from the British and other allies.[100] On 8 January, writing from Utrecht, Damas aired his concerns about the 'dangerous' situation of the legion's sick, about 40 in number, who were 'absolutely unable to serve at this moment' and remained at the city where they were joined by 16 sick from the Légion de Béon which was still with the Dutch field army. He had suggested that his sick could join the depot of the Légion de Béon at Harderwijk, north east of Amersfoort, on the shore of what was then the Zuiderzee, but had been informed that the local authorities there were unable and unwilling to receive them, so he asked Prins Frederik to provide a patent, or certificate, to transport them to another suitable place.[101]

The situation became even more critical as the days went by and on 12 January Damas wrote to the Stadholder asking for direction as to what to do about his legion. He stated that the infantry remained in the Grebbe Line, with a detachment of cavalry at Amersfoort, behind the line, and the depot was still at Utrecht; the main body of the cavalry, presumably, still on the Lek.[102] However this comparatively neat summary did not reflect the real situation on the ground. Defeat and retreat had caused confusion and disorder so, for instance, on 14 January, the garrison at Schoonhoven, on the north bank of the Lek, consisted of 25 officers and 356 other ranks, from eight different units including three officers and five men of the Damas infantry.[103]

On 15 January the Comte de Damas had an audience with the Stadholder, which included the following exchange:

> Damas: In the danger which menaces Your Highness & his family, the wish of the corps is that I put it at his disposal …
> Stadholder: You have nothing to ask; my youngest son gave the order to your corps to retire & follow the movements of the English army.
> Damas: Ah! Sire, I was going to ask precisely the contrary. In the name of the entire corps I was going to beg Your Highness to call us near to his person: gratitude, duty, our principles, all make it a duty for us to defend to the last Your Highness & his family. We came out of France for the defence of our Kings …
> Stadholder: No Colonel, my son gave the orders that he ought; if he had not done it, I myself would have given them …

100 Simon Schama *Patriots and Liberators, Revolution in the Netherlands 1780–1813*, 2nd Edition (London: Harper Collins, 1992), p.187.
101 NAN Archieven Prins Frederik, A34/256.
102 Letter of 12 January 1795 reproduced in Bittard des Portes, *Les émigrés*, pp.263–264.
103 Sabron, *De oorlog van 1794/1795*, Vol.II, p.212; the other soldiers were from the following regiments: 2e Orange-Nassau (1 officer, 19 men); Nassau-Usingen (1 officer, 5 men); Erfprins (19 men); Van Welderen (6 officers, 50 men); Bentinck (4 officers, 24 men); Bosc de la Calamette (5 officers, 89 men) and Plettenberg (5 officers, 145 men).

The Erfprins arrived and the Stadholder concluded the conversation, 'Adieu my Colonel: I have to work with my son; I wish you a good journey.'[104] The legion left Utrecht that very day to follow the retreat of the British army.[105]

On 16 January Utrecht capitulated to the French and when they entered the city the Patriot faction greeted them enthusiastically. The following evening, the Stadholder proffered his resignation to the States-General and the States of Holland, on the grounds that his continuing in office could be an impediment to peace; at the same time his sons resigned their military commands. The next day, 18 January, he sailed into exile in England, accompanied by his two sons. That day revolutionaries took over Amsterdam in a coup d'état. The cities of the province of Holland, with the exception of The Hague, had been the heartland of the Patriot movement and they quickly capitulated to the French; heralding the creation of the Batavian Republic, client of Republican France.[106]

The legion first concentrated on Amersfoort before marching to the Ijssel, through Barneveld and Apeldoorn. The legion's march was under the same conditions as the British, whose brigades and even regiments took separate routes, in order that the troops had some chance of shelter.[107] Tercier described it in his memoirs:

> Arrived one evening at a little town called Barneveld, we found fifteen thousand men packed into it. It was 15 January 1795. The next day we set off on the march again, through the most severe cold that I have ever experienced in my life. Several soldiers were dead on the way, above all English, who drank too much eau-de-vie. Only corpses were visible the whole length of the road. Leaving Barneveld, we made our way from eight in the morning until midnight when we arrived at Apeldoorn, … The weather had during the day turned to snow, and it fell in such quantity that we could not make out the roads. The country that we crossed is a land of moors, where we did not come across a village. There was no means to halt; we had to painfully drag ourselves to arrive dead or alive at this town …, where we hoped to obtain some succour to our many needs. But we found it so full of allied troops that it was not possible to get quarters. The legion had every difficulty to find a bad barn to take shelter from the rigour and severity of the weather. We had marched for sixteen hours. It was midnight when we arrived. We could receive no distribution of food, nor even procure some with our money; so that we remained hungry until next day at midday, when the commissariat brought some from the neighbouring villages.[108]

The retreat to the Ijssel was also recorded in British journals as being terrible due to the weather and the country that was being crossed. The Guards Brigade, marched from Lunteren on 16 January, taking a route, to the south, but parallel to that taken by the Damas Legion:

104 NAN Archieven van Willem V, A31/2136.
105 La Chanonie, *Mémoires*, p.89.
106 Schama *Patriots and Liberators*, pp.189–210.
107 Anon., *Journal*, p.163.
108 La Chanonie, *Mémoires*, pp.89–90.

> [A]fter a very tedious journey, about three o'clock in the afternoon [we] reached the verge of an immense desert, called the Welaw [Veluwe]; when, instead of having gained a resting place for the night as we expected, were informed that we had fifteen miles further to go. …
>
> For the first three or four miles such a dismal prospect appeared as none of us was ever witness to before; a bare sandy desert with a tuft of withered grass, or solitary shrub, here and there: the wind was excessive high, and drifted the snow and sand together so strong, that we could hardly wrestle against it; to which was added, a severity of cold almost insufferable. The frost was so intense, that the water which came from our eyes, freezing as it fell, hung in icicles to our eyelashes, and our breath freezing as soon as emitted, lodged in heaps of ice about our faces, and on the blankets or coats that were wrapped round our heads.[109]

Those who could not keep up, slumped to the ground and froze; at last, at 10:30 p.m., the column reached Beekbergen, south of Apeldoorn. However, the village was already occupied by Hessian troops who refused to share their quarters with the British guardsmen; the latter took what shelter they could find, 'partly by force, partly by stealth.'[110] The British army 'lived as if in an enemy country' during the retreat.[111] Lieutenant Colonel Frederick Keppel of the 88th Foot, Connaught Rangers, wrote that he was informed, 'that the plunder and outrages committed by the British in the different villages thro' which they retreated was so enormous as to stamp infamy on the name of Englishmen forever and render them odious to the Dutch.'[112]

Cavalrymen faced particular risks in the cold, as noted by a British officer:

> [T]he dragoons when on horseback for any considerable length of time were so benumbed, that they were frequently obliged to assist each other to dismount, in order by the exercise of walking, to promote the circulation of the blood in their half-perished limbs; otherwise their fingers or toes would soon, as the soldiers termed it, (as is usual with them to turn every misfortune to a jest) have been *returned missing*.[113]

One of the noble chasseurs, of the Damas cavalry, Louis de la Molliere suffered such a fate, losing his toes from a frost-bitten foot during the retreat.[114]

Some of the hardship was caused by the soldiers themselves, Tercier was not alone in remarking on British soldiers falling foul of the conditions through drunkenness, the Comte de Damas described another example of conduct that hampered the army.

109 Brown, *Corporal Brown's Campaigns*, p.156.
110 Brown, *Corporal Brown's Campaigns*, p.159.
111 Auzon de Boisminart, *Gedenkschriften*, Vol.I, p.44.
112 NRO ACC 2011/219 21 January 1795.
113 Anon., *Journal*, p 165.
114 BL Add MS 46710.

> On Sunday 18 January last, passing to Harderwijk and dining at an inn at the corner of the square where the church is, one of my people came to inform me horses were being sold very cheaply in the church, and that the master of the inn just bought one of them, I entered the church, there I found about twenty or twenty-four country horses, which the English dragoons actually sold to whoever presented themselves to buy one. There were about a dozen sold.
>
> The dragoons to whom I haggled, seeing my sash, hastened to leave and took with them the rest of the unsold horses. I did not know the cause of this rush; but I knew an hour later that the horses belonged to a convoy of eight, ten or twelve Dutch waggons (more or less) loaded with biscuits for the English army ; and when I left at 3 o'clock in the afternoon the waggons were still on the square, and could not possibly continue their journey for lack of horses.[115]

On 19 January the allies were established along the line of the Ijssel; the Légion de Damas marched north along the river, through Deventer and Zwolle, to the shores of the Zuiderzee. There the infantry was billeted for about a fortnight with the population of the small port of Blokzijl where, as Tercier noted, support for the Stadholder had not completely evaporated, 'we found good people strongly attached to the House of Orange.'[116] The Damas cavalry was quartered, along with the Légion de Béon, at nearby Vollenhove.[117]

The reception of the allied army elsewhere was not as hospitable; this, and a lack of supplies, is given as the reason that from 27 January the retreat continued towards the river Ems.[118] The legion retreated through Meppel and Coevorden to join the new position. The political situation in the provinces of the Netherlands remained patchy. At Zwolle the authorities supported the new regime, not only preventing the Loyal Emigrants from marching through the town but also threatening to resist them marching around it, whereas at Coeverdon the governor, *Generaal Major* von Drachstædt, loyal to the Prince of Orange, remained in control.[119]

115 BL Add MS 46703, letter dated Rhenen 4 February 1795.

116 La Chanonie, *Mémoires*, p.88; see also Corbehem, *Dix ans de ma vie*, p.146.

117 KHN Archieven van Stadhouder Willem V, A31/2120, Damas to the former Stadholder, 16 February 1795. Blokzijl and Vollenhove are no longer by the water side, following the creation of the Ijsselmeer and resultant land reclamation.

118 Fortescue *British Campaigns in Flanders*, p.399.

119 BL Add MS 46703, report of Colonel de Le Chastre [sic] dated 29 January 1795 regarding Zwolle; TNA WO 1/172, report of Major General Fox, 11 February 1795, regarding Coevorden.

6

Into the Service of His Britannic Majesty 1795

The British, with the German contingents, prepared to defend the German frontier, specifically the County of Bentheim, which was under Hanoverian control, and the Bishopric of Münster. The Légion de Damas joined the sector commanded by Sir Ralph Abercromby who established his headquarters, and principal position, at Bad Bentheim. His light troops manned a line of outposts to the west, over the river Dinkel, and in the Netherlands. The Damas infantry formed part of this line and was posted at Almelo, which Corbehem described as a 'large village entirely open, and which, above all on the side facing Holland, presents a fine plain, very suitable for cavalry combat.'[1] The legion's cavalry was posted in reserve behind the line.

Corbehem saw a number of minor skirmishes in front of Almelo between the opposing light cavalry. He also recounts an encounter in which a handful of the Damas infantry were also involved:

> About three quarters of a league from the village was situated, in the plain, a small village that was distinctly visible because of a slight rise in the ground, and halfway is a brook crossed by a wooden bridge. Wishing to ascertain if, as was suspected, the enemy occupied this village, a picket of light cavalry was sent to reconnoitre it. In order to protect its retreat, attached to it were a corporal and four men of my legion, who were to remain on the bridge, arrange everything to cut it and to only destroy it in case of pursuit and then after the picket had recrossed. The enemy who were in fact in force in the village saw what was taking place, and without showing themselves, quietly let our cavalry approach; but no sooner had they reached the first houses, than a strong squadron appeared and set off in pursuit chasing them back at a full gallop up to the bridge. The enemy even followed ours so closely, that there was not the time to cut the bridge. The loss of the five infantrymen thus appeared certain, but suddenly, throwing their axes and everything that could hamper them, with the exception of their muskets that they slung over their shoulders, they each grabbed with both hands the tail of a horse, and going along with

1 Corbehem, *Dix ans de ma vie*, p.147.

> the gallop of these animals, they arrived safely at the entrance to the village where we were placed in ambush: then the enemy retired and their safety was assured.[2]

In the meantime, Harcourt had begun the process of settling the status of the legion, as he described to the Duke of York:

> Before we left the Yssel [sic] and since that I received Proposals from several Corps in the Dutch Service to enter into His Majesty's, at the same time the most pressing Solicitations for an Advance of Money to relieve their present Wants. The Corps are Béon, Damas, Löwenstein and Wittgenstein.
>
> To the first Point it was impossible for me to give any Answer, till I had received Your Royal Highness's Instructions; but I thought myself justified in making Pecuniary Advances to them for the moment, had it only been with a View to prevent a number of Men without substance, or the means of procuring it, disbanding and plundering the Country; instead of which they are now doing Duty at our Out Posts ...[3]

He had provided an advance of £1,000 each for Béon, Damas and Löwenstein, of which the latter had not been issued yet, as well as £400 for Wittgenstein, which he described as 'unarmed and undisciplined, composed of Deserters from all Nations.'[4]

He also concluded a provisional capitulation with Etienne de Damas, dated 3 February, at Rheine. It provided an initial framework for the legion to enter service and receive British pay. At full strength it was to be formed of a staff, two companies of cavalry and six of infantry. The soldiers who were present were to be paid, backdated to 21 January, but officers would receive the pay, at the same rate as in the British Army, as soon as their company was at strength. In this regard Damas, prior to signing requested that consideration be made for the five officers who had been previously wounded and who would be without pay as they were not part of existing complete companies. From the wording of the capitulation, it appears there was only enough men for two complete companies and, significantly, no levy money was to be provided until a definitive capitulation was concluded.[5] On 14 February the provisional government, in Holland, announced the disbanding of the Légion de Damas and Béon along with all the other corps raised since the beginning of the conflict.[6]

On 16 February, Damas wrote to the former Stadholder, now in London, outlining what had happened to the legion in the preceding month and assuring him of its continuing loyalty. He stated that General Harcourt had provided subsistence and demanded a new

2 Corbehem, *Dix ans de ma vie*, pp.147–148; the nearest light cavalry, in British pay, were the Uhlans Britanniques, cantoned at Tubbergen, behind Almelo on the road to Neuenhaus; TNA WO 1/172, undated list but in sequence on or before 11 February 1795.

3 TNA WO 1/172, Harcourt, HQ at Rheine, to York, 11 February 1795.

4 TNA WO 1/172, Harcourt, HQ at Rheine, to York, 11 February 1795 (second letter).

5 KHN Archieven van Stadhouder Willem V A31/2124, TNA WO 1/172 and 24/1112; the last two copies appear to contain errors, that in WO 1/172 is dated 9 February and that in WO 24/1112 shows the infantry was to have 10 companies, see Appendix II.

6 *Decreeten van de Provisioneele Repræsentaten van het volk van Holland, 26 January tot 28 February 1795* (Den Haag: 1799), p.623.

capitulation to which he had provisionally agreed, having explained that he was dutybound to have the Stadholder's permission to enter into a new permanent capitulation. He finished his letter with further declarations of fidelity and confirmed that the legion retained their Dutch colours and distinctions, as he had insisted on 'keeping its colours that we have never quit'.[7]

The French had advanced towards the Ems to finally remove the allies from what was now the Batavian Republic in advance of imminent peace negotiations. The relationship between the French and Batavian Republics was, of course, never equal and was almost immediately strained when France demanded payment for the latter's liberation and the maintenance of the resident French army.[8] The Damas infantry were in action on 7 February as indicated by a brief note from Lieutenant Colonel George Churchill of the British 15th (King's) Light Dragoons, at Ootmarsum, 17 kilometres east of Almelo and on the road to Nordhorn, where the town's church was used as stables as well as housing a kitchen and hospital.[9]

> I have to inform you that the Post of [Wierden] in the Front of Amelo [sic] was forced this Evening, and that in consequence the Reg$^{t.}$ de Damas retired from Amelo this Evening. Col. Pigot of the Guards, who commands here, has reported the Circumstances to G$^{l.}$ Abercrombie [sic], and we wait his Orders. The Damas were ordered to take Post between this & Amelo.[10]

This and subsequent events were succinctly described by Bennes:

> We were very near being made prisoners at Hammelon [Almelo], and forced to retreat from the town. However, the next morning we were ordered to attack it again, and as we had no ammunition, to carry it with fixed bayonets, but the patriots had already evacuated the place, so that we entered it without any opposition. Two days after, they advanced, in order not to dislodge but to take us. They were very numerous and formed a blockade, and we must have either perished or surrendered at discretion, had it not been for the late heavy rains and melted snow, which covered part of the country, and through which we were happy enough to make our escape.[11]

A British soldier recorded that on 9 February 'a sudden thaw has set in, which lays the country afloat' and the next day, 'the thaw continuing, the river [Dinkel] rose to an amazing height' but the cold set in again on 13 February accompanied by 'a great fall of snow all this

---

7 KHN Archieven van Stadhouder Willem V, A31/2120. Béon, who was going through a parallel process and had also signed a provisional capitulation, informed the Stadhouder that his legion had retained these distinctions in a letter dated 25 February 1795 at Osnabrück, KHN Archieven van Stadhouder Willem V, A31/2124.

8 Schama, *Patriots and Liberators*, pp.189–210.

9 J. van Vloten *Bloemlezing uit de Nederlandsche Prozaschrijuers der Achttiende Euw* (Arnhem: Nijhoff, 1871), p.579.

10 TNA WO 1/172, Churchill, 7 February 1795.

11 Bennes, *Narrative*, p.33.

day.'[12] Tercier graphically describes the circumstances of what must have been the retreat from Almelo:

> We were menaced through the following day with a general attack. The thaw set in, and we hastened to leave in the night … We marched until eight o'clock in the morning, often having had water up to our waists. If we had delayed only two hours in evacuating the town, we were all taken, given the impossibility of us retiring with the sudden and unexpected appearance of so much water.
>
> Arrived in [a small town] … we rested two hours there, after which we were made to leave. We marched the whole day along dreadful and difficult paths. The rain had rendered them so bad that we sank into them knee deep while marching. Our young people, worn out with fatigue, could not drag themselves on anymore. They cried, sat down on the sides of the paths and refused to march further. Death, they said, was preferable to them to the punishment that they had endured for so long. We roused them as much as we could by our encouragement. It was only the fear of falling into the hands of the Republicans that reignited their efforts. At last, after an arduous march of twenty-four hours, we arrived at a Hanoverian village … it was midnight; we rested there for two days.[13]

It must be recognised that neither Bennes or Corbehem relate such a harrowing experience and there are a number of inconsistencies to Tercier's story, especially in chronology and location. An explanation may be that companies or detachments retreated separately and Catoire, a fusilier, recalled that, apparently during this retreat and being pursued by the enemy, a river had to be crossed by swimming.[14]

The Damas cavalry had moved up in support of the infantry passing through Ootmarsum, on their way to Almelo, on 7 February but did not take part in any action. They returned on 10 February, along with the Uhlans Britanniques, and Jacob van Loo, a resident of Ootmarsum, had two officers, apparently of the Légion de Damas, quartered in his house that day. They had with them two servants and three horses and Loo described them in very positive terms; they initially thought they would be staying some time but left that afternoon, ordered to continue their withdrawal.[15]

On 11 February the line of outposts had retracted a little behind Almelo and towards the border. The line around Ootmarsum and Oldenzaal was held by the York Rangers, Hompesch Chasseurs and infantry from the Damas, Salm and Rohan corps, along with the Salm Hussars. These units were to keep in contact with those at Neuenhaus and Losser, to their right and left respectively, their support was at Nordhorn and their line of retreat, if required, was on Denekamp.[16] It appears to be at this stage that Corbehem enjoyed hospitality offered by a local resident:

12 Brown, *Corporal Brown's Campaigns*, pp.164–165.

13 La Chanonie, *Mémoires*, p.90.

14 TNA HO 69/31, Catoire said it was the Rhine but, if it was indeed a river, it would have been the swollen Dinkel.

15 Vloten *Bloemlezing*, p.580.

16 TNA WO 1/172, dislocation dated 11 February 1795.

On leaving Almelo, we continued our retrograde movement, cutting after us all the bridges that were found on our path, and which were in great number. I recall an adventure that happened to us near one of these bridges and in which I myself played a role. Arrived a little before evening at the lodging that we were to occupy, I was ordered on duty with about twenty-five men of my legion to make a night reconnaissance. About eleven o'clock our unit arrived near a wooden bridge where one of our posts had been established and which for greater safety had raised the planks of the bridge. They were replaced on our approach and we crossed followed by a company of hussars, charged with supporting us. Arrived beyond a hamlet a short distance from the bridge, we advanced in a plain in the middle of which we were made to halt, while the cavalry went to explore. After about an hour, the cavalry returned without having seen anything. So, we were given the order to retrace our steps. We were dying of cold and hunger; as a consequence, we were allowed to stop in the houses of the hamlet. I knocked at a door with eight or ten of my comrades. The master of the house, opened and let us enter his home. Mistaking our uniform which was sky-blue with that of the Republicans, and deceived by our language, he took us for the latter, and as he no doubt belonged to the patriot party which desired the arrival of the French, he showed us all sorts of courtesies, lit a great fire and served us an excellent supper of hams and other meats, which he wetted with an abundance of beer and gin. When we were well restored and warmed, those amongst us who spoke the language of the country questioned our host about the enemy's position. He, always taking us for Republicans, told us all that he knew and described to us in a very exact manner the placement of our legion's post which was beyond the bridge. Not limiting his devotion to this simple revelation, he proposed to us to go to surprise and slaughter this post, offering to guide us himself and to carry on his back the planks needed to be able to cross this bridge. This offer was accepted joyfully by us. Our man immediately took a pile of planks on his shoulders and put himself at our head. The distance to cover was four to five hundred paces, and the night so dark, that in order to not go astray we were obliged to walk in file one after another, each holding the tails of the coat of the man in front, of whom only to the end of the bayonet could be seen. Finally, after a tiring march, carried out in the utmost silence, we arrived near the bridge; this was the critical moment for our guide. Unfortunately, the sentinel who was waiting for us and who despite our precautions heard us coming, shouted in a loud voice the regular challenge. At this shout, our guide who thought our project aborted, was seized with terror, and without waiting for our response, he hastily threw his load to the ground, saved himself at full speed and we lost him in the obscurity of the night. We regretted that this adventure ended so suddenly; not that we had the least intention of doing harm to our Dutch patriot, he had feasted us too well for that, but we would have liked to lead him to the guard room to enjoy at our leisure his embarrassment and to make a good joke of him.[17]

17 Corbehem, *Dix ans de ma vie*, pp.148–151.

The line behind Almelo was attacked on 25 February but the Légion de Damas does not appear to have been engaged. The main fighting of this, the very last stages of the campaign, took place further north. A British force, under Lord William Schaw Cathcart, which had retreated separately through the northern provinces of the Netherlands, was driven over the Ems on 3 April. This French advance prevented the British using the port of Emden and also raised the prospect that the estuaries of the Weser and the Elbe could also be closed to them. The British army was now on the east bank of the Ems from Emden to Rheine, with its headquarters at Osnabrück; Brunswick and Hanoverian troops now formed the cordon along the frontiers of Germany. Although the evacuation of British troops from the Continent was likely, since mid-February Lieutenant Popham had been reporting on the suitability of different ports for such an operation, Britain remained committed to the coalition; Harcourt, for one, did not know the British Government's intentions.[18] His army's situation became even more precarious when considerable Prussian forces arrived, ostensibly to take over the cordon line along the frontier. Prussia's loyalty to the coalition had been suspect for some time.

The Légion de Damas was, at this time, assigned cantonments in villages in Verden; the cavalry at Otersen and the infantry nearby at Wittlohe.[19] However it is likely that they did not occupy them, Corbehem for instance recalled that his company, at least, took provisional cantonments around Lingen and the Damas cavalry were shown as stationed around Meppen, in Westphalia, in early March.[20] It was at this stage, while withdrawing from the outposts on the frontier, that Catoire, by his own testimony, straggled and quit the unit; shortly afterwards he joined the Périgord Regiment at Cloppenburg, with which he served until it was disbanded.[21]

It was now that some regularity was brought to the formation and administration of the foreign units in British pay. The need for this had been identified for some time, indeed in November 1794 the Duke of York had pressed, not for the first time, for the appointment of an inspector of foreign troops, along with two deputies.[22] As the campaign unfolded the foreign troops in general were blamed for pillaging and other criminal behaviour and Wallmoden, writing to York on 19 February, vented his exasperation about them:

> I swear to Your Royal Highness that the services that they render are almost nil, the harm that they cause us is inexpressible and they will never be in order, never will they be worth something if one does not put at their head Officers of confidence, if one does not subordinate them to some special Inspector considered very strict.[23]

18 TNA WO 1/172, for example Popham to Harcourt, 13 February 1795, and Harcourt to 3York, 28 February 1795.

19 BL Add MS 46704, undated report, but apparently in March.

20 Corbehem, *Dix ans de ma vie*, p.151; *Neueste Ostfriesische Geschichte: von 1786 bis 1806*, Vol.10, N°1 p.159.

21 TNA HO 69/31.

22 TNA WO 1/171, York to Henry Dundas on 24 November 1794.

23 TNA WO 1/172, Wallmoden to York.

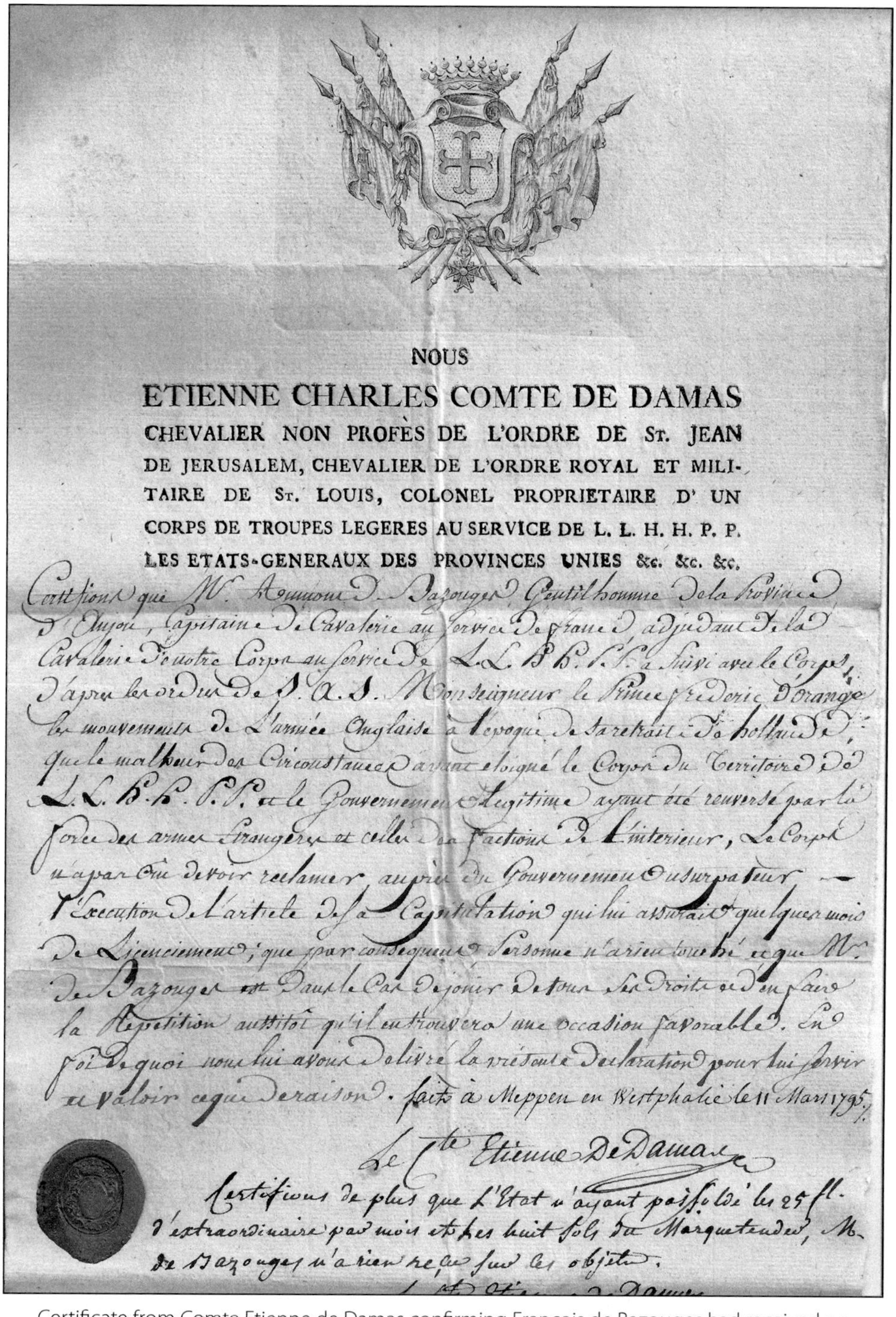

NOUS
ETIENNE CHARLES COMTE DE DAMAS
CHEVALIER NON PROFÈS DE L'ORDRE DE ST. JEAN DE JERUSALEM, CHEVALIER DE L'ORDRE ROYAL ET MILITAIRE DE ST. LOUIS, COLONEL PROPRIETAIRE D'UN CORPS DE TROUPES LEGERES AU SERVICE DE L. L. H. H. P. P. LES ETATS-GENERAUX DES PROVINCES UNIES &c. &c. &c.

Certifions que M. [illegible] de Bazouges Gentilhomme de la Province d'Anjou, Capitaine de Cavalerie au service de France, adjudant de la Cavalerie de notre Corps au service de L.L. H.H. P.P. a suivi avec le Corps, d'après les ordres de S.A.S. Monseigneur le Prince Frederic d'Orange les mouvements de l'armée Anglaise à l'époque de sa retraite de hollande; que le malheur des Circonstances ayant éloigné le Corps du Territoire de L.L. H.H. P.P. et le Gouvernement Legitime ayant été renversé par la force des armes Etrangères et celle des factions de l'interieur, Le Corps n'a pas cru devoir reclamer auprès du Gouvernement usurpateur l'Execution de l'article de sa Capitulation qui lui assurait quelques mois de Licenciement; que par consequent personne n'a rien touché et que M. de Bazouges est dans le Cas de jouir de tous ses droits et d'en faire la Repetition aussitôt qu'il en trouvera une occasion favorable. En foi de quoi nous lui avons delivré la presente declaration pour lui servir et valoir ce que de raison. faits à Meppen en Westphalie le 11 Mars 1795.

Le Cte Etienne De Damas

Certifions de plus que l'Etat n'ayant point soldé les 25 fl. d'extraordinaire par mois et les huit sols du Marquetender, M. de Bazouges n'a rien reçu sur ces objets.

Le Cte Etienne de Damas

Certificate from Comte Etienne de Damas confirming François de Bazouges had received no payment on the removal of the Légion de Damas from the service of the United Provinces, Meppen 11 March 1795. (Bazouges family archive)

In fact, Lieutenant Colonel Colebrooke Nesbitt had already been appointed to that very role on 1 January 1795 and he arrived at the army's headquarters at Osnabrück on 19 February. Reporting this to Henry Dundas, the Secretary of State for War, he assured him he would 'bring (as far as shall be within the reach of my situation) the different Corps into a state of order, economy & regularity'. He anticipated problems with some of the units' colonels, who did not follow 'the rules usually observed with officers in our service, and are very disobedient on many occasions, particularly where the order extends to their pecuniary concerns, and that they are ever attentive to take advantage of Government in all instance'.[24] Before Nesbitt's arrival Captain George Gordon had been responsible for inspecting and paying these units but had been hampered in his task by the different units' individual capitulations, their dispersal when the army was retreating and the fact that many were in the process of being raised. In the 61 days up to 23 February the foreign units, excluding those from Dutch service, had cost £29,810, Nesbitt was determined to bring this expenditure under control, or even reduce it.[25] Given his role it might be easy to caricature him as a mere petty functionary, however Nesbitt was a widely experienced and well-connected officer who had held command in the field in India during the Third Anglo-Mysore War and whose prudence and discretion was to earn him further commands from 1797. His task, as he identified, was to challenge the proprietors of the units, perhaps resulting in dispute.

He quickly set about his task and on 1 March submitted a detailed return of the foreign units in British pay. There were eight cavalry units: Uhlans Britanniques, Salm-Kyrburg Hussars, Hompesch Hussars, Rohan Hussars, Choiseul Hussars, York Hussars, Damas Chasseurs à Cheval, Béon Chasseurs à Cheval, and 11 infantry units: York Rangers, Salm-Kyrburg Light Infantry, Hompesch Chasseurs, Rohan Light Infantry, Power's Chasseurs, Périgord Light Infantry, Royal York Fuzileers, Damas Light Infantry, Béon Light Infantry, Wittgenstein Chasseurs, Löwenstein Chasseurs. They varied in size from the Salm-Kyrburg Hussars with 657 rank and file present for service, but only 400 horses, to the Hompesch Chasseurs with only 51 rank and file present, but three officers and 101 other ranks as prisoners of war. There were in all 374 officers, staff and quartermasters present and 7,744 other ranks, with 3,311 cavalry horses, as well as seven officers and 224 other ranks who were prisoners of war. The Damas and Béon Legions, infantry and cavalry, were amongst the smaller units.

Table showing the strengths of the Damas and Béon Legions, 1 March 1795

	Damas Chasseurs à Cheval	Béon Chasseurs à Cheval	Damas Infantry	Béon Infantry
Colonel	1	1	–	–
Major	1	1	–	–
Captain	1	1	2	2
Lieutenant	4	4	3	4
Ensign/Cornet	2	2	2	2
Staff	2	2	–	–

24 TNA WO 1/172, Nesbitt to Dundas, 22 February 1795.

25 TNA WO 1/172, Gordon's return, dated 1 December 1794, and account dated 23 February 1795 are attached to Nesbitt's letter of 22 February.

	Damas Chasseurs à Cheval	**Béon Chasseurs à Cheval**	**Damas Infantry**	**Béon Infantry**
Quartermaster	2	2	–	–
Sergeant	8	8	8	8
Trumpeter/ Drummer	2	2	2	2
Rank & File Present for service	163	113	173	160
R&F Sick	5	–	11	–
R&F On leave	7	–	5	–
R&F Recruiting	12	–	16	–
R&F Total	187	214*	205	216*
Horses Present in service	175	121	–	–
Horses sick	15	–	–	–
Horses Total	190	121	–	–

* The totals, for Béon, included recruits who were shown as having been passed but not yet armed or equipped, 101 in the cavalry and 56 in the infantry.

Source: BL Add MS 37872, the return gives the unit's names in French, they have been listed in English for consistency.

Nesbitt was bringing the accounting practices in line with those of the British forces. This was a somewhat drastic change, the Légion de Damas had after all been raised and commanded by French officers for the service of the United Provinces. Nesbitt took a strong line about the integrity of the numbers submitted as he noted that, 'The 40 Men returned in Damas's Corps as being on leave and recruiting will not be admitted'.There is no indication that he suspected fraud in this case, something which cannot be said of what he found in the Hompesch Hussars, a unit raised for British service. It had previously received money for 639 privates and 720 horses but Nesbitt found there to be only 459 rank and file and 481 horses.

This period was, for the members of the Légion de Damas, themselves, an opportunity to take much needed rest after the rigours of the winter. It was also a time for reflection, as described by Corbehem:

> I thought on my uncertain and precarious situation, on the calamities of my homeland, on the misfortunes of my family ... on the unparalleled triumphs of the Republicans. This last thought was one of those which occupied me the most. I could not conceive how a cause as just, as holy as that for which I fought, had been able to experience so many disasters; it appeared to me as struck with reprobation; it seemed that an irritated God rejected the sacrifices of His defenders, or that He had resolved to make them pass through the trials of a purification necessary to His justice and indispensable to the accomplishment of His impenetrable designs.[26]

26 Corbehem, *Dix ans de ma vie*, pp 152–153.

Although the campaign was now effectively over, the enemy continued to maintain pressure on the frontier and on 13 and 14 March Brunswick and Hanoverian troops, manning the cordon, were in action around Bentheim and Meppen. Since the end of February substantial numbers of Dutch army officers, as well as some soldiers, crossed the border to the allies and some of the latter were recruited into Légion de Damas.[27] Between 3 March and 11 June 1795, the Damas cavalry recruited 53 men of whom 35 came from the former army of the United Provinces:

Cavalry		
Van Tuyll van Serorskerken	13 men	All Dutch
Timmerman Hussars	8 men	4 Dutch, 2 Germans, 1 Swiss, 1 Belgian
Orange-Friesland	4 men	All German
Stavenisse Pous	1 man	Dutch
Gardes Dragonders	1 man	German
Gardes du Corps	1 man	Dutch
Orange Carabiniers	1 man	Dutch
Infantry		
Stuart	2 men	1 German, 1 Dutch
Wittgenstein	1 man	German
Waldeck	1 man	German
Horse Artillery	1 man	German

Twelve had come from French service: two Germans who had served in the Royal Deux-Ponts infantry, two Frenchmen from the Maréchaussée and eight, including a Dutchman and a German, whose unit was not specified. They had all served lengthy periods in the French army, between nine and 30 years. Finally, there were seven more, six Germans and a Belgian from Liège, who were shown without former service, most were skilled men: two farriers, two tailors and a shoemaker.[28]

The British Government eventually ordered the evacuation of its troops from the Continent. This would have to be undertaken in stages due to the numbers involved, access to ports and the availability of transports, as well as the warships to escort them. On 10 March Harcourt informed Wallmoden that he had 'positive orders' to embark the British infantry and artillery and from 15 March British transports began to arrive at Bremerlehe, now part of Bremerhaven, at the mouth of the Weser while others were sent towards the small Hanoverian port of Stade on the Elbe, downstream of Hamburg.[29] Harcourt was particularly concerned about the situation in which the British cavalry and the foreign corps in British pay would find themselves after the departure of the British infantry. So, he reorganised the British cavalry, making it more militarily effective by breaking up weak units and drafting men and horses to others, and left them some artillery support. The lack of senior officers with the army hampered his efforts, Major General David Dundas observed, when

27 TNA WO 1/172, Wallmoden to York 23 February.
28 TNA, WO 25/668, 'Recrues de remplacement du Régiment de Damas hussards', ff.62–63.
29 TNA WO 1/172, Harcourt to York 11 March 1795, and BL Add MS 46704.

writing to Henry Dundas, his distant familial relationship perhaps allowing him to be more candid than others: 'The Disorganization (as is the modern word) of this Army is without example' there were five brigades but only one general officer the 'next in command in the Corps, a Lt Col of 2 years' standing'.[30] Cathcart was appointed to command all the British cavalry and émigrés but on 22 March Harcourt reported that the emigrant corps needed brigadiers, writing, 'I am sorry to observe that notwithstanding the exertions used by Col. Nesbitt and myself the Excess and Insubordination still subsist in the Foreign Light Corps.' He took the immediate step of appointing Comte Charles de Sombreuil 'to restore order in the [Foreign] Depot.'[31]

Charles Eugène Gabriel de Virot de Sombreuil, born in 1770, after a military education, was appointed supernumerary *capitaine* in the Hussards d'Esterhazy in 1789. The next year he entered Prussian service, then that of Russia, and he served with Brunswick's army in the 1792 campaign. In February 1793 he was appointed *capitaine* in the Salm-Kyrburg Hussars, raised by Prince Moritz Gustaf Adolf von Salm-Kyrburg, former colonel commanding the Hussards d'Esterhazy; the regiment served with the Armée de Condé until it entered British pay on 22 October 1793. Despite his appointment Sombreuil was retained in Prussian service until the spring of 1794. On 17 June 1794, in Paris, his father and brother were both guillotined and his sister, 'Marie-Maurille', was the heroine of the tale, in which, whether fact or myth, she had to drink a glass of human blood to gain her father's life: she did so but only gained a temporary reprieve of his execution.[32] Sombreuil arrived to command the Salm Hussars in the final stages of the campaign in the Netherlands and he quickly gained admiration from the British as a trusted outpost commander.

Concern about the motives of Prussia, nominally still an ally and demanding to be treated as such by the British, continued to grow. Prussian troops had replaced the British at Emden and then abandoned the city without notice. On 22 March, Harcourt wrote that Prussia wanted its territories clear of British forces; he wondered 'how far it may be safe to leave the British Cavalry in a Country where they may fall a Sacrifice to the Duplicity of a perfidious Ally.'[33] His suspicions were well founded as, for many months, Prussia had been secretly negotiating a separate peace with Republican France which was concluded by the First Peace of Basel of 5 April 1795. Given the situation Harcourt decided to secure the evacuation by occupying Bremen where the Foot Guards, along with the artillery and ordnance, would embark. The rest of the British infantry were to leave from Bremerlehe, further north on the Weser; Stade, nearby on the Elbe, was to be the embarkation point for the foreign units.[34]

At this time the Damas infantry were around Diepholz, north east of Osnabrück, where a return, dated 25 March, was prepared in anticipation for its expected embarkation. Present were two captains, five subalterns and staff, eight quartermasters and sergeants with 186 drummers and rank and file; they were accompanied by 12 women.[35]

30 TNA WO 1/172 D. Dundas to H. Dundas 9 March 1795; despite the surname it was through DaviD. Dundas's mother's family that Henry was his half cousin (ODNB).
31 TNA WO 1/1/72 Harcourt to York 22 March 1795.
32 Bittard des Portes, *Les émigrés*, p.87.
33 TNA WO 1/172 Harcourt to York 22 March 1795.
34 TNA WO 1/172 Harcourt to York 28 March 1795.
35 BL Add MS 46710.

Nesbitt was still busy with the organisation, recruitment and discipline of the foreign corps; most of his time and efforts was expended on the newly-raised units, mainly of German recruits. However, he had also to negotiate a definitive capitulation with Etienne de Damas-Crux for the transfer of both his infantry and cavalry to British service. The main areas of contention involved financial issues but one, that was shared with Béon, was the oath that the British demanded the officers and men in their pay take. Despite both colonels being without any instructions from the Stadholder, they raised difficulties, jealous of their units' status as being of French émigrés who had sworn to serve the United Provinces and the House of Orange. On 31 March, Nesbitt, wrote to the adjutant general, Colonel George Don, and shared the problems he was having with the 'Dutch corps' which 'all shew [sic] a great disinclination to taking the oath of fidelity'; he did not expect that any more than 1,100 of them would embark. Clearly frustrated, he continued:

> I met Col Damas on the road on his way to annoy the General & torment me – he stopped me – I told him in very few words that one of the last questions I had put to the General was concerning the oath his people were to take, and that it would be insisted on whether they were embarked or not – I hope General Harcourt will not be led by anything he may say to alter his opinion – it is to be sure for redirection – a man at the head of a few Cavalry & a weak body of Infantry, to be attempting to balk in the way he does ...[36]

Nesbitt left the following day for Celle, where the foreign units were being massed prior to embarkation.[37] His task was far from easy, amongst the troops there was a great deal of suspicion and concern about where they were to be sent and crimps, who circled the depot, added to the unease in order to attract the men to Austrian or Prussian service. Wittgenstein's Chasseurs mutinied, refusing to embark; Nesbitt immediately disbanded the regiment:

> [T]he whole of the business was conducted with firmness & temper – & Colonel Sombreuil was on every occasion extremely alert and indefatigable not only in his conduct to the Officers of the Corps – for the men were not to blame, but in taking the necessary consequences to guard against any opposition on their parts ...[38]

Most of Wittgenstein's men were quickly drafted into the Salm infantry.

Although delayed by the mutiny, the first division of infantry, which included the Béon infantry, marched to Stade under Sombreuil's command on 4 April, Nesbitt retaining Löwenstein's Chasseurs at Celle, to protect the town from the remnants of Wittgenstein's corps. On the march to the coast, problems continued as the column was plagued by crimps not only working for other countries but also for other foreign corps in British pay, for example, trying to persuade men to desert an infantry unit to join a hussar regiment. The division reached Stade where on 8 April they were allocated quarters in the town.[39]

36 BL Add MS 46704.
37 TNA WO 1/172 Harcourt to York 2 April 1795.
38 BL Add MS 46704 Nesbitt to Don 3 and 6 April 1795.
39 BL Add MS 46704 6 and 8 April 1795.

Despite the distractions, Nesbitt concluded a definitive capitulation with the Comte de Damas on 2 April at Celle. The composition of the units remained as they were in the provisional capitulation but, despite there only being two infantry companies, a small staff was added to this arm as it was expected to embark imminently.[40] That the negotiations had not been easy is indicated by the details of the capitulation and also Nesbitt's report of 3 April when he wrote:

> I have not thought it expedient to press the taking of the oath on any of the Dutch Corps – but have told Colonels Beon [sic] & Damas that the ceremony must be gone through before the Corps can embark, much less land in England – they have consented to contrive the matter & reconcile it to their Men during the march – I have found it necessary with these Corps, as the Men must be enlisted for our service, to say they shall have 3 ½ Guineas for every Man whom they brought out of Holland – but that more cannot be given. The whole has long turned upon their circumstance, and I am rather inclined to think they will not accept it, in hopes of getting more on their arrival in England – nor can I by any argument convince them that they have no right to expect to be allowed the same as has been given to Salm & Rohan's Corps, who they say, were brought from another service, like themselves – Damas is extremely greedy after money.[41]

Salm and Rohan had signed their capitulations in early 1794, when their original corps had served with the Armée de Condé. Another area of contention was that Damas wanted the British to pay for the legion's horses and arms.

Both he and Béon appear to have wanted to press their claims, despite both signing capitulations, as they requested, in the first days of April, leave to go to England but their plans were frustrated when Harcourt instructed Nesbitt that both were to remain with their 'Corps of Cavalry' at Celle.[42] Nevertheless Damas persisted, writing, on 23 April, to the Stadholder, in England, asking him to provide him with title to the horses and arms. The grounds he gave for demanding the payment, and the request for the title, was that they were the property of Holland and the legion's possession of them indemnified the officers and men for the pay and allowances that they were owed by their former paymasters. Damas specifically mentioned that they were owed pay as well as the three months' advance due on the legion being disbanded. He apparently did not get satisfaction from the Stadholder or Nesbitt; all the capitulations the British signed with officers proposing to raise foreign units required the latter to provide not only the men but also their equipment and horses.[43] Although he had to leave it, Damas returned to this matter, claiming levy money for 355 men and horses, in 1802, apparently with the same result.[44]

There is no record of Harcourt's reason for specifying that both Damas and Béon remain with their cavalry rather than infantry, especially as the émigré and foreign infantry, in

40 TNA WO 24/1112, see Appendix II.
41 BL Add MS 46704 Nesbitt to Don 3 April 1795.
42 BL Add MS 46704 Nesbitt to Don 4 April 1795 annotated with Harcourt's instructions.
43 KHN Archieven van Stadhouder Willem V, A31/2120.
44 TNA WO 4/381, July and November 1802.

general, was short of senior officers. However, it is very likely that he was aware of the objections they would have had to serving under Sombreuil, having been much more senior to him in the former French army, and that these sensibilities would have been insurmountable.

Meanwhile Sombreuil returned to Celle to bring the rest of the infantry, including that of Damas, to the Elbe. The French *Gazette Nationale ou Le Moniteur Universel* of 10 Florèal an III (29 April 1795), perhaps gleefully, published a report from a German newspaper, dated 8 April:

> The émigrés in the pay of England have attracted on themselves the execration of all the lands where they stayed. At Celle, and in the surrounding area where their quarters were, they have seen several times the militia forced to march to repress their excesses. The Légion de Damas appears the only of which the most bitter complaints have not been made.

This time the march was very different to that of the first division. On 11 April, when Sombreuil wrote from Harburg that he expected to arrive at Stade two days later, he was able to report that there had been no desertions and morale was good. He ascribed the latter to the expectation the émigrés had that they would soon be fighting in their own country. The news of a planned expedition to France was now known. However, there were no transports in the Elbe when they arrived at Stade on 14 April.[45] That same day, the British infantry, including the Loyal Emigrants, embarked at Bremerlehe for England.

Another fleet, which was to sail from Hull on the East Coast of England, was to collect the troops at Stade but, in the meantime, Harcourt was ordered to halt the embarkation of the foreign troops. He referred to it on 18 April, before, he in turn, left for England.[46] Although no explicit reason for this decision is given, it came at a time when the transport service was particularly overstretched facing multiple and competing demands. In the first months of 1795 not only did troops need to be collected from Northern Europe, there were existing commitments such as on Corsica and in the West Indies as well as a pressing need to secure the Dutch colonies, particularly the Cape of Good Hope and Sri Lanka. These two colonies, given their key positions on the trade routes, would imperil British interests in India should they fall under French domination after the creation of the Batavian Republic. These theatres also required naval protection and all the while Britain needed to regularly re-supply its military and naval forces across the globe, on campaign and at sea.[47]

The command of the British contingent still in Germany now devolved to Major General David Dundas while Cathcart remained in command of the cavalry. Their position worsened as the peace between France and Prussia took hold and these countries now dictated the direction and pace of events; the Ems was declared to be a 'neutral boundary' and all the cavalry in British pay were expected to withdraw to the counties of Oldenburg and Delmenhorst, near Bremen.[48]

45 BL Add MS 46704 Sombreuil to Harcourt, 11 April 1795, and to Don on 14 April.
46 TNA WO 1/172, Harcourt to York, 5 and 18 April 1795.
47 See Roger Knight, *Britain Against Napoleon: The Organization of Victory 1793–1815* (London: Allen Lane, 2013), pp.153–210.
48 TNA WO 1/173 D. Dundas to York 25 April and to H. Dundas 2 May 1795.

Although problems continued in the formation and discipline of the foreign cavalry units, on 23 April Nesbitt was able to report that at Stade the infantry units were 'very Healthy, perfectly quiet & most with no desertion'.[49] It would appear that it was on this visit that the Damas and Béon infantry took the oath of allegiance, in the presence of their colonels, as Damas in a letter of the same date informed the Stadholder that they had done so.[50] Corbehem described the event:

> It was not long before we were subject to a general review by the English Colonel Nesbitt … During this review, a Lutheran minister passed along our ranks made us swear, on a fat book which he said was the Gospel, the oath to never bear arms against England, the House of Orange or that of Bourbon. I was astonished that Catholics were made to take such an oath on a heretical book to their eyes; but since I have reflected that the heresy is only in the interpretation and not in the text of this sacred book.[51]

Soon, in preparation for deployment, instructions were issued for the Damas infantry, along with that of Salm, Rohan, Béon and Löwenstein, to be 'completed' to a strength of 800 men, excluding officers, however, it was to fall far short of this aspiration.[52] Despite the preparations, the delay at Stade gave the officers and men time to enjoy some rest and social interaction, so on the birthday 'of the King of England, George III, all the officers of the French corps gave a superb festivity at Stade, to which were invited all the most distinguished persons of the Electorate of Hanover'.[53]

On 3 June Dundas received the order for the immediate embarkation of the five infantry units of Damas, Béon, Rohan, Salm and Périgord. Nesbitt travelled to Stade to oversee the final arrangements, including carrying out a final review, and Popham sent a division of nine transports to the port.[54] They arrived in the Elbe in mid-June and it took about a week for the troops to embark, the officer commanding the convoy was Captain Lawrence William Halsted, of HMS *Venus*. The division required seven ships for the 76 officer and 1,227 men and a further one for horses, the Damas infantry was allocated the *Silver Eel*, 374 tons, and was shown, on 17 June 1795, with sixteen officers and 200 other ranks.[55] The final return, signed by Nesbitt and dated 20 June, however showed less men, the result of 'the desertion that had taken place at the time of the embarkation.'[56]

The Damas infantry, now referred to as the Régiment de Damas, left Germany, on the *Silver Eel*, with 14 officers: a lieutenant colonel, two captains, four lieutenants, two ensigns,

49 BL Add MS 46704 Nesbitt to Don 23 April 1795.

50 KHN Archieven van Stadhouder Willem V, A31/2120, Damas to Stadholder, and A31/2124, Béon to Stadholder, 24 April, neither are explicit about when this happened.

51 Corbehem, *Dix ans de ma vie*, p.155.

52 BL Add MS 46711, letter from C. Crawford 6 May 1795.

53 La Chanonie, *Mémoires*, p.92.

54 TNA WO 1/173 D. Dundas to H. Dundas 4 June 1795 in it he acknowledges receipt of despatches dated 23 and 26 May, as only eight transports were required the ninth was sent to Bremerlehe to collect other French émigrés including civilians.

55 TNA ADM 1/1913.

56 Corbehem, *Dix ans de ma vie*, p.170.

three supplementary officers, a chaplain, an aide surgeon and 174 other ranks: 12 sergeants, three drummers, 159 rank and file along with six women and three children; its three horses were on board the *Kingston*.[57] Despite the intention to strengthen it, the unit sailed with only two companies, one of chasseurs and the other of fusiliers, as well as a reduced staff reflecting that envisaged in the capitulation. The officers were:

Staff	
Lieutenant Colonel	Charles Comte de Rouault de Gamache, with the appointments of a major reflecting the reduced staff for the two companies in compliance with the capitulation
Adjutant	Charles de Lavenne, with rank of ensign
Quartermaster	Jean-Baptiste Ducrozet, with rank of ensign, only a quartermaster sergeant was provided in the capitulation for the two companies
Surgeon	Urbain-Claude Vimar, as only an aide surgeon was provided in the capitulation and the same rank is given in the return of 20 June, Vimar, although a surgeon, would seem to have been serving with the appointments of an aide surgeon
Chaplain	*Abbé* Pierre-André-Wulfrand Langlois de La Heuse (or Heuze), as no such post was provided for in the capitulation for the two companies, it would appear he was serving on a voluntary basis
Chasseur Company	
Captain	Jean de Borassol
Lieutenants	Hugues Burgault de Montfort
	Alexis Chevalier de Chasteigner de Lagrange
Ensign	Claude de Tercier
Fusilier Company	
Captain	Louis d'Hébert de Boulon
Lieutenants	Joseph de Savignac
	Antoine Comte de Cardon de Vidampierre
Ensign	Thomas de Pressac

Two of the supplementary officers, in the return of 20 June, would have been Charles de Lavenne and Jean-Baptiste Ducrozet, respectively adjutant and quartermaster. Subsequent events show that the third was Jean-Louis-Alexis de Villeneuve-Laroche-Barnaud, formerly in the service of the United Provinces as an officer on the Bedaulx Infantry Regiment. His younger brother, Louis-Gabriel, serving in the same regiment, had witnessed the killing of the émigrés after the surrender of 's Hertogenbosch and was now an officer in the Régiment de Périgord.[58]

Finally, the transports dropped down the estuary to Cuxhaven from where, on 29 June, the wind having turned fair, they set sail escorted by the frigates HMS *Venus* and *Leda* and the ship sloop HMS *Lark*.[59] The troops on board were to join, as a second division, the

57 BL Add MS 46710.

58 AMC, Fonds Grouvel, Dossier "Légion de Damas", Hand written note by Vicomte Grouvel; Villeneuve-Laroche-Barnaud, *Mémoires sur l'expédition de Quiberon*, Part II, pp.142–143.

59 TNA ADM 1/1913 Halsted to Evan Nepean at the Admiralty, 4 July.

émigré troops that had landed in south eastern Brittany, however, they were already much later than had originally been planned. The convoy arrived at the Downs, off the Kent coast, late on 3 July and continued on to Portsmouth where it anchored at Spithead, the roadstead just outside the entrance to the harbour, at 7:00 p.m. two days later. The voyage had passed without any mishap for most of the Régiment de Damas, although Bennes was 'very ill with a putrid fever.'[60] The men on board the *Silver Eel*, which only carried the two Damas companies, had sufficient space as, at 374 tons, it was designated to carry a maximum of 249 troops on such a voyage.[61]

As his crew had not been paid since April, Captain Halsted had hoped to have three or four days at Portsmouth, however the Admiralty regarded his current service of 'so pressing a nature' that his instructions, which he received at 9:00 p.m. on 7 July, were to take on the necessary water and provisions and 'proceed ... without a moment's delay.'[62] The Admiralty was pressing urgency because the news of the émigrés' successful landing in Morbihan Bay had reached London in the evening of 5 July, the very same evening as the convoy, with the Damas infantry, had anchored at Spithead.[63]

The following day, 8 July, Halsted acknowledged receipt of his orders and reported that he, and the transports, would have sailed that morning but the loading of the ships with ordnance stores, which were to join his convoy, was yet to be completed.[64] The delay enabled the Damas officers to visit Portsmouth where they met some highlanders, presumably of the 78th Foot, with whom they had served in the Netherlands, Tercier recalled that, 'They showed much pleasure to see their brothers in arms again'.[65] The other ranks remained onboard where as Corbehem observed, they 'could at least contemplate at leisure the tableau of the immense maritime power of the English... Nearly sixty vessels of the line found gathered then in the Portsmouth roadstead.'[66]

Sombreuil, who had sailed separately from Stade to receive his instructions in London, had been ordered to join his division at Portsmouth without delay. He left immediately, not even delaying to marry, as planned; the evening he arrived at Portsmouth he came out to the *Silver Eel* and dined with the Comte de Rouault-Gamache and the other officers of the Régiment de Damas.[67]

With new orders to leave any ordnance vessel behind that was not ready, Halsted wrote, in the evening of 10 July, from Spithead:

60 Bennes, *Narrative*, p.35.

61 The capacity was calculated on the simple ratio of one soldier per one and a half tons for a voyage to the Continent or Gibraltar; it was 1:2 tons for troops sailing to a hot climate (Knight, *Britain Against Napoleon*, p.182).

62 TNA ADM 1/1913 Captain Halsted to Evan Nepean on 4 and 6 July 1795; ADM 1/1011 Admiral Parker to Nepean 7 July 1795.

63 Maurice Hutt, *Chouannerie and Counter-Revolution: Puisaye, the Princes and the British Government in the 1790s* (Cambridge: Cambridge University Press, 1983), Vol.II, p.278.

64 TNA ADM 1/1913 Halsted to Nepean on 8 July 1795.

65 La Chanonie, *Mémoires*, p.95.

66 Corbehem, *Dix ans de ma vie*, p.156.

67 Bittard des Portes, *Les émigrés*, pp.473–475; La Chanonie, *Mémoires*, p.105.

> The vessels with Ordnance stores being all ready this evening except the Grenville, which will not be ready before tomorrow evening, I intend sailing tomorrow at daylight, leaving her behind, with the hope, from the wish of their Lordships that I should get away as soon as possible, it may meet with their approbation.[68]

The next day, at 3:30 a.m., he reported that the convoy, the transports and six ordnance vessels, was putting to sea, the *Grenville* being left behind.[69] Again the voyage was uneventful, with light winds at best and in the evening of 15 July the convoy anchored in Quiberon Bay off the south east coast of Brittany.

Its arrival came at a key moment for the expedition, which had seen émigré troops landing on beaches at Carnac, in Quiberon Bay, on 27 June 1795 to be joyfully greeted by thousands. It was intended to support ongoing insurrections in Western France, in the Vendée and Brittany, where opposition to the enforcement of the *levée en masse* and the persecution of the clergy had coalesced with local grievances and tensions. The civil war that had ensued took broadly different forms: in Brittany, where it was known as the chouannerie, it mainly consisted of guerrilla actions by small local bands whereas the Vendéans, at least at first, engaged in open warfare in substantial, but inadequately equipped, numbers. The allies and, especially, French royalists saw these insurrections as a means to bring down Republican France from within and such an intervention had often been considered.

In Britain, the plans coalesced around Joseph de Puisaye. Before the Revolution he had risen, through family connections, to the rank of *lieutenant-colonel* in the French army, without active service or even a command at any level. In 1789 he was a deputy to the States-General for the nobility of his native province of Perche and had supported the development of a constitutional monarchy. He left the assembly in 1791 and involved himself in the raising of the National Guard in Normandy before joining, in the summer of 1793, an army formed in that province to oppose Robespierre's regime. When the army marched on Paris, Puisaye commanded the vanguard which was routed at the so-called Battle of Brécourt on 13 July. The army melted away and Puisaye took refuge in Brittany with a band of chouans in the Forest of Paimpont, west of Rennes. He soon established himself as a leading figure of the chouannerie through the development of a network that linked, and sought to give central direction to, the local bands. Finally, in September 1794, he travelled to London to press for Britain to support the chouans and intervene in Western France.[70]

There Puisaye built on the perception of leadership he had created and used his charm, energy and enthusiasm to gain the ear of influential government ministers. He submitted ambitious plans for a British landing on the north coast of Brittany, although these were rejected, he had arrived at an opportune moment. His proposal was attractive as the British Government wanted to divert French Republican attention from Germany but military resources were just not available at that time. He was not without opponents, despite his activity in furthering the royalist cause, he was distrusted, or worse, by the courtiers who surrounded the French Princes in exile as he had supported a constitutional monarchy and his ready co-operation with Britain only added to their prejudices.

68 TNA ADM 1/1913 Halsted to Nepean 10 July 1795.
69 TNA ADM 1/1913 Halsted to Nepean 11 July 1795.
70 Hutt, *Chouannerie and Counter-Revolution*, pp.23–97.

Finally, a division of four émigré infantry regiments was gathered in Southern England for the expedition. One was the Loyal Emigrants which had not had time to recover its numbers since arriving in England. The other three were newly raised and distinct from all other émigré and foreign units in British pay, which wore the black cockade of that service. They were raised under the authority of an Act of Parliament of 9 May 1794 which envisaged the formation of regiments modelled on the former French army and under the colonelcies of distinguished French émigré generals which would wear the French royal white cockade.[71] There was no difficulty in attracting suitable officers, and young gentlemen as volunteers, to these regiments, but by this stage of the war the only ready supply of Frenchmen for the ranks were deserters and prisoners of war. The Régiment d'Hervilly provided the largest element of the expedition, amongst its men were a considerable number from the Régiment Royal Louis, which had been raised and fought with distinction at Toulon, and as a result the regiment was often referred to by the latter name. Louis Charles Le Cat Comte d'Hervilly, the regiment's colonel, was firmly attached to the royalist cause, having remained with the King until after the taking of the Tuileries Palace and was to command the regular troops of the expedition's First Division. The Régiment d'Hector only had four companies, one of grenadiers, two of fusiliers and one formed of volunteers. All the officers had formerly served as such in the French Royal Navy and thus an alternative name for the regiment was the Marine Royale. Finally, the Régiment du Dresnay had strong links with Brittany with officers from the province and its recruits, many from prisoners of war held in England, were also principally Bretons. In addition to the infantry there was a half-battalion of the French Emigrant Artillery, under *Lieutenant-colonel* Pierre-Alexis Comte de Rotalier, which also contained many men who had previously fought against the republicans at Toulon, as well as around ten French engineer officers.

Immediately the émigrés had landed arms were distributed among the chouans and other Bretons who arrived to join the royalist cause and they were sent, on 28 June, to establish a defensive line, running from the area of Auray to Landévant. As early as 29 June, Captain Sir John Borlase Warren, who had commanded the convoy and remained with his squadron to support operations, wrote to England, 'I must … state that the number of regular troops are too small'.[72] There were less than 3,500 men, of all ranks, with the infantry, artillery and engineers, of which 1,442 were in the Régiment d'Hervilly. The other infantry regiments had a disproportionate number of volunteers, cadets and NCOs who were intended to provide leadership with the Bretons.[73]

The landing had initially caused panic amongst the French republicans in the immediate vicinity but *Général de Division* Louis-Lazare Hoche soon arrived to restore the situation, concentrating his forces and by 30 June Auray and Landévant had been recaptured. The royalists needed a bridgehead for their stores and hospital as well as a safe area in which

71 'An Act to enable Subjects of France to enlist as Soldiers in Regiments to serve on the Continent of Europe … and to enable His Majesty to grant Commissions to Subjects of France, to serve and receive Pay as Officers in such Regiments, or as Engineers …'

72 Julian S. Corbett (ed.), *Private Papers of George, Second Earl Spencer, First Lord of the Admiralty 1794–1801* (London: Navy Records Society, 1913), Vol.I p.79, Warren to Spencer 29 June.

73 TNA ADM 80/136, also WO 12/11708, 12/11741, 12/11681, 10/281, 1/388 and 12/11732 with BL Add MS 46710.

to equip and train the chouans, a port was essential for communication with, and support from, Britain.[74] The adjacent Quiberon peninsula appeared to offer the solution, its east coast having two small harbours, Port Haliguen, to the south, which was protected by a small coastal battery called Fort Neuf, and Port d'Orange at Saint Pierre-Quiberon, further to the north. The peninsula is, in effect, an island connected to the mainland by a low-lying, sandy isthmus stretching from a low escarpment on the mainland and, to the south, the Palice headland on which stands Fort Penthièvre, described at the time as 'an irregular polygon, covered, on the mainland side, by advanced works', that blocked access to the access to the peninsula.[75]

Quiberon peninsula was attacked on the morning of 3 July and after some brief negotiations Fort Penthièvre surrendered. About 400 to 500 republican soldiers at the fort, and perhaps a hundred more elsewhere on the peninsula, were taken prisoner; the majority enlisted in the regular émigré units, particularly the Régiment d'Hervilly.[76] Hoche, now with 13,000 men, again attacked the defensive perimeter on 4 July and it collapsed, the chouan defenders taking refuge on the peninsula. He then established himself at Sainte-Barbe, just north of the point where the connecting isthmus joined the mainland, and on 7 July his position was secured by the retaking of Carnac. That day Hoche declared that his enemies were, 'like rats, trapped in Quiberon, where the army keeps them confined.'[77] Nevertheless, the royalists were not passive as they carried out limited probing attacks, directed by Hervilly, on the Sainte-Barbe lines in the early mornings of 7 and 11 July. On 14 July news of the imminent arrival of Sombreuil's division reached Quiberon. The next day the transports dropped anchor offshore, in the bay, the last arriving around 11:00 p.m. and 'the shout of *Vive le Roi*, repeated three times, rose at the same instant, from all the ships of the convoy'.[78] Sombreuil immediately landed to confer with Puisaye, the troops of his division remaining onboard. Hervilly had planned an attack on the lines of Sainte-Barbe for the early hours of 16 July and, despite the arrival of the reinforcements, it was not postponed.

The plan involved columns of émigré troops and chouans advancing north, along the isthmus, to attack the western end of the republican lines. At 3:30 a.m. Puisaye gave the order to advance; Hervilly commanded the attack columns while Puisaye accompanied them, along with Sombreuil. The advancing columns drove in some forward positions and continued to vigorously attack the lines under sustained artillery and musketry fire, but mounting losses forced Hervilly to order the retreat. Just as he had done so he was seriously wounded and Puisaye instructed Sombreuil to command the withdrawal; 730 émigrés and chouans were killed or wounded of whom 'six hundred and sixteen ... remained on the field of battle.'[79]

74 TNA ADM 80/136.

75 Villeneuve-Laroche-Barnaud, *Mémoires sur l'expédition de Quiberon*, Part II, p.24.

76 TNA WO 12/11708 and 11681, PRO 30/11/225 and ADM 80/136.

77 Hoche to Chérin, 7 July, quoted in Patrick Huchet, *1795 – Quiberon ou le destin de La France* (Rennes: Ouest-France, 1995), p.99.

78 Villeneuve-Laroche-Barnaud, *Mémoires sur l'expédition de Quiberon*, Part I p.234 also see TNA WO 1/390, La Jaille to Dundas 18 July.

79 TNA ADM 80/136 and Jacques Scevola Cazotte *Témoignage d'un Royaliste* (Paris: Le Clere, 1839), p.231.

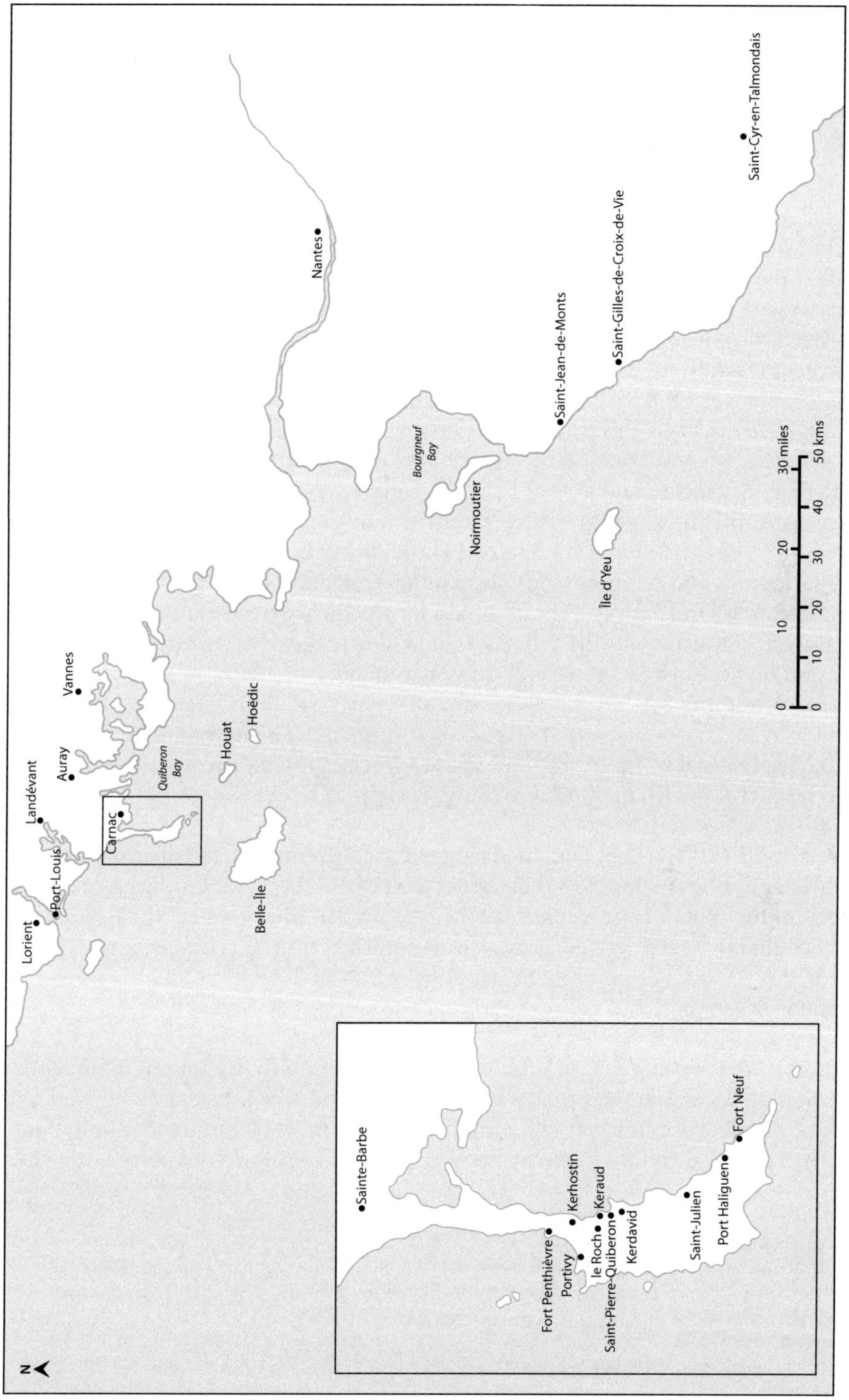

The Quiberon Expedition.

The Second Division remained on board the transports, without either news or orders to land, witness to the sight and sound of a battle that drew nearer as the morning progressed before finally dying away. At about 9:00 a.m. orders were received for the division's surgeons to land, with their equipment, to help treat the wounded who had managed to get away; those left on the field of battle were killed on the spot by the republicans. One of those who had been evacuated was Hervilly, his stomach wounded by a cannon shot; he hung on to die, in London, on 14 November. It was only at night when the surgeons and Sombreuil returned to the division that the full picture of what had occurred began to emerge.[80]

The next day, 17 July, the division started to land at Port d'Orange, the operation was undertaken with no urgency and the Régiment de Damas disembarked around midday on 18 July. The new arrivals were not greeted by Puisaye or even a senior member of his staff; the only officers present were those giving directions to where the troops were to be quartered. However Tercier remembered that, 'The good Bretons greeted us with joy; they embraced us and thanked us for coming to the aid of their land and their religion.'[81] As the men had no tents, the Second Division was distributed in the south of the peninsula, Corbehem recalling that, 'My legion and that of Béon were placed in a little hamlet dependent on the village of Saint-Julien, where we were crammed into the huts of the poor fishermen who inhabited it.'[82] The First Division remained at the fort and in hamlets at the northern end while the chouans, and refugees from the mainland, were between them

Only Sombreuil and Puisaye, the commander in chief, were commissioned as generals by the British Government. The latter was now determined to strengthen his control of the army so he declined to place both divisions under Sombreuil, retaining command of the First Division himself.[83] Whatever his faults may have been, Hervilly's conscientious application to military duty was sorely missed, measures for defence were neglected and discipline became slack. The defeat had severely rocked morale as described by an officer who had just arrived with the Rohan artillery detachment:

> This corps [First Division] remained plunged in consternation and discouragement, after having been exposed to dangers so fruitlessly. The news produced the same effect on the spirit of our soldiers: as their hopes had been exalted, their despondency could not be moderated; they were vanquished from this day.[84]

Corbehem recalled that:

> [M]ilitary duty was neglected, or to put it better totally forgotten. Sombreuil's division alone maintained that warlike attitude and strict discipline by which it was so highly distinguished in Germany… The hero who commanded it had too much experience and too perfect a knowledge of his calling, to not perceive to what

80 Villeneuve-Laroche-Barnaud, *Mémoires sur l'expédition de Quiberon*, Part I pp.236–239.

81 La Chanonie, *Mémoires*, p.106; see also Bennes, *Narrative*, p.35 and TNA ADM 80/136.

82 Corbehem, *Dix ans de ma vie*, p.160.

83 Bittard des Portes, *Les émigrés*, pp.515–528.

84 Joseph de Montbron, *Récit de l'Evasion d'un Officier pris à Quiberon* (Paris: Unknown Publisher, 1815), p.5.

> extent the lack of organisation in this ill-formed gathering of men, strangers to one another became harmful to the common cause ...[85]

The Régiment d'Hervilly remained in the garrison of Fort Penthièvre, which not only guarded access to the peninsula but also held most of the royalists' artillery, military stores and ammunition. The decline of morale and lack of attention to discipline soon manifested itself by renewed and increased desertion, especially amongst those with the flimsiest reasons for loyalty, the republicans recruited only a fortnight ago. On 17 July, a sergeant and four fusiliers deserted and, overnight 18/19 July, they were followed by two sergeants and 30 fusiliers.[86] Two of the sergeants, Nicolas Litté and Antoine Mauvage, both of whom had been recruited on 4 July, were interviewed by Hoche and they described their escape route which they recommended as the way to take the fort, offering to guide an attack themselves. They had got over the parapet to clamber down the west face of the cliff onto the beach and then avoided the attention of the patrols, by wading through the sea along the shore.[87]

Sombreuil proposed that the divisions exchange roles, and quarters, so that the Second garrisoned the fort and the First moved to the south of the peninsula, but Puisaye settled on a compromise which made things worse.[88] The Second Division was to send a detachment to join the guard at the fort for each tour of duty; thus, the risks Sombreuil hoped to mitigate remained whilst his own division was weakened. Tercier performed such a tour of duty:

> On 19 July, I mounted guard at Fort Penthièvre with four hundred men drawn from different corps. I distributed my posts in the manner that I thought the most suitable for the security of the army. I ordered the greatest watchfulness and a great attention in this duty. ... Throughout the night, I had patrols carried out one after the other. I held half of my unit awake. I did not allow myself any rest, constantly having an ear open to the sounds and eyes fixed on the seashore for fear of a surprise. All was quiet, that night. After the sun rose, I was able to take a few moments sleep on the platform of a battery. ... I stood down from the guard of the fort the next day, 20 July, at midday.[89]

Corbehem illustrated how the units were distributed during such a duty when he described a post at the fort being allocated to a Damas corporal and four soldiers, two from his unit and two more from Périgord. The reason for him recalling this particular occasion was that one of the Périgord soldiers was a young volunteer named César-René Comte de Choiseul-Praslin and the Damas corporal had previously been a *marmiton*, cook's boy, in his family's household.[90]

85 Corbehem, *Dix ans de ma vie*, p.162.
86 TNA WO 12/11681.
87 TNA WO 12/11681.
88 Villeneuve-Laroche-Barnaud, *Mémoires sur l'expédition de Quiberon*, Part II, p.109; Corbehem, *Dix ans de ma vie*, pp.162–163.
89 La Chanonie, *Mémoires*, pp.107–108.
90 Corbehem, *Dix ans de ma vie*, pp.163–164.

Very few cartridges were issued amongst the Second Division, indeed the Salm soldiers received none, this was not due to a lack of materials, but none had been prepared at the artillery park, another example of the lack of attention to duty and military competence reigning at the time on the peninsula.[91] That afternoon, 20 July, the weather turned wet and cloudy with a stormy night setting in when the men of the Second Division prepared for sleep, 'as custom, all dressed'.[92] The soldiers posted for duty that night at Fort Penthièvre were half a battalion, four companies, of the Régiment d'Hervilly and, from the Second Division, detachments from Rohan and Périgord, perhaps as few as 40 in all, as well as the 4th (Russey) Company of the Emigrant Artillery.[93] The positions in front of the fort, the advanced posts and the entrenched camp, were held by chouans supported by a contingent from the Loyal Emigrants and some gunners, in the entrenched camp. The fort's nearest reserve, the rest of Hervilly, were quartered at the settlement of Kerhostin.

Hoche now had more than 12,000 men around Sainte-Barbe, with a strong artillery arm consisting of 64 field pieces.[94] The royalists opposing them had around 4,500 regular troops, taking into account losses, detachments inland and the arrival of the Second Division, in addition there were 5,365 'peasants, including women, children and men' on the peninsula, of whom a half may have been capable of bearing arms; giving at most 7,255 potential combatants.[95]

The storm increased in strength and ferocity during the night; at about 11:00 pm., Sunday 20 July, the republicans began to march towards the peninsula. In front of the columns were 300 grenadiers, guided by another deserter who had just arrived, not only with that night's password but also the information that many men of Hervilly were ready to change sides at the first opportunity. The grenadiers waded into the rough seas to skirt the defenders' advance posts and get around to the west of the fort, the chouans, sheltering as best they could from the storm, did not see or hear them. Climbing the narrow, steep and slippery path which led to the parapet they were soon helped over it by men inside. Then the grenadiers and turncoats, whose numbers quickly grew, rushed to take the fort, attacking any who stood in their way. In the confusion the prearranged warning signal was only partly made, two cannon were fired rather than three. The fort was secured by about 1:30 a.m. The main republican columns, having driven in the advanced posts, attacked the entrenched camp. The defenders initially stood firm but were soon caught between two fires as the fort's guns were turned on them. After a short resistance, those still able to do so, fled from their positions. The main body of the Régiment d'Hervilly marched towards the fort but as it did so whole companies declared for the republicans and turned on their officers. A messenger was sent to Puisaye's headquarters and although the loyal survivors from the fort and outlying works rallied, they could not counter-attack as there was no ammunition. They had to retreat and the chouans melted away, many concerned to ensure the safety of their families on the peninsula.[96]

91 Villeneuve-Laroche-Barnaud, *Mémoires sur l'expédition de Quiberon*, Part II, p.129.

92 Corbehem, *Dix ans de ma vie*, p.165.

93 The evidence is not clear, the conclusion is drawn from comparison of that from La Chanonie, *Mémoires*, p. 110, Louis Marie de La Villegourio, *Ma Sortie de Quiberon* (Saint-Brieuc: Prud'homme, 1815), p.12 and TNA PRO 30/11/225, Rotalier to Lord Cornwallis, 29 July.

94 Bittard des Portes, *Les émigrés*, p 527.

95 Corbett (ed.), *Private Papers of George, Second Earl Spencer*, pp.90–91; see also TNA ADM 80/136.

96 Gérard de Contades, *Coblenz et Quiberon: Souvenirs du Comte de Contades* (Paris: Dentu, 1885), pp.202–206.

Royalist attempts to resist the republican offensive were confused, due to the lack of preparation as well as the dispersal of the troops. The messenger who arrived at the headquarters with the report of the taking of the fort was sent on to Sombreuil, with the order to bring up his division. Puisaye soon saw the effects of the attack as refugees and, later, the wounded, streamed past him heading towards Port d'Orange. He was to join them at the port from where he took a boat to Warren's flagship.

Many of the Second Division had been woken, at around 2:00 a.m., by the gun fire. Some, at first, thought it was the noise of the storm but any doubt was dispelled, at 2:30 a.m., by the arrival of the message from Puisaye and the call to arms was sounded. Units formed up at their respective quarters, in and around Saint-Julien, and the division soon marched north towards the fort. It marched through the centre of the peninsula, where the fields and enclosures were surrounded by low dry-stone walls, under *Lieutenant-colonel* Comte Boson-Jacques de Talleyrand-Périgord, commanding the Régiment de Périgord, while Sombreuil left to get further information and orders from Puisaye. Marching through the rain, the soldiers could make out the sound of combat but the noise gradually receded in time as they approached the fort. The Second Division arrived at le Roch, south of the fort, around 5:00 a.m. and deployed in battle lines just outside the village.[97] They were joined by the half-dozen or so survivors of the division's detachment that had been stationed in Fort Penthièvre.

Two 4-pounder field guns arrived at le Roch and were placed on the left of the village. The loyal remnant of Hervilly and a detachment of Loyal Emigrants also rallied at le Roch, without cartridges, along with a sizeable party of the Régiment du Dresnay.[98] Sombreuil now arrived and gathered his division's officers. He informed them of Puisaye's departure and that command now fell to him, he made no secret of how desperate their situation was, the conference concluded with unanimous shouts of 'Vive le Roi! Vive la France!'[99]

Corbehem stood with the volunteers of the Régiments de Damas and Béon in front of le Roch:

> [W]e saw leaving the fort and coming down into the peninsula battalions that a swarm of skirmishers preceded. At this sight ... all the volunteers were ordered to quickly get into skirmishing order. This order was executed instantly. ... despite our numerical weakness and the multitude of our enemies, we succeeded, by our valour and well-aimed fire, to make their skirmishers fall back onto the main body. It was on this occasion that on loading my musket, a ball grazed the fingers of my right hand and covered them with powder, presumably by the effect of the fine rain that was falling.[100]

At the same time troops were seen moving to the west of le Roch, around Portivy and the artillery park, it was not known if they were friends or foe. The Dresnay contingent was sent

97 Villeneuve-Laroche-Barnaud, *Mémoires sur l'expédition de Quiberon*, Part II, p.125 and Corbehem, *Dix ans de ma vie*, p.169.
98 TNA PRO 30/11/225, Rotalier, 29 July 1795.
99 Villeneuve-Laroche-Barnaud, *Mémoires sur l'expédition de Quiberon*, Part II, p.127.
100 Corbehem, *Dix ans de ma vie*, p 170.

towards them and finding they were republicans most of the Dresnay soldiers joined them; the few loyal men among them could do nothing more than return to le Roch in haste. The republican column advanced along the west coast, threatening to turn the émigrés' left and so cut off their retreat south.[101] At the same time Sombreuil was told that Port d'Orange could not be defended.[102] The order was given to fall back. Corbehem, in the skirmish line, was almost left behind:

> [T]he two legions received the order to fall back. I was not aware at first of this retrograde movement, being too busy with the enemy that I had before me; and it was only when the horn of the chasseur company of my legion had sounded the retreat, on turning around I saw that the legions were retiring. We started to run out of cartridges, and there was no one to give us any.[103]

The émigrés retreated to a position on heights above Saint-Julien, distinguished by two windmills and a flag post that stood there; possession of the site would protect embarkation, especially from Port Haliguen. While some elements retreated along the east coast, the main body of Sombreuil's division withdrew the way they had come, covered by a skirmish line of Damas and Béon chasseurs. Corbehem was among them:

> We executed our retreat always in skirmishing and protecting the corps which was before us. The enemy that we had repulsed, then returned on us in still even greater number than before and with an ardour difficult to contain; they were so close to us, that arrived at the gardens of the houses which we came to occupy, and which were enclosed by small stone walls about two feet in height, I only had time to leap without thought over one of these walls, to not be taken or killed. One of my comrades who was at my side having had the misfortune to take a false step fell against the wall and was instantly massacred with bayonet thrusts.[104]

The dry-stone walls, when hit by the enemy's artillery, threw fragments into the air causing casualties amongst those who had taken shelter behind them; they also hampered the two Emigrant Artillery guns which had to be abandoned. Damas lost four men killed in the day's fighting and it appears that it was around this time that Charles de Lavenne, the adjutant, was killed in a particularly brutal fashion. The normally very restrained Bennes noted that he was 'cut to pieces by the patriots' and Tercier related, 'The Chevalier Davesnes [sic], staff officer of my legion, was sent on reconnaissance; he fell in with a party of Republicans and was massacred in the same instant with all the barbarity possible.'[105]

---

101 TNA PRO 30/11/225, Rotalier, 29 July; see also Contades, *Coblenz et Quiberon*, p.205, Corbehem, *Dix ans de ma vie*, p.170 and Villeneuve-Laroche-Barnaud, *Mémoires sur l'expédition de Quiberon*, Part II, p.128.

102 La Villegourio, *Ma Sortie de Quiberon*, pp.13–14.

103 Corbehem, *Dix ans de ma vie*, p.171.

104 Corbehem, *Dix ans de ma vie*, p.171.

105 Bennes, *Narrative*, p.35; La Chanonie, *Mémoires*, p.114.

In the retreat some men from the regiment found themselves, by mishap or design, on the seashore amongst those seeking to get to the ships offshore and Rouault sent Tercier there 'to rally those of our soldiers that I found there'.[106] Meanwhile the troops with Sombreuil arrived at the heights and began to form a defensive line.

> His right, rested on the sea, was composed of the Régiment de Rohan; the *corps de la Marine* [Hector] formed the centre, with the remains of Damas, Béon and Loyal Emigrant; the left was confided to remnants of the Hervilly and Dresnay corps; a windmill formed the extremity of it, and the height where this mill was placed, presented the double advantage of observing the enemy's movements with success, and of bringing our forces to the most endangered spot.[107]

Apparently, some émigré officers now attempted to negotiate a capitulation. Much has been written about whether such an agreement took place, still dividing historians today, those with republican sympathies arguing that there never could have been one, the contemporary law being well known to both parties. Sombreuil quickly realised that he had too few troops, without sufficient ammunition or artillery, to hold his position so he ordered his men to withdraw to Fort Neuf, apparently in the hope he could negotiate surrender there.[108] Fort Neuf, built as a small coastal battery, had only rudimental, and neglected, defences; although, a few years before, it had been reconstructed as a redoubt and so promised some protection from a landward attack. It stands on a point just south of Port Haliguen which is separated from the port by a small bay, the Plage du Porigo. Despite its military inadequacies, it was to be the scene of the émigré troops' final stand at Quiberon.

Many of the émigré soldiers had not yet seen the seashore that morning but now, for all of them, the full horror of what was unfolding there became clear in graphic detail:

> [W]e could see different tableaux, each of which would have excited compassion in the hardest heart. On the rocks weeping women were to be made out, mixing their tears with those of their children, who all were in the most deplorable state; old men trembling and seeking refuge from the victorious enemy; men almost naked and ready to throw themselves into the sea, which was horribly rough, and covered with corpses that it hurled furiously against the jagged points of the rocks. On this stormy sea long-boats were seen wandering here and there to go to bring some help to the wretches who struggled against the violence of the waves; debris of several ship's boats scattered on all sides, and to which were attached other unfortunates, who, escaped from the enemy's sword, had come, in seeking their safety, to find a death even more cruel; along the coast, packs, haversacks, weapons, and other military effects which had been abandoned, the wretches we had seen, the corpses, floated at the mercy of the sea, that seemed, with our enemies, conspirators to our ruin; finally, in the middle of the bay, a strong squadron, with a hundred transport vessels battered by the tempest, rendered this spectacle as terrible as it was

106 La Chanonie, *Mémoires*, p.114.
107 La Villegourio, *Ma Sortie de Quiberon*, pp.15–16.
108 Contades, *Coblenz et Quiberon*, pp.207–210, supported by TNA PRO 30/11/225 Rotalier, 29 July.

> imposing. A secret horror seized our souls, but it was soon replaced to the feeling of our duty.[109]

At Fort Neuf the remnants of the First Division, officers with the few loyal soldiers, formed the front rank of the defenders, and the Second Division ranged behind them, in all there were between 500 and 1,000 of them within the small fort. Despite this show of defiance, they had little means to resist the republicans: each man probably only had one or two cartridges left.[110] However assistance now arrived from the sea, 'the Lark Sloop, and Pelter Gun Vessel having run close into a sandy bay' fired over the heads of the émigrés and went some way to keeping the republicans at bay.[111] These being prevented from approaching the flanks of the fort, could only form battle lines in front, about a musket shot's distance away.[112]

The sequence of subsequent events is somewhat confused. It appears that at first there was something of a stand-off with the opposing troops facing each other. Immediately the republican soldiers shouted to the émigrés to surrender and that no harm would come to them:

> [T]heir cries of peace, which they always repeated, produced a really dangerous effect on the soldiers of the First Division, who were the closest to the first outer wall. A great number among them threw their arms over the wall, crossed it and ran to the enemy who, at this first success, redoubled their shouts, to invite us to lay down our arms.[113]

It seems about 50 soldiers surrendered, or deserted, in this fashion. It was now, according to the émigrés who survived, that Sombreuil negotiated for a capitulation, apparently with Hoche in person. Whatever the truth about the contentious question of a capitulation, Sombreuil finally gave the order for his troops to lay down their arms and surrender. The order was passed on through the ranks, Bennes wrote that 'our major exclaimed to me, "Chevalier, throw down your musket."'[114] It is clear from memoirs of those in the Second Division, that most of the émigrés thought, or had convinced themselves, that they were to be treated as prisoners of war. Nevertheless, the order was received with consternation, including in Damas as Corbehem remembered, 'we received the order to put down our arms. At these words, a general murmur arose; we shuddered with anger; but it was necessary to obey. The order was executed, and each laid his arms at his feet in front of him.'[115] Tercier recalled that there was a more emotional reaction, 'Rather than surrender their weapons, they threw them in chagrin into the sea, or smashed them on the rocks.'[116]

---

109 Villeneuve-Laroche-Barnaud, *Mémoires sur l'expédition de Quiberon*, Part II, pp.131–132.
110 Villeneuve-Laroche-Barnaud, *Mémoires sur l'expédition de Quiberon*, Part II, p.138.
111 TNA ADM 1/103 Warren to Evan Nepean, *La Pomone*, Quiberon Bay, 22 July 1795.
112 Corbehem, *Dix ans de ma vie*, p.173.
113 Villeneuve-Laroche-Barnaud, *Mémoires sur l'expédition de Quiberon*, Part II, pp. 136–137.
114 Bennes, *Narrative*, p.35.
115 Corbehem, *Dix ans de ma vie*, p.176.
116 La Chanonie, *Mémoires*, pp.116–117.

The émigrés believed, as part of a capitulation, that they had been granted a period of about half an hour to try to embark. Corbehem wrote, 'As soon as M. de Sombreuil had informed us of this convention, many of the soldiers raising in the air, some their hats, others their handkerchiefs, made signs to the English to come and fetch us; some who knew how to swim threw themselves into the sea to get closer to them'.[117] Simultaneously the republicans arrived to secure Fort Neuf and the émigré troops it contained; it appears that they were commanded by *Général de Brigade* Louis Lemoine although Corbehem and Bennes, among others, state that Hoche also came to the fort. The action was necessary as some seem to have wanted to continue to resist and Corbehem recalled what happened among his companions:

> Général Hoche advanced ... to about six paces from me to the left, turning his back on his army and his face towards the sea. While he stared at the English vessels in front of him, the Marquis de Fo*****, ... who was immediately leaning against me, suddenly raised his musket, aimed the weapon at Général Hoche, and prepared to fire; but at that instant Wolf, hornist of the chasseur company of my legion, who was ten paces from us, saw the movement, jumped on the musket, tore it from the hands of the marquis and threw it on the ground. Fortunately, the general ... did not perceive this action, which nothing could excuse, and which would have had for us the most frightful consequences.[118]

The British vessels had continued to fire and the republicans demanded that the cannonade end, so *Sous-lieutenant* Gesril de Paspeu of the Régiment d'Hector swam out to her with the message from Sombreuil to cease firing. The guns fell silent and Paspeu returned to the shore. One of those who managed to get away, after the surrender, was Talleyrand-Périgord: reaching HMS *Pomone* he was able to inform Warren of what had happened.[119] The following day, the latter wrote,

> The regiments of Beon and Damas, who with the other troops had retreated from Fort Penthièvre the whole length of the island to the fort at the south end... stood upon their defence most nobly against the enemy; and I only discontinued the fire from receiving a messenger from Comte Sombreuil, who commanded them (and who has been the only active man since D'Hervilly's misfortune in being wounded), that he had made terms with the enemy, and that the two regiments were to be embarked.[120]

Jean-Louis-Alexis de Villeneuve-Laroche-Barnaud, with Damas, was the eldest of three brothers who found themselves at Fort Neuf; the others were François and Louis-Gabriel, lieutenants in, respectively, Rohan and Périgord. The latter wrote:

117 Corbehem, *Dix ans de ma vie*, p.174.

118 Corbehem, *Dix ans de ma vie*, p.177, the identity of this individual has not been established.

119 Anon. 'Biographical Memoir of Rear Admiral Sir John Borlase Warren, Bart. K.B.' *The Naval Chronicle*, Vol.III, January to July 1800 p.348.

120 Corbett (ed.), *Private Papers of George, Second Earl Spencer*, pp.87–88, Warren to Spencer 22 July 1795.

> My first care was then to seek my two brothers, when I saw them coming to meet me. ... in three different regiments ... on this unfortunate day, we had acted at three different points; my two brothers had met at Fort Neuf, and they found themselves in the most deplorable state. One cannot express the joy with which we embraced each other; each of us had done his duty, and we could only blame bad fortune.[121]

Warned by a captain of grenadiers, who was amongst the republicans who had entered the fort, that, as émigrés, they were in danger, the brothers looked to the British fleet:

> We went to the base of the fort, at the edge of the sea and on a rock, ... the Republican grenadiers had accompanied us there... Then some movements in the squadron, made us hope that they were disposed to send us ships boats from the transports. We then made out a long-boat under a flag of truce, which cut straight towards us; but soon, on slowing its course, it arrived at cannon range, and suddenly it went about and returned to the squadron. It is difficult to describe the sentiments that stirred in us; a half hour elapsed without us perceiving in the squadron any sign that they were coming to snatch us from a shore that was witness of our calamities.[122]

That the British did not send boats to collect them was, for many of the émigrés such as Corbehem, inexplicable; others like Tercier considered that the rough sea conditions prevented an attempt to carry out a final mass embarkation.[123] However, the explanation appears to be that the officers on the long-boat coming inshore under a flag of truce, as described above, had seen the republicans mixed with the émigrés in the fort and concluded that they were not free to leave having already been detained. Hence no boats were sent. The Villeneuve-Laroche-Barnaud brothers prepared to swim to safety and undressed to do so, but were persuaded by comrades, and some republican grenadiers, that this would mean their certain death 'while, by the capitulation, we were sure to keep our lives'. Persuaded the three climbed back up to the fort and joined their comrades.[124]

There are very different testimonies of the way the republican soldiers initially treated their disarmed prisoners. Corbehem stated that there was no triumphalism or undue rancour, and, in addition:

> [T]hey did not search any of us either and extract a contribution from anyone. I saw in truth some of our officers empty their pockets into the hands of the Republican soldiers, but I did not notice that they had been forced nor that any threat had been used against them. As for me, nothing was asked of me; but I also had nothing to

121 Villeneuve-Laroche-Barnaud, *Mémoires sur l'expédition de Quiberon*, Part II, pp.142–143; their youngest brother, Alexis, was serving as a lieutenant in the York Rangers, recently sent to the West Indies (*ibid*, Part I p.215).

122 Villeneuve-Laroche-Barnaud, *Mémoires sur l'expédition de Quiberon*, Part II, pp 146–147.

123 Corbehem, *Dix ans de ma vie*, p.175 and La Chanonie, *Mémoires*, p.113.

124 Villeneuve-Laroche-Barnaud, *Mémoires sur l'expédition de Quiberon*, Part II, pp.146–148.

> give. I kept my haversack containing my light baggage as a volunteer. This was all that I possessed in the world; again, I had the misfortune to lose it soon after.[125]

Tercier however related a different experience and view. 'All the émigré officers were searched and despoiled by the Republican soldiers and even the officers who, miserable with their *assignats* without value in Brittany, indemnified themselves a little with us. I found nevertheless the means to shield twenty guineas from their rapacity.'[126] Bennes was not so fortunate; she noted that, 'The Republicans carried away everything I possessed, both goods and money.'[127] Very soon the émigré prisoners were marched, in batches, to Fort Penthièvre:

> It was in this journey, that a soldier had wished to force M. du Croiset [sic], quartermaster of the Damas Regiment, to give him his silver spurs; Hoche, who passed in this instant, stopped, in fact to do justice on the spot, and declared that he will treat with the same severity anyone who permits himself the least act of violence contrary to the treaty that had just been signed, and by which we kept our effects.[128]

They arrived at the fort in the early afternoon. There they found other officers and soldiers, who had been captured piecemeal, as well as a large number of women, children and old men who had been unable to get away by boat. Everyone was tired and hungry, but the émigré soldiers were given nothing to eat.[129] The republican soldiers who guarded them were no better off, despite the capture of stores of food, drink and munitions at the fort. The severely wounded, along with the women, children and old men, were left at Quiberon while the other émigrés and chouans were soon on the move, initially to the republican camp of Sainte-Barbe and then onto Auray:

> While we sadly made our way towards Auray, the weather changed suddenly. A considerable rain arrived unexpectedly. We were soaked. Our escorts were themselves fatigued to such an extent, that they had difficulty to drag themselves along and follow us; the soldiers were starving and exhausted. There was no more order nor supervision, and still less when the night came. The roads were so bad that we sank knee-deep into the mud. Everything was pell-mell, soldiers and prisoners; some slipped or fell on their neighbours. It would have been very easy for us to take advantage in such favourable circumstances to escape. But all bound by the word of honour that had been asked of us, and that we gave on leaving, we would have thought ourselves dishonoured to break it ...[130]

The columns arrived at Auray during the night. Most of the prisoners, still without food or water, were immediately locked into the town's churches. Many of the chouans had taken

125 Corbehem, *Dix ans de ma vie*, pp.178–179.
126 La Chanonie, *Mémoires*, p.117.
127 Bennes, *Narrative*, p.35.
128 La Villegourio, *Ma Sortie de Quiberon*, pp.21–22.
129 La Chanonie, *Mémoires*, p.119, Corbehem, *Dix ans de ma vie*, p.179.
130 La Chanonie, *Mémoires*, p.121.

the opportunity to slip away into the countryside. However, the sense of duty and honour was so strong among the émigrés that those who had fallen by the wayside during the march made their own way to Auray. One of their number was a Damas chasseur, as related by a comrade, Jean-Baptiste-Joseph de Jacquier de Noyelle:

> We considered ourselves bound by honour, Sombreuil had answered for us; that was sufficient for us. The Chevalier Robert de Boisfossé, from Lower Poitou, thought he was doing a very unremarkable thing, when, the following morning, finding himself in a ditch where he had fallen with weariness and sleep, he returned without hesitation to the road to Auray. Some women however said to him: – Head along the short-cut, and, in three quarters of a league you will find the chouans. – That is impossible for me, he replied, I am engaged by the promise of my chief; I wish moreover to share the fate of my comrades. – And he arrived … without appearing even to suspect that he had performed a sublime act. Destined, at the time of the Revolution, to enter the [clerical] orders, circumstances made him follow a very different career …[131]

Warren, after being informed of Sombreuil's surrender, sent two Royal Navy officers, under a flag of truce, to negotiate a prisoner exchange but 'they were received very badly, and laughed at to their faces when they spoke of it' and the proposal was rejected.[132]

Despite everything almost a thousand troops, officers and men, and over 1,300 chouans 'capable of carrying arms' had reached the safety of the British fleet that morning, along with about 700 others: priests, women, children and other men.[133] The day after the defeat, 22 July, Warren issued instructions that all those rescued, who were scattered amongst the ships and boats of the fleet, should be re-distributed, in their units, and a proper count be made of their numbers. The émigré infantry was to be gathered in the warships and the artillery and chouans in transports; 'the remains of Dresnay, Salm & Damas', along with seven officers and 40 men of Hervilly, a total of 19 officers and 76 men, were allocated to go on board HMS *Venus*.[134]

The Régiment de Damas, as a military unit, no longer existed. Little more than a dozen of its men had found their way to the British feet. The most detailed return, dated 26 July, states that there were two sergeants and 12 fusiliers present and, by implication fit for duty, along with one wounded man, a woman and a domestic – 17 in all. Significantly no Damas officer was with them, no other unit in the expedition lost all its officers.[135] Less than seven percent of the unit was with the fleet, compared with an average of just over 13 percent for the Second Division as a whole.[136]

131 Eugène de La Gournerie, *Les Débris de Quiberon: Souvenirs du Désastre de 1795* (Nantes: Catholique Libaros, 1875), pp 4–5.

132 Contades, *Coblenz et Quiberon*, p.216; Corbett (ed.), *Private Papers of George, Second Earl Spencer*, p.88, 90 and 98.

133 Reconciling Corbett (ed.), *Private Papers of George, Second Earl Spencer*, p.91, returns in TNA WO 1/388, PRO 30/11/225 and ADM 80/136 and ADM 1/103, Warren to Evan Nepean, *La Pomone*, Quiberon Bay, 22 July 1795.

134 TNA WO 89/136.

135 TNA PRO 30/11/225.

136 Comparison of the average number of survivors (WO 1/388, ADM 80/136 and PRO 30/11/225) against average strengths (BL Add MS 46710 and ADM 80/136).

7

The Fate of the Infantry 1795

On 22 July, the officers and men of the Régiment de Damas who had sailed from Stade little more than a month ago, and who were still alive, were either on board the British ships in Quiberon Bay or on land, prisoners of the republicans. What happened to them will be described in this chapter, in that order, and the story of their comrades in Germany, especially the cavalry, will be covered subsequently.

The British Government reacted quickly once the news of the émigrés' landing had reached London and on 12 July arrangements began for 3,000 British troops to be immediately sent to Quiberon. They were intended to be the first wave of troops, to be commanded by Lord Moira, to secure the peninsula as a base from which the royalists could mount active operations. Puisaye was informed that these units, as well as the cadre corps of Williamson, Léon and Trésor, formed on the Channel Islands of émigré gentlemen intended to be officers for new regiments that would be recruited once landed, were on their way to join him.[1] Although embarked rapidly, contrary winds meant it was only on 26 July that the convoy reached Cawsand Bay, in Plymouth Sound, where the ships from the Channel Islands were waiting, and prevented further progress.[2] However, the same westerly winds hastened news of the disaster at Quiberon and initial reports reached the British Government on 29 July, becoming public knowledge two days later.[3] On 5 August the fleet, accompanied by the cadres, sailed from Plymouth Sound for the Solent, where most of them disembarked.[4]

On 31 July, Earl Spencer, the First Lord of the Admiralty, wrote a private and confidential letter to Warren. He explained that although the idea of operations on the coast of Brittany had not been abandoned, the nature of the defeat meant that some deliberation was needed. To do so, that very day, the Prime Minister and the Secretary at War, William Pitt and Windham, were in conference with Lord Moira. In the meantime, he was sending Captain Bertie, with HMS *Thunderer* (74) and some cutters, who 'will carry with him everything he can put on board that can be of most use.'[5] Warren had told Spencer, on 22 July, in the same letter in which he told of the defeat, 'I think it will be wrong to give up the business.' As part

1 TNA WO 1/390; Horse Guards to the Duke of York, 12 July, and Horse Guards to Puisaye, 14 July 1795.
2 TNA WO 1/176 and 12/12034; *The Times*, Monday 27 and Thursday 30 July 1795.
3 Corbett (ed.), *Private Papers of George, Second Earl Spencer*, p.96, Spencer to Warren (draft) 31 July 1795 and *The Times*, 31 July 1795.
4 *The Times*, Tuesday 4 and Thursday 6 July 1795.
5 Corbett (ed.), *Private Papers of George, Second Earl Spencer*, p.96, Spencer to Warren 31 July.

of his reasoning he particularly mentioned the renewed activity of the Vendéans who had again taken up arms, under François-Athanase Charette de la Contrie. His intention, in the meantime, was to take possession of the small islands of Houat and Hoëdic as well continue the blockade of Belle-Île. However, he was clear that 'eatables, canteens, tents, and forage for the horses must be had without a moment's loss of time.'[6] The condition of the survivors who had reached the British fleet was of immediate concern. The troops had lost most of their clothes and packs, indeed some had nothing, having stripped to swim to safety, so they were supplied with slops, coarse and loose working jackets and trousers issued to sailors, 'to cover their nakedness'.[7] Although they had only been ordered to join the *Venus* on 22 July, the Damas soldiers were soon transferred again as, on 26 July, as Halsted was ordered to be ready to command a convoy, which included the hospital ships with the wounded, that sailed on 29 July and arrived at Spithead on 7 August. At least three Damas soldiers were aboard these ships.[8]

By 31 July, Warren had taken possession of the islands of Houat and Hoëdic placing a garrison, of the Emigrant Artillery, in the fort on the first of these islands and had returned to the mainland 1,300 old men, women and children who were permitted to return home. This left 500 chouans with him. Wells were dug and, on Houat, ovens were enlarged so, within a week, soldier bakers were producing enough to supply the troops. However, supplies of beer and fresh food were urgently needed for the troops, chouans, ships' crews and population of the two islands to prevent scurvy.[9]

There was also further activity at sea. Operating with the British ships was a flotilla of Breton *chasse-marées*; fast-sailing sloops that not only acted as tenders to the British ships but also liaised with royalists on shore, bringing back not only messages and intelligence but also those who had escaped from the republicans. Some of the warships' launches, fitted as small gunboats, also harassed Republican forces on the shore, taking part in a number of skirmishes.[10] In addition two warships and other vessels landed a supply of gunpowder for the Vendéans on 'a bad beach for the purpose' between Saint-Gilles-Croix-de-Vie and Saint-Jean-de-Monts, opposite the Île d'Yeu, where it was received by 5,000 of Charette's men.[11] Warren considered the Vendée the only viable theatre for such operations due to republican reinforcements along the south coast of Brittany.

On 9 August the choauns were landed on Houat and armed ready to return to Brittany in line with Puisaye's plans.[12] The lack of provisions was becoming critical with Warren reporting, on 14 August, that there was only a month's supply remaining and that scurvy had appeared in his fleet.[13] Nevertheless he was 'unwilling to abandon these islands and this bay whilst offensive measures continue.'[14]

6 Corbett (ed.), *Private Papers of George, Second Earl Spencer*, p.89, Warren to Spencer 22 July.
7 TNA ADM 1/103 Warren to Admiralty 22 July 1795.
8 TNA ADM 1/1913.
9 Corbett (ed.), *Private Papers of George, Second Earl Spencer*, p.94 and TNA ADM 80/136.
10 TNA ADM 80/136 and ADM 1/103 Warren to Nepean 14 August 1795.
11 TNA ADM 1/103 Captain Sir Edward Nagle, *Artois*, to Warren 12 August 1795.
12 TNA ADM 80/136 and Corbett (ed.), *Private Papers of George, Second Earl Spencer*, p.98, Warren to Spencer 8 August 1795.
13 TNA ADM 1/103 Warren to Nepean 14 August 1795.
14 Corbett (ed.), *Private Papers of George, Second Earl Spencer*, p.100, Warren to Spencer 14 August 1795.

The *Thundrerer* finally arrived on 16 August and, although she brought no new orders for Warren, the supplies aboard, including tents, addressed some of the troops' immediate needs.[15] It appears that the remaining men of Damas had landed, perhaps with those of the Loyal Emigrants, on Houat the day before. The evidence for this is an order, dated 15 August 1795, written on a small piece of paper which reads: 'In case of an attack by the enemy, the Régiment de Damas will retire into the fort and will occupy the platform which is on the fort. On retiring, it will pass the general's [Puisaye?] house and there will take as much bread as it can.' A certificate at the end states that the order had been 'Read in front of the regiment' by 'Mercier des Pelle, fourrier, Commandant.'[16] This NCO, who now commanded the regiment, was Claude-Marie Mercier des Pelle-Saunier, who although apparently not an officer at the time of the Revolution had been a gentleman-cadet in the second battalion of the Régiment d'Aquitaine and had served in India at the same time as Damas. At the formation of the Légion de Damas in 1793, he had not been a chasseur but a soldier in Stack's fusilier company.

On 18 August, the troops who continued to be landed on Houat, were issued with tents, clothing, shoes, haversacks, 'muskets complete' and even drums.[17] On the island Erasme-Gaspard de Contades and Périgord took responsibility for the troops, despite Puisaye's presence. 'The General [Puisaye] and the army are not on good terms', Warren dryly observed.[18] Defeat had crushed the spirit of the émigrés as described by Contades, 'The greatest consternation reigned in the squadron; all our hopes had vanished.'[19] Although better clothed now, sickness emerged amongst the troops to dampen spirits further and on 28 August Warren wrote:

> I have remained in anxious expectation of receiving orders to send back the troops here, who are in a miserable state, ... and to return home, or to have seen Lord Moira with the British Army. ... There is a fever on those [ships] with the troops, and some have died, and near 115 of them in hospital. The rest are encamped as well as our means and circumstances would admit; but their fidelity, except the remains of three regiments, very little can be said, as I am persuaded they would not stand fire, and many of them join the enemy.[20]

Disaffection was not restricted to the units that had arrived with the First Division, on 3 October Warren considered that all the émigré troops 'except the artillery and La Châtre [Loyal Emigrants], Rohan, Salms, and Damas, have behaved very ill and are not to be trusted, one half of them republicans.' It is testament to the small band of Damas soldiers, without a single officer, that their loyalty was worthy of such recognition while their comrades of Béon had given concern and so were restricted on board on 22 August.[21]

15 The date of the *Thunderer's* arrival is given by Contades, *Coblenz et Quiberon*, p 222.
16 State Archive of the Russian Federation (GARF), Moscow, 758/2/52.
17 TNA ADM 80/136.
18 Contades, *Coblenz et Quiberon*, p.222 and Corbett (ed.), *Private Papers of George, Second Earl Spencer*, pp.102 and 104.
19 Contades, *Coblenz et Quiberon*, p.223.
20 Corbett (ed.), *Private Papers of George, Second Earl Spencer*, p.101, Warren to Spencer.
21 Corbett (ed.), *Private Papers of George, Second Earl Spencer*, p.104, Warren to Spencer 11 September 1795, and TNA ADM 80/136.

The troops were only on Houat for a few weeks and on 28 August orders were issued allocating transports for the troops 'when the signal is made'. Each unit was to embark with their camp equipment, stores and baggage. The Damas soldiers were allocated to the *Sarah* along with the remains of Salm, Périgord, Béon and the Warren Hussars, which had been raised in Brittany to provide cavalry for the expedition, in all 11 officers and 79 men.[22] The troops had to be ready to sail as food was running out, convoys from England taking around seven days to reach the bay, and there was a renewed threat of republican naval activity, particular from Lorient.[23] Nevertheless Warren remained reluctant to leave and there was no swift embarkation; it was to be 9 September before all the troops were onboard.[24]

In the meantime, faced with Warren's imminent departure, Puisaye left the fleet and went ashore at Carnac on 3 September, with some companions.[25] If Puisaye had always been controversial amongst the émigrés, an indication that British patience had been tested is given by *The Times* of Wednesday 16 September which reported his return to the mainland. The piece concluded, 'As he has to atone for great fault, some great effort may be expected from him.'[26] Warren, who had worked closely with Puisaye, in both success and failure, wrote, 'I believe he is, if I may be excused speaking freely upon a point in which my country is concerned, a character capable of doing much good or being no inconsiderable enemy and full of intrigue, and, I wish it were possible to say, possessed of equal bravery.'[27]

On 8 September, official confirmation arrived that reinforcements were on their way and the convoy arrived in Quiberon Bay four days later.[28] The British Government, after some deliberation, had decided to continue its support of the royalist risings in Western France. On 11 August Moira was instructed to embark four battalions of infantry, the 12th, 1/78th, 80th and 1/90th Foot, along with a detachment from the 14th Light Dragoons and some artillery, in transports at Southampton, and place them under the command of Major General Welbore Ellis Doyle. As soon as the troops had embarked the transports were to sail for Houat and Hoëdic, under the escort of a squadron commanded by Rear Admiral Sir Henry Harvey. Moira had been given clear and detailed instructions stipulating the orders he was to give Doyle. The latter was to take and hold Noirmoutier, in conjunction with and support of the Vendéans, but only attempt to do so if no risk was involved, this last stricture was reinforced at every stage. There was to be no large-scale deployment of British troops, they were now required elsewhere. Subsequently Doyle was told that the Île d'Yeu could be taken in addition, or as an alternative, to Noirmoutier.[29] Two days later the expedition's destination became public knowledge, and, disillusioned, Moira requested to be relieved of his command, which was duly granted.[30]

22 TNA ADM 80/136.
23 TNA ADM 1/103, Warren to Nepean 28 August 1795.
24 Corbett (ed.), *Private Papers of George, Second Earl Spencer*, p.103, Warren to Spencer 11 September 1795, and TNA ADM 80/136.
25 Hutt, *Chouannerie and Counter-Revolution*, pp.343–345.
26 *The Times* 16 September 1795.
27 Corbett (ed.), *Private Papers of George, Second Earl Spencer*, p.104, Warren to Spencer 11 September 1795.
28 Hutt, *Chouannerie and Counter-Revolution*, p.345; Fortescue *British Campaigns in Flanders*, p.419; Contades, *Coblenz et Quiberon*, p.228.
29 TNA WO 1/176 Horse Guards to Moira 11 and 12 August 1795.
30 TNA WO 1/176 Moira to Huskisson 14 August 1795.

On 18 and 19 August, the British units, about 3,300 strong, along with the cadre corps, embarked and their transports made their way to the rendezvous at Spithead.[31] Further troops, émigrés, were to sail with Doyle's division. Twenty-eight transports had sailed from Bremerlehe on 6 August with two more cadre corps, that of the Comte d'Allonville and *Colonel* de Quiefdeville, this last being of artillery officers, as well as a further 50 men to join Williamson's corps amongst whom were at least six former chasseurs of the Légion de Damas.[32] However the most significant elements were the Uhlans Britanniques and a detachment of the Choiseul Hussars, respectively of about 350 and 400 all ranks.[33] Their progress to Spithead was painfully slow, the transports were in the North Sea for 10 days, only reaching the Straits of Dover on 15 August and it took them a further week to reach the anchorage off Portsmouth.[34]

The reinforcement was graced by the presence of a prince of the French royal family. Since the death of his nephew, the Dauphin, from neglect in a Parisian prison, on 8 June, the Comte d'Artois was heir to the throne and so distinguished by the title of Monsieur. He had sailed from Germany just ahead of the convoy and on arriving at Spithead he went aboard HMS *Jason* on which there soon were about 40 senior officers with him 'of the staff, or better to say of the prince's court.'[35] He was unable to land in England, as he was liable to be arrested for unpaid debts.[36] Some of his suite had sailed with him from Germany and others joined him from London. One of the latter was Louis-Joseph-Jean-Baptiste de la Boëssière, Comte de Chambors and *major* of the Régiment de Damas. Born at court, he was *gentilhomme d'honneur* to Artois from 1773 and had rapidly risen through the ranks of the French army: *colonel en second* of the La Fère infantry, aged 23, and *mestre de camp* in 1788. He had served as an aide de camp to Artois in the 1792 campaign and had subsequently been appointed *capitaine* in one of the white cockade units, the Régiment de Vioménil. On 26 April 1795, when in London, he had received a letter from the Comte de Damas informing him of his nomination as *major* in the latter's infantry. Having arranged to join the regiment in Germany, Chambors was then advised to remain in England due to the impending departure of the regiment and so had missed the voyage to Quiberon. Now he again joined Artois, appointed *aide-major général*.[37]

The departure of the transports was delayed by contrary winds and they were forced to shelter in St Helen's Roads, off the Isle of Wight, until they were finally reported to be under sail on 30 August.[38] The reinforcement arrived in Quiberon Bay on 12 September. The number of vessels was impressive and the spectacle was enhanced by the 21-gun salute in honour of arriving royalty.

31 TNA WO 1/176, embarkation return, 19 August 1795, and *The Times*, 20 August.
32 They were Charles Angély de Lonne, Louis Charles Descorches de Saint-Blaise, François René de Hommet, Louis Vincent Le Lay Chevalier de Kermabain, Antoine Barthelemy d'Ormoy and Thomas François de Ronnay.
33 Bouillé, *Souvenirs*, Vol.II, p.264–265.
34 TNA ADM 12/67 and TNA WO 1/392.
35 Bouillé, *Souvenirs*, p.294; also see *ibid.*, p.275.
36 Hutt, *Chouannerie and Counter-Revolution*, pp.237–238.
37 BL Add MS 37859, ff.156–157 letter of Chambors to Windham, Hampstead, 16 June 1795.
38 *The Times* 1 September 1795.

Doyle was concerned about the émigré regiments he found waiting for him. 'The Commodore … agrees with me that it is better to send the remains of the Reg^{ts} of Hector, Du Dresnay & D'Hervilly who may perhaps be of more service elsewhere but cannot be employed here with the other French Reg^{ts} without great inconvenience & perhaps danger.'[39]

Meanwhile, on board the *Jason*, Artois carried out his royal duties, receiving the surviving senior émigré officers as well as those officers who managed to escape republican captivity. He also went to Houat where he attended a church service for the fallen and received the homage of not only the survivors but also loyal Bretons who travelled over from the mainland. Nevertheless, even after the recent arrivals, morale was poor, Contades observing, 'Confidence is lost from our side'.[40] Nevertheless preparations were made for a landing in Vendée, Warren and Doyle had written to Charette immediately after the latter's arrival, and on 15 September Artois wrote to the Vendéan leader to announce that within 48 hours he would be leaving Quiberon Bay for Noirmoutier.[41]

From 21 September boats were sent to explore Bourgneuf Bay and the approaches to Noirmoutier for possible landing points and to obtain intelligence of the enemy's strength and dispositions. Meanwhile transports left Quiberon Bay on 23 September; amongst the troops on board were the remnants of the Second Division and Loyal Emigrants who were fit for service.[42] Nevertheless, Noirmoutier was not attacked, Charette had not appeared on the mainland side and Doyle did not consider he had enough troops to hold the island even if he managed to capture it. 'The British are only 2870 including sick etc. and the remains of the French Reg^{ts} to about 200 soldiers. The Cadres are about 280 effective.'[43] The British commanders did not know that Hoche had renewed operations in the Vendée and Charette had been defeated at Saint-Cyr-en-Talmondais on 25 September.[44]

On the evening of 28 September seven warships left the fleet in Bourgneuf Bay with the transports carrying the 12th and 80th Foot and headed for Île d'Yeu. The next day the ships arrived off the island which surrendered and that evening the French royal banner with the British flag flew over the island.[45] However the lack of resources, including water, on the island was immediately recognised, and it was essential that supplies and equipment were landed as soon as possible as the weather was closing in with squalls and gales, but only shallow-draught vessels could enter the island's port. On 2 October Artois and his entourage landed on Île d'Yeu, Doyle and Warren were also on the island, hoping to make contact with Charette. However, on 13 October Doyle reported that nothing had been heard from the Vendéan leader and communication was hazardous due to the weather and the increasing presence of republican troops on the coast.[46]

39 TNA WO 1/176 Doyle to Dundas, 23 September 1795.
40 Contades, *Coblenz et Quiberon*, p.229.
41 TNA WO 1/176 Doyle to Dundas, 15 September 1795; Hutt, *Chouannerie and Counter-Revolution*, p.348.
42 TNA ADM 80/136 and Hutt, *Chouannerie and Counter-Revolution*, p 355.
43 TNA WO 1/176 Doyle to Dundas, 28 September 1795.
44 Hutt, *Chouannerie and Counter-Revolution*, p.358.
45 TNA WO 1/176 Needham to Doyle, 30 September 1795.
46 TNA ADM 80/136 Needham to Keats, 30 September 1795 and WO 1/176 Doyle to Dundas 13 October 1795.

Conditions for the troops on the island were bad and many quickly became sick, although more supplies were landed on 16 October it soon turned stormy again. During this weather the transports that had been anchored in Bourgneuf Bay had returned to Quiberon Bay. Warren commented:

> The cadres are anxious to return home again, and the cavalry … are half ill of the flux and horses dying in numbers, that the General [Doyle] … has requested I will return them home again, which I shall do by the first convoy. … I have a hard task to go through in combating the despondency and want of enterprise of the French …[47]

With the return of adverse weather, most of the émigré officers and men, on board ship in Quiberon Bay, appeared to only want to return to England and Captain Richard Goodwin Keats of HMS *Galatea*, who commanded there, informed Warren, on 20 October, that the 'complaints of the Cadres & other Corps multiplying makes me the more anxiously desirous of receiving your ultimate Commands respecting them …'[48]

On 14 October the British Government had decided that Doyle should return with his troops to England but protocol dictated that they had to wait for Artois to settle on what he was going to do before issuing their instructions. Meanwhile Doyle and Warren decided to send the émigré troops who remained in Quiberon Bay back to England but bad weather and westerly winds prevented them sailing. They only left the bay on 6 November and after a stormy passage they arrived piecemeal in England over the last weeks of that month.

The remaining soldiers of the Régiment de Damas were not aboard these transports. The order that the unit was to disbanded, along with all the others at Quiberon, had been issued by the War Office in London on 17 September 1795, with an effective date of 24 September.[49] Two days later a letter was sent by the department, 'to M de Damas, or the officer commanding the corps':

> The unfortunate event of Quiberon having reduced the regiment under your orders to a form insufficient to do active service, and no reasonable hope existing to be able to recruit it so as to be able to continue in your present form, your efforts for the cause of your King and your country, I have received the orders of the Secretary of War to inform you that it is the wish of His Majesty that your regiment be reformed following the plan confided to Mr Bird who is charged with communicating it to you.
>
> The Secretary of War orders me to add that he would be all the more anxious to announce to you this arrangement if he was not persuaded that it will contribute effectively to the good of the service, and that he will put the Government in a state to extend its benevolence to a greater number of those who have sacrificed so much to loyalty and honour.[50]

47 Corbett (ed.), *Private Papers of George, Second Earl Spencer*, p.110, Warren to Spencer (private) 16 October 1795.

48 TNA ADM 80/137 Keats to Warren, 20 October 1795.

49 TNA WO 4/735.

50 GARF, 758/2/52.

The men of all the former black cockade units, Damas, Béon, Périgord, Rohan and Salm, were to be incorporated into the Loyal Emigrants. The units were mustered on 8 October indicating that the order that they were to be disbanded was then known in Quiberon Bay. Unfortunately, no information is available for Damas but between them the four other units had nine officers, six staff and 147 other ranks.[51] On 23 October, Keats instructed that the soldiers from the five units be gathered together, in transports, ready to be sent to the Loyal Emigrants on Île d'Yeu.[52] The transfer took place soon after, as the return of 1 November, shows 112 men had joined in the previous month; five more joined in the following month.[53]

The pay lists of the Loyal Emigrants show that eight Damas soldiers joined the regiment at this time.[54] They were: Sergeant Jean Daniel (or D'Aniel); Corporals François Duvernay (or Duvernoy) and Jean-Baptiste Morel; Privates Joseph Belazord, Louis Beaujois, Charles Corvé, Hermans Casper and Pierre Schmith (who died on 2 December)

Some men had already returned to England among the wounded, to be treated at the hospital at Southampton. It was there that two men from Damas, Claude Berger and Jean Jessel, given as Jussel, were enrolled as sergeants in the Loyal Emigrants on 14 November and, apparently at the same time, another, Pierre Berthelot, as a corporal.[55] Two other members of the Régiment de Damas, who were shown as volunteers, also came to England, one was the unit's last commander, Mercier des Pelle-Saunier, who joined the cadre unit of the Prince de Léon, and the other was Jean de la Battud who was discharged with three months' pay.[56]

Although new supplies arrived at the beginning of November, the situation for the troops on Île d'Yeu led to many of them becoming ill and forty-five men in the British infantry died from dysentery.[57] In the final stage the garrison on Île d'Yeu consisted of the following units:

Units under the command of Major General Doyle, Île d'Yeu, 5 December 1795

British Army	**All ranks with women and children**	**Horses**
14th Light Dragoons	79	28
12th, 78th, 80th and 90th Foot	3,680	–
Loyal Emigrants	272	–
Royal Artillery	96	–
Civil Department and Horse Branch	247	60
'French Corps'		
Emigrant Artillery	130	–
Uhlans Britanniques	56	26
Choiseul Hussars	49	28
Warren's Hussars	25	3

Source: TNA WO 1/176, the monthly returns (WO 17/234) only show the British Army units which includes the Loyal Emigrants.

51 TNA WO 12/11732.
52 TNA ADM 80/137.
53 TNA WO 17/234.
54 TNA WO 12/11732; the date of their joining was backdated to 25 September, the official date of disbanding.
55 TNA WO 12/11732.
56 TNA WO 12/11981 and WO 4/377.
57 Fortescue *British Campaigns in Flanders*, p.423 also TNA WO 17/234.

Finally, Artois decided that his only realistic option was to leave the Île d'Yeu and sail with the British. On 17 November Artois sent a message, accompanied by a presentational sword, to Charette announcing his departure in a few days; the next day Artois left the island.[58]

The operation to evacuate the troops from the island faced some delays but began in earnest from 3 December.[59] Within the following week the troops were embarked onboard 18 warships and three *chasse-marées* of Warren's squadron; the stores, horses and equipment were taken onto 39 transports. The Loyal Emigrants, with 22 officers, 243 rank and file and two women or children, boarded the frigate HMS *Melampus* along with half the 14th Light Dragoon detachment and parties from the Emigrant Artillery and Uhlans Britanniques and sailed to Quiberon Bay.[60] Most of the troops were embarked by 10 December with the last going onboard five days later.[61]

Once in the bay there was some redistribution of the troops amongst the ships and the Loyal Emigrants transferred to the larger HMS *Tremendous*.[62] The fleet finally left the south coast of Brittany and sailed for England. HMS *Galatea*, sailing ahead, arrived at Plymouth, with Warren and Doyle, on 28 December accompanied by some *chasse-marées* under French Royal colours and the troops were reported to have arrived in Southampton Water on 8 January 1796.[63]

The Loyal Emigrants disembarked on the South Coast of England and spent the year, 1796, at Lymington in Hampshire. The following year the regiment was in Portugal, part of a brigade to support Britain's ally, where it remained until hostilities ended with the Peace of Amiens. The same year the Loyal Emigrants were disbanded on Jersey on 24 August 1802.

While these events had been taking place, the bulk of the Régiment de Damas, the officers and most of the soldiers, were prisoners at Auray after their march on the night of 21/22 July. The number of prisoners, most of whom had been brought to Auray, caused an immediate problem for the republican authorities, Hoche reported that 6,252 prisoners had been taken on 21 July: 278 émigré officers, 260 émigré soldiers, 492 Toulonnais, 1,632 French prisoners and 3,600 chouans.[64] The first task was to separate the different categories, so, mid-morning on 22 July the émigré officers were led away to the former church of Saint-Esprit which had been transformed into a prison with two floors and an attic. Later the rest of the prisoners were marched from the town so that the French and foreign soldiers could be divided from the émigrés, for the Damas personnel this meant, in effect, separating the chasseurs from the fusiliers. Sombreuil lodged separately, along with republican officers, at one of the town's inns.

58 Hutt, *Chouannerie and Counter-Revolution*, p.360; see also Bouillé, *Souvenirs*, p.309.

59 Corbett (ed.), *Private Papers of George, Second Earl Spencer*, pp.116–117, Warren to Spencer (private) 3 December 1795.

60 TNA ADM 80/137 'General List of the Embarkation of Troops taken off Isle Dieu between 3rd & 15th Dec 1795'.

61 Corbett (ed.), *Private Papers of George, Second Earl Spencer*, p.118, Warren to Spencer (private) 9 December 1795 and TNA ADM 80/137.

62 TNA WO 1/76 'State of the Forces … on board Rear Admiral Harvey's Fleet, Quiberon Bay 26th December 1795'.

63 *The Times* 1 and 13 January 1796.

64 G. Thomas de Closmadeuc, *Quiberon 1795 Émigrés et Chouans Commissions Militaires : Interrogatoires et Jugements* (Paris: Société d'éditions littéraires, 1899), p.161, report to the Directoire du département at Vannes, 5 Thermidor An III.

Other churches, chapels and convents were pressed into service for the other categories of prisoners.[65] Food was already in short supply in the town, with much of the countryside supplying the chouans, and it took some time for sufficient to be given to the prisoners. However local women, noble ladies, some of whom had family members amongst the prisoners, and townsfolk were permitted to bring food for the detainees. These visitors also brought news and information and, for some, provided help to escape when the time and opportunity arose.

The next significant step for the republicans was to establish the means to adjudicate on the culpability of individual prisoners and deal with them appropriately, the representatives of the Committee of Public Safety who were present, Jean-Lambert Tallien and Claude Blad, directed that military commissions be formed for this purpose. As the republicans did not consider themselves bound by any capitulation the process, for the émigré officers and volunteers, simply involved the commissions considering if there was any reason why they should not suffer the full force of the law. The law of 25 Brumaire An III was clear, all émigrés who returned to France and were taken armed in an assemblage were to be judged and condemned to death.[66]

Different laws covered other categories of prisoners, but the proscribed priests who had returned to France faced the same fate. The sheer number of chouans taken on 21 July, at other actions and those sent back from Houat, meant only those considered the most senior were to be condemned, the others were allowed to return home but not before many had died of typhus in prison.[67] As for the soldiers who had been captured – émigré soldiers, French prisoners as well as those who were identified as from Toulon – were also liable to be condemned either under the law of 25 Brumaire or under military law, if they had previously served in the republican forces, and deserted to the enemy. Those found to be foreigners were to be considered as prisoners of war, with the choice of joining the republican forces or waiting to be exchanged. Of the French soldiers, it appears that most of the soldiers never stood before a formal commission. Rotalier, after speaking to one of his men who had escaped, along with three Rohan soldiers, to re-join the British fleet in Quiberon Bay, later reported, 'as for the infantry soldiers the patriots make them submit to a sort of examination; they have shot those who do not give patriotic responses; and have incorporated into their regiments those in which they believe to find republican sentiments.'[68]

The first commission sat at Auray, on 27 July, 16 men were condemned including Sombreuil and they were immediately sent to Vannes to be shot the following morning. This commission was immediately disbanded and replaced by two more at Auray, while two were established at Quiberon with further ones at Vannes and Port Louis. The way individual émigrés chose to face the commissions varied greatly. Many refused to recognise their judges' authority or to sign the interrogations; others were more compliant. In the first days of the commissions many referred to the capitulation, saying this was the reason they had laid down their arms and so considered themselves prisoners of war. However, as it soon became clear the commissions

65 La Villegourio, *Ma Sortie de Quiberon*, p.25, Villeneuve-Laroche-Barnaud, *Mémoires sur l'expédition de Quiberon*, Part II, p.161, Closmadeuc, *Quiberon 1795*, pp.103 and 161.

66 Closmadeuc, *Quiberon 1795*, pp.51 and 150; Tallien left for Paris to inform the committee of the victory, leaving Blad to oversee the proceedings.

67 Closmadeuc, *Quiberon 1795*, p.145.

68 TNA PRO 30/11/225 Rotalier to Cornwallis 18 August 1795.

were not going to recognise the existence of any such capitulation, this approach was no longer used.[69] Many decided, 'It is better to die than live by a lie!'[70] The others chose to try to avoid being condemned by any means they thought might work, some stated that the British had tricked or forced them to serve against France and some tried to claim that they were foreigners or even told a combination of such tales. The commissions may have not been over zealous in their initial investigation of these stories but they did reject the suggestion raised by some, to avoid being shot, that they should be considered as foreigners simply on the basis that they were members of the Order of Malta.[71] Others described themselves as domestic servants or that they had served in some other non-combatant role and thus had not borne arms against the Republic. A number sought reprieve on the basis that they had emigrated, along with a father or other relative, as a boy. Many of the young, or young looking, officers, cadets and volunteers lied about their age to allow them to use this exception when it became known that Blad had directed the commissions to take a lenient interpretation of the law, namely not to condemn anyone who had emigrated before the age of 16. He had however written to the Committee of Public Safety for confirmation of this decision.[72]

It was at Quiberon that the first members of Damas were interrogated and condemned, on 28 July by the commission, presided by *Chef de Bataillon* Dinne of the Tirailleurs Belges, sitting at Kerdavid, just north of Saint Pierre-Quiberon. They were a chasseur, Louis-Guillaume de Varin, aged 46, a former garde-du-corps de Monsieur who had served in Damas since its formation, and a 20-year-old fusilier, Florentin-Ignace-Marie Dussautoir, who had previously deserted from the Bataillon de Saint Omer before joining Damas.[73] The location of the hearing, and the mixed group of those condemned at the session, seems to indicate that these prisoners had remained at Quiberon, probably among the sick or wounded. They were duly taken to a natural ditch to the west of the village and shot.[74]

The next day, 29 July, saw the largest number of Damas personnel appear before a commission, with *Chef de Bataillon* Jean-Germain Lalène de Laprade as president, sitting in a former chapel, which is now the tourist office, at Auray. They were the surgeon Urbain-Claude Vimar, two NCOs, Charles-Gabriel-Germain Chevalier de Chenu and Jean-Nicolas Legris, the Chasseur hornist Jean-Nicolas Wolf and 22 of the chasseurs. Except for one or two of the chasseurs who were reprieved by reason of their actual, or claimed, youth, all were executed the following day. They were marched a few kilometres north of the town and shot, beside the tidal reaches of the Auray River, in a field which was to become known as the Champ des Martyrs.[75]

69 Closmadeuc, *Quiberon 1795*, p.195.

70 Montbron, *Récit de l'Evasion d'un Officier*, p.54, quoting an old officer.

71 Villeneuve-Laroche-Barnaud, *Mémoires sur l'expédition de Quiberon*, Part II, p.208.

72 Closmadeuc, *Quiberon 1795*, pp.216–218.

73 The condemned have been identified by use of the lists compiled by Eugène Le Garrec, *Les Vrais Martyrs de Quiberon (1795)* (Vannes: Lafolye et Lamarzelle, 1935), Closmadeuc, *Quiberon 1795*, and La Gournerie, *Les Débris de Quiberon*, which do not always coincide.

74 La Gournerie, *Les Débris de Quiberon*, p.81. Nicolas Joseph Noël, formerly of the Damas infantry and serving with the Loyal Emigrants, was condemned, as were two others who may have served in Damas, but whose identification is not definite, Pierre Joseph La Brousse, Veteran Loyal Emigrants, and Charlemagne Joseph Mathurin François de Courson de Kernescop, Rohan cadet.

75 La Gournerie, *Les Débris de Quiberon*, p.90.

Chenu also gained a reprieve, through an intercession made on behalf of an old comrade. He and Pierre-Paul Botta had served together as *capitaines* in the Régiment de Normandie. Botta, now *général de brigade*, lost his leg in the attack on Fort Penthièvre and when he was brought to Auray he learnt of the capture of Chenu. Before he died from his wound, on 28 July, Botta had asked a republican official to see what he could do for Chenu but, despite his best efforts, the official only managed to obtain a short stay of execution of two days or so. A fellow prisoner later described Chenu, when the order for his execution arrived, thanking the official for his efforts and recommending the other prisoners to him, 'Admirable deed of self-sacrifice, courage, kindness and resignation. As he expresses all the good sentiments, all the motions of a noble heart, the lofty manners of a fine soul!'[76]

It was soon the turn of the main body of the Damas officers to face their judgement. They, with other captured officers, about a hundred in all, were marched back to Quiberon. Jean-Louis-Alexis de Villeneuve-Laroche-Barnaud, of Damas, had not resigned himself to captivity, previously proposing that they set the prison at Auray alight to perhaps provide a means to escape and looked forward to the march as it might give an opportunity to do so, but none arose as the prisoners were well guarded.[77] Tercier was amongst them:

> We were marched between a triple row of soldiers … We arrived about four hours after midday at Quiberon; we were made to enter into a field closed and surrounded by a barely raised dry-stone wall. We had all brought in our pockets a miserable morsel of bread which was to be sufficient for us in the few moments that we had still to groan in this country, once so sweet. We slept in this field. We were very thirsty. It was with the greatest difficulty that we could obtain some glasses of water from our enemies…[78]

The next day the Damas officers went before the commission, sitting in a house at Keraud, outside Saint Pierre-Quiberon. One of the prisoners wrote,

> It ought to be acknowledged, we were disposed of promptly. Your name, your age, place of your birth, had you emigrated? This is to what the questions to us were restricted posed by M. Dubois, *chef de bataillon* from Arras and president of the military commission that judged us. The affirmative response to this last question was the signal for your condemnation. From the chamber where the commission sat, you were made to go up into a bad attic; and at the approach of the night, twenty soldiers, sad executors of the vengeance of a few scoundrels, led to the seashore, and there shot twenty victims whose corpses were borne away on the ebbing waves.[79]

76 Claude Berthier de Grandry, *Récit Sommaire de la Déplorable Affaire de Quiberon* (Nantes: Forest, 1861), pp.41–42.

77 Villeneuve-Laroche-Barnaud, *Mémoires sur l'expédition de Quiberon*, p.186 and 202 and La Villegourio, *Ma Sortie de Quiberon*, p.36.

78 La Chanonie, *Mémoires*, pp.142–143.

79 La Villegourio, *Ma Sortie de Quiberon*, pp.36–37.

In general, the Damas officers were not passive in their appearances before the commission: most were defiant, especially regarding their reasons for leaving France, while some actively tried to avoid being condemned. Captains de Boulon and Borassol said they had left France due, Boulon said, to persecution by political clubs and, in Borassol's case, bad treatment in his home town of Toulouse. Lieutenant de Montfort simply stated that he had emigrated in 1791 having been permitted to retire after refusing to swear the oath required by the new regime but that he did not know of the laws against émigrés. Lieutenant Joseph de Savignac, when asked, said that he had left in 1792 because of the insurrection of the battalion under his command. Both Lieutenants de Chasteigner de Lagrange and Cardon de Vidampierre referred to a capitulation. Lagrange said he had left France through persecution, and being refused leave that he needed, and that he had laid down his arms after the capitulation. Although Vidampierre had explained that he only served in the Régiment de Damas out of necessity and he had had no idea he would be brought to France, the commission noted his defiance:

> [He] further observed that he only finds himself here by virtue of the proposition made by the general and the officers of the bataillon de la Gironde, that it would be nothing to them ... Without this capitulation, he would have embarked with his soldiers or would have been killed at their head.[80]

Ensign de Pressac took a penitent line, saying that he left France due to a personal affair and, unaware of the law, he had joined Damas through necessity. He 'further observed that before his leaving France, he had served the Republic with all possible zeal; that part of his family still serves it and that an unfortunate circumstance alone had been able to force him to quit his position.' His fellow ensign, and quartermaster, Jean-Baptiste Ducrozet said that he had left France after refusing to make the required oath and that he did know about the law but had believed that he was in fact sailing to Jersey. In common with all the Damas officers who acknowledged their rank, Ducrozet made no mention of his Dutch service, only dating his service with the unit from that of his British commission. Villeneuve-Laroche-Barnaud gave the same reason for leaving France but denied serving in any regiment, explaining that he was only attached to the Régiment de Damas in order to go to England, never thinking he would end up in France.[81]

While at Auray Lieutenant Colonel de Rouault de Gamache had actively tried to find the means for the officers to escape and then liberate the other prisoners. His case features in several of the memoirs and subsequent histories, leading to some colour being added to what happened, but the official record provides a fairly straightforward turn of events. He gave his name as Charles Genhaut and that he was Swiss, there was a grain of truth to this as he had been born at Nyon, Switzerland, when his parents were there as visitors, so he should be treated as a prisoner of war. Inexplicably he, correctly, said he had been second *major* in the Chasseurs à Cheval de la Lorraine but, when his rank was suppressed, he had gone to England where he married and was appointed to the Régiment de Damas. Finally,

80 Le Garrec, *Les Vrais Martyrs de Quiberon*, pp.133–134.

81 Closmadeuc, *Quiberon 1795*, pp.261–331 (quotes pp.261 and 284) and Le Garrec, *Les Vrais Martyrs de Quiberon*, pp.131–136.

he signed the interrogation, Charles Rouault. He was executed along with his domestic, François Vaudin, who had refused to leave him.[82]

Two of the Damas officers were successful in passing this, their first, test and their cases were adjourned. Claude de Tercier later recounted that being impatient he voluntarily went first when the commission began its hearings at 8:00 a.m.

> I replied that I was Liegois, born in that place. Examined why I found myself in the assemblage, I said that I had embarked at Hamburg, as a merchant, on the English fleet, persuaded, as the rumour had spread, that it was to land in Belgium, from where I intended to reach the lands of the Indes. I contested for a long time with the judges of the commission, of whose reasoning, fallacious questions and quibbles I confounded.[83]

An even more imaginative story was given to the commission by *Abbé* Langlois de la Heuse, who appeared as a deported priest who had been captured on the beach at Quiberon. He explained:

> Having learned from the papers, in England, that a decree of the Convention gave full latitude to the liberty of religion and conscience, he had taken a passage which was said to be destined for Jersey and Guernsey; from there, he had the intention to take a fisherman's boat to return to France.
>
> The merchant vessel on which he was contained no émigrés; instead of taking him to Jersey it received the order to come to the coasts of France, where he was disembarked *despite him and to his great astonishment.*
>
> He observed that having one day landed from his ship at Quiberon and having remarked that the island [sic] was occupied by the émigrés and that they were waging war with the republicans, he re-embarked on the spot to not be compromised and it is only by force that he was obliged to land on the eve of the taking of Fort Penthièvre.[84]

He added that he had had the opportunity to embark during the republican offensive on 21 July but had chosen not do so 'full of confidence in the generosity of his fellow citizens *who he wished to re-join*.' His offer to tend the wounded had been accepted and he had not been treated as a prisoner.

Both Tercier and Langlois de La Heuse were marched to Auray to await a further interrogation. The commissions at Quiberon soon closed, other prisoners had been sent to Vannes and it was there, as well as at Auray, that the commissions continued their work in early

82 Closmadeuc, *Quiberon 1795*, pp.308–309; Le Garrec, *Les Vrais Martyrs de Quiberon*, pp.133–135, also see Montbron, *Récit de l'Evasion d'un Officier*, pp.67–68, Villeneuve-Laroche-Barnaud, *Mémoires sur l'expédition de Quiberon*, p.202 and La Chanonie, *Mémoires*, pp.149, 151–154.

83 La Chanonie, *Mémoires*, p.150 also pp.412–414.

84 Closmadeuc, *Quiberon 1795*, p.364. Le Garrec, *Les Vrais Martyrs de Quiberon*, p.159 states that the chaplain appeared before the Dinne Commission and not that chaired by Dubois, this is conceivable given his explanation of his role at Quiberon.

August. A small number of the chasseurs and other soldiers who had served in the Damas infantry seem to have been condemned during these weeks, however conclusive identification is difficult as the commissions, as time went on, appear to have been less concerned to record the units to which their victims had belonged.[85]

In Paris, on 9 August, the Committee of Public Safety overturned Blad's decision and ordered that judgements be made on those who had quitted France before they were 16 years old and had been taken with arms.[86] This brought many young émigrés before the commissions again. At Auray the brothers Pierre and Théodore du Garreau de La Seinie were condemned and executed. The three brothers had been the first to join the Légion de Damas at Maastricht in 1793 but Joseph, the eldest, had joined the Austrian army as an infantry officer in February 1795. They, along with Pierre Sevestre who shared the same fate, had previously appeared before the Lalène Commission with the other Damas chasseurs, but their cases had been adjourned in compliance with Blad's directive. The same commission condemned the *Abbé* Langlois de La Heuse, he had had only a brief reprieve. The last member of the Régiment de Damas executed at Auray was a fusilier, Pierre Arnault or Arnoult, condemned on the last day of August.

Most of the young émigrés had been held in the Tour du Connétable at Vannes, but only three of them were Damas chasseurs, the brothers Florentin and Fidèle du Laurent de La Barre and Louis-François de Vélard; all three were condemned. Another pair of brothers, Louis-Henry and Pierre-Abel de Savatte de Genouillé, were condemned by the Legrand Commission; both had joined the Damas infantry in 1793 but later transferred to the Loyal Emigrants. Other than these young chasseurs, three more men from the unit were condemned at Vannes at the end of August and the first few days of September. Despite their different backgrounds, all came from the Perpignan area. François Bassou, described as a 19-year-old saddler, a fusilier sergeant, Joseph de Pontich de Roig, aged 28, had previously been a junior officer in the royal Army and so was probably a chasseur, and the last was 51years old armourer Jean Noël. François Gervais Eudes de Boiseudes who had been a chasseur in Damas in 1793, but who may have transferred to another unit afterwards, was also condemned at Vannes, on 31 August.

The last of the Régiment de Damas to be executed was the chasseur, Jean-Baptiste-François-Marie Pallet d'Antraize, he had continued to try to avoid execution by claiming, in addition to being younger, that he had been a republican soldier who, having been captured by the Austrians, had only joined the émigrés after almost a year's imprisonment. His ruse succeeded at first, however the ages he claimed were inconsistent and, after some delay, he was condemned on 14 September.[87]

Some Damas personnel, of course, escaped execution. Late in 1796 the War Office issued instructions 'to pay Mr de la Nugarde late a Serjeant attached to the Regiment of Béon and Mr de la Coulange late a Volunteer attached to the Regiment of Damas both of whom were taken prisoner at Quiberon, the whole of their appointments during their Absence viz:

85 The condemned being Fusilier Louis Chatel; Marie-Charles Petit de la Pichonniere, Jean de Sanzillon, Jean-Baptiste-Germain de La Chevière of the Chasseurs and Jean-Antoine Daurout, a former Chasseur, who was serving in the Loyal Emigrants as a veteran.

86 Closmadeuc, *Quiberon 1795*, pp.230–232.

87 Closmadeuc, *Quiberon 1795*, p.307.

– from 21st July 1795 to 1st August 1796.'[88] It is not clear how they had escaped and what had happened to them before arriving on England. However, this is not the case for those of the regiment who survived to write their memoirs. Those of Jacquier de Noyelle are somewhat opaque in places; however, he appears to have been taken to Vannes where he was held with the other young émigré volunteers. There he fell ill and was taken to one of the hospitals for some time. Having recovered his health, he was again held in a prison within the city walls; before being taken before a commission at which he was absolved and told he would be taken into the French Republic's army. He managed to obtain a certificate of convalescence for a fortnight from the doctor who had previously treated him, enabling him to obtain a passport with which he travelled to Nantes and made his escape.[89]

Tercier's account provides more details as well as mentioning others from the Régiment de Damas. He was the only officer to escape, having managed to have his immediate judgement adjourned. At Auray he appeared before the Lalène Commission and maintained his identity as a merchant from Liège; his nationality was finally accepted but he found himself considered a prisoner of war. He was soon marched under escort to Vannes where, he relates, much to his consternation he was imprisoned with the prospect of being brought before another commission to be condemned. He was accompanied, on the march to Vannes, by Madame de Bennes, on arrival they were initially housed together, 'A chapel, the name of which I forget, served as a place of detention for a hundred or so prisoners, Prussians, Austrians and French deserters. That is the place where we were locked up.'[90]

Bennes made her escape and Tercier was questioned about it, but soon, in turn, he was able to slip away unseen. He was given sanctuary by well-wishers, before being taken to a house on the edge of town where he found 'six to eight people' including one of the Damas chasseurs, Emmanuel de Guéfontaine. After three days both Tercier and Guéfontaine were guided away to join the chouans; they requested the means to re-join their unit, and the British fleet, but Puisaye not only refused to help but also blocked their departure. As a result, Guéfontaine joined a 'company' of émigrés who had escaped and served with the chouans. Both men subsequently joined Marie-Paul Vicomte de Scépeaux's division operating in Maine, there Tercier became a *chef de division*, and followed the path of the chouannerie in the region; Guéfontaine met his death at Ballée on 20 October 1799.

Further evidence that many of the soldiers captured whilst serving with the émigrés were placed in republican units and then deserted to the chouans is provided by Corbehem. He found himself among the few émigrés imprisoned alongside the captured French and foreign soldiers at Vannes. After being held in various churches and other buildings these prisoners were soon assembled in an expansive walled enclosure, without protection from the elements, in the grounds of a suppressed religious community, the Père-Éternel, alongside the canal and outside the city walls. Three other Damas volunteers were there also, held amongst this class of prisoner: Bennes, the 'marquis de Fo*****' who he had noted at Fort Neuf and another of which he could not recall the name or fate. They initially received visits and comforts from a lady visitor, a Madame du Portail, but fearing this particular attention

88 TNA WO 4/353.
89 Closmadeuc, *Quiberon 1795*, pp.4–48.
90 La Chanonie, *Mémoires*, p.169.

would mark them out as émigrés these soon stopped. Their benefactor, however, provided the means for both Bennes and 'marquis de Fo*****' to escape.[91]

Each morning a republican a detachment, with a drummer, attended the enclosure to march a party of prisoners out to be interrogated by a commission. As there was no list of the prisoners, those who considered that they had least to fear from the proceedings went first. Initially Corbehem stayed behind as he desperately sought a story that would save him. As he was held as an ordinary soldier, he had to convince the commission that he was either a foreigner or a Frenchman who had been forced to serve in the émigré ranks. One day, as he was walking in the enclosure, he heard a Rohan soldier talking in a familiar accent. The soldier came from the village of Troisvaux, just outside Corbehem's home town of Saint-Pol-sur-Ternoise; he explained that having been conscripted into the local battalion, the 3e du Pas-de-Calais, but had deserted to the émigrés near Lille. The soldier's story inspired Corbehem to pass himself off as a similar conscript, from Artois, who had been captured and forced to serve with the émigrés. He thus tried to obtain as much information about the same Saint-Pol battalion, its personnel and service, as he could.

After two days, Corbehem felt he had to take his chance, considering that the commission would take a more jaded view of those prisoners who had waited until the last to appear before it. On questioning, he gave his own name, but that he was only 20 years old and had been conscripted into the battalion before it left Saint-Pol at the end of 1793. He explained that he had been captured by the Austrians while on patrol near Lille and was kept in such awful conditions at Antwerp that he succumbed to the blandishments of the Dutch recruiters, but only with the intention of deserting. However, he was taken to Maastricht and enrolled in an émigré unit from which he could not escape, always posted far from republican lines such as with the baggage guards, his first chance was at Quiberon. He managed to maintain his composure during supplementary questioning so that the commission accepted his story. He was to be taken into the Republic's army.

> On leaving the presence of the commission, and becoming free again, was led to the bivouac outside the town, where all the absolved prisoners were collected… We were three to four hundred in this bivouac; at the end of a few days, the commanders of the different corps stationed in the town, and whose battalions were not complete, came to review us, and to each take a certain number of men. I was chosen with many others for the 42e régiment d'infanterie, formerly the régiment de la Reine, and we were transferred to a location encompassed with walls, also situated outside the town, and which the regiment occupied. Some tents had been erected for it; others were for us, at a certain distance. It seemed that we were not worthy of being approached, or that, novice Republicans, we would have a trial period to pass before being called to the honour of fraternising with them.[92]

He remained in this situation for about a fortnight during which time parties of new recruits were assigned fatigue duties under the supervision of two NCOs armed with batons. He

91 Corbehem, *Dix ans de ma vie*, p.207.
92 Corbehem, *Dix ans de ma vie*, pp.215–216.

wanted to join the chouans and, hearing from Madame du Portail, he was told of a house in Vannes in which he would obtain sanctuary if he could escape. One day when, as usual, his party was marching through the town to collect the regiment's food rations he slipped away unseen and reached the safe house. There he was taken to a room in which there were five other escapees, all unknown to him. As night fell, they were joined by Madame du Portail and some other women and they soon strolled out of the town unchallenged, dressed as townsfolk, each with a female companion on their arm, to a house in the country. Later a guide led them through the night to the lodgings of the chouan leader, Georges Cadoudal.

Cadoudal joined them in a meal, asking about their experiences at Quiberon, and they agreed to serve under his orders. The party was then guided to a country house outside the village of Grand-Champ in which there were about thirty fellow émigrés, two of whom Corbehem knew personally. These were Guéfontaine and a sergeant from one of the Damas fusilier companies, who Corbehem identified by the name of 'Chaumont.'[93] Corbehem, who served with them for about three months, described the émigrés as forming a band of volunteers who served without formal structure or assigned duties. They always served together, 30-40 strong, joining chouans who had gathered for an operation and continually on the move. They received no pay but their needs were provided by the country folk. However, they were without news from the outside world and surrounded by people who only spoke and understood the local Breton tongue, receiving their orders directly from Cadoudal or the other chouan leaders. The band took part in several operations which had limited success.

In the last action Corbehem took part in with the volunteers, they were joined by chouans which raised their number to about a hundred men. Moving from Méradec, a hamlet to the north, an ambush was laid on the Vannes-Auray road. After two hours wait a small republican infantry detachment of about 50 men came into view; fired upon the republicans fled towards Vannes, leaving a few of their number dead. After a short pursuit, the volunteers and choauns returned to Méradec to eat. They had just sat down to their meal when a warning shout arose, 'There are the blues!'; they were attacked by republican cavalry from Vannes. Everyone seized their arms and in chaos ran to save themselves. The volunteers were unfamiliar with the area and Corbehem, only by luck stumbled into a marsh, north of the hamlet, in which he hid from the cavalry. Many of the chouans, and volunteers, tried to reach the substantial buildings of the Manoir de Kérango some way off to the east of Méradec and across open ground. Several of them were cut down by the republican cavalry including Chaumont, 'who saw the end, on this day, of his honourable career. This brave man, whom we all regretted, had not ceased, during the whole course of his life, to give proofs of the most complete devotion to the royal cause. He merited a more fortunate fate.'[94] Corbehem was by now disillusioned with the chouannerie so, taking his leave from Cadoudal, he walked through Brittany and Normandy before eventually reaching his home, after an absence of four years.

Corbehem had always been worried about being denounced by one of the soldier prisoners he had been held with, men of different nationalities and from different units, all

93 Corbehem, *Dix ans de ma vie*, pp.224–225; although it is not conclusive, it appears that 'Chaumont' was André Froment de Chau-du-Mont, formerly *capitaine* in the Orléans infantry and sergeant in Stack's Fusilier Company.

94 Corbehem, *Dix ans de ma vie*, p.236.

wishing to save themselves. There were some instances of prisoners succumbing to republican persuasion and denouncing the émigrés amongst them, but he had 'very sweet satisfaction in certifying that not one informer was found among the soldiers, either of my legion, or all those who had formed part of Sombreuil's division.'[95] Indeed Bennes owed her life to such loyalty. Despite her unique situation, her account which was written so soon after the events provides some fascinating glimpses into how the republicans tried to uncover the evidence to condemn the émigrés. When the prisoners were initially separated, émigrés from the others, she was designated to remain with the soldiers. This was because she identified herself as a woman who worked for the men, only wearing a uniform as a convenient, and cheap, form of attire. Imprisoned at Auray she describes the soldiers as only receiving a pound of coarse bread a day and not even straw to lie on. After three weeks, the soldier prisoners were marched to Vannes where they were 'again confined in different churches. Two days after, we were taken to a place called Le Pere Eternel [sic], and, three weeks after, I was brought before the Tribunal.'[96]

There she gave a false name, saying she was from the Sittard region, near Maastricht, and that she and her husband had fled on the approach of the French. Without money, her husband enlisted in the first regiment they encountered which, by chance, was an émigré unit. After the death of her husband, in the previous year, she had remained with the regiment only because it allowed her to make a living. The initial hearing ended after this brief examination. However, after a month she was confronted in prison, the republicans apparently having discovered her identity. She stuck to her story despite being challenged including with a document bearing her true name and home – she calmly returned it, claiming she could not read. The republican officer, 'turning to a soldier who stood by me, and belonged to the same regiment, offered to grant him his pardon, and to let him at liberty that very day, if he would declare who I was. This honest fellow, (who by the bye was a Dutchman) replied, that he could not tell, as he himself had never enquired.'[97]

Her situation appeared more ominous when she was prevented from going with other women prisoners who were permitted to leave to wash clothes, she was being treated as a special case. A few days later she was again brought before the commission and robustly challenged over her story but she would not shift. It was decided to see if other Damas soldiers would undermine her position:

> Accordingly, three of my companions were sent for, but great care was taken to prevent me from speaking to them. I have been informed since, that when they were asked who I was, they said they knew not; whether I was not one of the *ci-devant Nobles*? They answered in the same manner. What was my business with them? That I was a semptress and a washer-woman. Whether my husband was an officer or a private? That he was dead before they had entered the regiment, so that they were not certain, but that they had heard that he was a private. They were offered a bribe in case they would inform against me, but they persisted in saying, that they

95 Corbehem, *Dix ans de ma vie*, p.202.
96 Bennes, *Narrative*, p.37.
97 Bennes, *Narrative*, p.39.

> could not tell things they were ignorant of. Yet these good fellows knew everything about me. Their generosity cannot be too much admired.[98]

A few days later she heard that she was to be executed the following day, she had to escape as soon as possible and was told of a safe house should she succeed. The unit performing the guard duties changed overnight and hoping that the soldiers may not have been told of the restrictions on her, she loaded a basket with dirty laundry and went to leave the prison to do the washing; this time she was permitted to go. She immediately made her way to the safe house where she hid from the republicans and received women's clothing. Moved to another house in the city for three days she then went into the countryside, going from house to house; lastly, she sheltered in a hollow in the ground near the seashore for 10 days before getting out to the British fleet in a boat.

She boarded HMS *Arethusa*, on which she sailed for England, landing at Plymouth on 20 November.[99] She had no money, she had not wanted to take charity from the naval officers, but by luck she met the former *chirurgien major* of the Légion de Damas in Plymouth who gave her half a guinea. The surgeon, Georges Couturier, formerly of the Régiment de Berwick, had been appointed to the Légion de Damas on 19 February 1794, after Niel's resignation, and then had joined the Uhlans Britanniques, to be replaced in Damas by François Couturier, previously his assistant in Berwick and almost certainly a relation.[100] Having been with his new regiment in Quiberon Bay, he was at Plymouth after its piecemeal return. Madame de Bennes continued her journey, on foot, to London where she found somewhere to live and soon wrote her memoirs.

Her story and those of the other survivors of Quiberon bear witness to the fate of the infantry of the Légion de Damas, the Régiment de Damas. The story of the legion's cavalry, which had remained in Germany, had further to run.

98 Bennes, *Narrative*, pp.40–41.

99 TNA ADM 51/1102, Captain's Log of HMS *Arethusa*, does not mention or allude to her arrival. However, the ship operated in Quiberon Bay from 8 September until 6 November and had frequent contact with *chasse-marées* carrying Chouans. The *Arethusa* left the bay on 6 November and reached Cawsand Bay, Plymouth Sound, on 16 November.

100 François is shown as surgeon at the review of the Damas infantry on 27 October 1794 but did not accompany the infantry to Quiberon. Although unclear, it is likely that he was the same man who remained with the cavalry, but known as Louis Couturier.

8

From the Elbe to the Rhine 1795–1796

In Germany, the foreign cavalry units in British pay had, by the end of March 1795, been placed in cantonments in the region of Celle, about 50 kilometres to the north-east of Hanover. The Damas cavalry were at Burgdorf along with the legion's depot, which was commanded by the Comte de La Grange, formerly of Boulon's fusilier company.

Under the terms of the definitive capitulation, signed on 2 April, the two Damas cavalry companies were each to have four officers and 111 other ranks. It is of note that they had been entitled chasseurs à cheval in February's provisional version, but no specific designation was used in the definitive capitulation. Armed and equipped as hussars, they, as well those of Béon, soon became known as such.[1] The 'List of the Officers of Foreign Corps' of 1796 listed the officers of the 'Damas Hussars' although as some of their names had been given incorrectly on their commissions these errors were replicated in this list:[2]

Colonel	Comte Damas
Major	Vicomte Montjustin
Captains	Raimond Comte de Boisseulh
	Marquis de Bongars
Lieutenants	Chevalier de Bazonges [Aumont de Bazouges]
	Comte de Couan d'Oloo [Conan d'Ocor]
	J.B. Vidal
	Brandin de Saint-Laurent
Cornets	Vicomte de Lentilhac
	Lewis Plantière
Chaplain	Abbé de Chilleau [du]
Adjutant	J.B. de Moizés [Moisez de Souslatour]
Surgeon	Lewis Couturier
Mate	Meyer

1 For example, Puisact noted in his *Journal*, on Friday 8 May 1795: 'I wrote a note … that I inserted in a letter from La Hourrerie to his cousin, hussar with Damas'.

2 TNA WO 65/167, list dated 24 April 1796.

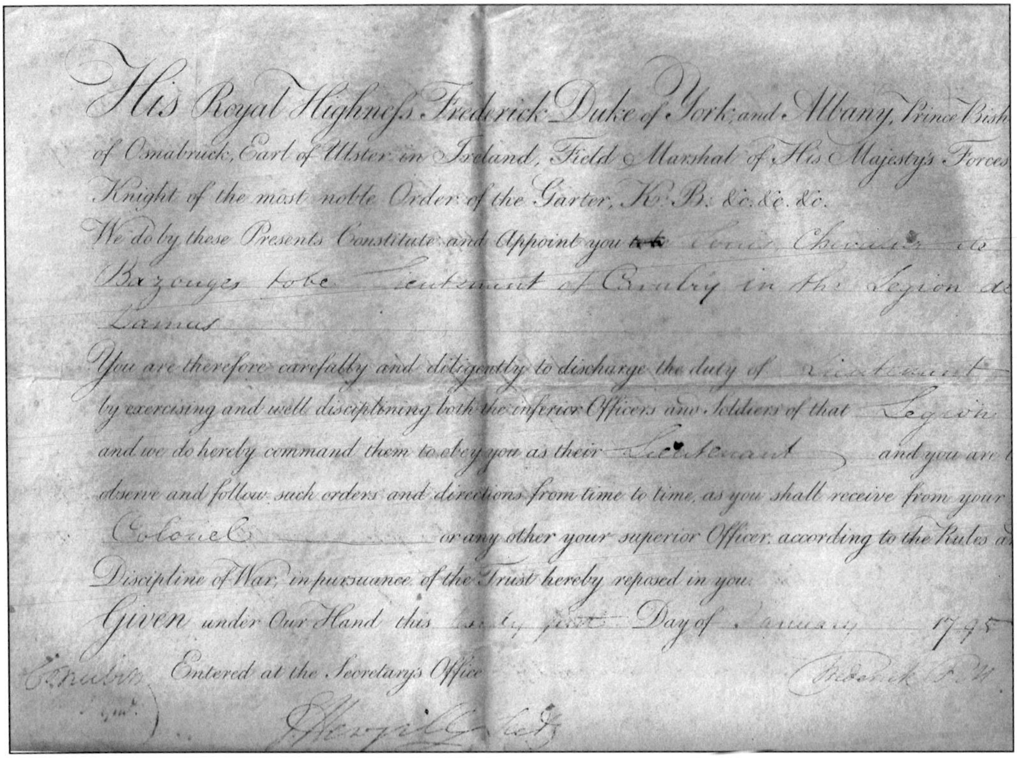
His Royal Highness Frederick Duke of York and Albany, Prince Bish[op]
of Osnabruck, Earl of Ulster in Ireland, Field Marshal of His Majesty's Forces
Knight of the most noble Order of the Garter, K. B. &c. &c. &c.
We do by these Presents Constitute and Appoint you Louis Chevalier de Bazouges to be Lieutenant of Cavalry in the Legion de Damas
You are therefore carefully and diligently to discharge the duty of Lieutenant by exercising and well disciplining both the inferior Officers and Soldiers of that Legion and we do hereby command them to obey you as their Lieutenant and you are to observe and follow such orders and directions from time to time, as you shall receive from your Colonel or any other your superior Officer according to the Rules and Discipline of War, in pursuance of the Trust hereby reposed in you.
Given under Our Hand this twenty first Day of January 1795
Entered at the Secretary's Office

British commission to the Chevalier de Bazouges, 21 January 1795. (Bazouges family archive)

The commissions were dated 21 January 1795 which was, whether symbolically or by chance, the anniversary of the execution of King Louis XVI.

When a separate peace between France and Prussia was signed on 5 April and ratified 10 days later, it was followed on 17 May by an additional convention fixing a line of neutrality across Germany, from the North Sea to the Rhine. It was then for Prussia, in the following three months, to convince the states of Northern Germany, particularly those supplying troops to Britain, and those of the Rhine that they could also benefit from the same conditions. At the strategic level, this measure allowed France to strengthen its forces before a new decisive offensive across the Rhine to force the increasingly isolated Austria to abandon the banks of the river and retire into Southern Germany, with its position at the head of the German Empire severely shaken. In particular it was incumbent upon Prussia to pressurise Hanover to drive out the British troops and émigrés who were still present.

As soon as it was known that such an accord was imminent, the British considered sending a part of their foreign cavalry to reinforce the Austrian forces under *Feldmarschall* Clerfayt, or those of the Prince de Condé, on the Rhine; the changed situation drawing Britain and Austria closer once more.[3] However, due to the diplomatic consequences of

3 TNA WO 1/173.

such a deployment, the project to send these troops remained under study. The best route to Hanau and Frankfurt not only passed through the territory of Hanover and Hesse but also crossed the frontiers of Prussia. The Hanoverians were increasingly complaining about the foreign corps in the region of Celle, accusing them of every evil. If some of these complaints were justified, they were often exaggerated to be rid of the troops in anticipation of the map of Europe being redrawn. Rumour suggested that the King of Prussia had proposed to the French to seize Hanover and give it to the House of Orange, with the British royal family compensated by adding the two Bishoprics of Paderborn and Hildesheim to their lands in Germany. The Hanoverians had convinced themselves that the foreign troops and émigrés were in their territory specifically to control them in case of revolt.

Although they had been in British pay from 1 March, the Damas and Béon cavalry had retained the insignia of the Dutch service, 'It is good to see that the émigrés and other corps which have passed from the service of Holland to that of England have had the order to keep the orange cockades and sashes.'[4] However a month later they changed to British insignia as Béon informed Willem V on 24 April, 'Today I have had to change the colours that we have worn with such happiness and gratitude.'[5]

Around this time dissatisfaction emerged amongst Damas's cavalry as shown by the 'Burgdorf incident' when noble volunteers claimed their horses in compensation for the Dutch discharge payment, which they of course had not received. They wanted to secure their horses so that they could individually join the Armée de Condé. Eighty gentlemen presented their resignations to the Comte de Damas but he refused them but accepted those of the four volunteers who had been chosen by their comrades to present their grievances.[6]

This step was all the more ill-received given the projected expedition to the coasts of France which honour demanded all émigrés capable of bearing arms should support. Puisaye had requested that he have a significant contingent of cavalry join the expedition, to which the Prime Minister Pitt had replied 'he could count on four thousand of the best cavalry in Europe. Those who recall the services of the chasseurs of Béon, Damas, Rohan, Salm, etc, and who know the composition of the English cavalry, and the manner with which it is mounted, know enough that this compliment had nothing of exaggeration then.'[7] This change of plan suited the new situation in Germany as the Landgrave of Hesse no longer concealed his intention to join Prussia in making peace with the French Republic so would undoubtedly also hinder any movement to reinforce the Austrians or Condé on the Rhine. In the first days of May 1795, all the foreign cavalry regiments, categorised as either German or émigré, were sent towards Bremen. The future expedition to Brittany was widely known and some gentlemen left Damas to join the cadre corps, including three who joined Williamson's corps.[8]

4 Jean Kaulek and Alexandre Tausserat-Radel, *Papiers de Barthélemy, ambassadeur de France en Suisse, 1792–1797, publiés sous les auspices de la Commission des Archives des Affaires étrangères, Tome V (septembre 1794–septembre 1795)* (Paris: Alcan, 1894), p.155 (Sturler to Barthélemy, Bremen 23 March).

5 KHN A31 2124, letter Stade 24 April 1795.

6 AMC Series Y carton XXIII.

7 Joseph-Geneviève de Puisaye, *Mémoires du comte Joseph de Puisaye … qui pourront servir à l'histoire du parti royaliste françois durant la dernière révolution* (London: Cox and Baylis, 1803–8), Vol.IV p.415.

8 TNA WO 12/12034, muster roll Williamson's corps, London, 17 June 1798, 'Du Ruel' and 'de Rosnay' on 5 May and 'Descorches' the next day. They are all shown as being from Damas cavalry but the

At the same time troops still loyal to the Stadholder who had quit the Batavian Republic also converged on Bremen, as reported by Sturler, one of the agents employed by François Barthélemy, the French Ambassador at Basel:

> There are here and in the surrounding a great assembly of lackeys of the Stadholderate and intrigues of all hues are plotted to cause movements in the United Provinces. Above all they work on Friesland, Groningen and Overijssel. The points from where the brands of discord are launched are Emden, Leer and several other small places on the frontiers. But the greatest chancellery of intrigues is at Bremen where the Orange cockade is the most fashionable. It is from here that reports are sent every day to London via Cuxhaven. The Stadholder has just ordered all his agents, the headquarters of his army etc. to remain in our region without moving and to hold themselves ready for the first signal.[9]

The French renewed pressure on Prussia to secure Bremen and impede any further embarkation but the former was again playing something of a double game. Instead of marching her troops into Hanover or to the shores of the North Sea, the Berlin court returned them to its own territory to reap substantial economies from the peace. Augusta, the King of Prussia's daughter, was on the point of marrying the Prince of Hesse-Cassel, an essential pawn in Prussia's project; her sister was married to the Stadholder's eldest son, the Erfprins, and her half-sister to the Duke of York, in whose army Hessian troops had, and still, served. Despite French insistence Prussia sought to shut its eyes to the embarkation of the émigrés or at least hasten as slowly as possible to impede it.

Britain's war policy which consisted of several, often incompatible, strands was confused with no project being consistently prioritised. In early June, it was decided to identify the foreign troops which would be sent overseas, particularly to the West Indies; those which would participate in the descent on the coast of Brittany and, finally, those which would remain employed on the Continent. To this end on 3 June Lieutenant General David Dundas conferred with Colonel Nesbitt and Lieutenant Colonel Charles Craufurd. The latter was attached to Clerfayt's headquarters as well as that of the Prince de Condé, whose corps was now paid for by Britain. Given the scale of his task, Craufurd managed to have his younger brother, Robert, later of Peninsular War fame, appointed as his deputy and so he attached him to Condé. Among other things, it was decided, at this conference, that Craufurd would liaise with Clerfayt to find out his views about the foreign cavalry moving to the Rhine to join him or Condé. The principal difficulty which was anticipated was the need to cross the line of demarcation, or as Dundas put it 'the Prussian Magic Circle,' near Hanau and Frankfurt.[10] The more pressing demand was, however, Brittany so Dundas gave, on 17 June, the order for five foreign cavalry regiments – Hompesch, Uhlans Britanniques, Rohan, Choiseul and Salm – to move to Hoya, on the Weser, 'to form part of a cavalry camp that is formed near this town, in the plain of Schwarme, between Verden and Bremen … under

second has been identified as Thomas François de Ronnay of the Damas infantry who received a certificate of service from Rouault on 7 June.

9 Kaulek and Tausserat-Radel, *Papiers de Barthélemy*, p.254, Sturler to Barthélemy, Bremen 3 May.

10 TNA WO 1/173, D. Dundas to Henry Dundas 4 June 1795.

the orders of Major General Lord Cathcart'.[11] It was planned that the émigré cavalry would embark at the next opportunity, expected to be on the transports which would bring the British cavalry remounts into the Weser. Henry Dundas wanted Rohan's Hussars to be the first to embark as it was considered that local royalists would rally to the cause particularly as the Prince de Rohan traced his ancestry to the ancient Kings of Brittany.[12] Meanwhile the British, especially the Foreign Secretary, William Grenville, was pursuing a policy of strengthening the Armée de Condé and his agent, William Wickham, on 25 June recommended that the Prince's corps, which already was to be increased by eight infantry battalions and two regiments of cavalry, should be joined by 'the Regiments of Rohan, Beon (?), Bouillé, Choiseul and Damas now in our pay'.[13]

It is clear that individual Béon volunteers had left to become officers in the newly raised foreign and émigré cavalry regiments while others had even been encouraged to leave, as a body, to form a noble company in the Uhlans Britanniques. It is likely that those of Damas were similarly approached as, prior to 22 June, the volunteers of the two companies wrote a letter to their colonel. Although they did not directly complain of the stricter disciplinary measures that he had taken towards them in response to the 'Burgdorf incident' they assured him of their complete loyalty while reminding him that he himself had undertaken to treat them on an equal footing, as fellow French gentlemen, in spite of their differences of rank.[14] At the same time the companies continued to increase in strength. The British capitulation had not specified the background of the personnel in the companies, many of the recruits had formerly served in the army of the United Provinces, as already seen above.

On 6 July, Lieutenant General Dundas wrote to the Secretary of State for War:

> [T]he Corps of Rohan's Hussars ... will be ready to march and embark at Bremerlehe as soon as the transports arrive there for them ... The Corps may certainly embark 600 men. If any others are to follow for French Service, Lord Cathcart recommends preferably the Corps of Damas, Beon & Uhlans, as being composed chiefly of Frenchmen ... Damas and Beon's have many Gentlemen in the ranks who have served well and would be particularly useful in a new destination. As we understand that the remount Transports have been applied to another Service we cannot expect that this embarkation of Rohan's can take place till towards the end of the month.[15]

Five days later, in a memorandum to Wallmoden, he indicated that the first to embark would be 'the Damas and Rohan Hussars to the Amount of 700, at least' and the second would be the corps of Choiseul, Béon and the Uhlans, having resolved that the Salm and

11 Bouillé, *Souvenirs*, Vol.II, p.256. Schwarme was near the frontiers of both Prussia and the Duchy of Brunswick.

12 TNA, WO 1/173, in his letter of 6 July, in reply to that of 26 June from the Secretary of State, he stated that the corps would be able to embark 600 men.

13 William Wickham (ed.), *The correspondence of the Right Honourable William Wickham from the year 1794* (London: Bentley, 1870), Vol.I p.109.

14 BL, *Don Papers*, Add MS 46711.

15 TNA, WO1/173.

Hompesch Hussars, two German corps, would remain with the rest of the British cavalry until further orders.[16] The French had reduced their strength in Holland and so would not oppose these movements, but Dundas, in the same message of 6 July, noted that another enemy had appeared; the Regency of Hanover not only made difficulties with regards the army he commanded but also displayed open hostility!

Now that it was clear that soon Hessian troops would no longer be available, the raising of new units on the Continent was essential for the pursuit of Britain's war and foreign policy. The King had informed the Regency that he had 'thought proper to order a considerable Number [of units] to be raised in Germany for the service of Britain' but prohibited not only recruiting but also the placing of permanent depots in the electorate. On the other hand he expected the Regency to provide 'all means that can facilitate the Passage of the new Corps destined to embark'; however, instead, Lieutenant General Dundas reported 'direct Opposition to the Execution of His Majesty's Intentions.'[17] As evidence he forwarded some reports relating to incidents including one, raised on 2 July, involving the Duc de La Force, who commanded the Béon Hussars. Lieutenant Bernard Simon of the York Rangers had complained to him about the actions of the Hanoverian commander of Celle who had had one of his recruits, obtained in Prussian territory, arrested and thrown in prison. Lieutenant Hunter, assistant to Colonel Nesbitt, added:

> According to the report that has been given to me this morning by M. Simon … on the subject of a man who had been engaged near Hildesheim in the service of His Britannic Majesty, and who on his way to Celle had been arrested by order of the Hanoverian Commandant, I asked M. de La Hautière [sic], officer commanding the detachment of Damas cavalry, to go with Lieutenant Simon to the Commandant, to point out to him that the man in question not having been engaged on His Majesty's territory and not having been even born there, he could not under any account be considered as engaged contrary to the laws, and to beg him to deliver him to his officer.
>
> The Hanoverian colonel refused to hand over the man, but returned the passport with which he had been supplied, signed by the commander of the regiment.

The Hanoverian officer argued that he had received the order to oppose all recruitment and the bringing of any recruits into Hanoverian lands. As a result, Dundas was to propose that all the foreign corps be gathered at Stade and in the surrounding area, in order to reduce the chance of interference by the Hanoverian Regency and also to take the earliest opportunities to embark for their intended destinations. In expectation of an imminent embarkation the cavalry assembled at Hoya was reviewed on 9 July and then, six days later, again in a formal ceremony attended by the Comte d'Artois and the Duc d'Angoulême. On this

16 TNA, WO1/173.

17 TNA WO/173, Dundas to Wallmoden 11 July 1795. The Comte de Damas was, later to write, 'the government of Hanover, which wished to make its peace with France, had opposed the passage of British troops across its territory. The prohibitions were so rigorous that even convoys of recruits for the black cockade corps were dispersed with weapons in hand by the Hanoverian troops and peasants.' (AMC, Series Y, carton XXIII – June 1796).

occasion Artois addressed the hussars of Choiseul, Rohan and the Uhlans Britanniques, as they were due to embark first; it is perhaps significant that those of Damas and Béon were not there.[18]

The émigrés on the right bank of the Rhine, with the Austrian forces, were unaware of this imbroglio, and remained convinced that all the corps were destined to reinforce them, as indicated by a personal letter written on 9 July by Duc Charles-Ferdinand de Berry who was at Condé's headquarters, at Müllheim, 'matters are at their best, our army is going to increase very quickly by the arrival of the Hohenlohe, Rohan and other regiments'.[19]

Dutch deserters continued to arrive in Germany as Sturler, reported, on 12 July:

> The émigrés who returned from Holland eight days ago, and who had been allowed to come back very sloppily on the part of the French commanders in Holland, have executed a very clever coup to strengthen their corps camping, at Celle and Stade, which was very successful for them. They made the Dutch soldiers believe that the Prince of Orange was on the frontier with Westphalia where he raised an army under the protection and the pay of the King of Prussia, and distributed many letters accordingly in different garrisons on these borders, and caused by this manoeuvre such desertion that there arrived here on Friday 400 Dutch deserters together, and yesterday 700, even having wagons and haversacks with them. There were about 200 of the Swiss Guards among the others Walloons. But these poor dupes not finding the Prince of Orange, have been engaged by the émigrés, who by this find themselves completely up to strength in several corps ...

Among the men who had arrived were 250 from the Van Tuyll cavalry regiment who had deserted from the border with Westphalia, bringing their arms and mounts.[20]

The plans to reinforce the expedition in Brittany were widely known so that on 24 July the *Bayreuther Zeitung* noted that Monsieur, the Comte d'Artois was to embark at Bremen on 29 July accompanied by 'the 4,200 men of the Rohan Hussars and legions of Choiseul, Damas and Béon'.[21] Artois was to sail for England on HMS *Asia*, that, according to Sturler, had brought 'some forty officers and adventurers of every type who come to help in the affair of the Prince Frederik of Orange.'[22] Deluding himself as to the support that his brother-in-law, the King of Prussia, would provide, the Stadholder Willem had, on 19 July, appointed Prince Frederik, to gather in the lands around Osnabrück a corps of Dutch émigré troops, ready to reconquer the United Provinces: this was to be known as the *rassemblement*. These Orangist forces were to attack Zeeland, with the support of British and Russian ships, or invade from Gelderland with the support of Prussian troops. On 22 July, the Prince of Orange had written to King Friedrich Wilhelm hoping to repeat the coup of 1787, when the Duke of

18 Abel Hugo, *Vie anecdotique de S.M. Charles X* (Paris: Maurice, 1824), pp.59–61.

19 Père P.C. Sommervogel, *Correspondance pendant l'émigration (1792–1797), 48 lettres inédites du prince de Condé, du duc de Berry et du duc d'Enghien* (Paris: Author, 1867), p.28.

20 Kaulek and Tausserat-Radel, *Papiers de Barthélemy*, p.380, Sturler to Barthélemy, Bremen 12 July.

21 The Uhlans Britanniques were not included although without them such a number seems improbable.

22 Kaulek and Tausserat-Radel, *Papiers de Barthélemy*, p.408 Sturler to Barthélemy, Bremen, 30 July.

Brunswick had marched at the head of 12,000 Prussian troops to restore the Stadholder.[23] Eight days later, Sturler reported on the progress of the *rassemblement*:

> Prince Frederik was at Hanover and he is at Osnabrück where he forms his nucleus. The unit grows each day, and it ought to be joined shortly by the English cavalry and other units in the pay of England. All his adjutants and other actors received considerable sums to run around the country and to enrol anyone; and people have been sent everywhere in Holland to engage troops with money to join the prince. It is a blessing to see with what profusion Pitt rolls out guineas for this business. I have seen such and such Dutch officers who in their life had not possessed a hundred ducats, and who have received twenty and thirty thousand écus [crowns] at a time for this recruitment.[24]

Despite the financial support the *rassemblement* at Osnabrück gathered barely more than 2,200 men, including 839 officers. There was competition for these men from several other units. As early as 22 June, the Comte de Damas had proposed to Colonel Nesbitt to raise six fusilier companies 'of 150 men each, including the Sergeants, Corporals & Drummers coming from Holland' to form the second battalion of his infantry, the officers of which had to have been previously in the service of the United Provinces. On 2 August, Damas asked for authorisation to move its establishment from Stade to Osnabrück, but this movement was dependent on the possible embarkation of his cavalry which he was required to command. At the same time Damas suggested that this battalion should be augmented by a chasseur company and one of artillery; although agreed to by Nesbitt these proposals were annulled a few days later.[25]

Jean-Victor de Constant-Rebecque learning of the raising of this new battalion wrote to Damas from Brunswick, on 8 July 1795, and requested a position in it, while at the same time, as a former Dutch Foot Guards and staff officer, he wrote to the Erfprins for his approval of this request. Ten days later Damas informed him that he had been appointed captain in 'his 2[d] Dutch battalion' and Constant-Rebecque was to go to Stade where he was to receive the recruits and take command of the depot. His appointment as captain indicates that, in accordance with the capitulation, at least 150 men had already been recruited. He arrived at Stade on 24 July where he found the Damas cavalry in garrison, alongside foreign regiments in British service and some Hanoverians. The following day, after dining with the Comte de Damas, he left for Bützfleth and Assel, villages just to the north of Stade, where the troops he was to command were in cantonments.[26]

On 26 July Constant-Rebecque was joined at Assel by the infantry adjutant, André Boucher de Courson, and took up lodgings in a nearby farm. Two days later he had the recruits assembled and a roll called before they were exercised and then issued with clothing,

23 TNA WO 1/617.

24 Kaulek and Tausserat-Radel, *Papiers de Barthélemy*, p.409 Sturler to Barthélemy, Bremen, 30 July.

25 See Appendix II.

26 NAN 2.21.008.01 – 19, Jean-Victor Constant-Rebecque Journal Vol.I; the units in British pay at Stade he gave as the 'Royal Liégois, Royal York, York Chasseurs, the [cavalry of] the corps of Salm and of Damas.'

footwear and pay; Constant-Rebecque spent most of the next three weeks at his duties, at Stade and Assel. Finally, on 21 August, he received a reply from the Erfprins, at Windsor, who wanted Constant-Rebecque to serve alongside Prins Frederik. In response, two days later, the Comte de Damas not only sent him to Frederik but also offered the prince his Dutch battalion. On 26 August Constant-Rebecque joined the prince at Nienburg, on the Weser, and resumed his place as an officer in the Dutch Guards, which was to be formed again in the *rassemblement*, resigning from the Légion de Damas as from 1 September 1795.[27]

There is no record of Prins Frederik's reply to Damas's offer of the battalion, the progress of its recruitment or its final fate. However, it seems that the Second Battalion disappeared very quickly, certainly before the infantry regiment was disbanded. On 8 October 1795 Damas wrote to Nesbitt, from Stade, asking to appoint a chaplain to his cavalry. The reason for this request was that article five of the April capitulation prevented the appointment of any officer to the staff until there were two cavalry and three infantry companies present. Damas wrote, 'The disaster of Quiberon renders this Article unachievable on my part for the Infantry'.[28] He would not have had to make such a request if his Second Battalion, which was apparently of at least of company strength three months earlier, still existed; he made no mention of the Second Battalion at all. Presumably the project had been abandoned, like several similar ones, and the men had joined the *rassemblement*, been recruited into other newly raised units in British pay or simply drifted away.

This project took place while the Damas Hussars waited to join the infantry in Brittany or the Vendée. Lieutenant General Dundas had to juggle with the issues of embarking the troops to their respective destinations, while a shortage of transports meant they only arrived intermittently, co-operating with the *rassemblement* and reinforcing the Prince de Condé which resulted in a series of orders and counter-orders. At the end of July, he was informed that transports with the British remounts had arrived at Bremerlehe, rather than the Elbe, so he intended to send the ships on to Stade 'to receive Damas, Rohan, and as many of the Infantry as they can contain'. However, Captain Popham, the transport agent, suggested the hussars embark at Bremerlehe so they could get off as quickly as possible, to which he agreed; the units at Stade would then have to follow in ships Popham was hiring in the Elbe.[29] In pursuit of this plan, divisions of the Uhlans Britanniques and Choiseul Hussars, encamped at Wulmstorf, were ordered to march to Bremerlehe; Rohan and Damas would have to remain at Stade to embark from there.[30] He did not explain the reason he had made this decision, as Wulmstorf is no closer to the embarkation point than Stade. The two units boarded about 30 transports on 4 and 5 August, 'and the convoy, which was also composed of quite a large number of other ships, steered, on 6 August, for the coast of England'.[31]

They sailed without knowing about the tragic events of Quiberon, but the news finally leaked out at Stade, as described by Sturler:

27 NAN 2.21.008.01 – 19, Jean-Victor Constant-Rebecque Journal Vol.I.
28 See Appendix II.
29 TNA WO 1/173, D. Dundas to H. Dundas, 26 July 1795.
30 TNA WO 1/173, D. Dundas to H. Dundas, 2 August 1795
31 Bouillé, *Souvenirs*, Vol.II, p.265.

> The news from Quiberon had been so well hidden from the troops who were aboard at Bremerlehe, that they had been three days in the roadstead and left without knowing it on 7th. It was not so successful at Stade. The gazettes got through there, there was a complete insurrection: they refused to embark. General Dundas had to say to them that they will be employed on the continent …[32]

However, his report about the Duc de Bourbon at Bremen, on his way to join Artois in Vendée, did not reflect such disaffection:

> The Duc de Bourbon is still here with his fleur de lysed generality. … they await Monsieur's orders from Spithead. The duke and his generality are full of hope that the great expedition will still take place and succeed; the one which failed at Quiberon was only an accessory … These people do not give up the part lost at all, and flatter themselves very much for the success of this campaign.[33]

On 16 August, at Stade, the Damas Hussars were reviewed by Colonel Nesbitt. The unit was complete, under the capitulation, but for two men (197 were present or in quarters, eleven sick or wounded and two men absent), and 17 horses, but also had two hautboists, musicians, as supernumeraries.[34] Since the previous return, of 1 July, two men had deserted but four had been received as recruits; it is of note that the other cavalry units present for the review were the Rohan, Choiseul and York Hussars, but not Béon.[35] The same day Lieutenant General Dundas acknowledged receipt of the order 'to stop the Embarkation of the 2d Division of Cavalry and hasten that of the Infantry … Rohan, Damas, Choiseul Hussars will remain in consequence of Your Dispatch cantoned or encamped near Stade …'[36]

Four days later the Damas Hussars were reviewed by the Duc de Bourbon, with the following composition:

	Staff	
Colonel	Comte de Damas	
Major	Vicomte de Montjustin	
Adjutant	Moisez	
Surgeon Major	Couturier	
Supernumerary – Paymaster*	Bertemy	
Supernumerary	Augustin	
	First Company	**Second Company**
Captain	Marquis de Bongars	Comte de Boysseulh
Lieutenant	de Bazouges	de Conan

32 Kaulek and Tausserat-Radel, *Papiers de Barthélemy*, p.426, Sturler to Barthélemy, 13 August.
33 Kaulek and Tausserat-Radel, *Papiers de Barthélemy*, pp.426–427 Sturler to Barthélemy 13 August.
34 AMC Series Y, carton VIII.
35 AMC Series Y, carton VIII.
36 TNA WO 1/173, D. Dundas to H. Dundas, 17 August 1795.

Second Lieutenant	de Saint-Laurent	de Vidal
Cornet	de Lentilhac	de Plantières
Quartermaster	de Bouillé	de Gaunel
	4 sergeants, 6 corporals, 65 gentlemen	4 sergeants, 6 corporals, 59 gentlemen
	1 sergeant, 2 corporals, 32 *flanquers*	1 sergeant, 2 corporals, 38 *flanquers*
	1 farrier	1 farrier
	1 hautboist, 1 trumpeter	1 hautboist, 1 trumpeter

* The term that was used was 'paye-meester' apparently from Dutch.

Source: AMC Series Y carton VIII, Etat de situation de la cavalerie de la Légion de Damas présentée à S.A.S. Mgr le duc de Bourbon, le 20.8.1795 à Stade.

It is noteworthy that each company now contained two types, indeed classes, of men, noble hussars or 'volunteers' who were all French gentlemen and regular paid cavalrymen, designated as *flanquers* (literally flankers), the majority of whom were foreigners, especially Dutch and Germans. A memorial written in June 1796 relates how some of these *flanquers* came to be in the unit:

> When the regiment left Holland, some of the Timmerman Hussars followed a detachment of volunteers, commanded by the Marquis de Bongard [sic], to Amersfoort. These men could doubtless be considered deserters, since their regiment had remained in the interior of the country. Also, the Cte Etienne in engaging them bought their horses. However, when he found himself in the last summer in the Dutch *rassemblement*, at Osnabrück, MM. Van de Hoop, Major, and Dangely [sic], captain of the Timmerman Regiment, claimed the men and the horses in the situation where they would have formed their companies, and he would have undoubtedly been obliged to give them up if the *rassemblement* had actually taken place.[37]

The Dutch initiative, the *rassemblement*, ran counter to the interests of Prussia. King Friedrich Wilhelm had procrastinated while he attempted to get France to compensate the Orange-Nassau family while also trying to avoid a complete rupture with Britain, but he was forced, on 4 August, to order *Generalmajor* von Schladen to clear the Stadholder's adherents from Osnabrück and prevent them rallying in not only Westphalia but also Hanover. On 12 August 'all the Dutch with orange cockades' were driven from Osnabrück:

> These people dispersed in the province, but the majority went to Hamburg and Bremen where the Prince Frederik of Orange is. He ordered his people to stay to wait for orders by return of the messenger that he sent to London. He hopes to form his *rassemblement* in these surroundings on Hanoverian land…[38]

37 AMC Series Y carton XXIII.

38 Kaulek and Tausserat-Radel, *Papiers de Barthélemy*, p.437 Sturler to Barthélemy, Bremen 20 August. The King of Prussia sent a copy of his response to the Stadholder to the Duke of Brunswick who, on

At the same time the Prussian representative in London tried to convince King George, as Elector of Hanover, to accede to the Peace of Basel in exchange, among other things, for the temporary maintenance of the debris of the *rassemblement* in the Bremen region.

The British Government had just decided on a new expedition to the West Indies and to disentangle itself from direct military intervention on Continental Europe so wanted to embark all the foreign corps as soon as possible. On 28 September Lieutenant General Dundas acknowledged orders to send 'the French Corps towards Ireland' and the German regiments to Spithead and Cork.[39] The situation had become urgent with Austrian reverses in Germany, hostilities now declared against the Batavian Republic, and clear evidence that Hanover itself would negotiate to sign the pact of neutrality. Only two ports were available for embarkation, Bremerlehe for the British and Stade for the foreign troops. However, by 29 September, of the latter, only the York Hussars, York Fuzileers and York Rangers and three companies of 2nd Regiment, or New, Rohan Hussars were embarked, although their departure for England was still postponed for a week. The Damas Hussars remained in Germany and one French source suggested that they would be sent to Corsica as, 'following some bloody fracas, between the Corsican and British battalions, it had been resolved to recall a part of the latter to Gibraltar, and have them replaced by the émigré regiments of Damas and Rohan, coming from Holland.'[40] However, no reports of such incidents have been found and, furthermore, it is doubtful such royalist troops would have been welcomed given the fractious nature of politics, and society, on the island. After all it had only been conquered by the French King in 1769.[41]

The infantry had already been disbanded and as Damas put it his hussars remained 'on the point of embarking,' when he was requesting the appointment of a chaplain.[42] It seems that it was not only the colonel who took an interest in matters spiritual as, while at Stade, 'some Damas hussars gave a living to an elderly superior and the whole group of nuns; until the day that they could collect for them the cost of a crossing to England.'[43]

On 5 October the British staff estimated that there were still more than 11,300 people to be embarked: 4,800 men, women, children and servants; 257 officers; 3,900 horses; six cannon and 700 tons of ammunition with the British units and 3,600, 310 and 2,020, respectively, with the foreign units, as well as an estimated 600 additional recruits and 100 Dutch officers and 1,700 men, although it was expected that hardly any of the Dutch would in fact leave.[44] Five days later a detailed return was completed of the foreign regiments in British pay, so not including the Dutch, showing that there were still 6,776 people and 3,315 horses from such corps still in Germany, with the Béon and Damas Hussars there were:[45]

the 16th, wrote to Prince Fredrik to remind him of its terms and to dissuade him from pursuing this venture – see TNA WO 1/617.

39 TNA WO 1/173, D. Dundas to H. Dundas, 28 September 1795.

40 Jomini, *Histoire critique et militaire*, Vol.I, p.327.

41 Furthermore, it is also highly unlikely that infantry regiments would have been replaced on the island by cavalry. The only reason sending the émigré cavalry to Corsica might have been considered was to make up for the absence of British cavalry and the lack of success in raising local cavalry units on the island.

42 See Appendix II.

43 Bittard des Portes, *Les émigrés*, p.301.

44 TNA WO 1/173.

45 TNA WO 1/173. It is noted on this return that La Tour's regiment is not included. The total for people with Damas has been corrected from 308 as shown on the original.

	Béon	Damas
Officers	16	16
Other ranks	173	224
'Followers and Servants'	32	36
Women and Children	36	36
Total number of persons	257	312
Horses	221	272

That very day, 10 October, Henry Dundas, the Secretary of State for War, informed the Duke of York that the army in Germany was to be dissolved and that the repatriation of the British cavalry was the first priority. The intention had been to send the Salm-Kyrburg, Choiseul, Rohan, Damas and Béon Hussars, along with their horses, to the French coast but any cavalry transports in the Weser and Elbe that might have carried them were now allocated to the British cavalry which was to leave by the end of the month. Thus 'no provision remains for the embarkation of the Horses of the five Corps of foreign light cavalry': instead, the units were to be dismounted, the horses sold and the men brought to Spithead. Dundas considered that the five corps were 'liable to serve in the West Indies' so they could be sent to Haiti, although no final decision had been made, indeed it might be considered better to send them to France after all, or the Channel Islands. Finally, he wrote, 'It would be very desirable that one of the two Corps of Damas or Béon should be drafted into the other' and, unless the duke had a 'material objection' he should give orders for this to take place.[46] Four days later, Henry Dundas wrote directly to Nesbitt to set these measures in motion. If Choiseul and Salm agreed to embark – Nesbitt had pointed out that the Salm Hussars were limited by their capitulation to only serve in Europe – their horses were to be sold, and they would be offered the same benefits as other units already departing for the West Indies; this proposition was also to be offered to Rohan, Damas and Béon.[47]

In the febrility, not to say confusion, then reigning, the Secretary of State soon wrote a bad-tempered letter to Nesbitt blaming him for not taking measures required, in particular the amalgamation of understrength foreign corps to avoid the cost of reorganisation elsewhere. Cavalry regiments were to be dismounted to make the best use of space on the shipping, especially as it was expected many horses would not survive the Atlantic crossing. Dundas repeated the orders that the émigré cavalry of Salm, Rohan, Damas and Béon, were 'to be completely dismounted and sent to Spithead, where they will receive orders as to their future proceedings.' He reiterated that they could receive the additional gratuities if they agreed to serve in the West Indies or in any other part of the world required.[48]

Nesbitt quickly undertook Dundas's instructions, this is shown by a letter the Comte de Damas addressed, on 26 October, to Béon's officers and volunteers:

> The Duc de La Force had the goodness to send me a letter from Colonel Nesbitt dated yesterday, regarding the orders of H.B.M. to unite the corps of Béon and

46 TNA WO 6/25.
47 TNA WO 6/25, 14 October.
48 TNA WO 6/25, 20 October.

> Damas, being henceforth to form three companies under my command. I make it a duty to express to you, Sirs, how I consider myself honoured by an event so little awaited on my part and also flattering for me. The glory that you have gained, in so many ways, instructs me to appreciate the honour of being at your head, and to the Damas corps the satisfaction to have you for companions in its labours.
>
> You will find, Sirs, in the chief and in your future comrades, an equal eagerness to show you the esteem which is due to you, and to acquire your friendship. On my part, I will employ all my care to mollify the just regrets that you must have to be separated from a chief under whose name and leadership you have gained such a distinguished reputation.[49]

The Comte de Béon, who was then in London, apparently learned of this development by chance and immediately lobbied to have it rescinded, writing on 13 November to William Windham, 'The Béon corps is the first of all armed for the service of the allies. On 21-1-1795, it passed like that of Damas to the service of H. Britannic M. It is to be incorporated on 24-11 into a corps less senior than it and which passed at the same time into the pay of England'.[50] He was, to some extent successful, leading Henry Dundas to write Nesbitt a letter on 17 November in which he reversed the instructions he had so testily given him less than a month before without, of course, acknowledging that he was doing so:

> In consequence of several favourable circumstances which have been stated to me by the Count de Béon respecting his corps which I find was formed at a much earlier period than that of Damas, and has served with the greatest distinction from the commencement of the present war, and the extreme concern with which several Emigrant Gentlemen serving in the Ranks as Volunteers under him appear to have received the notification of this measure, I have been induced to recommend to the King that the proposed measure of Drafting Colonel de Béon's Corps should not for the present be carried into execution, and I am to signify to you His Majesty's pleasure that you are after dismounting the said Corps in the same manner as the others, to cause it to be embarked upon its present establishment and in case this letter should not reach you before the 24th Instant, the day I understand you have fixed upon for Drafting it, you will after receiving it return the men to their former situation under Colonel de Béon.[51]

However, Béon's efforts were to no avail, on his return to Germany, at the end of the month, he found his cavalrymen had themselves dispersed, the greatest number, in particular the former *Gardes du Corps*, to join the Armée de Condé by their own means, as the Comte de Damas explained later, 'Béon dissolved itself. There were only 17 horses left'.[52]

The region was in turmoil. It was feared the continuing presence of men from the *rassemblement* could be used as a pretext for a Batavian and French offensive which would further

49 GARF 758/2/52.
50 BL Windham Papers, Add Ms 37850.
51 TNA WO 6/25, Dundas to Nesbitt, 17 November 1795.
52 AMC Series Y, carton XXIII, June 1796.

imperil the British embarkations, while the Orangists would have withdrawn to Jeverland under the protection of Russia.[53] In October, Sturler, at Bremen reported:

> [S]ince the 15th, every day convoys of the Prince of Orange's troops pass through here, eight to twelve hundred at a time with their officers well mounted. The troops are superb, well dressed, although without uniforms or weapons. Each corps is followed by 20 to 30 covered wagons in which are the uniform coats and weapons, and loaded besides with quantities of women and several sick. They come from different assembly points, and go, as the princes' generals say, to canton in the region of Bremerlehe, while waiting for them to be embarked for the East or West Indies ...[54]

However, within days Prince Frederik received notice of the end of the project and he soon left for England. Many of the soldiers left behind now sought a future in British service, others joined the recruits, deserters, refugees and other adventurers passing from one dominion to another, often to offer themselves to the highest bidder.

For the British the main objective remained the embarkation of their last troops, British and foreign, at least those that could be redeployed in other theatres. Time was now pressing not just for military or diplomatic reasons; winter was closing in and the Weser was expected to be closed to navigation from 15 November by ice. On 9 November, Lieutenant General Dundas reported that half of the British cavalry had just been embarked and was likely to set sail within a few days while it was hoped that the dismounted Hompesch and Rohan Hussars, along with three infantry units, would be onboard ships and ready to set sail a week later.[55] On 17 November 56 transports arrived in the Elbe from Newcastle and were sent to Stade and 32 more appeared a week later in the Weser to embark almost all of the remaining British units.[56] With the ships already charted and these directed to Stade, Dundas considered that all the foreign corps could be embarked in one go.

The Prince de Rohan had agreed a new capitulation, receiving £8,000 to do so, for his two regiments to serve in the West Indies. His regiments still had about a thousand men in Germany, including 900 of the 1st Regiment, and they were to embark, apparently on 1 or 2 December, but two companies escaped, sword in hand:

> As soon as the order for embarkation became known, a great number of Frenchmen abandoned their corps and rendered themselves to the Armée de Condé. A part of the officers of the Rohan Legion were for the embarkation, the other was against, as well as the soldiers who, all, wanted to go to the Armée de Condé with arms, baggage and horses. While they deliberated, the British government, had, during the night, the legion surrounded by Hanoverian regiments; the hussars mutinied, but they were forced to embark with the officers of good will; most of the mutineers were hung on the seashore.[57]

53 Kaulek and Tausserat-Radel, *Papiers de Barthélemy*, p.465 Sturler to Barthélemy, Bremen 17 September.
54 Kaulek and Tausserat-Radel, *Papiers de Barthélemy*, p.491 Sturler to Barthélemy, Bremen 18 October.
55 TNA WO 1/173, D. Dundas to H. Dundas 9 November 1795.
56 TNA WO 1/173, D. Dundas to H. Dundas 20 November 1795.
57 Bernard de La Frégeolière, cited by Vicomte Robert Grouvel, *Les Corps de troupe de l'émigration* (Paris: La Sabretache, 1961–1965), Vol.I pp.53–54.

Among the officers who quit the Rohan Hussars was Jean-Baptiste de Constantin de Pressac who immediately joined the Damas Hussars.[58] Then as Sturler, noted, on 3 December, 'What happened with the Rohan Hussars also came to take place with those of Salm. They were to be embarked at night. More than 250 decamped … But these hussars not knowing anymore what to do to live, turned to theft and murder. Several have been arrested in the act.'[59] Finally, the last squadron was disbanded, with three pounds per man, and each soldier authorised to keep his horse but some of the Salm officers and hussars opted to be drafted into the Hompesch Hussars.

By 2 December, all the British troops on the banks of the Weser had been embarked and were ready to sail, but the situation on the Elbe remained chaotic. Unable to be embarked on the Weser the 16th Light Dragoons were ordered to Stade, soon followed by the 11th and a hundred men of the 15th Light Dragoons who would be embarked instead of the Salm Hussars. In addition to the last foreign units, space had to be also found for 120 returned prisoners of the 55th Foot, the last foreign recruits, and 300 to 400 Dutch who had agreed to serve in the British forces. Men still came to join the *rassemblement*, 'Over three days, there arrive in the Dutch quarters entire bands of Germans who had served in the Dutch Swiss units.'[60] Seeking to keep and employ them, on 5 December the Erfprins instructed Constant-Rebecque to take a confidential letter to Clerfayt in which he proposed that the Nassau territory be mobilised by using the Orangist troops but the Austrians refused. Britain then undertook to continue to pay the troops until 12 January 1796 when the *rassemblement* was finally disbanded; the soldiers given three months' pay and the officers transferred to half pay.[61] Considering himself betrayed, Prince Frederik refused to join his father and elder brother in England and obtained a command in the Austrian army, serving until his death, by fever, in 1799.

The last transports apparently left the Continent on 15 December and it was only on 8 or 9 December that the Comte de Damas had been informed that he could not be embarked and that he should do his best to preserve his unit. According to the last return, dated 18 November, it had 14 officers, 10 NCOs, two trumpeters, 200 soldiers, 17 domestics and seven women, a total of 250 individuals, along with 26 officers' and 215 troop horses.[62] However perilous their current situation, the soldiers were unaware of the deadly fate that would have awaited had they sailed. On 8 December Henry Dundas sent the Duke of York his precise orders about what was to be done with the foreign troops that had been in Germany. They were all to be sent to the West Indies and the Damas Hussars, with those of Béon, 1st Rohan and Salm, all dismounted, as well as La Tour's infantry were, 'To be drafted and reduced, and the Men to be appropriated to the completion of the other Corps … or to the other Services'.[63]

58 P. Louis Lainé, *Archives généalogiques et historiques de la noblesse de France* (Paris: author, 1829), Vol.II, p.22. He had served in the 1792 campaign in the Armée des Princes (company of the *Royal-Vaisseaux* officers) before passing 'into the Rohan-Montbazon Hussar Regiment in which he served in Holland in the 1794 and 1795 campaigns. In November of the latter year, he entered the Damas hussars'.

59 Kaulek and Tausserat-Radel, *Papiers de Barthélemy*, p.522 Sturler to Barthélemy, Bremen 3 December.

60 Kaulek and Tausserat-Radel, *Papiers de Barthélemy*, p.522 Sturler to Barthélemy, Bremen 3 December.

61 TNA WO 6/195.

62 BL Add MS 46710.

63 TNA WO 6/25, Dundas, unaware, of events in Germany included Béon in these units. La Tour's infantry continued, as the Royal Foreigners, to serve in the West Indies until it was amalgamated into

The regiment could not remain at Stade but the puzzle was how to reach the Austrians at Mannheim and from there to join the Armée de Condé at Offenburg. The solution the Comte de Damas-Crux used was to persuade Prince Ernst von Mecklenburg, military governor of Celle and brother-in-law of King George III, to convince the Hanoverian Regency that his cavalry unit no longer existed, and to provide his men with Hanoverian passports that bore the words 'disbanded and disarmed'. These allowed the hussars to leave the electorate in small groups of five to 10 men, visibly unarmed, having rid themselves 'of the inconvenient weight of the pouches and carbines' and concealing their other weapons, and taking all the corps' remounts and equipment with them.[64] One such passport was provided at Stade on 11 December to five volunteers – de Chastenay, the Chevalier de Chastenay, de Champied, de Longneval and de Bois-Marin – and four hussars – Morel, Hougervine, Le Comte and Seguin.[65] The subterfuge was aided by reports such as that published several days later:

> Germany – Münster, 20 December 1795. Stade, and the whole country, is finally fortunately delivered from the vagabondage of the émigrés and free corps. The disbanding of the émigré bands of Damas and Béon being achieved, the corps of the Salm Hussars deported to the frontiers ...[66]

To reach the Armée de Condé, the Comte de Damas had to take advantage of the myriad of little states, sometimes with entwined possessions, in this part of Germany. Fortunately, a safe haven existed nearby. After commanding the Prussian army in the campaigns of 1792 and 1793, the Duke of Brunswick had resigned and made his dominion, the principality of Brunswick-Wolfenbüttel, a haven for the émigrés. His territory bordered Hanover to the south-east and its capital, Brunswick, was only 56 kilometres from Celle, a journey of one or two days. The Damas cavalry took up its new winter quarters, in the middle of December 1795, near the city of Brunswick providing the Comte de Damas the respite required to either reorganise or, if no financial support could be found, to finally dissolve his unit.

The situation, as far as the British were considered, was clarified on 20 December when Colonel Nesbitt wrote to the Comte de Damas from Stade to inform him of his decision on the future employment of the unit. That the corps had not been able to embark with the last troops could be put to advantage, Nesbitt continued:

> [O]n bringing my attention onto the composition of your corps, on the distress that the gentlemen would experience if they embarked without their horses and on the impossibility nevertheless of embarking them otherwise, I had to think that it would be equally advantageous for the government and agreeable for the corps to have them march to the Rhine keeping their arms, horses and equipment and consequently an existence useful and worthy for a corps of which the conduct can only warrant eulogies ...[67]

the 60th Foot in 1798.

64 AMC Series Y, carton XXIII, letter from the Volunteers to the Prince de Condé, June 1796.

65 AMC Series Y, carton XXIII.

66 *La Gazette nationale* or *Moniteur universel* N°111, 21 Nivôse An IV or 14 Janvier 1796.

67 AMC Series Y, carton XIII.

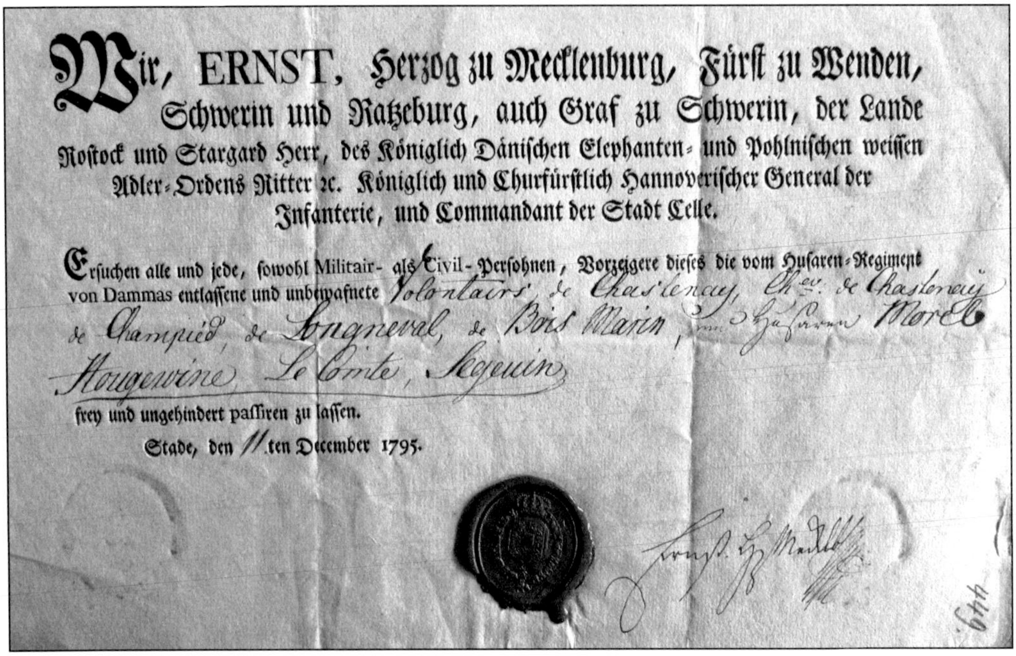
Wir, ERNST, Herzog zu Mecklenburg, Fürst zu Wenden, Schwerin und Ratzeburg, auch Graf zu Schwerin, der Lande Rostock und Stargard Herr, des Königlich Dänischen Elephanten- und Pohlnischen weissen Adler-Ordens Ritter ꝛc. Königlich und Churfürstlich Hannoverischer General der Infanterie, und Commandant der Stadt Celle.

Ersuchen alle und jede, sowohl Militair- als Civil-Persohnen, Vorzeigere dieses die vom Husaren-Regiment von Dammas entlassene und unbewafnete Volontairs de Chastenay, Chev. de Chastenay, de Champied, de Longneval, de Bois Marin, [illegible] Morel, Hougevine, Le Comte, Segauin frey und ungehindert passiren zu lassen.

Stade, den 11.ten December 1795.

Passport issued by Ernst von Mecklenburg, military governor of Celle, 11 December 1795. (Bazouges family archive)

Thus, the Damas Hussars were to join the Armée de Condé, which was paid for by Britain. The officers were provided with six months' pay and the other ranks that of three, instead of the two agreed in the capitulation, but the unit was to remain 'liable to be recalled to the service of His Britannic Majesty, if he judges at a point to employ it against his enemies … to combine to the glory of his arms a corps the presence and example of which will be always sure guarantee of success.'[68] The Damas cavalry had distinguished itself in Dutch and British service by its conduct and excellent discipline, and its officers received the recognition of the new King of France, Louis XVIII. Comte Etienne de Damas-Crux was promoted *maréchal de camp* and in the same period its former major, Nantouillet, had been made Chevalier of Saint-Louis on the saint's day, 25 August.[69] Other officers and NCOs, nominated that August, received the coveted cross of Saint-Louis on 15 December 1795: 'Guillaume-Catherine-Judith, Vicomte de Montjustin, *capitaine* in the Royal Lorraine cavalerie, *lieutenant-colonel* … Jean-François Marie, Marquis de Bongars, *chef d'escadron* in the régiment de Noailles, *capitaine* … François Aumont de Bazouges, *capitaine* in the Orléans Cavalerie, *capitaine* … Louis-Alexandre de Culant, *lieutenant* in the Royal Piémont cavalerie, *maréchal des logis* … Louis-Alexandre Carrey d'Asnières, *lieutenant* in the Dauphin Infanterie, *maréchal des logis*.'[70]

68 Grouvel *Les Corps de troupe de l'émigration*, Vol.II, p.253.

69 AMC Series Y carton II-3 – f.271.

70 AMC Series Y carton XXII and AG, 'Nominations in emigration in the Order of Saint-Louis' carton E.13. The ranks mentioned were those then occupied in the Damas Hussars. The official presentation

Despite his corps having ceased to exist through the volition of its own personnel and Nesbitt's decision, the Comte de Béon, with some licence, wrote directly to the Prince de Condé at the end of December 1795:

> The corps of cavalry of the Colonel Comte de Béon, after having made war during three successive years, having always been at the advanced posts and conducted itself in a manner to receive the esteem and consideration of the army, has been disbanded after the return from the unfortunate affair on the coasts of Brittany. The Comte de Béon had immediately gone to HRH the Duke of York and the Minister for War and represented to them that following the conduct of his corps, it ought not expect a disbandment. HRH had regard for the claim and finding it just, the disbandment was revoked. The Comte de Béon hastened to go to learn news of his corps which was in the Electorate of Hanover, but unfortunately, he arrived too late. The disbanding having been done before the second orders from the Ministry for War had been received, each individual had taken his share. He therefore found no more than 180 volunteers that he sent to the Armée de Condé asking Your Serene Highness to be kind enough to receive them.
>
> The Comte de Béon being able to have at this time almost 300 men, has the honour of asking Your Serene Highness to be so kind as to accord him a capitulation as for the Damas Regiment. This corps will soon be complete, the Comte de Béon bringing with him 300 men and those with whom he fought would certainly come to find him again, having informed him that they would come to re-join him if he had a new capitulation.
>
> The Comte de Béon has the honour to lay his request at the feet of Your Serene Highness and begs him to be kind enough to have regard to a corps which for 3 years made every effort to serve its King and Country. He does not come himself to present his memorial to Your Serene Highness because he is retained in London to finish with the government business of interest which will enable him to lead 300 men to the Armée de Condé and to equip his corps. If Monseigneur has the goodness to grant the capitulation and there was something to obtain from the English Government following the protection of Your Serene Highness and the manner in which the Béon corps served the English army, he has every reason to hope that he will come across no opposition. But if Monseigneur cannot grant him a capitulation, as soon as his business is completed, he hopes to have the honour to pay court to Your Serene Highness and ask him for permission to serve under his banners.[71]

The Prince is sure to have regarded the approach with scepticism and wondered how an officer who had failed to retain 180 men could claim to lead 300. Béon gained some compensation in England, being retained on full pay despite having no command.[72] The Comte de

ceremony of the crosses took place on 14 February 1796 at Pyrmont, as shown by the certificate from the Comte de Damas-Crux to François Aumont de Bazouges (Bazouges family archive).

71 AMC Series Y carton VI, this letter is doubtless following the final disbanding which was ordered on 24 December 1795.

72 TNA WO 25/167.

Damas, on the other hand, had maintained the cohesion and discipline of his cavalry corps and indeed, with the guarantee of employment from Britain, brought his corps back into an operational condition, as the Duke of Brunswick later certified, 'Comte Etienne de Damas maintained at his own expense this regiment ... which he had remounted and equipped on his account from suppliers of arms and equipment in the lands of Hanover and Hildesheim, as well as here in the city of Brunswick'.[73]

The Comte de Damas, in his turn, wrote to the Prince de Condé to propose three ways his troops could join the army. One was by disbanding, and the proprietor being compensated, with the men joining the Armée de Condé individually and paid from 20 January to 1 March 1796 (one, 40-day, month). This would cost the prince 54,936 livres and, on the basis that they would be neither mounted nor armed, they would be then placed either in the noble companies or cadres. On the other hand, they could be 'delivered' under a contract by which he provided the equipment – clothing, breeches, boots, cloak, saddle and bridle, portmanteau, small mount – and pay at the monthly (40 days) rate of 240 livres for a noble hussar and 270 for a *flanquer*. With 126 gentlemen present on 1 December, and a further 30-40 expected to join, and 90 paid hussars, this would cost 70,000 livres.

However, if the men arrived as a unit, the cost would only be 12,180 livres, 'in accordance with the formation rules and rate of appointments and pay of His army'. This calculation was made on the basis of the squadron being formed of only two companies, but as there were extra men present, serving as supernumeraries without appointments, and 30-40 more were expected to join, it was feasible that the unit could join the Armée de Condé four companies strong. Even in this circumstance, this would still result in a saving of 30,576 livres.[74]

The problem was how the regiment could join the prince's army. On 24 January 1796 Damas informed him that having failed to obtain permission to cross Hesse, it had taken refuge in the County of Pyrmont ruled by Prince Friedrich Karl August of Waldeck, a former general in the service of the United Provinces, who readily greeted his former comrades in arms.[75] The city of Pyrmont became the assembly point for all those who wished to join the Damas Hussars. Situated in Lower Saxony, the spa offered many advantages including its proximity to the Imperial headquarters at Mannheim, where the British commissioner Lieutenant Colonel Charles Craufurd, was placed, as well as that of the Prince de Condé which had been at Bühl, in Baden, since the beginning of December 1795.

The enforced halt meant the funds Nesbitt had allocated for the corps to get to the Rhine had been exhausted. Initially Damas had negotiated with the noble volunteers and the officers to get them to agree to provide for themselves, at their own expense, while he was responsible for the remounts and equipment of the whole corps, as well as the pay of the ordinary hussars. He approached Craufurd for additional travelling expenses but this was refused and the Comte de Damas solicited the Prince de Condé himself for funds. The latter also being unable to provide them, Damas undertook to cover the new expenses, estimated at 36,000 livres, from his gratification of six months' pay and sought loans using

73 AMC Fonds Grouvel, Dossier Légion de Damas, 'Collection Robert von Arnoldi, at Berlin' certificate of 14 March 1803.

74 AMC Series Y carton XXIII.

75 AMC Series Y carton XXIII, letter from Bühl, 24 January 1796.

his possessions as security, asking the prince to engage himself to reimburse him as soon as possible. He also asked Craufurd for an enhanced rate of pay for his volunteers, at first the commissioner agreed to pay them at the same rate as the Gardes du Corps but subsequently had had to retract and declared that the Damas Hussars would be paid on the same basis as the newly-formed Baschi Hussars. However, that regiment had no gentlemen volunteers serving with it, so Damas warned that his volunteers might well leave to engage, individually, in regiments where they would be better paid, observing that 'the Béon Volunteers, after having objected to the incorporation ordered by HM are almost all noble chasseurs and paid as such'.[76] Nevertheless, on 26 January 1796, he was pleased to inform the Prince de Condé of the result of the negotiation:

> I hasten to report to Your Serene Highness that at last I can deliver myself up to the hope of seeing my wishes fulfilled, Colonel Crawfurd [sic] undertakes to include my corps on the statements of expenditure for the army on the 1st March in addition to those of the old army of Monseigneur, and the funds will be released for the Damas corps on the basis of the Baschy Regiment; that is what he has just undertaken. It remains to me to obtain the distinction of a noble squadron and a paid squadron. I hope to get away tomorrow, but I did not want to lose a moment to inform Your Highness of the actual state of things. M. de Nantouillet is going to report to him in detail, and to take his orders relative to the route of march ...[77]

Damas had thus managed to secure not only the financial support of his corps by Britain but also its augmentation, to two squadrons each with two companies, so he would join the Armée de Condé at the head of a modest-sized, but celebrated, regiment. While at Pyrmont the Damas Hussars received an unexpected recruit, Bernard de Corbehem, the chasseur who had escaped execution in Brittany. After leaving the chouans he had travelled home on foot to his parents at Saint-Pol, near Dunkirk, but after only a week, and fearing for his family should he be denounced, he left at the end of December 1795. He then walked through Flanders and Belgium, crossed the Rhine and reached Münster where he learnt that the cavalry of his old legion was no longer in Hanover but Pyrmont. So, it was there that Corbehem engaged in the Damas Hussars, arousing much excitement and curiosity by his arrival, 'in the absence of the colonel, I was greeted by my commanders and my new comrades with the respect due to great misfortunes. ... I had to satisfy people eager for news'.[78] He had arrived at a propitious time:

> [O]n arriving at Pyrmont, I learned of the fate of my regiment, an uncertain moment, had just been determined by the generous efforts of its colonel, the Comte de Damas, who had signed, with the British Government, a capitulation by virtue of which the regiment ceased to be his property, passed into the pay of Britain, on

76 AMC Series Y carton XXIII.
77 AMC Series Y carton XXIII.
78 Corbehem, *Dix ans de ma vie*, p.296.

> the same basis and under the same conditions as the other corps of the Armée de Condé of which it was, in the future, to make an integral part.[79]

Planning began for the regiment to join the prince's army. On 9 February the Comte de Damas, at Mannheim, informed Condé's headquarters, 'the Etienne Damas cavalry regiment, today 300 men strong and as many horses, and which soon will be at 400, should be put on the road and arrive in March with the army. Monseigneur desires that it be placed near Bühl.'[80] However, due to a lack of space, the staff directed that it be cantoned in the area of Rottenburg, on eastern side of the Black Forest. With the destination established, the route, with staged halts where forage could be obtained for the horses, needed to be decided in consultation with Craufurd and then passports obtained to permit passage from one state to another. However, certain German princes did not hesitate to take petty vengeance on the French nobility, held responsible for bringing the misfortunes of war to the German Empire, now assailed or occupied by the revolutionary troops. The Comte de Damas, travelling back to Pyrmont from the Imperial headquarters, personally requested the Landgrave of Hesse for such passports but was categorically denied, as he reported to Condé's representative at Mannheim:

> I have the honour to report to you that having obtained without difficulty from the Baron Lillyen the march route that Colonel Crawfurd [sic] and you had kindly asked from him for my corps, I have been myself to Cassel [sic] to ask for the passage through the Landgraviate. The Prince gives his audiences at the parade, and they are short; at least that is what I experienced. After having explained the object of my trip to him, I had for my first response: 'Sir, I do not believe myself in the situation of granting what you ask.' So, I wanted to show him the march route, I had the second response: 'Sir, make your request in writing, and I will send you my response.'[81]

The written request was rejected in the same fashion so the regiment would have no 'other resort than to pass through the lands of Paderborn, Waldeck and Hesse-Darmstadt', country that the Comte considered 'ruined in fodder because the magazines of the King of Prussia had stripped them,' which would not only incur additional cost, of a third on the initial estimate, but also further delay. However, on 8 March, *Feldmarschall* von Wurmser, commanding the Imperial forces on the Rhine, wrote, 'Comte Etienne de Damas … [who] ought to arrive today at Friedberg with his corps, is to receive there through the commissariat a further march route to bring him directly to Rottenburg', where enough food would easily be found for its 1,200 horses.[82] While the regiment had been at Pyrmont, horses had been bought in other parts of Germany, as shown by a passport issued on 9 March 1796 on behalf of the Duke of Brunswick:

---

79 Corbehem, *Dix ans de ma vie*, p.297.
80 AMC Series Y carton XXII.
81 AMC Series Y carton XXII, dated Pyrmont 13 February 1796.
82 AMC Series Y carton XII.

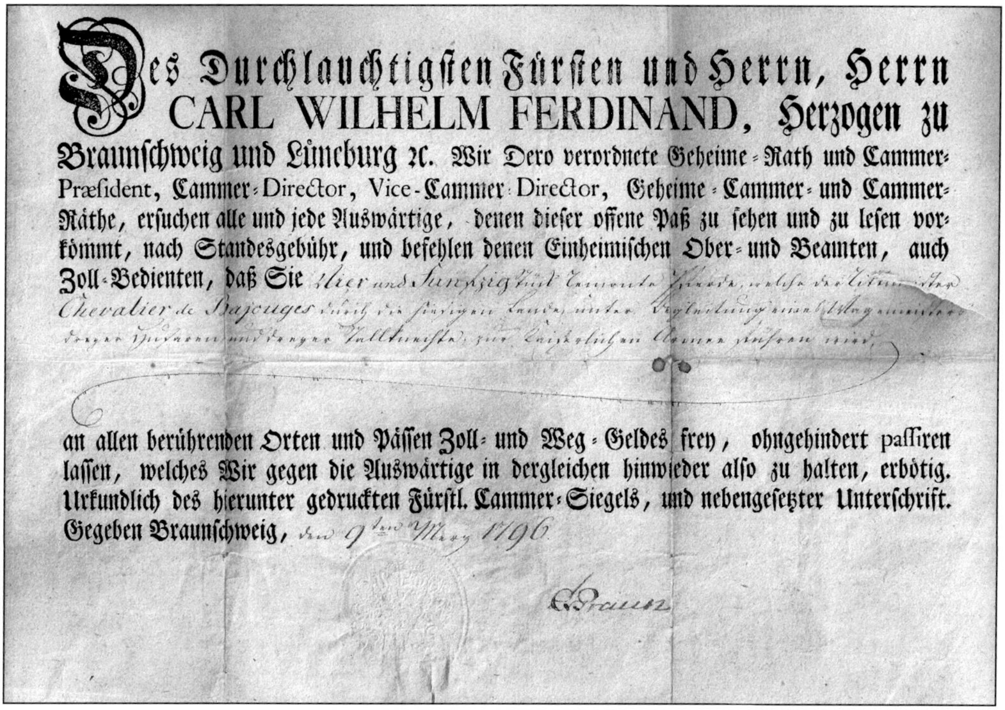

Des Durchlauchtigsten Fürsten und Herrn, Herrn CARL WILHELM FERDINAND, Herzogen zu Braunschweig und Lüneburg 2c. Wir Dero verordnete Geheime-Rath und Cammer-Præsident, Cammer-Director, Vice-Cammer-Director, Geheime-Cammer- und Cammer-Räthe, ersuchen alle und jede Auswärtige, denen dieser offene Paß zu sehen und zu lesen vorkömmt, nach Standesgebühr, und befehlen denen Einheimischen Ober- und Beamten, auch Zoll-Bedienten, daß Sie [illegible] Chevalier de Bazouges [illegible]

an allen berührenden Orten und Pässen Zoll- und Weg-Geldes frey, ohngehindert passiren lassen, welches Wir gegen die Auswärtige in dergleichen hinwieder also zu halten, erbötig. Urkundlich des hierunter gedruckten Fürstl. Cammer-Siegels, und nebengesetzter Unterschrift. Gegeben Braunschweig, den 9ten Marz 1796.

[illegible]

Passport issued on behalf of the Duke of Brunswick to François de Bazouges's detachment, 9 March 1796. (Bazouges family archive)

> We order every citizen, employed or dignitary in the public service, as well as the members and officers of the customs that they accord without obstruction the right of passage to 54 horses which will be conducted across our territory; for the Chevalier de Bazouges, accompanied by a sergeant, three hussars and three grooms, in order to join the Imperial army …[83]

Finally, the corps moved to the neighbouring principality of Waldeck and Corbehem recalled, 'this march was carried out in the best order, and such that one might expect from a corps as distinguished by its good composition as by its admirable discipline.' There Prince Friedrich Karl August greeted them at Arolsen Castle where 'graces and pleasures, banished from France, seemed to have taken refuge'; in fact, 'in the middle of the general agitation that reigned in Europe' this prince had been able to preserve in his little court 'a physiognomy of grandeur and gaiety that was difficult to find elsewhere'. Among those present were several émigrées who had been among the leading women of the court of Louis XVI and Marie-Antoinette, including Mesdames de Polastron, Pardaillan and la Roche-Lambert. 'The latter' adds Corbehem, 'who combined beauty with spirit, making herself particularly remarkable by the vivacity of her witticisms and the delicacy of her thoughts.

83 Bazouges family archives.

She had composed on the passage of our legion a very pretty song that we all learnt by heart, and that we did not cease to sing on the journey, until our arrival with the Armée de Condé.'[84] After a brief halt in Waldeck the regiment continued its march, nearly 440 kilometres, to its destination, the small city of Rottweil, south of Rottenburg, in a meander of the Neckar. The bulk of the Armée de Condé was stationed around Freiburg im Breisgau on the far side of the Black Forest.

The Damas Hussars had continued to recruit, and by 1 March had 345 men, in a 30-strong staff and two squadrons of two companies each; the companies of the 'noble' squadron having 72 and 75 men and those of the so-called 'ordinary' squadron 93 and 96 men. Indeed later, in 1801, the Comte de Damas-Crux claimed from the British Government the reimbursement of expenses 'for conducting … his cavalry from Stade to the Armée de Condé where Colonel Crawfurd [sic] admitted it once again into His Britannic Majesty's pay' and specifically for 'compensation to be granted for the two months and more that this corps remained entirely at the expense of Comte Etienne de Damas, to the value of 355 men mounted, armed and equipped in every respect'.[85]

One recruit was François de Cézac, formerly of the Régiment de Maëstricht, who came with his friend du Gauthier. They had been serving in the Bercheny Hussars since February 1793 and had decided to join the Armée de Condé in the Breisgau. When they presented themselves to the Prince de Condé, the Duc de Berry and the Duc d'Enghien, the Comte de Damas-Crux 'hastened (after having taken note of our certificates) to obtain from the old prince that we would be incorporated among his gentlemen'. This being arranged Damas:

> [O]ffered a place in his carriage to go to join his corps, cantoned in a small Black Forest town. The next day with this new colonel, who showed us infinite bounty and benevolence on route, we arrived at our destination. In a few days, we were well mounted and equipped, and the fine Damas Hussar Regiment came in full to join the Armée de Condé, camped not far from the banks of the Rhine …from the same day, we were part of the noble squadron of the Damas Hussars; there were two other squadrons [sic] that were called those of the flanquers.[86]

It was on 24 March 1796 that the regiment was conclusively taken into British pay to serve as part of the Armée de Condé on its new establishment of two squadrons, each with two companies. The former corps was now officially dissolved by the British, dated 1 April 1796.[87] The Comte de Damas provided a list of the new regiment's officers which he signed at Bühl:

84 Corbehem, *Dix ans de ma vie*, p.298.

85 GARF Armée de Condé Dossier n°52 British Service 'Two written pieces from the Cte E. de Damas on the subject of the officers of the corps de Béon and de Damas'. The date of 1801 is given as the letter bears on the second page a note from the Duc de Bourbon, dated 2 December 1801, supporting this demand.

86 Cézac de Belcayre, *Dix ans d'émigration (1791–1801)*, pp.193–194. Evidence of the Comte de Damas's travels to and from Condé's headquarters is provided by his valet, Guy Halouze, from Normandy, dying at Biberach on 10 March 1796 (AMC Armée de Condé – Carton n°356-1 – Register of deaths, baptisms and marriages of the Bourbon Grenadiers/Losses of the Damas Hussars).

87 TNA WO, 65/167 and 168, Army Lists, Foreign corps, 1793 to 1816.

Etat-Major (Staff)		
Colonel Propriétaire	Comte Etienne de Damas	
Colonel commandant	Comte de Nantouillet	
Colonel en Second	Marquis de Sourdis	
Lieutenant-colonel	Vicomte de Montjustin	
Major	Marquis de Bongars	
Capitaine aide-Major	Comte d'Andelarre	
Lieutenant sous-aide Major	Moisez	
Porte Etendard	Sainte Marie	
Aumônier (chaplain)	Abbé du Chilleau	
Chirurgien (surgeon) *major*	Couturier	
	Compagnies Nobles	**Compagnies d'engagés**
Capitaines	de Bazouges	de Maumigny
	de Conan	Vicomte de L'Entilhac
Lieutenants	de St Laurent	Marquis de la Haye
	Plantières	Chevalier d'Hoffelise
	Augustin	Lageard
	Bouillé	de Rosières d'Euvezins
Sous-Lieutenants	La Craie	Vicomte de Charry
	d'Esmottes	Chanteirac
	Brugières	Comte de Monteclerc
	Montagnac	Carré de Verneuil

This list was completed by a 'nominative state of the officers of the said Regiment to whom the King accords the brevets of the ranks in which they have been admitted to the army.'[88]

The unit was henceforth designated as the Régiment d'Etienne-Damas Hussards, and some officers of the 'old' Damas gained advancement under the new establishment. External appointments had been limited to the staff in the person of the Marquis de Sourdis, promoted *colonel en second*, and the Marquis d'Andelarre, nominated as *capitaine aide-major*. Antoine-René d'Escoubleau Marquis de Sourdis had the advantage of not only having been aide de camp to the Duc de Berry but also was a nephew of the Comte d'Avaray, a long-time favourite of King Louis XVIII. While Antoine d'Andelarre had, at the time of his emigration, been a longstanding *chef d'escadron* in the Noailles dragoons, he had then served briefly in the Armée de Condé before joining the 2e Compagnie noble d'ordonnance, the 'red company' intended to be the continuation of the two former musketeer companies of the King's Household, in the Armée du Centre. He served as *sous-aide major* in the 1792 campaign and when the army was disbanded, he managed to be appointed *lieutenant* in the Régiment de Broglie, a white cockade regiment. Leaving in May 1795, he joined the Dragons de Fargues in the Armée de Condé, as *aide major*, but soon served as an ordinary cavalryman in the Noble Cavalerie, despite his place as *sous-aide major* in the

88 AN O3 2571 Regt Etienne Damas Hussars, n°5. In AMC Fonds Grouvel, Légion de Damas and Series Y carton XXIII.

2e Compagnie noble d'ordonnance, in accordance with the custom and regulations of the King's Household, ranking him as *lieutenant-colonel* of cavalry. Andelarre had his former comrade, the Marquis de Bongars, to thank for his new appointment, they had together been the *chefs d'escadron* in the Régiment de Noailles and then *sous-aide majors* in the 2e Compagnie noble d'ordonnance of the Armée du Centre in 1792.

The unit's officers thus remained particularly homogenous and although the regiment had incorporated nearly 150 recruits since the previous summer, it had lost nothing of its identity preserved by a core of volunteers or noble hussars who had for the most part served in every campaign since 1792. Its arrival in the Armée de Condé was eagerly awaited, many gentlemen rejoicing to rediscover a friend, a family member or simply someone from his own province, there was also the chance that news might be obtained of a family member who had been lost from sight that a Damas noble hussar had perhaps come across in his travels.

As part of its incorporation into the prince's army, the regiment was inspected at Rottweil on 28 March 1796, it was composed thus:

Staff: *colonel propriétaire, colonel commandant, colonel en second, lieutenant-colonel, major, aide-major, sous-aide-major, quartier-maître, porte-étendard* (standard bearer), *chirurgien-major, aide-chirurgien, aumônier, maréchal expert* (master farrier), *maîtres sellier* (master saddler) *armurier* (armourer), *tailleur* (tailor), *vivandier* (sutler) and six carters – 23 men; 50 horses for the officers and troops, 26 horses for vehicles.

Each company had: a *capitaine*, two *lieutenants*, two *sous-lieutenants*, four *maréchaux-des-logis* (equivalent to sergeants), a *fourrier*, four *brigadiers* (corporals), four *sous-brigadiers* and a trumpeter.

Of the noble companies: The 1st Company had 46 noble hussars, a musician (the only one in the regiment), a farrier and five grooms – 72 men plus seven on leave or recruiting; 76 horses including twelve remounts. The 2nd Company had the same structure, with 50 noble hussars and four grooms but had two farriers – 75 men plus three on leave or recruiting; 78 horses including 12 remounts. Of the 'ordinary' companies: The 3rd Company had 74 hussars and 81 horses including twelve remounts. The 4th Company had 77 hussars and 78 horses.

Since the beginning of month, the regiment had gained seven recruits and one horse, four were allocated to the 3rd Company and three men and the horse to the 4th; furthermore, at the end of the review 11 gentlemen were admitted into the 2nd Company. This addition meant that the regiment had a total of 370 men and 389 horses present.[89]

The Etienne-Damas Hussars remained established as a paid regiment, which meant that the gentlemen volunteers received the same pay as the ordinary hussars. Damas raised the subject later when he wrote to the prince requesting compensation for his noble volunteers who considered that they received 'humiliating pay' and repeated their claims to ownership of their mounts, as compensation. Although the decision fell in Damas's favour in relation to the horses, the Prince de Condé could only promise it would be done as soon as circumstances would allow, a promise he was never able to fulfil.[90]

89 AG Armée de Condé carton n°357.

90 AMC, Series Y, carton XXIII, Riegel 10 May 1796 and 18 June 1796.

Nevertheless, the Damas Hussars had escaped the disasters of the expeditions to Brittany and Vendée and destruction in the West Indies. The prestige of its colonel, its appearance and still more its valour, would lead to the Régiment d'Etienne-Damas Hussards being considered among the finest corps of the prestigious Armée de Condé.

9

The Régiment d'Etienne-Damas Hussards in the Armée de Condé 1796–1798

In 1793 the Armée de Condé had suffered terrible losses in Alsace, particularly at Berstheim, on 2 and 8 December, and then, in the following spring, the infantry regiment of Hohenlohe and the Salm Hussars left to go into the pay, respectively, of the United Provinces and Britain. On top of these losses, many gentlemen left the army to join the insurrection in Western France or numerous émigré corps raised by Austria or Britain, in particular as officers in the white cockade regiments raised by the latter in the summer of 1794. Some of these reductions were offset by the formation, in the summer of 1794, of a new hussar regiment by the Comte de Baschi du Cayla, *maréchal de camp* and first gentleman to the Prince de Condé. Funds were extended to this unit while the rest of the army did without, as the Marquis de Toustain, then serving in the Légion de Mirabeau, observed, 'They were covered with silver and us with coats of holes and patches'.[1] The army's situation was particularly difficult as the Austrians, with whom they had to operate and by whom they were paid, viewed the '*Condeischens*' with ill-feeling. After having spent the preceding winter in the Rottenburg region, in May 1794 the prince's army had been brought up to the Rhine, around Rastatt, where it simply stood guard until the end of the year. Their treatment by the Austrians as well as the enforced inactivity, in sight of France, was to drive more gentlemen to quit the army to try to find a better future.

By the end of the year the Prince de Condé feared his army may dissolve through lack of funds. He approached the British Government for financial support in October and some was immediately provided, so he soon pressed for his army to pass fully into British pay, requesting that 'the arrangements to that effect might be completed as expeditiously as possible'.[2] Initially prospects of this looked fair but the prince, on 25 December, learned that the Austrians wanted to keep his army in their pay.[3] Over the next few months, the prince continued to receive contradictory indications, in the meantime, the French completed the

1 Marquise de Perry de Nieüil, *Mémoires du marquis de Toustain (1790–1823)* (Paris: Plon, 1933), p.49.
2 TNA FO 37/55, Foreign Office to Lord St Helens, 24 October and reply of 31 October 1794; FO 37/56, Lord St Helens, 16 December 1794.
3 Comte de Ribes, *Journal d'Émigration du Prince de Condé 1789–1795* (Paris: Société Bibliophile François, 1924), p.502.

invasion of the United Provinces and on 19 January 1795 they entered Amsterdam to be greeted as liberators.

The coalition armies were in retreat and rumours of peace, and a wholescale redrawing of the map of Europe, were rife. The Armée de Condé received the order to withdraw from the banks of the Rhine and returned to Rottenburg and the Neckar valley. As the winter drew on, the army's financial situation only worsened until, on 4 April, the Prince was informed by William Wickham, Britain's acting chargé d'affaires in Switzerland, that he had been instructed to make funds available for it. However, this was immediately put into jeopardy with the news, received on 12 April 1795, that Berlin had unilaterally agreed peace raising the possibility that Britain may gave up the struggle against the Revolution in Europe leaving the prince no other recourse than to seek asylum in Russia. However, soon, fortune finally smiled on the Prince de Condé as money arrived from both Vienna and Wickham.

In the following days the *Condéens* were ordered to again deploy along the Rhine attached to *General der Kavallerie* von Wurmser's 45,000 strong Corps of Observation covering from Basel to Karlsruhe. The Armée de Condé, estimated to only have 4,700 men present, its lowest strength, was stationed between Freiburg im Breisgau and Basel, with its headquarters at Müllheim.[4] The British Government had decided to finally settle the funding of the prince's army with the Austrians, who were themselves seeking a subsidy from Britain. 'There seems to be so little Reason to expect that any real Assistance will at least be afforded by the Court of Vienna to the Prince of Condé', so the prince was to be given £10,000 for 'the immediate and pressing Wants of his Army' and an officer would be sent as a commissioner to arrange its supply as well as to co-ordinate plans with the prince to reorganise and augment the army; furthermore Windham, of the British War Office, also 'apprized the Court of Vienna of this Intention.'[5] The Armée de Condé effectively passed into British pay on 15 June when Colonel Charles Craufurd arrived at the prince's headquarters as the commissioner with the aim of enlarging it to at least 10,000 men.

On 17 June, it was decided that eight new regiments, four cavalry and four of infantry, would be created: the cavalry being the Chasseurs de Noinville and d'Astorg, Dragons de Clermont-Tonnerre and the Régiment d'Ecquevilly and the infantry, cadre regiments that took the names of their colonels: Bardonnenche, Roquefeuil, Alexandre de Damas and Montesson. The *Condéen* cavalry were also soon joined by a squadron of hussars raised by the Vicomte de Carneville, previously in Austrian service, and another of dragoons under the *Commandeur* de Fargues, all the officers of this last were, like their colonel, to be Knights of Malta. In addition, existing units were augmented, the Chevaliers de la Couronne were increased to 400 horse and brigaded with the Dauphin-Cavalerie, which was increased from a squadron to a regiment; a second regiment of Cavalerie Noble was also created at the end of June 1795, uniting the former Gardes du Corps, at the request of the new sovereign Louis XVIII. The famous Légion de Mirabeau which, in 1792 and 1793, had made up a third of the *Condéen* forces was now a shadow of what it had been. Comte Roger de Damas had bought the legion in May 1795 from the Vicomte de Mirabeau's widow and it was in turn reorganised in the summer to have an infantry regiment and 400 hussars.

4 TNA FO 74/6, undated estimate of all units.
5 TNA FO 74/7, Windham to Wickham 12 May 1795.

During the campaign of 1795, the Armée de Condé again remained inactive on the banks of the Rhine in the anticipation of a possible thrust into Franche-Comté or against Strasbourg. With the disaster of the Quiberon expedition and the failure of that to the Île d'Yeu, the Armée de Condé again attracted gentlemen and nobles as the last vestige of the royal army to which to rally. Furthermore, active recruiting amongst republican prisoners had gone some way to filling the ranks of his paid soldiers. These were reinforced at the end of the year by the arrival of some of the hussars who had quit their regiments in Germany as well as the Hohenlohe-Bartenstein Regiment and, at the end of November 1795, the remnants of the white cockade regiments still in Germany. The year ended with an armistice, the Rhine separating the opposing forces.[6]

At the beginning of March 1796, with the truce coming to an end, the Armée de Condé returned to the banks of the Rhine and concentrated around Riegel, where the prince established his staff in the castle of this small city, situated about 20 kilometres from Freiburg. It is at this period that arms and munitions were finally delivered and the troops were put in a condition to enter a campaign. It was also about now that many of the Béon volunteer hussars joined the 2e Régiment de Cavalerie Noble, the Noble Chasseurs or even the cadres of the various new units that were being raised or completed.

On the 23 March, the Prince de Condé placed the Duc de Berry, the young second son of the Comte d'Artois, in command of the cavalry and his own grandson, the Duc d'Enghien, *maréchal de camp* since 1 February 1794, at the head of the vanguard of his army. The last appointment was ill received by *Maréchal de Camp* de Vioménil who had hoped to return to this command, having held it until the beginning of 1794 before he had quit to command one of the white cockade regiments. In the weeks that followed, the cavalry of the Armée de Condé was reorganised into two brigades, one of heavy and another of light cavalry, the latter was to be formed of the two new régiments des chasseurs: de Noinville and d'Astorg. The principle reason for this reorganisation was to provide Vioménil, without doubt the best tactician among the royalist generals, with the command of the light cavalry brigade which would act with the vanguard. However, at the start of the campaign the Astorg Chasseurs had less than 50 men under arms so the Prince de Condé added the Etienne-Damas Hussars to the formation leading to it being often called the Etienne-Damas Hussar Brigade. The regiment, the 'Old Damas', as the Duc de Berry liked to affectionately call it, remained at Rottweil for a month after its review. It was a welcome addition to the army, Toustain remarking, 'this corps had been distinguished in all the campaigns in Brabant and Holland; it was superb in men and very well mounted … the regiment was complete.'[7] On 27 April 1796 the regiment numbered 384 all ranks with 364 horses.[8]

It had arrived just at the right time, when the Armée de Condé was at its greatest strength, 'Never, since its formation, had it been as strong, neither in so fine a state;' with 'about 9,000 men under arms, including 3,000 cavalry.'[9] Although Rottweil was hospitable, Damas's hussars continually faced hostility from the population in the countryside, in

6 Adolphe Thiers, *Histoire de la Révolution française* (Paris: Lecointe, 1823–1827), Vol.II, p.254.

7 Corbehem, *Dix ans de ma vie*, p.299; Perry de Nieüil, *Mémoires du marquis de Toustain*, p.63.

8 AG, Armée de Condé, Carton n°357-1.

9 Perry de Nieüil, *Mémoires du marquis de Toustain*, p.64 and Hyrvoix de Landosle, *Souvenirs du chevalier d'Hespel d'Hocron, volontaire à l'armée de Condé (1794–1797)* (Paris: Roger, 1927), p.47.

the Margraviate of Baden and even more so in the neighbouring Duchy of Württemberg, and several men only escaped from assault by the peasants by the swiftness of their horses. Desertion prevailed especially in the army's newly raised units during the suspension of arms and it was exacerbated by attempts to solicit men for other regiments or even the service of other powers. The Prince de Condé took severe measures against this:

> [A] gentleman having demeaned himself to the point of taking the trade of crimp for the British units, and having engaged to this end as dragoon in the Régiment de Clermont-Tonnerre, was arrested on 9 March, and condemned to be hung; but Monseigneur having commuted the sentence, had his head cut off.[10]

On the eve of the campaign the Armée de Condé was organised thus:

		Coy.	Bn.	Sqn.	Strength
	VANGUARD **HSH Duc d'Enghien**				
Lanau Brigade	Légion de Roger de Damas		2		800
	Régiment de Hohenlohe-Bartenstein		2		1,000
Thumery Brigade	Hussards de Roger de Damas			2	400
	Hussards de Baschi			2	400
	Hussards de Carneville			1	100
	Total		4	5	2,700
	ARMY CORPS **HSH Prince de Condé**				
	Infantry				
Mazancourt Brigade	Régiment noble à pied		2		1,200
Salgues Brigade	Régiment de Bardonnenche		1		600
	Régiment d'Alexandre de Damas		1		600
	Régiment de Roquefeuil		1		600
	Régiment de Montesson		1		500
	Garde Française du quartier-général	1			120
	Garde Suisse du quartier-général	1			120
	Artillerie noble	1			50
	Artillerie soldée		1		450
	Total	3	7		4,270
	Cavalry				
Boisseson Brigade	Régiment de Dauphin			1 ½	250
	Dragons de Clermont-Tonnerre			1 ½	250
	Dragons de Fargues			½	100

10 Marquis d'Ecquevilly, *Campagnes du corps sous les ordres de Son Altesse Sérénissime Monseigneur le prince de Condé* (Paris: Unknown Publisher, 1818), Vol.II, p.6.

Vioménil Brigade*	Chasseurs de Noinville			2	400
	Hussards d'Etienne-Damas			2	400
	Prévôté				50
	Total			8	1,450
	CAVALRY RESERVE HSH Duc de Berry				
	Régiment Noble à Cheval (1e)			2	400
	Régiment des Gardes du Corps (2e noble)			2	400
	Régiment des Propriétaires			½	100
	Chevaliers de la Couronne			2	400
	Total			6 ½	1,300
	General total	3	11	19 ½	9,720
	Of which 8,000 under arms				

* The Chasseurs d'Astorg are not included in this list, but other evidence shows that its few men served with the Vioménil Brigade.

Table based on the list in Comte de Castres, *Relation d'un voyage sur le bord septentrional de la mer d'Azof et en Crimée, dans la vue d'y établir une colonie d'émigrés* (Paris: Killian, 1826), pp.VIII–IX; another in Perry de Nieüil, *Mémoires du marquis de Toustain*, pp.416–418, shows variations in the distribution of the units.

On 1 May 1796 the new King Louis XVIII arrived at the Prince de Condé's headquarters at Riegel. He had been asked to leave the city of Verona, as the ruling Republic of Venice was afraid of displeasing the advancing French revolutionaries, and he arrived declaring that he had come to serve as a simple volunteer under the orders of his cousin alongside his beloved nobility. 'He was then hardly forty-two years old; his head was superb his carriage marked with dignity; he was fat and his legs were already swollen … he wore the iron grey coat of the staff of Condé's Corps, and the epaulettes decorated by a crown, as he wore later when he was on the throne.'[11]

The vanguard under the Duc d'Enghien, who was adored by his men for his personal courage, chivalric spirit and military talents, was deployed along about 28 kilometres of the Rhine, from 12 kilometres above Kehl to Emmendingen. Vioménil had rapidly re-established good relations with the duke, 'too sincerely disciplined not to set an example, he was soon to obey in the vanguard corps.'[12] His three regiments, the Etienne-Damas hussars and the Noinville and Astorg Chasseurs, more soberly dressed in dark-green coats and breeches or overalls, were installed at Teningen, Nimburg and Bötzingen, to the north of Freiburg and west of Emmendingen, in order to rapidly support the vanguard.

On 21 May the Armée de Condé was warned that the armistice was to end, with hostilities to recommence after 10 days, and either side could take the offensive:

11 Comte Alexandre de Puymaigre, *Souvenirs sur l'émigration, l'Empire et la Restauration, publiés par son fils* (Paris: Plon, 1884), p.28.

12 Bittard des Portes, *Histoire de l'armée de Condé* (Paris: Dentu, 1896), p.240.

> Mainz and Mannheim were in the power of the Austrians. These two important points assured them a sure passage and a solid fulcrum point on the left bank of the Rhine. But the French occupied Düsseldorf and had a formidable bridgehead before Neuwied, which gave them a foothold in Germany.[13]

The Imperial troops were commanded to the north, between the Moselle and Rhine, by the Emperor's brother, Archduke Charles, and to the south, from Mannheim to Basel, by the Graf von Wurmser. The defence of the bridge and fort at Kehl, opposite Strasbourg, was entrusted to the Schwäbisches-Kreis-Contingent, troops who had been recently and reluctantly raised by the princes of the Swabian, Southern German, Circle of the Empire. The Duc d'Enghien described its 12 to 15,000 men as 'badly commanded, so to speak without officers, and of whom not one soldier had fought in war and had the least idea of service'.[14]

The armistice had been ended to enable Carnot, the French Minister for War, to enact his plan to march on Vienna through the two valleys of the Danube and Main and so bring Austria to the negotiation table. A diversionary offensive in Italy was launched under the young *Général de Division* Bonaparte and, on 10 April 1796, he made his first attack into Piedmont against the Austrians under *Feldzeugmeister* Beaulieu. What was to have been a distraction rapidly turned into a brilliant campaign that, at the end of May, caused *Feldmarschall* von Wurmser to be sent with 25,000 men to Italy, as Bonaparte laid siege to Mantua. Appointed to the command in Italy, Wurmser was replaced in Germany by *Feldzeugmeister* Comte de Latour. With their opponents on the Rhine weakened, the French offensive could begin.

The Austrians initially sought to take the initiative and, at the beginning of June, moved troops towards Huningue, near Basel, one of the principal crossing points of the Rhine, to strike into Upper Alsace. The Armée de Condé was to take part in this operation and moved, from 2 to 4 June, into the region of Steinenstadt, south-west of Müllheim. However, to the north, *Général de Division* Kléber, with a wing of the Armée de Sambre-et-Meuse, attacked the Imperial troops near Mainz and at the Battle of Altenkirchen on 4 June 1796 forced them to abandon their position. In response, the *Condéens* were ordered, on 6 June, to return to their previous positions, with their headquarters at Riegel, the infantry camped behind Kappel-Grafenhausen, north-west of Ettenheim and on the bank of the Rhine, the cavalry in its former cantonments and the vanguard again facing the Rhine near Nonnenweier.

Kléber's offensive allowed Jourdan to cross the Rhine on 12 June, at Neuwied, however the Austrians soon forced Kléber to fall back on 19 June and Jourdan to abandon Neuwied and the right bank of the Rhine. Moreau, the new commander of the Armée du Rhin et Moselle, then feigned to cross the Rhine near Mannheim while he sent the bulk of his troops to Strasbourg. From midnight 23/24 June, the initial wave of republican troops commanded by Desaix crossed the Rhine on boats around Kehl while a deafening cannonade was unleashed from 1:00 to 9:00 a.m., along the length of the river from Huningue to Mannheim. Some republican troops came up against *Condéens*, 'posts of the Légion de Mirabeau [sic] [and]

13 Comte Boulay de La Meurthe, *Correspondance du duc d'Enghien (1801–1804) et documents sur son enlèvement et sa mort*, Récit de la campagne de 1796 par le duc d'Enghien, Vol.IV (Paris: Picard, 1913), p.220.

14 Boulay de La Meurthe, *Correspondance du duc d'Enghien*, p. 222.

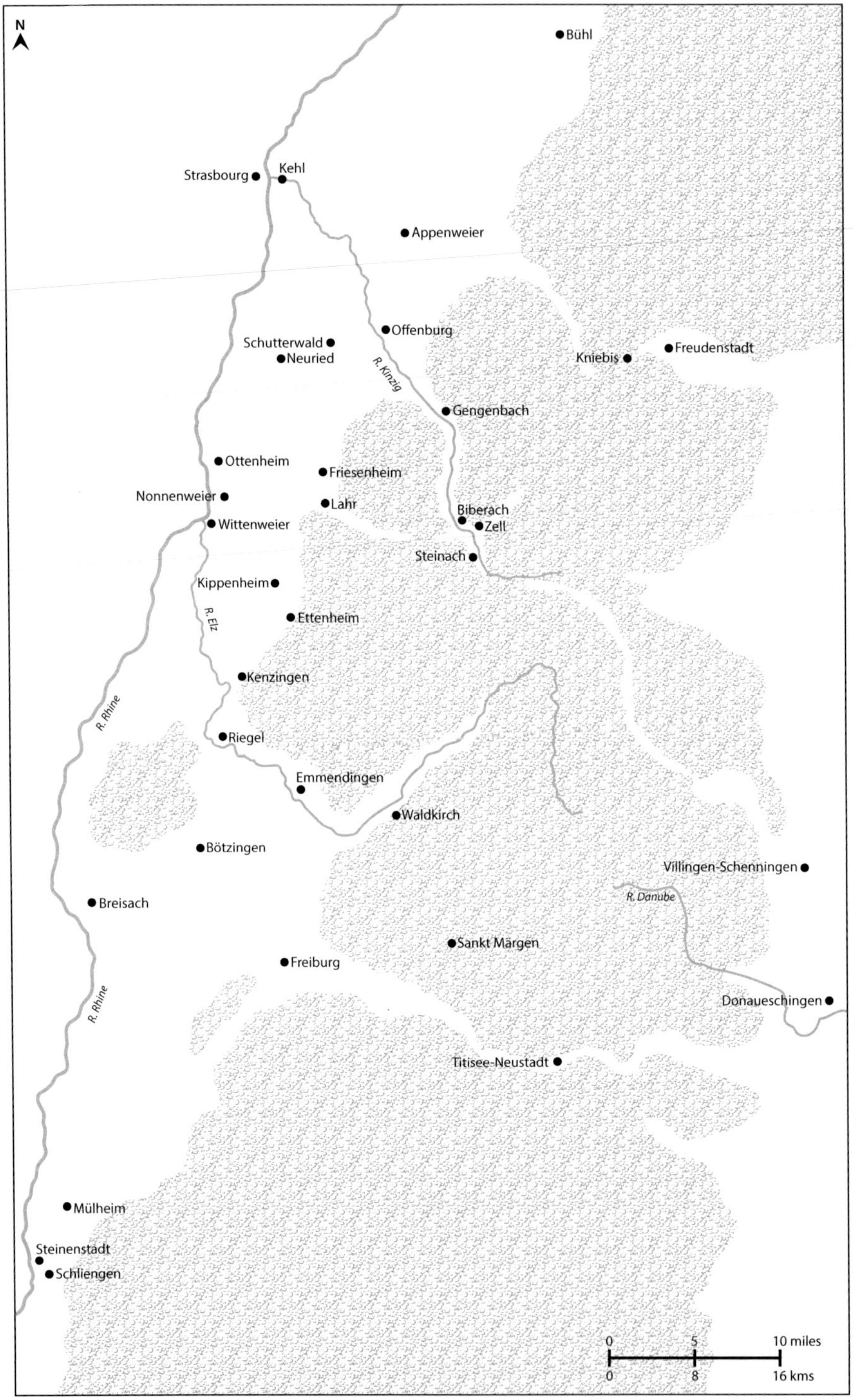
N
Bühl
Strasbourg
Kehl
Appenweier
Offenburg
Schutterwald
Neuried
R. Kinzig
Kniebis
Freudenstadt
Gengenbach
Ottenheim
Friesenheim
Nonnenweier
Lahr
Biberach
Zell
Wittenweier
Steinach
Kippenheim
R. Elz
Ettenheim
Kenzingen
R. Rhine
Riegel
Emmendingen
Waldkirch
Bötzingen
Villingen-Schenningen
R. Danube
Breisach
Sankt Märgen
Freiburg
R. Rhine
Donaueschingen
Titisee-Neustadt
Mülheim
Steinenstadt
Schliengen
0 5 10 miles
0 8 16 kms

Breisgau.

were vigorously received by them'. However, Kehl was their target where, 'The disembarkation of the Patriots was in fact carried out, apparently, without resistance on the part of the Württembergers'.[15] It was attacked at 10:00 a.m. and taken in half an hour, with little opposition from the Kreistruppen who then abandoned the Rhine, retreating in the greatest disorder towards the city of Offenburg on the River Kinzig.

Shocked by the news of the fall of Kehl, which reached Riegel that afternoon, 24 June, at around 4:00 p.m., Condé's troops were immediately placed under arms, ready to move. The republican vanguard crossed the Rhine the next day and at 7:00 a.m. the prince sent Vioménil's brigade towards Offenburg, while the main corps marched for Nonnenweier to replace the Duc d'Enghien who had left to place himself in front of Offenburg. Having filled the void left by the German troops, he expected to be joined by an Austrian corps of 8,000 men that the Comte de Latour had promised him. Yet no such corps appeared and, although reinforced by a large part of the paid regiments of his grandfather's army, Enghien found himself extended between Offenburg and the village of Marlen, on the Rhine, eight kilometres south of Kehl. Skirmishing took place all day with enemy's forward troops and the *Condéens* strove to prevent the republicans infiltrating between their vanguard and the Prince de Condé's position to the north. This task fell to Vioménil's brigade and the Régiment d'Etienne-Damas hussards 'united with that of the chasseurs de Noinville, executed manoeuvres that, by their continual and sustained activity, clearly aimed at tricking the enemy by multiplying to their eyes the apparent strength of the *Condéen* cavalry'.[16] Meanwhile, Enghien asked for reinforcements from the small Austrian corps of *Feldmarschalleutnant* Sztáray, as well as the Swabians, to drive the republicans back to the left bank of the Rhine and retake Kehl. However, Sztáray, who was certainly not a timid commander, only had 4 to 5,000 men and considered such an operation too risky, however he did send Enghien the 1,200 strong free corps commanded by Ignaz Graf Gyulai. In the evening of 26 June Enghien pushed back the republicans beyond Marlen, but was counter-attacked and after some fierce fighting he disengaged to move to a new position, two kilometres in front of Altenheim, to the north of Neuried and west of Offenburg This brought him closer to his grandfather who had just arrived at Ottenheim with the noble infantry and cavalry but Enghien immediately received the order to fall back onto Schutterwald, a small village a league to the west of Offenburg, with his staff installed further to the south in the Abbey of Schuttern.

The order had come from *Generalmajor* von Stein, commanding the Kreistruppen, and it meant that the Rhine had been abandoned to the French who were quickly reinforced on the river's right bank. The Prince de Condé had also received an order, at 2:00 a.m. that night, to withdraw. There was a suspicion among the royalists that the republicans had secretly negotiated with the German princes to allow the crossing of the Rhine and withdraw their forces so creating a breach in the Austrian centre which now threatened to cut the *Condéen* vanguard from the rest of their army. This presentiment was confirmed by events that same day, 27 June. It began with cavalry skirmishes, in which Corbehem witnessed an incident that showed the changing relations between republican and royalist soldiers although, when

15 AMC Fonds Grouvel, Dossier Légion de Damas, Mémoires inédits du comte de Vioménil.

16 Corbehem, *Dix ans de ma vie*, p.301.

Enghien heard of it, he condemned it not wishing to encourage further fraternisation in the future:

> Our headquarters was still at Schuttern when one day we took a position on a plain in front of the bridge at Offenburg, with the intention to dispute the passage of this bridge. A quite singular circumstance happened to us at this time: the regiment with which we had most particularly to deal with was that which formerly had the name of Conti, and of which the dragoons had become chasseurs. While some amongst us skirmished with this regiment, the two parties driven by some sort of gaiety of spirit which only is to be met among the French, suddenly ceased fire, approached together and drank to the health of each other; at the end of a few moments they separated and the fire started again ...[17]

In the afternoon, Desaix's corps attacked Enghien's position at Schutterwald and, unable to resist, he fell back while skirmishing onto the Schwäbisches-Kreis-Contingent that was placed in a defensive position, to the rear and on his right, along the Offenburg to Appenweier road. Vioménil was sent with his brigade by the Prince de Condé to Offenburg to discover the republican movements and the attitude of the German troops:

> [Vioménil] crosses through Offenburg, asks subsistence for his men and horses who had not eaten for 24 hours. The Fürst zu Fürstenberg, second in command of the Swabians, refuses them at first, but, menaced with pillage by Vioménil, ends by granting them.
>
> Vioménil moves onto the bridge; he sees three republican columns marching against the Swabian positions; the Württemberg artillery fires on them with blanks. Having understood the situation, Vioménil prepares to re-join Condé but, called to defend the Offenburg plain by the quartermaster general of the Swabian cavalry, he moves there and places himself in the interval of the 8 squadrons of the troops of the Circles. Sharply cannoned, Vioménil sends Lieutenant-colonel de Dortan [of Noinville] to reconnoitre his rear and ... [sensing that his brigade is being trapped by the Swabians] gives the order to retreat; he has to put his pistol in his hand in order to make a passage through the Swabians [when a troop of Württemberg cavalry tries to block his path] ... and re-joins the Duc d'Enghien near the bridge beyond Offenburg.[18]

Corbehem had been sent by Vioménil with a note reporting the situation to the headquarters, four leagues away. The prince had him brought some refreshment while an answer was prepared, with which Corbehem left immediately:

> I returned with as much promptitude as I had come, and although the day was already at its close, I found my regiment approximately in the position that I had

17 Corbehem, *Dix ans de ma vie*, pp. 304–305.
18 Grouvel *Les Corps de troupe de l'émigration*, Vol.II, pp.221–222.

> left it, which is to say a little closer to the Offenburg bridge; but after a few moments had passed, the storm that I had foreseen that the enemy's manoeuvre threatened burst on us; they suddenly debouched with impetuosity on the Swabian cavalry's flank, and the latter, solely at their appearance, fled at full speed and in the greatest disorder towards the bridge, the passage of which it blocked by its extreme confusion. Our danger was imminent, and it took all the presence of mind of the general who commanded us to extract us from the bad situation. Our retreat was made with as much order as the circumstances permitted; we left Offenburg by a gate at the same moment that the enemy entered it by another.

In the retreat Corbehem lost one of his comrades, 'Duménil, a Norman gentleman as brave as distinguished through his moral qualities.'[19] The Marquis de Toustain, serving with the staff of his uncle, Vioménil, recalled:

> [T]he horrible affair of Offenburg, where the brigade of M. de Vioménil having had the fight not only against enemies, but also against traitors, overcame so many obstacles and owed its safety only to the foresight of the general who had made a reconnaissance of a route of retreat in the [Kinzig] valley, did not cost us as much as we would have thought: few men were killed or wounded, which we attributed to the great order which did not cease to reign in the brigade during the retreat.[20]

Desaix's troops had continued their advance and:

> [O]verflowed the Circles' position who, seized by terror, did not delay to retreat in disorder without firing a musket shot. They abandoned with precipitation redoubts that they had provided with cannons, and a magnificent position in which, superior in number as they were, they had nothing to fear. This army marched through Offenburg all night, gaining the highroad to Gengenbach [in the Kinzig valley that cut into the western flank of the Black Forest][21]

Enghien withdrew to take a position to defend the bridge at Offenburg and his artillery did not stop cannonading the enemy until nightfall, but threatened with being outflanked he was forced to cut the bridge and retreat in the middle of the night in the pouring rain. He had to choose between following the routed Schwäbisches-Kreis-Contingent along the Kinzig valley or withdrawing south to join his grandfather in front of Friesenheim. He chose the first option as he had more chance to reach the Gengenbach Abbey in the Kinzig valley before the French republicans who may have already begun to encircle him via other valleys. Nevertheless, he had reason to fear the 12,000 German troops ahead of him who could at any moment try to deliver him to his pursuers, estimated to be at least 30,000 men, in the mountains. Enghien, with the vanguard and Vioménil's brigade, reached Gengenbach at the break of day where he detached himself from the Kreistruppen who

19 Corbehem, *Dix ans de ma vie*, pp.305–306.
20 Perry de Nieüil, *Mémoires du marquis de Toustain*, p.66.
21 Boulay de La Meurthe, *Correspondance du duc d'Enghien*, p.227.

were now preoccupied in pillaging. He then continued south to the village of Biberach then Steinach, while Graf Gyulai, with his free corps, installed himself at Zell at the entrance of the Harmersbach Valley. The Duc d'Enghien remained the next day, 29 June, at Steinach and succeeded in re-establishing communication with his grandfather who ordered him to maintain his position, with Gyulai on his right.

Corbehem had a narrow escape during the retreat, on the morning of 29 June. The regiment had lodged in a large village at the entrance of the gorge of the Kinzig valley, perhaps Gengenbach. Exhausted, he slept there for a few hours but when the march resumed his comrades simply could not wake him. At daybreak, when the republicans entered the village Corbehem was finally wakened by his host who patently did not share their revolutionary ideas:

> I was laid down fully dressed behind my horse, which he had saddled and loaded. At the first noise that my host made, I mounted with haste and saved myself at the gallop. The moments were indeed precious; for scarcely had I left the house that I heard the shouts of the enemy infantry who were making their entrance into the village. Escaped from danger, I followed the valley and I was not long in joining at first a unit of *Condéen* infantry, and further on my regiment who were astonished to see me again, thinking me killed or taken in the fight.[22]

The Prince de Condé, having united with the Austrian troops of *Feldmarschalleutnant* von Fröhlich, commanding in the Breisgau, had received, at 1:00 a.m. on 28 June, the order to fall back to hold a defensive line from Lahr to the villages of Nonnenweier and Wittenweier, on the Rhine, with his headquarters at Kippenheim. On 29 June, the Austrian command agreed that the vanguard, at Steinach, should re-join the *Condéen* troops around Kippenheim, on the condition of leaving the Régiment de Hohenlohe and a squadron of the Baschi Hussars as reinforcements for Gyulai holding the Kinzig Valley. The vanguard re-joined the Prince de Condé at 9:00 a.m. on 30 June and was immediately deployed as the Duc d'Enghien described, 'Arriving on the ground that my grandfather occupied with his corps, I found his advanced posts skirmishing with the enemy behind Friesenheim. The Régiment de Carneville charged three times, and took some horses. I threw myself onto the left with the rest of my vanguard, in order to scout this part as far as the Rhine'.[23] The Etienne-Damas Hussars took part in this operation as Corbehem related, 'Thus a few leagues from Schuttern Abbey, my regiment took part in a brilliant affair, led by the Duc d'Enghien, and in which the Carneville Hussars particularly distinguished themselves.'[24]

The following day, on 1 July, the Etienne-Damas Hussars were ranged in battle order, by echelons, in a plain, under the fire of the republican artillery, when a rider suddenly appeared who was to say the least unexpected:

> His Majesty … alone, without followers, without guards, without escort, and despite the balls which rained down around us, came to pass before each platoon of

22 Corbehem, *Dix ans de ma vie*, pp.306–307.
23 Boulay de La Meurthe, *Correspondance du duc d'Enghien*, p.230.
24 Corbehem, *Dix ans de ma vie*, p.302.

> cavalry, addressing us with all those so flattering words which seem to trip so naturally from the mouth of the Bourbons. "Messieurs," said the King to the platoon in which I was, "you have yesterday shared the glory of my cousin Enghien; I congratulate you." These words raised our enthusiasm to such a point that we would have at this time defied forces ten times greater than ours, but our courage was not put to the test.[25]

According to the Marquis de Toustain:

> The King, with the Duc de Berry and all his suite, spent a day before our front, and stayed there quite some time, despite the fire of the enemy. He complimented the general [Vioménil] and said the kindest things to the brigade. This brave prince was as calm and gay, in this situation where balls almost brushed him, as he would have been in his palace of Versailles.[26]

Several days later, Louis, under pressure from the Viennese court, was to leave the Armée de Condé. At midnight, 1 to 2 July, the army marched to join Fröhlich who had installed himself in a firm defensive position around Kenzingen, on the River Elz, to await reinforcements that the Archduke Charles was to bring to Breisgau. Enghien's troops joined Fröhlich at Kenzingen while the main body of the army was placed, in the rear, around Riegel. On 3 July patrols explored the country in front of the positions:

> Comte Etienne de Damas, returning from the reconnaissance that he had been charged to make, reported that having advanced to Mahlberg, his scouts had encountered those of the enemy between this village and that of Kippenheim where, from the information that he had been able to gather, he had reason to believe that there could be seven to eight hundred men there. His detachment on the left had moved up to Kappel[-Grafenhausen], where the republicans had appeared to him to be in small numbers; besides, all this part of the Rhine was so flooded that it had become impracticable.[27]

The position around Kenzingen was precarious and while the vanguard, strengthened by the Régiment de Bardonnenche and the infantry of the Légion de Roger de Damas, remained there the rest of the Armée de Condé was sent to Villingen, a key point on the eastern side of the Black Forest. The reason for *Feldmarschalleutnant* von Fröhlich ordering this move was explained by the Duc d'Enghien thus:

> It was twelve days since the French had crossed the Rhine at Kehl. The complete success of this first attempt had made them hasten the arrival of their reinforcements; they were already more than 50,000 on the right bank. The Austrian corps that had been sent against them had been beaten near Renchen [28 June]; they

25 Corbehem, *Dix ans de ma vie*, p.302.
26 Perry de Nieüil, *Mémoires du marquis de Toustain*, p.67.
27 Ecquevilly, *Campagnes*, Vol.II, p.38.

> occupied Rastatt, and the archduke in person had just experienced a violent check [further north] around Ettlingen and Karlsruhe ...[28]

The Schwäbisches-Kreis-Contingent had given further proof they could not be trusted by abandoning, without the least resistance, the key positions in the Black Forest at Kniebis and Freudenstadt. This left open to the republicans the gorges immediately in front of Strasbourg that led into Württemberg and on to Bavaria and Austria. Furthermore, to the north, Jourdan, at the head of 80,000 men, had crossed the Rhine around Mainz and was now marching south-eastwards by way of Frankfurt on Franconia and the left bank of the Danube.

Enghien's vanguard, with the Etienne-Damas brigade and the two attached infantry units, remained in the Breisgau, on the Elz, with Fröhlich for twelve days despite being attacked on 6 and 9 July. However, learning that Moreau had crossed the Rhine with the bulk of his forces on 13 July, the Austrian general ordered a retreat to Villingen that night, as described by Enghien:

> I left at two o'clock in the morning, and following the order that I had received, I passed through Riegel, the bridge of which I found already broken. The Austrians, on leaving, had taken this precaution without checking if I had already crossed or not. I sent by the Gorge of Freiburg, as I had been ordered, the Etienne-Damas brigade, under the orders of the Comte de Vioménil, and I went with the rest of my troops through Emmendingen and Waldkirch,[29]

The Marquis de Toustain, however, remembered that the order to evacuate the Breisgau was given 24 hours later. On 14 July, when the French attacked, Fröhlich defended his position supported by Vioménil's brigade:

> We sent pickets to support the Austrians; some Noinville chasseurs, men we had taken from the French and who had engaged in this regiment, deserted and took with them, by force, a Damas volunteer. Then M de Vioménil drove from the ranks all the prisoners that we had made and who were still found under his command.[30]

According to him, it was at 1:00 a.m. on 15 July that the general received the order to march by way of Freiburg towards Titisee-Neustadt, forming the rear-guard of all the corps withdrawing from the Breisgau, and that Vioménil gave the order to break the bridge at Riegel.

To the north, Jourdan's advance forced Archduke Charles to withdraw on Stuttgart in the direction of Ulm and the Danube, it was now clear that Jourdan sought to push the archduke before him towards Moreau to trap him between pincers. It was essential that the two Austrian armies, of the archduke and Latour, to which Condé's corps was now attached, always remained level to each other.

28 Boulay de La Meurthe, *Correspondance du duc d'Enghien*, p.234.
29 Boulay de La Meurthe, *Correspondance du duc d'Enghien*, p.234.
30 Perry de Nieüil, *Mémoires du marquis de Toustain*, p.70.

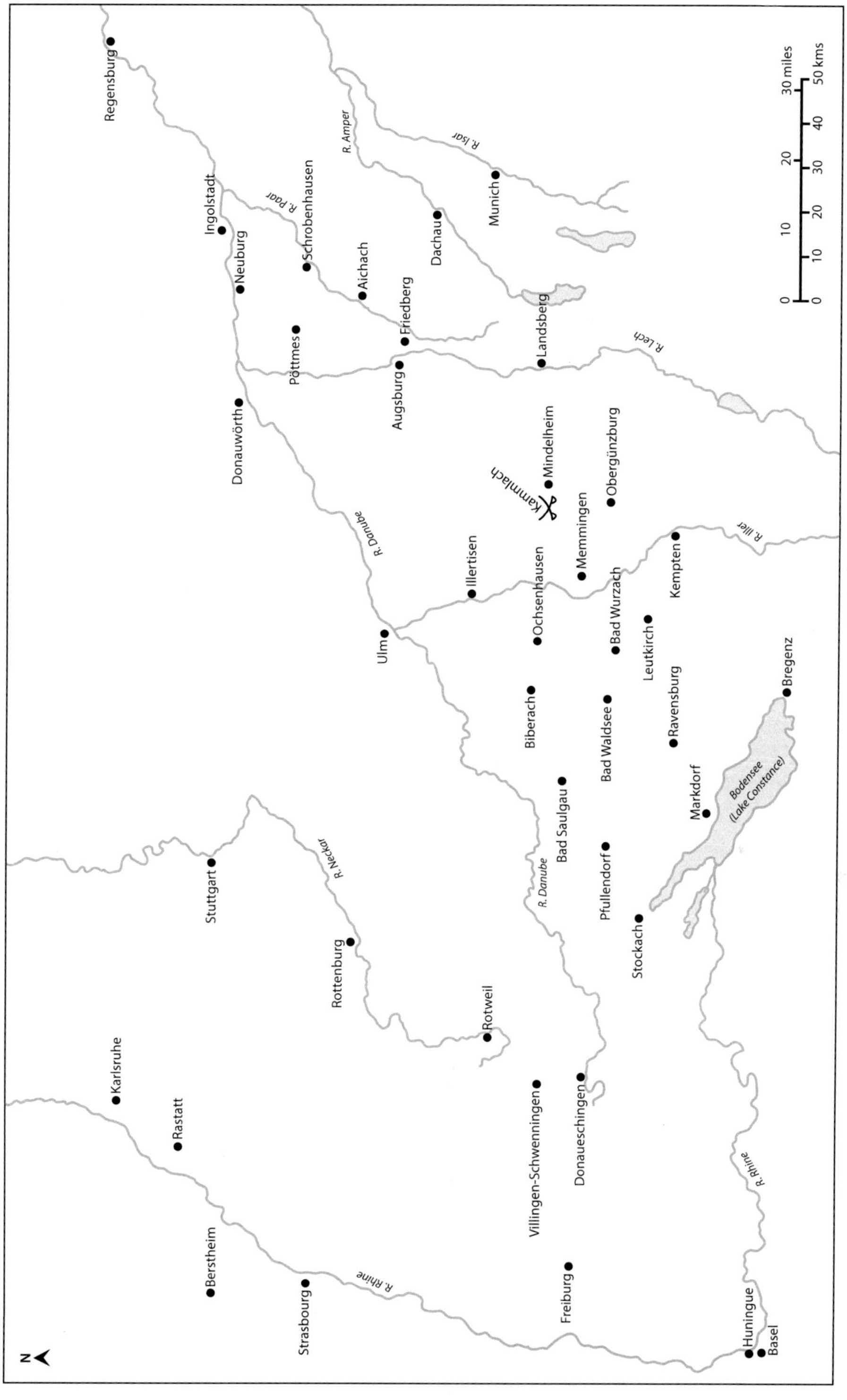

Southern Germany.

Vioménil's brigade arrived at Titisee-Neustadt at about 6:00 p.m. on 15 July and left around 10:00 a.m. the next day for Donaueschingen, south of Villingen. The retreat resumed from there on 18 July with the Armée de Condé split into columns to use different routes, Vioménil's brigade going directly to Stockach on the north of the Bodensee (Lake Constance). It was in the region of the lake that the army was reunited. In the meantime, Moreau had concluded an armistice with the Duke of Württemberg, followed on 17 July by the rest of the Swabian Circle, and was known to be on the point of signing another, separately, with the Margrave of Baden, 25 July. The remains of the Schwäbisches-Kreis-Contingent, about 4,000 men, were near Biberach an der Riß, north-east of the Bodensee, and on 29 July they were disarmed, which was done 'with the least resistance.'[31]

On 24 July Fröhlich had requested a reinforcement of 200 horse from the Prince de Condé and 'a detachment from the Etienne-Damas brigade, under the orders of the Comte de Noinville, was commissioned for this service.'[32] In the following days the whole army moved northwards via Markdorf, Bad Waldsee, Ravensburg, Weingarten Abbey, Bad Wurzach on 30 July to reach Memmingen, just east of the River Iller, on 1 August where 'the brigade of Etienne de Damas was detached four leagues in advance at Ochsenhausen [north-west of Memmingen, halfway between it and Biberach], where the detachment commanded by the Comte de Nonville re-joined it.'[33]

The Prince de Condé was entrusted with the forward defence of Memmingen and the banks of the River Iller, with Enghien at Leutkirch, to the south and Vioménil at Ochsenhausen. Over the next few days, with the enemy probing towards Wurzach, Enghien reduced his front confining himself to defending the Iller.[34] Vioménil's brigade remained around Ochsenhausen but on 6 and 7 August his outposts had contact with the enemy. It was clear that the French were about to deliver the knockout blow and Memmingen was abandoned. The Armée de Condé was now to be a link between the two Austrian corps of *Feldzeugmeister* de Latour, who was withdrawing towards Ulm and then Augsburg to be closer to Archduke Charles, and *Generalmajor* von Wolf who was directed to the southern end of the Bodensee, around Bregenz, to protect the Tyrol. Condé had to provide 1,300 of his men to *Generalmajor* Klinglin von Hadtstadt who was placed around Kempten, between him and Wolf. Before retreating Latour had instructed Condé to cover Landsberg am Lech, a strategic crossroads on the road to Munich, by holding Mindelheim, midway between Memmingen and Landsberg, with the 4,000-5,000 men he still had available.

In the night of 8/9 August the troops of the Duc d'Enghien retreated, in the wake of those of the Prince de Condé, but halted at Erkheim 'a good position in front of the forest which descends to Kammlach [or Oberkammlach].'[35] The village was half-way between Memmingen and Mindelheim, and Enghien established his headquarters just to the south at Sontheim. Vioménil, withdrew from Ochsenhausen 'harassed by the enemy, who had taken a patrol of five men.'[36] In the afternoon of 8 August he had retired to Memmingen and

31 Ecquevilly, *Campagnes*, Vol.II, pp.60–61.
32 Ecquevilly, *Campagnes*, Vol.II, p. 58.
33 Ecquevilly, *Campagnes*, Vol.II, p. 62.
34 Boulay de La Meurthe, *Correspondance du duc d'Enghien*, p.237.
35 Boulay de La Meurthe, *Correspondance du duc d'Enghien*, p.238.
36 Ecquevilly, *Campagnes*, p.68.

left there on the morning of 9 August to get to Obergünzburg, to the south in the direction of Kempten. 'In this new position, we had the Duc d'Enghien to our right, at Sontheim, and to our left, General Klinglin, who occupied Kensten [Kempten]. So that, in a country where cavalry is good for nothing, we were obliged, with our two regiments, to keep ground seven leagues in extent.'[37]

The Prince de Condé's troops arrived at Mindelheim at 4:00 a.m. on 9 August and deployed in front of the village, to the west, facing the highroad from Memmingen. At the village the émigrés found some consolation after their retreat, receiving, 'upon the archduke's authorisation … a considerable quantity of wagons loaded with camp equipment, several consignments of arms, and of what could be found of the horses belonging to the Swabian army, of which the number amounted to a hundred and eighty'.[38] However, they were isolated, Fröhlich's corps was almost 40 kilometres to the north and that of Wolf, an even greater distance to the south-west.

In the evening of 10 August, the republican vanguard emerged from Memmingen and pressed Enghien's outposts the next day. In the morning of 12 August, the enemy advanced and cannonaded his front while sending columns to turn his flanks.[39] One of the columns encountered Vioménil's brigade:

> On the 12th, at eight in the morning, we saw a considerable French column which, directing itself on our right, attacked the Duc d'Enghien. One of his aides de camp came from him to ask the general to move, with his cavalry, into the plain of Sontheim, and to take the enemy in the rear. M de Vioménil refused this, knowing that he would be undoubtedly cut off. There debouched from a village in front of Sontheim, a column of 2,000 infantrymen, 800 horse and cannon, commanded by Général Abbatucci, that headed for us. M de Vioménil having neither infantry, nor artillery, found himself unable to resist this attack, but, before retiring, he wanted to wait for the enemy to be at a hundred paces. The retreat was then all the more difficult as the country that we had to traverse for two leagues to re-join the Prince de Condé, was all covered with woods. To add to our misfortune, we received notice that the enemy had moved on our left another column that could occupy Mindelheim before the prince, he having no troops on this side. The general ordered me to go with the greatest speed possible to warn him of the danger that threatened him. I found him, at the head of his cavalry, in a great plain, before the village of Ansbach [Oberauerbach], and reported my mission to him. He received me testily and sent me back to tell the general to retire into the plain and to cover his left. M de Vioménil thus deployed his cavalry in line, facing the road from Sontheim. The French who pursued us did not dare to advance. We lost some men in this retreat, as well as several horses.[40]

37 Perry de Nieüil, *Mémoires du marquis de Toustain*, p.73.
38 Ecquevilly, *Campagnes*, p.69.
39 Boulay de La Meurthe, *Correspondance du duc d'Enghien*, p.238.
40 Perry de Nieüil, *Mémoires du marquis de Toustain*, pp.73–74.

This movement permitted Enghien to retreat east unmolested as the republicans did not follow him into the plain, about a kilometre in width, before Mindelheim for fear of the *Condéen* cavalry. This respite allowed the Prince de Condé to plan a battle that he would doubtless not have considered had he not been notified, that evening, 12 August, of the Austrian staff's displeasure with his retreat from Memmingen, and also that Wolf and Klinglin had had to abandon Bregenz, and Kempten, so uncovering his left flank.

The prince's army was camped in the wide plain in front of Oberauerbach, just before the road entered Mindelheim; it was not a good position as the road dropped into a steep valley between the two and Mindelheim, itself, was without defences. Facing them, the republicans held the wood, about eight kilometres long, north to south, on the other side of the plain, as well as the village of Oberkammlach in front of this wood behind it they occupied the zone between Memmingen and Sontheim. Thus, the republicans could mass their forces behind Oberkammlach for an attack on Mindelheim, once the bulk of Ferino's division, 8,000 men, had joined his vanguard under Abbatucci.

Cézac de Belcayre of the Etienne-Damas Hussars was, in the evening of 12 August, a vedette sentry, within musket range of the wood held by the republicans, having performed the duty on the plain throughout the day. He was, like the republicans, convinced that once night fell the émigrés would disengage under the cover of darkness to withdraw, perhaps even to Landsberg.

> [T]hey finally came to relieve our picket and tell us that we were ordered to each return to our respective companies, doubtless, we thought, to make our accustomed retreat. We re-joined our units and I saw, to my great astonishment, that mine was in line and battle array like all our army: the noble cavalry, the Fargues dragoons, those of Enghien and the Mirabeau hussars formed the division on the right; the infantry on the right was formed by the noble chasseurs, those of Mirabeau, the Grenadiers de Bourbon, and the Régiment de Hohenlohe. The division on the left was composed of the Chevaliers de la Couronne, Damas hussars and the Noinville chasseurs; its infantry comprised the four cadre regiments.[41]

Shortly beforehand, the Prince de Condé had conferred with his generals, 'The impossibility of defending our position being well known, there was only two choices: that of retreat during the night, or that of a very sharp attack on our part, which, thanks to the darkness, would make us appear more numerous than we really were. This last opinion prevailed'.[42] The troops were formed into three columns, the prince commanded that in the centre composed of the two battalions of the Nobles à Pied, 1,080 men, and the cavalry reserve; the vanguard, under Enghien, formed the right column. Vioménil commanded that on the left, mainly of cavalry, its only infantry being the two companies, French and Swiss, of the headquarters guard: he 'had instructions to turn the left of the forest and to disturb the enemy's right flank, while the two others attacked head on.'[43]

41 Cézac de Belcayre, *Dix ans d'émigration (1791–1801)*, pp.199–200. The writer made a mistake as the Bourbon Grenadiers were only raised in 1798 in Russian service.

42 Ecquevilly, *Campagnes*, pp.72–73.

43 Boulay de La Meurthe, *Correspondance du duc d'Enghien*, p.240.

The centre and right columns set off at 1:00 a.m. on 13 August. The centre, advancing along the main road attacked the village of Oberkammlach which, after some hard fighting, was taken at the point of the bayonet. It then continued to the forest edge where a deadly fire-fight took place, at close range. Fierce fighting continued, the republican 89ème Demi-Brigade de Ligne contesting every step as the noble infantry continued into the trees. Enghien's column, on the right, advanced in support of the centre through Unterkammlach to the forest. The first resistance it encountered was approaching the edge of the forest, from the 3ème Demi-Brigade Légère, and the fight became fierce as the *Condéens* worked their way forward, friend and foe intermingled in the darkness and trees. Both columns were weakening as casualties mounted while their foes were continually reinforced, by this stage 'Nearly three quarters of the Noble battalions were wounded, killed, or occupied in transporting the wounded'.[44] Nevertheless the *Condéens* had almost reached the western fringe of the wood when another line of republicans was seen on a height by Erkheim massed to receive them when they emerged into the intervening open ground. Victory was impossible particularly as it was learnt that Ferrino's division was only three leagues away and approaching fast, so the Prince de Condé gave the order to retreat, it had to be repeated several times before it was affected.

Meanwhile, Vioménil's column, about 650 sabres, including the Etienne-Damas Hussars, had moved forward towards the village of Stetten which was occupied as soon as the cannon, signalling the opening of the general attack, was heard.

> The general had the village which was in front of us, on the Sontheim road, searched and, being assured that it did not contain any adversaries, he had us advance, his infantry in skirmishing order, to the right and left of the road into the wood, and his cavalry in column by squads on the road. After a short distance, we encountered the French outposts that retired on our approach, but always disputing the ground.[45]

Vioménil was to stay level with the centre column but, unable to see its progress due to the darkness and trees, had to judge its advance by the noise of the fighting.

> [Considering] that the centre column had the best of them, he had us move in front, always pushing the troops to which were opposed. We had gone a league and a half, and we had no more than a quarter of a league to reach the plain at Sontheim, where our cavalry could break out and obtain great success. When we arrived at the spot where the enemy had concentrated all their forces, that they had placed in the woods to the left of the road, they sent towards us an army of skirmishers who opened a terrible fire on ours and made them give way somewhat. Then, the general had the column halt. In the same instant, we heard, on the right, battalion fire followed by fire by file and most lively, which remained in the same place for a long time and appeared to us then to advance on Kammlach. The general judging

44 Boulay de La Meurthe, *Correspondance du duc d'Enghien*, p.240.

45 Perry de Nieüil, *Mémoires du marquis de Toustain*, p.76.

> that the centre column was repulsed, prepared to withdraw, when he received the order from the prince.[46]

The centre and right-hand columns finally managed to extract themselves from Oberkammlach and withdraw to Oberauerbach under the protection of the Duc de Berry's reserve cavalry. The French attempted to exploit the retreat, as seen by one of the Chevaliers de la Couronne: 'Abbatucci seeing the disorder in our infantry and wishing to profit from it, launched his cavalry. We then saw emerging from the village of Oberkammlach towards us the republican 4e Dragons: we were already stood on our stirrups; but the eight-pounder pieces sufficed, to our great regret, to make this cavalry disappear.'[47] Once through Oberauerbach, at about 7:00 a.m., the Prince de Condé withdrew the Noble cavalry and ordered Vioménil to protect the rear with his brigade.

> The enemy seeing this movement, sent skirmishers into the plain; we opposed them with ours. They also placed two artillery pieces at the head of the village of Kammlach and opened a very lively fire on our cavalry. When that of the gentlemen had passed through Ansbach [Oberauerbach], the general had his men retire to the left of the village. He remained in this position, despite the repeated orders that he received to retire, until the army had entirely passed through the gorge that led to Mindelheim, for he felt strongly that, if he made his movement too soon, the enemy would take advantage of it to move, with artillery, on the position which he left, and it would have been easy for them to destroy, by the fire of their artillery, the troops who would have been caught in the gorge. The French did not dare to descend into the plain, and we cleared this passage at the gallop, with the result that they could not establish their pieces in enough time to reach us.[48]

The Etienne-Damas hussars rode towards Mindelheim through woods where the infantry rested:

> On continuing our route, we finally joined the baggage and the wagons in which the unfortunate wounded were; their lamentations and cries that pain rendered from them made us shudder and pierced us with tribulation and sorrow. Our cavalry had, among the noble chasseurs (where there were the greatest number of wounded) brothers, relatives, friends who gave us, so to speak, their last farewells! This situation was so painful that the Comte de Damas, our colonel, wanting to remove from our eyes the spectacle of desolation, to which we could not provide any remedy, ordered a full trot.[49]

With a little more than 4,000 men, the Armée de Condé as a whole had lost 720 killed or wounded but few prisoners; the French had comparable casualties, estimated at between

46 Perry de Nieüil, *Mémoires du marquis de Toustain*, pp.76–77.
47 Landosle, *Souvenirs du chevalier d'Hespel d'Hocron*, p.65.
48 Perry de Nieüil, *Mémoires du marquis de Toustain*, p.78.
49 Cézac de Belcayre, *Dix ans d'émigration (1791–1801)*, p.204.

700 to 800 men.[50] Vioménil's losses were comparatively light, twenty or so infantrymen and a handful of hussars killed, although the loss of horses were more significant. The the Etienne-Damas Hussars lost 14 men: two hussars killed, 11 wounded and one missing. Three of the wounded were volunteers, Claude Louis Suzanne Comte de Sarrazin, Jean-Baptiste-Louis de Verdal and Jean-Jacques Goislard de Villebresme de Constantin.[51] What happened to Villebresme was related by his brother:

> Our cavalry, placed to the right and left of the highroad, covered the retreat; the last echelon formed by the Damas cavalry performed a charge to stop the hussars who followed us too closely and repulsed them … The Damas cavalry of which he made part after its charge turned into foragers; one of Jean's comrades led a hussar who he had taken prisoner and who he had left with his arms doubtless in regard for a compatriot, but the latter, not thinking himself seen, took advantage of what his vanquisher had allowed him to traitorously run his sabre through his body and try to escape. But Jean had witnessed the drama, he rushed on the wretch who, badly mounted, was soon caught and sabred, not without having defended himself well …

Jean de Villebresme's hand was wounded in the encounter. He had served with the unit since 1794, and had had a horse killed under him before Nijmegen and now, only 19 years old, he was reportedly on the point of being awarded the cross of Saint-Louis. However, that evening one of his comrades made light of his wound, a simple slash on the hand according to him, leading to them, at 6:00 the following morning, duelling with pistols in a Mindelheim garden. Jean was wounded and left the Armée de Condé, he only received his brevet for the cross on 24 September 1814.[52] The Marquis de Sourdis, *colonel en second* of the Etienne-Damas hussars would not have to wait so long, he was nominated Chevalier de Saint-Louis for his distinguished conduct in the action.

The next day, 14 August, the army retreated 13 kilometres, eastwards, to the village of Türkheim. On 16 August *Feldzeugmeister* de Latour came and informed the Prince de Condé that his army was to be part of his command, of 30,000 men, deployed from Augsburg to Kempten.[53] The following day the Armée de Condé withdrew from behind Türkheim towards Landsberg am Lech, from where the Duc d'Enghien, was charged with maintaining contact with *Generalmajor* Klingin to the south-west. An unfortunate clash, involving the Etienne-Damas Hussars, appears to have taken place around this time as reported by Cézac de Belcayre:

50 C.L.F. Panckoucke (ed.), *Victoires, conquêtes, désastres, revers et guerres civiles des Français, de 1792 à 1815* (Paris: Panckoucke, 1817–1821), Vol.VI, p.292, described the *Condéens'* heavy losses (many killed and 1,000 to 1,100 wounded or prisoners) and underhand tactics in contrast to the prodigies of valour by the republicans who nevertheless only lost fifty men killed and 160 wounded. This was refuted, in detail, by an anonymous émigré general in a pamphlet, *Journée d'Oberkamlach*, published in 1818.

51 AG, Armée de Condé, Carton n°351-1, Pertes d'Oberkamlach.

52 Vicomte Maurice de Villebresme, *Souvenirs du Chevalier de Villebresme, Mousquetaire de la Garde du Roi 1772–1816* (Paris and Nancy: Berger-Levrault, 1897), p.176.

53 Ecquevilly, *Campagnes*, pp. 87–88.

> A few days later, in a type of squall, our French style uniforms and our language caused us a fatal mistake: several regiments of our cavalry, masked by a whirlwind of dust, mistaken and, thinking themselves to be engaged with some republicans, cut themselves up in dreadful manner. One officer, named M de Mominil, [sic] received a horrible wound which almost parted his face and cost him an eye.[54]

He was undoubtedly referring to *Capitaine* Comte Paul de Maumigny, born in 1735, a veteran of the Seven Years War in Germany, who had been *colonel* of the 4e Régiment de Chasseurs à Cheval (former Franche-Comté) when he emigrated in 1791. In 1797 he had to give up his company although he remained listed as supernumerary officer with the regiment.

On 21 August, the Prince de Condé received the order to fall back behind the Lech as Latour had already crossed the river abandoning Augsburg, to go to Friedberg on the opposite bank. Having crossed the river, the brigade was deployed on outpost duty south of Landsberg and on 22 August the Comte de Damas-Crux, temporarily in command as Vioménil was sick, reported its activities to the Prince de Condé:

> I have the honour to report to Your Serene Highness, that it is camped in a small plain before the village of Pflugdorf and behind that of Haden [sic?]. The country is very much covered by woods; the roads are very difficult. The village of Mundraching is in front of the position, very close to the Lech. This river, according to the report of the country folk, is not fordable at any point, up and down. A path from Kaufbeuren ends opposite Mundraching. I have placed a post there of 12 men with an officer. He has the order to collect under his guard two small boats that were on the left bank, and others that must be at Hirschau up river, and at Pitzling down it. I am going to verify the thing myself tomorrow morning. It was too late today ...[55]

The following day, the Comte de Damas-Crux dispatched patrols in the direction of Apfeldorf in order to keep in communication with *Feldmarschalleutnant* von Fröhlich, and proposed on 24 August the posting of some volunteers to ensure communication between the prince and Pflugdorf.

That same day, 24 August, Latour was attacked at Friedberg and forced to withdraw towards Munich causing the Armée de Condé to do likewise the next day, through Inning and then Weichselbaum, to reach the western suburbs, around the Nymphenburg Park where the prince's headquarters were installed in the magnificent country house of the Elector of Bavaria. The same evening, the order was given to withdraw that night to the east of Munich; Bavaria having declared its neutrality, neither the Austrians nor *Condéens* could enter the city. Munich had to be bypassed to establish, on 30 August, positions behind the Isar, facing the city, with the Etienne-Damas brigade bivouacked near the village of Berg with the rest of the army nearby in what is now suburbs of Munich. The *Condéen* troops who had been attached to Klinglin having re-joined on 28 August, the army was now united.

54 Cézac de Belcayre, *Dix ans d'émigration (1791–1801)*, p.205.
55 AMC, Series Y, carton XXIII, f. 161/91, Hussards de Damas, 1796, 22 August, at 'Pfuldorff,' 11:00 p.m.

On 4 September the allies learnt that the Armée de Sambre-et-Meuse had been beaten and was in full retreat towards the Rhine. Jourdan had pushed deep into Bavaria before Archduke Charles audaciously turned north and, uniting with *Feldzeugmeister* Wartensleben, he defeated Jourdan in a pitched battle at Würzburg on 3 September 1796. All Jourdan's messages had been intercepted by the Austrians so Moreau was now isolated in the south and ignorant of the situation. It was thought he was already preparing to retreat and perhaps had already sent his artillery and baggage away, so the Fürst zu Fürstenberg, who had replaced Latour, called to the north by Archduke Charles, asked the Prince de Condé to send 'at the break of day, a strong detachment of cavalry that should cross the Isar four leagues above Munich and observe the enemy's movement.'[56] At 4:00 a.m. on 5 September, the Comte de Vioménil marched at the head of 300 horse from the Etienne-Damas brigade with orders to cross the Isar at Schäftlarn (which he reached at 11:00 a.m.), observe the enemy's right flank and, if possible, harass its retreat that was thought to have begun. The bridge was broken but it was repaired the next day and the horsemen crossed one by one, on foot, each holding his mount by the bridle; the brigade then established itself near the Schäftlarn Abbey. The same day, on Fürstenberg's request, the Prince de Condé sent 400 infantry, 100 cavalry and a cannon towards Starnberg. This detachment joined Vioménil in the morning of 7 September and he made his junction with *Generalmajor* Klinglin but the latter would only guard the Schäftlarn bridge, refusing to go further as he needed to keep his forces ready to move to the south-west to shield the Tyrol. In the afternoon, Vioménil's brigade moved north towards Munich, with the Isar on the right, 'we pushed the enemy outposts to a league from Munich, where we found their united forces much superior to ours. Their infantry occupied a wood that was only separated from that in which we were by a small plain, in which quite a large number of their cavalry was ranged in battle order.'[57]

Meanwhile the Prince de Condé received the order to make a demonstration against the Munich bridge, as a diversion, and this was in progress when a courier arrived from Vioménil reporting that:

> [H]aving followed the left bank of the Isar, the Comte de Nantouillet, colonel commanding the Régiment d'Etienne-Damas, who he had detached from him in advance with a hundred horse, had encountered two republican squadrons and had charged them with success; he had killed several, made some prisoners, and had lost three or four men. M d'Arrot, first capitaine of the Noinville Chasseurs, had been quite gravely wounded by three sabre blows to the head.[58]

Corbehem remembered this as 'a brilliant affair with the former Conti chasseurs, those with whom we had already fought near Offenburg, an affair which only cost us a few men and several wounded.'[59]

During the night, Vioménil received the order from Condé to attack the following day, 8 September, although Vioménil considered the mission impossible with only 400 infantry,

56 Ecquevilly, *Campagnes*, pp.104–105.
57 Perry de Nieüil, *Mémoires du marquis de Toustain*, p.82.
58 Ecquevilly, *Campagnes*, p.107.
59 Corbehem, *Dix ans de ma vie*, pp.310–311. He mistakenly placed this action as on 13 September.

the terrain being unfavourable to cavalry, against the republicans' 5 or 6,000. Nevertheless, he advanced at 5:00 a.m.:

> [A]nd posted himself in column in front of Baierbrunn, where we encountered the enemy who occupied the woods on the other side of this village. M de Vioménil brought forward a cannon, and fired on their outposts. He took a position in front of Baierbrunn and had the men eat. We had not been in this position for a quarter of an hour when we received a new order to march. M de Vioménil then summoned around him all the superior officers and gave them instructions in case he was killed. It was three o'clock. The general distributed his infantry, half on the right, half on the left of the main road, having skirmishers in front and on the flanks. The cavalry marched along the road, having the artillery at their head.[60]

The enemy did not dispute the wood and withdrew to a strong position on the south of the city where even more infantry were massed so Vioménil fell back, the way he had come, onto Schäftlarn to reunite with Klinglin.

The next day, the *Condéens* remained in their positions but, 'the Comte de Vioménil sent in the evening several prisoners who had been taken by his patrols, and who told us nothing new on the position and enemy forces.'[61] The momentum of the campaign had definitely turned. If 10 September was particularly quiet, a certain agitation reigned the next day and it was soon confirmed that Moreau had finally received the news of Jourdan's precipitative flight towards the Rhine with Archduke Charles in pursuit. In anticipation of forthcoming movements, Fürstenberg had Vioménil's troops, who faced the right flank of the enemy, reinforced, Condé sending the Dauphin cavalry and 400 more infantry. A local armistice was agreed and some of the *Condéen* officers went into the city:

> The day when I went to Munich, with some of brothers in arms, we learnt that a military ball was to take place the same evening. All the French officers who we met soliciting us very much to come, we did not think we ought to refuse their pressing politeness; about twenty of us went; some senior officers presented us; so we were, on our entrance, surrounded by a crowd which overwhelmed us with kindness and attention to the point of obliging us to take punch and other refreshments. Nothing was more pleasing for the Bavarians than to see Frenchmen who fought each other, finding themselves gathered at a ball, drinking, clinking glasses together and appearing to converse in the greatest intimacy; our hats with the white cockade and plume were mixed on the tables with those of the republican officers which bore the tricolour ones. We danced all night and, in each quadrille, one saw represented Frenchmen serving under both banners![62]

Fürstenberg's preparations were justified when it was found Moreau's army had slipped from the city undetected. Most of the Austrian units he had were weak or inexperienced,

60 Perry de Nieüil, *Mémoires du marquis de Toustain*, p.83.
61 Ecquevilly, *Campagnes*, p.108.
62 Villebresme, *Souvenirs*, p.211.

some made up of recruits drawn from the depots of various regiments, so he relied on the *Condéen* vanguard for the immediate pursuit of the French troops. Enghien marched to the western suburbs of the city where, at Dachau, he was joined by Vioménil with his brigade and attached infantry and cavalry:

> Our adversaries had broken the Dachau bridge and defended the approach to the river until night. When they had retired, the bridge was repaired and our vanguard cantoned in the town. On 13 [September], we parted from the duke who marched to Klingen on the Donauwörth road, while we followed that of Augsburg, as far as Adelzhausen where we lodged in a castle that the French generals had occupied two hours before. The French having seized the village of Klingen very close to Aichach where the general was to take position, he resolved to profit from the gloom of the night to chase the enemy whose strength there we did not know. He detached three companies and fifty horse under the command of Colonel Marquis de Roquefeuil.[63]

The pursuit continued on to Friedberg, Aichach and Pöttmes, until contact was made with Moreau's army at Neuburg an der Donau, where he doubtless intended to cross the Danube. This was prevented, on 15 September, when the Austrians initially achieved a minor victory but they were soon beaten and forced to retreat. The Duc d'Enghien was vigorously attacked on 16 September and retreated a league the following day, bringing the Eteinne-Damas brigade with him, 'On 17, at 02:00 in the morning, we retired along the Schrobenhausen road, and we took an advantageous position a league from Aichach.'[64] Nevertheless, Vioménil maintained the pressure and some of his infantry captured a village but the enemy, being reinforced, counter-attacked and in the fighting the Marquis de Roquefeuil, *colonel* of his own regiment, could not be found. It was initially thought he had been killed but, the following morning, 18 September, he was found by the republicans, 'gravely wounded, having received a musket shot in the jaw and a broken arm.'[65] Immediately informed and particularly concerned about his fate, Vioménil sent a parley to enquire about his condition, 'M de Moisez, from the Damas hussars, was charged with this perilous mission, and left with a trumpeter and four hussars for the enemy's outposts.'[66] The mission was especially delicate as the fighting continued:

> On 18, at 08:00 in the morning, M de Vioménil received the order to unite with the Duc d'Enghien at Schrobenhausen. At the moment that we marched, the French attacked us; we opposed them with our skirmishers and continued our march. They followed us, but did not interfere with us. Arrived at Schrobenhausen, we found the duke there struggling with the enemy; he asked the general to send a detachment of infantry and cavalry to the Hörzhausen bridge, to defend this crossing; M de Vassé [Dauphin cavalry] commanded this detachment. The general placed the division to the left of the duke's troops, to prevent the enemy attacking him on this point. This

63 Perry de Nieüil, *Mémoires du marquis de Toustain*, p.84.
64 Perry de Nieüil, *Mémoires du marquis de Toustain*, p.85.
65 Ecquevilly, *Campagnes*, p.120.
66 Perry de Nieüil, *Mémoires du marquis de Toustain*, p.86.

> affair took place by lively cannonading one on another. At 06:00 in the evening, M de Vassé received the order to retire from the bridge and to come to re-join the division; as he had to traverse a quite vast plain, the passage was difficult for his infantry which, effectively, while entering into the plain, was charged and captured by the French hussars, but M de Vassé charged in his turn the enemy and disengaged the infantry.[67]

Moreau had remained at Neuburg but on 20 September resumed his march westward, having learnt that two divisions from the army of Archduke Charles were advancing on the Danube. Augsburg was evacuated by the French as they sought to reach the gorges of the Black Forest, the immense Breisgau plain and then the Rhine as fast as possible. Vioménil re-joined Enghien:

> On 21, united to the duke, we marched through Friedberg to Augsburg. The enemy rear guard left the city when we presented ourselves to enter it. It is impossible to testify more joy than these brave people showed at our passage in Augsburg; they hugged our horses, called us their liberators and made the air resound with their shouts of joy and of "Long live the Emperor! Long live the Prince de Condé!" All the streets were so crowded, that we had a great deal trouble and spent a great deal of time in crossing the city. We feared that all our division would emerge drunk, as wine, beer and liquors of all kinds were distributed. In the evening, all the city was illuminated.'[68]

M de Roquefeuil was found in the city's hospital, left behind by the French, *Lieutenant* de Moisez, *sous-aide-major* of the Etienne-Damas hussars, having already re-joined the brigade:

> Before our arrival at Augsburg, the officer who we had sent on the 17 under a flag of truce, to have news of M de Roquefeuil, and of whom we were very uneasy, as he was absent for four days, had re-joined us. He reported to M de Vioménil that, having reached the French outposts, he had been led to *Général* Jordis [sic Delmas?]. The latter, after having listened to him, had introduced him into the neighbouring chamber to his where he had found M de Roquefeuil laid in a very good bed, having two soldiers occupied in swatting the flies that bothered him. The general had then retired to let them talk together. M de Roquefeuil praised the good treatment from *Général* Jordis, who had just returned him a belt containing two hundred gold pieces and his cross of Saint-Louis, that had been taken from him when he had fallen into the enemy's hands, after having received two musket shots. *Général* Jordis had invited our officer to dinner, but when the latter had wished to return, he had said to him that, as he knew the talents of M de Vioménil, having served with him in America, and that he was going to make at the same instant a movement of

67 Perry de Nieüil, *Mémoires du marquis de Toustain*, pp.86–87.
68 Perry de Nieüil, *Mémoires du marquis de Toustain*, p.87.

> retreat, of which he would not want his adversary to be informed, he would not let him return to his men until his march had been assured.[69]

The Marquis de Roquefeuil did not survive, dying of his wounds on 30 September. Cézac de Belcayre, going into some detail, gives a different version of the event, according to him the Comte de Damas having received the Prince de Condé's permission sent an officer with a volunteer, Elie du Cheyral de la Fleunie who was a former cavalry *capitaine*, and a trumpeter named Louis, to reclaim M de Garodès, a *maréchal des logis* of his regiment, a distinguished man and much loved by his peers, who had been taken prisoner during a skirmish. The general, who Cézac identifies as *Général de Division* Lecourbe, invited the three émigrés to dine with his staff. At the meal he declared that he was laying a trap to seize Condé's corps and that his guests would not be released in time to give a warning. At that moment, the general was informed that a gravely wounded émigré colonel was brought on a stretcher who the hussars recognised through a window as being the Comte de Roquefeuil.[70] Cézac was, of course, not party to what happened and may have merged two separate incidents in later memoirs. As for Corbehem, he recalled the event with the place of the French general officer as being none other than the commander, 'Some days later, Moisez, an officer of my regiment, was sent in parley to *Général* Moreau, with two of my comrades. This general was not content to welcome them with the greatest distinction, he even wished that all three dine at his table'.[71]

On 23 September Vioménil's brigade resumed its march and arrived at Roggenburg Abbey, only two hours after Moreau had left.[72] This same day it was learnt that, in the north, Archduke Charles had pushed the French over the Lahn, and that Fröhlich had gained the upper hand over the republicans in the south, retaking Memmingen. Enghien's vanguard, attached to that of the Austrians, set off along the Ulm road shadowing the enemy without making contact. On 24 September, Enghien joined the Etienne-Damas brigade at midday and the next day his division reached the Iller:

> On 25, we marched on Illertissen, situated on the right bank of the Iller. We saw Moreau's army parade on the left bank. It marched in close column, in very good order, less than a quarter of a league from us. We could not attack it, firstly because all the bridges were destroyed, then because we were not strong enough …[73]

The bridges being quickly repaired, several cavalry detachments crossed the river and attacked the enemy rear-guard, taking some prisoners. The next day, 27 September, was spent in the same position Vioménil having to be more cautious as the detached infantry, dragoons and Dauphin cavalry were no longer with his brigade.[74]

69 Perry de Nieüil, *Mémoires du marquis de Toustain*, p.88; Antoine-Guillaume Delmas (1768–1813), commanding a division of the Armée du Rhin, had served in America in the Régiment de Touraine. The Austrian *Feldmarschalleutnant* Alexander von Jordis retired from service in 1796.

70 Cézac de Belcayre, *Dix ans d'émigration (1791–1801)*, p.210.

71 Corbehem, *Dix ans de ma vie*, p.313.

72 Perry de Nieüil, *Mémoires du marquis de Toustain*, p.88.

73 Perry de Nieüil, *Mémoires du marquis de Toustain*, p.89.

74 Perry de Nieüil, *Mémoires du marquis de Toustain*, p.89.

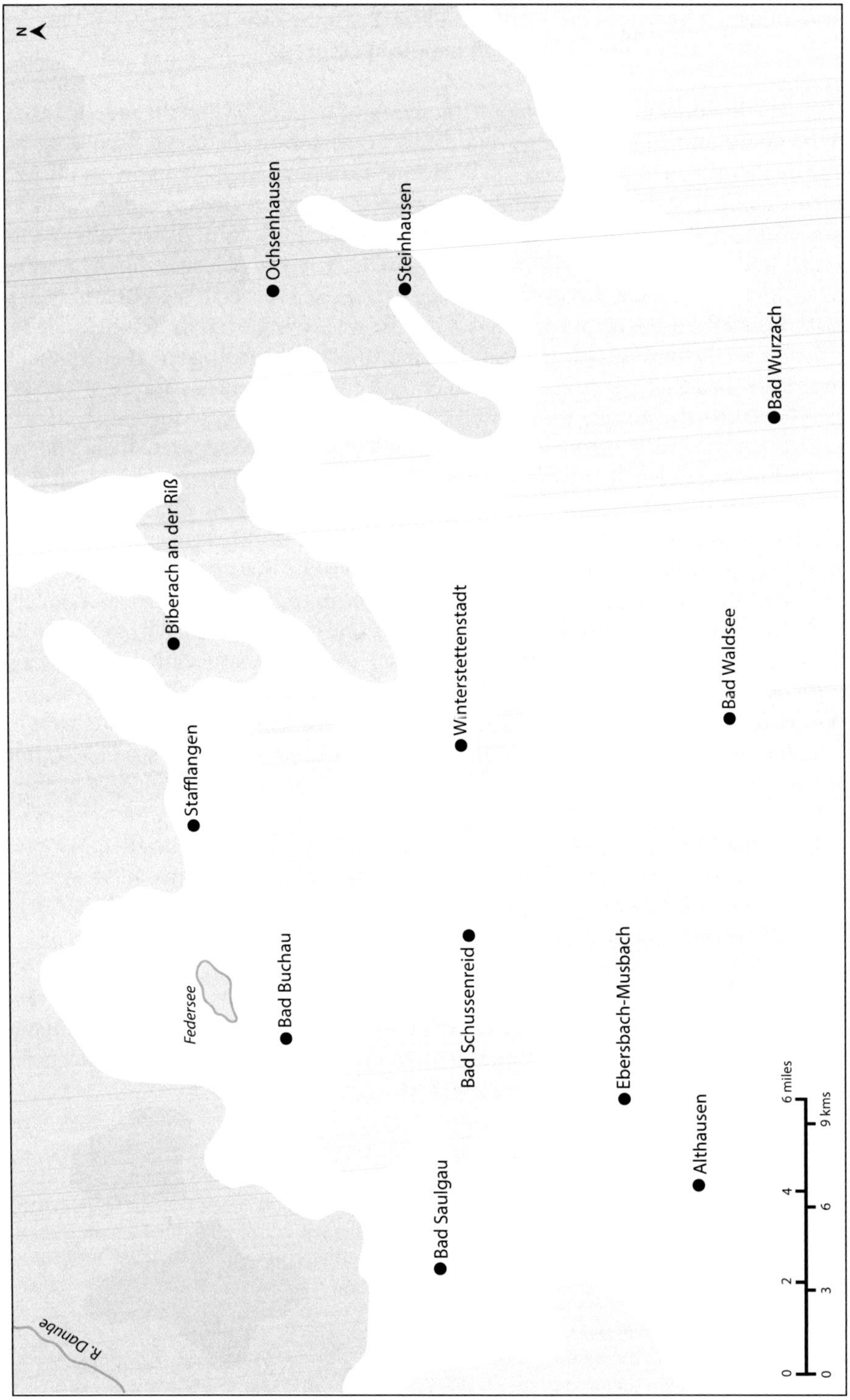
N
R. Danube
Ochsenhausen
Steinhausen
Bad Wurzach
Biberach an der Riß
Winterstettenstadt
Bad Waldsee
Stafflangen
Federsee
Bad Buchau
Bad Schussenreid
Ebersbach-Musbach
Althausen
Bad Saulgau
0 2 4 6 miles
0 3 6 9 kms

Biberach.

On 28 September, in the afternoon, the Condé Corps crossed the Iller on a pontoon bridge. Moreau now moved south-west heading for Stockach via Biberach, and Pfullendorf. To protect his rear, he had Bad Schussenried and other villages to the west of Biberach strongly occupied. It was here that the Austrians and *Condéens* made contact with part of Moreau's considerably stronger force on 29 September, Corbehem remembered that, 'Almost no day passed that the vanguard of which my regiment made part did not attack the enemy or was not attacked by them; but these affairs had in general nothing very remarkable, except for that of Schussenried which preceded by two days the great battle of Biberach.'[75]

At 4:00 a.m. on 30 September the Duc d'Enghien was ordered to advance westwards in advance as far as Ebersbach-Musbach, north-east of Altshausen, in the direction of Bad Saulgau; the enemy was known to be nearby and an engagement was anticipated. Desiring to make contact with the enemy, the duke pushed ahead with the cavalry, from his vanguard and Vioménil's brigade. Two kilometres in front of Schussenried, he found the enemy, thought to be the republicans' rear-guard, installed on a wooded height and the duke reconnoitred the French position, accompanied by Vioménil and their staffs, including the Marquis de Toustain:

> Their advance posts occupied the village of Steinhausen, to the left (in relation to them) of which was an escarped mountain, on which they had posted a battalion. To the right of the village were to be found other less elevated heights, but covered with woods, which they had occupied in force; in front stretched the plain where our cavalry was deployed, and which was ended by a wood placed behind us. The general pushed his reconnaissance quite far by our left, and decided that the enemy could only be attacked by this point. The bulk of their army occupied Schussenried, their right resting on the abbey and their left on [Bad] Buchau, having before it the Federsee [a lake] and many marshes on all their front.[76]

While the émigré officers re-joined their cavalry in the plain, a division of the Austrian Hussar Regiment Nr 3 Erzherzog Ferdinand belonging to Latour's vanguard launched an assault on the height on the left of Steinhausen, held by the republican battalion; despite the slope and defenders the Austrian hussars seized the position and drove the French from it. In the meantime, the infantry of the *Condéen* vanguard had caught up and Enghien sent the two battalions of the Légion de Roger de Damas to attack the republican right but the wood was strongly held by the enemy and they had to fall back under well-directed fire. Vioménil convinced him to resume the attack with two columns, Roger de Damas on the left and Hohenlohe on the right:

> It was taken in an instant. M de Vioménil had two cannons brought to the right of the position from which the enemy had just withdrawn, so that when they came out of the wood from which our troops chased them, they again lost many more by the fire of our artillery. Those who occupied Steinhausen, seeing their right completely

75 Corbehem, *Dix ans de ma vie*, p.311.
76 Perry de Nieüil, *Mémoires du marquis de Toustain*, p.90.

> uncovered, retreated in haste and were charged by pickets from our cavalry. The general then had the cavalry advance which deployed between the village and the height which was on the right.[77]

The republicans then received reinforcements and pushed Enghien back to his starting point but he now committed the rest of his infantry, who were joined by two Austrian battalions. The duke, who fought amongst the first line of his infantry, described the engagement as 'brisk, long and murderous'.[78] Exchanges of fire lasted until the end of day leaving the Austrians holding the wood and the Duc d'Enghien in a position facing the abbey, which was still held by the French. The actions cost him 300 men killed or put out of action, and left a strong impression on the memory of Corbehem: 'three times we attacked the enemy positions without being able to take them and Monseigneur the Duc d'Enghien performed prodigies there.'[79]

Once again, acts of humanity occurred which would have been unthinkable only a year before:

> The day of the engagement at Schussenried, some men from my regiment, among others the abbé du Chilleau, who was its chaplain, lost their way and were taken. The abbé, without seeking to hide his role, clearly declared who he was, at the risk of what could happen, and he had no reason to regret his frankness. He was in the same instant sent back with every possible regard. As to the men who were known to be émigrés, and who had been taken while armed, they were not returned, but they were given every sort of opportunity to escape, and they all returned to the regiment, with the exception of one alone who preferred to freely return to France ...[80]

The next day was tense with the troops in some places only 50 paces apart. Moreau had decided that the opportunity was ripe to turn on his weaker pursuers. Latour's position was a line extending north to south in front of Biberach; his right was at Stafflangen behind Federsee, a considerable distance from his centre at Steinhausen which was alongside his left, posted immediately facing Schussenried. The left was much the strongest of his line and the *Condéens* formed part of the troops here, although the Dauphin cavalry with the Fargues and Clermont-Tonnerre dragoons reinforced Latour's reserve closer towards Biberach. The *Condéens* were attending religious service, on Sunday 2 October, when two French cannons signalled the attack at 11:00 a.m. The Austrians on the right were quickly overrun and five battalions surrendered; their centre faced a frontal assault while being outflanked on the right and was soon forced to retreat onto the reserve. The planned attack on the left, held by the émigrés with Austrian troops, did not develop as the republican column was delayed but they nevertheless were forced to withdraw:

---

77 Perry de Nieüil, *Mémoires du marquis de Toustain*, p.91.
78 Boulay de La Meurthe, *Correspondance du duc d'Enghien*, pp.259–260.
79 Corbehem, *Dix ans de ma vie*, pp.311–312.
80 Corbehem, *Dix ans de ma vie*, pp.312–313.

> The French attacked with boldness and impetuosity, swept the Austrians from the wood that had cost us so dear to take on 30th, and followed them swords in their backs. The latter did not even try to rally; the flight was general as far as beyond Biberach. We stayed in our position until the last extremity, and we only made a retrograde movement when the Austrians, by their retreat, uncovered our right. The proof of it is that we were forced to cross the great meadow behind Winterstettenstadt under the fire of three French flying artillery pieces, which had arrived before us. Nothing could rally the frightened Austrians, who had already passed by Biberach, abandoning baggage, artillery and everything that could not run like them.[81]

Latour tasked the Prince de Condé to cover the retreat and he skilfully deployed his infantry and artillery to hold a position behind Steinhausen and another protecting the bridge on the highroad, his cavalry he placed in a fold in the terrain. While Vioménil's brigade covered the retreat of the centre, republican skirmishers and dragoons who rushed into the plain in pursuit of the Austrians were dispersed by the royalist artillery and cavalry. The émigré troops greeted their fleeing allies with boos as they ran or galloped through their ranks. It was only in the middle of the night that the *Condéens* disengaged in good order and re-joined Latour at dawn the next day.

The Austrians had lost 300 killed and wounded but 4,000 men had been captured along with 18 cannons and two standards while, by comparison, the Armée de Condé only had three officers killed and seven wounded, as well as 20 or so soldiers. Although their contribution has been largely ignored in later works, Moreau paid homage to the *Condéens*, 'Without this handful of émigrés, the Austrian army was mine'.[82] For Corbehem it was one of its greatest feats of arms. 'I do not need to recall how much this battle of Biberach was glorious for our army. That of the Imperials was destroyed without the valour and presence of mind of the Prince de Condé, and without the admirable conduct of our artillery which performed prodigies there.'[83] Indeed it was undoubtedly this incident that William Windham referred to in a later speech in the Houses of Parliament, 'the army of the Austrians had been saved by the exertions of this corps, who had many of them gallantly fallen while defending their allies.'[84]

The French army retreated the same night, 2 to 3 October, they had three days head start as the Austrian army had fallen back behind Ochsenhausen and defeat ensured Latour would now exercise greater prudence. Moreau retreated towards Stockach but, as the French had just been driven from there by Fröhlich's troops, he continued on to Donaueschingen and Latour followed with Vioménil's brigade at the forefront of his troops:

81 Boulay de La Meurthe, *Correspondance du duc d'Enghien*, pp.263–264.

82 Jean-Baptiste Pierre Jullien de Courcelles, *Dictionnaire historique et biographique des généraux français*, Vol.III, (Paris: Bertrand, 1821), p.92.

83 Corbehem, *Dix ans de ma vie*, pp.312.

84 Thomas Aymot, *Speeches in Parliament, of the Right Honourable William Windham; to which is prefixed, some account of his life* (London: Longman, 1812), Vol.I, p.318, speech of 24 April 1798.

> Moreau continued his retrograde movement towards the Rhine, we still had an affair with his rear guard in the plain that is in front of Donaueschingen. I cannot refrain to say here that during all of this action, we were in echelon in the plain, having in front of us our tirailleurs who skirmished with those of the enemy, and while balls quite frequently landed at the feet of our horses, we quietly played macao on the pommel of our saddles.[85]

It was here that, on 14 October, the Armée de Condé left Latour's command and was again attached to that of Fröhlich to pursue Moreau through the Black Forest towards Freiburg im Breisgau via Titisee-Neustadt. Vioménil was on Moreau's heels as indicated by a message he sent from Löffingen, at 9:00 p.m. on 14 October, to *Capitaine* de Bazouges, of the first noble company of the Etienne-Damas hussars, in advance at Rötenbach:

> Remain quietly my dear Basouge [sic] in the village where you are until tomorrow at 5 o'clock in the morning. M de Nantouillet is going to take you to go to take post at Neustadt. He will place your picket in the barns until the arrival of the vanguard. The picket which replaces you will scout with its patrols the road from Neustadt to Freiburg, while waiting for our arrival.[86]

Moreau in fact evacuated Neustadt at dawn on 15 September and, after a rest day, the Austrian corps continued its progress on the principal road leading from this village to Freiburg. The enemy was pressed by the *Condéens* and attacked on 18 October, in the heart of the Black Forest at Sankt Märgen and the following day the Etienne-Damas hussars were in action. 'A brilliant affair … near the abbey of Saint Peter, and where my regiment distinguished itself in a particular manner, hastened the retreat of the enemy division which was opposed to us.'[87]

Once Moreau had reached the Breisgau plain he tried to reach Kehl but immediately ran into Archduke Charles who defeated him at Emmendingen on 19 October. This forced him to turn south to reach the Rhine crossing at Huningue. Thus, on 21 October when Enghien's vanguard reached Freiburg the republicans had just left. The following day Moreau halted at Schliengen, opposite Mulhouse in Alsace, where the plain narrows between the Rhine and the Black Forest. He placed his troops on a row of hills running from Steinenstadt, on the river, south-east, through Schliengen to the mountains. At 7:00 a.m. on 24 October Archduke Charles launched a four-pronged attack along Moreau's front. The Armée de Condé advanced against the positions immediately beside the Rhine, the occasion to distinguish itself one last time in this campaign. Having quickly seized their objective, the royalists in the same manoeuvre moved to the south of Steinenstadt while securing the bridge there. The republicans remained at Schliengen, only separated by a low valley, with strong forces particularly artillery on the heights of that village and an adjacent hillside. From there, they subjected the *Condéens* to constant artillery and infantry fire for seven hours,

85 Corbehem, *Dix ans de ma vie*, pp.312–313. Macao, Macau or Makaó is a card game of Hungarian origin.

86 Fonds Grouvel/Dossier Légion de Damas.

87 Corbehem, *Dix ans de ma vie*, p.314.

that only ceased with the arrival of night. This last major engagement of the campaign cost the Armée de Condé about 250 men.

The Austrians planned to renew the attack the next day, 25 October, but at dawn it was found that Moreau's army had slipped away, crossing the Rhine at Huningue the following day. Moreau, however, maintained a bridgehead on the right bank opposite the town and, at the same time Archduke Charles moved against the other French bridgehead on the right bank of the Rhine, the fort at Kehl. The Armée de Condé was not involved, taking up winter quarters from 29 October to 8 November, as Corbehem recalled, 'While the Austrians, despite the rigour of the season, laid siege to Kehl and the Huningue bridgehead, we took provisional cantonments in the Breisgau, in the region of Freiburg. Lodged in a village three leagues from this city, we were somewhat spectators of the events that marked these two sieges.'[88] Both Moreau and the Archduke Charles favoured an armistice that would enable troops to be released for other fronts, particularly Northern Italy where an Austrian garrison was trapped in Mantua. However, court politics in Vienna demanded that all efforts be made to secure the two bridgeheads of Kehl and Huningue.

The Etienne-Damas hussars was inspected by the Comte d'Ecquevilly on 12 December 1796.

Review of the Régiment d'Etienne de Damas, 12 December 1796

Colonel Propriétaire	Comte Etienne de Damas	
Colonel commandant	Comte de Nantouillet	
Colonel en second	Marquis de Sourdis	
Lieutenant-colonel	Vicomte de Montjustin	
Major	Marquis de Bongars	
Aide-major	Marquis d'Andelarre	
Sous-aide-major	de Moisez	
Quartier-maître	de Bertemy	
Porte-étendard	Comte de Sainte Marie (absent)	
Aumônier	*Abbé* du Chilleau	
Chirurgien major	Couturier	
Aide chirurgien	Meyer	
Master farrier	1	
Master saddler	1	
Master bootmaker	1	
Master tailor	1	
Officers' horses	39 including 2 to M. de Nantouillet	
Troop horses	3	
	Compagnie noble de Bazouges	*Compagnie noble de Conan*
Capitaine	de Bazouges	de Conan
Lieutenant	de Saint-Laurent	de Plantière
Lieutenant	de Bouillé	d'Augustin

88 Corbehem, *Dix ans de ma vie*, p.315.

Sous-lieutenant	de La Craye	Desmottes
Sous-lieutenant	de Brugière	vacant
Fourrier	1	1
Maréchaux des logis	4	4 (incl. 1 at depot)
Brigadiers	4	4 (incl. 1 in hospital)
Sous-brigadiers	4	4
Trompettes	2	1
Maréchal ferrant (farrier)	1	1
Volontaires	42 (incl. 3 at depot, 2 in hospital, 3 detached, 1 in prison)	42 (incl. 3 at depot, 1 in hospital, 3 detached)
Total	58	57
Officers' horses	12	9
Troop horses	53 (incl. 1 absent, 3 at depot, 3 detached)	55
Company grooms	3	3
Officers' domestics	5	4
	Compagnie ordinaire de Lentilhac	*Compagnie ordinaire de Maumigny*
Capitaine	de Lentilhac	de Maumigny
Lieutenant	de La Haye	d'Hoffelize
Lieutenant	de Lageard	de Rozières
Sous-lieutenant	de Charry	de Monteclair
Sous-lieutenant	de Chanteirac	de Verneuil
Fourrier	1	1
Maréchaux des logis	4 (incl. 1 at depot)	4 (incl. 1 at depot)
Brigadiers	4	4 (incl. 1 in hospital)
Sous-brigadiers	4	4
Trompettes	1	1
Maréchal ferrant	1	1
Hussards	54 (incl. 1 at depot, 5 in hospital, 1 orderly)	56 (incl. 1 at depot, 2 in hospital, 1 orderly)
Total	69	71
Officers' horses	11	9
Troop horses	50	51
Company grooms	–	–
Officers' domestics	5	5

Source: AG, Armée de Condé, Carton n°357-1.

The regiment had 31 officers and 259 other ranks while eight months earlier, on 27 April, it had 32 officers and 352 other ranks. In the intervening time it had recruited 37 men but lost 131. The reason for the one officer casualty, presumably *Sous-lieutenant* Montagnac, is not specified. Of the other ranks, 47 were killed, 45 deserted, 11 had been captured by the enemy, seven transferred to other units, 10 were discharged or driven from the unit, one was hanged and nine died, of sickness or accident. The soldier who was executed, Louis

Hourdequin, aged 22, from Valenciennes, was probably a deserter as he was executed on 19 August at Tittmoning on Bavaria's border with Austria; he had had his fist cut, first, before being hanged. In the same period the regiment also lost 73 horses from various causes, including 22 troop horses that had been killed.

As for the equipment and armament, the following table indicates its state and the repairs or replacements required.

Clothing	Good to last for a year	Good but for repair	Mediocre and requiring repairs	Unfit for service	Missing	Total to be replaced
Shakos	167	29	14	2	47	49
Pelisses	85	57	17	30	69	99
Dolmans	133	14	6	24	82	106
Sashes	142	17	10	24	90	90
Breeches	68	68	6	37	80	117
Drawers	68	42	25	76	116	192
Boots and spurs	91	45	62	14	57	71
Bonnets de police	20	35	28	15	161	176
Stable waistcoats	97	45	36	10	71	81
Cloaks	103	56	29	10	71	71
Sabretaches	63	35	18	37	106	143
Arms						
Carbines	31	4			191	
Pairs of pistols	104	38			117	
Sabres	108	81			70	
Pistol ramrods	135	81			124	
Men's Equipment						
Belts	175	17			67	
Swordknots	177	17			82	
Pouches	146	19			81	
Carbine belts	115	9			96	
Horse Equipment						
Saddles	144	45		45	22	22
Shabracques	60	61		68	22	90
Covers	133	36		34	8	42
Portmanteaux	79	86		34	95	95
Bridles	111	64		34	36	36
Bits	124	49		34	38	38
Snaffles	139	24		1	47	48
Lanyards and halters	98	69		4	40	44

The hussars certainly would not have appeared in a uniform and pristine state at the review, however Ecquevilly concluded:

> I will confine myself by observing here that all the objects are in general much better maintained in the squadron of volunteers than in that of the soldiers of which repairs are very urgent. The horses are in general good and well cared for ... the chief of this unit ... serves with great zeal and exactitude as well as all the officers among whom reigns a very good spirit.

The regiment was soon on the move, 'the cavalry of our army left the Breisgau where forage began to run short, and went to take cantonments beyond the mountains of the Black Forest. My regiment took its quarters in the neighbourhood of the small town of Pfullendorf ... After the fall of the Huningue bridgehead [5 February 1797], our cantonments became permanent.'[89] In the meantime the news from Italy was calamitous for the Austrians, Wurmser had surrendered at Mantua on 2 February and so Archduke Charles was sent, with 25,000 men, from the Rhineland to try to rectify the situation. On 9 March, Vioménil's brigade received the order to prepare to move to Stockach, north of the Bodensee, apparently in anticipation of the Armée de Condé being also sent to Italy.

The move was delayed as the army was at this time being reorganised as a result of instructions from London, brought by Robert Craufurd on 1 March. Those paid regiments which were understrength were to be disbanded and their men drafted into the remaining units. One of the units which was disbanded was the Régiment des Dragons de Fargues from which a significant number of men were incorporated into the Etienne-Damas hussars and on 9 March the regiment had 425 men and 346 horses. The amalgamation, which took place in the Rottweil region, was completed on 13 March 1797; some of the dragoon officers also joined the regiment, including, as an additional *colonel*, *Commandeur* Jean-Barthélemey de Méallet de Fargues along with other members of his family.[90] Soon, after 20 March, the Etienne-Damas hussars were sent with the Noinville chasseurs and Dauphin cavalry to the Stockach region where forage was more abundant.[91]

Bonaparte defeated Archduke Charles at the Battle of Tagliamento on 16 March 1797 and then drove him into Carinthia, seizing Klagenfurt on 29 March. When Bonaparte had reached Leoben, in Styria, just 30 leagues from Vienna, on 7 April, Charles agreed to an armistice and it was here that on 18 April the preliminaries for peace between the Emperor and the French Republic were agreed, though the definitive treaty of Campo-Formio would not be signed until 18 October 1797. Bonaparte's success had been so swift that it outpaced the long-planned French operation on the Rhine, intended to coincide and support those in Italy, as well as exploit the removal of Austrian units from the Breisgau. In the night of 19/20 April Moreau's Armée du Rhin et Moselle crossed the Rhine just north of Strasbourg and, as Corbehem described, went on to 'flood the Breisgau with their troops. The Austrians, too weak to resist an enemy which had the advantage over them of numbers and the ascendancy of victory, started at the greatest speed, and in all directions, a retreat which alone could save them from

89 Corbehem, *Dix ans de ma vie*, p.351.

90 The officers of the Dragons de Fargues included three of the colonel's brothers (a *capitaine*, a *lieutenant* and the *aumonier*) and two of his nephews (both *lieutenants*). See Grouvel *Les Corps de troupe de l'émigration*, Vol.II, pp.204–205.

91 The Dauphin cavalry and Noinville chasseurs had received, respectively, the men of the Clermont-Tonnerre dragoons and the Astorg chasseurs which were disbanded.

total destruction.'[92] The main body of the Armée de Condé was still in the Breisgau, dispersed around Müllheim and was in jeopardy but was saved when the armistice became known. On 15 April the Etienne-Damas hussars had been ordered to re-join the army and had reached Donaueschingen when the news of the armistice arrived. They immediately returned to the region around the Bodensee, receiving remounts there on 27 April. Although the armistice had been an immediate relief it also caused a sense of unease amongst the émigrés.[93]

Suspecting that the consequent treaty under negotiation by Austria and France might include a secret article banishing his army from Imperial territory, the Prince de Condé had immediately sent one of his aides de camp to Russia. As early as 1792, Catherine the Great had given financial support for the Counter-Revolution, in particular the Armée de Condé, even proposing that the émigrés settle in Crimea. When she died suddenly, on 16 November 1796, the Prince de Condé had sent one of his officers to the coronation of her successor, Tsar Paul I. The prince had welcomed the tsarevich as a guest at his château at Chantilly in 1782 and they had maintained a cordial correspondence since. The prince felt he could no longer rest his future in the hands of Britain which, with no ally on the Continent of Europe would doubtless seek to convince the *Condéens* that there remained no other expedient than pursuing the war in British uniforms overseas, something which the prince, cousin to the King of France, would never accept. Fortunately, the new tsar provided a very favourable response, not only granting the same conditions his mother had offered but also proposing to take the Armée de Condé into his pay.

Nevertheless, the armistice might not hold and the troops had to be ready. The Etienne-Damas Hussars were at Pfullendorf when, on 10 May 1797, *Colonel* de Damas listed its officers.[94]

Colonel propriétaire	Comte Etienne de Damas-Crux
Colonel commandant	Comte de Nantouillet
Colonel attaché	Commandeur de Fargues
Lieutenant-colonel	Vicomte de Montjustin
Major	Marquis de Bongars
Capitaine aide-major	Marquis d'Andelarre
Sous aide-major	Moisez
Quartier-maître trésorier	Bertemy
Porte-Etendard	Comte de Sainte-Marie de Saint-Martin
Capitaines	de Bazouges, de Conan d'Ocor, Vicomte de Lentilhac, J-J. de Fargues
Lieutenants	de Saint-Laurent, de Plantières, Augustin, de Bouillé, Marquis de La Haye, Comte d'Hoffelize, H. de Fargues, J. de Fargues, Marquis d'Anjony
Sous-lieutenants	de La Craie, Chevalier de Brugières, Chevalier des Mottes, Marquis de Lageard, Vicomte de Charry, de Chanterac, Comte de Sedages
Capitaine réformé	Comte de Maumigny
Lieutenant réformé	Comte de Rosières d'Euvezin
Sous-lieutenants réformés	Comte de Monteclerc, de Verneuil

92 Corbehem, *Dix ans de ma vie*, p.318.
93 See Corbehem, *Dix ans de ma vie*, p.318.
94 AG, Armée de Condé, Carton n°357-1.

The *réformé* (retired) officers although no longer able, due to their state of health, to serve within the companies carried out other duties in the regiment such as with the baggage or in the depot.

From the 16 May the Armée de Condé was, in its entirety, around the Bodensee. This was a time when other pursuits could be enjoyed and Vioménil arranged for the Duc de Berry to enjoy the thrill of the chase, 'The area around Pfullendorf offering magnificent hunting country, abundant in big game, he organised it for him, preparing fine halts for him where the musicians of the Damas hussars serenaded during his meals.'[95] On 1 June a general review was carried out at Stockach by *Generalmajor* Friedrich Nauendorf, apparently he was surprised by the number present, 'He had been told that a very great number among us had returned to France and he did not think that we were more than 4,000. Instead of that, we were 7,000 in perfect condition.'[96]

There had been, on 10 February 1797, a distribution of crosses of Saint-Louis in the army, three of the recipients were members of the Régiment d'Etienne-Damas: *Colonel en second* de Sourdis, and two noble hussars, *Brigadier* Chevalier Louis-Théodore de Josne Contay and François Millard de La Croste, a volunteer. Others were rewarded with brevets of promotion, these either confirmed the grade an officer held in the Armée de Condé or one that, despite the rank they currently held, would take effect in the royal army in the case of a future restoration. On 26 January 42 officers were made *maréchal de camp*, one was Comte Etienne de Damas-Crux and he was joined by another relative, Comte Charles de Damas, who had distinguished himself throughout the campaign at the head of the legion of his brother, Roger. Two of the officers who received brevets as cavalry *colonel*, thus confirming their rank in the regiment, were the Comte de Nantouillet, who had been a *major en second* of dragoons at the time of his emigration and had served as *colonel* since 16 November 1793, and *Commandeur* de Fargues, cavalry *capitaine* at the time of the Revolution and previously proprietary *colonel* of his own regiment from 25 July 1795. Among those breveted as *lieutenant-colonels* were the Vicomte de Montjustin, cavalry *capitaine* when he emigrated and later *lieutenant-colonel* of the Etienne-Damas Hussars, and also the Marquis de La Haye, a former retired cavalry *lieutenant* who served in the same rank in the 2nd Squadron (Lentilhac's Company).[97] Furthermore two volunteers were breveted on 1 July 1797, François de Guisard de Montarnal, as *lieutenant*, and Jean de Vauvillé as *sous-lieutenant*.[98]

There was also the opportunity for other officers to seek promotion, or rather their colonel to ask for it on their behalf. Among these were the Marquis d'Andelarre, *capitaine aide-major*, and Aumont de Bazouges, the senior *capitaine*, of the Etienne-Damas hussars. The latter had his nomination delayed as further information was required but his brevet as *major* was granted on 24 October 1797, backdated to 31 July, and the Marquis d'Andelarre,

95 Perry de Nieüil, *Mémoires du marquis de Toustain*, p.105.

96 Villebresme, *Souvenirs*, p.181.

97 AMC, Archives of the Armée de Condé, Series Y/I-2-316, 'Statement of the Colonels employed in the Cavalry department.'

98 AMC Series Y/I-2-299/300, 'General nominative statement giving right to the brevets, letters and commissions/gentlemen'

who was by then serving as *chef d'escadron*, received that of *lieutenant-colonel*.[99] However, Bazouges would have to wait sometime before he was officially notified.

The Etienne-Damas hussars were now entirely re-equipped and ready for the field, under the command of *Commandeur* de Fargues, and 'a report dated 18 July from Pfullendorf shows that the corps at the strength of 406 men, and 392 horses, with 3 carters and drivers, 5 cart and 3 pack horses, 2 valets of the noble maréchaux-des-logis, 3 sutlers and 6 horses, 58 remount horses.'[100] Despite having no indication from the British Government of its intentions, the Prince de Condé became impatient for news from Russia. On 20 July he received confirmation that one of the tsar's aides de camp would come, probably in mid-September, to take the Armée de Condé to Russia.[101] In the meantime, Vioménil was invited to go directly to St Petersburg and he soon left accompanied by his nephew, Toustain, 'After the touching farewells that the Damas and Noinville officers gave to my uncle at Pfullendorf, we left on 1 August 1797, at two o'clock in the morning'.[102]

Prince Gorchakov, the tsar's aide de camp, finally arrived on 3 October bringing the conditions under which the Armée de Condé would pass into Russian pay. The rates of pay offered by Britain would be retained, as well as the ranks obtained in the French army, and the Condé's corps, which would keep its name and be under the command of the prince, was to take an oath of loyalty to the tsar and adopt the Russian cockade. It was to receive Russian training in Volhynia, or Polish Russia, a region which had been incorporated on the third partition of Poland in 1795 and is today north-west Ukraine. In addition, the French nobility were to enjoy the same prerogatives as their Russian counterparts and retain their coats of arms which would be integrated into the heraldry of the Empire, moreover, any émigré who wished to settle in Russia would be granted a hereditary property. Finally, the French émigrés would enjoy the freedom to practice Catholicism.

The Armée de Condé now left British pay and the officers and noble volunteers, including those of the Etienne-Damas Hussars, were generously granted six months' pay from 16 September 1797, the date of their discharge. This award prompted the Comte de Damas-Crux to write to the Prince de Condé on 24 September, asking that his regiment's noble hussars be paid at the same rate as other noble soldiers on the transfer to Russian service; the request was supported by both Robert Craufurd and Prince Gorchakov.[103] The paid NCOs and soldiers however only received one months' pay which led a number of them, especially from the cavalry, to leave and enter Austrian service particularly in the Bussy Chasseurs and Rohan Hussars. The Austrians also gained men when all foreigners were discharged, including a large number of the paid Etienne-Damas hussars, the exceptions were those in the Régiment de Hohenlohe, the personal property of a prince of the Empire and thus a 'German regiment'. In addition, all the cavalry horses were to be returned to the British commissioner on 29 September to be sold, but the Comte d'Ecquevilly, later wrote:

99 AMC, Archives of the Armée de Condé, Series Y/I-2-305, 'Work of the King with the Prince de Condé – favours granted.'

100 Grouvel *Les Corps de troupe de l'émigration*, Vol.II, p.255 and AG, Armée de Condé, carton 357, f.1.

101 Castres, *Relation d'un voyage*, p.XIX.

102 Perry de Nieüil, *Mémoires du marquis de Toustain*, p.107.

103 AMC, Series Y, carton XXIII, Überlingen 24 September 1797.

> I must not omit to render homage to the nobility with which HBM's commissioner conducted himself in this circumstance ... granting horses not only to all the fourriers and maréchaux-des-logis of the noble cavalry, but also all the noble cavalrymen who, by their age or their services, had some title to keep them, and of whom I gave him the state. He added to this favour from his government, which had doubtless given him carte blanche to this effect, that of providing a quite considerable sum, intended to be distributed among the women and children who needed this help for the great journey that they were going to undertake.[104]

Condé's corps passed into Russian pay on 1 October 1797. The Duc d'Enghien was in command as the Prince de Condé was preparing to leave directly for St Petersburg:

> The order for the departure of the different columns was sent on 4 [October] to the units. It was decided that that of the train would take place on the 8th; that one formed of the general officers, those of the mounted troops, and generally all those who were authorised to keep their horses and to travel by land, would leave on the 9th, and that destined to embark on the Danube, composed of the headquarters, all the infantry, except a battalion of the Hohenlohe Regiment escorting the train, the artillery and all the dismounted cavalry, marching on the 10th.[105]

The Etienne-Damas Hussars, 213 men, marched to the Danube with the paid infantry and cavalry regiments of Noinville, Dauphin and Chevaliers de la Couronne, in a column of 990 officers and soldiers.[106] They embarked at Regensburg on 27 October and Corbehem described the journey from there:

> We went down the river as far as Linz, capital of Upper Austria, where we were granted a stay of twenty-four hours. We made it an occasion to enjoy a pleasure that we were rarely called to share: for we ordinarily lodged in villages. Here we were on the contrary in one of the prettiest cities of the Austrian monarchy. We had neither sorrows, nor worries; no service to do, no horses to care for, as we had been dismounted before leaving Swabia; no other arms to maintain than our sabres which had been left with us; and, to add to our satisfaction, each having money in his pocket ... From Linz, continuing on our way still on rafts, we reached the little city of Krems, fifteen leagues from Vienna. There we left the Danube to take the land route. We soon came out of the territory of Austria proper, to traverse the fertile and well-cultivated fields of Moravia.[107]

Their progress is indicated by a letter written by the Comte de Damas-Crux to *Capitaine* de Bazouges from Olomouc on 20 November 1797:

104 Ecquevilly, *Campagnes*, p.226.
105 Ecquevilly, *Campagnes*, p.227.
106 AMC, Fonds Grouvel, dossier *Hussards de Damas/Légion de Damas*, return for the regiment, 21 October.
107 Corbehem, *Dix ans de ma vie*, pp.326–327.

> It is with the most extreme pleasure, my dear Bazouges, that I announce to you the accomplishment of your desires and mine. Nantouillet and the Cte d'Ecquevilly tell me from Blankenburg that the King has granted you the brevet of major. M. the Prince de Condé left for St Petersburg with the new work, which he will only announce when he joins the Corps in Volhynia…[108]

The march was made in quite poor weather which only turned worse in the final six days, with heavy snow and temperatures tumbling.

> [The army then] crossed the Bug on 1 January [1798], a small river that separates the Austrian lands from those of the Russian emperor, entered the Russian territory of Kladniv, where it formed a square, at the centre of which was erected an altar. The oath of loyalty to the Emperor of Russia … was read in a loud voice by a chaplain, the soldiers having raised a hand. It was then signed by all the officers individually.[109]

The army's headquarters were placed at Volodymyr-Volynskyi on 4 January but there was not enough accommodation, as the city had recently suffered a fire, so it moved to Lutsk before being finally established at Dubno, ten leagues away, around 20 January. The units were distributed among the small towns and villages of the region; the Etienne-Damas hussars were scattered in twelve villages along the Styr River, north of Lutsk: Myl's'k, Dukhche, Sokil, Kopyllya, Vyshen'ky, Lukiv, Naviz, Hruzyatyn, Borovychi, Chetvertnya, Hodomychi and Kolky.[110]

The Prince de Condé had arrived at St Petersburg on 2 November 1797 and six days later the tsar decreed the new organisation of the Condé Corps. It was to be reduced to six regiments: three of infantry, the Infanterie Noble, Grenadiers de Bourbon and Mousquetaires de Durand (formerly Hohenlohe), two of cavalry, the Dragons Nobles de Berry and Dragons d'Enghien, and one of artillery; in addition, the guard of the prince's headquarters, the French and Swiss companies, would be maintained. However, it was only after the Prince de Condé and his suite arrived at Dubno on 30 March 1798 that the reorganisation was put into effect; like the other units, the Régiment d'Etienne-Damas hussards was disbanded on 10 April. The following day, 'the Chevaliers de la Couronne and the company of noble volunteers of Etienne de Damas were incorporated and formed the régiment noble à cheval de Berry' which was cantoned at Lokachi and Khorokhoryn; 'the régiment des dragons d'Enghien was formed of the remains from the Dauphin, Noinville, Baschi, Carneville, the paid men of Etienne de Damas and the [Roger de Damas] legion's hussars' and installed at Lutsk.[111]

Isolated in the depths of Volhynia, with no other distractions than sleeping, gaming and hunting, and without remounts, arms and equipment, the *Condéens* made the best of the

108 Bazouges family archive.
109 Ecquevilly, *Campagnes*, p.233.
110 AMC, Series Y, Carton n° XX (Russian service) 'Carte de l'établissement du Corps de Condé dans les districts de Wlodimier [Volodymyr-Volynskyi], Kowel Kovel et Lutzck [Lutsk].'
111 Ecquevilly, *Campagnes*, p.297.

situation. Here they waited for their Russian uniforms, but it was to be the end of 1798 before they were all clothed and equipped. The men of the 'Old Damas' were not at the close of their military adventures. New political twists and turns were to save them from their planned fate as military colonists in Crimea, bring them back to the heart of Europe and finally enable the survivors from the Légion de Damas to return home to France.

Epilogue

Almost 30 volunteers and officers from the Etienne-Damas hussards, foremost of whom was the Comte de Damas-Crux, continued to serve in the Armée de Condé until its final disbanding, in February 1801. A dozen or so of the volunteers stayed together in the fourth squadron of the Dragons Nobles de Berry but only two of the 'Old Damas' officers, Bazouges and Lentilhac served with them, reduced in rank to *sous-lieutenants*, although those in this squadron benefitted from the ministry of the *Abbé* du Chilleau who had asked to remain with them. The Comte de Damas-Crux commanded the second squadron and a dozen of the specialists from Etienne-Damas were in the corps: Couturier, the *chirurgien major*, and Vasseur, *maréchal-expert*, on the staff; in the first squadron there were five trumpeters, along with a saddler and tailor, Müller and Louis, from the regiment while another tailor was in the fifth squadron. The remaining gentlemen had been scattered in the other companies of the Dragons Noble de Berry and Comte Paul de Maumigny, promoted *maréchal de camp* in 1797, was present on the list of supernumerary officers as *lieutenant* but Moisez soon transferred to the Compagnie de la Prévôté. At least four men joined the Dragons d'Enghien as officers, so serving with the former paid soldiers from the Etienne-Damas hussars: Marquis Jean-François-Marie de Bongars, *major*, Hyppolite de la Cropte de Chanteraie and Jacques-Joseph de Faget de Renol, *sous-lieutenants*. The last was the Vicomte de Montjustin who, having broken his arm severely, had had to remain at Regensburg, accompanied by Couturier, until joining the regiment at the end of 1797; although left disabled by the break, he commanded a squadron from 1798 to 1800 and then was *lieutenant-colonel* commanding the Enghien depot in 1800 and 1801.[1]

All participated in the Swiss Campaign (1799–1800) with Marshal Suvorov's troops and when the Condé Corps was dismissed by Tsar Paul I, in 1800, the army passed for a second time into British pay, the Berry Dragons being renamed the Régiment Noble à Cheval d'Angoulême. The last of the Damas volunteers, including Cézac, served in the fourth squadron along with the *Abbé* du Chilleau. The only Damas officer to remain in the squadron was François Aumont de Bazouges, still a *lieutenant*, as Lentilhac had been promoted *sous-aide major* on the regimental staff in 1799. On the announcement of the suspension of arms, signed at Rosenheim in early January 1801, the Comte de Maumigny, still a supernumerary officer with the rank of *lieutenant*, retired to Krieglach, in Styria, Austria but, his health shattered, he died suddenly died on 10 January. His death preceded the final disbanding of the Armée de Condé and thus the inevitable and final dispersal of

1 AG, Armée de Condé, carton n°355-1.

the last survivors of the Légion de Damas. Most took advantage of the conditions offered to finally return to France, some did immediately while others, like the Vicomte de Lentilhac, encountered difficulties in obtaining the documents required to benefit from the amnesty now available to those who had emigrated. Only a few continued to serve against France. When the Dragons d'Enghien were disbanded on 1 May, some of the NCOs and dragoons formed a company in the newly raised Chasseurs Britanniques and doubtless some of the former paid soldiers of the Hussards d'Etienne-Damas were among them. Faget de Renol certainly passed into the Chasseurs Britanniques as lieutenant and served in the Egyptian Campaign, in 1801 and 1802. Furthermore, in 1811 two former members of Damas units were commissioned as ensigns in the same regiment: Epiphane-Etienne Julien (1767–c.1846) who had joined the legion in 1793 as a noble chasseur and Barnabé-Silvain de Foulogne de Précorbin (1778–1858) who was one of the Béon volunteers who had joined the Damas Hussars in 1795.[2]

Madame de Bennes, had soon found that she could not afford to live in London and so, speaking German well, she left to settle in Hamburg. She was only able to return to France in 1803 where she was reunited with her two children who she had not seen for 12 years. She then took possession of her family home, Bois-Manselet, near the village of Lonlay-le-Tesson, north-west of Alençon in the Orne and peacefully waited there for the return of the Bourbons. Such was not the case for Tercier who, after Quiberon, had pursued the struggle in the West, at first in Anjou where he had been named chief of one of the divisions of Scépeaux's army (1796) before going into Maine as adjutant to *Général* Rochecotte, in 1797. When the latter was shot, Tercier replaced him as general in chief but was arrested and imprisoned at the Temple in the same year. Freed in 1799, he returned to Maine where he raised the army again but, after the pacification of 1800, he retired to his home. He was called in 1803 to Paris by his friend Georges Cadoudal, who had remained fiercely committed to the royalist cause culminating in his involvement in a plot against Napoleon in 1804 involving Pichegru and implicating Moreau. When the conspiracy was uncovered Tercier was once again arrested and thrown into prison but he was released that same year and put under surveillance at Amiens, where he was to remain until 1814.

Only three former members of the Damas infantry appear to have gone on to serve under the Emperor Napoleon. William or Guillaume O'Meara (1764–1828), and his twin brother Daniel Joseph, had been born at Dunkirk in 1764, sons of a former officer in the Régiment de Clare of the Brigade Irlandaise in French royal service. William joined his father's former regiment as cadet in 1770 and progressed to be *capitaine* in the Régiment de Berwick in 1790. He emigrated with the other officers of this regiment and subsequently entered the Légion de Damas in 1793 as a volunteer in O'Moore's Company, involved in recruiting. The following year he received a captaincy in the 6th (Conway) Regiment in the Irish Catholic Brigade in British service; when the brigade was disbanded in 1797, he was placed on half pay. He reverted to full pay, as a captain in the 62nd (Wiltshire) Foot in 1801 but retired the next year, when the British Army was rapidly reduced following the Peace of Amiens. He returned to France and was later appointed *capitaine* in Napoleon's Légion Irlandaise

2 See Alistair Nichols *Wellington's Mongrel Regiment: A History of the Chasseurs Britanniques* (Staplehurst: Spellmount, 2005), pp.192, 197–198.

and then aide de camp to *Général de Division* Clarke, the future Duc de Feltre, in 1804. Guillaume married one of Clarke's sisters-in-law and his career, and that of his brother, benefited from this connection, especially after Clarke became Minister of War in 1807. O'Meara was appointed *major* and then *colonel* of the Régiment d'Isembourg in 1806 and 1807. Employed in various staff duties he was made a baron of the Empire in 1809 and *général de brigade* in 1813; he ceased to be active after the First Restoration of 1814.

Henry-Philippe Marquis de Ségur-Bouzely (1770–1829) was *sous-lieutenant* in the Chasseurs des Cévennes à Pied in 1786 and *capitaine* in 1791. He emigrated in 1792 and joined the Armée de Bourbon and then Condé before serving as a noble chasseur in the Légion de Damas from November 1794 to October 1795. Having returned to France in 1800, he served as a gendarmerie officer, attached to the Vicomte de Noailles, in *Général de Division* Leclerc's Haiti expedition in 1802. He fell afoul of Napoleon's displeasure due, apparently, to his opposition to the latter's coronation as emperor in 1804, and was removed from active service in disgrace but, in 1807, was appointed aide de camp to Joachim Murat and quickly promoted *capitaine*. He was severely wounded at the Battle of Heilsberg that year and lost his left arm but returned to serve alongside Murat, being promoted in the Neapolitan Army to *adjutant commandant* in 1810. He was taken into French retirement pay, as *colonel*, on 13 January 1815 and appointed honorary *maréchal de camp* on 31 October 1827. In 1814 he applied for the cross of the order of Mérite Militaire, being inadmissible for that of Saint-Louis as he was Protestant, and, despite some resistance as the former order was considered for foreign and not French officers, his request was acceded to.

The Comte de Chambors, appointed major in the Damas Regiment, had been unable to join the unit but served with the Comte d'Artois on the Île d'Yeu. In October 1796 he joined the Portuguese service and commanded two brigades in the confrontation with Spain in 1801. The following year he was appointed inspector of the infantry and strongholds and, in 1807, *coronel* of the 15º Regimento de Infantaria. That same year the French, under Junot, invaded the kingdom and Chambors joined the French general's staff; he continued to serve in staff and command roles during the Peninsular War until 1813, despite not having been removed from the list of those proscribed as émigrés. In 1815 he returned to his place at court as Artois's gentleman of honour and then gentleman of the chamber when the latter succeeded to the throne as Charles X; he had been promoted *général de division* in 1820 and died at his country set in 1846.

It seems that only two former Damas hussar officers served Napoleon's Empire, one had been present in 1794 at the formation of the hussars of the Légion de Damas and the other had joined the Régiment d'Etienne-Damas Hussards in the Armée de Condé in 1796. The latter was the Marquis de Sourdis, who returned to France on 1 July 1801. He chose to do so despite having been equerry in the Household of King Louis XVIII in 1798 and serving during his stay in the former palace of the Dukes of Courland, at Jelgava (then called Mittau). Born in 1767 and then only 34 years old he had had a rich and varied military career. At 16 years old he had been enrolled as a supernumerary in the King's Gardes du Corps before serving in the artillery then the Dauphin Dragons, he was *capitaine* in the Guyenne Chasseurs à Cheval at the time of the Revolution before he transferred to the 16e Régiment de Cavalerie (former Royal-Lorraine). He emigrated in 1791 with the unit's officers and joined the Armée des Princes, serving in the 1792 campaign as aide de camp to the Comte d'Artois. Discharged and without employment, he apparently engaged in the

Loyal Emigrant Regiment before passing briefly to the Rohan *hussards talpaches* in Austrian service.[3] He joined the Armée de Condé at the end of 1795 and was named aide de camp to the Duc de Berry before being promoted in 1796 *colonel en second* of the Etienne-Damas Hussards. When Napoleon formed the Gendarmes d'Ordonnance in 1806, almost entirely of returned émigrés and their sons, Sourdis was appointed *capitaine* commanding the third company and served in this ephemeral unit's only campaign (1806–1807). He then entered the Chasseurs à Cheval de la Garde as *capitaine* then instructor of the Mameluke Squadron (10 September 1808). Returning to France in 1809, Sourdis was immediately named as head of the Paris Riding School, charged, with the rank of *chef d'escadron*, with the instruction of the Chevau-légers de Paris, the cavalry of the capital's *Garde Nationale*. Although struck from the strength of the Guard in 1811, he nevertheless retained his functions at the head of the Riding School.

The former was the Marquis de Bongars who, in 1803, went into the service of the Prince of Hohenzollern-Hechingen and in 1807 was attached to the headquarters of Prince Jérôme, Napoleon's brother and King of Westphalia from 1807 to 1813. By Imperial decree, dated 1 June 1807, he was nominated as commander of a Silesian battalion of light infantry (called Hohenzollern) which passed into the service of the Kingdom of Westphalia in January 1808. Bongars was not only authorised to remain in the service of the German kingdom, while retaining his French nationality, but he was also appointed, on 8 February 1808, *colonel* aide de camp to King Jérôme and, three days later, commander of the gendarmerie legion. He was promoted *général de brigade* and *capitaine* in the King's Guard on 28 April 1809, but retained the senior command of the gendarmerie, at the head of which he served in the 1809 Saxony campaign; promoted inspector of gendarmerie, in July 1810, and finally *général de division*, in January 1813, he was however reduced to *général de brigade* at the end of the year, when he passed into French service. Appointed to the command of the *départements* of Meuse then Marne, to organise the mass levy there in 1814, he did not play an active role during this campaign and sought to place himself at the disposal of the Bourbons, at the First Restoration (April 1814–March 1815).

The Comte de Damas-Crux was appointed first gentlemen of the Duc d'Angoulême's chamber in 1798 and at Jelgava, in June 1799, he married Anne-Félicité-Simone, the daughter of the Duc de Sérent, chevalier of the orders of the king, former governor to the Ducs de Berry and Angoulême, and member of Louis XVIII's court. Damas followed the royal family in its exile at first at Warsaw (until 1804), Blankenberg, Jelgava, once again (1804–1807), and finally in England. Disembarking at San Sebastian with the Duc d'Angoulême on 1 February 1814 he returned to France in March accompanying the British troops sent to secure Bordeaux and remained attached to the prince until the final return of the Bourbons, at the conclusion of Waterloo and Napoleon's abdication. He was covered with honours at the First Restoration, appointed *lieutenant-général* and Grand Croix of Saint-Louis, then peer of France on 17 July 1815, and created duke on 3 February 1816. He was, however, considered as politically inept by the King. Nevertheless, he remained, for his

3 See Hughes de Bazouges 'Des hussards tolpaches de Rohan aux Chasseurs de Rohan-Brunswick' *Carnet de La Sabretache* Nos. 198, pp.40-44 and 199 (2015), pp.31-36.

former comrades in arms, 'a man of perfect bounty and quality,' never failing to come to their aid or support their efforts.'[4]

The first who benefited from this was Tercier, in the first days of July 1814:

> M. Comte Etienne de Damas, *lieutenant-général* and *cordon rouge*, lately presenting some officers to H.M. wished that M. de Tercier, former Vendéan general, and even earlier officer of his legion, put himself at the head of the presentation. This brave general was presented to the King as being the only officer from the Damas Legion who escaped from the Quiberon affair; as having by miracle escaped in the affair of Georges, Pichegru and Moreau; having also escaped three military commissions. The King greeted him with extreme kindness; he was subsequently presented to Madame the Duchesse d'Angoulême, who knew his devotion, his misfortunes and his bravery, and who testified to him the most honourable interest.[5]

Tercier was indeed rewarded for his merits and fidelity as he was nominated *maréchal de camp* in 1816 and given retirement in the same year.

Shortly before, when he was travelling with the Duc d'Angoulême between Angers and Le Mans, in the summer of 1814, the Comte de Damas learnt at La Flèche that his friend François Aumont de Bazouges had died of exhaustion in 1808. His tomb is still to be found in the cemetery at Bazouges-sur-Loir. *Seigneur* at the time of the Revolution, his family having purchased the château in 1756 and provided the 29th, 30th and 31st *seigneurs*, he had found his family and managed to regain his lands again in 1801. He had just been elected mayor of his commune only weeks before his death but his widow had no relative, or any other kind of assistance, for support. Damas ensured that she and her daughters were received by the King, at the Tuileries Palace, on 12 September and that she benefited from the reversion of the *lieutenant-colonel* of cavalry's pension, the rank which had been granted to her husband at the time of the disbanding of the Armée de Condé.[6]

Survivors of the Légion de Damas received the cross of Saint-Louis from 1814 including a half dozen of the former members of the Irish companies. However, it was only in May 1817 that Madame de Bennes went to Paris to claim a pension and the cross of Saint-Louis, in consideration of her service in the Hommes d'Armes à pied in 1792 and three continuous years of campaigning as a volunteer in the Légion de Damas, both posts which had entitled her to the rank of *lieutenant*, and also her three wounds two of which were received at the Leuven Canal. Her application was supported by certificates from, among others the Duc de Damas-Crux and the Duc de Berry, but was rejected by the Minister of War on the grounds of her gender with the recommendation that she approach the King's Household, which would not be constrained by having to apply law and custom, for 'special graces'.[7] She repeated her application in 1820 and Jacquier de Noyelle describes meeting her by chance as he was about to take a stage coach. Madame de Bennes was about to board another public

4 Etienne-Léon Baron de Lamothe-Langon, *Mémoires de Louis XVIII* (Brussels: Hauman, 1823–1833), Vol.VII, p.275.

5 *La Gazette de France* n°186 Tuesday 5 July 1814 p.740.

6 Bazouges family archives

7 SHD GR 1 Yi 3

carriage when she recognised in this officer the young Damas chasseur of 25 years before; overwhelmed with joy, she kissed him and introduced him to her grandchildren who were with her.[8]

In his memoirs, the Comte de Neuilly reports that he encountered her at the same period and by the greatest chance, at the Palais Royal, still dressed as a man.[9] Although there is no trace of her nomination, Neuilly states that she received the cross of Saint-Louis as did the Comte de Contades who, in his writing, relied on witness statements from the 1850s. The latter related that each year, on 25 August, the royal fete of Saint-Louis, Madame de Bennes donned her old uniform and sported her decoration, whether it had indeed been granted by the King's 'special graces' or was in fact the less prestigious, and strictly administered, Ordre du Lys. For a day, she was again the Chevalier de Haussey, former noble chasseur of the Légion de Damas.[10]

The Duc de Damas-Crux's concern did not stop with only the survivors as, from 1821 to 1830, he was also president, and instigator, of the commission for the monument at Auray erected in memory of those shot after Quiberon in what became the 'Field of Martyrs', honouring the memory of his former comrades in arms of the Légion de Damas who had fallen for God and King, and to whom Napoleon himself was to render justice in his memoirs: 'They were paid by our enemies, that is true, but they were or ought to have been for the cause of their King. France furnished death for their action and tears to their courage. All devotion is heroic.'[11]

Updated lists of personnel from the Légion de Damas and Etienne-Damas Hussards, with biographical notes, as well as other related material are available at the website fortisetfidelis.com.

8 La Gournerie, *Les Débris de Quiberon*, p.33.

9 Barberey, *Dix années d'émigration*, p.91.

10 Contades *Emigrés et chouans* p.42. In his less extravagant *Notice sur la Commune de Lonlay-de-Tesson* (Paris: Champion, 1881), p.24, Contades stated Bennes received the Decoration du Lys after 29 October 1814.

11 Gaspard Gourgaud, *Mémoires pour servir à l'Histoire de France sous Napoléon, écrits à Sainte-Hélène par les généraux qui ont partagé sa captivité et publiés sur les manuscrits entièrement corrigés de sa main* (Paris: Didot, 1823), Vol.VIII p.249.

Appendix I

Organisation of the Armée du Centre, or Armée des Princes, 1792

VANGUARD

Infantry

Chasseurs royaux des Princes

Chasseurs carabiniers de Wittgenstein (1/2 battalion)

Chasseurs royaux de Provence

Cavalry

Hussards de Bercheny (2 squadrons)

Hussards de Saxe (4 squadrons)

Hussards de Chamborant-Lauzun (1 squadron)

Chasseurs étrangers de Polignac (2 squadrons)

FIRST LINE

Cavalry of the left wing

Hommes d'armes à cheval
(4 squadrons)

Compagnies nobles d'ordonnance
(8 squadrons)

Attached Infantry

Régiment de Wittgenstein
(1/2 battalion)

First Infantry Division

1st Brigade

1st battalion:
Companies of officers: Colonel général, la Reine,
Normandie, Vintimille, Flandre,
Vivarais, Lyonnais-la-Sarre, Beaujolais

Cavalry of the right wing

Grenadiers d'ordonnance à cheval
(1 squadron)

Gardes du corps du Roi
(12 squadrons)

Gardes du corps des Princes
(2 squadrons)

Attached Infantry

Régiment de Vexin
and Company of Chasseurs nobles de Rouault
(1/2 battalion)

Second Infantry Division

3rd Brigade

1st battalion:
Régiments de Dillon and Walsh

2nd battalion:
Companies of officers: Champagne, Dauphiné, Agenois, Lorraine, Poitou, Languedoc, La Marck-Royal, Deux-Ponts, Bouillon

2nd Brigade

1st battalion:
Companies of officers: Armangac, La Couronne, Béarn, Vermandois, Brie, Royal-Comtois, Anjou, Chartres

2nd battalion:
Coalition of Bretagne
(7 companies)

2nd battalion:
Régiment de Berwick
Artillerie des Colonies attached

4th Brigade

1st battalion:
Coalitions of Saintonge and Angoumois, Poitou, Périgord, Languedoc

2nd battalion:
Compagnies of officers : Navarre, Royal Vaisseaux, Forez-Angoumois, Royal Roussillon, Dauphin, Bourgogne, Limousin, Penthièvre

SECOND LINE

Cavalry of the left wing

1st Brigade

1st Squadron:
Companies of officers: Monsieur-Angoulême Dragons, Artois Dragons, Chasseurs à cheval de Flandre

2nd Squadron:
Company of officers: Chartres-Penthièvre Dragons
Coalition of Périgord

3rd Squadron:
Companies of officers: Chasseurs à cheval de Franche Comté and Picardie

4th Squadron:
Companies of officers: Chasseurs à cheval du Hainault and Champagne

2nd Brigade

1st Squadron:
Companies of officers: Commissaire général, Royal Picardie

2nd Squadron:
Coalition of Poitou
(2 companies)

3rd Squadron:
Coalition of Bretagne
(2 companies)

4th Squadron:
Carabiniers de Monsieur
(2 companies)

Cavalry of the right wing

1st Brigade

1st Squadron:
Companies of officers: Colonel général, Royal Champagne, Royal Piémont

2nd Squadron:
Coalition of Auvergne
(2 companies)

3rd Squadron:
Coalition of Auvergne
(2 companies)

4th Squadron:
Companies of officers: Royal Lorraine-Orléans, Royal Guyenne

2nd Brigade

Régiment Royal Allemand
(3 squadrons)

RESERVE

Infantry

Marine royale
(1/2 battalion)
Hommes d'armes à pied
(2 battalions)
Institution de Saint-Louis
(1/2 battalion)

Cavalry

Marine royale
(1 squadron)
Coalition of Languedoc
Coalitions of Saintonge and Angoumois
(1 squadron)

Artillery
Engineers
Provost
General Administration
Medical Service

Source: Grouvel *Les Corps de troupe de l'émigration*, Vol.III pp.23–24.

Appendix II

Poster advising of the raising of a Corps by Comte Etienne de Damas

---

1 June 1793

NOTICE TO FRENCH ÉMIGRÉ GENTLEMEN

Comte ETIENNE DE DAMAS, Infantry Colonel, has, with the permission of Monsieur Regent of FRANCE, obtained from THEIR MIGHTIEST LORDS & the Prince of ORANGE, the agreement to assemble a Corps intended to serve the cause that arms Europe. He hastens to inform the French Émigré Gentlemen, in order that those who would honour him sufficiently with their confidence to wish to serve with him during this Campaign, know in advance by what right they could give new proof of their fidelity to God, Honour & the King.

The Corps will have the name RÉGIMENT DE MAESTRICHT, in memory of the defence of this place.

It will be composed of Companies of Chasseurs & Companies of Fusiliers.

The places as Officers, Chefs de Section, Chefs d'Escouäde & Chasseurs are intended for Émigré Gentlemen. Nevertheless, distinguished NCOs who have emigrated with their Officers, & whose Conduct makes them worthy of commendation, will be eligible for the places of Chefs d'Escouäde in the Fusilier Companies, & to be promoted in turn to those of Chefs de Section of the said Companies.

The Fusiliers will be enrolled Soldiers, who will spare the Chasseurs from the more arduous duties such as manual labour, ground working, in war, guards, fatigues, etc.

The Corps will be clothed, armed & equipped by means of advances that T M Lords made for this purpose. One will follow for repairs & replacement of items, what is practised among the Troops of the Dutch Republic.

The Officers will be appointed, for the first time, by HSH the Prince of ORANGE, on the recommendation of the Comte de DAMAS.

On 15 July next at the latest, the seniority of each Member of the Corps will be established on a General Register. All those who enter the Corps after the said time, will be added onto the end of the General List.

Once the first Appointments are made, all replacements will be made rank by rank after the table of seniority of Service of the entire Corps: thus, the most senior Lieutenant of the Corps will become Capitaine of the vacant Company, as the most senior Chasseur will become Chasseur Chef d'Escouäde.

Seniority will be determined by the active Service of each, those who had retired previously, only being able to count the years that they had actively served, & the intervening years being considered as void.

On equal seniority, age will determine the Rank.

One of the principal Clauses of the Capitulation is the Condition positively expressed & signed to be able at any time to be recalled by the Princes, Uncles of the King, for His Majesty's Service or by His Majesty himself.

At the time of the Corps ceasing Service, each of the individuals who compose it will receive as Gratification three 42-day moths' salary attached to his rank, after the following Table:

		Florins		
Chasseur & Fusilier Officers	Capitaine	158	0	0
	Capitaine-Commandant	83	0	0
	Premier Lieutenant	60	0	0
	Second Lieutenant & Enseigne	54	0	0
Chasseur Companies	Chef de Section	28	6	0
	Chef d'Escouäde	22	11	0
	Chasseur	18	1	0
	Drummer	14	1	0
Fusilier Companies	Chef de Section	24	0	0
	Chef d'Escouäde	17	13	0
	Fusilier	14	1	0
	Drummer	14	1	0

all these salaries are per 42-day Month.

Comte ETIENNE DE DAMAS will receive with readiness, all those Émigré gentlemen who will present themselves furnished with a Certificate of Service in one of the three Armies of Our Princes, during the last Campaign. He is conscious of the accolade to be at the Head of such a Corps. His greatest care will be to combine his duties as Commander, for the exactitude of the Service and good Military spirit, with the consideration that will be due to those Émigré gentlemen who come to array themselves beneath the flags of the RÉGIMENT DE MAESTRICHT.

The assembly point is at MAASTRICHT; sooner the Corps will be formed, & sooner it will have the advantage of joining the Armies.

Source: Poster printed at The Hague, dated 1 June 1793. Translated from BL Add Ms 8069.

Appendix III

British Capitulations

These are translated from the original copies, in French. They are from TNA WO 24/1112, unless stated otherwise; the other sources being TNA WO 1/172 and KNH A31/2124.

Provisional Capitulation

Rheine 3 February 1795 *[the copy in TNA 1/172 is dated 9 February]*

I have the honour to receive the propositions that you have made to me to enter into the pay and service of His Britannic Majesty a corps of cavalry and one of infantry which has been until present under your orders in the service of Their Mightiest Lords.

I will only be able to accept men who compose these two corps under the following conditions up until I have received HBM's orders on this subject. Namely –

1 – The number of men that you actually have will be taken into the pay of England (dated 21 January) after having been approved by an inspector appointed to this effect.

2 – The men will be formed in companies each of one hundred and eleven men, including four sergeants and six corporals. For each company which will be formed in this manner, four officers will be accorded namely 1 Captain, 2 Lieutenants and 1 Cornet.

3 – The pay of the officers will begin from the day of the completion of their respective companies and each rank will be granted the appointments customary with the English troops.

4 – One will not take into our pay any officer of the major or minor staff until when the two companies of cavalry or three of infantry are formed or that it will please the commander in chief to grant it to you. *[The WO 1/172 version ends '... to grant it sooner.']*

5 – It ought to be well understood that notwithstanding that all the men who you have at present will be paid from 21 January, one will accord nothing to the number that are

lacking to form a second, third or fourth company until when it is found that this company is complete in men and passed by the inspector.

6 – Neither the officers nor soldiers will have any right to make demands of the English government than for pay, bread and forage; these last two articles will commence to be issued to each officer and soldier from the day when they will be paid; but one cannot back claim food rations or forage, according to the regulations of the army.

7 – The commander in chief reserves the right to confirm this capitulation by another which will be more detailed and more favourable for the two parties or to break the present immediately that it will please HBM to give his orders thereupon the Comte de Damas will be able while waiting to name officers to the posts. *[The WO 1/172 does not include the passage 'and more favourable for the two parties']*

8 – We do not engage to pay any money for the recruitment of men until we are in the instance of making a second capitulation.

9 – The officers and soldiers will be subject to all the orders and disciplinary Regulations customary for the British army.

10 – These articles will be as much for the cavalry as for the infantry.

Mutatis, mutandis.[1] The formation of each arm will be as it is in the margin.

Cavalry corps composed of two companies – Each company will be composed of		Infantry corps composed of six* companies each company composed of	
Captains	1	Captain	1
Lieutenants	2	Lieutenants	2
Cornet	1	Ensign	1
Quarter Master	1	–	
Sergeants	4	Sergeants	4
Corporals	6	Corporals	6
Trumpeter	1	Drummer	1
Chasseurs à Cheval	100	Fusiliers	100
Total of a company	111	Total of a comp.	111
When two companies will be complete in men and horses major and minor staff will be granted, namely		When a major and minor staff will be accorded, it will have	
Colonel Commandant	1	Lieutenant Colonel	1
Major	1	Major	1
Adjutant	1	Adjutant	1
Surgeon Major	1	Surgeon Major	1

1 Meaning things being changed that have to be changed.

Assistant	1	Assistant Surgeon	1
		Chaplain	1
		Sergeant-Major	1
		Quarter-Mr-Sergeant	1

* *The WO 24/1112 version shows 'dix' (ten) which is clearly an error in copying as the other two copies of this provisional capitulation and the final capitulation all show six infantry companies; this conclusion is also supported by the text of the capitulation.*

It is indicated that Lieutenant General Harcourt signed all three versions, but only on that in WO 24/1112 is it indicated that Comte Etienne de Damas had done so as well. This was after he had added the following passage:

Accepted the present provisional capitulation signed by the Honourable Lieutenant General Harcourt commanding the British troops in recommending to the English generosity the officers actually existing in the corps, coming to the number of five, who find themselves deprived of their employment and of their means of subsistence, because of musket shots, fatigues and the excess of the services of the Corps during this Campaign reduced it at this moment below the number present for the formation of three infantry Companies.

Definitive Capitulation, Celle, 2 April 1795

1 – The number of men of which your corps is actually composed will be taken (as it said in the provisional capitulation) into the pay of England dated 21 January, having been approved by the inspector appointed to this effect.

2 – I will only be able to accept the men who compose your corps under the following conditions.

Namely

3 – The men will be formed in companies each of one hundred and eleven men, including four sergeants, six corporals and a trumpeter. For each company which will be formed in this manner, one will grant four officers, namely a captain, two lieutenants and a cornet.

4 – The pay of the officers will commence from the day of the completion of their respective companies, and one will grant to each rank the customary appointments of the English troops.

5 – One will not take into our pay any officer of the major or minor staff until the two cavalry companies and three of infantry have formed. *[More restrictive than article 4 of the provisional capitulation].*

6 – It is intended that the complete companies will be paid as from 21 January. The surplus of the men destined to form others, except for those who left Holland with you, will only be paid when they have been passed in companies by the inspector.

7 – The officers or soldiers will have no right to make claims to the English government except for pay, bread and forage. These last two articles will commence to be issued to each officer from the day when they will be paid, but one cannot claim back food rations, nor forage according to the army regulations, when bread is not issued to the soldiers one and a half sols will be given to them as equivalent.

8 – It is accorded to each infantry company, for the maintenance and repair of the arms, the pay of three men per day, which in English is called contingent-men, and which is paid every six months. (Note: 3 Contingent men per company to be allowed for Reparation of Arms).

9 – According to our Regulations only effective men will be paid.

10 – Although I cannot think that you have claims to make relative to the levy money for the men who left Holland with you, and who have been received into the service of England, it will be accorded to you for each of them the sum of three and a half pounds sterling for the purpose that by this means they can be engaged into the service of HBM following the ordinary forms (Note: £3.10- to be allowed per Man) meanwhile if at such time that there is an increase of levy money accorded for these men, the three and half pounds mentioned above will be considered as an advance payment already received and will be counted with the increase.

11 – The English service does not admit the distinction of colonel proprietor so that all the powers and prerogatives which are assumed ought to be attached to this distinction are without weight. The authority and powers of a colonel in the English service being in every possible case sufficient with regards discipline and subordination.

12 – No soldier can leave without the consent of the commander in chief, or of the inspector general. This is indispensable according to the rules of the English service.

13 – The officers and soldiers will take the oath of fidelity and will be subject to all the orders and disciplinary rules of His Britannic Majesty.

(Note: Intended that we would never be employed against the legitimate heirs of the House of Bourbon nor against the House of Orange our Benefactor (signed) Le Col Cte Etienne de Damas and below, was written, as agreed (signed) C Nesbitt Insp General)

14 – Each officer like each soldier ought to receive without any deduction the pay which he is accorded by the Rules of the Army.

You cannot have a company in ownership, nor in any case that it can be appropriated by you nor advantage you when the rules and customs of the army do not permit it: by this one does not intend meanwhile to prevent that by contributions or other honourable means, one seeks to assist disbanded officers, on the contrary every assistance that they will receive until they are placed will give consideration and credit to the Regiment which will have granted it to them.

15 – In case of death or vacancies, the King, or his general in chief, will name appointments.

16 – The Corps will regard itself as engaged in the Service of His B M without time limit being at the wish of the said Majesty to retain it in his service after the war if he judges it appropriate. As also to employ them [sic] where he will judge proper for the Good of his service; but if His Majesty wants in some time to reform the said corps, he engages himself to forewarn it of this two months in advance during which they will continue to receive the normal pay, and when it will be reformed, the NCOs and soldiers, will receive two months' pay, and the officers that of six to retire to their homes.

17 – One has not spoken of clothing, armament, equipment and maintenance of your soldiers, because one works at this moment to make a general arrangement for all the corps.

It is intended that that will only involve those of cavalry that are in the Pay of England for two years and those of infantry that are in it for one year; to begin from the moment of their formation.

As for the Regiments de Damas and Béon this article is applicable to the men who came out of Holland with their respective commander.

18 – The formation of each arm will be as it is to be found in the margin.

Cavalry corps composed of two companies each company will be composed of		Infantry corps composed of six companies each company composed of	
Captains	1	Captain	1
Lieutenants	2	Lieutenants	2
Cornet	1	Ensign	1
Quarter Master	1	–	
Sergeants	4	Sergeants	4
Corporals	6	Corporals	6
Trumpeter	1	Drummer	1
Privates	100	Privates	100
Total of a comp.	111	Total of a comp.	111
When two companies will be complete in men the staff will be granted, namely		When a staff will be accorded, there will be	
Colonel	1	Lieutenant Colonel	1
Major	1	Major	1
Adjutant	1	Adjutant	1
Surgeon Major	1	Surgeon	1
Assistant Surgeon	1	Chaplain	1

	Sergeant-Major	1
	Quarter-Mr-Sergeant	1
	Although the third company is not complete as the infantry has to embark it will be accorded	
	A Major or Lieut. Colonel with the appointments of Major	1
	Adjutant	1
	Assistant Surgeon	1
	Sergeant-Major	1
	Quarter-Mr-Sergeant	1

19 – The sick and wounded will be taken care of as the troops of His Majesty and one will take care of the crippled.

20 – As for regards the recruitment of the two companies already formed, or the raising of the four to be formed, twelve pounds, or gold louis, will be paid to you for each NCO or soldier clothed, armed, equipped etc. after having been approved by a Commissioner; it is understood that the companies to be formed will be passed in Companies as it is stated in the present Capitulation.

21 – It will be accorded to you the subsistence of a month paid in advance for each company to be formed, this is to say when your company, for example your third, will be approved, you will receive again the pay for 30 days of another; and thus in succession until all are raised.

22 – As to the replacement recruits, you will be granted to provide for all the charges, being those in relation to subsistence, forage, or to all other expenses, six weeks of subsistence for each man who will be raised and sent to the places that will be indicated to you from time to time, and which will always be at the option of the commander in chief or Inspector general. These replacement recruits cannot be sent to the depot in a smaller number than twenty and to arrive there from the 20th to the end of each month. Directly they will have arrived there, and passed, they will be considered as forming part of the Regiment.

23 – You should furnish your corps everything which will be necessary for it to campaign; except tents and camping utensils.

24 – It is expressly forbidden for you to engage men who are deserters either from your corps or from any other in the Pay of Great Britain, and in case of contravention, I reserve myself as well as my assistants the power to act as the case requires.

Signed by C Nesbitt, as Inspector General, and Damas, dated Celle 2 April 1795. It is followed by the following note:

You will know that the Regulations of the English Army, of which you make part, decide that any man who received pay during 48 hours is recognised as a soldier as if he had signed the more formal engagement.

Capitulation accorded to Comte Etienne de Damas for the levy of six Dutch companies, dated 22 June 1795

Art 1 – It will be formed of Six Companies of 150 men each, including the Sergeants, Corporals & Drummers coming from Holland.

Art 2 – Each Company will be composed of a first Sergeant; four other Sergeants; eight corporals, one hundred and thirty-five sentries [sic] and two Drummers.

Art 3 – The Recruits will be paid on the basis of £15 each for any costs whatever even the subsistence, until when the men have been passed as Recruits and approved by an Inspector appointed to the Effect.

Art 4 – For £19 the recruits will be engaged for four years in the service of HBM and to be employed anywhere it is the wish of HM.

They will be clothed, armed and equipped as follows; a coat, waistcoat and breeches of cloth; a pair of gaiters; a hat; a collar; a cockade; a musket with its bayonet; a haversack supplied the day of the Review with a pair of shoes which are new and fit the feet; a new shirt, not comprising that on the Body; a pair of stockings; two handkerchiefs; a comb; a bag of powder; a shoe-brush; a pouch and its shoulder belt.

Art 5 – The Recruits thus clothed, armed and equipped will be passed in review, received, sworn [?] and paid by the number of fifty, from this moment they will no longer be at the expense of the recruiter. Their subsistence, and losses and replacement of men, will be at the expense of the British government.

Art 6 – The day when the first third of a Company will have been passed in review, a lieutenant will be attached to it. A second lieutenant will be attached at the second third, and a captain with an ensign when the Company will be formed. The Officers will be paid in the progression above and at the same periods.

Art 7 – When there are three companies thus formed, there will be attached to them a staff composed of a Major, an Adjutant, a Sergeant-Major, a Quarter-Master Sergeant and an assistant Surgeon. An Officer of one of the three Companies will commence to have the title and receive the salary assigned to the Paymaster of Foreign Infantry.

Art 8 – When there are five Companies formed, there will be added to the staff mentioned above, Lieutenant Colonel, a Quarter-master, a Surgeon Major and a Chaplain.

Art 9 – The Officers, NCOs and soldiers will enjoy the appointments, pay, treatment and advantages which are enjoyed by the foreign Corps in the pay of His Britannic Majesty.

Art 10 – In case of disbandment, the corps will be forewarned two months in advance, during which it will continue to be paid, and it will receive subsequently, namely the Officers six months of their salaries, and the NCOs and Soldiers two months of their pay in gratuity.

Art 11 – The levy proposed by the present Capitulation will be part of the Infantry of the Légion de Damas will present the subjects of the Royal appointment for the posts of Officers which can only be occupied by Officers coming from the service of Holland.

Letter dated Stade 2 August 1795

Damas requests Nesbitt's approval for him to move his depot for the raising of the 'Dutch Battalion' from Stade to Osnabrück and proposes the following changes to the capitulation of 22 June:

The Circumstances existing that the assembly of the Battalion being made in the Principality of Osnabrück instead of taking place in the town of Stade, each man will only be paid thirteen pounds sterling instead of fifteen as it was stated by article 3 of the Capitulation.

The rest of the Capitulation will have its full and entire effect.

There will be added to the six companies of fusiliers, a Company of Chasseurs and one of Artillery.

Each of these Companies will be of the same strength and paid on the same basis as the Company of Chasseurs and that of Artillery accorded to Mr Crookceus.

[in the capitulation with Crookceus [sic] dated Stade 23 July 1795]

Artillery Company		Chasseur Company	
Captain	1	Captain	1
1st Lieutenant	2	1st Lieutenant	2
2nd Lieutenant	2	2nd Lieutenant	2
Sergeants	6	Sergeants	6
Corporals	6	Corporals	8
Bombardiers	6	Hornists	2
Drummer	1	Chasseurs	134
Gunners	102		
Horse grooms	50		
Total	176	Total	155

Damas asks to be given £500 on account, payable at Bremen, for the levy of the battalion as well as the continuing recruitment of his cavalry. All changes, and the last request, are shown as agreed by Nesbitt.

Letter of service dated Stade 8 October 1795

Damas refers to Article 5 of the capitulation of 2 April:

The disaster of Quiberon renders this Article inoperable on my part for the Infantry.

As the Cavalry is on the point to embark, I venture to supply you to accord me a chaplain to fix his salary and to determine the period which you judge to be the point from which this it would be shown on the abstracts.

Nesbitt agrees stating that the chaplain should be paid as assistant surgeon, dated from 24 August 1795.

Appendix IV

Uniforms: 1793–1798

If there is no illustration, or more precisely no complete representation, of a *jager*, or *chasseur*, and of a *musquettier*, or *fusilier*, of the Légion de Damas between 1793 and 1795, there are on the other hand sources of information available to reconstruct what they looked like. The principal source consists of two colour plates each depicting two silhouettes of uniforms, one for Béon and another for Damas. These plates are part of a collection in the Dutch military archives, the *Jassenboekje* (Military Coats Book) which depicts uniforms of the forces of the United Provinces. These drawings were apparently owned, and may even have been produced, by Duncan Macalester Loup, a former officer of the Scots Brigade, who was a *solliciteur-militair*, or agent, between 1785 and 1795. This can explain both the great accuracy in the representation of the cut of the uniforms, and the realisation of uniforms that appeared between the summer of 1793 and the following spring.[1]

The Légion de Béon having been the first raised and serving as the model for that of Damas, this major source can be compared with other primary evidence. Thanks to a picture 'taken from life' at Brugge by the Belgian painter Gregorius, dating from the summer of 1793, doubtless June or July, it is shown that the first Béon infantry companies wore a sky blue or '*bleu céleste*' uniform, the colour of the last royal legions, taken from the German regiments in the French monarchy's service. The cut was that of the 1786 model with orange collars, round cuffs and lapels, the distinctive colour of the province of Holland that paid the legion, seven white metal buttons, a tricorn hat of black felt and an orange national cockade, white waistcoat and coat lining. Serving as light infantrymen, the soldiers of Béon wore 'Hungarian' style breeches with half-gaiters and they were 'lightly armed' which signifies that they would have been armed with a shorter and lighter musket than that of the line fusiliers and that they wore black leather equipment.

Gregorius's illustration fully confirms the plate from the *Jassenboekje* dedicated to the Légion de Béon and so the validity of that for Damas representing the two uniforms of the *fusiliers* and *chasseurs*. That of the *fusiliers* was distinguished by three chevron-shaped, or herringbone, buttonholes placed on the pointed cuff, that was, at the time of the Revolution, only seen on the coats of the Brigade Irlandaise as well as that of the light troops of Hesse-Darmstadt. It appears that there may have been three uniforms for the fusiliers and that the

1 Joep van Hoof *Military Uniforms in the Netherlands, 1752–1800: The Jassenboekje (The Military Coats Book) and the drawings of uniforms by Duncan Macalester Loup* (The Hague and Vienna: Netherlands Institute of Military History, 2011), pp.6–7, 24–26.

first, that of the French 'bourgeoise' company, was identical but with round cuffs of the 1786 Model, like Béon. The *Jassenboekje* plate would then be the uniform of the Irish companies in Damas, more precisely the two Berwick companies, unless they were reserved for only the 'native Irishmen' serving as cadets or volunteers in them. However, it is also possible that in giving this new unit this distinction, then only seen among Hessian troops, it was hoped that the men would be taken for German troops in the service of the United Provinces. It was very difficult to discern the third: if the ordinary fusiliers had buttonholes of white thread, those of the officers were silver, like those of the gentlemen who served as fusiliers while waiting for a vacant place in the chasseur companies which were limited to 200. It is conceivable that this measure was extended to the Irish officers and cadets present in the ranks of O'Moore and McDermott's fusilier companies.

All the staff officers and *capitaines* were mounted and the chasseur subalterns were also armed with carbines. Gorgets were not worn but all bore the colours of the House of Orange, the cockade like the soldiers as well as, in the fusiliers, the orange sash of command knotted to the left, the chasseur officers not wearing it. The officers' grade was indicated by silver epaulettes, as in France, except when the officers were not under arms, the grade was then denoted by aiguillettes, worn on the right and different according to the rank.

As for the cavalry of the Légion de Damas, there is no 'historic' description of their first uniform, for lack of detail of the capitulation, illustration of the time or even a contemporary description; although the uniform appeared in February 1794 it does not figure in the *Jassenboekje*. It can however be reconstructed by deduction. Indeed, it is attested by different documents of 1794 and 1795 that, although the Damas cavalry had been initially raised as chasseurs à cheval, being formed of noble volunteers or chasseurs, they were designated as hussars. The first uniform was represented by the French illustrator JOB (Jacques Onfroy de Bréville) in Issue n°15 of the *Tenues des troupes de France* (January 1903) and the accompanying text states that he had as his source 'a considerable series of naïve pictures of the time.' This same uniform was represented three years later in Plate n°84 of Volume V of Lienhart and Humbert's *Les Uniformes de l'armée française – Recueil d'ordonnances 1690–1894* (Leipzig, 1897–1906), one of the principal reference works of uniformology at the time.

Two contemporary illustrations do, however, allow the reconstruction of the successive uniforms worn between 1794 and 1796 by the Damas Hussars in Dutch then British service. They appear in the Berlin Album in the Military Collection at the Brown University Library (Rhode Island, USA) in which at least 30 of the plates illustrate the émigré troops gathered in Hanover, and in particular around Stade, in 1795.[2] It is clear, by two tracings of the hussar plates held in the Archives of the Musée Condé (Château de Chantilly, France), that the Vicomte Grouvel, author of *Corps de Troupe de l'émigration*, knew of the Album before it was acquired by what was to become the Brown Collection in 1962, as Volume I (Service of Great Britain and the Netherlands) of his work was published a year earlier.[3] The two

2 The authors thank Brown University in the person of Peter Harington, curator of this precious collection. Thanks to him, they have been able to obtain the illustration which they lacked to make this identification. A part of these plates was photographed by René Chartrand, in 1999, then reproduced in *Emigré & Foreign Troops in British Service (1) 1793–1802*.

3 At the time of the drafting of Vol.IV of his famous work dedicated to the uniforms of the British Army, in 1966, Cecil C.P. Lawson only had to hand a black and white sketch of the first plate, sent by

pictures are almost identical but in fact show marginal differences illustrating the evolution of the uniform of the Damas Hussars during their stay in Germany and of their passage into British service.

The Berlin Album also provides a representation of the new uniform adopted in Germany before the expedition to Brittany, which is of British style for the *fusiliers* and 'émigré' for the *chasseurs*, close to that the *chasseurs* of the Légion de Béon adopted after the massacre at 's Hertegonbosch (October 1794) and shared by several foreign corps in British service, like Löwenstein's Chasseurs. The infantry wore the black cockade although some modern sources suggest it was replaced by a white one prior to landing at Quiberon, none of the memoirs of the Damas Regiment, or indeed other units in the Second Division, describe this when it is inconceivable that the adoption of such a royalist symbol would have passed without mention.

The hussars wore four different versions of uniform during their short existence:

1st uniform – in the service of the United Provinces (1794–1795): we know that the colonel commanding a legion was responsible for the cut and colour of the uniform that he proposed, but that he was obliged to adapt to the details of uniform of his employer for the reason of identification in combat. Raised at Maastricht, when the Austrians occupied Limburg, the Damas Hussars adopted the uniform of the Austrians hussars or, more specifically, of the émigré hussars in Austrian service, Légions de Carneville and Bourbon, of the distinctive sky-blue colour like the legion's infantry, while the two units of Dutch hussars wore a Prussian style uniform. The rank distinctions may have followed this style as well but it is certain that the corps bore the distinctive insignia of the Stadholder's troops: sabretache with the arms of the United Provinces and the orange cockade for all, the officers wearing the orange sash of command and sword knots of a mix of silver and orange. Of particular note is a detail which was shared by only four émigré hussar units in the allied army: the braided cords of two colours. Originally a characteristic of the Austrian hussars alone (in yellow and black), this cord was adopted by the Légion de Carneville, which had served in the 1792 campaign in the Armée de Bourbon, when it passed in 1793 to the Austrian service as the *Freikorps Carneville* and it was soon shared by the Légion de Bourbon.[4] This detail was adopted a few months later, and almost simultaneously, by the Damas Hussars in Dutch pay (white and black cord), and the Choiseul Hussars (yellow and red cords) in the service of Britain. The latter corps wore a very slightly different model of shako, that of Damas is of the Austrian style as is shown by the woollen lace at the top of the headgear, the type of white and black cockade in the centre and the cord and raquettes worn on the right side. In contrast, the type of black and white plume is completely Dutch in style.

The horse furniture of the Damas Hussars would have been similar to that of the Béon Hussars, reconstructed from contemporary testimonies and the Berlin Album, which is to say a cloth cover of sky blue bordered with black wolf teeth with the interior edged in white,

Vicomte Grouvel, and also mentioned JOB's picture as the only other source.

4 Brons, *Journal d'émigration*, p.192.

completed by a sky-blue portmanteau edged with white and a half-shabracque of black or white sheepskin for the troops.[5]

2nd uniform – in British service (March–April 1795): this is the same uniform as before and is represented in the first picture from the Berlin Album, doubtless made at Stade or the Hoya camp, the only occasion in which all the units depicted were together. It is identical to JOB's illustration, except for one detail: the colour of the pelisse was not chestnut but cinder grey. Article 17 of the definitive capitulation of 2 April 1795 (see Appendix III) makes it clear that the men retained the uniform they had worn in Dutch service until there was a 'general arrangement for all the corps …' In addition, we know thanks to the testimony of Comte de Béon that the two legions retained the Stadhouder's colours until 23 April. It may be supposed that, for the sake economy and standardisation, they adopted a simple sheepskin shabracque, without wolf teeth edging, also depicted for the two Rohan Hussar Regiments.

3rd uniform (May 1795–January or February 1796): the new uniform was only distinguished from the preceding one by details which appear in the second plate from the Berlin Album dedicated to the Damas Hussars:

- plume entirely white.
- metallic pieces of the horse's harness in brass and not in steel.
- same for the sabre sheath and guard which is of brass and no longer of steel.
- Hungarian knots at the top of the cuffs and bastion, rather than knot, shaped lace on the thighs.

It can be assumed that by this period the unit used British marks of rank to go with the adoption of ranks of the same nation. The sabretaches used by the Damas hussars are not shown in the relevant Album plates but those of the Salm and Hompesch Hussars, regiments raised directly as British troops, as well as the First Rohan Hussars, like Damas an émigré unit, are all shown as bearing the royal cypher of King George III surmounted by a crown.

Thanks to the testimony of Cézac de Belcayre who joined the Damas Hussars in mid-March 1796, we know the precise description of the uniform worn between March 1795 and March 1796, before the corps joined the Armée de Condé on a new formation, indeed, his squadron 'composed of the élite nobles, were distinguished from the others by a uniform which, although the same, had on the chest a frame of silver lace the width of two fingers and another of the same size at the top of the shako; the flanquers had this lace in wool. The colour of the dolman was sky blue and the pelisse the colour of cinder with black fur.'[6]

Charles Hamilton Smith (1776–1859), celebrated illustrator who created *Costume of the Army of the British Empire according to the Last Regulations*, had also produced a series of plates representing the uniforms of the émigré corps in British service between 1794 and

5 Hughes de Bazouges 'L'uniforme des Hussards de Béon (1793–1795)' *Le Carnet de La Sabretache n°207*, June 2016, pp.26–31 and *n°208*, September 2016, pp.27–30.

6 Cézac de Belcayre, *Dix ans d'émigration (1791–1801)*, p.193.

1802.[7] That of the 'Emigrant Hussar Regiment of Damas – 1794' for this period shows the hussar with a sabretache with George III's cypher and the letters HOD (Hussars of Damas) in the centre of the portmanteau. Even if Hamilton Smith had really seen the Damas Hussars during his stay in Hanover in 1795, we now know that this illustration was produced in the 1820s from official documents.[8] Indeed, the title is an error as this uniform conforms to that worn by the émigré corps between the summer of 1795 and February 1796.

4th uniform – Armée de Condé (March 1796-April 1798): the uniform worn in the Armée de Condé, last survivor of the royal army, was of the 1786 model and thus practically the same, with the exception of the shako of the émigré hussar type, with the royal distinctive insignia. This is confirmed by the different testimonies gathered by the Vicomte Grouvel, in particular descriptions from 1796 by *maréchal de camp* the Comte d'Eon de Cély, inspector general of troops in the Armée de Condé, or the description of a painting which has now disappeared representing the Comte Roger de Damas dressed as colonel of his legion's hussars, as well as a miniature of a subaltern of the Mirabeau/Damas hussars, in 1796 or 1797, which came up for sale about 10 years ago.

Although we have not found any formal evidence, we consider the horse furniture was a saddle cloth of the regiment's distinctive colour, like the other light cavalry units of the army, the hussars of the vanguard and light cavalry brigade, with a white fleur de lys in the corners. The sabretache was also decorated with a large fleur de lys in the centre although, according to Grouvel, those of the officers would have borne the royal coat of arms of France. The troopers and gentlemen had retained the previous brassard, with one or three black fleur de lys, but that of the officers had edging and three embroidered fleur de lys in gold.

7 This series is conserved in the collection of engravings in the Bibliothèque nationale de France, Paris.

8 After having served in the 1794 campaign in the United Provinces as a volunteer in the 8th Light Dragoons, he was appointed cornet in the Hompesch Hussars transferred in December 1795 to the Isle of Wight before embarking in March 1796 for the West Indies.

Bibliography

Archives

France

Archives de la guerre (AG) (now held in SHD)
Archives nationales (AN)
Archives du Musée Condé, Château de Chantilly (AMC)
Service historique de la Défense (formerly Service historique de l'Armée de Terre) (SHD)

The Netherlands

Koninklijk Huisarchief, courtesy of HM the King (Royal Archives) (KHN)
National Archief, The Hague (NAN)
Stichting Historische Maastricht, courtesy of Jos Notermans (SHM)
Het Utrechts Archief, Staten van Utrecht, Utrecht (HUA)

Russia

State Archive of the Russian Federation, Moscow (GARF)

United Kingdom

British Library, London (BL)
The National Archives, Kew (TNA)
Norfolk Record Office (NRO)
Royal Archives, Windsor, De Budé Papers, courtesy of HM the Queen (RAW)

Venezuela

Archivo del General Miranda, Volume V published Caracas: 1931 (MIRANDA)

Contemporary Newspapers and Journals

Bayreuther Zeitung
Bulletin des Amis de la vérité (Volume I 1793)
La Gazette de France
La Gazette de Leyde or *Nouvelles extraordinaires de divers endroits*
La Gazette des Gazettes
La Gazette des Pays-Bas
La Gazette nationale or *Le Moniteur universel*
Hampshire Chronicle
Journal des débats et des décrets
Journal politique de Bruxelles

Journal général de la guerre
London Gazette
Le Mercure de France
Mercure Français Historique, Politique et Littéraire
Nieuwe Nederlandsche Jaarboeken, of Vervolg der Merkwaardigste Geschiendenissen, die voorgevallen zyn in de Vereenigde Provinicien, de Generaliteits Landen, en de The Times,
Ommelander Courant
The Times
Volkplantingen van den Staat (Leyden and Amsterdam 1793)

Contemporary Registers

Britain – *A List of the Officers of the Army and Marines, with an Index, a Succession of Colonels; A List of the Officers of the Army and Marines on Half-Pay, also with an Index* ('The Army List') (annual editions).
France – *Etat Militaire de France* (annual editions 1753–1793).
United Provinces – *Naamregister der Heeren militaire Officieren, den Capitein generaal, de Generaals, Lieutenant-Generaals, Generaals-Major, Colonels, Lieutenant-Colonels, Majors, Capiteins, Lieutenants en Vaandrigs... Vermeerded mit eene Lyste der Chefs van alle de Regimenten, zo Cavallery, als Infantery, zedert den Jaare 1713. Mart 1794* (The Hague: 1794).

Published works

Abrantès, Laure Junot d', *Mémoires de Madame la duchesse d'Abrantès, ou Souvenirs historiques sur Napoléon, la Révolution, le Directoire, le Consulat, l'Empire et la Restauration* (Paris: Mame-Delaunay, 1833).
Arcq, Alain, *Fleurus, 26 juin 1794* (Plougastel: Historic'One, 2007).
Anon., *A concise narrative of all the actions in which the British forces were engaged during the present war on the Continent of Europe* (Manchester: 1797).
Anon., Decreeten *van de Provisioneele Repræsentaten van het volk van Holland, 26 January tot 28 February 1795* (Den Haag: Unknown Publisher,1799).
Anon., *Journal kept in the British Army, from the landing of the troops under the command of Earl Moira, at Ostend, in June 1794, to their return to England the following year* (Liverpool: Unknown Publisher, 1796).
Anon., *Journée d'Oberkamlach, ou Parallèle du récit de cette Affaire par un Officier Général de l'Armée de Condé, avec celui qui en avait été fait par les Rédacteurs des Victoires, Conquêtes, etc. des Français* (Paris: Le Normant, 1818).
Anon., MAASGOUW (Local history magazine, Maastricht) Volume V, May 1907.
Anon., Notice *Historique sur La Maison de Cardevac d'Havrincourt avec ses alliances et sur la Terre d'Havrincourt* (Cambrai: J. Renaut, 1885).
Atkinson, C.T., 'Foreign regiments in the British Army 1793–1802', *Journal of the Society for Army Historical Research*, Part II Vol. XXII No.85 (Spring 1943) pp.2–14 and Part III Vol. XXII No.86 (Summer 1943) pp.45–52.
Auzon de Boisminart, Willem Pieter d', *Gedenkschriften* (Gravenhage and Amsterdam: De Gebroeders van Cleef, 1841).
Aymot, Thomas, *Speeches in Parliament, of the Right Honourable William Windham; to which is prefixed, some account of his life* (London: Longman, Hurst, Rees, Orme and Brown, 1812).
Barberey, Maurice de, *Dix années d'émigration – Souvenirs et correspondance du comte de Neuilly* (Paris: Charles Douniol, 1865).
Barrière, François, *Mémoires du Marquis de Bouillé, avec une notice historique sur sa vie, des notes et des éclaircissements historiques* (Paris: Librairie Firmin Didot Frères, Fils et cie., 1859).
Barruel, *Abbé* Auguste de, *Mémoires pour servir à l'Histoire du Jacobinisme* (London: Chez Ph. Le Boussonier & Co, 1798).
Bas, François de, *Prins Frederik der Nederlanden en Zijn Tijd* (Schiedam: H.A.M. Roelants, 1887).
Bazouges, Hughes de, 'Des hussards tolpaches de Rohan aux Chasseurs de Rohan-Brunswick' *Carnet de La Sabretache n°198*, March 2014, pp.40-44, and *n°199*, June 2014, pp.31-36.

Bazouges, Hughes de, 'L'uniforme des Hussards de Béon (1793–1795)' *Le Carnet de La Sabretache n°207*, June 2016, pp.26–31, and *n°208*, September 2016, pp.27–30.
Beauchet-Filleau, H, *Tableau des émigrés du Poitou aux armées des Princes et de Condé* (Poitiers: Charles Pichot, 1845).
Bennes, Louise Françoise de Houssay de, *A narrative of the sufferings of Louise Françoise de Houssay, de Bennes, who served in the army as a volunteer, from 1792 to July 21, 1795, when she was made a prisoner at Quiberon* (London: Unknown Publisher, 1796).
Berthier de Grandry, Claude, *Récit Sommaire de la Déplorable Affaire de Quiberon* (Nantes: Vincent Forest, 1861).
Biarda, Lileman Dothias, *Neueste Ostfriesische Geschichte, 1ère Partie (1786–1806)* (Leer: Unknown Publisher, 1817).
Bittard des Portes, René, *Histoire de l'armée de Condé* (Paris: E. Dentu, 1896).
Bittard des Portes, René, *Les émigrés à la cocarde noire, en Angleterre, dans les provinces belges, en Hollande et à Quiberon* (Paris: E. Paul, 1908).
Bodinier, Gilbert, *Les gardes du corps de Louis XVI* (Versailles: Service historique de l'armée de Terre, 2005).
Bonnart, Médard, *Histoire de Médard Bonnart* (Epernay: Mme V. Fiévet, 1838).
Bouillé, Louis-Joseph-Amour Marquis de, *Souvenirs et fragments pour servir aux mémoires de ma vie et de mon temps* (Paris: Société d'histoire contemporaine, 1908).
Boulay de La Meurthe, Comte Alfred, *Correspondance du duc d'Enghien (1801–1804) et documents sur son enlèvement et sa mort* (Paris: Librairie Alphonse Picard, 1913).
Bricard, Alfred and Jules, *Journal du canonnier Bricard (1792–1802)* (Paris: Librairie Delagrave, 1891).
Broc, Hervé Vicomte de, *Dix ans de la vie d'une femme pendant l'émigration Adélaïde de Kerjean Marquise de Falaiseau* (Paris: Librairie Plon, 1893).
Brons, Jean-Antoine de, *Journal d'émigration* (Saint-Quentin-de-Baron: Chez Entre-deux-mers, 2014).
Broster, D.K., 'The Black Cockade' *The Cornhill Magazine* Volume XVIII, May 1910, pp.716–732.
Brown, Robert, *Corporal Brown's Campaigns in the Low Countries: Recollections of a Coldstream Guard in the Early Campaigns Against Revolutionary France 1793–1795* (Milton Keynes: Leonaur, 2008, first published 1795).
Brown, Steve, *The Duke of York's Flanders Campaign Fighting the French Revolution 1793–1795* (Barnsley: Frontline Books, 2018).
Brumauld de Beauregard, Jean, *Mémoires de Monseigneur J. Brumauld de Beauregard, évêque d'Orléans, précédés de sa vie, écrite sur des notes et des documents authentiques* (Poitiers: Saurin frères, 1842).
Buchez, Philippe-Joseph-Benjamin and Roux, P.-C., *Histoire parlementaire de la Révolution française ou Journal des Assemblées nationales depuis 1789 jusqu'en 1815*, Volume XXVII (Paris: Paulin Librairie, 1836).
Cacqueray de Valménier, Charles Georges, *Mémoires inédits – Tome II « L'émigration » 1791–1794* (Cholet: Editions Pays & Terroirs, 2006).
Capellen de Maarsch, Robert-Gaspard de, *Mémoires et discours politiques sur la république batave* (Paris: Lavillette, 1793).
Castres, Comte de (Charles de La Croix de Castries), *Relation d'un voyage sur le bord septentrional de la mer d'Azof et en Crimée, dans la vue d'y établir une colonie d'émigrés* (Paris: A.J. Killian, 1826).
Cazotte, Jacques-Scevola, *Témoignage d'un royaliste* (Paris: Librairie d'Adrien Le Clere et Cie, 1839).
Cécille, Lucien, Charlet, Philippe, and Pattyn, Jean-Jacques, *Mont-Saint-Jean 6–7 juillet 1794* (Plougastel: Historic'One, 2015).
Cézac de Belcayre, Charles-François de, *Dix ans d'émigration (1791–1801), Souvenirs de François de Cézac, Hussard de Bercheny, Volontaire à l'Armée de Condé* (Paris: A. de Maricourt, Emile Paul, 1909).
Charlet, Philippe, '1794 Les Français Victorieux à Waterloo' *Traditions: Guerriers et Militaires de l'Époque Moderne* (February 2018), pp.26–39.
Chartrand, René, and Courcelle, Patrice, *Emigré and Foreign Troops in British service (I) 1793–1802* (Botley: Osprey Publishing, 1999).
Chateaubriand, François-René de, *Mémoires d'outre-tombe* (Paris: Eugène et Victor Penaud Frères, 1849).
Choiseul, Duc de, *Histoire et procès des naufragés de Calais* (Paris: Bossange Frères, 1824).
Chuquet, Arthur, *Lettres de 1793, première série* (Paris: Librairie Honoré Champion Editeur, 1911).
Chuquet, Arthur, *Dumouriez* (Paris: Hachette, 1914).
Closmadeuc, G. Thomas de, *Quiberon 1795 Émigrés et Chouans Commissions Militaires: Interrogatoires et Jugements* (Paris: Société d'éditions littéraires, 1899).
Contades, Comte Gérard de, *Émigrés et Chouans* (Paris: Perrin et cie, 1895).
Contades, Comte Gérard de, *Coblenz et Quiberon: Souvenirs du Comte de Contades* (Koblenz: E. Dentu, 1885).
Contades, Comte Gérard de, *Notice sur la Commune de Lonlay-le-Tesson* (Paris: H Champion, 1881).

Corbehem, Bernard de, *Dix ans de ma vie ou Histoire de mon émigration* (Paris: A. Phian Delaforest, 1827).

Corbett, Julian S. (ed.), *Private Papers of George, Second Earl Spencer, First Lord of the Admiralty 1794–1801* (London: Navy Records Society, 1913).

Courcelles, Jean-Baptiste Pierre Chevalier de, *Histoire généalogique et héraldique des pairs de France, des Grands Dignitaires de la couronne, et des principales familles nobles du royaume, précédée de la généalogie de la Maison de France* (Paris: Arthus Bertrand, 1822).

Courcelles, Jean-Baptiste Pierre Chevalier de, *L'art de vérifier les dates depuis 1770 jusqu'à nos jours* (Paris: Arthus Bertrand, 1821).

Courcelles, Jean-Baptiste Pierre Chevalier de, *Dictionnaire historique et biographique des généraux français* (Paris: Arthus Bertrand, 1821).

Crossard, Jean-Baptiste-Louis Baron de, *Mémoires militaires et historiques pour servir à l'histoire de la guerre depuis 1792 jusqu'en 1815 inclusivement* (Paris: Chez Migneret, 1829).

Daly, D.D., 'Brigadier-General Sir Charles MacCarthy, KT. 1764–1824' *Journal of the Society for Army Historical Research* Volume X No.39b (July 1931), pp.143-149.

Damas, Ange-Hyacinthe de, *Mémoires du Baron de Damas* (Paris: Plon-Nourrit et cie, 1922–1923).

Daudet, Ernest, *Histoire de l'Émigration pendant la Révolution Française* (Paris: Hachette, 1905).

Davidson, Major H, *History and services of the 78th Highlanders, Ross-shire Buffs, 1793–1881* (Edinburgh and London: W & A K Johnston, 1901).

Debrett, John (ed.), *A Collection of State Papers relative to the War against France now carrying on by Great Britain and the several other European Powers* (London: J. Debrett, 1794–1797).

Demet, Paul, *'We are accustomed to do our duty': German Auxiliaries with the British Army 1793–95* (Warwick: Helion & Co, 2018).

Diesbach, Ghislain de and Grouvel, Vicomte Robert, *Histoire de l'émigration, 1789–1815* (Paris: Perrin, 1984).

D.P., Comte de (Laroche-Poncié), *Correspondance condéenne précédée d'une notice sur l'armée de Condé, de Lettres et Proclamations des princes étrangers pendant leur émigration et d'autres documents authentiques et importants* (Paris: Chez Dentu, 1850).

Dumas, Comte Christian, *Souvenirs du Lieutenant-général comte Mathieu Dumas, de 1770 à 1836* (Paris: Charles Gosselin, 1839).

Dumouriez, Général, *Correspondance avec Pache, ministre de la Guerre, sur la campagne de Belgique en 1792* (Paris: Chez Denné, 1793).

Dumouriez, Général, *Vie privée et politique du général Dumouriez, pour faire suite à ses Mémoires* (Hamburg and Leipzig: B.G. Hoffmann, 1794).

Dumouriez, Général, *La vie et les mémoires du général Dumouriez écrits par lui-même* (Paris: Librairie Historique, 1822).

Dupuis, Commandant Victor, *Les opérations militaires sur la Sambre en 1794* (Paris: R. Chapelot et cie, 1907).

Dupuis, Commandant Victor, *La campagne de 1793. L'Armée du Nord et des Ardennes. D'Hondschoote à Wattignies* (Paris: R. Chapelot et cie, 1909).

Ecquevilly, Armand François Hennequin, Marquis d', *Campagnes du corps sous les ordres de Son Altesse Sérénissime Mgr le Prince de Condé* (Paris: Unknown Publisher, 1818).

Ferguson, James, *Papers illustrating the history of the Scotch Brigade in the service of the United Netherlands 1572–1782* (Edinburgh: Scottish History Society, 1899).

Fieffe, Eugène, *Histoire des troupes étrangères au service de la France* (Paris: Dumaine, 1854).

Fortescue, The Honorable John W., *British Campaigns in Flanders 1690–1794* (London: Macmillan and Co, 1918).

Garland, John L, 'Genealogical details from the Grouvel Dossiers' *The Irish Genealogist* (Volume 6, N°6, November 1985), pp.771–778.

Gleig, G.R. (ed.), *The Hussar* (London: Henry Colburn, 1841).

Goethe, Johann Wolfgang von, *Campagne in Frankreich* (1822) translated as *Campagne de France* (1898) modern edition (Lausanne: La Guilde du Livre, 1968).

Gould, Robert W., *Mercenaries of the Napoleonic Wars* (Brighton: Tom Donovan Publishing, 1995).

Gourgaud, Gaspard, *Mémoires pour servir à l'Histoire de France sous Napoléon, écrits à Sainte-Hélène par les généraux qui ont partagé sa captivité et publiés sur les manuscrits entièrement corrigés de sa main* (Paris: F Didot, 1823).

Grazebrook, R. M., 'The Campaign in Flanders of 1793–1795: Journal of Lieutenant Charles Stewart, 28th Foot' *Journal of the Society for Army Historical Research (JSAHR)*, Spring, 1951, Vol. 29, No. 117 pp.2–17.

Green, Jorgen, *Jean Baptiste Xavier Carpentier de Colbaut. Un émigrant loyal et son combat contre la Révolution, 1792–1794* (Denmark: Editions Grifo, 2011).

Gros, Albrecht David Gabriel de, *Journal des principales opérations de la campagne de 1794 dans les Sept Provinces-unies et pays de la Généralité, principalement de ce qui s'est passé pendant le blocus et le bombardement de la ville de Grave jusqu'à sa reddition* (Unknown Publisher, 1795).

Grouvel, Vicomte Robert, *Les Corps de troupe de l'émigration* (Paris: La Sabretache, 1961–1965).

Habets, Joseph, 'De Fransche Emigranten te Maastricht' *Publications de la Société historique et archéologique dans le duché de Limbourg* (Volume XXVIII 1891), pp.133-228.

Harrington, Peter (ed.), *With the Guards in Flanders; The Diary of Captain Roger Morris 1793–1795* (Warwick: Helion & Co, 2018).

Haussonville, Paul Gabriel de, 'Souvenirs de l'émigration et de l'Empire' *Revue des Deux Mondes* (Volume XXV 1878), pp.91-123.

Hauterive, Ernest d', *Journal d'émigration du comte d'Espinchal* (Paris: Perrin, 1912).

Hoof, Joep van, *Military Uniforms in the Netherlands, 1752–1800: The Jassenboekje (The Military Coats Book) and the drawings of uniforms by Duncan Macalester Loup* (The Hague and Vienna: Netherlands Institute of Military History, 2011).

Huchet, Patrick, *1795 - Quiberon ou le destin de La France* (Rennes: Ouest-France, 1995).

Hugo, Abel, *Vie anecdotique de S.M. Charles X* (Paris: J.M. Maurice, 1824).

Hutt, Maurice, *Chouannerie and Counter-Revolution: Puisaye, the Princes and the British Government in the 1790s* (Cambridge: Cambridge University Press, 1983).

Jarry, Abbé Pierre-François-Théophile, *Discours sur la délivrance de la ville de Maestricht* (Maastricht: Unknown Publisher,1793).

'JOB' (Jacques Onfroy de Bréville), *Tenues des troupes de France* (Paris: Martin, 1900–1904).

Jomini, Antoine Baron de, *Histoire critique et militaire des Guerres de la Révolution, 1793–1797* (second edition Paris: Anselin et Pochard, 1816–1820).

Jouan, Louis, *La campagne de 1794–1795 dans les Pays-Bas, Tome I, La conquête de la Belgique (mai–juillet 1794)* (Paris: L. Fournier, 1915).

Juste, Théodore, *Histoire de la révolution belge de 1790* (Brussels: A. Jamar, 1846).

Kaulek, Jean and Tausserat-Radel, Alexandre, *Papiers de Barthélemy, ambassadeur de France en Suisse, 1792–1797, publiés sous les auspices de la Commission des Archives des Affaires étrangères, Tome V (septembre 1794--septembre 1795)* (Paris: F. Alcan, 1894).

Knight, Roger, *Britain Against Napoleon: The Organization of Victory 1793–1815* (London: Allen Lane, 2013).

La Chanonie, Charles de, *Mémoires politiques et militaires du général Tercier, (1770–1816)* (Paris: Plon, 1891).

Lafayette, Gilbert de, *Mémoires, correspondance et manuscrits du général Lafayette* (Paris & London: sa famille, 1837.

La Gournerie, Eugène de, *Les Débris de Quiberon : Souvenirs du Désastre de 1795* (Nantes: Catholique Libaros, 1875).

Lainé, P-Louis, *Archives généalogiques et historiques de la noblesse de France* (Paris: Lainé, 1829).

Lamothe-Langon, Etienne-Léon Baron de, *Mémoires de Louis XVIII* (Brussels: Louis Hauman et Cie, 1823–1833).

Landosle, Hyrvoix de, *Souvenirs du chevalier d'Hespel d'Hocron, volontaire à l'Armée de Condé (1794–1797), accompagnés d'une notice sur la famille d'Hespel, publiés et annotés* (Paris: Pierre Roger, 1927).

La Rochefoucauld, François, Duc de, *Souvenirs du 10 août et de l'Armée de Bourbon* (Paris: Calman-Lévy, 1929).

Lawson, Cecil C.P., *A History of the Uniforms of the British Army* (London: Norman Military Publications, 1966).

Las Cases, Emmanuel-Auguste-Dieudonné Las Cases Comte de, *Mémorial de Sainte-Hélène: Journal de la vie privée et des conversations de l'Empereur Napoléon, à Sainte-Hélène* (London: Henry Colburn & Co, 1823).

Lavergne, R, 'Les émigrés au siège de Maëstricht' *Revue des questions historiques* (Volume n°63, 1 January 1898), pp.516-531.

La Villegourio, Louis Marie de, *Ma Sortie de Quiberon* (Saint-Brieuc: Prud'homme, 1815).

Le Garrec, Eugène, *Les Vrais Martyrs de Quiberon (1795)* (Vannes: Lafolye et J. de Lamarzelle, 1935).

Legrand, Louis, *La révolution française en Hollande: la république batave* (Paris: Hachette, 1894).

Lenotre, Gaston (Théodore Gosselin), *Paris révolutionnaire. Vielles maisons, vieux papiers* (Paris : Perrin et cie, 1912).

Lejeune, Baron Louis-François, *Souvenirs d'un Officier de l'Empire* (Toulouse: Viguer, 1851).

Malmesbury, James Howard Harris, Earl of (ed.), *Diaries and Correspondence of James Harris, First Earl of Malmesbury* (London: Richard Bentley, 1844).

Marmottan, Paul, *Le Général Fromentin et l'Armée du Nord (1792–1794)* (Paris: Dubois, 1891).

Martinant de Préneuf, G Jacques, *Huit années d'émigration : souvenirs de l'abbé G.-J. Martinant de Préneuf 1792–1801* (Paris: Perrin et cie, 1908).

Mazas, Alexandre, *Histoire de l'ordre royal et militaire de Saint-Louis depuis son institution en 1693 jusqu'en 1830* (second edition Paris: Firmin Didot Frères, Fils et cie, 1860).

Meisel, August Heinrich, *Cours de style diplomatique* (Paris: J.P. Aillaud, 1826).

Mirabeau, Honoré-Gabriel, Comte de, *Aux Bataves sur le stathoudérat* (London: Unknown Publisher, 1788).

Moleville, Bertrand de, *Mémoires particuliers pour servir à la fin du règne de Louis XVI* (Paris: G.L. Michaud, 1821).

Montbron, Joseph de, *Récit de l'Evasion d'un Officier pris à Quiberon* (Paris: Unknown Publisher,1815).

Muret, Théodore, *Histoire de l'armée de Condé* (Paris: Dentu, 1844).

Nichols, Alistair, *Wellington's Mongrel Regiment: A History of the Chasseurs Britanniques Regiment, 1801–1814* (Staplehurst: Spellmount, 2005).

O'Connell, Mrs Morgan John, *The last Colonel of the Irish Brigade Count O'Connell and Old Irish Life at Home and Abroad 1745–1833* (London: Kegan Paul, Trench, Trübner & Co, 1892).

Orléans, Louis-Philippe d', *Mémoires (1789–1793)* (Paris: Plon, 1973).

Pancoucke, C.L.F. (ed.), *Victoires, conquêtes, désastres, revers et guerres civiles des Français, de 1792 à 1815* (Paris: C.L.F. Panckoucke, 1817–1821).

Parra-Pérez, Caraciollo, *Miranda et la Révolution française* (Paris: Pierre Roger, 1925).

Peltier, Jean-Gabriel, *Dernier tableau de Paris, ou Récit historique de la Révolution du 10 août 1792, des Causes qui l'ont produite, des Événements qui l'ont précédée, et des Crimes qui l'ont suivie* (London: Chez l'Auteur, Hôtel de la Sablonière, Leicester-fields, 1793–1794).

Peltier, Jean-Gabriel, *Histoire de la Restauration de la Monarchie française ou La Campagne de 1793. Publiée en forme de correspondance sur les affaires du tems, et servant de suite à l'Histoire du 10 Août et du 2 Septembre 1792* (London: Unknown Publisher, 1793).

Perry de Nieüil, Marquise de, *Mémoires du marquis de Toustain (1790–1823)* (Paris: Plon, 1933).

Piérart, Zéphyr-Joseph, *La Grande épopée de l'An II* (Paris: Revue Spiritualiste, 1864).

Pinguad, Léonce, *L'invasion austro-prussienne (1792–1794) Documents publiés pour la Société d'histoire contemporaine* (Paris: Alphonse Picard et fils, 1895).

Plowden, Alison, *Caroline and Charlotte Regency Scandals 1795–1821* (Stroud: Sutton, 2005).

Poissonier-Desperrières, Adrien-Marie-Gabriel, *Vie politique et militaire du général A.M.G. Poissonier-Desperrières* (Paris: C.J. Trouvé, 1824).

Popham, Hugh, *A Damned Cunning Fellow, The Eventful Life of Rear-Admiral Sir Home Popham KCB, KCH, KM, FRS, 1762–1820* (Tywardreath: Old Ferry Press, 1991).

Pradel de Lamase, Paul and Martial de, *Nouvelles notes intimes d'un émigré (le chevalier de Pradel de Lamase, officier à l'armée de Condé)* (Paris: Émile-Paul frères, 1914–1920).

Publicola-Chaussard, Jean-Baptiste, *Mémoires historiques et politiques sur la révolution de la Belgique et du pays de Liège en 1793* (Paris: Buisson, 1793).

Puisaye, Joseph-Geneviève de, *Mémoires du comte Joseph de Puisaye … qui pourront servir à l'histoire du parti royaliste françois durant la dernière révolution* (London: Cox and Baylis, 1803–8).

Puymaigre, Comte Alexandre de, *Souvenirs sur l'émigration, l'Empire et la Restauration, publiés par son fils* (Paris: E. Plon, Nourrit et cie, 1884).

Raichas d'Aiglun, A de, 'D'Arçon, sa vie et ses écrits' *Mémoires de la Société d'émulation du Doubs* (Fourth series, Second volume, 1867), pp.208-336.

Rambaud, Jacques (ed.), *Mémoires du comte Roger de Damas (1787–1806)* (Paris: Plon-Nourrit, 1912).

Rial, Sébastien, et al, *De Nimègue à Java: les soldats suisses au service de la Hollande XVIIe-XVIIIe siècles* (Morges: Centre d'Histoire et de Prospective Militaires, 2014).

Ribbe, Claude, *Alexandre Dumas, le dragon de la Reine* (Paris: du Rocher, 2002).

Ribes, Comte de, *Journal d'Émigration du Prince de Condé 1789–1795* (Paris: Société Bibliophile François, 1924).

Rochambeau, Jean-Baptiste Donatien de Vimeur, Comte de, *Mémoires militaires, historiques et politiques* (Paris: Pillet Ainé, 1809).

Romain, Félix de, *Souvenirs d'un Officier Royaliste, contenant son entrée au service, ses voyages en Corse et en Italie, son émigration, ses campagnes à l'armée de Condé, et celle de 1815, dans la Vendée* (Paris: Égron, 1824).

Rösselet, Abraham and Steiger, Rudolf von, *Souvenirs de Abraham Rösselet* (Neuchâtel: J Attinger, 1857).

Sabron, Frederik Henri Alexander, *De oorlog van 1794–1795 op het Grondgebied van de Republiek der Vereeenigde Nederlanden* (second edition Breda: Koninklijke Militaire Academie, 1893).

Saint-Gervais, Antoine de, *Histoire des émigrés français depuis 1789 jusqu'en 1828* (Paris: L.F. Hivert, 1828).

Schama, Simon, *Patriots and Liberators: revolution in the Netherlands (1780–1813)* (London: Harper Collins, 1977).

Schoell, Maximilien Samson-Frédéric, *Cours d'histoire des Etats européens* (Paris: author, 1833).
Ségur, Louis-Philippe, *Histoire des principaux événements du règne de Frédéric-Guillaume II, roi de Prusse, et tableau politique de l'Europe, depuis 1786 jusqu'en 1796, ou l'An 4 de la République, contenant un précis des Révolutions de Brabant, de Hollande, de Pologne et de France* (Paris: F. Buisson, 1800).
Ségur, Louis-Philippe, *Politique de tous les cabinets de l'Europe, pendant les règnes de Louis XV et de Louis XVI* (Paris: Buisson, 1793).
Smith, Digby, *The Greenhill Napoleonic Wars Data Book* (London and Pennsylvania: Greenhill Books, 1998).
Sommervogel, Carlos (ed.), *Une correspondance pendant l'émigration 1792–1797, quarante-huit lettres inédites de Louis-Joseph de Bourbon, prince de Condé, du duc de Berry et du duc d'Enghien* (Paris: author, 1867).
Soult, Nicolas-Jean de Dieu, *Mémoires du Maréchal-général Soult, duc de Dalmatie* (Paris: Librairie d'Aymot, 1854).
Stewart, David, *Sketches of the Character, Manners and Present State of the Highlanders of Scotland; with details of the Military Service of the Highland Regiments* (Edinburgh: Archibald Constable, 1822).
Thiers, Adolphe, *Histoire de la Révolution française* (Paris: Lecointe, 1823–1827).
Thiboult de Puisact, Jacques de, *Journal d'un fourrier de l'armée de Condé* (Paris: Didier et cie, 1882).
Tornare, Alain-Jacques, *10 août 1792 – Les Tuileries. L'été tragique des relations franco-suisses* (Lausanne: PPUR, 2012).
Tozzi, Christopher, 'Between Two Republics: American Military Volunteers in Revolutionary France' *The Proceedings of the Western Society for French Revolution* (Volume 39, 2013), pp.166-176.
Tranié, Jean and Carmigniani, Juan Carlos, *La patrie en danger 1792–1793, Les campagnes de la Révolution* (Paris: Lavauzelle, 1987).
Uzureau, V., 'Prêtres français en exil à Maëstricht, 1792–1793' *Revue belge de philologie et d'histoire* (Volume II, 1923), pp.709-711.
Vauban, Jacques Anne Joseph Le Prestre Comte de, *Mémoires pour server à l'histoire de la Guerre de la Vendée* (Paris: Baudouin Frères, 1830).
Vermeulen, Dr. P.J., *Tijdschrift voor oudheden, statistiek, zeden en gewooten, regt, genealogie en andere deelen der Geschiedenis van het Bisdom, de Provincie en de Stad Utrecht* (Utrecht: Kemink en Zoon, 1852).
Verney, Sir Harry, *The Journals and Correspondence of General Sir Harry Calvert* (London: Hurst and Blackett, 1853).
Villebresme, Vicomte Maurice de, *Souvenirs du Chevalier de Villebresme, Mousquetaire de la Garde du Roi 1772–1816* (Paris and Nancy: Berger-Levrault et cie, 1897).
Villeneuve-Laroche-Barnaud, Louis Gabriel de, *Mémoires sur l'expédition de Quiberon, précédés d'une notice sur l'émigration de 1791 et sur les trois campagnes de 1792, 1793 et 1794* (second edition Paris: C. J.Trouvé, 1824).
Vloten, J. van, *Bloemlezing uit de Nederlandsche Prozaschrijuers der Achttiende Euw* (Arnhem: Nijhoff en Zoon, 1871).
Wickham, William (ed.), *The correspondence of the Right Honourable William Wickham from the year 1794* (London: Richard Bentley, 1870).

Unpublished Works

Bazouges, Hughes de, *La légion de Damas au service des Provinces Unies, 1793–1795* (MA La Sorbonne, Paris 1995).

Online Sources

Anon, 'Etat nominatif du Régiment de Maëstricht' *La Sabretache* <http://lasabretache.fr/produit/regiment-de-maestricht-1793/> (accessed 17 December 2019).
Anon, 'Histoire' *Ham-sur-Heure-Nalinnes* <http://www.ham-sur-heure-nalinnes.be/crbst_116.html> (accessed 11 July 2016).
Anon, Home *grebbelinie.nl* <http://www.grebbelinie.nl/page/home> (accessed 2 January 2020).
Endfield, Georgina, 'Cold weather records: reflections from the bus stop' *University of Nottingham* <http://blogs.nottingham.ac.uk/weatherextremes/2015/01/19/> (accessed 20 June 2017).
Evert Kam, Evert (ed.) 'Dagboek van Nijmegen 1794–1795' *Dagboek van Nijmegen 1794–1795* <http://www.noviomagus.nl/Gastredactie/Kam/Hulst/Hulst.htm> (accessed 13 April 2015).

Index

From Reason to Revolution – Warfare 1721-1815

http://www.helion.co.uk/series/from-reason-to-revolution-1721-1815.php

The 'From Reason to Revolution' series covers the period of military history 1721–1815, an era in which fortress-based strategy and linear battles gave way to the nation-in-arms and the beginnings of total war.

This era saw the evolution and growth of light troops of all arms, and of increasingly flexible command systems to cope with the growing armies fielded by nations able to mobilise far greater proportions of their manpower than ever before. Many of these developments were fired by the great political upheavals of the era, with revolutions in America and France bringing about social change which in turn fed back into the military sphere as whole nations readied themselves for war. Only in the closing years of the period, as the reactionary powers began to regain the upper hand, did a military synthesis of the best of the old and the new become possible.

The series will examine the military and naval history of the period in a greater degree of detail than has hitherto been attempted, and has a very wide brief, with the intention of covering all aspects from the battles, campaigns, logistics, and tactics, to the personalities, armies, uniforms, and equipment.

Submissions

The publishers would be pleased to receive submissions for this series. Please contact series editor Andrew Bamford via email (andrewbamford@helion.co.uk), or in writing to Helion & Company Limited, Unit 8 Amherst Business Centre, Budbrooke Road, Warwick, CV34 5WE

Titles

- No 1 *Lobositz to Leuthen: Horace St Paul and the Campaigns of the Austrian Army in the Seven Years War 1756-57* (Neil Cogswell)
- No 2 *Glories to Useless Heroism: The Seven Years War in North America from the French journals of Comte Maurés de Malartic, 1755-1760* (William Raffle (ed.))
- No 3 *Reminiscences 1808-1815 Under Wellington: The Peninsular and Waterloo Memoirs of William Hay* (Andrew Bamford (ed.))
- No 4 *Far Distant Ships: The Royal Navy and the Blockade of Brest 1793-1815* (Quintin Barry)
- No 5 *Godoy's Army: Spanish Regiments and Uniforms from the Estado Militar of 1800* (Charles Esdaile and Alan Perry)
- No 6 *On Gladsmuir Shall the Battle Be! The Battle of Prestonpans 1745* (Arran Johnston)
- No 7 *The French Army of the Orient 1798-1801: Napoleon's Beloved 'Egyptians'* (Yves Martin)
- No 8 *The Autobiography, or Narrative of a Soldier: The Peninsular War Memoirs of William Brown of the 45th Foot* (Steve Brown (ed.))
- No 9 *Recollections from the Ranks: Three Russian Soldiers' Autobiographies from the Napoleonic Wars* (Darrin Boland)
- No 10 *By Fire and Bayonet: Grey's West Indies Campaign of 1794* (Steve Brown)
- No 11 *Olmütz to Torgau: Horace St Paul and the Campaigns of the Austrian Army in the Seven Years War 1758-60* (Neil Cogswell)
- No 12 *Murat's Army: The Army of the Kingdom of Naples 1806-1815* (Digby Smith)
- No 13 *The Veteran or 40 Years' Service in the British Army: The Scurrilous Recollections of Paymaster John Harley 47th Foot – 1798-1838* (Gareth Glover (ed.))

No 14 *Narrative of the Eventful Life of Thomas Jackson: Militiaman and Coldstream Sergeant, 1803-15* (Eamonn O'Keeffe (ed.))

No.15 *For Orange and the States: The Army of the Dutch Republic 1713-1772 Part I: Infantry* (Marc Geerdinck-Schaftenaar)

No 16 *Men Who Are Determined to be Free: The American Assault on Stony Point, 15 July 1779* (David C. Bonk)

No 17 *Next to Wellington: General Sir George Murray: The Story of a Scottish Soldier and Statesman, Wellington's Quartermaster General* (John Harding-Edgar)

No 18 *Between Scylla and Charybdis: The Army of Elector Friedrich August of Saxony 1733-1763 Part I: Staff and Cavalry* (Marco Pagan)

No 19 *The Secret Expedition: The Anglo-Russian Invasion of Holland 1799* (Geert van Uythoven)

No 20 *'We Are Accustomed to do our Duty': German Auxiliaries with the British Army 1793-95* (Paul Demet)

No 21 *With the Guards in Flanders: The Diary of Captain Roger Morris 1793-95* (Peter Harington (ed.))

No 22 *The British Army in Egypt 1801: An Underrated Army Comes of Age* (Carole Divall)

No 23 *Better is the Proud Plaid: The Clothing, Weapons, and Accoutrements of the Jacobites in the '45* (Jenn Scott)

No 24 *The Lilies and the Thistle: French Troops in the Jacobite '45* (Andrew Bamford)

No 25 *A Light Infantryman With Wellington: The Letters of Captain George Ulrich Barlow 52nd and 69th Foot 1808-15* (Gareth Glover (ed.))

No 26 *Swiss Regiments in the Service of France 1798-1815: Uniforms, Organisation, Campaigns* (Stephen Ede-Borrett)

No 27 *For Orange and the States! The Army of the Dutch Republic 1713-1772: Part II: Cavalry and Specialist Troops* (Marc Geerdinck-Schaftenaar)

No 28 *Fashioning Regulation, Regulating Fashion: Uniforms and Dress of the British Army 1800-1815 Volume I* (Ben Townsend)

No 29 *Riflemen: The History of the 5th Battalion 60th (Royal American) Regiment, 1797-1818* (Robert Griffith)

No 30 *The Key to Lisbon: The Third French Invasion of Portugal, 1810-11* (Kenton White)

No 31 *Command and Leadership: Proceedings of the 2018 Helion & Company 'From Reason to Revolution' Conference* (Andrew Bamford (ed.))

No 32 *Waterloo After the Glory: Hospital Sketches and Reports on the Wounded After the Battle* (Michael Crumplin and Gareth Glover)

No 33 *Fluxes, Fevers, and Fighting Men: War and Disease in Ancien Regime Europe 1648-1789* (Pádraig Lenihan)

No 34 *'They Were Good Soldiers': African-Americans Serving in the Continental Army, 1775-1783* (John U. Rees)

No 35 *A Redcoat in America: The Diaries of Lieutenant William Bamford, 1757-1765 and 1776* (John B. Hattendorf (ed.))

No 36 *Between Scylla and Charybdis: The Army of Friedrich August II of Saxony, 1733-1763: Part II: Infantry and Artillery* (Marco Pagan)

No 37 *Québec Under Siege: French Eye-Witness Accounts from the Campaign of 1759* (Charles A. Mayhood (ed.))

No 38 *King George's Hangman: Henry Hawley and the Battle of Falkirk 1746* (Jonathan D. Oates)

No 39 *Zweybrücken in Command: The Reichsarmee in the Campaign of 1758* (Neil Cogswell)

No 40 *So Bloody a Day: The 16th Light Dragoons in the Waterloo Campaign* (David J. Blackmore)

No 41 *Northern Tars in Southern Waters: The Russian Fleet in the Mediterranean 1806-1810* (Vladimir Bogdanovich Bronevskiy / Darrin Boland)

No 42 *Royal Navy Officers of the Seven Years War: A Biographical Dictionary of Commissioned Officers 1748-1763* (Cy Harrison)

No 43 *All at Sea: Naval Support for the British Army During the American Revolutionary War* (John Dillon)

No 44 *Glory is Fleeting: New Scholarship on the Napoleonic Wars* (Andrew Bamford (ed.))

No 45 *Fashioning Regulation, Regulating Fashion: Uniforms and Dress of the British Army 1800-1815 Vol. II* (Ben Townsend)

No 46 *Revenge in the Name of Honour: The Royal Navy's Quest for Vengeance in the Single Ship Actions of the War of 1812* (Nicholas James Kaizer)

No 47 *They Fought With Extraordinary Bravery: The III German (Saxon) Army Corps in the Southern Netherlands 1814* (Geert van Uythoven)

No 48 *The Danish Army of the Napoleonic Wars 1801-1814, Organisation, Uniforms & Equipment: Volume 1: High Command, Line and Light Infantry* (David Wilson)

No 49 *Neither Up Nor Down: The British Army and the Flanders Campaign 1793-1895* (Phillip Ball)

No 50 *Guerra Fantástica: The Portuguese Army and the Seven Years War* (António Barrento)

No 51 *From Across the Sea: North Americans in Nelson's Navy* (Sean M. Heuvel and John A. Rodgaard)

No 52 *Rebellious Scots to Crush: The Military Response to the Jacobite '45* (Andrew Bamford (ed.))

No 53 *The Army of George II 1727-1760: The Soldiers who Forged an Empire* (Peter Brown)

No 54 *Wellington at Bay: The Battle of Villamuriel, 25 October 1812* (Garry David Wills)

No 55 *Life in the Red Coat: The British Soldier 1721-1815* (Andrew Bamford (ed.))

No 56 *Wellington's Favourite Engineer. John Burgoyne: Operations, Engineering, and the Making of a Field Marshal* (Mark S. Thompson)

No 57 *Scharnhorst: The Formative Years, 1755-1801* (Charles Edward White)

No 58 *At the Point of the Bayonet: The Peninsular War Battles of Arroyomolinos and Almaraz 1811-1812* (Robert Griffith)

No 59 *Sieges of the '45: Siege Warfare during the Jacobite Rebellion of 1745-1746* (Jonathan D. Oates)

No 60 *Austrian Cavalry of the Revolutionary and Napoleonic Wars, 1792–1815* (Enrico Acerbi, András K. Molnár)

No 61 *The Danish Army of the Napoleonic Wars 1801-1814, Organisation, Uniforms & Equipment: Volume 2: Cavalry and Artillery* (David Wilson)

No 62 *Napoleon's Stolen Army: How the Royal Navy Rescued a Spanish Army in the Baltic* (John Marsden)

No 63 *Crisis at the Chesapeake: The Royal Navy and the Struggle for America 1775-1783* (Quintin Barry)

No 64 *Bullocks, Grain, and Good Madeira: The Maratha and Jat Campaigns 1803-1806 and the emergence of the Indian Army* (Joshua Provan)

No 65 *Sir James McGrigor: The Adventurous Life of Wellington's Chief Medical Officer* (Tom Scotland)

No 66 *Fashioning Regulation, Regulating Fashion: Uniforms and Dress of the British Army 1800-1815 Volume I* (Ben Townsend) (paperback edition)

No 67 *Fashioning Regulation, Regulating Fashion: Uniforms and Dress of the British Army 1800-1815 Volume II* (Ben Townsend) (paperback edition)

No 68 *The Secret Expedition: The Anglo-Russian Invasion of Holland 1799* (Geert van Uythoven) (paperback edition)

No 69 *The Sea is my Element: The Eventful Life of Admiral Sir Pulteney Malcolm 1768-1838* (Paul Martinovich)

No 70 *The Sword and the Spirit: Proceedings of the first 'War & Peace in the Age of Napoleon' Conference* (Zack White (ed.))

No 71 *Lobositz to Leuthen: Horace St Paul and the Campaigns of the Austrian Army in the Seven Years War 1756-57* (Neil Cogswell) (paperback edition)

No 72 *For God and King. A History of the Damas Legion 1793-1798: A Case Study of the Military Emigration during the French Revolution* (Hughes de Bazouges and Alistair Nichols)

No 73 *'Their Infantry and Guns Will Astonish You': The Army of Hindustan and European Mercenaries in Maratha service 1780-1803* (Andy Copestake)